DATE DUE

			PRINTED IN U.S.A.

THE MACMILLAN COMPANY
NEW YORK · BOSTON · CHICAGO
DALLAS · ATLANTA · SAN FRANCISCO

MACMILLAN AND CO., LIMITED
LONDON · BOMBAY · CALCUTTA
MADRAS · MELBOURNE

**THE MACMILLAN COMPANY
OF CANADA, LIMITED**
TORONTO

THE YOUNG
SHELLEY

GENESIS OF A RADICAL

BY

KENNETH NEILL CAMERON

NEW YORK

THE MACMILLAN COMPANY

1950

To BESS

PREFACE

A series of studies on Shelley's later works, conducted between 1939 and 1947, convinced me of the need for a fuller study of the earlier period. Using some of the material gathered in these years as a base, I began such a study in the spring of 1948 at the Henry E. Huntington Library, after some preliminary research at the Rare Book Room of the University of Texas Library, and completed it with additional work at the Indiana University Library and the New York Public Library. During the course of the work, I consulted on sociological and psychological problems with Professor Alfred E. Lindesmith and Mr. Wardell B. Pomeroy at Indiana University, and Dr. Julius I. Steinfeld of The Forest Sanitarium, Des Plaines, Illinois, and had many helpful discussions with my wife, formerly of the Sociology Department at Indiana University. The manuscript was typed by Mrs. Elsie Dosch, who heroically battled with innumerable interlineations and interpaginations. The final manuscript was checked by Mr. and Mrs. Jack Marken and Mrs. Robert D. Brown. Mrs. Brown also assisted in the compilation of the index. The Librarian of the Huntington Library kindly gave me permission to make use of the Shelley family papers in the possession of the library, Longmans, Green & Co. to quote from *The Town Labourer* by J. L. and Barbara Hammond, Alfred A. Knopf, Inc. to quote from *Shelley* by the late Newman I. White, and Routledge and Kegan Paul Ltd. to quote from *Shelley in England* by Roger Ingpen. Especial thanks are due to the administrative officials of Indiana University, who granted me a semester's leave of absence, a series of generous research grants, and a reduction in teaching hours in order that I might complete this work.

Bloomington, Indiana.

CONTENTS

INTRODUCTION

Shelley has suffered, as perhaps no other poet has suffered, from anthologizing. The most popular anthologies reprint, year after year, lyrics which, excellent though they are in their genre, are yet unrepresentative of the main streams of his thinking and writing. And it is, unavoidably, from the anthologies that the general reading public derives its impressions.

Shelley, as George Bernard Shaw pointed out in a brilliant but forgotten essay, was not only a poet but a thinker, and not only a thinker but a radical thinker: in politics, in religion, in morals. The foundations of this thinking were laid down in the years 1809–1813, the years covered in this study; and in some of the works of this period, notably *Queen Mab,* this thinking is transmuted into powerful creative expression. But Shelley was not born a radical thinker, he developed into one; and it is in watching the unfolding of this development that one gets insight into his works—the later as well as the earlier works. For Shelley did not, contrary to the widely held opinion, change fundamentally in his later period. The theme of *Queen Mab* is the theme of *Prometheus Unbound;* the revolutionary spirit of *A Letter to Lord Ellenborough* is the spirit of *Hellas.*

The ideas of Shelley are, moreover, important ideas, and largely relevant today; for Shelley, living, as we do, in an age of social ferment, achieved a sharpness of perspective denied to those in more quiescent times. Victorian misunderstandings have continued, anachronistically, into the present, from Arnold to Eliot, from the old to the new critics, until a real need exists for an objective re-analysis, an analysis, which, if it is to possess relevance, must view these ideas in their developmental relations to the social and ideological patterns of their age. For one cannot, as is so often done, view Shelley as a unique phenomenon. He was the product of a school of thought—its most penetrative creative thinker, in fact—stretching from Jefferson to Cobbett, from Diderot to Godwin; a school arising out of the American and French Revolutions and the English reform movement. If at times Shelley states his, and their, views with a startlingly iconoclastic directness, the function of the critic is not apology but interpretation.

Shelley has suffered, too, in the popular biographies. His life, replete, as it was, with the romantic and the dramatic, has provided a happy hunting ground for the sentimentalist and the humorist. And the most common view of him held today is that expressed in André Maurois' *Ariel,* with its skillfully caricatured distortion of motive and personality, a picture duplicated, ad infinitum, in textbook and other shorter accounts.

The examination of Shelley's personality must proceed, as with that of his works, in relation to formative forces and must attempt to ascertain the basic patterns of behavior. Here, even in the better studies, oversimplifications have crept in. Sympathetic biographers, correctly feeling that Shelley was essentially lovable and admirable, have often (anticipating hostile distortions) metamorphosed these qualities into absolutes in relation to which the total character must be viewed. But modern clinical psychiatry has amply revealed personality structure as a complex of antithetical forces which defy analysis in terms of rigid moral abstractions. In this field, although I have, from time to time, consulted with specialists in the problems of human behavior, I have attempted little more than to search out major directions. Shelley is essentially important not for his life but for his works. And a predominately biographical approach leads, of itself, to false perspectives.

I VOTARY OF ROMANCE

Zastrozzi
Original Poetry by Victor and Cazire
The Wandering Jew
St. Irvyne

In the ancient, peaceful, sheep-raising county of Sussex there had long existed two Shelley families, the Michelgrove Shelleys and the Fen Place Shelleys, the former "an ancient house," hallowed by a pedigree traceable—with some stretching—to William the Conqueror and a baronetage bestowed by James I; the latter a middle-class farming family with no pretension either to lineage or to wealth. In the middle eighteenth century, indeed, their fortunes were so modest that one younger son, Timothy, underwent the final degradation of emigration to the colonies. There, after marrying the widow of a New York miller, working "in trade," falling into debt, producing two sons, and perhaps practicing as a "quack doctor," he was finally rescued by the death of one brother and the insanity of another, and hastened back to manage the modest family estate. In 1752 one of his sons, born in Newark, New Jersey, Bysshe Shelley, eloped with the sixteen-year-old daughter of a Sussex clergyman of considerable means (and had her make a "settlement" whereby the estates she was to inherit were to be turned over to him when she became twenty-three, a precaution that turned out to be unnecessary as she died at twenty-five). Nine years later he remarried (again eloping), this time with the daughter of a wealthy, aristocratic family possessed of extensive estates in several counties. In the fullness of time (and by proper use of his wealth), Bysshe achieved the honor of a baronetage and began building a huge mansion, Castle Goring, as a suitable home for the new-found family prestige. When he died in 1815, he left a fortune of £200,000, a modest fraction of it reserved for an unstated number of bastard offspring, but the bulk of it going to his son Timothy (named after Sir Bysshe's father). Thus, in the final decades of the eighteenth century were the lowly Fen Place Shelleys, thanks to the matrimonial enterprise of Sir Bysshe, metamorphosed; and when, on August 4, 1792, a son was born to Timothy, he was not born, contrary to the widely held belief, into an old aristocratic family, but a nouveau riche "county" family, regarded perhaps with some apprehension by their remote Michelgrove kin.[1]

"Shelley," writes Santayana, of this son of Timothy's, "was one of these spokesmen of the a priori, one of these nurslings of the womb, like a bee or a butterfly . . . a finished child of nature, not a joint product, like most of us, of nature, history and society. . . ."[2] But for the treader in less transcendental realms, the vision, with all its temptations of simplification of procedure, has to be eschewed. Shelley was, alas, "like most of us," the product of society, and of a family within that society. And the enquiring biographer must see what clues he can find in that early environment to the development of a mind and personality later of unusual complexity and richness.

Timothy Shelley—he became Sir Timothy on the death of Sir Bysshe in 1815—was brought up, via Oxford and the Grand Tour, to be a country gentleman and Member of Parliament; and he presumed that his son would follow the same path.

As a lad Shelley was "exceedingly fond" of his father, and his sisters remembered him, when the good squire was laid up with the gout, "watching and listening at the door of the sickroom to try to discover how his father was."[3] And Timothy, for his part, took a genuine pride in his talented youngster. He used to read to him in the vacation ("in the full hopes of making him a good and Gentlemanly Scholar"),[4] and on first taking him to Oxford he marched with him to the shop of Henry Slatter, the town's leading bookseller; twenty years later Slatter well remembered the occasion:

Thither Sir Timothy repaired with his son, and gave him a particular injunction to buy whatever he required in books and stationery of the aforesaid parties. Sir Timothy, moreover, said, "My son here," pointing to him, "has a literary turn; he is already an author, and do pray indulge him in his printing freaks."[5]

Later, it is true, after the twin scandals of the expulsion and elopement, Timothy hardened his heart, but that in this early, formative period he attempted any authoritarianism beyond the normal bounds of a father-and-son relationship in nineteenth-century England is unlikely. The theory that he did rests mainly on Shelley's derogatory statements in some letters to Godwin in 1812, but these letters were written immediately following the elopement controversy and, furthermore, are tinged by Shelley's attempt to provide a satisfactorily Godwinian picture of parental tyranny.[6] Timothy's view was different. "I never before oppos'd or closely pursued him," he wrote, in sad bewilderment, to his family attorney at the time of the elopement; and Shelley's early letters bear him out, for while they reveal some feeling that his father is too strict (for instance, he would not allow the boy to visit alone in London), yet they show the two as going to dances together, and imply a predominately friendly relationship.[7] Indeed, as some of Shelley's later actions and statements reveal, far from having been unduly disciplined he was, as first son in a family of girls, unduly indulged and allowed too much to have his own way.[8] Timothy, in his personal life, was a good-natured, kindly man, loved by his children, and apparently well liked by the laborers on his estates.[9] His business letters show him as a competent and fairly clear-thinking country gentleman with a genuinely warm feeling for his family and family tradition. But when faced by a crisis, his easy-going but definitely circumscribed personality floundered and he became weak and indecisive.

Thus, while the picture of parental tyranny is false, and while father and boy were on good terms, there certainly existed barriers to a really intimate relationship based on high mutual respect and coincidence of interests. Shelley, although attached to his father, early developed a somewhat fondly condescending attitude toward him, which probably reflects that of the family—an attitude the later overflowing of which into moods of exuberant disrespect should not be allowed to obscure the underlying fondness.

A more important influence on the boy's personality came from his mother. Mrs. Shelley was celebrated, we hear, for her "admirable letters" and "keen observation of character," which, in the opinion of a "popular writer," "if it had had a wider field might have made her a Madame de Savigne or Lady Wortley Montague."[10] She was, as was also her son in later life, famed for her philanthropic kindness,[11] and she was a woman of liberal views. "My mother is quite rational; she says, 'I think *prayer* and thanksgiving are of no use. If a man is a good man, atheist, or Christian, he will do very well in whatever future state awaits us.' This I call liberality."[12] Furthermore, she had the confidence of her son in his own radical thinking as his father did not. He ordered that no copy of the *Posthumous Fragments of Margaret Nicholson,* with its revolutionary opening poem, be sent to his father, but he sent one himself to his mother.[13] She was deeply attached to her son, protecting him, with typical maternal concern, from the wrath of his father, and Shelley, his friend Hogg informs us, "had a warm affection for his mother." [14] When Shelley was expelled from Oxford, she sent him money secretly and intercepted hotheaded letters she feared might arouse her husband.[15] After the elopement with Harriet, she opposed Timothy's decree forbidding him entry to the family estate and conspired to have him and his bride welcomed home, informing him the while of the moves and moods of his father.[16] She felt their later separation keenly. "Mrs. Shelley often spoke to me of her son; her heart yearned after him with all the fondness of a mother's love." [17]

In view of these facts, the neglect of Shelley's mother by the biographers is extraordinary.[18] True, we do not have as much information as we would like, but we have enough to perceive that we are dealing with a formative factor of a fundamental nature. There was nothing inevitable in the fact that Shelley became a poet. He was, as we shall see, brought up to be a politician. And if he entered the profession of letters instead of that of politics, it was probably due to the influence of his mother, herself interested in writing and no doubt sympathetically encouraging her son's creative efforts; without this early molding of his mind it is doubtful whether later influences would have taken effect. It was perhaps from his mother, too, that Shelley got his never failing drive and persistence. Mrs. Shelley, aware of the contrast between her capacities and her production, may have attempted to execute her own unfulfilled ambitions through her son (one of the more common forms of psychological "projection"). And, finally, it must have been from his mother's affection that Shelley developed those underlying qualities of confidence and stability that enabled him to weather, without breaking, the most extreme crises—the breakup of his marriage, the legal abduction of his children, the death of other children, persecution, poverty, failure. Biographers have often stressed the instabilities and eccentricities in Shelley's character, but fundamentally there was not instability but stability.

In addition to these, some other character patterns of a different nature can, perhaps, also be traced to his mother; for, as modern psychiatry has shown us, ambivalence is inevitable in any deep emotional relationship. Two patterns, in particular, stand out: a phobia of the withdrawal of love (e.g. in *Alastor*); the acquisition of some feminine characteristics (as we shall see, at school). The basis for the first of these may lie in a partial rejection of the boy by his mother. Mrs. Shelley, although giving affection and drive, may have failed to give that warm and continuous love which her son's nature required, or, perhaps, shut him (and his father) out of a more intimate inner circle of herself and his sisters. His unusual pranking at school, essentially an attention-getting mechanism, may also reflect an early partial rejection. The acquisition of feminine characteristics—his love of romantic intrigue and gossip, for instance, was lifelong—implies a rejection of a male pattern. I have suggested that Shelley's condescension toward his father reflected the attitude of his mother and sisters. Does it not also reflect an actual rejection, conscious or unconscious, of the father, the male, by the mother? Shelley certainly grew up without a male ideal and so, perhaps, did his sisters, for three out of four of them (all apparently, handsome girls) remained single. One would like to know more of Mrs. Shelley, and her deeper relationship to the man (aged thirty-nine at the time) that she had married.

One unusual factor stands out in Shelley's early environment: until the age of ten he was not in the normal atmosphere of association with other boys.[19] The first ten years of his life, 1792–1802, were spent at the country home of the Shelleys in Sussex, Field Place (acquired in the reign of Sir Bysshe), a lovely old mansion surrounded by large grounds and beautiful gardens, about two miles from the small town of Horsham and one from the village of Warnham. Here he was educated by a private tutor and spent his leisure hours at play with his four sisters, all of whom were younger than himself, and, later, with his baby brother.[20] His sister Hellen has given us, in her letters, an interesting picture of this life at Field Place:

I went to school before Margaret, so that she recollects how Bysshe came home in the midst of the half-year to be nursed; and when he was allowed to leave the house, he came to the diningroom window, and kissed her through the pane of glass. She remembers his face there, with nose and lips pressed against the window, and at that time she must have been about five years old. In the holidays, he would walk with us, if he could steal away with us; and on one occasion he walked with us through the fields to Strood; where, in those days, there was a park stile to encourage good neighborhood: there was a sunk fence to divide the lawn from the meadows, and gates were despised, where difficulty would augment the pleasure; and we were assisted up this perpendicular wall. I was big enough to be pulled over, but Margaret was gently thrown across on the grass. Our shoes were sadly soiled, and the little one of the party was tired and required carrying;

but she was to be careful to hold her feet so that the trousers [i.e. Shelley's] might not be damaged.[21]

The picture is that of a devoted older brother, worshiped by his sisters, gently shepherding them in their frolics; an idyllic, sheltered existence.

To the other pleasures of Field Place were added those of fishing and hunting in its extensive domains. When his friend Hogg first met Shelley at Oxford, he informs us that he was "tanned and freckled by exposure to the sun, having past the autumn, as he said, in shooting." [22] And on this his cousin Medwin commented:

And he said rightly, for he had, during September, often carried a gun in his father's preserves; Sir Timothy being a keen sportsman, and Shelley himself an excellent shot, for I well remember one day in the winter of 1809, when we were out together, his killing at three successive shots, three snipes, to my great astonishment and envy, at the tail of the pond in front of Field Place.[23]

Shelley, then, was brought up as the son of a country gentleman, being trained to become, in turn, the squire of the estates. "As a boy he would ride through the Sussex lanes and roads with Lucas, his father's steward." [24] The boy, however, showed one changeling trait that might have warned a more perceptive father. Cut off from the extroverting influences of other boys (and perhaps encouraged by his mother) he had turned to the world of his imagination. Many and fantastic were the tales—of an "Alchemist old and gray" who secretly inhabited the garret, of "a 'Great Tortoise' that lived in Warnham Pond"—that almost every evening he recited to his little sisters, seated on his knees. Sometimes, indeed, he would invent more prosaic episodes:

On one occasion he gave the most minute details of a visit he had paid to some ladies, with whom he was acquainted at our village: he described their reception of him, their occupations, and the wandering in their pretty garden, where there was a well-remembered filbertwalk and an undulating turfbank, the delight of our morning visit. There must have been something peculiar in this little event, for I have often heard it mentioned as a singular fact, and it was ascertained almost immediately, that the boy had never been to the house.[25]

Syon House Academy, the middle-class boys school to which Shelley was sent at the age of ten,[26] provided a bitter contrast to the private Arcadia of Field Place; and in this contrast lies more than one clue to the development of his personality. Fortunately, we have a first-hand account of the school and Shelley's life there, for his cousin who later became his biographer, Tom Medwin, was also a pupil at the school.[27]

We were about sixty school-fellows [writes Medwin]. I well remember the day when he was added to the number. A new arrival is always a great excitement to the other boys, who pounce upon a *freshman* with the boldness of birds of prey. We all had had to pass through this ordeal, and the remembrance of it gave my companions a great zest for torture. All tormented him with questionings. There was no end to their mockery, when they found that he was ignorant of pegtop or marbles, or leap-frog, or hopscotch, much more of fives or cricket. One wanted him to spar, another to run a race with him. He was a tyro in both these accomplishments, and the only welcome of the Neophyte was a general shout of derision. To all these impertinences he made no reply, but with a look of disdain written in his countenance, turned his back on his new associates, and when he was alone found relief in tears.[28]

From the *Autobiography* of another pupil at the school (Sir John Rennie, later a famed Victorian engineer) we get a further picture:

During the time that I was there the most remarkable scholar was the celebrated poet, Percy Bysshe Shelley, who was then about twelve or thirteen (as far as I can remember), and even at that early age exhibited considerable poetical talent, accompanied by a violent and extremely excitable temper, which manifested itself in all kinds of eccentricities. His figure was of the middle size, although slight, but well made. His head was well proportioned, and covered with a profusion of brown locks; his features regular, but rather small; his eyes hazel, restless, and brilliant; his complexion was fair and transparent; and his countenance rather effeminate, but exceedingly animated. The least circumstance that thwarted him produced the most violent paroxysms of rage; and when irritated by other boys, which they, knowing his infirmity, frequently did by way of teasing him, he would take up anything, or even any little boy near him, to throw at his tormentors. His imagination was always roving upon something romantic and extraordinary, such as spirits, fairies, fighting, volcanoes, etc., and he not unfrequently astonished his schoolfellows by blowing up the boundary palings of the playground with gunpowder, also the lid of his desk in the middle of schooltime, to the great surprise of Dr. Greenlaw himself and the whole school.[29]

Nor was the boy tormented by his fellows only. The pupils in schools in those days were subject to brutal punishment, and still another student, who was at Syon House with Shelley, supplements the picture. Shelley is recalled as "like a girl in boy's clothes, fighting with open hands, and rolling on the floor when flogged, not from the pain, but 'from a sense of indignity.' " [30] "Yet," as Rennie testified, "with all this, when treated with kindness, he was very amiable, noble, high-spirited and generous."

Life at Syon House, however, was not entirely fruitless and unhappy. Medwin tells us that Shelley became famed for his skill as a writer of Latin verse and that he developed an interest in science; and Rennie tells us that he was an outstanding scholar. The headmaster, Dr. Green-law, whom Shelley later described to his friend Hogg as "a man of liberal opinions," [31] engaged a famed amateur scientist named Adam Walker to lecture to the boys.

The second or third year after Shelley's domicile at Syon House, Walker gave a course of lectures in the great room at the academy, and displayed his orrery.[32] This exhibition opened to Shelley a new universe of specula-tions; he was, till then, quite ignorant of astronomy . . . but if he was astonished at the calculations of the mathematician, and the unfolding of our System, he was still more delighted at the idea of plurality of worlds.[33]

This theory of the "Plurality of worlds," Shelley always retained (*Hellas, On The Devil and Devils*) [34] and his interest in astronomy spread to embrace chemistry and physics (we have the amusingly pathetic picture from sister Hellen of her and the other children being "placed hand-in-hand around the nursery table to be electrified").[35]

That Shelley should not know how to fight or play boys' games may have been partly due to his isolated rural upbringing, but it cannot have been mainly due to this. Parents, and especially a mother—for Timothy was busy about his estates or in Parliament in London—interested in producing masculine characteristics could have put a son into situations in which he could have learned these games and known more of boys. That he did not was unfortunate, because it meant that from a very early age he was ill-adjusted to normal group relationships and this inevitably accentuated whatever psychological instabilities had previ-ously existed. Among these was that phobic sense of isolation and perse-cution which comes out so strongly later in his fictional characters (e.g. Lionel and Laon) and an abnormal violence of retaliation. His reaction to persecution was not at all that of Christian meekness, as Medwin in 1847, attempting to present a sympathetic picture to a Victorian audience, wished to imply, but was closer to the "rage and resistance and redress" of another embattled poet of the age. Shelley was, throughout his life, as the biographers have failed sufficiently to note, a fighter. When he was attacked by the pack, whether the boys at Syon House or the Tories of the *Quarterly,* he struck back with whatever weapons were at hand, physical at Syon House, intellectual in *Adonais.* Rennie does not, however, we may note, state that Shelley habitually threw smaller boys at larger boys. The implication is that occasionally, perhaps, once only, he picked up a smaller boy and gestured with him when tormented beyond endurance. This early persecution not only produced a sense of isolation and retaliation, it also laid the psychological basis for that hatred of tyranny which Shelley later integrated—using the Whig outlook of his family as intellectual foundation—into his political philosophy.[36]

\ Shelley could not tolerate frustration or suppression. Not that he was habitually irascible; on the contrary, he was easygoing, humorous, and agreeable in his daily living. But any powerful frustration produced an emotional crisis, a reaction doubtless having its base in some early "spoiling" of a first son in a family of girls. Fundamentally, as all his friends agree, he was unusually warm-hearted, loving, and generous. But along with this capacity to love went an equally strong capacity to hate. And Shelley turned on those whom he considered to have injured him, with cold fury—e.g. the Lord Chancellor, Southey, the Westbrooks; others he seems to have deliberately blotted out of his life. The lack of any kindly mention of his parents in his later letters, for instance, is remarkable, and it is hard to forget or to forgive the comment on the "foolish dedication [of *Queen Mab*] to my late wife." [37] We seem to be confronting a rejection pattern with deep roots.

The reasons for these and other patterns may doubtless be ascertained by socio-psychological analysis. Rennie's description, however, emphasizes another factor which we must not lose sight of. The "exceedingly animated" face with its "restless and brilliant" eyes, the abnormal intensity of the reactions, the intellectual superiority, all these show us that we are dealing with a neurological and emotional structure of unusual fineness. The directions of Shelley's reactions we can analyze in terms of environmental moldings; the strength of these reactions, however, grows out of inherited capacities, and these, in turn, modify the nature of the directions. That Shelley became a poet may have been due to his mother's influence. That he became a great poet was due to his biological inheritance. One does not proceed very far with the study of Shelley without realizing that we are dealing with a highly sensitive organism.

From the middle-class confines of Syon House, Shelley, in 1804, at the age of twelve, passed to the aristocratic demesnes of Eton, where he remained until he was almost eighteen.[38] There he was, in his early years, subjected to the same kind of treatment as at Syon House, and he reacted in much the same patterns. Unfortunately Medwin did not accompany him to Eton and so we have to rely on the scattered letters and memoirs of a few of his schoolfellows, which have become colored by the passing of years and Shelley's subsequent reputation.

Shelley, the poet, cut off at so early an age, just when his great poetical talents had been matured by study and reflection, and when he probably would have produced some great work, was my friend and associate at Eton. He was a boy of studious and meditative habits, averse to all games and sports, and a great reader of novels and romances. He was a thin, slight lad, with remarkably lustrous eyes, fine hair, and a very peculiar shrill voice and laugh. His most intimate friend at Eton was a boy named Price, who was considered one of the best classical scholars amongst us. At his tutor, Bethell's, where he lodged, he attempted many mechanical and scientific experiments. By the aid of a common tinker, he contrived to make something like a steam-engine, which, unfortunately, one day suddenly exploded, to the great consternation of the neighborhood and to the imminent danger of a severe flogging from Dr. Goodall.[39]

Shelley and I used to amuse ourselves in composing plays, and acting them before the other lower boy,—who constituted our sole audience. Shelley entered with great vivacity into this amusement. . . . I think I hear, as if it were yesterday, Shelley singing, with the buoyant cheerfulness in which he often indulged, as he might be running nimbly up and down stairs, the Witches' songs in "Macbeth." [40]

We used to wander for hours about Clewer, Frogmore, the Park at Windsor, the Terrace; and I was a delighted and willing listener to his marvellous stories of fairyland, and apparitions, and spirits, and haunted ground; and his speculations were then (for his mind was far more developed than mine) of the world beyond the grave. Another of his favourite rambles was Stoke Park, and the picturesque churchyard, where Gray is said to have written his *Elegy,* of which he was very fond. I was myself far too young to form any estimate of character, but I loved Shelley for his kindliness and affectionate ways: he was not made to endure the rough and boisterous pastime at Eton, and his shy and gentle nature was glad to escape far away to muse over strange fancies, for his mind was reflective and teeming with deep thought.[41]

But there was another practice infinitely more galling. The particular name of some particular boy would be sounded by one, taken up by another and another, until hundreds echoed and echoed the name. . . . The Shelley! Shelley! Shelley! which was thundered in the cloisters was but too often accompanied by practical jokes,—such as knocking his books from under his arm, seizing them as he stooped to recover them, pulling and tearing his clothes, or pointing with the finger, as one Neapolitan maddens another.[42]

Shelley, it is clear, did not fit into the atmosphere of a school designed to train an aristocracy in the twin patterns of domination and conformity. He had no desire to dominate younger boys (for which the "fag" system, whereby the lower form boys were semi-servants to the upper form boys, gave unlimited scope); instead of conforming he took intense and unorthodox interest in science and in reading, shunned most sports (except rowing and hunting),[43] and delighted in walks with solitary companions. For his lack of conformity he was subjected to collective bullying, but his tormentors never succeeded in breaking him into line. When he was left alone he was of a friendly, cheerful nature, warm-hearted to all who would befriend him, but driven by his lack of recognition from his fellows into mischievous pranking.

The stresses and strains of these early years at Eton, however, cannot have been as continuous as some of his contemporaries remembered (for highlights tend to stand out in recollection), and Shelley later had happy memories of picnics on the grass and evenings on the river.[44] In his later years at Eton the picture underwent considerable change. One cannot, as is too often done, view the Eton period as a whole. In the final two years of a public school—especially having achieved the envied heights of the "sixth"—a boy is a much different person to what he was in the lowly "third" or "fourth," and while he may still be subject to some collective persecution [45] his life achieves a new dignity and authority. And from Shelley's few extant letters in these years (1809–1810) we get the impression of a typical young English gentleman, interested in girls and dancing and in going off to London from time to time for sprees with his fellows or to the opera, chafing, in the vacations, at the monotony of country life, solacing himself with reading and hunting:

Dear Tisdall,

For reasons best explained at meeting it would have been impossible to have dined with you on Wednesday, had the punctilios of my Father suffered me to accept your obliging invitation: I hope we shall have the pleasure of your Company at Easter; my Father has promised me that he will write to you to invite you when you are at Eton, so by that means any objections will be done away with. But I have really some scruples of Conscience about making you perform penance in this temple of Solitude in the dullest time of the year, & am afraid you will conceive a very disadvantageous opinion of our residence. But self-interestedness overcomes these scruples, & I hope you will find at least novelty to make up for grandeur. Your task is not forgotten & you may depend upon my fidelity in that respect. Tell me in your next when you propose to come to Eton. I hope it will be as soon as me, or despair!!! Tuite is well; he writes better than he does any thing else tho' now and then I find a little ghostly admonition. Dissipation and Pleasure are stagnant at Horsham, & after a few Balls, ill attended, every thing is now silent. I hear they are to be unusually gay at Easter, & your presence now [no] doubt will add to the brilliancy.— Here are thousands of wild Ducks and Geese in our River and Lake. I have shot at numbers but killed only one. But this is such shocking weather that to dissipate the stagnation of my spirits I like you am writing letters &, what you have given up, read Novels & Romances all day, till in the Evening I fancy myself a Character.

A letter so full of ennui as this can be of no possible further Entertainment to you—so with best wishes believe me your[s] affectionately,

PERCY BYSSHE SHELLEY [46]

And again: "I shall be in London on the 16th, at the *Opera* on Tuesday: observe *who* I am with, & I will ask your opinion at some future period. Very little to do in the country, & a most excellent time to go mad for want of better employment; you will see me quite wild on the 20th." [47] It is clear that the maturing young gentleman who penned these letters was a very different person from the youngster of the lower form "Shelley Baits."

It was in these final years at Eton, too, that Shelley began to achieve fame as a youthful author. In March, 1810, he published a horror novel, *Zastrozzi,* and one of his contemporaries remembered that "with part of the proceeds he gave a most magnificent banquet to eight of his friends, among whom I was included." [48] In the same period he wrote (in conjunction with his sister Elizabeth) a volume of juvenile verses, *Original Poetry* by "Victor and Cazire," and a blood-and-thunder narrative poem, *The Wandering Jew,* which contained a scene from a now fortunately lost horror novel *The Nightmare,* which he and cousin Medwin had previously composed; and a second "Gothic" tale, *St. Irvyne, or The Rosicrucian,* which was not published until after he had taken up residence at Oxford.[49]

In spite of his continued writing in this vein he had, at least by the time of his final year at Eton, begun to direct his reading into more serious channels. Medwin informs us that Southey (whose style is evident in *Queen Mab*) was his "favorite poet in 1809"; that Chatterton (celebrated later in *Adonais*) was "one of his favorites," but that he did not care for Wordsworth.[50] He had turned, too, to an interest in philosophical speculation in Pliny and Lucretius, and to a combination of philosophical with social speculation in Benjamin Franklin and Condorcet.[51] He must have achieved considerable proficiency in his studies, for he embarked upon a translation of Pliny's *Natural History*[52] and, just before going down from Eton, delivered "on Election Monday, July 30, before his Compeers in oratory" one of Cicero's speeches against Cataline,[53] thus continuing his skill acquired at Syon House. ("He used to write verse, English and Latin," Rennie recalled, "with considerable facility, and attained a high position in the school before he left for Eton.")[54] The young scholar and author who was graduated from Eton in July, 1810, preparatory to going to Oxford, must, in spite of his nonconformities, have been recognized as one of the most talented members of his class.

In his turning to more serious reading at Eton, Shelley received encouragement from one who was not a master at the school but who had all the learning of the best of them and had, in addition, the invaluable gift of appreciation for an unorthodox and original student. This was Dr. James Lind, physician to King George III at nearby Windsor Castle. That Lind made a vivid impression on the young Shelley we know from Shelley's own comments and from the later pictures of him in *The Revolt of Islam* and *Prince Athanase*.[55] From these we would gather that Lind was a kindly man of liberal ideas both in political and scientific thinking. It was by him, apparently, that Shelley was first introduced to Godwin's *Political Justice*.[56] His scientific interest is revealed in three papers published for the Royal Society (one on a transit of Venus, one on an eclipse of the moon, and one on a portable wind gauge) and his (Edinburgh) M.D. thesis on "the Fever of 1762 at Bengal."[57] Of his political opinions we know less. Hogg's story of his cursing George III is apparently untrue,[58] but he may have been the author of an anonymous work of 1769—he was born in 1736—which has been described as "a cautious plea for political equality and natural rights."[59] Shelley depicts him as an advanced humanitarian in *The Revolt of Islam,* but the portrait there is clearly shaded with characteristics from William Godwin.

During this final period at Eton, Shelley was undergoing his first love affair, with his cousin Harriet Grove (whose mother was Mrs. Shelley's sister). Harriet was, according to Medwin,[60] an extremely beautiful girl, but her journal (unearthed by Ingpen) reveals her as an average adolescent, interested in parties and dances and "Percy."[61] As

Harriet lived near Hindon in Wiltshire, about eighty miles from Horsham, the two saw each other only on the occasions of family visits, but in 1809 they began a correspondence (probably mostly on religious and political subjects).[62] For the first nine months of 1809, Shelley wrote to her about once a week and she replied about once every two weeks; and on one ecstatic occasion, as the young lover later remembered in sorrow, the two plighted their troth:

> Again you say, "Confide in me,
> For I am thine, and thine alone,
> And thine must ever, ever be." [63]

In September, 1809, the correspondence suddenly ceased,[64] as the Grove family had stepped in and ended whatever "understanding" had existed between the two. The reason for this interference is given by Harriet's brother, Charles: "But she became uneasy at the tone of his letters on speculative subjects, at first consulting my mother, and subsequently my father also on the subject. This led at last, to the dissolution of an engagement between Bysshe and my sister, which had previously been permitted, both by his father and mine." [65]

Following this edict in the fall of 1809, the two, although not allowed to correspond regularly, were permitted to see each other as before on the apparently rather rare occasions of family visits (only one such visit is recorded for 1809 and one for 1810).[66] In April, 1810, the Grove family spent a week at Field Place and when they went on to London were joined by Shelley, his mother, and his sister Elizabeth.

During this period of the dissolution of their "engagement," Shelley, although disturbed,[67] gives no evidence of going through an extreme crisis. Six months or more later, however, he does go through such a crisis, deep and tumultuous enough, though less so than his self-dramatizing letters to his friend Hogg indicate. He implied that he had "followed" Harriet to Wiltshire (which is almost certainly untrue) and "would have followed her to the ends of the earth," but his efforts to get her back were vain.[68]

I am but just returned to Field Place from an inefficient effort. Why do you, my happy friend, tell me of perfection in love? Is she not gone? And yet I breathe, I live! But adieu to egotism; I am sick to death at the name of *self.* . . .

I have wandered in the snow, for I am cold, wet, and mad. Pardon me, pardon my delirious egotism; this really shall be the last. My sister is well; I fear she is not quite happy on my account, but is much more cheerful than she was some days ago.[69]

She is no longer mine, she abhors me as a Deist, as what she was before. Oh! Christianity, when I pardon this last, this severest of thy persecutions, may God (if there be a God), blast me! . . .

I am afraid there is selfishness in the passion of love, for I cannot avoid feeling every instant as if my soul was bursting; but I *will* feel no more! It is selfish. I would feel for others, but for myself—oh! how much rather would I expire in the struggle! Yes, there were a relief! Is suicide wrong? I slept with a loaded pistol and some poison, last night, but did not die. . . .[70]

She is gone! She is lost to me forever! She is married! Married to a clod of earth; she will become as insensible herself; all those fine capabilities will moulder.[71]

The reason for this crisis, coming more than a year after the official severing of ties, is, it seems to me, to be found in the final excerpt given above. Following her return from London in April, 1810, Harriet's journal records occasional visits from a Mr. William Helyer, scion of a nearby farming family; in the fall of 1811 she and Helyer were married. It was doubtless the engagement leading up to this marriage that so upset Shelley, for this engagement put a final end to his hopes as the previous break had not,[72] and, even more important, it meant that he had been supplanted by another. Shelley, as we have seen, brought up as the older brother in a family of girls, was used to having his own way, and throughout his life, from the "rages" of Syon House to the quarrel recorded in *Julian and Maddalo,* the one thing that inevitably produced an extreme reaction was a serious blocking of his will. Hence, the roots of this crisis are to be found not in a genuine love disappointment but in frustration and jealousy. His relationship with Harriet Grove went through four stages: occasional visits and (later) correspondence, 1805–1809, Shelley being then aged twelve to sixteen; an official breaking of relations (September, 1809); renewed acquaintance in April, 1810; a final break (October–December, 1810). The relationship was extremely immature and resulted in no deep emotional involvement on either side. The fact that, except for his sisters, he appears to have known no other girls accentuated its immaturity, and accounts, in part, for the sentimental idealizations with which it was attended. Shelley saw Harriet Grove on only two occasions following childhood, once in April, 1809, once in April, 1810.

One of the effects of this crisis on Shelley may have been the sharpening of a psychological pattern already present, the phobia of the withdrawal of affection, already aggravated, as I have suggested, by his sudden shunting from Field Place to Syon House, a pattern which is, perhaps, ultimately responsible for that unmasculine dependence in love which is sometimes present in his love poetry. ("Let thy love in kisses rain On my lips and eyelids pale.") [73] It may be, too, that his later search for the ideal had some roots in this early phobic insecurity in love, that is in earthly, human love: security might perhaps be found only in a transcendental love, a love of permanence—not failing and wounding like human love—and of supreme beauty. And, perhaps, Shelley's interest in incest between brother and sister (*vide: Laon and Cythna* and *Rosalind and Helen*) [74] can be traced to the same roots; for the rebuff by Harriet Grove sent him grasping for stability back to the old pre-Syon House emotional patterns and produced a love-dependence on his sisters well beyond the normal. This was especially true of his sister, Elizabeth. "His resemblance to his sister Elizabeth," Captain Kennedy remarked, "was as striking as if they had been twins." [75] And Shelley, as we can tell from his letters, swung to Elizabeth for aid with unusual vehemence:

I could not come on Monday, my sister would not part with me, but I must, I will, see you soon. My sister is now comparatively happy, she has felt deeply; had it not been for her, had it not been for a sense of what I owed to her, to you, I should have bid you a final farewell some time ago.[76]

Elizabeth watched over him anxiously and intervened in his behalf with his lost inamorata. At least an unconscious desire to consummate so intimate a relationship between brother and sister must have existed, and, later, as Shelley began to develop his free love theories, the nature of these past emotions perhaps became clearer to him and he questioned the ethics which forbade their expression.[77]

This emotional complex, too, perhaps increased Shelley's inevitable tendency, as elder brother to three sisters, toward intellectual domination. He tried to convert his sisters into deists; "divine little scion[s] of infidelity"; [78] and he assisted Elizabeth with her poetry. He was, in fact, continually, and often with an abnormal intensity of purpose, attempting to shape the thinking of the whole female group. And this pattern persisted throughout his life, later becoming integrated with his feminist social philosophy.

OXFORD

When we reach the Oxford stage of Shelley's career, we are once more favored by the presence of a future biographer as schoolfellow. Thomas

Jefferson Hogg, born the same year as Shelley (1792), was the son of a Tory barrister, Deputy Lieutenant for the county of Durham. He entered University College in February, 1810, became Shelley's most intimate friend, and was expelled with him in March, 1811. From that time until Shelley's departure for Italy, he was—despite a temporary alienation—one of Shelley's closest friends, and in after years remained a friend of Shelley's widow. In 1817 he was called to the bar, but achieved no particular distinction in his profession, although he was recognized as a man of ability and was promised the post of Professor of Civil Law at London University (a promise unfulfilled). In 1827, he made another link with the Shelley tradition by living with Jane Williams, the widow of Captain Edward Ellerker Williams, who was drowned with Shelley in Italy in 1822. Both the Williamses had known Shelley intimately in Italy.[79]

In 1832 Hogg wrote a series of articles on Shelley at Oxford, and in 1858 published the first two volumes of a biography including these earlier articles. A third volume is known to have been written but was not published as Shelley's son and daughter-in-law, Sir Percy Florence and Lady Jane Shelley, objected to the first two and withdrew the documents they had placed at Hogg's disposal.[80]

This biography is our main source for Shelley's life at Oxford and an important source for his early life as a whole. From it, more than from any other single work, the popularly held concept of Shelley has been formed; for its racy descriptions—in *Pickwick Papers* style—have proved irresistible to later biographers and from them have stemmed out into the anthologies, textbooks, and popular accounts (notably Maurois' *Ariel*). Yet it is important in dealing with Shelley's early life to recognize that Hogg's book presents a fundamentally distorted picture. It is not genuine biography but semi-fiction in which the author feels free to reconstruct conversations—forty-eight years later—and to slant episodes in line with his shallow concept of his subject. The reason for this distortion is not to be found, as some critics have contended, in personal malice, for Hogg had a genuine fondness for Shelley and would not have deliberately embarked upon a harmful satire. The reason lies in the fundamental divergence of philosophy between the two, aided by Hogg's unconscious resentment at the contrast between Shelley's posthumous fame and his own obscurity. Hogg's family was, he informs us with pride, "of the highest Church and of the high Tory party"; he would not, exemplifying his creed, "walk across Chancery Lane in the narrowest part, if by doing so I could at once redress all

the wrongs and grievances of Ireland." [81] As to Shelley: "He gave himself up too much to people, who have since been called radicals; these
were necessarily vulgar." [82] Between the radical humanitarianism which
was the essence of Shelley and the snobbish Toryism of Hogg there
was a great gulf, a gulf that no biographer, however well meaning,
could cross. Shelley's motivating philosophy, the philosophy behind his
actions and his poetry, was genuinely ridiculous to Hogg, and Hogg
reveals him either in isolation from this philosophy or in relation to a
caricatured version of it, placing the emphasis on personal eccentricities.
We do not anywhere get the sense of watching the unfolding of the
mind and life of a great poet but of an amusing though lovable eccentric. "*Our* Book," Hogg wrote to Lady Jane Shelley, "*must* be *amusing*." [83] The book was to reveal Hogg to the age as an undiscovered
humorist (it is almost as much about Hogg as Shelley), fulfilling, at
last, the promise of his early articles. And it is in the scrambling pursuit
of this object that Shelley, a man for whom he had fondness but no
veneration, is victimized. Once this fundamental warping of framework is realized, however, the critic, by selection and placing of material in perspective, can make important use of the work, for Hogg,
within his limits, was a keen observer.

Shelley had first been brought to Oxford by his father in April, 1810,
to be "admitted" to Timothy's old college (University); he then returned to complete his final term at Eton, and entered Oxford in
October. On his first dinner in the college hall he met Hogg who remembered him as "remarkably youthful" in appearance and rather
"absent and thoughtful" in manner:

> His figure was slight and fragile, and yet his bones and joints were large
> and strong. He was tall, but he stooped so much that he seemed of low
> stature. His clothes were expensive, and made according to the most ap-
> proved mode of the day; but they were tumbled, rumpled, unbrushed. His
> gestures were abrupt, and sometimes violent, occasionally even awkward,
> yet more frequently gentle and graceful.[84]

When Hogg engaged him in conversation, he proved a lively and
stimulating talker, discoursing on both literature and science. The next
day Hogg saw him again, and again was charmed by his eloquence
(especially, this time, on science) though he had little sympathy (at
least in 1832) for his views. The two boys became fast friends, and went
for many walks, read together, and held endless discussions. On one
walk Shelley was attacked by a dog (but fortunately had Hogg along

to rescue him); on another they came across a boy beating an ass (and perhaps he would have beaten Shelley also had not Hogg intervened);[85] on a third occasion they met a lost and hungry child:

In one of our rambles we were traversing the bare, squalid, ugly, corn-yielding country, that lies, if I remember rightly, to the southwest of Oxford: the hollow road ascended a hill, and near the summit Shelley observed a female child leaning against the bank on the right: it was of a mean, dull, and unattractive aspect, and older than its stunted growth denoted. The morning, as well as the preceding night, had been rainy: it had cleared up at noon with a certain ungenial sunshine, and the afternoon was distinguished by that intense cold which sometimes, in the winter season, terminates such days. The little girl was oppressed by cold, by hunger, and by a vague feeling of abandonment. It was not easy to draw from her blue lips an intelligible history of her condition. Love, however, is at once credulous and apprehensive; and Shelley immediately decided that she had been deserted, and, with his wonted precipitation (for in the career of humanity his active spirit knew no pause), he proposed different schemes for the permanent relief of the poor foundling, and he hastily inquired which of them was the most expedient. I answered that it was desirable, in the first place, to try to procure some food, for of this the want was manifestly the most urgent. I then climbed the hill to reconnoitre, and observed a cottage close at hand, on the left of the road. With considerable difficulty—with a gentle violence, indeed—Shelley induced the child to accompany him thither. After much delay, we procured from the people of the place, who resembled the dull, uncouth and perhaps sullen, rustics of that district, some warm milk.

It was a strange spectacle to watch the young poet, whilst, with the enthusiastic and intensely earnest manner that characterizes the legitimate brethren of the celestial art—the heaven born and fiercely inspired sons of genuine poesy—holding the wooden bowl in one hand and the wooden spoon in the other, and kneeling on his left knee, that he might more certainly attain to her mouth, he urged and encouraged the torpid and timid child to eat. The hot milk was agreeable to the girl, and its effects were salutary; but she was obviously uneasy at the detention. Her uneasiness increased, and ultimately prevailed: we returned with her to the place where we had found her, Shelley bearing the bowl of milk in his hand. Here we saw some people anxiously looking for the child—a man and, I think, four women, strangers of the poorest class, of a mean, but not disreputable, appearance. As soon as the girl perceived them she was content, and taking the bowl from Shelley, she finished the milk without his help.

Meanwhile, one of the women explained the apparent desertion with a multitude of rapid words. They had come from a distance, and to spare the weary child the fatigue of walking farther, the day being at that time sunny, they left her to await their return; those unforeseen delays, which harass all, and especially the poor, in transacting business had detained them much longer than they had anticipated.

Such, in a few words, is the story, which was related in many, and which the little girl, who it was said, was somewhat deficient in understanding, as well as in stature, was unable to explain. So humble was the condition of these poor wayfaring folks, that they did not presume to offer thanks in words; but they often turned back, and with mute wonder gazed at Shelley, who, totally unconscious that he had done anything to excite surprise, returned with huge strides to the cottage, to restore the bowl and to pay for the milk.[86]

The anecdote is interesting in revealing Shelley's warm humanitarianism, and it is even more interesting as a study in Hogg's method. Hogg, we note, plays himself up and plays Shelley down. His assertion, that Shelley after seeing the child went off into a series of Utopian generalities—"he proposed schemes for the permanent relief of the poor foundling"—and had to be told by Hogg that she needed milk, is either sheer invention or, more likely, an exaggeration of a pose Shelley half-humorously adopted for Hogg's benefit. From all we know of Shelley's character in similar situations—Hunt's anecdote of him carrying the poor woman on his back to the shelter, or his charities in Marlow or his dyke building in Wales—his conduct was immediately practical; and this is the picture we get also from his letter to Hunt from Oxford.[87] Whatever the explanation, the central fact remains that Hogg has to fit Shelley into his preconceived portrait of the eccentric madcap. "Ordinary rules may guide ordinary men," he writes, "but the orbit of the child of genius is essentially eccentric." [88] So Shelley is put in the orbit; and in concentric and satisfying contrast stands the practical man-of-the-world Hogg. And along with this invention of detail come the ironical overtones of such phrases as "in the career of humanity his active spirit knew no pause," "the legitimate brethren of the celestial art," "the heaven born and fiercely inspired sons of genuine poesy." This is typical of Hogg. Shelley is always "the Poet," "the son of fancy," or, in contrast, "the poor fellow." As Humbert Wolfe remarks: "Hogg, as a matter of routine, refers to Shelley as 'the divine poet,' but in the same way as Antony referred to Brutus as 'an honourable man.' The more he exhibited the ridiculous aspects of Shelley, the more fervently he asserted his belief in his divinity." [89]

Of Shelley's academic work at Oxford we know little. He came up from Eton with a reputation as a classical scholar, and Hogg testifies that he had not lost his skill,[90] but the depressing routine and intellectual narrowness that was typical of academic Oxford in those days [91] had little to offer him. Of his extracurricular activities, however, there can be no doubt. He began immediately to continue the reputation he had achieved in his final months at Eton as a budding author by publishing two books of verse, *Original Poetry* by Victor and Cazire and *The Posthumous Fragments of Margaret Nicholson,* and a novel, *St. Irvyne;* and he entered upon a new career, that of political radical, by championing the cause of a persecuted Irish journalist, Peter Finnerty. These and other activities we find recorded in an interesting contemporary letter by Charles Kirkpatrick Sharpe, M.A., of Christ Church:

Talking of books, we have lately had a literary Sun shine forth upon us here, before whom our former luminaries must hide their undiminished heads—a Mr. Shelley, of University College, who lives upon arsenic, aquafortis, half-an-hour's sleep in the night, and is desperately in love with the memory of Margaret Nicholson. He hath published what he terms the Posthumous Poems, printed for the benefit of Mr. Peter Finnerty, which, I am grieved to say, though stuffed full of treason, is extremely dull; but the author is a great genius, and if he be not clapped up in Bedlam or hanged, will certainly prove one of the sweetest swans on the tuneful margin of the Cherwell . . . Shelley's style is much like that of Moore burlesqued; for Frank is a very foul-mouthed fellow, and Charlotte, one of the most impudent brides that I ever met with in a book. Our Apollo next came out with a prose pamphlet in praise of Atheism, which I have not as yet seen, and there appeared a monstrous Romance in one volume, called St. Irvyne or the Rosicrucian. Here is another pearl of price! all the heroes are confirmed robbers and causeless murderers, while the heroines glide *en chemise* through the streets of Geneva, tap at the palazzo doors of their sweethearts, and on being denied admittance leave no cards, but run home to their warm beds, and kill themselves. If your lordship would like to see this treasure I will send it. Shelley's last exhibition is a poem on the State of Public Affairs. I fear, my dear lord, you will be quite disgusted with all this stuff.[92]

Sharpe—later a writer for the *Quarterly Review*—had no more sympathy for Shelley's radical activities or writings than did Hogg, and his air of amused condescension is due in part to this and in part to the traditional feeling of M.A.'s toward freshmen. In spite of his amusement, however, Sharpe is clearly a little startled by the phenomenon of a freshman producing, within his first few months, two books of poems, a novel, and a pamphlet, and engaging in a "free speech" campaign. We learn from Sharpe's letter, as we do not from Hogg, that Shelley had made his mark on the intellectual atmosphere of Oxford. He was clearly being regarded by the powers that be with some wonderment and doubtless also with some apprehension; and by his fellow students with a mixture of awe and amusement.

Sharpe's picture of Shelley's reputation is confirmed in another account of him as he appeared at this time, in the (1841) reminiscences of Joseph Gibbons Merle, later a London editor, who met Shelley through a mutual acquaintance, Edward Graham, a protégé of Timothy:

Shelley had been frequently described to me by his admiring friend Graham as a very superior being—as a poet, as a philosopher. Shelley, I knew, had already published several effusions which had attracted considerable notice; I was the poor parent of one solitary production, and that a string of wretched verses in an ephemeral publication. My pride dreaded humiliation; and such was the effect of the contrast which I had made in my own mind between Shelley and myself, that when Graham, who received me at the door of the house in which he lodged, opened the door of the room on the first floor, where Shelley was waiting for me, my legs trembled with nervous agitation. But short indeed was the suffering inflicted upon me by the terrors of my imagination, and the absurd pride with which I had in vain endeavoured to arm myself. The impressive eye of the young poet beamed upon me in all the radiance imparted by his benevolent heart; he grasped my hand with the fervour of old acquaintance, and in a second we were friends.

I have no *technica memoria* to assist me in a description of our first interview. I remember, however, that we passed three hours in free and unrestrained conversation. Shelley discoursed much of literature, and urged me to persevere in my poetical wanderings.[93]

Merle's picture has a special value as a balance to Hogg and Sharpe. Merle had no impression of a volatile eccentric but of an earnest young intellectual, enjoying considerable repute among his fellows. He is of a warm and open nature and, although unmistakably a gentleman, completely unaffected in manner. And Merle's picture is no doubt true. This is Shelley as he must have appeared to any intelligent, sympathetic observer. But the pictures of Sharpe and Hogg possess truth also; for Shelley, in his drive for recognition, had certainly added eccentricities to his natural intensity. What neither Hogg nor Sharpe perceived, however, was that these characteristics were peripheral and not central.

Shelley's fame had spread well beyond the walls of University College and brief though his career at Oxford was, he must have been recognized as one of its outstanding undergraduate intellectuals, a radical in politics and religion, a promising author. And this radical reputation is borne out in the observations of others. Elizabeth Grant, the niece of the master of University College, noted that Shelley was "the ringleader of every species of mischief within our grave walls," was "very insubordinate, always infringing some rule," and "proceeded so far as to paste up atheistical squibs on the chapel doors."[94] The worthy Slatters, booksellers of Oxford, were alarmed and brought in "a literary friend, then residing in Oxford, to meet him in order to canvass and combat his extraordinary opinions."[95] J. J. Stockdale, London publisher of *St. Irvyne,* was alarmed also and wrote to inform Sir Timothy that his son intended to publish "a Metaphysical Essay, in support of atheism."[96]

Sharpe's letter was written on March 15. On March 25, there occurred the culminating event of Shelley's brief career at Oxford—his expulsion.

Shelley, we are informed by Hogg, carried on an extensive correspondence on controversial matters.[97] He would, for instance, write to a clergyman under an assumed name naively asking certain leading questions. When the clergyman, in all innocence, answered, he would be subjected to a barrage of sulphurous dialectic. It was apparently to further this activity that Shelley and Hogg wrote *The Necessity of Atheism.* This little pamphlet was to be included in letters to divines and others throughout the country. Unfortunately Shelley also filled up the store window of his Oxford booksellers with copies while the proprietors were out, and the display was noted by the Reverend John Walker, fellow of New College and later vicar of Hornchurch, Sussex. This gentleman immediately summoned the proprietors and demanded that the offending pamphlets be destroyed; "whereupon," Slatter solemnly records, "they proceeded into a back kitchen and burned them, in this gentleman's presence."[98] Even here, perhaps, the incident might have rested had not Shelley sent a copy to the Reverend Edward Copleston, professor of poetry and fellow of Oriel. Copleston was famed as the champion publicist of Oxford conservatism, a reputation he had achieved the previous year (1810) when the *Edinburgh Review* attacked the university as the intellectual fortress of medievalism. Copleston rushed to the defence with several pamphlets from which the following may be culled as representative: "The scheme of Revelation, we think, is closed, and we expect no new light on earth to break in upon us. Oxford must guard that sacred citadel."[99]

This vigorous crusader, discovering the pamphlet was Shelley's, took it around to the master and fellows of University College, and Shelley was summoned before the college authorities. Several accounts exist of the succeeding interview, one by Hogg, and some emanating from Shelley himself.[100] Hogg's account, as Edmund Blunden points out,[101] is obviously colored; and those coming from Shelley contain varying degrees of self-dramatization (especially that told to Peacock, where the interview becomes metamorphosed into a public trial with Shelley delivering a Ciceronian oration). The most faithful account seems to be one written down but a little time after the event by C. J. Ridley, a fellow student of Shelley and later a junior fellow of the college:

It was announced one morning at a breakfast party, towards the end of Lent Term (March 25, 1810 [an error for 1811]), that Percy Bysshe Shelley, who had recently become a member of University College, was to be called before a meeting of the common room for being the supposed author of a pamphlet called "The Necessity of Atheism." This anonymous work, consisting of not many pages, had been studiously sent to most of the dignitaries of the university and to others more or less connected with Oxford. The meeting took place the same day, and it was understood that the pamphlet, together with some notes sent with it, in which the supposed author's handwriting appeared identified with that of P. B. S., was placed before him. He was asked if he could or would deny the obnoxious production as his. No direct reply was given either in the affirmative or negative. Shelley having quitted the room, T.J. Hogg immediately appeared, voluntarily on his part, to state that if Shelley had anything to do with it, he (Hogg) was equally implicated, and desired his share of the penalty, whatever was inflicted. It has always been supposed that Hogg wrote the preface. Towards the afternoon a large paper bearing the college seal, and signed by the Master and Dean, was affixed to the hall door, declaring that the two offenders were publicly expelled from the college *for contumacy in refusing to answer certain questions put to them*. The aforesaid two made themselves as conspicuous as possible by great singularity of dress, and by walking up and down the centre of the quadrangle as if proud of their anticipated fate. I believe no one regretted their departure for there were but few, if any, who were not afraid of Shelley's strange and fantastic pranks, and the still stranger opinions he was known to entertain; but all acknowledged him to have been very good-humoured and of a kind disposition. T.J. Hogg had intellectual powers to a great extent, but unfortunately, misdirected. He was not popular.[102]

Shelley, then, was ostensibly expelled for refusing to affirm or deny that he had written *The Necessity of Atheism,* and Hogg, co-author of the pamphlet, was expelled for his own generous admission that if any guilt fell on Shelley it should be shared by him. Behind these formal charges, however, the picture is pretty clearly that of a group of conservative administrators getting rid of a couple of young radicals. Medwin informs us that when Shelley told him the news he was not surprised, "having been led to augur such a close to his collegiate career from the Syllabus [*The Necessity of Atheism*] and the Posthumous Works of Peg Nicholson" [103] and Hogg's account of his own appearance before the master and fellows is revealing:

> The angry and troubled air of men, assembled to commit injustice according to established forms, was then new to me; but a native instinct told me, as soon as I entered the room, that it was an affair of party; that whatever could conciliate the favour of patrons was to be done without scruple; and whatever could tend to impede preferment was to be brushed away without remorse.[104]

No doubt Shelley's radical poetry in the *Margaret Nicholson* volume had disturbed the authorities, as well, perhaps, as had certain designedly shocking passages in his novels; but a much more important factor must have been his championing of the Irish radical, Peter Finnerty. The Finnerty case—to be further noted in the next chapter—was a national issue, one that was rocking the country and which helped to bring about the downfall of the Tory ministry. Shelley's attempts to establish a center of controversy on it in Oxford, parallel to that in London, must have been viewed with displeasure in high places, and Hogg's hint—"an affair of party"—that political motives were behind the expulsion probably had foundation. The publication of *The Necessity of Atheism* was only the culminating step in a series of affronts to authority, all of which led cumulatively to the expulsion.

Putting together our information from Hogg, Sharpe, Slatter, Merle, Miss Grant, and Ridley, we can build up a picture of Shelley at Oxford. He is famed, as he had been in his last months at Eton, as an undergraduate novelist and poet, but is now becoming known as an active young radical. An observer meeting him would see an abnormally slim, bright-eyed young gentleman, his speech and manners those of the English upper class, yet lacking all affectation, and understandingly quick to put others at their ease. He is generally in high spirits, his humor bubbling and puckish. Yet, in argument—which he loves—he is sharp, logical, dialectical, a formidable opponent. His reading knowledge seems unbelievable for a boy of eighteen as he ranges easily from chemistry to politics to metaphysics to literature. As the argument grows his voice rises to an unpleasant pitch in excitement; a shrewd observer might perceive behind the excitement a ceaseless drive to penetrate to truth in every field. A drive strangely combined, at times, with a tendency to dramatize and invent. He might sense, too, an unusual capacity for tense emotions. The boy, however, seems completely fearless, not only intellectually but morally, and he has a true dignity arising from his convictions: "He had great moral courage, and feared nothing, but what was base, and false, and low . . . Shelley said to me when leaving Oxford under a cloud: "'Halliday, I am come to say good-bye to you, if you are not afraid to be seen with me.'" [105] He has, one finds, a reputation for eccentricity; he is, at times, quick and erratic in his movements; he sleeps little; he delights in "fantastic pranks"; he makes sudden exits and entrances; he gives the impression of a kind of coiled-spring energy. Beneath these surface eccentricities and mannerisms one finds sincerity, honesty, strength of character, and a real friendliness of spirit—"good-humoured and of a kind disposition." "I never saw Shelley but once," wrote Thomas Barnes, later editor of *The Times,* "he was then a student of Oxford. A friend of mine who was fellow of Wadham invited me to spend a few days with him: he was a townsman of Shelley and very intimate with him: the consequence was that we spent a long evening together and I received an impression of the frankness and uprightness of Shelley's character which I have retained ever since. He was then a fine-looking youth, with one of those ingenuous countenances which ought never to look old." [106]

EARLIEST WRITINGS

During the period we have been considering biographically Shelley underwent an intellectual transformation. He entered Syon House a wide-eyed youngster obsessed with the mysteries of the occult; he left Oxford a young radical dedicated to the service of humanity. And, although he was to go through many developments in his life, was to add vastly to his knowledge, and to develop new subtleties of understanding and taste, it was in this period that the foundations were laid. And of this Shelley himself was aware.

I am [he wrote to William Godwin in 1812] the son of a man of fortune in Sussex. The habits of thinking of my father and myself never coincided. Passive obedience was inculcated and enforced in my childhood. I was required to love, because it was *my duty* to love; it is scarcely necessary to remark, that coercion obviated its own intention. I was haunted with a passion for the wildest and most extravagant romances. Ancient books of Chemistry and Magic were perused with an enthusiasm of wonder, almost amounting to belief. My sentiments were unrestrained by anything within

me; external impediments were numerous, and strongly applied; their effect
was merely temporary.

From a reader, I became a writer of romances; before the age of seventeen
I had published two, "St. Irvyne" and "Zastrozzi," each of which, though
quite uncharacteristic of me as now I am, yet serves to mark the state of
my mind at the period of their composition. I shall desire them to be sent
to you: do not, however, consider this any obligation to yourself to mis-
apply your valuable time.

It is now a period of more than two years since first I saw your inestimable
book on "Political Justice"; it opened to my mind fresh and more extensive
views; it materially influenced my character, and I rose from its perusal a
wiser and a better man. I was no longer the votary of romance; till then I
had existed in an ideal world—now I found that in this universe of ours
was enough to excite the interest of the heart, enough to employ the discussions of reason; I beheld, in short, that I had duties to perform. Conceive
the effect which the "Political Justice" would have upon a mind before
jealous of its independence and participating somewhat singularly in a peculiar susceptibility.[107]

Shelley, then, realized that the main development in his life during
the 1808–1811 period was the transformation from an ivory tower
romanticism to a consciousness of social problems and duties.

But, while he states the central point well, the transformation itself,
he does not accurately represent the stages of that transformation. He
implies that it was Godwin's book alone which changed him and that
he moved overnight from his "votary of romance" stage to that of Godwinian egalitarianism. But this was not so. Shelley went through at
least two intermediary stages between these extremes, and we can take
his failure to mention them here as part of the desire of a young disciple
to flatter the master as "the onlie begetter" of his views. In a later letter
to Godwin, Shelley himself informs us of one of these stages:

I did not truly *think* and *feel*, however, until I read "Political Justice,"
though my thoughts and feelings, after this period, have been more painful,
anxious and vivid—more inclined to action and less to theory. Before I was
a republican: Athens appeared to me the model of governments; but afterwards, Athens bore in my mind the same relation to perfection that Great
Britain did to Athens.[108]

Shelley did not leap straight from the Gothic novel to egalitarianism.
He was a "republican" before he was an egalitarian, and republicanism
was, next to Godwinism, the most radical doctrine of the age. The republican advocated the abolition of the monarchy and the House of

Lords, by revolution if necessary, and the transformation of England into a democratic republic on the American model. Shelley, therefore, before he had encountered Godwin at all had advanced to a high point of radical thought.

But how did Shelley arrive at so advanced a position as republicanism in the first place? A man would not normally go from horror novels to republicanism without some intermediate stage. In Shelley's case there clearly was such a stage, a stage which I shall call the Whig-Reform stage. In this stage, Shelley was a follower of the Whigs and then of the "moderate" reformers, Sir Francis Burdett and Leigh Hunt. The objectives of this group were not nearly so drastic as those of the republicans. They advocated the extension of the franchise to all taxable property owners, the abolition of the rotten borough system, and certain other measures designed to weaken the hold of the aristocracy on the House of Commons, but they were for retaining the monarchy and the House of Lords. They were, indeed, simply reviving the old demands of the Whigs, which the Whigs themselves had repudiated.

"Votary of romance," Whig-reformer, republican, Godwinian egalitarian; we must not expect to find a simple transition from stage to stage; the "votary of romance" was also a young Whig (but one to whom political affairs seemed of secondary importance); the Godwinian egalitarian was still a reformer and republican (and still, indeed, something of a Whig); but these are the essential components and stages of the young Shelley.

The works Shelley produced as a "votary of romance," we have already noted: *Zastrozzi* and *St. Irvyne or the Rosicrucian; Original Poetry* (by Victor and Cazire) and *The Wandering Jew*.[109] The novels are "Gothic" novels; the poems "terror" narratives (*The Wandering Jew* and some of *Original Poetry*) and sentimental lyrics (others of the Victor and Cazire volume). That Shelley, as a youngster, was genuinely interested in the mysterious and the occult, we have ample evidence, and in his novels he was, from time to time, carried away by his subject—especially by the character of Ginotti in *St. Irvyne*—but he wrote largely with his tongue in his cheek—delighting, at times, in parodying his own style— [110] aware, as he was writing the novels, of their inherent ridiculousness, but interested in a quick, schoolboy fame. Less than two years later he was apologetically describing them as "distempered" and "unoriginal," the product of an "intellectual sickness." [111] They have interest only as illustrating the early development of a great poet.

It is, however, important also to recognize that the Gothic novel was an established literary genre in the early nineteenth century. Shelley was writing in a tradition that had attracted some of the most talented writers of the age.

The main conventions and devices for the genre were established in its first important specimen, Horace Walpole's *Castle of Otranto:* the winding underground passage, the gloomy, Gothic castle, the skeleton, daggers, and stabbings, the avenging ghost (here of gigantic size), the persecuted heroine. The most famous example of the type in Shelley's day was Matthew Gregory Lewis's *The Monk,* and it was from Lewis and his school (especially "Rosa Matilda") [112] that Shelley learned the tricks of the trade. Lewis—also the author of Shelley's favorite *Tales of Terror*—was, in fact, the most important single influence in the "votary of romance" period. In *The Monk,* Ambrosio, the Monk, is seduced by the evil Matilda (who enters the monastery disguised as a boy), revels in her voluptuous charms (in some detail), pursues, and after two unsuccessful attempts finally rapes the virtuous Antonia in an underground vault.

With every moment the friar's passion became more ardent, and Antonia's terror more intense. She struggled to disengage herself from his arms. Her exertions were unsuccessful; and, finding that Ambrosio's conduct became still freer, she shrieked for assistance with all her strength. The aspect of the vault, the pale glimmering of the lamp, the surrounding obscurity, the sight of the tomb, and the objects of mortality which met her eyes on either side, were ill calculated to inspire her with those emotions by which the friar was agitated.

He clasped her to his bosom almost lifeless with terror, and faint with struggling. He stifled her cries with kisses, treated her with the rudeness of an unprincipled barbarian, proceeded from freedom to freedom, and in the violence of his lustful delirium, wounded and bruised her tender limbs. Heedless of her tears, cries and entreaties, he gradually made himself master of her person, and desisted not from his prey, till he had accomplished his crime and the dishonour of Antonia.[113]

In the end Matilda turns out to be not a human being at all but an agent of the devil, and in the final scene the devil himself appears to claim the monk for his own.

Here we have the essence of the Lewis method of neurotic sensation-mongering, for which the youthful Shelley scornfully passed by the more genteel horrors of Lewis's main rival, Mrs. Radcliffe.[114] Shelley, however, although he made full use of the shocking and voluptuous, never achieved the tumescent heights of sadistic horror scaled by the master.

The plot of *Zastrozzi* (probably written between March and August, 1809, when Shelley was sixteen) [115] runs as follows: Zastrozzi, a towering and darkly scowling villain (in the Gothic tradition), is pursuing the unfortunate Verezzi, whose father long ago had wronged Zastrozzi's mother. Verezzi is also being pursued (though with a different purpose) by the shameless Matilda, but he will not yield to her advances because he is in love with the gentle Julia. Matilda and Zastrozzi collaborate on their plans; Zastrozzi is to find Verezzi for her and to murder Julia. (He intends, all the time, to murder Verezzi when he does get him, but he does not tell Matilda that.) He does not succeed in murdering Julia, but Matilda falsely informs Verezzi that Julia is dead anyway and Verezzi marries her. After their marriage, however, Julia shows up one night; Verezzi, stricken with horror at the thought of his marriage to Matilda which prevents him from possessing the noble Julia, commits suicide, and Matilda murders Julia on the spot. Matilda and Zastrozzi are taken before the inquisition and are executed.

The flavor of this not untypical production of the horror school can, perhaps, best be communicated by an extract from the climactic scene of the murder of Julia. Verezzi has just expired, and Matilda regards his corpse with horror; Julia has fainted.

She [Matilda] advanced to the lifeless corse of Verezzi—she plucked the dagger from his bosom—it was stained with his life's-blood, which trickled fast from the point to the floor. She raised it on high, and impiously called upon the God of nature to doom her to endless torments, should Julia survive her vengeance.

She advanced towards her victim, who lay bereft of sense on the floor; she shook her rudely, and grasping a handful of her dishevelled hair, raised her from the earth.

"Knowest thou me?" exclaimed Matilda, in frantic passion—"knowest thou the injured Laurentini? Behold this dagger, reeking with my husband's blood—behold that pale corse, in whose now cold breast, thy accursed image revelling, impelled to commit the deed which deprives me of happiness for ever."

Julia's senses, roused by Matilda's violence, returned. She cast her eyes upwards, with a timid expression of apprehension, and beheld the infuriate Matilda convulsed by fiercest passion, and a blood-stained dagger raised aloft, threatening instant death.

"Die! detested wretch," exclaimed Matilda, in a paroxysm of rage, as she violently attempted to bathe the stiletto in the life-blood of her rival;

but Julia starting aside, the weapon slightly wounded her neck, and the ensanguined stream stained her alabaster bosom.

She fell on the floor, but suddenly starting up, attempted to escape her bloodthirsty persecutor.

Nerved anew by this futile attempt to escape her vengeance, the ferocious Matilda seized Julia's floating hair, and holding her back with fiend-like strength, stabbed her in a thousand places; and, with exulting pleasure, again and again buried the dagger to the hilt in her body, even after all remains of life were annihilated.

At last the passions of Matilda, exhausted by their own violence, sank into a deadly calm: she threw the dagger violently from her, and contemplated the terrific scene before her with a sullen gaze.[116]

The plot of Shelley's second novel, *St. Irvyne or The Rosicrucian,* by "a Gentleman of the University of Oxford" is more complicated. The reason is that Shelley really has two plots in one novel, plot number one concerning the pursuit of the hero, Wolfstein, by the sorcerous Ginotti; plot number two detailing the misadventures of one Eloise de St. Irvyne. The novel was probably written in the main between the fall of 1809 and the spring of 1810.[117]

Plot number one runs roughly as follows. In the opening scene Wolfstein stands on a high precipice contemplating suicide but is prevented by the entry of a band of monks; the monks are attacked by bandits who lead Wolfstein to their underground cavern and he becomes one of them. One day the bandits capture the beautiful Megalena; Wolfstein poisons the bandit chieftain and is saved from death only by a mysterious member of the band called Ginotti. Wolfstein and Megalena escape together. One night they are confronted by Ginotti, who makes Wolfstein swear that he will, when requested, listen to his life's story and give him proper rites of burial.

The reason for this strange oath is not immediately apparent and becomes so only when we learn that Ginotti is a Rosicrucian. As a Rosicrucian he has learned the secret of eternal life, but, like the Rosicrucian in Godwin's novel *St. Leon* (from which Shelley took the idea) [118] and the hero of Maturin's *Melmouth the Wanderer* (1820), he has grown tired of eternal life. However, in accordance with Rosicrucian rules and regulations, he cannot die unless he finds someone to whom he can pass on the secret.

Ginotti, having extracted the oath from Wolfstein, leaves, and his occasional and sinister appearances and disappearances do not constitute more than a minor diversion in Wolfstein's life (which turns out to be

quite a merry one). He first seduces Megalena and is, in turn, almost
seduced by the shameless Olympia. One evening Megalena catches them
together and demands that Wolfstein murder Olympia. Wolfstein
obediently goes to Olympia's house to carry out his deed but the sight
of her white bosom distracts him and he is unable to conclude his
mission. Olympia, however, awakes and on being informed that he
does not love her obligingly commits suicide.

Following this domestic disturbance the sinister Ginotti (suitably
cloaked) comes to demand fulfillment of his bargain. He tells Wolfstein his life story and demands that he meet him at the "ruined abbey"
near the castle of St. Irvyne, there to receive the dread secret of eternal
life. Wolfstein proceeds thither, but things do not go according to plan.
He first stumbles across the dead body of Megalena (there is no intimation as to how she got there), and then, when Ginotti gives him the
secret elixir, instead of Ginotti alone dying and Wolfstein receiving
eternal life, they both die. The reason for this reversal of customary
Rosicrucian procedure seems obscure.

Such is plot number one. Chapter VII begins rather abruptly (chapters V and VI are simply omitted) with the introduction of one Eloise
St. Irvyne who is pictured as returning to the castle of St. Irvyne [119]
after six years of terrible misfortunes, the history of which we are now
to witness. We are, therefore, invited to return to the beginning of the
six-year period. The first misfortune to befall Eloise was the death of
her mother in Geneva. Her second is to be seduced by the villainous
Nempere. Her third is to be handed over by Nempere for a gambling
debt to an Englishman named (rather strangely) Chevalier Mountfort,[120] who, in turn, hands her over to an Irishman named Fitzeustace,
and then, for some unknown reason, murders Nempere. Her life, however, ends happily (as Shelley confirmed in a letter to his publisher),
for she and Fitzeustace marry and settle in England: so we are to suppose that Shelley changed his plot somewhere in the middle but then
omitted to take out the touching scene in Chapter VII of Eloise (six
years later) crawling back in misery to the castle of St. Irvyne. It remains only to be noted what we are informed rather startlingly in the
final paragraph that Eloise of plot number two is the sister of Wolfstein of plot number one and that the villainous Nempere of plot number two is the same person as the villainous Ginotti of plot number
one. The only difficulty with this interesting legerdemain is that if
Nempere and Ginotti are the same person, he is killed twice, once by
Mountfort in plot two and then again by the secret elixir in plot number

one. Nor is there any indication how this suddenly revealed relationship of characters makes any real connection between the two plots. There does not seem to be any interrelationship, either in action or in motivation, between the two even if Eloise is Wolfstein's sister and Nempere is really Ginotti.[121]

What is the explanation for these discrepancies, the double death of Ginotti, the inconsistency in the real and indicated conclusion of the story of Eloise, the hurried attempt (in two bald sentences "Ginotti is Nempere. Eloise is the sister of Wolfstein") to link the two plots in the final paragraph? There can be no doubt that Professor A. M. D. Hughes is correct in his suggestion that during the composition of the novel Shelley's interests in political and philosophical subjects began to rise and the whole thing began to seem rather futile to him, so that he desired only to finish it up as rapidly as possible and get on to work which seemed of some significance[122] (the campaign for Finnerty, the anti-war poem of the Margaret Nicholson group, *The Necessity of Atheism,* the political organization of which he wrote to Hunt, etc.). There are, we may note, no such inconsistencies in the earlier *Zastrozzi.*

The earlier novel, however, in spite of this advantage is not superior to *St. Irvyne* on all counts. The style of *St. Irvyne* is noticeably more mature than that of *Zastrozzi* and the situations more roundly developed; some scenes, such as the opening scene of Wolfstein on the precipice, contain a certain Gothic luridness that would rank with some of the better passages in Lewis or Mrs. Radcliffe or (later) Maturin,[123] and the character of Ginotti has a compelling mysteriousness which the shallower Zastrozzi does not. On the other hand *Zastrozzi* contains a schoolboyish verve which is lacking in *St. Irvyne,* whose tangle of plots and patched inconsistencies often give it a rather dragging pace. One other point of difference between the two novels is the increased attempt at the exploitation of voluptuous sensationalism in *St. Irvyne.* In *Zastrozzi* there is only one seduction; that of Matilda by Verezzi; in *St. Irvyne* there are three: Megalena by Wolfstein, Eloise by Nempere, Eloise by Fitzeustace; and one attempted seduction: Wolfstein by Olympia. That Shelley is here following the "Monk" Lewis tradition and hoping to exploit its type of sex melodrama for added sales there can be no doubt, especially in view of his comment to his friend Graham that the (rather heated) "Epithalamium" in the Margaret Nicholson volume would "make it sell like wildfire."[124]

If Shelley's Gothic novels are bad, his horror poetry written in the same period is worse. Of *Original Poetry* by Victor (Shelley) and

Cazire (Elizabeth Shelley) [125] a correct judgment was given by an outspoken contemporary critic in *The Poetical Register* for 1810–1811: "There is no 'original poetry' in this volume; there is nothing in it but downright scribble." [126] The poems fall into four classes: two girlish "Letters" by Elizabeth; ten sentimental lyrics; four "horror" poems; and one poem on a political theme—"The Irishman's Song." Of the lyrics, three are clearly by Elizabeth as they are paralleled in some verses which Shelley gave to Hogg as examples of Elizabeth's poetry.[127] Two of them (often taken as by Shelley) [128] are apparently assurances to Harriet Grove by Elizabeth of the love of her brother. (Elizabeth later, we remember, attempted to bring Harriet back to Shelley.) As this gives a total of five out of sixteen poems to Elizabeth, it is probable— if "Victor's" name in the first place means anything—that the remaining eleven are by Shelley. These eleven include the four horror poems (the last of them interpolated in *St. Irvyne*),[129] "The Irishman's Song," and seven lyrics. Of the lyrics, only one—"Come——! sweet is the hour" —is clearly to Harriet Grove, and the rest (with the exception of a feebly rollicking imitation of Scott, "Ah! grasp the dire dagger and couch the fell spear") are adolescent *Weltschmerz:* "Despair," "Sorrow," "Hope," "Oh! what is the gain of restless care," "Fierce roars the midnight storm." The main influence on the lyrics—also apparent on the young Byron—is Moore's *Irish Melodies.* They are no better and no worse than most adolescent verse. The main influence on the horror poems is "Monk" Lewis; *Saint Edmund's Eve,* indeed, was simply lifted from Lewis's *Tales of Terror and Wonder* (more probably by Shelley than by Elizabeth); *Ghasta or The Avenging Demon* is based on the incident of the exorcism of the bleeding nun by the Wandering Jew in *The Monk* (even to the echoing of the lines: "Thou art mine and I am thine"); and a third poem *The Revenge* is also derived from *The Monk.*[130]

The Wandering Jew, although combining the worst features of *Original Poems* in long narrative form, is important as Shelley's first attempt at a full length poem, and one which he regarded with considerable seriousness, for, although it was completed in the main in the winter and spring of 1810—when he was also at work on *St. Irvyne*— he revised it as late as November, 1810, when he was "a Gentleman of the University of Oxford" and beginning to turn his mind to higher things, and he almost certainly took it with him to Edinburgh in August, 1811, to seek a publisher.[131]

The poem falls into four cantos. Canto One reveals a mysterious horseman approaching a convent in which four nuns are dragging a novice to the altar in a scene slightly reminiscent of *The Monk*. The novice escapes their clutches and is seized by the mysterious horseman who gallops off with her to a mountainous castle, promising eternal love as they go.

In Canto Two, Paulo (for such was the stranger's name) and his "bride" (Rosa) are joined in the castle by Paulo's friend Victorio. Paulo is moody but is soothed by the music of Rosa, who sings him a mournful ballad of the specter of a betrayed girl who committed suicide. He then announces that he will tell his life story.

Canto III deals with this story. Paulo, it turns out, is, in reality, the Wandering Jew.[132] Sixteen hundred years before he had cursed Christ and was condemned by God to wander endlessly on the earth. He tells— in a versified form of a prose story Shelley quotes in the notes—of his futile attempt to achieve death:

> I have cast myself from the mountain's height,
> Above was day—below was night;
> The substantial clouds that lower'd beneath
> Bore my detested form;
> They whirl'd it above the volcanic breath,
> And the meteors of the storm; . . .
> Oh! would that I had waked no more!
> Vain wish! I lived again to feel
> Torments more fierce than those of hell!!

But still he cannot die, for he is "doomed by fate to stand, a monument to the Eternal's ire." He has a vision of an angelic form (really the devil) who tempts him to sell his soul to Satan (a scene paralleled in *St. Irvyne* and perhaps suggested by *The Monk*) [133] but he refuses.

In Canto Four, the poem ends rather obscurely. Victorio has fallen in love with Rosa and to save her from the Wandering Jew visits a monstrous witch (an incident, Medwin tells us, from the now lost juvenile novel, *The Nightmare,* that he and Shelley wrote together),[134] who summons up Satan who gives Victorio a "potent drug." This, one would presume, he intended to use on the Wandering Jew, but, in the end, it is Rosa who dies, and Victorio curses the "futile power" of the "false fiend." We can only assume that the devil's poison would not kill the Wandering Jew, but did, by some misadventure, kill Rosa, a confusion and motif paralleling the ending of *St. Irvyne*. Both works, we may note, deal with the theme of the undying mortal, a theme which continued to fascinate Shelley.

All in all, as we look back on Shelley's "votary of romance" period it is a dreary spectacle in spite of glimmerings, here and there, of the Shelley to come; and as we view his macabre collection of avenging demons, sinister Rosicrucians, and seductions by the brace, we cannot but heave a sigh of relief that he finally (via Godwin or any one else) found that he had social "duties to perform" which would, henceforth, form the basis for his thinking and writing.

II   FROM FOX TO GODWIN

The Posthumous Poems of Margaret Nicholson
The Necessity of Atheism

"To defecate life of its misery and its evil was the ruling passion of his soul; he dedicated to it every power of his mind, every pulsation of his heart. He looked on political freedom as the direct agent to affect the happiness of mankind. . . . These characteristics breathe throughout his poetry." [1] So wrote Shelley's widow, some seventeen years after his death. And she wrote truly. The core of Shelley's poetry is his philosophy of social revolution. This philosophy takes many forms. Sometimes it centers around the theme of the ascent of humanity, as in *Queen Mab* or *Prometheus Unbound* or *The Triumph of Life;* sometimes it manifests itself in more or less subtle forms of social protest, as in *Adonais* or *The Cenci* or *Charles I;* sometimes it directly takes political shape, as in *The Mask of Anarchy* or *Swellfoot the Tyrant;* sometimes, as in *Hellas* or *The Revolt of Islam* or the "Ode to Liberty," it expends itself in panoramic surveys of a world passing through the birth pangs of war and revolution; it weaves its way, sometimes directly, sometimes indirectly, into the personal poems, *Rosalind and Helen, Julian and Maddalo, Lines Written Among the Euganean Hills, Epipsychidion;* it is the very spirit of the "Ode to the West Wind," and its breath is present in the eternal soarings of the skylark. Our present task is to uncover the roots from which this flowering grew: without which it would not have grown.

WHIG AND REFORMER

The first fact to strike one in this search is that Shelley came from a Whig family. His grandfather, Sir Bysshe, was, as we are informed in *The Shelley Memorials,* "a staunch Whig, and on that ground obtained a baronetcy from the short-lived Whig administration of that year" [2] (i.e., the famous "all the talents" ministry of 1806, the last Whig ministry until Grey's in 1830). Sir Bysshe, as one of the great landowners in Sussex, aligned himself with one of the leading Whigs of the county, the Duke of Norfolk. "The family connections of Mr. Shelley," writes Leigh Hunt, "belonged to a small party in the House of Commons, itself belonging to another party. They were Whig aristocrats, voting in the interest of the Duke of Norfolk." [3]

That Sir Bysshe moved to the liberal side in politics simply because of the Duke's influence is unlikely. The Whigs, although traditionally the mercantile party and opposed by the large landed interests, were supported by a minority of these interests connected with the wool trade, for this trade had brought about a community of agricultural and manufacturing objectives. [4] And Sussex in the years of Shelley's boyhood "supported about three hundred thousand of the best sheep in England" many of them doubtless on the extensive Shelley estates, estates well filled also with another product for manufacture—timber. [5]

Furthermore, Sir Bysshe was far from being a traditional English aristocrat. His fortune, as we have seen, had been built up rapidly, and he must have been looked down upon by his more elegantly pedigreed contemporaries. He had been born in America, the younger son of a younger son who had there worked "in trade," his mother was an American (perhaps not too happily received in England), and he himself had spent his formative first eight years in America. And this American influence was apparently feared by the Shelley family, for Bysshe's grandmother, in her will, made the year after his return from New Jersey as a boy, ordered that he be given a "gentleman-like education" and never "be sent or put to sea on any account or pretence whatsoever, or by any persons whomsoever." [6] These combined influences would certainly suffice in themselves to move Sir Bysshe toward the Whigs rather than the Tories, and even to the end of his life, we learn from Merle, who visited Horsham in 1811, he exhibited strange "democratic" ways:

Sir Bysshe, although a man of large property, rarely mingled with persons of his own rank in society. . . . The baronet lived in a small house near the town-hall at Horsham, almost without attendance. Sir Bysshe was as indifferent to his personal appearance as he was to his style of living. He wore a round frock, and spent a portion of his time in the tap-room of the Swann Inn at Horsham,—not drinking, indeed, with its frequenters, but arguing with them in politics. [7]

Something of the flavor of his talk can be gathered from a letter that his erring grandson sent to him after the double crisis of expulsion and elopement:

I am accustomed to speak my opinion unreservedly; this has occasioned me some misfortunes, but I do not therefore cease to speak as I think. Language is given us to express ideas . . . he who fetters it is a BIGOT and a TYRANT, from these have my misfortunes arisen . . .

I expect from your liberality and justice no unfavourable construction of what fools in power would denominate *insolence*.[8]

Shelley would not have written thus, in endeavoring to win his grandfather over to his side, if such terms as "bigot" and "tyrant" and "fools in power" had not been part of the old democrat's habitual talk.

As a result of the family connection with the Duke of Norfolk, Bysshe's son, Timothy, not only joined the Whig Party but became a Member of Parliament. The story of his securing this seat is an interesting one and may be found recounted in detail in the voluminous *Parliamentary History of the Ancient Borough of Horsham*.[9] The Horsham seat had for many years belonged to a local aristocratic family whose representative in the late eighteenth century was a Lady Irwin. In the year 1787, Thomas Charles Medwin—father of Shelley's cousin and biographer—then a young lawyer at Horsham ("an expert on Manorial Law and Custom")[10] and steward for the Duke of Norfolk, informed the Duke that it might be possible, by buying up sufficient vote-carrying property in the town, to wrest the control of the borough away from the Irwin interest. The Duke, following his advice, began buying up property and decided on Timothy Shelley as his candidate; unfortunately Lady Irwin got wind of the scheme and began buying also. The result can be gathered from the following item in the *Sussex Advertiser* for September 8, 1788:

The "free" Burgesses of Horsham, we hear, have determined at the next general election to try their strength on behalf of Timothy Shelley Esq. against the interests of Lady Irwin, who has heretofore had the disposal of that Borough; in consequence of which, houses have increased near a thousand per cent of their value; in proof of which we need mention only one instance. A house that before the starting of Mr. Shelley was offered for sale at £40 has since been purchased at the enormous price of £400.[11]

Medwin had, in the meantime, by various Gilbertian maneuvers, secured for himself the key positions of chief poll clerk and town clerk. As poll clerk, he disqualified a number of Lady Irwin's voters, and Timothy Shelley was elected, a great celebration being held in his honor with the Duke of Norfolk (according to the *Sussex Advertiser*) making a "long and animated speech on their privileges as Burgesses and rights as Englishmen."[12] Lady Irwin, however, refused to accept defeat and demanded a parliamentary investigation. The investigating committee ruled that Medwin had wrongly disqualified Lady Irwin's voters and deprived Timothy of his seat. Later, the Duke put him in Parliament for another of his boroughs, New Shoreham, and Sir Timothy enjoyed a long career in Sussex politics, always as a Whig, and, although claiming a continuing interest in parliamentary reform, swinging toward the right wing of his party and ultimately losing the confidence of the reform voters. He made a final appearance in 1835, opposing the reform candidate, Robert Henry Hurst:

> Sir Timothy Shelley, now 82 years of age, then came forward and proposed Mr. Broadwood, and was at once assailed by the most vigorous yells and outcries from the Blue party. He claimed to be a Reformer himself, and indirectly charged Mr. Hurst with being more intent as a candidate upon a position at St. James' Palace than as a Member of the House of Commons. Upon this his feeble voice was drowned by the hootings and shoutings of the Blues.[13]

Shelley's home county may traditionally have been, as Professor White declared, "the most conservative county in England," [14] but certainly Horsham had a goodly bloc of progressive votes; Hurst was elected at least twice, and the whole county was a center of reform agitation in the 1830's. In 1814, Horsham petitioned Parliament to abolish the slave trade, and, in 1817, "a large reform meeting was held in front of the old 'Lamb Inn,'" the magistrates having refused permission to hold it in the Town Hall because the notice for the meeting did not restrict it to property owners but invited "all labourers, mechanics, and apprentices." [15] The meeting was considered sufficiently important to warrant comment in the House of Commons and Sir Timothy arose to testify to its orderliness.[16] Shelley, as a boy, may well have come in contact with some of these Horsham reformers.

The significance of the Whig connections of the Shelley family does not generally seem to have been recognized by Shelley's biographers.[17] These connections mean, for one thing, that Shelley from an early age lived and breathed a political atmosphere. In most English upper-class families, politics is a major subject of discussion; in a family, the father of which is a Member of Parliament, it is likely to become a daily diet. Sir Timothy, even though not distinguished for his volubility in Parliament—a search through *Hansard* reveals only the brief speech on the Horsham reform meeting—was nevertheless a loyal party man and doubtless discussed the daily events of the House and the issues of the day in the bosom of his family; and young Percy probably also got liberal doses of Whigism from Sir Bysshe and the Duke of Norfolk (whose nearby estate he visited).[18] Most significant of all, Shelley himself was brought up to succeed his father as Whig M.P., and had, indeed, anticipated such a career for himself up to the time of his expulsion from Oxford. A few weeks before leaving Oxford, Shelley wrote to Leigh Hunt: "My father is in parliament, and on attaining twenty-one I shall in all probability fill his vacant seat."[19] The evidence from Hogg, garbled as usual, is nevertheless intelligible and gives added information.

Without expecting an answer, he continued—"A certain nobleman (and he named him) advised me to turn my thoughts towards politics immediately. 'You cannot direct your attention that way too early in this country', said the Duke; 'they are the proper career for a young man of ability and of your station in life. That course is most advantageous, because it is a monopoly. A little success in that line goes far, since the number of competitors is limited; and of those who are admitted to the contest, the greater part are altogether devoid of talent, or too indolent to exert themselves; so many are excluded, that, of the few who are permitted to enter, it is difficult to find any that are not utterly unfit for the ordinary service of the state. It is not so in the church; it is not so at the bar; there all may offer themselves. The number of rivals in those professions is far greater, and they are, besides, of a more formidable kind. In letters, your chance of success is still worse. There none can win gold, and all may try to gain reputation; it is a struggle for glory—the competition is infinite—there are no bounds—that is a spacious field, indeed—a sea without shores.' The Duke talked thus to me many times, and strongly urged me to give myself up to politics without delay, but he did not persuade me. With how unconquerable an aversion do I shrink from political articles in the newspapers and reviews! I have heard people talk politics by the hour, and how I hated it and them! I went with my father several times to the House of Commons, and what creatures did I see there! What faces!—what an expression of countenance!—what wretched beings!— Here he clasped his hands, and raised his voice to a painful pitch, with fervid dislike. Good God! what men did we meet about the House—in the lobbies and passages! and my father was so civil to all of them—to animals that I regarded with unmitigated disgust."[20]

Hogg, exaggerating for effect, represents Shelley's disgust with the do-nothing Whigs as an aversion to politics in general. That he had no such aversion, but, on the contrary, was seriously thinking of a political career—probably as a lone wolf Independent of the Burdett stripe—and was well versed in political issues, is clear from the letter to Hunt, a letter which, as we have noted, Hogg fails to quote in his account of Shelley's Oxford career.[21] Merle, visiting Shelley shortly after his expulsion from Oxford, found him holding forth in "animated" style on "politics," "the social condition of man," the "tyranny of the aristocracy," and "the lamentable position of the lower orders." [22] It was doubtless this interest in political and social questions, plus his obviously unusual talents, that caused the Duke of Norfolk to regard the boy as one of the young hopefuls for the Whig party. And it was, doubtless, in such a role also that Timothy showed him off to his colleagues in the House.

The Whigs, in Shelley's day, were living in the shadows of past greatness. The party had been born, in the late seventeenth century, of a compromise whereby a combination of great merchants and land-owners, opposed both to the middle-class dictatorship of the Common-wealth men and the aristocratic church state of James, seized power in the so-called Revolution of 1688, and held it, with only minor Tory interludes, for more than a century. In the later eighteenth century, as the party became more and more infiltrated by middle-class capitalist interests—which were increasing with the rise of industry—the Tory party, hitherto under the taint of Jacobitism, emerged as the "respect-able" party, and the major financial interests, both of town and country, coalesced around its banner, and that of its brilliant leader, William Pitt. The Whigs, thus left as a minority party with its center of gravity swinging toward the town petty bourgeoisie and finding itself caught, in the first decade of the nineteenth century, between the upper and nether millstones of Tory-military dictatorship and a turbulent move-ment of the people, decided on a course of do-nothing compromise and ceased to be a major political force. In the late 1820's, it was to emerge to greatness again, this time as the political vehicle of the new, industrial capitalists, and press on to the victory of the Reform Bill, but in the early 1800's it had little to offer a young liberal interested in a parlia-mentary career. Its inactivity, however, did not mean that its members did not still hold as their theoretical faith the radical creed enunciated by its leaders Grey, Fox, and Sheridan, in the great reform and anti-war battles of the 1790's. And it was this creed in which the young Shelley was nurtured. "That great and good man Charles Fox," he later wrote to the Irish people, ". . . was your friend and the friend of freedom. . . . He never flattered or disguised his sentiments, but spoke them *openly* on every occasion . . . . He saw the truth and he believed it . . . . " [23]

We tend to forget nowadays just how radical this creed became as the Whigs' demands for their own class interests achieved universal implications. The great split in the party had come in 1792 when Burke and the right wing deserted to the Tories on the issue of the French Revolution and the more advanced Whigs under Fox were left to hold the fort. The "Foxites" stuck to three basic points of policy: reform of Parliament (by abolishing rotten boroughs and extending the franchise); Catholic emancipation (aimed mainly at alleviating the subjugation of Ireland); and peace with France. During these years Fox carried with him about forty or fifty members of the Commons and half a dozen peers in the House of Lords. A small group of the Commons members, led by Grey and Erskine, were somewhat to the left of Fox himself and it was this group that, in the two celebrated debates of 1793 and 1797, fought the issue of parliamentary reform. The best way to get something of the flavor of this early Whig doctrine is to glance at a typical Whig debate in the Commons as given in *Hansard*. One can learn more from such debates than from many pages of generalized discussion. Let us take the debate of 1797 on parliamentary reform, which is especially revealing.[24]

The debate is opened by Lord Grey,[25] then the promising young radical of the party: "The right of election instead of being confined to freeholders, as it now is, he thought, should be extended to copyholders and leaseholders"—a move designed to transfer some political power from the aristocracy to the middle classes. "In France," Grey continues, "a revolution had taken place, the principles, at least, in which it originated, whatever others might think of them, he should always defend." In regard to Ireland: "God grant that a convulsion may not happen, but it can only be prevented by measures of reform and conciliation." (The following year revolution broke out in Ireland.)

Grey's motion is seconded by Thomas Erskine,[26] who makes an especially vigorous speech. He calls for a union of liberals against Toryism: "to raise a standard around which the leaders of English liberty might proudly rally,[27] to which all wanderers from it might return." The tides of progress cannot be dammed: "But the insolence with which the mighty changes of the rising world were denounced within these walls is an awful lesson to mankind.— It has taught us, that there is an arm fighting against the oppressors of freedom stronger than any arm of flesh;[28] and that the great progressions of the world, in spite of the confederacies of power and the conspiracies of corruption, move on with a steady pace, and arrive at the end at a happy and glorious consummation." [29] He warns the Tories of approaching doom: "It [a corrupt government] stands for a season upon the mass of national subjection, shaking from time to time by irritated and indignant feelings which terror may suppress, but can never subdue or extinguish, till the moment of explosion arrives which so suddenly overwhelms it in ruin: for know, that in some form or other the original rights of mankind will surely be reassumed, and the monuments of tyranny and injustice be overthrown. (Here there was a loud cry from the Treasury bench of 'Order!')." [30]

Erskine's speech makes such an effect that Pitt himself arises to answer it.[31] He charges that the Whigs by agitating for reform are irresponsibly building up a destructive revolution, and urges that they rather "check their wishes than to risk the inrush of Jacobin principles and the impudence of affording to the enemies of the constitution the means of accomplishing its destruction." This is the usual Tory strategy of "redbaiting" the Whigs by associating them with the reformers and republicans; and Pitt is assailed in a brief but fiery address by Sir Francis Burdett.[32] The war against France, he declares, is but "another edition" of the war against colonial America: "It is another bold and daring, but unsuccessful attempt to stifle the flame of liberty." He expresses sympathy for the common people: "Indeed with all our boast of wealth, the mean and hard lot of poverty falls to the share of the mass of the people; and that comfort which ought to be the reward of honest labour, is seized by the griping hand of a rapacious government." Following a vigorous speech by Richard Brinsley Sheridan,[33] attacking rotten boroughs, defending the French Revolution, and calling for universal suffrage (i.e. the vote of all adult males), Fox arises to conclude the debate.[34] He immediately answers Pitt's charge that the Whig efforts for reform will result in "anarchy" (mob rule). The boot, he claims, is on the other foot: it is the stubbornly reactionary policies of the Tories which are driving the people to revolution; the situation can be saved only by the gradualist program of the Whigs; but, in either case, "between the alternatives of base and degraded slavery on the one side, or the tumultuous though, probably, short lived anarchy on the other . . . no man would hesitate to make a choice." [35] He attacks the Tory policy of building up the national debt; [36] he is for the vote for "householders," but he opposes "universal suffrage," and ridicules the notion of woman suffrage.[37] He does not wish for a fundamental change: "Sir, I have done. I have given my advice. I propose the remedy, and fatal will it be for England if pride and prejudice much longer continue to oppose it. The remedy which is proposed is simple, easy and practicable; it does not touch the vitals of the constitution; and I sincerely believe it will restore us to peace and harmony." The Whigs lost, 256–91.

Those who are acquainted with Shelley's political thinking will see many of the germs of it in these Whig doctrines (some of which I have pointed out in the notes): the sympathy for the French and American Revolutions; the advocacy of the extension of the franchise; the championing of the Irish; the preference of brief "anarchy" to prolonged "despotism"; the faith that the "mighty changes of the rising world," will overthrow "the monuments of tyranny and injustice," and move on to "a happy and glorious consummation." It is clear that any impressionable youngster being indoctrinated along these lines would be well on his way to a radical political philosophy.

I have mentioned that only about six peers in the upper house were faithful to Fox and his group. Prominent among these was the Duke of Norfolk. The Duke—his borough mongering, which was a commonly accepted practice, notwithstanding—belonged to the left and not to the right wing of the Whig party, the wing that precipitated the debates of 1793 and 1797 on reform. He came from a Catholic family and his first wife was Irish; he himself renounced his Catholic faith in 1780 in order to be allowed legal entrance to politics before succeeding to the dukedom (but was said while "under the dominion of wine" to reassert his old faith).[38] In 1778 he—and his father—signed "the petition of the English Catholics to George III";[39] in 1808, 1810, and 1815 (and perhaps in other years also) he supported Catholic emancipation in the House of Lords;[40] in 1812 he refused the order of the Garter in protest against the Prince Regent's turncoat policy toward the Irish Catholics.[41] His interest in parliamentary reform is attested to by one who knew him: "His active zeal for the rights and liberties of the country, and his eagerness for a reform in our representation, are well known; and though he, by much exertion and expense, sought for parliamentary influence and weight, yet he constantly and unhesitatingly declared and proved that his interest in this was to obtain the Reform which we have now acquired."[42] In addition to this reform interest, he was a staunch supporter of the movement for the abolition of the slave trade and, in the general election of 1807, "strongly supported" an abolitionist candidate for Parliament from Sussex.[43] That, at times he could go beyond these issues into dangerous radicalism is revealed in a celebrated incident of the year of the Irish Revolution,

1798. At a dinner given in that year at that haven of radical meetings, the Crown and Anchor Tavern, in honor of Fox's birthday, the Duke, in proposing the toast of the evening, daringly compared Fox to Washington: "Not twenty years ago the illustrious George Washington had not more than two thousand men to rally round him when his country was attacked. America is now free. This day full two thousand men are assembled in this place; I leave you to make the application." This, in view of the current bloody events in Ireland, was deliberate treason. Later in the evening, the Duke made another toast, this time directly subversive of the monarchy itself: "our Sovereign's health—the Majesty of the People." [44] For this offense he was deprived of his post as colonel of the militia and his lord-lieutenancy of the West Riding. Fox, in indignation, repeated the toast and consequently was removed from the Privy Council. (Pitt thought he should be sent to the Tower.) Fox wrote to the Duke: "The toast relating to the sovereignty of the people will be universally and I believe truly considered as the cause of your removal, and thus you will be looked up to as the marked champion of that Sovereignty, under which alone King William and the Brunswick Kings have held their throne." [45]

This, then, was the man to whose political fortunes Shelley's father and grandfather were attached, and it was certainly through him, either directly, or indirectly, that Shelley imbibed much of the Whig philosophy. It is, however, difficult to isolate a definite Whig stage in Shelley's thinking because he had by the early age of seventeen come under the influence of Sir Francis Burdett, and Burdett incorporated in his own more "leftish" philosophy the essentials of the Whig outlook.

There are, however, two early pieces of writing which may indicate exclusively Whig influence. The first is "The Irishman's Song," in the *Victor and Cazire* volume. This song is dated October, 1809, earlier than any evidence we possess of an interest in Burdett. Its theme is the injustices done by the English to Ireland:

> See! the wide wasting ruin extends all around,
> Our ancestors' dwellings lie sunk on the ground,
> Our foes ride in triumph throughout our domains,
> And our mightiest heroes lie stretched on the plains. [46]

It concludes by implying that the Irish will (and should) fight to regain their freedom, urged on by the spirits of those slain by the English. In view of the Foxite Whigs' position on the Irish question and the Duke of Norfolk's consistent championing of Catholic emancipation, we need infer no other than Whig influence to account for this poem.

The second piece of evidence indicating Whig influence is Shelley's support of Lord Grenville for the chancellorship of Oxford in the fall of 1809. Both Hogg and Medwin tell us of Shelley's enthusiasm for Grenville, and Medwin informs us that he wrote a letter—"I think in the Morning Chronicle, under the signature of A Master of Arts of Oxford"—in which he supported Grenville.[47] Now, Grenville was a right-wing Whig, so right wing, indeed, as to be almost indistinguishable from the Tories. He not only split from the Foxites on the issue of the war with France; he advocated prosecuting that war to the uttermost at a time when even Pitt felt a respite was needed; and in 1797, he introduced into the House the infamous Treasonable Practices Bill and the Seditious Meetings Bill. By 1809, he was one of the leading Whig opponents of parliamentary reform.[48] It is, therefore, unlikely that Shelley would have given ardent support to such a man after he had come under the more radical influence of Burdett. He might have given him tacit support as preferable to his main Tory rival, Lord Eldon (of *Mask of Anarchy* fame), but he would certainly have gone no further. His enthusiasm for Grenville late in 1809 (the contest ran from October 30 to December 14), then, indicates an essentially Whig outlook.

Following the celebrated debate of 1797 on parliamentary reform the Whigs dropped the reform issue, and, in fact for a time, dropped everything else as well. From 1797 to 1800 they boycotted the House and spent their time managing their country estates or attending to their city businesses. In the year 1809, a revival of the reform issue was initiated in Parliament, not by the Whigs but by Burdett and his Independent Whigs.[49]

Burdett, in spite of his later backsliding, was, during his heyday, one of the great figures in that long struggle for the democratization of the British Parliament that had begun in the 1770's with the Wilkes' reform agitation, reached a climax in the Reform Bill of 1832, but was not finally completed until all adult women were granted the vote in 1928. Graciously aristocratic in manner, famed as a lover of the liberal Lady Oxford (into whose circle Byron was drawn in 1812), Burdett was essentially a lone wolf politician constantly defying the wrath of both Whigs and Tories by his courageous exposés of social evils (from the flogging of soldiers to the oppression of the Irish). During the years in which we are here interested (1809–11), he achieved national fame on two counts, his proposal for parliamentary reform in 1809 and his imprisonment in the Tower in 1810.

Burdett introduced his famous reform plan into the House of Commons on June 15, 1809. In this plan (which followed the old Whig pattern) he advocated: (a) the extension of the franchise to those "subject to direct taxation"; (b) the reduction of the seven year duration period for Parliament; (c) the subdivision of the counties in accordance with the "taxed male population"; (d) the abolition of sinecures; (e) the reduction of the civil service and the standing army.[50] This plan was seconded by one William Madocks, M.P. for Boston, but resident of Tremadoc in Wales.

Hardly had the plan been proposed than it acted as a rallying cry for liberals, who had become disgusted by the inactivity of the Whigs. Burdett was supported by two important weeklies, the *Political Register* of the redoubtable William Cobbett and *The Examiner* of John and Leigh Hunt. The effect of the plan on the Whigs was to split them into a pro-reform and an anti-reform faction. Burdett and his plan, we can be sure, were well talked over in every Whig household in the country. That they formed part of the general conversation at the Shelley home at Field Place is revealed in the second of the Victor and Cazire poems (dated April 30, 1810):

> Then to politics turn, of Burdett's reformation,
> One declared it would hurt, t'other better the nation,
> Will ministers keep? sure they've acted quite wrong,
> The burden this is of each morning-call song.

Shelley and his sister [51] then, had come in contact with Burdett's views at least as early as the spring of 1810. By the summer of the same year he seems to have become an ardent admirer of Burdett, for to *The Wandering Jew,* sent, as we have seen, to Edinburgh for publication that summer, is prefixed the following dedication: "To Sir Francis Burdett, bart., M.P., in consideration of the active virtues by which both his public and private life is so eminently distinguished, the following poem is inscribed by the author." [52]

In order to understand the significance of this dedication we must look at the political maelstrom in which Burdett was involved in the spring and summer of 1810. Parliament had decided on an inquiry into the disastrous Walcheren expedition, which had had as its object the hemming in of the French fleet at Antwerp, and had ended in complete defeat for the British. A London radical, John Gale Jones by name, was imprisoned by the House for attacking its decision to hold this inquiry in secret, and Burdett (on March 12, 1810) demanded his release in a speech in which he made an excoriating attack on the House. When this speech was reprinted in *Cobbett's Political Register,* the House, in a fury, voted, on April 6, to commit Burdett to the Tower. Burdett, however, defiantly barricaded himself in his London mansion, his friend, Lord Cochrane, adding a dramatic touch to the proceedings by the purchase of a keg of gunpowder. Great crowds gathered in the streets, beating up everyone who would not hurl his cap in the air and cheer Burdett, who had become a popular hero such as England had not seen since the stormy days of "Wilkes and Liberty." Finally, on April 9, Burdett was escorted to the Tower by two squadrons of the Fifteenth Light Dragoons, two troops of Light Guards, "marching in open order," and a party of Light Dragoons, followed by an immense mass of the London populace, shouting, "They have taken him! They have dragged him out of his house!" [53] Finally, after a great storm of protest—headed by Hunt's *Examiner* and *Cobbett's Political Register*— Burdett was released with the prorogation of Parliament on June 21.

Shelley, therefore, in dedicating *The Wandering Jew* to Burdett in the summer of 1810, was associating himself with this campaign. More, he was defying the Whigs; for the Whigs had been quick to repudiate Burdett. "Indeed," writes Michael Roberts, "the Whigs lost no opportunity of publicly disavowing all connexion with Sir Francis and his principles; and openly mocked his demand for annual parliaments and universal suffrage." [54] By the time of this dedication, Shelley was clearly making the transition from Whig to Burdett reformer, i.e. to the group which was actually carrying out the old Whig creed. Two years later, as we shall see, he was suspected of radicalism because he was sending so many letters to Burdett, and a letter from his wife, Harriet, scornfully declared: "We know what men the Wigs [sic] are, now." [55]

One other incident in Shelley's life during these early years (1809– 1811) was connected with the activities of the Burdett-Hunt group. This was the famous Peter Finnerty case previously mentioned. Finnerty was an Irish journalist who had fought the British government's Irish policies for some twelve years previous to 1810. [56] In 1809, he was granted permission to accompany the Walcheren expedition as a correspondent for the Whig *Morning Chronicle,* but was ordered home by the government without being allowed to report the expedition. When the venture failed and 20,000 British dead lay strewn on the Walcheren marshes, Finnerty was conspicuous in a protest movement which gathered rapid momentum and threatened the life of the government. [57] The Tories hastened to prosecute so dangerous a publicist. On Feb. 7,

1811, he was sentenced to eighteen months' imprisonment. Sir Francis Burdett and *The Examiner* began a campaign for his relief, Burdett holding a protest meeting at the Crown and Anchor Tavern on February 20, *The Examiner* publishing articles and editorials on the case.

The movement spread from London to Oxford. On February 23, the liberal *Oxford University and City Herald* championed Finnerty's case and opened a subscription for him.[58] On March 2, in a list of four courageous subscribers appeared: "Mr. P. B. Shelley, 1£ 1s. od." In the same paper for March 9, appeared the following advertisement:

Literature.
Just published, Price Two Shillings,
A POETICAL ESSAY
on the
Existing State of Things.
AND FAMINE AT HER BIDDING WASTED WIDE
THE WRETCHED LAND TILL IN THE PUBLIC WAY,
PROMISCUOUS WHERE THE DEAD AND DYING LAY,
DOGS FED ON HUMAN BONES IN THE OPEN LIGHT OF DAY.

Curse of Kehama.

by a
GENTLEMAN of the University of Oxford.
For assisting to maintain in Prison
Mr. Peter Finnerty,
imprisoned for a libel.
London: Sold by B. Crosby and Co.,
and all other booksellers.
1811.

That this advertisement announces a poem by Shelley there can be no doubt. The pseudonym "a Gentleman of the University of Oxford," was the one he had used for *St. Irvyne;* two years later an Irish paper stated that Shelley had once written a poem for the aid of Finnerty;[59] Charles Kirkpatrick Sharpe, in his letter from Oxford, accepts it as Shelley's[60] and an Oxford fellow, Phillip Bliss, lists it among Shelley's works.[61] But, whether the poem ever actually appeared is not known. No copy has yet turned up.[62] The advertisement, however, indicates that the poem would have dealt, to some degree, with conditions in Ireland—"the wretched land"—and establishes the important fact that Shelley wished to play a part in the Finnerty campaign in Oxford similar to that of Burdett and Hunt in London. He had identified his interests with theirs and was, by this time, well to the left of the official Whigs. (In view of the political storm stirred up by this case, it can hardly be doubted, as I have suggested, that Shelley's efforts to spread the agitation to Oxford played a part in his expulsion.)

The final manifestation during these years of Shelley's allegiance to this reform group comes in his letter to Hunt, as editor of *The Examiner,* from Oxford on March 2, 1811:

Permit me, although a stranger, to offer my sincerest congratulations on the occasion of that triumph, so highly to be prized by men of liberality; permit me also to submit to your consideration, as one of the most fearless enlighteners of the public mind at the present time, a scheme of mutual safety, and mutual indemnification for men of public spirit and principle, which if carried into effect, would evidently be productive of incalculable advantages: of the scheme the following is an address to the public, the proposal for a meeting, and shall be modified according to your judgment, if you will do me the honour to consider the point.

The ultimate intention of my aim is to induce a *meeting* of such enlightened unprejudiced members of the community, whose independent principles expose them to evils which might thus become alleviated; and to form a methodical society, which should be organized so as to resist the coalition of the enemies of liberty, which at present renders any expression of opinion on matters of policy dangerous to individuals. It has been for want of societies of this nature, that corruption has attained the height at which we now behold it; nor can any of us bear in mind the very great influence, which some years since was gained by *Illuminism* without considering that a society of equal extent might establish *rational liberty* on as firm a basis as that which would have supported the visionary schemes of a completely-equalized community.

Although perfectly unacquainted privately with you, I address you as a common friend to *liberty,* thinking that in cases of this urgency and importance, that etiquette ought not to stand in the way of usefulness.

My father is in parliament, and on attaining twenty-one, I shall in all probability fill his vacant seat. On account of the responsibility to which my residence in the University subjects me, I of course, dare not publicly avow all I think, but the time will come when I hope that my every endeavour, insufficient as this may be, will be directed to the advancement of liberty.[63]

The reference in the first sentence to "that triumph" was to the recent trial of *The Examiner* editors for an article in which they had attacked the army system of flogging.[64] The Hunts were brilliantly defended by the liberal barrister Lord Brougham and, in spite of the Tory judge's (Lord Ellenborough) demands for conviction, were freed by the jury.

In order to understand the rest of the letter it is necessary to know something of the immediate political background. Burdett's plan for reform, as we have noted, split the Whigs into pro-reform and anti-reform factions. In January, 1810, the *Edinburgh Review* came out in an article entitled "Short Remarks on the State of Parties at the Close of the Year 1809," [65] with a strong plea for the pro-reform group. The essence of the *Edinburgh's* argument was that if the Whigs did not take up the reform issue the reformers would withdraw their following from them. Especially was it necessary that the reform movement be taken from the hands of such extremists as Burdett and placed into the safekeeping of moderate Whigs. But the reform the *Edinburgh* proposed was of the mildest and vaguest kind. It was careful to point out that it stood solidly for "the monarchy and aristocracy as the only sure supports of a permanent and regulated freedom"; in order to achieve this ideal the "Whig leaders" must "first conciliate and then restrain the people." [66]

This Tory casuistry (dressed up as liberalism) received a sharp answer in the same year from Leigh Hunt in his pamphlet "Reformist's answer to the Article entitled 'The State of Parties' in the last 'Edinburgh Review.'" [67] In this work, one of Hunt's most penetrating political essays, he begins by pouring ridicule on the Whig leaders whom the *Edinburgh* imagined could lead a reform movement—the sinecurist Grenville, the apostate Grey, the fence-sitting Windham. These men, Hunt pointed out, had no connection with the people but were a small group of isolated aristocrats who had no real interest in reform. What then was to be done? Hunt proposed a union between the Burdett reformers and "left" Whigs. Such a group, he contended, would be a truly formidable force in the cause of reform.

Shelley's letter is, in part, an attempt to give Hunt's plan more specific form. He advocates a meeting at which all sincere reformers—"enlightened and unprejudiced members of the community"—should form a united organization—"a methodical society"—to fight against the union of Tories and right-wing Whigs which was in control of the government—"the coalition of the enemies of liberty"—and supporting the system of rotten boroughs and sinecures—"corruption." Inclosed with this letter were "an address to the public" and a "proposal for a meeting," both of which have been lost. By this support of Hunt, Shelley is indicating that he has no faith in the ability of the Whigs alone—the *Edinburgh Review* plan—to carry through reform; reform can be achieved only by the union of the reformers—especially the Independent Whigs—with the left Whigs (Whitbread, Madocks, Brand, William Smith, and others).[68] The letter shows remarkable political acumen for a young man of eighteen. Shelley had not only been following the political situation in some detail but the remedy which he proposes is an eminently practicable one; for the greatest need of the reform forces at the time was unity; the Whigs feared the Burdett-ites as dangerous radicals and the Burdettites looked askance at the Whigs as feeble moderationists. In this situation, the Tories and the right Whigs had nothing to fear. A year or so later, we may note, just such an organization as Shelley here advocates did originate in the Hampden Clubs, which enrolled among its members reformers from the extreme left (Major Cartwright) through such advanced Whigs as Byron to moderate Whigs.[69]

REPUBLICAN

In the letter to Hunt, Shelley is dealing only with the practical policy of the reform movement. And this position he never abandoned. His general political theory, however, had even at this time passed beyond the reformism of Burdett or the left Whigs into republicanism. Of this he informs us himself in his letter to Godwin of June 3, 1812, quoted in the last chapter. But just how early he had entered this republican phase, how long he remained in it (before passing over to Godwinism), or how much or what reading in republican literature he did at this time, we cannot accurately tell. We have Hogg's statement that at Oxford he read "certain popular French works, that treat of man, for the most part in a mixed method, metaphysically, morally and politically"; and these probably included: Condorcet's *Esquisse d'un tableau historique des progrès de l'esprit humain,* Volney's *Les Ruines, ou méditations sur les révolutions des empires,* and Rousseau's *Discours sur l'origine . . . de l'inégalité parmi les hommes.*[70] We know, from Medwin, that he was enthusiastic about Benjamin Franklin,[71] and to these others we are safe in adding the name of Tom Paine. In Feb-ruary, 1812, less than a year after his expulsion from Oxford, Shelley thought of editing a selection from Paine's works, and so considerable an interest indicates a good many months' acquaintance with Paine;[72] a few months later he protested in an open letter to the Chief Justice, Lord Ellenborough, the prosecution of a printer (Daniel Isaac Eaton) for having published Paine's works; and in 1819 he made a similar protest against the prosecution of the famous radical, Richard Carlile on the same charge.[73] In view of this interest, it seems likely that Shelley had encountered Paine's works in his early republican period. And two other republicans whom he later read he might also have met with at this time: Mary Wollstonecraft and the Coleridge of the *Conciones ad Populum*.[74]

To Shelley's own statement and the remarks of Hogg and Medwin we have only one piece of evidence of republicanism to add during this period from his works: two of the *Margaret Nicholson* poems, the first poem (later entitled "War") and the second, "Fragment Supposed to be an Epithalamium of Francis Ravillac and Charlotte Corday." This little volume of verse (written in October and November, 1810) [75] was issued under an amusing but wisely precautionary subterfuge. We are informed in the sub-title and advertisement of a rare literary discovery—that of the posthumous fragments of Mrs. Margaret Nicholson "that noted female who attempted the life of the King in 1786." Mrs. Nicholson had been declared insane and committed to Bedlam, her poetic talents having remained undisclosed until her "nephew," John Fitzvictor—son, perhaps, of the Victor of a previous poetic enterprise—had discovered these poems among his "aunt's" papers. The advertisement—whose impish sardonics may be placed in early evidence against the obtuse theory that Shelley was devoid of humor—concludes with a happy augury of more to come:

In case the sale of these Fragments evinces that the Public have any curiosity to be presented with a more copious collection of my unfortunate Aunt's Poems, I have other papers in my possession which shall, in that case, be subjected to their notice.[76]

"War" is a stormy attack on monarchy as a system breeding war abroad and exploitation at home, but its main purpose (and hence the "Margaret Nicholson" subterfuge) lies in its implied criticism of George III and his ministers as the instigators of the war with France. Shelley is not attacking war and monarchy in general, but the British monarchy and the current war. It is an anti-war poem written in the midst of a war hysteria and would have been so taken by Shelley's readers. The poem opens with a characterization of the Napoleonic Wars, implying condemnation of both British and French governments:

> Ambition, power, and avarice, now have hurled
> Death, fate, and ruin, on a bleeding world.

It denounces monarchies (i.e. the Allied powers in particular) as the cause of the war and looks forward to the time of their overthrow and the fraternization of the troops:

> Monarchs of earth! thine is the baleful deed,
> Thine are the crimes for which thy subjects bleed.
> Ah! when will come the sacred fated time,
> When man unsullied by his leaders' crime,
> Despising wealth, ambition, pomp, and pride,
> Will stretch him fearless by his foemen's side?
>
> Kings are but dust—the last eventful day
> Will level all and make them lose their sway;
> Will dash the sceptre from the Monarch's hand,
> And from the warrior's grasp wrest the ensanguined brand.

Such lines as these go beyond the pallid anti-war sentiment of the Whigs and the reformist views of the Burdett-Hunt group, both in their doctrine and in their emotional ardor. Shelley is here placing the blame for social evils such as war not upon a mere "corruption" of some aspects of the existing governmental system but upon the very nature of that system itself, and he is envisaging the abolition of such evils not by a simple extension of the franchise but by the abolition of the monarchist-aristocratic state and the "leveling" of all people. And the "Epithalamium" has similar republican implications.[77] (We might note also that some of Elizabeth Shelley's poems of 1810–11 are anti-war and republican.) [78]

The republican influence on Shelley has, as a result of the almost exclusive emphasis on Godwin, been underestimated. It is, however, a difficult influence to trace or limit, for there is much republican influence in Godwin and Burdett, with the ideas of both of whom Shelley was familiar before going to Oxford (although the full significance of Godwin's doctrines was somewhat later in dawning). But one characteristic of Shelley's works, in addition to certain points of doctrine, is definitely republican, that radical fervor of style which distinguishes his handling of social themes whether in prose or verse. The republicans were revolutionaries, not retired radicals engaged in the intellectual dissection of society; their theory came hot from the firing line and was enunciated with vigor and passion. And the fountainhead of republicanism in England was Paine.

With the outbreak of the French Revolution, the older English radical movement, stemming largely from Wilkes and led by such men as

Major Cartwright, the reformer, and Thomas Holcroft, the dramatist, was transformed from a rather quiescent, theoretical movement into an active, political force. Clubs and societies of all kinds—notably the Correspondence Societies (formed to correspond with the French republicans)—sprang up everywhere and new leaders and new ideas began to appear. The weakness of the movement, however, was its lack of a unified series of principles: it was a turmoil of left Whigism from Fox and Sheridan, mechanical reformism from Major Cartwright, half-formulated republicanism from Priestley. The great service of Paine to the movement was to provide these principles. Fresh from his experiences in the American and French Revolutions, Paine had an insight into the workings of social movements keener than that of his English colleagues and a capacity for sharp, pungent phrasing easily understood by the masses. The result was that *The Rights of Man* had a success, as Paine himself declared, "beyond anything in the history of Printing." [79] It went through three editions in a fortnight and spread rapidly from one end of the kingdom to the other (even in faraway Dundee it inspired the inhabitants to plant a tree of liberty), and by 1793 had sold 200,000 copies.[80] It laid the base for the republicanism of the young intellectuals and writers; its ideas dominated Coleridge's *Conciones ad Populum,* Wordsworth's *Letter to the Bishop of Llandaff,* and Southey's *Wat Tyler.* Either directly, or through such works as these, it permeated also the thinking of the next generation of intellectual radicals, Byron, Hazlitt, Hunt, and Shelley.

The Rights of Man falls into two parts. In the first, Paine is mainly concerned with answering the slanders of Burke on the French Revolution and only indirectly indicates his own republican creed. In the second, he explains this creed and applies it to the situation in England. He opens with a vigorous attack upon hereditary right:

The vanity and presumption of governing beyond the grave, is the most ridiculous and insolent of all tyrannies.

Man has no property in man; neither has any generation a property in the generations which are to follow.[81]

He champions, with equal vigor, the revolutionary people of France (Burke's "swinish multitude") and their taking of the Bastille (a concept of the French people similar to that in *The Revolt of Islam*):

The incredible numbers with which they assembled the next morning, and the still more incredible resolution they exhibited embarrassed and astonished their enemies. Little did the new ministry expect such a salute. Accustomed to slavery themselves, they had no idea that liberty was capable of such inspiration, or that a body of unarmed citizens would dare face the military force of thirty thousand men.[82]

That there were excesses Paine does not deny, but he contends—as did Shelley in his Preface to *The Revolt of Islam* and Wordsworth in his *Letter to the Bishop of Llandaff*—that such are only to be expected when an oppressed people arise:

In the tremendous breaking forth of a whole people, in which all degrees, tempers and characters are confounded, and delivering themselves by a miracle of exertion, from the destruction meditated against them, is it to be expected that nothing will happen? When men are sore with the sense of oppressions, and menaced with the prospect of new ones, is the calmness of philosophy, or the palsy of insensibility to be looked for? [83]

If some of these excesses are due to the fact that the people are brutal and ignorant (*vide: A Philosophical View of Reform*), the social system and not the people are to blame:

It is by distortedly exalting some men, that others are distortedly debased, till the whole is out of nature. A vast mass of mankind are degradedly thrown into the background of the human picture, to bring forward, with greater glare, the puppet-show of state and aristocracy.

And politically linked up with the aristocratic state is the church: "By engendering the church with the state, a sort of mule animal, capable only of destroying, and not breeding up, is produced, called, the church established by law." [84]

Toward the end of the first part, he quotes the French *Rights of Man* (paralleled in Shelley's *Declaration of Rights*),[85] the most interesting of which, for our purpose, is the final "right":

The right to property being inviolable and sacred, no one ought to be deprived of it, except in cases of evident public necessity legally ascertained, and on condition of a previous just indemnity.[86]

Paine, was no economic egalitarian (as were Godwin and Shelley). He believed in political democracy and a curtailing of extreme fortunes but went no further.

The second part [87] opens with Paine's perspective of world-wide republican revolution (which is similar to Shelley's—and the young Coleridge's):

As revolutions have begun, (and as the probability is always greater against a thing beginning, than of proceeding after it has begun) it is natural to expect that other revolutions will follow. The amazing and still increasing expenses with which old governments are conducted, the numerous wars they engage in or provoke, the embarrassments they throw in the way of universal civilization and commerce, and the oppression and usurpation acted at home, have wearied out the patience, and exhausted the property of the world. In such a situation, and with such examples already existing, revolutions are to be looked for. They are become subjects of universal conversation, and may be considered as the order of the day.[88]

He then goes on to develop the basic proposition (also taken over by Shelley—possibly via Godwin) that government should be subordinated to society: "Government is no farther necessary than to supply the few cases to which society and civilization are not conveniently competent; and instances are not wanting to show that every thing which government can usefully add thereto, has been performed by the common consent of society, without government."[89] Government is a man-made product and evil, whereas: "All the great laws of society are the laws of nature."[90] Government has thus—as Rousseau had claimed and Shelley later preached—broken the kinship between man and nature. Insofar, however, as government is at all necessary it should be "a delegation of power for the common benefit of society," and not "an assumption of power for the aggrandizement of itself."[91]

Paine attacks, as in part one, the principles of monarchy and aristocracy, indicating that these evils cause not only domestic oppression but international war (as Shelley does in "War"): "But I might go further, and place also foreign wars, of whatever kind, to the same cause. It is by adding the evil of hereditary succession to that of monarchy, that a permanent family interest is created, whose constant objects are dominion and revenue." It is vain to hope for a correction of these evils from the old parties: "It is not whether this or that party shall be in or out, or whig or tory, or high or low shall prevail; but whether man shall inherit his rights. . . ."[93] He indicates the shallowness of Whig reformism by asserting a fundamental injustice in the mere existence of a House of Lords: "No reason can be given, why a house of legislation should be composed entirely of men whose occupation consists in letting landed property, than why it should be composed of those who hire, or of brewers, or bakers, or any other separate class of men."[94] "The only use to be made of this power, (and which it has always made,) is to ward off taxes from itself, and throw the burden upon such articles of consumption by which itself would be least affected."[95]

He condemns the weaknesses and injustices of the British monarchy, tying up the corruption of the whole system and its array of pensioners and job holders with the national debt (an argument later taken over by Cobbett, and via Cobbett, by Shelley).[96]

He concludes with a simile of a type favored by Shelley (notably in "An Ode to the West Wind" where it appears with similar application):

It is now towards the middle of February. Were I to take a turn into the country, the trees would present a leafless, wintry appearance. As people are apt to pluck twigs as they go along, I perhaps might do the same, and by chance might observe, that a single bud on that twig had begun to swell. I should reason very unnaturally, or rather not reason at all, to suppose this was the only bud in England which had this appearance. Instead of deciding thus, I should instantly conclude, that the same appearance was beginning, or about to begin, everywhere; and though the vegetable sleep will continue longer on some trees and plants than on others, and though some of them may not blossom for two or three years, all will be in leaf in the summer, except those which are rotten. What pace the political summer may keep with the natural, no human forsight can determine. It is, however, not difficult to perceive that the spring is begun.[97]

We might summarize Paine's political philosophy as follows: in the beginning of history, government was the servant of society; but this "natural" position has been reversed and society has become the servant of government; the specific form which this servitude has taken is that of the enslavement of the people by a monarch, a class of aristocrats and a reactionary church; this oppressive state power cannot be overthrown by engaging in mere Whig-Tory party politics but only through building a popular movement; if one objects that the people are brutal and corrupt, the answer is that people are whatever the system has made them and that in a new order they would be different; when this movement is aroused it must overthrow the monarchy, the aristocratic class, and the church and establish a democratic republic on the American model; as this change, in itself, will solve most of the great evils of society, egalitarian economic reform is not necessary.

While Paine was expounding these principles, another republican thinker, Condorcet, was providing the movement with something almost equally important—a perfectibilian vision of the new order; for without such a vision of a goal men will not work and die in a cause. Medwin informs us that Shelley read to him with enthusiasm the following passage:

Is it absurd to suppose this quality of amelioration in the human species as susceptible of an indefinite advancement; to suppose that a period must one day arrive, when death will be nothing more than the effect either of extraordinary accident or of the slow and gradual decay of the vital powers; and that the duration of the middle space, of the interval between the birth of man and his decay, will have no assignable limit?

The passage will be found toward the end of the famous final chapter of Condorcet's *Esquisse d'un tableau historique des progrès de l'esprit humain.*[98]

Condorcet's career, the dramatic circumstances under which this particular work was written, and the nature of that work itself, were all such as to attract the rapturous attention of the young Shelley. Condorcet, one of the most brilliant of the younger encyclopedists, had turned early to an interest in science, writing on mathematics, and in 1777 was elected permanent secretary of the Academy of Sciences. With the coming of the Revolution he joined the republicans and was elected to the Legislative Assembly and later to the National Assembly. However, he fell foul of the Girondists for voting against the execution of the King, and fled to escape punishment. While in hiding he wrote the *Esquisse* as a summary of his political creed, and shortly afterwards was captured and died in prison.

The following passages will serve to illustrate Condorcet's impassioned perfectibilian vision and its inevitability in terms of the "laws of history" which so deeply impressed Shelley (blending later with similar concepts in Godwin):

From these observations on what man has hitherto been, and what he is at present, we shall be led to the means of securing and accelerating the still further progress, of which from his nature, we may indulge the hope. Such is the object of the work which I have undertaken; the result of which will be to show, from reasoning and from facts, that no bounds have been fixed to the improvement of the human faculties; that the perfectibility of man is absolutely indefinite; that the progress of this perfectibility, henceforth above the control of every power that would impede it, has no other limit than the duration of the globe upon which nature has placed us. The course of this progress may doubtless be more or less rapid, but it can never be retrograde. . . .[99]

If man can predict, almost with certainty, those appearances of which he understands the laws; if, even when the laws are unknown to him, experience of the past enables him to forsee, with considerable probability, future appearances; why should we suppose it a chimerical undertaking to delineate with some degree of truth, the picture of the future destiny of mankind from the results of its history? [100]

Such are the questions with which we shall terminate the last division of our work. And how admirably calculated is this view of the human race, emancipated from its chains, released alike from the dominion of chance, as well as from that of the enemies of its progress, and advancing with a firm and indeviate step in the paths of truth, to console the philosopher lamenting its errors, the flagrant acts of injustice, the crimes with which the earth is still polluted? It is the contemplation of this prospect that rewards him for all his efforts to assist the progress of reason and the establishment of liberty. He dares to regard these efforts as a part of the eternal chain of the destiny of mankind; and in this persuasion he finds the true delight of virtue, the pleasure of having performed a durable service, which no vicissitude will ever destroy in a fatal operation calculated to restore the reign of prejudice and slavery. This sentiment is the asylum into which he retires, and to which the memory of his persecution cannot follow him; he unites himself in imagination with man restored to his rights, delivered from oppression, and proceeding with rapid strides in the path of happiness; he forgets his own misfortunes while his thoughts are thus employed; he lives no longer to adversity, calumny and malice, but becomes the associate of these wiser and more fortunate beings whose enviable condition he so earnestly contributed to produce.[101]

❧ THE INFLUENCE OF GODWIN

Next to Paine's *Rights of Man,* Godwin's *Political Justice* (1793) was the most influential work in the formation of early British radical theory. Although the book was originally published at 3 guineas (later reduced, for the second edition, to 14 shillings), its ideas received a wide circulation not only by word of mouth but by numerous pamphlets reprinting its essential doctrines and by cheap pirated editions in Scotland and Ireland.[102] Its impact upon the intellectuals was especially strong. Coleridge published a sonnet in the liberal *Morning Chronicle* (Jan. 10, 1795) on Godwin as one "form'd t'illumine a sunless world forlorn"; Southey "all but worshipped" the book (which he got from the Bristol public library); Crabb Robinson wrote of it as a work "which directed the whole course of my life"; [103] and in 1825, Hazlitt—protesting the current neglect of Godwin—wrote:

No work in our time gave such a blow to the philosophical mind of the country as the celebrated Enquiry concerning *Political Justice.* Tom Paine was considered for the time as a Tom Fool to him; Paley an old woman; Edmund Burke a flashy sophist. Truth, moral truth, it was supposed, has here taken up its abode; and these were the oracles of thought. "Throw aside your books of chemistry," said Wordsworth to a young man, a student in the Temple, "and read Godwin on Necessity." [104]

Hogg informs us that Shelley first read *Political Justice* in a copy borrowed from Dr. Lind while at Eton and that it had an almost immediate effect on his thinking.[105] That this information came directly from Shelley a few months later is indicated by the references to Godwin in his letters to Hogg during the Oxford period. The two must have had many discussions on Godwin. Hence, Hogg is almost certainly right. Of Shelley's two statements on the subject, one places the first reading prior to January, 1810, the second subsequent to the spring of 1810, both within the Eton period.[106] It is, it seems to me, this early reading of *Political Justice* that, more than any other single factor, accounts for the change in Shelley's writing that took place between the spring and fall of 1810, between *The Wandering Jew* and *Posthumous Fragments*. Its initial effect was probably to synthesize his previous radical thinking, but the realization of the full significance of its doctrines was doubtless a longer process. Shelley's letters in the winter of 1810–1811 show admiration for Godwin but take issue with him on several counts.[107] In the fall of 1811 he recommends Godwin's works to a correspondent, but seems to place *The Enquirer* above *Political Justice*.[108] Captain Kennedy, on his visit to Field Place in the summer of 1814, quoted him as saying that he "had derived all that was valuable in knowledge and virtue" from *Political Justice*.[109] Godwin's book, therefore, while far from being the exclusive source of Shelley's views that it is often represented as being [110]—and Shelley himself tended to exaggerate on this score—is nevertheless the most important single influence among the many works that molded his political thinking.

It has for so long been the custom of writers on Shelley to ridicule Godwin (a somewhat easier task than refuting him) that few Shelley students today have much idea of what his beliefs really were. I shall outline them as they appear in *Political Justice,* under four heads: social and political theories; economic analysis; the future state; methods of achieving the future state. All or most of these theories we shall find embodied in Shelley's works.

Godwin's social and political thought is distinguished by several assumptions; first, that national morality is rooted in the political structure and that a higher morality can be achieved only by changing that structure as a whole and not by moral or religious education for their own sakes (hence, the title of his book):

May it not be found, that the attempt to alter the morals of mankind singly and in detail is an erroneous and futile undertaking; and that it will then only be effectually and decisively performed, when, by regenerating their political institutions, we shall change their motives and produce a revolution in the influences that act upon them? [111]

It is, we may note here, from a failure to grasp this concept that the false idea arose that Shelley advocated attaining social change by individual moral conversion. Shelley's views on the matter are the same as Godwin's.

The second of Godwin's assumptions is that mankind is "perfectible," the concept that Condorcet was developing at about the same time.[112] Godwin—as his (and Shelley's) critics have not always perceived—is careful to give an exact definition to this term:

Lastly, man is perfectible. This proposition needs some explanation. By perfectible it is not meant that he is capable of being brought to perfection. But the word seems sufficiently adapted to express the faculty of being continually made better and receiving perpetual improvement; and in this sense it is here to be understood. The term perfectible, thus explained, not only does not imply the capacity of being brought to perfection, but stands in express opposition to it. If we could arrive at perfection, there would be an end of our improvement. There is however one thing of great importance that it does imply: every perfection of excellence that human beings are competent to conceive, human beings, unless in cases that are palpably and unequivocally excluded by the structure of their frame, are competent to attain.[113]

By perfectibility, then, Godwin and Shelley mean only that man has a capacity for progress and not—as is frequently assumed—that man can become "perfect." [114] He has this capacity because his mind is not a set entity but is molded by the environment and, hence, capable of change (progressively as the environment progresses), and his actions are determined *basically* not by emotional fluctuations but by reason:

Under this branch of the subject I shall attempt to prove two things; first, that the actions and dispositions of mankind are the offspring of circumstances and events, and not of any original determination that they bring into the world; and secondly, that the great stream of our voluntary actions essentially depends, not upon the direct and immediate impulses of sense, but upon the decisions of the understanding.[115]

And these propositions hold good for all classes of society. The mind of the lord and the peasant have equal equipment at birth and are equally capable of development. "What," Godwin enquires sarcastically, "are the sensations that the lord experiences in his mother's womb, by which his mind is made different from that of the peasant? Is there any variation in the finer reticulated substance of the brain, by which the lord is adapted to receive clearer and stronger impressions than the husbandman or the smith?" [116]

For the rest, Godwin's political theory is similar to that of the republicans. He is as violent in his denunciations of monarchy and aristocracy, and as favorable to democratic government: "Democracy restores to man a consciousness of his value, teaches him by the removal of authority and oppression to listen only to the suggestions of reason." [117] He agrees that government should be reduced to a minimum: "since government even in its best state is an evil, the object principally to be aimed at is, that we should have as little of it as the general peace of human society will permit." [118]

It is on the question of the economic analysis of the social order that Godwin first makes a fundamental break with Paine and the republicans. "Republicanism," he bluntly declares, in a passage that clearly affected Shelley, "is not a remedy that strikes at the root of the evil. . . . However great and extensive are the evils that are produced by monarchies and courts, by the imposture of priests and the iniquity of criminal laws, all these are imbecil and impotent, compared with the evils that arise out of the established administration of property." [119] ". . . in the most refined states of Europe, the inequality of property has arisen to an alarming height. Vast numbers of their inhabitants are deprived of almost every accommodation that can render life tolerable or secure." [120]

Inequality of property, resulting in the exploitation of the mass of the poor by a rich minority, breeds class conflict:

The superiority of the rich, being thus unmercifully exercised, must inevitably expose them to reprisals; and the poor man will be induced to regard the state of society as a state of war, an unjust combination, not for protecting every man in his rights, and securing to him the means of existence, but for engrossing all its advantages to a few favoured individuals, and reserving for the portion of the rest want, dependence and misery.[121]

The rich, however, exploit the masses not only by direct economic means. They oppress them also by their control of the political and judicial systems (which they use, among other things, to prevent the formation of trade unions—"combinations"):

First then, legislation is in almost every country grossly the favourer of the rich against the poor. . . . The rich are encouraged to associate for the execution of the most partial and oppressive positive laws; monopolies and patents are lavishly dispensed to such as are able to purchase them; while the most vigilant policy is employed to prevent combinations of the poor to fix the price of labour . . .[122]

Another evil arising from the property system is psychological distortion: "But accumulation brings home a servile and truckling spirit, by no circuitous method, to every house in the nation."[123] And this distortion affects not only the lower classes but upper and lower classes alike:

Hereditary wealth is in reality a premium paid to idleness, an immense annuity expended to retain mankind in brutality and ignorance. The poor are kept in ignorance by the want of leisure. The rich are furnished indeed with the means of cultivation and literature, but they are paid for being dissipated and indolent.[124]

As to the republican view (e.g. in point XVII of *The Rights of Man* as quoted by Paine) that the rights of property are sacred, Godwin boldly answers that these rights are subordinate to "the principles of universal morality," and that wherever it is clear that property rights infringe upon human happiness they are no longer valid.[125] All wealth, all property comes ultimately from human labor and there is no such right, in terms of human morality, as that of inheriting property.

The spontaneous productions of the earth are few, and contribute little to wealth . . . property is produced by the daily labour of men who are now in existence. All that their ancestors bequeathed to them was a mouldy patent, which they show as a title to extort from their neighbours what the labour of these neighbours has produced.[126]

In all these economic theories Godwin goes beyond the republicans but falls below the socialistic analysis which some two decades later Robert Owen was to propose to a startled bourgeoisie. Godwin did not, as did Owen, with a more fully developed capitalism before him, see the system as a dynamic whole, producing alternately booms and depressions, but as a static framework of property inequality.

On the basis of these theories, both economic and political, Godwin worked out his picture of the state of the future. This state was, as we should expect, to be built upon economic equality and political democracy, and in it, human nature, under these changed conditions, would be transformed. In this world wide egalitarian society, mankind, aided by science, would progress to heights hitherto undreamed of. The following passages give the essence of Godwin's vision:

> The spirit of oppression, the spirit of servility, and the spirit of fraud, these are the immediate growth of the established administration of property. They are alike hostile to intellectual and moral improvement. The other vices of envy, malice and revenge are their inseparable companions. In a state of society where men lived in the midst of plenty, and where all shared alike the bounties of nature, these sentiments would inevitably expire. The narrow principle of selfishness would vanish. No man being obliged to guard his little store, or provide with anxiety and pain for his restless wants, each would lose his individual existence in the thought of the general good. No man would be an enemy to his neighbour, for they would have no subject of contention; and of consequence philanthropy would resume the empire which reason assigns her. Mind would be delivered from her perpetual anxiety about corporal support, and free to expatiate in the field of thought which is congenial to her. Each would assist the enquiries of all.[127]

> In reality the constitution of a state governed either in whole or in part by a political monopoly, must necessarily be complicated. But what need of complexity in a country where the people are destined to govern themselves? The whole constitution of such a country ought scarcely to exceed two articles; first, a scheme for the division of the whole into parts equal in their population, and, secondly, the fixing of stated periods for the election of a national assembly; not to say that the latter of these articles may very probably be dispensed with.[128]

Godwin's Utopia is neither socialistic nor communistic. He did not, as did Owen, look to state regulation of a unified economic system, balancing production and consumption, nor, as did Marx, to a communist society based on a high level of industrial production. In fact, he has little conception of economic progress at all, least of all industrial progress. The essence of his plan is a society of small agricultural and manufacturing units, privately owned and of equal value, with a common sharing of produce and a minimum of governmental direction. And if he regarded the coming of a new order as inevitable, he regarded it, not as Marx did, as arising from the development of productive forces and the class struggle, but as the result of the quiet workings of "Necessity."

By the doctrine of Necessity (a doctrine much misrepresented by his critics), Godwin meant that there were laws operating in the physical universe, in history, and in the human mind which made for consistent and unalterable patterns of movement in all three realms. "This view of things presents us with an idea of the universe as connected and cemented in all its parts, nothing in the boundless progress of things being capable of happening otherwise than it has actually happened." [129] In the realm of history, the pattern has become one of continuous or almost continuous improvement, and once this pattern has so begun it must continue:

First, there is a degree of improvement real and visible in the world. This is particularly manifest, in the history of the civilised part of mankind, during the three last centuries. The taking of Constantinople by the Turks (1453) dispersed among European nations, the small fragment of learning, which was, at that time, shut up within the walls of this metropolis. The discovery of printing was nearly contemporary with that event. These two circumstances greatly favoured the reformation of religion, which gave an irrecoverable shock to the empire of superstition and implicit obedience. From that time, the most superficial observation can trace the improvements of art and science, which may, without glaring impropriety, be styled incessant. Not to mention essential improvements which were wholly unknown to the ancients, the most important characteristics of modern literature, are the extent of surface over which it is diffused, and the number of persons that participate in it. It has struck its roots deep, and there is no probability that it will ever be subverted. It was once the practice of moralists, to extol past times, and declaim without bound the degeneracy of mankind. But this fashion is nearly exploded. The true state of the fact is too gross to be mistaken. And, as improvements have long continued to be incessant, so there is no chance but they will go on. The most penetrating philosophy cannot prescribe limits to them, nor the most ardent imagination adequately fill up the prospect.[130]

The law of Necessity by which the human mind operates is simple: a seeking of pleasant sensations and a shunning of unpleasant ones. That these pleasant sensations have, in past ages, especially in primitive society, been largely self-centered, Godwin does not deny, but he asserts that, as a result of the general advancement of society, pleasurable sensations are becoming more unselfish—"benevolent." When we "promote the happiness of our child, our family, our country or our species," we are "actuated by the most perfect disinterestedness." [131] The continuation of this tendency over a long period of time—Godwin, his critics to the contrary, had no belief in a speedy millennium—would pave the way for the egalitarian society:

The change we are here contemplating, consists in the disposition of every member of the community, voluntarily to resign that, which would be productive of a much higher degree of benefit and pleasure, when possessed by his neighbour, than when occupied by himself. Undoubtedly, this state of society is remote from the modes of thinking and acting which at present prevail. A long period of time must probably elapse, before it can be brought entirely into practice. All we have been attempting to establish is, that such a state of society, is agreeable to reason, and prescribed by justice; and that, of consequence, the progress of science and political truth among mankind, is closely connected with its introduction. The inherent tendency of intellect is to improvement. If therefore this inherent tendency be suffered to operate, and no concussion of nature or inundation of barbarism arrest its course, the state of society we have been describing, must, at some time, arrive.[132]

This quiet vision of a slow unfolding in the reaches of time, however, left without any satisfactory answer the question of what should be done in the present. And here we come to the Achilles heel of the Godwinian system. Godwin rejected the methods of the reformers and republicans, the building and activation of political associations. The new society would be achieved by small bands of enlightened philosophers who would, little by little, convert their fellows—including "the rich and great" [133]—to the justice of their views:

The indefatigable votary of justice and truth, will . . . fear to attach himself in his intercourse to any particular set of men, lest his thoughts should become insensibly warped . . . associations, instead of promoting the growth and diffusion of truth, tend only to check its accumulation, and render its operation, as far as possible, unnatural and mischievous.[134]

The reason for this rejection of political organization was Godwin's fear of revolution. Godwin, a retired scholar, had none of the enthusiasm for the people which is so marked in the works of professional revolutionaries like Paine or Mary Wollstonecraft but hoped to achieve his goal by peaceful, educational means. Any organization of the people, he argued, would but precipitate violence and all would be lost:

Every attempt of this sort, even if menaced only and not carried into act, tends to excite a resistance which otherwise would never be consolidated. The enemies of innovation become alarmed by the intemperance of its friends. The storm gradually thickens, and each party arms itself in silence with the weapons of violence and stratagem. Let us observe the consequence of this. So long as the contest is merely between truth and sophistry, we may look with tolerable assurance to the progress and result. But, when we lay aside arguments, and have recourse to the sword, the case is altered. Amidst the barbarous rage of war, and the clamorous din of civil contention, who shall tell whether the event will be prosperous or adverse? The consequence may be, the riveting on us anew the chains of despotism, and insuring through a considerable period the triumph of oppression, even if it should fail to carry us back to a state of torpor, and obliterate the memory of all our improvements.[135]

While Paine's revolutionary tactics could—as the American and French examples showed—produce results, Godwin's genteel propaganda campaign would have produced precisely nothing. In this opposition to political organization Shelley and Godwin parted ways. Shelley's letter to Hunt from Oxford is based on the establishment of political organization, although he had by then read *Political Justice,* and the following year he vigorously challenged Godwin's view.[136]

In spite of this weakness in Godwin, however, in many ways he penetrated deeper than did the republicans. By emphasizing economic inequality, as they had not, he gained a deeper insight into many aspects of the existing order, including its psychological effects, and projected a vision of a new order, both moral and cultural, higher in its standards than any they had conceived of. And his doctrine of Necessity, despite its mechanistic oversimplifications, provided a philosophic basis for radical theory.

Such, in brief, was the thinking that laid the foundations of Shelley's philosophy. What he later learned from such political thinkers as Cobbett or Hunt or Bentham did not change this fundamental pattern but was assimilated into it, and his later experiences, in England, Ireland, and Italy, confirmed its correctness. These foundations, indeed, had been laid, in the main, by the time of Shelley's expulsion from Oxford, in March, 1811. From his father and grandfather he had early imbibed the liberal creed of Whiggism: parliamentary reform, Catholic emancipation and the cause of Ireland, the folly of the war against France. At the time these ideas did not capture his imagination, which was wrapped up in the fascinations of science and the occult, and to balance the monstrosities of *Zastrozzi* and *St. Irvyne, Original Poetry* and *The Wandering Jew* (March, 1809–September, 1810) we have but the solitary "Irishman's Song" (October, 1809). But many seeds were then laid which later came to fruition. Without this early Whig pattern, Shelley's mind could not have become receptive to the more extreme radicalism of Burdett and the republicans, and these later ideas, especially Condorcet's perfectibilian visions, gave new meaning to the earlier ones. During the spring and summer of 1810, political concepts began to achieve a new meaning, probably as a joint result of the Burdett case and a first reading of *Political Justice;* and *The Wandering*

Jew was defiantly dedicated to Sir Francis Burdett in that summer. But as late as September the old fascination for the occult and mysterious still lingered and we have the horror-mongering of *Original Poetry*. By November, however, the new pattern, hitherto minor, began to become major; in November, *St. Irvyne*, still regarded with enthusiasm in April, had so palled that its author could not bring himself even to make minor revisions in it; and in the same month appeared the *Posthumous Fragments of Margaret Nicholson*. In February came the campaign for Finnerty and the "Poetical Essay"; in March, the letter to Hunt. The "votary of romance" has become a reformer and a republican; he believes in extra-parliamentary action for the achieving of parliamentary reform, allying himself with Burdett and Hunt; and he believes that final solutions to such evils as war and exploitation lie in the establishment of a republic. To these rapidly developing views, now beginning to grasp his imagination (and not his intellect only) with the same force as the old occult romanticism they had expelled, the new thrilling perspective of *Political Justice* began to open out. All his previous political views began to coalesce into the greater vision of Godwin and to receive new meaning in the process. The history of man was not a mere cycle back to a republic "on the Athenian model" but a progress toward hitherto unachieved goals; history was no haphazard play of men and forces; behind history as behind nature, was law; and this law—Necessity—guaranteed ever greater futures for humanity. One could now battle for parliamentary reform, the freedom of Ireland, the abolition of the monarchical system with a new strength, for these things were not goals in themselves but part of a vaster picture.

➤ THE NECESSITY OF ATHEISM

In these early years, too, Shelley laid the base for his future thinking in religion, ethics, and science.

Shelley as a boy had accepted such general religious tenets as God and prayer—

> I called on poisonous names with which our youth is fed;
> I was not heard—I saw them not— [137]

but seems to have turned toward skepticism in regard to Christian doctrine at quite an early age; and, as was the case with his political radicalism, the seeds from which his views sprang may be found in the intellectual environment of his home. Of his grandfather, the formidable Sir Bysshe, Shelley wrote: "He is a complete Atheist, and

builds all his hopes on annihilation." [138] And Timothy, we may judge
from the following comment by Medwin, who, as a member of a
Horsham family well acquainted with the Shelleys, was in a position to
know, did not exert himself to turn his son's mind toward the light:
"Indeed, his religious opinions were also very lax; although he occasionally went to the parish church, and made his servants regularly
attend divine service, he possessed no true devotion himself, and inculcated none to his son and heir, so that much of Percy Bysshe's scepticism
may be traced to early example, if not to precept." [139] Before Shelley's
expulsion he discussed unorthodox principles openly with his father; [140]
and Dowden records that Timothy subscribed for "two copies of the
Rev. Mr. Sadler's Sermons (Unitarian) under the title 'A friend to religious liberty.' " [141] All this does not, of course, mean that Timothy was
an agnostic or a deist but it does indicate that he believed himself to be a
liberal Christian; the voluminous *Natural Theology* of Bishop Paley
with which he attempted to proselytize his son, was—in spite of that
son's explosive reactions—considered a very liberal work.[142] Timothy
was certainly not over-zealous in his religious observances and Shelley
probably received only the most general kind of religious instruction at
Field Place (mingled, perhaps, with periodic blasts of atheism from
Sir Bysshe). Nor was this situation likely to be protested by a mother
who thought prayer of "no use" and good atheists as likely to land in
Heaven as good Christians.[143] His sister Elizabeth, he informed Hogg,
"is no more a Xtian than I am, but," he added scornfully, "she regards
as sacred criterion the opinion of the world." [144] To a boy of unusual
intelligence, thus brought up without any outside influence until the
age of ten (when he first went to school), catechismal instruction from
that choleric divine, Dr. Greenlaw, master of Syon House, probably
served only to alienate him further from religious views.[145] At Eton
the atmosphere seems to have smacked more of the Inferno than the
Paradiso. On the one hand, there was a rule forbidding religious instruction (so that one master complained that he was practically de-
barred "from saying a word about God to his pupils"); and, on the
other hand, there was a galling compulsory chapel twice every Sunday,
the sermons "mumbled and jumbled by old men with weak smothered
voices, not one word of which could be heard." [146]

According to Shelley, himself, he first began to question religious
truth through reading the classics:

The first doubts, which arose in my boyish mind concerning the genuine-
ness of the Christian religion, as a revelation from the divinity, were excited

by a contemplation of the virtues and genius of Greece and Rome. Shall
Socrates and Cicero perish, whilst the meanest hind of modern England
inherits eternal life? [147]

These doubts took more positive form during his final years at Eton:
During the last two years of his stay at Eton [writes Medwin] he had, as
I have already stated, imbued himself with Pliny the Elder, especially being
struck with the chapter *De Deo,* and studied deeply Lucretius, whom he
considered the best of the Latin poets, and with him he referred at that
time . . . all creation to the power of Nature.[148]

This "De Deo" section of Pliny's *Natural History,* he not only read
but translated, and in it, says Medwin, found "the first germ of his ideas
respecting the nature of God." When we turn to the section and find
arguments such as the following there can be little doubt that Medwin
is right: "That that supreme being, whatever it be, pays heed to man's
affairs is a ridiculous notion"; "Frail toiling mortality, remembering
its own weakness, has divided such deities into groups, so as to worship
in sections, each the deity he is most in need of." [149] In *A Refutation of
Deism* Shelley quotes Lucretius, *De Rerum Natura,* I, 146–150,—
printing the final line—"no thing is ever by divine power produced
from nothing"—in capitals—and this was doubtless a passage that
early impressed him.[150]

At Oxford he turned to modern skeptics. Of Hume's famous *Essays,
Literary Moral and Political,* Hogg informs us, he and Shelley "made
a very careful analysis." [151] Then came the "certain popular French
works" [152] we have noted previously, and which doubtless included
the acid anti-clericalism of Volney's *Les Ruines* and Condorcet's *Esquisse.*[153] It seems likely, too, that Shelley used the empirical reasoning
of another favorite work of his, Locke's *Essay concerning Human Understanding,* for anti-Christian purposes (as some of the deists had done
before him).[154] And, in a letter to his father from Oxford on February
6, 1811, he lists among the famous "deists," who were not Christians:
"Voltaire, Lord Kames, Mr. Hume, Rousseau, Dr. Adam Smith, Dr.
Franklin" (i.e. Benjamin Franklin).[155]

Among the first works of Shelley's in which we find evidence of anti-
religious views are the terror novels *Zastrozzi* and *St. Irvyne.* As these
novels were written while he was still at Eton, and as we learn from
Hogg that he was known at Eton as "Shelley the Atheist," [156] it appears
that his thoughts had turned in this direction at least by his last year at
Eton and perhaps even earlier. And this is confirmed by the anti-reli-

gious nature of his correspondence with Harriet Grove (January to September, 1809).[157]

In both *Zastrozzi* and *St. Irvyne* the dominant characters, Zastrozzi and Ginotti are atheists. Zastrozzi attempts to convert Matilda to atheism, and, at the end of the novel, when faced by the inquisition, he reaffirms his belief:

"Matilda," replied Zastrozzi, whilst a smile of contemptuous atheism played over his features—"Matilda, fear not; fate wills us to die; and I intend to meet death, to encounter annihilation, with tranquillity. Am I not convinced of the non-existence of a Deity? . . . Why need I then shudder at death? Why need anyone, whose mind has arisen above the shackles of prejudice, the errors of a false and injurious superstition." [158]

Ginotti (Nempere) similarly utters atheistic sentiments to Eloise [159] and, at the end urges Wolfstein to "deny his creator." [160] Shelley's motives in bringing these elements into the novels is to spread anti-religious propaganda and to add to the general flesh-creeping paraphernalia of the horror story.[161] That he (or his publishers) were nervous even of these comparatively minor doses of sulphur seems indicated by the vaguely religious sentiments scattered throughout both books (mainly by Matilda and Eloise).[162]

In *The Wandering Jew* (probably written at about the same time as *St. Irvyne*) a new anti-religious note is apparent. Whereas in the novels these sentiments were rather general, in *The Wandering Jew* they take the specific form of an attack upon God as presented by the theologians. This is indicated, first, in the alternate title for the poem Shelley proposed—*The Victim of the Eternal Avenger*—and in the sarcastic references in the preface to "the equally groundless superstitions of the battle of Armageddon, the personal reign of J[esus] C[hrist], etc." [163] In the poem itself, he is largely concerned with displaying the ruthlessly vengeful character of God in his persecution of the Wandering Jew:

> I knew it was the avenger's sway,
> I felt it was the avenger's ire! [164]

But that, in spite of these anti-Christian sentiments and the atheistical horror-mongering of the novels, Shelley's development was not at first toward atheism but anti-clerical deism we can tell from his views a few months later at Oxford. Of these views we have a fairly complete record in his correspondence with Hogg during the Christmas vacation in December and January, 1810–1811, a correspondence which throws a revealing light upon *The Necessity of Atheism*. The correspondence opens with a letter on December 20, in which Shelley informs Hogg that Stockdale, publisher of *Original Poetry* and *St. Irvyne,* has told Sir Timothy that his son is "a supporter of deistical principles"; he thinks, therefore, that Stockdale will not do as a publisher for a work which Hogg apparently thought of sending him. Even if Stockdale did believe Hogg's "assertion" about this work, and published it; "There exist numbers who will find out its real tendency." [165] Hogg's work was evidently ironically anti-religious; and from later letters we gather that it was probably his now lost novel *Leonora.*[166] He did not accept Shelley's advice and sent the manuscript to Stockdale.[167]

On December 30, Shelley received a letter from Hogg in which Hogg had apparently argued against the existence of a deity. On January 3, Shelley replied with a deistical argument: "I may not be able to adduce proofs; but, I think, that the leaf of a tree, the meanest insect on which we trample, are, in themselves, arguments more conclusive than any which can be advanced, that some vast intellect animates infinity." [168] Yet, while he will not follow Hogg into atheistical speculation, he is bitter in his denunciations of Christianity, denunciations tangled up with the psychological shock of the loss of Harriet Grove because of his anti-religious sentiments.

On January 6, came a further refutation from Hogg—an "argument against the existence of a Deity"—to which Shelley again countered with deistical reasoning:

Then admitting, that this actuating principle is such as I have described, admitting it to be finite, there must be something beyond this, which influences *its* actions and all this series advancing, as if it does in one instance, it must to infinity, must at last terminate, if it can terminate, in the existence which may be called a Deity.[169]

Hogg replied in turn, Shelley receiving his "argument" on January 11— "you disbelieve the existence of an eternal and omnipresent spirit"— and attempted, in answer, again to "prove the existence of a Deity" by the argument of a "First Cause." But the Christian religion he hates as bitterly as ever: "Hideous! Hated trait of Xtianity! Oh Xt., how I hate thy influence." [170]

In the meantime, Stockdale, sniffing out, as Shelley had feared he might, the brimstone in Hogg's novel, made enquiries about Hogg (through Mrs. Stockdale who had relations in County Durham) and found that he was suspected of anti-religious sentiments. Now convinced, as he had not been previously, that Hogg was "the master spirit

... lead[ing] him astray," and having heard from Shelley himself that he intended to write a "Metaphysical Essay in support of atheism ... which he intended to promulgate throughout the university," Stockdale hastily wrote to Timothy, warning him of "the precipice, over which he [Shelley] was suspended by a hair." [171] He apparently disclosed the anti-religious nature of Hogg's manuscript and retailed the information he had picked up from Hogg's neighbors.[172] Of these disasters, Shelley informed Hogg on January 14. On January 14, too, there arrived from Hogg a letter attacking religion which was to be forwarded to a Mr. Wedgewood after perusal by Shelley. Shelley's answer gives us an insight into the propaganda campaign that he and Hogg were conducting, the climactic blow of which was to be *The Necessity of Atheism.*

Your letter and that of Wedgewoods came today; yours is excellent, and, I think, will fully (in his own mind) convince Mr. W. I inclosed five sheets of paper full this morning, and sent them to the coach with yours. I sate up all night to finish them; they attack Xtianity's very basis, which at some future time, I will explain to you; and I have attempted to prove, from the *existence* of God the futility of the superstition upon which he founds his whole scheme.[173]

On January 17, Shelley writes: "Your systematic cudgel for Christianity is excellent. I tried it on with my father, who told me that thirty years ago he had read Locke, but this made no impression." [174] This "cudgel" was either a new argument from Hogg, perhaps similar to that transmitted to the beleaguered Mr. Wedgewood on the 14th, or, less likely, that received on the 11th.[175]

In the final letter of the series, apparently written on about January 23, Shelley informs Hogg that he will "be at Oxford on Friday or Saturday evening," that is on January 25 or 26, and that he did arrive at Oxford on one of those dates is probable, for he addressed a letter to Stockdale from Oxford on January 28.[176]

In the *Oxford University and City Herald* for February 9, there appeared the following advertisement:

Speedily will be published,
To be had of the Booksellers of London and Oxford,

The
NECESSITY OF ATHEISM.

"Quod clara et perspicua demonstratione caveat pro vero habere, mens omnino nequit humanae." Bacon de Augment. Scient.[177]

By at least February 13, the speedy publishing had been accomplished, for on that day Shelley sent a copy to his friend Graham in London.[178] On March 25, Shelley and Hogg were expelled.

It has generally been believed that *The Necessity of Atheism* was either entirely or almost entirely the work of Shelly, but this belief is not tenable. Professor Frederick L. Jones has demonstrated, in an article which succeeding scholars appear to have forgotten, that it was at least as much the work of Hogg as of Shelley. And this is clear, not only from the evidence which Professor Jones presents, revealing that Shelley himself and all observers in his confidence refer to it as a joint production, but from the Shelley-Hogg correspondence which I just outlined. The correspondence reveals that Shelley was not an atheist but a deist at least as late as January 12, whereas Hogg was an atheist, denying not only Christian doctrine but "the existence of an eternal and omnipresent spirit." Nor is it probable that Shelley had become a convinced atheist between January 12 and February 9. Shelley, I suspect, found himself sufficiently struck by the revelatory logic of Hogg's argument, and his own inability to answer it, to decide to put it in along with some of his own. And this procedure is implicit in the "through deficiency of proof, an atheist" of the prefatory "Advertisement." The decision to actually print the work, Hogg intimates, was taken by Shelley without consulting him and before returning to Oxford. Thus, although the central atheistic argument of the work is Hogg's, Shelley was the moving spirit behind its public appearance in the world.[179]

The arguments of this little work, almost the first in England openly to champion atheism,[180] revolve around the proposition that knowledge of God can come from three sources only: (a) from the senses; (b) from reason; (c) from the testimony of others (arguments which go back to Hume rather than, as is sometimes suggested, to Locke).[181]

(a) From the Senses: "If the Deity should appear to us . . . this revelation would necessarily command belief;—those to whom the Deity has thus appeared have the strongest possible conviction of his existence"[182] (to which, when reprinting this sentence in the Notes to *Queen Mab,* Shelley sardonically added the nullifying clause,—"But the God of the Theologians is incapable of local visibility").[183]

(b) From Reason: This falls into two parts: reason applied to the origin of the universe and the origin of the person. In regard to the first, the mind has two choices: to believe that the universe was created or to believe that it has existed forever. The authors of *The Necessity of Atheism* favor the latter: "it is easier to suppose that the Universe has existed from all eternity, than to conceive a being capable of creating it." [184] This Humean conclusion, [185] we may note, is one which Shelley is arguing against in his letters—"Was not this first cause a deity?"

In regard to the origin of the person, it is true that this presupposes a creative force, but there is no reason to consider this force a Deity: "we admit that the generative power is incomprehensible, but to suppose that the same effect is produced by an eternal, omniscient, Almighty Being, leaves the cause in the same obscurity, but renders it more incomprehensible." [186]

(c) From Testimony: Here Shelley and Hogg take the argument from Hume's essay *Of Miracles* that it is more likely that the observers (here, specifically the apostles) were mistaken or lied, than that the miracles actually took place, and this they link with the argument that disbelief is not a sin. "The testimony that the Deity convinces the senses of men of his existence can only be admitted by us, if our mind considers it less probable that these men should have been deceived than that the Deity should have appeared to them . . . our reason can never admit the testimony of men, who not only declare that they were eye-witnesses of miracles but that the Deity was irrational, for he commanded that he should be believed, he proposed the highest rewards for faith, eternal punishments for disbelief . . . we can only command voluntary actions, belief is not an act of volition, the mind is even passive. . . ." [187]

The essay then concludes that as none of the three sources of conviction produces any real proof of the existence of God the mind cannot accept such a belief. This argument we find repeated in Shelley's letter to his father on February 6—just three days before the advertisement of *The Necessity*:

. . . the testimony of the twelve Apostles is insufficient to establish the truth of their doctrine, not to mention how much weaker the evidence must become when filtered thro' so many gradations of history, so many ages.

Supposing twelve men were to make an affidavit before you that they had seen in Africa a vast snake three miles long, suppose they swore that this snake eat nothing but Elephants, and that you knew from all the laws of nature, that enough Elephants could not exist to sustain the snake, would you believe them? The case is the same . . . it is clearly therefore proved that we cannot, if we consider it, believe facts inconsistent with the general laws of Nature, that there is no evidence sufficient, or rather that evidence is insufficient to prove such facts.[188]

And with this argument is linked, as in *The Necessity,* the argument on punishment and the non-ethical nature of a lack of belief:

The coming of Christ was called εὐαγγελλιον [sic] or good tidings; it is hard to believe how those tidings *could* be *good* which are to condemn more than half of the world to the Devil, for as St. Athanasius says, "He who does not believe should go to eternal fire"—As if belief were voluntary, or an action, not a passion (as it is) of the mind.[189]

In *The Necessity* we find: "it is also evident that as belief is a passion of the mind, no degree of criminality can be attached to disbelief."[190]

The indication is that of the two main arguments of *The Necessity,* the second and the third, the second, on the non-existence of a deity, was Hogg's and the third, on belief and disbelief, was Shelley's. Shelley, considering himself as having been labeled a moral criminal by the Grove family for his lack of belief, was especially interested in this question, and Hogg, as we can tell from Shelley's letters, in the arguments on the non-existence of a deity.

ETHICS AND SCIENCE

The radical pattern of Shelley's thinking in politics and religion is early evident in his ethical views. By the time of the writing of *Zastrozzi* (*ca.* March–August, 1809), he had already become interested in free love theories. "Love like ours," exclaims Verezzi to Matilda, "wants not the vain tie of human law."[191] By the time of *St. Irvyne,* some months later, free love has become a major doctrine in the plot. Every love affair—Wolfstein and Megalena, Eloise and Ginotti (Nempere), Eloise and Fitzeustace—is accompanied by little sermons on the injustices of chaining free spirits by legal ties, usually, however (as was the case with Verezzi and Megalena also), with the added qualification that it is best, in the interests of happiness, to submit to the dictates of society. As Fitzeustace solemnly concludes at the end of *St. Irvyne:*

But before we go to England, before my father will see us, it is necessary that we should be married—nay, do not start, Eloise; I view it in the light that you do; I consider it an human institution and incapable of furnishing that bond of union by which alone can intellect be conjoined; I regard it as but a chain, which, although it keeps the body bound, still leaves the soul unfettered: it is not so with love. But still, Eloise, to those who think like us, it is at all events harmless; 'tis but yielding to the prejudices of the world wherein we live and procuring moral expediency, at a slight sacrifice of what we conceive to be right.[192]

We find, too, in this early period that Shelley's thinking was going beyond the confines of a simple free love morality into general theories of love and selflessness, love as a renunciation of the ego and the antithesis of lust, theories which, in more developed form, became a permanent part of his later ethical views. Each individual, he contended, countering Hogg, ought to aspire to happiness "more for other than self."

But adieu to egotism; I am sick to death at the name of self. Oh, your theory cost me much reflection . . . Is it not, however, founded on that hateful principle? Is it self which you propose to raise to a state of superiority by your system of eternal perfectibility in love? No! . . . What then, shall happiness arise from? Can we hesitate? Love, dear love, and though every mental faculty is bewildered by the agony, which is in this life its too constant attendant, still is not that very agony to be preferred to the most thrilling sensualities of epicurism? [193]

We get a further glimpse of his thinking in his final letter to Hogg before returning to Oxford:

You have very well drawn your line of distinction between instinctive and rational motives of action; the *former* are not in our own power, yet we may doubt if even these are *purely* selfish, as congeniality, sympathy, unaccountable attractions of intellect, which arise independent frequently of any considerations of your own interest, operating violently in contradiction to it, and bringing on wretchedness, which your reason plainly foresees, which yet, although your judgment disapproves of, you take no pains to obviate. All this is not selfish. And surely the operations of reason, of judgment, in a man whose judgment is fully convinced of the baseness of any motive, can never be consonant with it.[194]

Hogg had apparently been arguing along Hobbist lines on the inherent self-centeredness of all motives deriving from emotional reaction and hence implying the "natural" selfishness of man. This Shelley denies, pointing out that such unselfish reactions as "congeniality" and "sympathy" are also natural; indeed (and he is perhaps referring to his own experience with Harriet Grove) they sometimes overcome the intellect. And he emphasized, apparently more strongly than did Hogg, the Godwinian doctrine that conscious reason in the "disinterested" thinker is always unselfish.

In addition to politics, philosophy, and ethics Shelley also had, as we have seen, a considerable interest in science. Unfortunately he did no writing on this subject and does not refer to it in his letters of the period, so that we have to rely mainly on Medwin and Hogg for our information. As we have already noted, he seems to have been started in this direction by the lectures of Adam Walker at Syon House and was doubtless encouraged in it by Dr. Lind. Just what reading he did in the subject we do not know. Of ancient authors interested in science he knew Pliny and Lucretius.[195] We hear of a chemistry book which Timothy returned to Medwin's father as it was "a forbidden thing at Eton," [196] and in his second letter to Godwin, Shelley informs him that he had early read "ancient books of Chemistry and Magic." [197] That among the "magic" were Albertus Magnus and Paracelsus we can gather from a later letter on the same subject,[198] but we do not know what the chemistry books were. By the end of July, 1811, he was reading Erasmus Darwin, who, as Professor Grabo has shown, had considerable influence on his scientific thinking, and he may have read him before that date.[199]

Whatever his reading, however, there can be no doubt of the intensity of his interest in science. This emerges clearly, even through Hogg's caricatured account, if one does a little judicious reading between the lines. Here, for instance, is Hogg's picture of Shelley's rooms at Oxford on the occasion of his first visit to them:

Books, boots, papers, shoes, philosophical instruments, clothes, pistols, linen, crockery, ammunition, and phials innumerable, with money, stockings, prints, crucibles, bags, and boxes, were scattered on the floor and in every place; as if the young chemist, in order to analyze the mystery of creation, had endeavoured first to re-construct the primeval chaos. The tables, and especially the carpet, were already stained with large spots of various hues, which frequently proclaimed the agency of fire. An electrical machine, an air-pump, the galvanic trough, a solar microscope, and large glass jars and receivers, were conspicuous amidst the mass of matter. Upon the table by his side were some books lying open, several letters, a bundle of new pens, and a bottle of japan ink, that served as an inkstand; a piece of deal, lately part of the lid of a box, with many chips, and a handsome razor that had been used as a knife. There were bottles of soda water, sugar, pieces of lemon, and the traces of an effervescent beverage. Two piles of books supported the tongs, and these upheld a small glass retort above an argand lamp. I had not been seated many minutes before the liquor in the vessel boiled over, adding fresh stains to the table, and rising in fumes with a most disagreeable odour. Shelley snatched the glass quickly, and dashing it in pieces among the ashes under the grate, increased the unpleasant and penetrating effluvium.[200]

Two corrections need to be made in this account. This cannot be, as Hogg claims, a picture of his first visit to Shelley's rooms as Shelley would scarcely have had time in the few days he had been at Oxford to have wrought such extensive havoc.[201] The second is a correction in perspective. Hogg's attitude toward science is one of cynical tolerance, and, toward Shelley, one of amused condescension. And while the main facts of his picture are doubtless correct (and, indeed, are corroborated by Medwin),[202] the overall picture, if it had been given by one with a genuine interest in science, would have been greatly different. We are witnessing here the early efforts of a boy who might, as A. N. Whitehead has asserted, have become one of the world's greatest scientists:

What the hills were to the youth of Wordsworth, a chemical laboratory was to Shelley. It is unfortunate that Shelley's literary critics have, in this respect, so little of Shelley in their own mentality. They tend to treat as a casual oddity of Shelley's nature what was, in fact, part of the main structure of his mind, permeating his poetry through and through. If Shelley had been born a hundred years later, the twentieth century would have seen a Newton among chemists.[203]

The reason for Shelley's interest in science was twofold. In the first place, he believed that it afforded a way to philosophic truth. The study of languages, he once commented to Hogg, was merely the study of "the names of things"; but by means of "the physical sciences and especially through chemistry," one could investigate "things themselves." [204] In the second place, he believed that science provided an instrument for the amelioration of the human race, and that, by his Oxford period, this was the main motive behind this interest is shown in a talk on the subject which Hogg records. While this cannot, as Hogg implies, represent Shelley's own words, it certainly reflects his ideas.

"Is not the time of by far the larger proportion of the human species," he inquired, with his fervid manner and in his piercing tones, "wholly consumed in severe labour? . . . What is the cause of the remarkable fertility of some lands, and of the hopeless sterility of others? A spadeful of the most productive soil, does not to the eye differ much from the same quantity taken from the most barren. The real difference is probably very slight; by chemical agency the philosopher may work a total change, and may transmute an unfruitful region into a land of exuberant plenty. Water, like the atmospheric air, is compounded of certain gases: in the progress of scientific discovery a simple and sure method of manufacturing the useful fluid, in every situation and in any quantity, may be detected; the arid deserts of Africa may then be refreshed by a copious supply, and may be transformed at once into rich meadows, and vast fields of maize and rice. . . . What a comfort would it be to the poor at all times, and especially at this season, if we were capable of solving this problem alone, if we could furnish them with a competent supply of heat! These speculations may appear wild, and it may seem improbable that they will ever be realised, to persons who have not extended their views of what is practicable by closely watching science in its course onward; but there are many mysterious powers, many irresistible agents, with the existence and with some of the phenomena of which all are acquainted. What a mighty instrument would electricity be in the hands of him who knew how to wield it, in what manner to direct its omnipotent energies? . . . The balloon has not yet received the perfection of which it is surely capable; the art of navigating the air is in its first and most helpless infancy; the aerial mariner still swims on bladders, and has not mounted even the rude raft: if we weigh this invention, curious as it is, with some of the subjects I have mentioned, it will seem trifling, no doubt—a mere toy, a feather, in comparison with the splendid anticipations of the philosophical chemist; yet it ought not altogether to be contemned. It promises prodigious facilities for locomotion, and will enable us to traverse vast tracts with ease and rapidity, and to explore unknown countries without difficulty. Why are we still so ignorant of the interior of Africa?—why do we not despatch intrepid aeronauts to cross it in every direction, and to survey the whole peninsula in a few weeks? The shadow of the first balloon, which a vertical sun would project precisely underneath it, as it glided silently over that hitherto unhappy country, would virtually emancipate every slave, and would annihilate slavery forever." [204]

As we look back over Shelley's thinking during this period we find that, once he emerged from his "votary of romance" stage, his thinking began to fall into a consistently radical pattern, a pattern given unity by the dominant concept of assisting the progress of humanity. These different realms of thought, of course, developed internal logics of their own, but this concept was the central point around which the system as a whole revolved.

III A SEVERING OF CORDS

The Devil's Walk
Letters to Elizabeth Hitchener

FATHER AND SON

On March 26, 1811, Shelley and Hogg arrived by stagecoach in London, following their expulsion from Oxford, and settled down in lodgings in Poland Street, chosen by Shelley because it reminded him of the Polish struggle for national freedom. The next few weeks in Shelley's life were taken up by a conflict with his father over the expulsion and his radical views. In this controversy Timothy Shelley was torn between genuine affection for his "young man" and the necessity for asserting parental authority. Shelley, for his part, was outwardly defiant, but inwardly deeply troubled, indulging in some romantic posturing in the role of the rebel son but determined to stick to his guns. On March 29, he wrote with ironic naïveté to inform his father of his "misfortune":

> The case was this:—You will know that a train of reasoning and not any great profligacy has induced me to disbelieve the scriptures:—this train myself and my friend pursued, we found to our surprise that (strange as it may appear) the proofs of an existing Deity were as far as we had observed defective.
> We therefore embodied our doubts on the subject and arranged them methodically in the form of "The Necessity of Atheism," thinking thereby to obtain a satisfactory or an unsatisfactory answer from men who had made Divinity the study of their lives.
> How then were we treated? not as our fair, open, candid conduct might demand, no argument was publicly brought forward to disprove our reasoning, and it at once demonstrated the weakness of their cause, and their inveteracy on discovering it, when they publickly expelled myself and my friend.[1]

In reply, Timothy put forward the following propositions:

1st. To go immediately to Field Place, and to abstain from all communication with Mr. Hogg, for some considerable time. 2nd. That you shall place yourself under the care and society of such gentlemen as I shall appoint and attend to his instructions and directions he shall give.[2]

To this the rebels replied with a fairly conciliatory set of counter proposals:

They will not obtrude Atheistical opinions upon anyone whatever, they will refrain from publishing Atheistical Doctrines or even speculations. They will return immediately to their respective homes. The parties feel it their duty to demand an unrestrained correspondence.[3]

If these propositions had been accepted the situation would probably have resolved itself satisfactorily.[4] Instead of accepting them, however, Timothy Shelley, after a fruitless interview with the two recalcitrants on April 7,[5] turned the whole matter over to his attorney, William Whitton, a man of decidedly Tory mentality, and demanded that all future correspondence be through him. Whitton pointed out that the situation was more serious than Timothy realized: blasphemy was a legal offense, and his family position might be jeopardized in a public trial.[6] Greater firmness was necessary. The immediate result of Timothy's frightened indecisiveness in thus handing matters over to Whitton was the following curt note from Shelley to the lawyer:

Sir,

As common report and tolerably good authority informs me that part of Sir Bysshe Shelley's property is entailed upon me; I am willing by signature to resign all pretensions to such property in case my father will divide it equally with my sisters *and my Mother,* and allow me now 100 pounds per an: as an annuity which will only amount to 2000 pounds, perhaps less.

Your obt. humble sert.[7]

This cool proposal to sacrifice his family fortune shocked Whitton to the marrow of his feudal bones:

Sir,

I am not a willing instrument by which insult may be offered to your father and I must therefore decline acting in any manner under the paper you have sent to me. I most sincerely wish you to reflect on the tendency of the proposal you have thought proper to make before you offer it to your father's consideration.[8]

This, Shelley—eighteen, republican, and Godwinian—answered with some heat:

I will not listen to the suggestions of family pride; to interest, to fortune, I am indifferent; and I desire that when I am addressed again, a less authoritative manner be used, or subsequent letters are returned unopened.[9]

Whitton then sent Shelley's proposal to Timothy Shelley. Timothy was greatly upset, perhaps realizing for the first time the gravity of the situation. On April 22 he replied to Writton:

I never felt such a shock in my life, infinitely more than when I heard of his expulsion, for I could not then have thought it of so hidious [sic] a cast. . . . The insulting ungentlemanly letter to you appears the high-ton'd, self-will'd dictate of the Diabolical Publications, which have unluckily fallen in his way, and given this Bias to his mind, that is most singular. To cast off all thoughts of his Maker, to abandon his Parents, to wish to relinquish his Fortune and to court Persecution, all seems to arise from the same source. . . . I hear he has corresponded with Lucien B[onaparte] and it is thought he did with Finnerty. Perhaps I have not heard half.[10]

At about this time, the Duke of Norfolk, either voluntarily or by the request of Timothy, entered the picture and arranged to have both Shelley and his father to dinner and tried to persuade Shelley to adopt a political career. But this proposal Shelley recognized as an attempt to get him into the House as a supporter of the Duke's mild Whiggism and he turned it down.[11] In the middle of April, Hogg departed, leaving Shelley alone in the Poland Street lodgings. On April 23, Timothy again came to London—hearing that his son was "woefully melancholy" —and opened negotiations through the Grove family, generously offering an allowance of £200 a year and freedom of action. He returned to Field Place on April 28, and on the same day—perhaps after consulting Sir Bysshe, who was for "unconditional submission"—withdrew his offer. There was, however, no real barrier to Shelley's return to Field Place, and Hogg was surprised to learn on about May 4 that he was still in London: "You have reason—you have a right to be surprised that I am not at Field Place, that I did not fly instantly thither in spite of everything. I will explain as soon as possible." [12] Shelley, however, continued to remain in London for another four or five days and the "explanation" never materialized. When he finally did leave, he did not go directly to Field Place but selected the house of his uncle Captain John Pilfold (Royal Navy, retired) as a base of operations. And he selected wisely. Pilfold had first seen action at sea in 1794, in 1797 had captured "several privateers" and helped to put down a mutiny "sword in hand," in 1800 "commanded the boats in the destruction of the

French corvette Insolente," and had received his captaincy for commanding H.M.S. *Ajax,* a seventy-four gun battleship, at Trafalgar. The father of two daughters but no sons, he had a warm feeling for his blacksheep nephew, whom he considered to have been too harshly treated. The combination of the horny veteran and the mettlesome prodigal, acting in a spirit of militant camaraderie, soon had Field Place furling its flags. By May 15, Shelley was re-established on his family domains, his £200 per annum restored. Timothy, he gleefully informed Graham, after the victory, "looks rather blue today but the captain keeps him in tol[erable] order." [13]

Looking back over this controversy—which was soon to renew itself in a more violent form and result in a permanent estrangement—it becomes evident that the essence of the problem, so far as Timothy and the Duke were concerned, was the rescuing of Shelley as a potential Whig landed-gentleman and Honorable Member for New Shoreham. [14] This is made clear by Medwin (who is probably giving an impression derived from his father):

Sir Timothy, who, proud of his son's talents, had looked forward to his acquiring his academical distinctions, felt deeply, not so much the disgrace of the expulsion, as an apprehension that the circumstance might tend hereafter to affect the brilliant worldly career he had etched out for his heir, marring his prospect of filling the seat in parliament which he then occupied, and intended one day to resign in favour of Percy Bysshe. . . . The Duke of Norfolk, who was a friend of his father, and to whom his grandfather owed his title, often engaged him, when dining, as he occasionally did, in St. James's Square, to turn his thoughts towards politics.—"You cannot direct your attention too early to them," said the Duke. "They are the proper career for a young man of ability and of your station in life." . . . This holding up of politics as the το καλον, was natural in one, who had renounced his faith for political power. I was present at a great dinner of Whigs, where one of them, an M.P., speaking of the nominees of election committees, who act as advocates on the side of their nominators, though they take the same oath as the other members of the committee, and his saying how easy it was for a man determined to *believe,* bending his mind to believe any thing, *alias,* making up his mind beforehand how he should vote. Such casuistry would have been lost on Shelley, to whom I detailed these sentiments, which he highly reprobated. The Duke of Norfolk talked to him many times, in order to convert him to politics, but in vain. [15]

And these political machinations of the Duke and Sir Timothy are confirmed by Shelley's cousin, Charles Grove:

In the course of the spring, when his father was attending Parliament, an effort was made by the Duke of Norfolk to persuade my cousin to become a politician, under his auspices. By the duke's invitation Bysshe met his father, at dinner at Norfolk House, to talk over a plan for bringing him in as member for Horsham, and to induce him to exercise his talents in the pursuit of politics. I recollect the indignation Bysshe expressed after that dinner, at what he considered an effort made to shackle his mind, and introduce him into life as a mere follower of the duke. His father was puzzled what to do when that plan failed.[16]

These political and social considerations do not, of course, signify that Timothy Shelley had no personal fondness for his son. His letters, as well as the comments of Medwin and Hogg, indicate that he loved his son, and took pride in him, and was genuinely upset by the expulsion and consequent rebellion. But the disgrace of expulsion and threat of further disgrace—to a family but recently risen in the world—had both hardened Timothy and driven him to distraction. Merle, visiting Field Place at this time, gives us a revealing picture of the situation there:

I had received a letter from Shelley, dated from Horsham, in which he announced his intention of paying me an early visit. Two days afterwards, however, I had business in the Neighborhood of Horsham, and resolved to go there. As soon as I had made myself comfortable "at mine inn," I walked down to Field Place, the residence of Mr. Timothy Shelley, distant about a mile from the town, and asked for Bysshe. The servant who answered me said his young master was in the town, and that he did not expect him to return until late. It was then seven in the evening. Mr. Shelley, who was in the diningroom, having heard his son asked for, came out, and rudely, as I thought, told me that his son was from home, and that it was not the custom to receive his acquaintances at Field Place. Feeling that I did not belong to the class of acquaintances proscribed by Mr. Timothy Shelley, I told him that he was mistaken, and that if all his son's associates were like myself, he would have little to fear as to his principles. On this Mr. Shelley invited me into the house, and we had a long conversation, in the course of which he almost shed tears when alluding to the doctrines which his son professed, and took a pleasure in promulgating. Mr. Graham had spoken of me in such favourable terms, that Mr. Shelley no sooner knew who I was than he made many apologies for his mode of receiving me, and was as anxious that I should see his son as he had previously been to keep him from me. As the time at which Bysshe would return home, however, was uncertain, Mr. Shelley promised that his son should call upon me at my inn, if he should not return too late in the evening. As I did not expect that Bysshe could call much before nine o'clock, I profited by the fineness of the weather for walking, and arrived at the Swan Inn, where I had put up, soon after nine. The Swan was a second or third-rate inn, which had been recommended to me as more comfortable than any other house of public entertainment in Horsham; but the entrance to the coffee-room was not very inviting, for it was through a taproom. As I was passing I saw, to my astonishment, Shelley seated by the tap-room fire at a table, on which he was writing, with a glass of brandy-and-water before him. "Bysshe," said I, "this is not a place for you; come into my bed-room." He left the spot immediately, and we went up-stairs together. I ordered tea; and for some time our conversation was mere tea-table gossip. When the tray had been removed, he asked me how I had been received by his father, expressing his fear that I had been treated with rudeness. I did not conceal from him that it was certainly the reverse of friendly in the first instance, but that Mr. Shelley had handsomely atoned for it by his subsequent behaviour. "Ah! I understand," said Shelley; "you told him that you were not one of my freethinking friends: and this accounts for the readiness with which he announced your being at Horsham, and almost insisted that I should immediately call on you. It really astonishes me that he can be so silly. I am quite old enough to select my own acquaintance; and I am vain enough, if it be vanity, to believe that there is not one of my friends from whom I have anything to learn, good or bad, on the subjects which excite my father's anxiety. If there be a seducer, it is myself; and I know that some of the young fellows have received much paternal admonition to avoid my company." [17]

The picture is unmistakable: on the one side, the distraught father on the ancestral estates, on the other, the rebellious son brooding at the village inn; the father, a shaken man, flying from extreme to extreme, blindly hitting out at the ideas which, as his letter to Whitton reveals, he believed to be at the root of the trouble, determined to shut his son off from intercourse with those purveying such ideas, yet almost pathetically grateful at any glimmering of help; the son intractable, embittered and scornful, his old filial affection dissolving under attacks which seemed the embodiment of that narrow, prejudiced tyranny to the extirpation of which he had dedicated his life, the old, humorous condescension toward his father's limitations rapidly changing to contempt. It was a soul-shaking crisis for both father and son, a crisis inevitably headed for a complete break.

ELOPEMENT

The break was not long in coming. Indeed, the elements for it were already maturing although Timothy was unaware of them. It was not until the latter part of August that the rumor reached him that his son was interested in the daughter of a retired coffeehouse keeper, and he asked Whitton to investigate. But Whitton was too late. He could not in August stop a train of events that had started in January, a train of events which, ironically enough, had resulted from Timothy's own quarantining tactics.

Shelley's sister Hellen, twelve years of age, had a school-girl friend, fifteen years of age, Harriet Westbrook, who used to receive letters for her from Shelley, as Timothy, fearing the spread of Shelley's radicalism, had forbidden correspondence between the brother and sister.[18] Probably on January 1 or 2, Shelley, accompanied by his cousin, Charles Grove, called on Harriet; and on January 11 he requested Stockdale to send her a copy of *St. Irvyne*.[19] Shelley requested that they correspond on matters philosophical and political, and, from that time on, letters—which have all now disappeared—passed back and forth.[20] This correspondence not only began a new period in Shelley's life but precipitated in its outcome one of the most violent controversies in English literary biography.

Of the Westbrook family we know comparatively little. John Westbrook was born in 1750 or 1751, and at the time of his marriage in 1780 was described as a "vintner." [21] He made a comfortable fortune from the ownership of an establishment known as the "Mount Coffee House" in Grosvenor Square,[22] "a noted coffee-house" according to Wheatley's *London*.[23] When Westbrook obtained this business, we do not know, but it must have existed before his proprietorship because Laurence Sterne addressed a letter from it in 1765.[24] By 1782 it was apparently quite well known, for it is represented in that year as the scene of a political debate in William Mason's satire "The Dean and the 'Squire,'" which opens:

> In Coffee-house of good account,
> Not far from Bond-street, call'd *The Mount,*
> Soame Jenyns met the Dean of Gloucester . . .[25]

It must have been a flourishing and quite extensive business. When Westbrook died in 1835 his personal estate was sworn under £60,000,[26] and he had been in retirement since at least 1811; in 1817, he was prepared to put up £2000 for the Shelley children and he owned a country house in Wales.[27] The Westbrooks, therefore, were not, as one might gather from Hogg's jibes,[28] a disreputable, lower-class family, but prosperous representatives of the London middle class. Their wealth, however, did not mean that a certain taint did not accrue to them from the nature of the business, for a coffeehouse in early nineteenth century

London was not the genteel establishment of an earlier day described by Addison and Steele, but had evolved into a kind of combination tavern, club, and gambling house.[29] Some of them (such as that so riotously visited by Tom and Jerry) [30] were the haunts of professional sharpers and prostitutes; and while Westbrook's was not one of these but a large establishment "of good account," his designation of "vintner" shows that coffee was not the only beverage sold, and he would certainly not be acceptable in the higher circles of society.

Of Mrs. Westbrook we know nothing beyond Hogg's remark that she sat "as dignified as silk and satin could make her" all day long "with her hands before her"; but "utterly incapable of aught beside." [31] Hogg may have had some basis for his picture, although he was never in the Westbrook household, for Mrs. Westbrook seems to have played curiously little part in subsequent events, but she was, at any rate, capable of producing four children, one son and three daughters, of whom we are concerned only with Eliza, born in 1782, and Harriet, born on August 1, 1795.

Following Shelley's visit to the Westbrook home (at 23 Chapel Street, within a block or so of the Mount Coffee House) in January 1811, we hear no more of the Westbrooks until a letter to Hogg on April 18: "Miss Westbrook [Eliza] has this moment called on me, with her sister [Harriet]. It certainly was very kind of her." [32] Shelley can hardly have seen much, if anything, of the Westbrooks between his January visit and March 26, for he was in Oxford during that period. They cannot have called on him between March 26, when he arrived in London, and April 17, for Hogg left London on April 17 and had not seen them.[33] On the other hand, it is likely that Shelley had called on the Westbrooks during this period, for they knew that Hogg was leaving and ostensibly called to cheer up the now lone bachelor. From this date until Shelley's elopement with Harriet on August 25, there is scarcely a letter to Hogg which does not mention the Westbrooks. On April 24, we hear that "my little friend Harriet W. is gone to her prison house. She is quite well in health, at least so she says, though she looks very much otherwise. I saw her yesterday, I went with her sister to Miss H.'s, & walked about Clapham Common with them for two hours." [34] The "prison house" and "Miss H.'s" are identical, namely the school at Clapham run by a Miss Hawkes, attended by both Harriet and Shelley's sisters, and at which Shelley believed they were harshly treated.[35] On the same day he is going to the Westbrooks for dinner, and a day or so later is "called" to Miss Westbrook's, and has been with her visiting Harriet at school. He has heard that Harriet is being ostracized by the other pupils for being the friend of the "atheist" Shelley.[36] By April 28, this "persecution" has so worn Harriet down that she is back for a day at her father's house:

My poor little friend has been ill, her sister sent for me the other night. I found her on a couch pale; her father is civil to me, very strangely; the sister is too civil by half. She began talking about *l'amour*. I philosophized, and the youngest said she had such a headache, that she could not bear conversation. Her sister then went away, and I stayed till half-past twelve. Her father had a large party below, he invited me; I refused. Yes! The fiend, the wretch, shall fall! Harriet will do for one of the crushers, and the eldest (Emily), with some taming, will do, too. They are both very clever, and the youngest (my friend) is amiable. Yesterday she was better, to-day her father compelled her to go to Clapham, whither I have conducted her, and I am now returned.[37]

On May 8, Shelley writes: "I spend most of my time at Miss Westbrook's," and he addresses a letter from their house at about the same time: "I am now at Miss Westbrook's. She is reading Voltaire's *Dictionnaire Philosophique*." [38] His strange dallying in London from the middle of April to the middle of May, which so surprised Hogg, was, therefore, probably motivated by his interest in Harriet (and, indeed, his mysterious hintings at it in conjunction with his comments on the Westbrooks and his love poetry included in the letters seem intended to convey as much to Hogg); and when he finally did leave, he "arranged a correspondence" with Eliza and Harriet, to be addressed not to Field Place, but to the home of Captain Pilfold at Cuckfield.[39] On May 19, he there received a letter from Eliza,[40] and on June 11, another letter:

It gives me pleasure to see from the trend of your last letter that your mind has greatly recovered its accustomed cheerfulness, and that you are otherwise amended by a change of residence.

I am obliged to you for your proposition in regard to Harriett, but I am in hopes she will leave school for good—there has been another little misunderstanding between the friends at Clapham, which has rendered the situation of my sister so completely uncomfortable my Father has now determined upon her not returning there again; he talks of wholly retiring into the country, but not to any distant part. It is so much my wish to leave this busy scene that I shall do all in my power to expedite his plan.

You will not take any notice to your sister Mary, or indeed any of your family, of your intimacy with us; for particular reasons which I will explain to you when next I have the pleasure of seeing you.[41]

By June 21, and probably by June 16, Shelley had received an invitation from Mr. Westbrook to spend a vacation with them at their country home at Aberystwyth in Wales. Knowing that his family would not consent, he also accepted a previous invitation from his cousin Thomas Grove to visit his estate near Rhayader in Wales, some thirty miles from Aberystwyth. From there he intended to visit the Westbrooks, without the knowledge of his family, and also to visit Hogg in York.[42]

While on one of his visits to his uncle's (on which he picked up the mail from the Westbrooks), Shelley met a schoolteacher from a nearby town, Elizabeth Hitchener, with whom he opened a correspondence on political and religious matters, similar to that with Harriet. Miss Hitchener was in London later in June, and Shelley told her on June 25 that he would visit her there on his way to Wales.[43] When he arrived in London, we do not exactly know. He addressed a letter from Field Place on July 4, and his next letter is from his uncle's estate in Wales on about July 15.[44] That he spent several days of the intervening period in London we know, and it is likely, as Professor Hughes speculates, that he spent them with the Westbrooks.[45] He had failed to write to Hogg from London and he had failed to visit Miss Hitchener as promised, both omissions that require a powerful counter-motive to explain. That this counter-motive was indeed Harriet is indicated in Shelley's purposely mystifying account of his activities in London, stating (to Miss Hitchener) that he was there for some "days" of "pressing and urgent business" such as would "admit of neither delay or rest" during which, he hints, his mind was "subdued" by his "body," an experience which resulted in "several nights of restlessness" and "a short but violent nervous illness."[46] A few days later he is still preparing to meet the Westbrooks in Aberystwyth; and he has received a novel from Harriet, *Adelina-Mowbray, or the Mother and Daughter* by Amelia Opie.[47] The plot of this book (according to Professor White's summary) concerns a young author, of good family but with radical views on religion and marriage, who falls in love with the beauteous Adelina. They become united in a free-love union, which results in persecution and exile. "The remaining two-thirds of the book emphasized the disastrous consequences of unmarried love. . . ."[48] A few days later, annoyed at Hogg's continued bantering, Shelley wrote:

Your jokes on Harriet Westbrook amuse me: it is a common error for people to fancy others in their own situation, but if I know anything about love, I am *not* in love.[49]

But on about the fifth of August, Hogg received the following extraordinary communication:

You will perhaps see me before you can answer this; perhaps not; Heaven knows! I shall certainly come to York, but *Harriet Westbrook* will decide whether now or in three weeks. Her father has persecuted her in a most horrible way, by endeavouring to compel her to go to school. She asked my advice: resistance was the answer, at the same time that I essayed to molify Mr. W[estbrook] in vain! And in consequence of my advice *she* has thrown herself on *my* protection.

I set off for London on Monday. How flattering a distinction!—I am thinking of ten million things at once.

What have I said? I declare, quite *ludicrous*. I advised her to resist. She wrote to say that resistance was useless, but that she would fly with me, and threw herself upon my protection. We shall have £200 a year: when we find it run short, we must live, I suppose, upon love! Gratitude and admiration all demand that I should love her *for ever*. We shall see you at York. I will hear your arguments for matrimonialism, by which I am now almost convinced. . . . I shall come to live near you, as Mr. Peyton.[50]

And Shelley wrote in similar strain to his cousin Charles Grove.[51] If Shelley left Wales on Monday, August 5, as he told Hogg he would, he must have arrived in London on about August 7. He remained there "several days," mostly with Harriet, took a flying trip to Field Place, August 14–15, returned to Field Place on about August 17 and remained there until about August 24. While there he made a trip to Cuckfield, where he saw Miss Hitchener and informed her he was thinking of entering medical school, and another trip to Horsham where he borrowed £25 from Medwin's father, Thomas Charles Medwin.[52]

His letters to Hogg show that in his first few days in London (i.e. *ca.* August 7–14), after his enthusiastic trip from Wales, he met with a "perplexing" situation and reveal him as in a state of unstable depression. Harriet has turned him down.

My arguments [i.e. to persuade Harriet] have been *yours*. They have been urged by the force of the gratitude which this occasion excited. But I yet remain in London; I remain embarrassed and melancholy. I am now dining at Grove's. Your letter has just been brought in; I cannot forbear just writing this. *Your* noble and exalted friendship, the prosecution of your happiness, can alone engross my impassioned interest. I never was so fit for calm argument, as now. This, I fear, more resembles exerted action than inspired passion.[53]

A day or so later he is more explicit:

The late perplexing occurrence which called me to town, occupies my time, engrosses my thoughts. I shall tell you more of it when we meet, which I hope will be soon. It does not, however, so wholly occupy my thoughts, but that you and your interests still are predominant. . . . My father is here, wondering, possibly, at my London business. He will be more surprised soon, possibly!

My unfortunate friend, Harriet, is yet undecided; not with respect to me, but herself. How much, my dear friend, have I to tell you! In my leisure moments for thought, which since I wrote have been few, I have considered the important point on which you reprobated my hasty decision. The ties of love and honour are doubtless of sufficient strength to bind congenial souls—they are doubtless indissoluble, but by the brutish force of power; they are delicate and satisfactory. Yet the arguments of impracticability, and what is even worse, the disproportionate sacrifice which the female is called upon to make—these arguments, which you have urged in a manner immediately irresistible, I cannot withstand. Not that I suppose it to be likely that *I* shall directly be called upon to evince my attachment to either theory.[54]

But all difficulties were ultimately resolved, for on the morning of August 25, following his return from Field Place the day previously, he met Harriet at a coffeehouse in Mount Street—whether or not that previously owned by her father is not recorded. From there, accompanied by his cousin, Charles Grove, they went to an inn where they waited all day until the mailcoach for the north left at 7 in the evening.[55] On August 28, after three days of continuous travel, they arrived in Edinburgh, obtained a license, and were married the following day.[56]

Such, in brief, were the events leading up to one of the most discussed elopements in literary history. The motives behind these events are more complex than would appear on the surface. Considering first the Westbrook side of the picture, the inference is clearly that Eliza Westbrook is engineering a marriage. This is clear from her own letter of June 11 to Shelley, a letter addressed not to his home but to that of Captain Pilfold and specifically warning him against mentioning "your intimacy with us" to his family. It is inferable also from the attention she paid Shelley in London and from Shelley's letter of April 28. The technique Eliza used to excite Shelley's interest is apparent also in her June 11 letter—to play up Harriet's "persecution" and to hint of her removal from school (and from Shelley) by her father.[57] That she was assisted by Mr. Westbrook, to some degree, is apparent from his strange "civility" and his invitation to Shelley to spend a vacation at their home in Wales. And Whitton was of the opinion that he was "at least passive if not aiding in the intercourse between the young persons." [58] What part Harriet played in the scheme is not clear, but we have to remember that Harriet was a girl of fifteen (just turned sixteen at the date of the elopement), who had led a sheltered existence: "When I lived with my father, I was not likely to gain much knowledge, as our circle of acquaintance was very limited, he not thinking it proper that we should mix much with society." [59] Her dependence on her sister was abnormal: "She is my more than Mother. What do I not owe to her gentle care? Everything." [60] Harriet, during this period, cannot be treated as an adult or judgments made about her in adult terms. Her level of emotional maturity was about that of a highschool sophomore today even though her intellectual interests were unusually extensive. That she was actually persecuted at school for her admiration of the "atheist" Shelley we know to be true from another source,[61] and she doubtless believed herself to be "in love" with the dynamic, rebellious youth of nineteen. On the other hand, it is a reasonable assumption that Eliza's main motive was social and economic, i.e. to unite the Westbrooks' family fortunes with those of the prospective heir to £200,000, Field Place, and a baronetcy. And, in view of Harriet's apparently rather passive character and her abnormal dependence on her sister, the probability is that she worked mainly under Eliza's guidance, although perhaps from time to time taking the initiative, writing letters to Shelley, sending Mrs. Opie's anti-free love novel, exaggerating her disturbance over her "persecution."

So much for the Westbrooks. What of Shelley? Shelley gave his version of the story some two months later to Elizabeth Hitchener:

The frequency of her letters became greater during my stay in Wales, l answered them; they became interesting. They contained complaints of the irrational conduct of her relations, and the misery of living where she could *love* no one. Suicide was with her a favorite theme, her total uselessness was urged as its defence. [This I] admitted, Supposing she could *prove* her inutility, [and that she] was powerless. Her letters became more and more g[loomy] at length one assumed a tone of such despair, as induced me to quit Wales precipitately.—I arrived in London. I was shocked at observing the alteration of her looks. Little did I divine its cause; she had become violently attached to *me,* and feared that I should not return her attachment . . . prejudice made the confession painful. It was impossible to avoid being much affected, I promised to unite my fate with hers. I staid in London several days, during which she recovered her spirits. I had promised at her bidding to come again to London. They endeavoured to compel her to return to a school where malice and pride embittered every hour; she wrote to me. I came to London. I proposed marriage for the reasons which I have given you, and she complied.[62]

Shelley's version as gathered from this letter and those to Hogg is that, although he was not in love with Harriet, Harriet fell in love with him and to save her from "persecution" at school he married her. But this version is clearly suspect, for Shelley, as Professor White has pointed out,[63] had motives for distortion. He did not wish Hogg to feel that their friendship was being relegated to a secondary position by his interest in Harriet, and he was sensitive in explaining to Elizabeth Hitchener how he, one of the anti-matrimonial enlightened, came to marry and, furthermore, married without informing her in advance: "You will enquire how I an *Atheist* chose to subject myself to the ceremony of marriage,—how my conscience could consent to it." [64] Thus Shelley's tendency in explaining his actions to both of these correspondents would inevitably be to play down his own initiative. And, in doing so, he fell into contradictions. In his letter of August 15 to Hogg, he admits in his opening sentence that the affair with Harriet "occupies my time, engrosses my thoughts," and then, sensing that this might hurt Hogg's feelings, adds "you and your interests are still predominant." In the same letter, after announcing that he is now "a perfect convert to matrimony" and that his father is due for a "surprise," he hastily adds that he does not feel that he will have to put his views into practice.[65] In the letter to Hogg on *ca.* August 3, he states that Harriet's proposal came by mail to Wales and that it was its receipt that decided him to return to London; in the letter to Elizabeth Hitchener, he represents the proposal as coming verbally after his return to London and represents that return as due to Harriet's "gloom" and threats of suicide. In view of these motives and contradictions, Shelley's statements to Hogg that he is "not in love" and is forcing himself to act become suspect, and the whole story to Elizabeth Hitchener requires examination.

In the first place, it is clear that Shelley was no passive victim of circumstance but was in active pursuit of Harriet. In this pursuit he was driven by two sets of motives, social and sexual. He had decided upon a career as social propagandist for a new order and to make a break with his family. Eleven days before the elopement he wrote with anger to Elizabeth Hitchener of "this detestable coil of primaeval prejudice, that I will free myself from," and Merle, visiting him at Horsham, found him dissatisfied and bitter.[66] In this career he believed that Harriet would make a suitable partner: "Harriet will do for one of the crushers." "I am," he wrote some months later to Godwin, "married to a woman whose views are similar to my own." And again: "My wife is the partner of my thoughts and feelings." [67]

Shelley's sexual instincts were normally strong and he had a good deal of insight into them. His interest in sex is eloquently attested by *Zastrozzi* and *St. Irvyne* (not to mention the rascalities of *Epithalamium*), and his letters to Hogg a few months later, apropos of Hogg's interest in Harriet, provide an interesting revelation, by implication, of his own state prior to the elopement:

I attach little value to the monopoly of exclusive cohabitation . . . if you lived with us you would be driven to this last consummation of your love for Harriet . . . You would fancy it was virtue, & passion prolific in excuses would coin thousands when so great was the purchase.

How can I tell, how can you tell that passion will not urge this love to its extremest consummation, for I do not believe that sensation is something other than terribly strong.

It is strange to me that you, who know the human mind so well, should think so lightly of sensation. If you have loved, I can believe you have not felt it lightly.

I don't know that absence will certainly cure love; but this I know, that presence will terribly augment the passion.[68]

There can be little doubt that Shelley is here analyzing Hogg's motives in terms of his own of a few months previously. He begins with the premise that the sexual drive ("sensation") is a "terribly strong" force. Not wishing to recognize this strength, one tends to rationalize, to invent other motives ("passion prolific in excuses"). The sexual instinct can be aroused without love (which is the implication in regard to Hogg), but, on the other hand, if love is present the two are intermixed ("if you have loved . . ."). And while it may exist when the object of desire is not present, nothing arouses it so violently as the "presence" of this object. And here Shelley is doubtless thinking of the "augmenting" of his own "passion" by the "presence" of Harriet during his final days with her in London.

In other letters of the same period he elaborates to Elizabeth Hitchener his theories on lust and love: on the one hand, a "passion of animal love," on the other, a "disinterested" love, a love which considers not the desires of the lover but the "happiness of its object"; the one "self-centred, self-devoted, self interested . . . the parent of jealousy," the

other a love "which seeks the good of all, the good of its object first . . .
loving virtue for virtue's own loveliness." [69] In his pursuit of Harriet,
Shelley believed that he was motivated by this second love, i.e. a genuine
love as distinct from simple lust. But this did not mean, as his comments
to Hogg indicate, that genuine love was not combined with the sexual
drive, a drive, however, not turned inwards toward self-gratification,
but outwards toward the pleasure of the beloved. "Love! Adore!" he
enjoined Hogg in another letter, ". . . Combine it if you will with
sensation; perhaps they are inseparable." [70] (And seven years later he
had developed the concept further, referring to the sexual act as "the
act which ought always to be the link and type of the highest emotions
of our nature.") [71]

Shelley, therefore, in spite of his comments to Hogg in August, did
believe himself to be in love with Harriet at the time of the elopement;
this love he considered "disinterested" but realized its sensuous aspects.
In its pursuit he was ardent: "engrosses my thoughts." And he believed,
too, as we have seen, that he and Harriet were intellectually compatible.
Thus, in the person of Harriet the sexual and the social motives
blended.

The initial declaration of love between Harriet and Shelley came, in
all probability, neither, as he informed Hogg, by letter at Harriet's
initiative, nor, as he told Elizabeth Hitchener, in London after his
return to Wales, but during his visit to London in July before proceeding to Wales. This and its ramifications was the mysterious "business"
in London during that visit which produced "sleeplessness" and a
"nervous illness"; it was perhaps then, too, that the scene described in
the letter to Elizabeth Hitchener took place; and it was then that he
first urged Harriet to run away with him.[72] This initial proposal, moreover, was not for marriage but for a free-love union: in the August 3
letter, he implies that Harriet has accepted his previous proposition and
this was obviously not one of marriage; Hogg has been writing to warn
Shelley of the follies of a free-love adventure—which he clearly presumed was Shelley's intention—and urging him to marry; [73] Harriet
sent the anti-free-love novel to Shelley shortly after he left London for
Wales. The free-love proposal had either been rejected or held over
for consideration when Shelley left London in July. On August 2 or 3
came Harriet's letter which Shelley interpreted as an acceptance of this
proposal. His intention then, as he told Hogg, was to elope with Harriet
to York, live there under the name of "Peyton," and discuss with Hogg
the pros and cons of "matrimonialism."

When Shelley arrived in London on about August 7, he presumably made the proposal to Harriet, as he had outlined it to Hogg, and was rejected. He, then, as he told Elizabeth Hitchener, "proposed marriage." [74] This proposal had been made by *ca.* August 14 as the letter to Hogg of that time reveals: "My arguments have been *yours*" (for Hogg's arguments had been for marriage).[75] Even this proposal, however, left Harriet "undecided" and her indecision made Shelley "embarrassed and melancholy," but he devoted all his "time" to a solution. That the reason for the indecision was psychological in Harriet, as Shelley indicates, may be partly true, but it probably reflects a crisis in the Westbrook family. A regular marriage was impossible as Shelley's father would have withheld consent; and Mr. Westbrook must have been opposed to an elopement, for he put up no money for it and later refused funds to the honeymooners, whereas Eliza must have been in favor of it as the subsequent elopement was too well regulated for it to have been entirely directed by Shelley and Harriet.[76] When Shelley saw Elizabeth Hitchener on about August 17, he talked of going into medicine, and this may have been a blind or it may indicate that he feared that the elopement would not materialize. But within a day or two he received a letter from Harriet that all was well, borrowed £25 from Mr. Medwin, and rushed to London.[77] He had not, it seems, intended to elope until September 1 when his £75 quarterly allowance came due,[78] but the £25 decided him to act immediately. Thus, if it is true that Eliza had been setting a trap for Shelley, it is true also that he entered it with his eyes open—"the sister is too civil by half"—and, in the final stages, with impetuous eagerness: "occupies my time, engrosses my thoughts."

Shelley and Harriet honeymooned in Edinburgh from the end of August until the end of September, being joined by Hogg a few days after their arrival. And it is from Hogg that we first begin to get a picture of Harriet. Harriet, he informs us, was "always pretty, always bright, always blooming; smart, usually plain in her neatness; without a spot, without a wrinkle, not a hair out of its place. The ladies said of her that she looked as if she had just that moment stepped out of a glass case; and so indeed she did." "She was," he continues, "fond of reading aloud; and she read remarkably well, very correctly, and with a clear distinct agreeable voice, and often emphatically. She was never weary of this exercise, never fatigued; she never ceased of her own accord, and left off reading only on some interruption." Moreover, her reading was mainly in "grave and excellent books"; unlike most young ladies of the day, she eschewed devotional reading: "I never once saw a Bible, prayer book or any devotional work in her hand . . . I never heard her say that she had been at church . . . her music was wholly secular." She was skilled enough in French to translate a novel (or at least a part of it): "She rendered the two volumes exactly and correctly; and wrote the whole out fairly, without blot or blemish, upon the smoothest, whitest, finest paper, in a small, neat, flowing and legible feminine hand." [79] She was a "gentle" and "modest" girl, "always most unwilling to show her ankles." [80] She was usually in good spirits but not deeply emotional—"bright, blooming and placid." [81] One strange characteristic Hogg noted: a tendency to talk of suicide:

She often discoursed of her purpose of killing herself some day or other, and at great length, in a calm, resolute manner. She told me that at school— where she was very unhappy, as she said, but I could never discover why she was so, for she was treated with much kindness and exceedingly well in- structed—she had conceived and contrived sundry attempts and purposes of destroying herself. . . . She spoke of self-murder serenely before strangers; and at a dinner party I have heard her describe her feelings, opinions, and intentions with respect to suicide with prolix earnestness; and she looked so calm, so tranquil, so blooming, and so handsome that the astonished guests smiled.[82]

From this picture, a psychological pattern begins to emerge. The unhappy childhood with its suicide fantasies reveals an early malad- justment, a sense of isolation from the group, which was doubtless nurtured by a child's sensitiveness, in a better-class girls' school, to the nature of her father's business and must have had early roots in the home environment. Harriet retreated to her books and her fantasies, and turned, in her retreat, toward an abnormal dependence on a domi- nant elder sister. The result was the formation of a dependent "compul- sive" personality; the unusual "neatness" in dress, the exactness and correctness of the translation, the "small, neat" handwriting, the "cor- rect" reading which continued mechanically, the extreme modesty; and underneath this rigid structure, unmistakable schizoid foundations: "She spoke of self-murder *serenely* . . ." There were weaknesses in the skeleton of the personality, weaknesses which would not withstand strain; but the personality as a whole, the living personality, was friendly and lovable and goodnatured and sincere; a "pure and truthful nature," wrote Peacock, remembering forty-seven years later, "her speech the essence of frankness and cordiality . . . once to be in her company was to know her thoroughly." [83] And her letters reveal her as having been a friendly, intelligent, and observant girl, interested in social problems but strangely lacking in emotional or intellectual initiative. To Hogg, in Edinburgh, she and Shelley appeared to be a devoted young couple, happy in their love, with mutual interests, and full of fun and jests. From the top of a coach, Hogg pointed out to them fields of turnips and barley. "Poor Harriet was not much of a farmer . . . 'Pray tell me, Bysshe,' she asked, 'which are the turnips and which is the barley?' 'Why, you little Cockney,' Shelley, the heir of entail to broad lands, exclaimed, 'surely you know turnips from barley!' " [84] And the picture is borne out by Shelley's letters. "I am devoted to her happiness," he wrote a few weeks later to Hogg.[85] ". . . Assist me," he urged Elizabeth Hitchener, "to mould a really noble soul into all that can make its nobleness useful and lovely. Lovely it is now, or I am the weakest slave of error." [86]

WANDERINGS AND EXCISIONS

By the end of September, Hogg had to get back to his legal apprenticeship at York and all three journeyed there, probably arriving on October 5, traveling on funds provided by Captain Pilfold.[87] Ten days later, Shelley departed for Pilford's house at Cuckfield, Sussex,[88] leaving Harriet and Hogg behind together; for while the honeymooners had been sojourning in Edinburgh, other events had taken place elsewhere. About the middle of August, Timothy had learned that machinations were afoot and commissioned the trusty Whitton to investigate.[89] But Whitton hesitated—"I shall not like to meddle with such a chicken, for he has much confidence" [90]—and Timothy first heard of the elopement via an insultingly casual note en route from his erring son:

Doubtless you will be surprised at my sudden departure; you will be more surprised at its finish; but it is little worth the while of its inhabitants to be affected at the occurrences of this world.[91]

Receipt of this letter sent him scurrying to London, apparently with the intention of disinheriting his heir (perhaps with a scheme of making him a "Ward of Chancery").[92] On being informed that this was legally impossible, and after interviewing Westbrook—an interview unfortunately unrecorded—he decided, once more, to cut off Shelley's allowance and to refuse to accept his letters. All correspondence, again, was to be through Whitton.[93]

To the disgrace of expulsion from Oxford was now added the disgrace of marriage out of caste. And this, let it be clear, was the point at issue. Stockdale, encountering Timothy's protégé, Graham, about this time, learned from him "that Mr. Bysshe Shelley had run away with and married an inn-keeper's daughter, I think from Wales, and that they came to London, together, in a stage coach, with scarcely any pecuniary resources." [94] Stockdale's memory (after fifteen years) is hazy on the details of Graham's account, but the social attitude it conveyed is clear. "She was respectably connected," wrote De Quincey, "but had not moved in a rank corresponding to Shelley's." "His family," he continued, probably retailing gossip he heard in the Lake District following Shelley's visit there a few months later, "were now thoroughly irritated by what they regarded as a *mésalliance*." [95] If Shelley had run away with Harriet Grove, the young couple would have been welcomed back to Field Place with a few waggish remonstrances.

Shelley at first had little concept of how seriously Timothy would regard the elopement and continued to address him in ironical style (similar to that later brought to perfection in *A Refutation of Deism*): "To distrust your own mind . . . which the duties of legislation demands to be unruffled . . . is certainly as wrong as it is inconsistent with the Christian forbearance and forgiveness with which you are so eminently adorned." [96] But, as Timothy remained firm, and, more important, as the allowance failed to materialize, ironical insult turned to frantic rage:

I shall take the first opportunity of seeing you; if *you* will not hear my name *I* will pronounce it. Think not I am an insect whom injuries destroy . . . Had I money enough I would meet you in London and hollow in your ears Bysshe, Bysshe, Bysshe . . . aye, Bysshe till you're deaf.[97]

Such was the mood in which Shelley advanced on Field Place on October 20. He demanded his £200 allowance, accused his father of having broken his word that this allowance would be permanent (to which Timothy replied that it was granted only on condition that Shelley enter some profession), accused his mother wildly of an affair with Graham, declaring, indeed, that this threat to her honor was his sole reason for leaving York. His raging and accusations "frightened his mother and sisters exceedingly, and now if they hear a Dog Bark they run up stairs." So Timothy, belaboured but unmoved—"he must be humbl'd"—informed Whitton a few days later.[98] A letter and visit to the aging Sir Bysshe in his tavern lair were equally unavailing.[99] A threat to Whitton to confront him with the formidable Captain Pilfold left the lawyer unimpressed.[100]

On October 21, Shelley was back at Cuckfield with his uncle, and from there wrote to Mr. Thomas Charles Medwin at Horsham informing him that he intended to remarry Harriet, as he was apparently doubtful of the legality of the Scottish ceremony, and requested that he, as an attorney, draw up a marriage settlement of £700 a year for her "in case of my death." Medwin was to address his reply to him care of Mr. Westbrook, 23 Chapel street.[101] On the 22nd, Shelley and his uncle went to London.[102] There Shelley stayed until the 24th or 25th, negotiating with Whitton and probably discussing the marriage settlement with the Westbrooks.[103] He had intended to bring Eliza back to York with him,[104] but she left one day ahead of him, perhaps at his suggestion.[105] On the 22nd, Timothy also in London, met the Duke of Norfolk at a banquet, and the Duke agreed once more to try his hand with Shelley. "The Duke of Norfolk felt much and wished something might be settled, but His Grace said, 'Mr. S[helley], you cannot do it.' "[106] On October 24, the Duke called and asked Whitton to contact Shelley but Shelley had already left for York—from where he addressed a calm but troubled reply to the Duke—when Whitton's letter was delivered.[107]

Shelley arrived at York on October 26. The previous day, as we have noted, Eliza had arrived to unite her person and her fortunes with those of the happy couple.

The arrival of Bysshe [writes Hogg] was acknowledged by Harriet, but it was plain that he had been superseded; Eliza once or twice betrayed a faint consciousness of his presence, as if the lamp of her life had been faintly glimmering in its socket, which fortunately it was not; that was all the notice she took of her sister's husband. His course, therefore, was plain; his peace might have been assured; whether his happiness would ever have been great, may be well doubted. It was absolutely necessary to declare peremptorily, "Either Eliza goes, or I go"; and instantly to act upon the declaration. This so necessary course the poor fellow did not take; and it is certain that the Divine Poet could not have taken it, for with superhuman strength, weakness less than human was strangely blended; accordingly, from the days of the blessed advent, our destinies were entirely changed. The house lay, as it were, under an interdict; all our accustomed occupations were suspended; study was forbidden; reading was injurious—to read aloud might terminate fatally; to go abroad was death, to stay at home the grace! Bysshe became nothing; I, of course, very much less than nothing— a negative quantity of a very high figure.[108]

Even more revealing than Hogg's striking picture is Shelley's comment, a few months later, to Elizabeth Hitchener that "Eliza keeps our common stock of money, for safety, in some hole or corner of her dress" and "gives it out as we want it." [109] With the coming of Eliza, the marriage was put on a new basis, indeed, one might say under new management. It was transformed from a union of two young people who could learn and grow together into that of two dependents and an overseer. If we ask, as Hogg did, why Shelley did not take a firm stand with Eliza, we have first to consider the possibility that Shelley himself had urged Eliza to join them. Shelley, at this time, as his letters show, had considerable regard for Eliza [110] (and probably Eliza for Shelley), and the evidence, as has been noted, indicates that they consulted before she left for York. Hogg's implication, therefore, that Eliza forced her way into the household or was urged in by Harriet alone is almost certainly untrue. It is more likely that we are faced with the first manifestation of Shelley's penchant for a household containing two or more women, a penchant which perhaps had some psychological basis in an unconscious attempt to reconstruct his childhood home. And, when Shelley later grew to dislike Eliza, he faced a difficult situation, for a break would, in view of Harriet's psychological dependence on her sister, have threatened a major domestic crisis. We have to remember, too, that Eliza was ten years older than Shelley.

How long Shelley had intended to remain at York we do not know, but within a week he, along with Eliza and Harriet, had left for Keswick in the Lake District,[111] where the Duke of Norfolk had extensive estates. Hogg, typically, attributes this unannounced departure to Shelley's eccentricity, but the real reason for it we learn from a letter to Elizabeth Hitchener from Keswick shortly after Shelley's arrival: "Hogg is a mistaken man—vilely, dreadfully mistaken. . . . You know the implicit faith I had in him. . . . Can you then conceive that he would have attempted to *seduce my wife*." [112]

From a later letter we learn that Hogg had first attempted to seduce Harriet in Edinburgh but was rebuffed, but when Shelley left the two alone at York, "he urged the same suit, urged it with arguments of detestable sophistry. 'There is no injury to him who knows it not.'" [113] When Harriet broke the news to Shelley, he took Hogg for a walk out into the fields near York: "Our conversation was long . . . he was silent, pale, overwhelmed." [114] But if Hogg was overwhelmed, Shelley was overwhelmed also, and the letters that passed between the two from Keswick to York reveal a psychological crisis of first rate dimensions. Hogg asked that he be allowed to live with them again in "intimacy on the same happy terms as formerly" and prove that he was superior to temptation; he threatened suicide: "I *will* have Harriet's forgiveness, or blow my brains out at her feet"; he challenged Shelley to a duel, and, when refused, sarcastically commented on Shelley's "consistency in despising religion, despising duelling, and despising sincere friendship." [115] Shelley's letters were equally frenzied. He at first described Hogg's conduct as "disgusting and horrid," but later, perhaps having been reminded that as a champion of free love his arguments were inconsistent, he took the line that while he himself would not object to Hogg having relations with Harriet, Harriet would object and her "prejudices" must be taken into account:

Heaven knows that if the possession of Harriet's person, of the attainment of her love was all that intervened between our meeting again tomorrow, willingly would I return to York, aye willingly, to be happy thus to prove my friendship. Jealousy has no place in my bosom; I am indeed at times very much inclined to think the Godwinian plan is best, particularly since the late events. But Harriet does not think so. She is prejudiced; tho' I hope she will not always be so,—and on her opinions of right & wrong alone does the morality of the present case depend. If she was convinced of its innocence, would I be so sottish a slave to opinion as to endeavour to monopolize what if participated would give my friend pleasure without diminishing my own?" [116]

Hogg is deceiving himself if he believes that his motive is other than directly sexual: "I wish you would investigate the sources of this passion, my dear friend,—you would find it derived its principal source from sensation." This passion Harriet cannot "return" and "if she could she ought to stifle her desire to do so." Hogg is now fallen, degraded: "How terrible, how complete has been the perversion of that reason I *once* fancied almost omnipotent." [117] He is deceiving himself if he believes that he could live with them and not again be tempted: "presence without satisfaction will kindle the passions to an inextinguishable flame." [118] Hogg must under no circumstances visit them.

But at other times Shelley wavered, deeply disturbed, almost incoherent:

Are we parted, you . . . I . . . Forgive this wildness. I am half mad. I am wretchedly miserable. I look on Harriet. [Illeg: ? I think] she is before me . . . Has she convinced you? In what a spot Nature has exhausted the profusion of her loveliness. Will you come . . . dearest, best beloved of friends, will you come. Will you share my fortune, enter into my schemes . . . love me as I love you; be inseparable as once I fondly hoped you were . . . Yes, all's past, like a dream of the sick man which leaves but bitterness to a fleeting vision.

Ah! how I have loved you. I was even ashamed to tell you how! & now to leave you forever . . . no, not forever. Night comes, . . . Death comes . . . Cold, calm death, almost I would it were to-morrow. There is another life . . . Are you not to be the first there . . . Assuredly.

Dearest, dearest friend, reason with me . . . I am like a child in weakness . . . Your letters came directly after dinner. How could anyone read them unmoved . . . How could I forbear wishing that Death would yawn.[119]

That Shelley believed Hogg's action to be a violation of the principles they had both sworn allegiance to is true, and it is true that much of his emotional disturbance came from this belief, for, to Shelley, principles were all important. But all his disturbance, or even most of it, did not come from this belief. He is reacting primarily on an emotional and not an intellectual level; his first reaction is one of jealousy, even though his belief in principle will not allow him to admit this to himself. He is clearly not going to give Hogg and Harriet a chance to find out the nature of their "love" but has decided that it is based on "sensation." Harriet is whisked away from the tempter and he is abruptly told that even if she could conceive a passion for him she should not.

But an even deeper element than this is present, namely a strong and unmistakable homosexual attraction between Shelley and Hogg. This is evident not only in the frenetic letter just quoted—"Ah! how I love you"—and in other letters in the same series, but in Shelley's protestations during his courtship of Harriet that Hogg will still be "predominant." To Elizabeth Hitchener he contrasts Hogg's "animal passion" for Harriet with friendship:

How much worthier of a rational being is *friendship,* which tho' it wants none of the impassionateness which some have characterized as the inseparable of the other, yet retains judgment, which is not blind tho' it may chance to see something like perfection in its object, which retains its sensibility, but whose sensibility is celestial and intellectual, unallied to the grovelling, passions of the Earth.[120]

The attraction is evident, too, in his description of Hogg: "but never could you conceive, never having experienced it, that resistless and pathetic eloquence of his, never the illumination of that countenance, on which I have sometimes gazed till I fancied the world could be reformed by gazing too." [121] The explanation for this worship of Hogg, for the tortured neuroticism of the letters, for Hogg's wild threats of suicide and duels, and Shelley's frenzied waverings, can hardly lie within the normal bounds of disillusion in friendship. Shelley and Hogg are passing through a shattering emotional crisis, the root of which is the breakup of their relationship by Shelley's marriage.

But, although the homosexual emotion is unmistakable neither Shelley nor Hogg was predominately homosexual: Shelley did break with Hogg to marry Harriet; we know of no other homosexual episodes in his life; both he and Hogg married and had children (six in Shelley's case); Shelley's main interest in his writings, both emotionally and theoretically, is in normal love. What we are apparently dealing with is a passing postadolescent attraction between two college students in an exclusively male institution; such attachments, as recent researches have shown, are not uncommon, and those involved usually have a later predominantly or exclusively normal sexual and emotional history.[122] In Shelley's case, we can receive further illumination by consulting his introductory essay to his translation of Plato's *Symposium* (1818) in which he gives his views on sexual relations with special attention to the homosexual arguments Plato advances. Shelley, here, as elsewhere, condemns the Greek exaltation of homosexuality as part of a social repression of women:

. . . represent this passion as you will, there is something totally irreconcilable in its cultivation to the beautiful order of social life, to an equal participation in which all human beings have an indefeasible claim, and from which half the human race, by the Greek arrangement, were excluded.[123]

As a result of this degradation of women, the love instincts of the Greeks "deprived of their natural object, sought a compensation and a substitute . . . beautiful persons of the male sex became the object of that sort of feelings, which are only cultivated at present as towards females." [124]

But [he continues] let us not exaggerate the matter. We are not exactly aware,—and the laws of modern composition scarcely permit a modest writer to investigate the subject with philosophical accuracy,—what the action was by which the Greeks expressed this passion. I am persuaded that it was totally different from the ridiculous and disgusting conceptions which the vulgar have formed on the subject, at least except among the more debased and abandoned of mankind. It is impossible that a lover could usually have subjected the object of his attachment to so detestable a violation or have consented to associate his own remembrance in the beloved mind with images of pain and horror. If we consider the facility with which certain phenomena connected with sleep, at the age of puberty, associate themselves with those images which are the objects of our waking desires; and even that in some persons of an exalted state of sensibility, that a similar process may take place in reverie, it will not be difficult to conceive the almost involuntary consequences of a state of abandonment in the society of a person of surpassing attractions, when the sexual connection cannot exist, to be such as to preclude the necessity of so operose and diabolical a machination as that usually described. This is the result apparently alluded to by Plato.[125]

Thus, while Shelley rejects the Greek elevation of homosexuality as unnatural, "a substitute" resulting from their reactionary treatment of women, he does not condemn all forms of homosexual expression. He applies a similar criterion to that which he applies to love between a man and woman, namely that the relationship should be on a high emotional and intellectual level, and result in mutual pleasure. If the sexual act between a man and woman is part of an intense emotional complex, its physical aspect is minimized: "the perfection of this intercourse consisting, not perhaps in a total annihilation of the instinctive sense, but in the reducing it to as minute a proportion as possible, compared with the higher faculties of our nature, from which it derives its value." [126] In the case of two persons of the same sex, normal intercourse is impossible and any attempt at duplication is "ridiculous and disgusting," but, if the emotional "sensibility" is sufficiently intense, an even greater minimization of the physical is possible than in normal love. The concept, we may note, is similar to that in the letter on Hogg to Elizabeth Hitchener in which he upholds a "friendship" free from "animal passion" but which lacks none of the "impassionateness" of regular love and "retains its sensibility" to an even greater degree. The essay, therefore, tends to confirm the relationship with Hogg and places it in the perspective of Shelley's total views and life.

After a few weeks, the correspondence with Hogg ceased and Shelley's letters to Elizabeth Hitchener show Hogg taking up less and less of his interest and his beloved speculation on philosophical and political problems more and more, until by the end of his stay at Keswick, Hogg has dropped out of his letters entirely.

When the Shelleys and Eliza arrived in Keswick, they must have been almost without money. They had received a "small sum" from Mr. Westbrook, but, within a few weeks of their arrival, Shelley informed

Mr. Medwin that "we are now so poor as to be actually in danger of every day being deprived of the necessaries of life." [127] In these precarious circumstances, he began to realize the seriousness of the rift with his family, and turned, almost in desperation, to the Duke of Norfolk as a last hope for a settlement. Shortly before leaving York he had written to the Duke, and the tone of his letter, in striking contrast to the ironical or enraged epistles previously dispatched to his father, reveals his anxiety:

My situation is consequently most unpleasant: under these circumstances I request your Grace to convince my father of the severity of his conduct, to persuade him that my offence is not of the heinous nature that he considers it, to induce him to allow me a sufficient income to live with tolerable comfort.[128]

On November 7, the Duke replied to Shelley, under the impression that he was still at York, recording his letter in his journal:

To Mr. B. Shelly in answer that I should be glad to interfere, but fear with little hope of success; fearing that his father, and not he alone, will see his late conduct in a different point of view from what he sees it.

That I propose going into the North next week, and will come to York to see him, provided he will inform me when I may find him there.[129]

Thomas de Quincey, then living at nearby Grasmere, was, therefore, almost certainly right in believing—apparently on the basis of local rumor—that Shelley's choice of Keswick as a destination was influenced by his desire to continue negotiations through the Duke:

His Grace possessed the beautiful estate of Gobarrow Park on Ullswater and other estates of greater extent in the same two counties; his own agents he had directed to furnish any accommodations that might meet Shelley's views; and he had written to some gentlemen amongst his agricultural friends in Cumberland, requesting them to pay such neighbourly attentions to the solitary young people as circumstances might place in their power. This bias, being impressed upon Shelley's wanderings, naturally brought him to Keswick, as the most central and the largest of the little towns dispersed amongst the Lakes. Southey, made aware of the interest taken in Shelley by the Duke of Norfolk, with his usual kindness, immediately called upon him; and the ladies of Southey's family subsequently made an early call upon Mrs. Shelley.[130]

On November 10, the Duke "dined at Horsham," presumably with Sir Bysshe and Timothy.[131] On November 23, he invited Shelley, Harriet, and Eliza for a visit to his castle at Greystoke some fourteen miles from Keswick and invited a number of other guests also, including the liberal Whig, William Calvert (a friend of Wordsworth's), whom he had apparently requested to look after Shelley's interests.[132] The Duke of Norfolk, in 1811, was a man of sixty-five, drawing to the close of his stormy political career and known throughout the country as one of the most powerful and one of the most unorthodox members of the Whig aristocracy. In appearance, a large, ungainly man, noted both as a convert from Catholicism and a bon vivant—rumor had it that he had incongruously secreted within his castle both a priest and a mistress—he was as strange and "democratical" in his ways as his old crony Sir Bysshe, defiantly continuing the radical tradition of wearing his hair short and unpowdered (originally a sign of opposition to the powder tax used to promote the war against France) and "always appearing in a plain blue coat" in disregard of the fashions of the day.[133] That this eccentric but powerful man intervened once more to assist Shelley reveals not only his regard for the family but reflects also his own and the family's opinion that the young man might even at this last hour be saved for Field Place and Whigdom. The interest, as is clear from the Duke's diaries and from De Quincey, was not all on Shelley's side. And of this Shelley was aware:

The Duke is far from the best of the English Noblemen: he is not a moral man, but certainly is not attached to Catholicism. He desires and votes for Reform, tho' he has not virtue enough to begin it in his own person. He is in every respect a character of mediocrity, depend upon it, I have nothing to fear either from him or his emissaries. The Duke is as [little] my friend as he is yours—he merely desires to gratify thro' our family, his own borough-interest.[134]

The comments, made to Elizabeth Hitchener, of whose sensitivity to his upper-class position Shelley was acutely aware,[135] doubtless present a more unfavorable picture of the Duke than he really felt. But even here, Shelley admits that the Duke is a liberal thinker in politics and religion, a supporter of parliamentary reform and Catholic emancipation; and his strictures on the ducal morality are borne out by other accounts of him.[136]

We have no detailed account of Shelley's stay at Greystoke but we can imagine that the Duke and his guests had their hands full. For Shelley was a great believer in the stimulus of intellectual argument. "I explain my opinions with coolness and moderation," he informed his father shortly after returning from Greystoke,[137] and doubtless the ducal court was treated to a staggering barrage on the non-existence of God, the "detestable" nature of the marriage laws, the corruptions of Christianity, the horrors of aristocracy, and the necessity for economic equality.[138] Calvert, the Whig, Shelley liked, but the rest of the honored guests were dismissed as embodiments of "aristocratical insipidity"—"senseless monopolizers of time." [139]

The Shelleys and Eliza remained at Greystoke from December 1 to December 8 or 9 [140] and returned to Keswick. There, on December 13, at the Duke's suggestion, Shelley wrote to his father, apologizing for the "uneasiness which I have occasioned" and hoping for a "reconciliation," but standing firm on his principles. "I think it my duty to say that, however great advantages might result from such concessions, I can make no promise of concealing my opinions in political or religious matters." [141] To this Timothy replied on December 18, leaving open the door for further negotiations, but closing ominously: "I can never admit within my Family of the Principles that caus'd your expulsion from Oxford." [142] In his reply Shelley expressed filial gratitude that he was no longer regarded "in an unfavorable light" (which was hardly a legitimate deduction from Timothy's letter), noted, for his father's benefit (not, one may surmise, without some modicum of malicious pleasure) that they were now receiving £200 per annum from Mr. Westbrook, and held firm on his principles: "My principles still remain those which caused my expulsion from Oxford." [143] Within a month, however, Timothy, while keeping to his resolve not to receive him into the family unless he recanted, had restored his allowance of £200 ("to prevent your cheating strangers"),[144] an act of prime importance. The break with Field Place, with the comfortable post in one of the professions that his father had urged, with the career in the Lords or the Commons, was now complete. The final cord with his past was severed. Shelley was free to pursue his own life in his own way.

Shortly after his return from Greystoke, Shelley met Robert Southey —pensioned and two years away from his laureateship—at Calvert's home. Southey was deeply impressed both by Shelley's personality and talents: "He is brimfull and overflowing with everything good and generous—though the Oxford men were as much shocked at him as if he had hoofs and horns . . . but . . . when they expelled him they sent away more genius and better principles than they kept behind." [145] "Shelley," he wrote, "acts upon me as my own ghost would do." [146] And well he might so think, for Southey had been expelled from Westminster School for writing a radical article in opposition to flogging, had proceeded to Oxford where he had been noted as a young radical, a supporter of the French Revolution, with hair short and unpowdered. And on leaving Oxford he had written the revolutionary *Wat Tyler,* depicting the peasant's revolt of 1386 with direct reference to contemporary conditions and events:

> Our ministers, panders of a king's will,
> Drain all our wealth away, waste it in revels,
> And lure, or force away our boys . . . to fill their armies
> And feed the crows of France.[147]

But the ghost of the Southey of 1793 must have looked askance at the Southey of 1811, now a Tory supporter of war abroad and dictatorship at home, reviewer for the *Quarterly,* writer of odes to the Prince Regent and the Czar of Russia, supporter of punishment in the navy—"there will always be some subjects so vicious and brutal, that nothing but the fear of bodily pain may be powerful enough to deter them from guilt"— [148] advocate of political sinecures and placemen, implacable foe of parliamentary reform and democracy: "If all elections were made popular and the influence of wealth and power destroyed . . . it is easy to see who would be the successful candidates . . . not men whose names and families are older than the old oaks upon their estates . . . but the unsuccessful, the disappointed, and the desperate." [149]

Southey seems to have taken kindly to Shelley (not unaware of the Duke of Norfolk's interest),[150] invited him to his home, placed his extensive library at his disposal, and immediately got to work to put his youthful feet on the laurel-strewn path to orthodoxy and Toryism. His descriptions of Shelley in his letters are of unusual biographical interest for they reveal him as he appeared to a perceptive observer at this stage of his life. He was, of course, completely unknown to the general reading public but was perhaps remembered in some Eton and Oxford circles as an undergraduate writer; to Southey he appears essentially as a radical young prodigal, probably destined for a political career.

. . . Do you know Shelley the member for Shoreham? (not the Lewes Member). His eldest son is here under curious circumstances. . . . His father has cast him off,—but cannot cut off £6000 a year, tho' he may deprive him of as much more,—her's allows them £200 a year, and here they are. The D. of Norfolk is trying to bring about a reconciliation. I, liking him as you may suppose the better for all this, am in a fair way of convincing him that he may enjoy £6000 a year when it comes to him, with a safe conscience, that tho' things are not as good as they will be at some future time, he has been mistaken as to the way of making them better, and that the difference between my own opinion and his is—that he is 19 and I am 8 and 30. No other harm has been done than the vexation to her from her family, for as for the early marriage I consider that rather a good than an evil, seeing—as far as I have yet seen—that he has chosen well. If you know the father well enough to speak upon such a subject—endeavour to make him understand that a few years will do everything for his son which he ought to wish. He is got to Pantheism already, and in a week more I shall find him a Berkeleyan, for I have put the Minute Philosopher at his hands. He will get rid of his eccentricity, and he will retain his morals, his integrity and his genius, and unless I am greatly deceived there is every reason to believe he will become an honour to his name and his country. No possible chance [could] have thrown him in the way of a better physician, nor of one who would have taken a more sincere interest in the patient. . . .[151]

Southey's confidence in his therapeutic talents might have been somewhat shaken if he could have seen his would-be disciple's comments on him to Godwin ten days later as "the paid champion of every abuse and absurdity. . . . I do not feel the least disposition to be Mr. S.' proselyte." [152]

In spite of this unfavorable reaction—perhaps exaggerated somewhat for Godwin's benefit—Shelley's acquaintance with Southey must have left a deep impression on him. Southey was the first man of letters, indeed the first important intellectual, he had known, and to have such a man greet him with kindness in his wandering exile and open his library to him must have moved him strongly. The effect, however, was probably exactly the opposite to that which Southey intended. We do not know what books (except Berkeley) he urged upon him, but it is not likely that he would omit his own early radical works, *Joan of Arc, Wat Tyler, The Devil's Walk,* for he would naturally not wish to appear in too stodgy a light before the young radical. If so, Southey may have inadvertently given Shelley his first lesson in the art of expressing a radical creed in an extended literary medium, a lesson Shelley did not forget, for the sentiments of these works were soon to appear in his own poetry. Southey, in short, may have been a more important influence on the young Shelley than has been realized, for, while his stylistic influence has long been recognized, his ideological influence has not. Shelley's disgust with Southey's current philosophy, however, was genuine, and while he appreciated Southey's personal kindness and personal virtues, with this philosophy he was prepared to make no compromise.[153] When, in February, he left for the political maelstrom of Ireland, the two parted on amiable terms, although Southey "regretted" his action.[154] The two never met again; but their brief acquaintance was to have strange repercussions in future years.[155]

❧ REBEL AND ATHEIST

The stormy months from Shelley's expulsion from Oxford to the elopement and its aftermath of alienation from his family were scarcely conducive to literary effort, but he did embark upon a remarkable number of projects, the most ambitious of which have not survived. His first work was a political satire on the Prince Regent, inspired by his scornful contemplation of the gaudy fête held by the prince at Carlton House on June 19. At this fête—held in a London racked by war and haunted by the hideous impoverishment of its newly-developing industrial masses—there were entertained two thousand guests, 400 of them in the house, 1600 in the gardens under canvas. "All these walks in the gardens," the *Times* reported, "were closed in by walls, and covered over by awnings made for the occasion. In each of these cross walks were placed long supper tables, and at the end of each walk were communications to circular marquées, in which were tables containing all the necessary refreshments for the company, with space for the numerous servants and assistants in attendance. The Great Walk from the house southward had in it six tables, leaving those spaces quite open where other walks crossed it. . . . The interior sides of these grand walks were lined with festoons of flowers, yielding the most odoriferous perfumes, and relieved by the verdant and softer beauties that more towering plants and shrubs could bestow. The arched roofs were ornamented in the liveliest manner, and, from them, were suspended thousands of lights. . . . In the front of the Regent's seat there was a circular basin of water, with an enriched Temple in the centre of it, from whence there was a meandering stream to the bottom of the table, bordered with green banks. Three or four fantastic bridges were thrown over it, one of them with a small tower upon it, which gave the stream a picturesque appearance. It contained also a number of gold and silver fish." [156]

Shelley's indignation at this vulgar gaudiness bursts out in a lettter to Elizabeth Hitchener:

What think you of the bubbling *brooks* and mossy *banks* at Carlton House—the *allees vertes,* etc.? It is said that this entertainment will cost £120,000. Nor will it be the last bauble which the nation must buy to amuse this overgrown bantling of Regency. How admirably this growing spirit of ludicrous magnificence tallies with the disgusting splendours of the stage of the Roman Empire which preceded its destruction! Yet here are a people advanced in intellectual improvement wilfully rushing to a revolution, the natural death of all great commercial empires, which must plunge them in the barbarism from which they are slowly arising.[157]

"Bysshe," Charles Grove remembered, ". . . wrote a poem on the subject of about fifty lines, which he published immediately, wherein he apostrophized the prince as sitting on the banks of his tiny river; and he amused himself with throwing copies into the carriages of persons going to Carlton House after the fête." [158]

In August, shortly before his elopement, Shelley was engaged on a series of "moral and metaphysical essays," and he continued work on them after settling in Keswick, but they were later left behind in Ireland.[159] At Keswick, too, he was at work on a political novel, *Hubert Cauvin,* dealing with "the cause of the failure of the French Revolution, and the state of morals and opinions in France during the latter years of the monarchy." [160] But of this novel, although Shelley claimed to have written two hundred pages, all trace has been lost.[161] The only important extant work of the period is *The Devil's Walk.* In 1799 Coleridge and Southey printed in the *Morning Chronicle* a political ballad entitled *The Devil's Thoughts,* later reprinted as *The Devil's Walk,* in which the devil, viewing England as his farm, and himself as overseer, visits its inhabitants. The ballad, in detailing his adventures, hits at such current evils as the slave trade, taxation, prison conditions, church corruption. The only remembered line in the work is that on the devil's "favorite sin" being "the pride that apes humility," but it struck a sufficiently popular note for Byron to imitate it in 1813 and for Professor Porson's admirers later to claim it as his.[162] It seems likely that Southey showed Shelley this old squib of his and Coleridge's, for in a letter of January 20, 1812 (but a few weeks after meeting Southey), Shelley sent his own version of the poem to Elizabeth Hitchener.[163] Later he rewrote this early version and had it printed as a broadside (for the distribution of which his servant was arrested in August). Shelley adopts the general plan from the Southey-Coleridge original—the devil visiting England as his farm—and imitates some of their stanzas but brings the matter up to date.[164] Instead of attacking slavery, which, following Wilberforce's efforts, was no longer a live issue, he attacks the war against France, specifically Wellington's current campaign in Spain, the foreign policy of Castlereagh in Ireland, economic exploitation—

> And they thrive well who from the poor
> Have snatched the bread of penury—

the obese decadence of "the first gentleman in Europe":

> Fat as that Prince's maudlin brain,
>   Which, addled by some gilded toy,
> Tired, gives his sweetmeat, and again
>   Cries for it, like a humoured boy.[165]

The poem is deliberately written in the loose, over-simplified style of the political ballads of the time, and, although it lacks the cohesive sparkle of the best works of the genre, is an effective piece of mass political propaganda. It is important, too, in the history of Shelley's development, as the first work in the strain later so successfully developed in *Peter Bell* and *Swellfoot the Tyrant*.

Although the extant works of this period are of no literary value, they are of importance as revealing a further development of the pattern begun in the Finnerty campaign at Oxford. The "votary of romance" period has perished and perished for good, and Shelley is now committed to his new career of social and political propagandist. This propaganda is directed to two different classes of readers, the working people and the liberal intellectuals. The former, Shelley is attempting to arouse to a realization of their wrongs through the medium of popular, political ballads distributed as broadsheets; the latter, he is endeavoring to instruct in their political duties through novels and essays. The essence of this instruction, as embodied in *Hubert Cauvin,* was, as we can gather from Shelley's comments on the "lessons" of the French Revolution in his first Irish pamphlet composed in the same period, to urge the intellectuals to assume their place as the political leaders of the people and guide them through the coming social upheavals, which would be similar, he believed, to the French Revolution. In this stage of his career Shelley did not regard himself primarily as a writer or poet but a social thinker using poetry and fiction as propaganda media.

In the extant works, however, we have little direct indication of Shelley's actual intellectual development during this period. If the essays and novels had survived, they, doubtless, would have provided such a guide. As it is, however, we have to turn to his letters in order to supply the gap. And, fortunately, these letters, especially those to Elizabeth Hitchener, are remarkably rich in such material.

From these letters we learn that that Godwinian egalitarianism, which we noted as an influence at Oxford, had become, by the summer of 1811, the foundation of Shelley's political philosophy. He believed with Godwin that social evils were fundamentally caused by economic inequality (and not by a mere lack of political rights), and that these evils could only be abolished by the establishment of an egalitarian system; complete equality perhaps, could not—any more than could "perfectibility"—be attained, but man should strive to come as close to it as possible:

Equality is natural, at least many evils totally inconsistent with a state which symbolizes with Nature prevail in every system of inequality. I will assume this point, therefore, even although it be your opinion, or *my* opinion that equality is unattainable except by a parcel of peas or beans, still political virtue is to be estimated in proportion as it approximates to this ideal point of perfection, however unattainable.—But what can be worse than the present aristocratical system? Here are in England ten millions, only 500,000 of whom live in a state of ease; the rest earn their livelihood with toil and care.—If therefore these 500,000 aristocrats, who possess resources of various degrees of immensity, were to permit these resources to be resolved into their original stock; that is, entirely to destroy it, if each earned his own living (which I do not see is at all incompatible with the *height* of intellectual refinement,) then I affirm that each would be happy and contented, that crime and the temptation to crime would scarcely exist.—"But this paradise is all visionary."—Why is it visionary? Have you tried? The first inventor of a plough doubtless was looked upon as a mad innovator: he who altered it from its original absurd form doubtless had to contend with great prejudices in its disfavor. But is it not worth while that (altho' it may not be *certain*) the remaining 9,500,000 victims to its infringement (should) make some exertions in favour of a system evidently founded on the first principles of natural justice? [166]

In examining the evils of the existing property system, he condemns not only the aristocracy, with its great estates, but the capitalists also (a point emphasized by Mary Wollstonecraft among the republicans but not prominent in Godwin):

I here see palaces the thirtieth part of which would bless with every requisite of habitation their pampered owners . . . theatres converted from schools of morality into places for the inculcation of abandonment of every moral principle, whilst the haughty aristocrat, and the commercial monopolist unite in sanctioning by example the depravities to which the importations of the latter give rise. All monopolies are bad. I do not, however, when condemning commercial aggrandizement, think it in the least necessary to panegyrise hereditary accumulation.—Both are flagrant encroachments on liberty, neither can be used as an antidote for the poison of the other. . . . [167]

Shelley, however, not only disapproves of the rulers of the system but has an active sympathy for its victims, the industrial workers, who were subject to virtual military rule under the barracks system (whereby barracks for soldiers were established in manufacturing centers). He felt that in time the extreme misery of the working classes would result in revolution. As he wrote to Elizabeth Hitchener on December 26, 1811:

The manufacturers [workers] are reduced to starvation. My friends the military are gone to Nottingham. . . . Curses light on them for their motives, if they destroy one of its famine-wasted inhabitants.—But if I were a friend of the destroyed, myself about to perish, I fancy that I could bless them for saving my friend the bitter mockery of a trial.—Southey thinks that a revolution is *inevitable:* this is one of his reasons for supporting things as they are. But let us not belie our principles. They may feed and may riot and may sin to the last moment.—The groans of the wretched may pass unheeded till the latest moment of this infamous revelry,—till the storm burst upon them, and the oppressed take ruinous vengeance on the oppressors.[168]

He hoped that a revolution might be avoided; but if it came he would—and here he veered more to Paine than to Godwin—support the cause of the people: "Popular insurrections and revolutions I look upon with discountenance. *If such things must be,* I will take the side of the People; but my reasonings shall endeavour to ward it from the hearts of the Rulers of the earth, deeply as I detest them." [169]

In Shelley's religious views, the waverings and uncertainties of his letters to Hogg of the *Necessity of Atheism* period have disappeared and he is now an atheist, speaking of deism as a stage through which he has passed: "I *once* was an enthusiastic Deist, but never a Christian." [170] "I find there can be bigots in Atheism as well as Religion; I perhaps may be classed with the former." [171] When he encountered the deism of Leigh Hunt, combining a disavowal of Christian theology with a "veneration for the Deity," he hoped to rescue him—for he was "a man of cultivated mind"—from "this damnable heresy from reason." [172] His belief in a creative Deity has vanished and the concept of "some vast intellect" animating the universe is now modified into that of an indefinable "cause":

What then is a "God"? It is a name which expresses the unknown cause, the supposititious origin of all existence. When we speak of the soul of man, we mean that unknown cause which produces the observable effect evinced by his intelligence and bodily animation, which are in their nature conjoined, and (as we suppose, as we observe) inseparable. The word God then, in the sense which you take it analogises with the *universe,* as the soul of man to his body, as the vegetative power to vegetables, the stony power to stones. . . . In this sense I acknowledge a God, but merely as a synonime [sic] for *the existing power of existence. . . .*[173]

God, according to this concept, seems to be simply a name for the power of life and motion in the universe, a view somewhat akin to that of Spinoza, whom Shelley admired.[174] This God has no directive force external to the laws of nature and takes no interest in human affairs (in fact cannot, as a mere objective *force,* be said to take an interest in anything). The common concept of God, Shelley believed, along with Voltaire and others, to be purely anthropomorphic: "It [his own concept of the word God] is another *word* for the essence of the universe. You recognize not in this an identical being to whom are attributable the properties of virtue, mercy, loveliness—imagination delights in personification; were it not for this embodying quality of eccentric fancy we should be to this day without a God."[175]

Shelley had thus, within a few weeks of his expulsion, accepted the atheistic arguments of Hogg and had blended them with his general philosophical concepts. One question that he and Hogg strangely enough had not discussed was immortality.[176] What Hogg thought on the subject we do not know, but Shelley at this time of his life believed that the survival of the soul was probable, not because of supernatural intervention and not in its individual being, but as a new entity and in accordance with the general law of the indestructibility of all things:

Yet one of the properties of animal soul is consciousness of identity. If this is destroyed, in consequence the *soul* (whose essence this is) must perish. But as I conceive (and as is certainly capable of demonstration) that nothing can be annihilated, but that everything appertaining to nature, consisting of constituent parts infinitely divisible, is in a continual change, then do I suppose—and I think I have a right to draw this inference—that neither will soul perish; that in a future existence it will lose all consciousness of having formerly lived elsewhere,—will begin life anew, possibly under a shape of which we have now no idea.[177]

His old opposition to organized Christianity continued, but he now is less subjectively emotional and bases his attack on social-historical grounds, the connection of the church with reactionary political and social trends, its persecutions and religious wars, its association with dictatorial rule:

You are willing to dismiss for the present the subject of Religion. As to its influence on individuals, we will. But it is so intimately connected with politics, and augments in so vivid a degree the evils resulting from the system before us, that I will make a few remarks on it. Shall I sum up the evidence? It is needless . . . the persecutions against the Christians under the Greek Empire, their energetic retaliations, and burning each other, the excommunications bandied between the popes of Rome and the patriarchs of Constantinople, their influence upon politics, wars, assassination, the Sicilian Vespers, the Massacre of St. Bartholomew, Lord G. Gordon's mob, and the state of Religious things at present, can amply substantiate my assertions. . . . And Liberty!—Poor Liberty! even the religionists who cry so much for thee use thy name but as a mask, that they alone may seize the torch, and show their gratitude by burning their Deliverer. . . . I should doubt the existence of *a* God who if he cannot command our reverence by *Love, surely* can have no demand upon it, from Virtue, on the score of terror. It is this empire of terror which is established by Religion, Monarchy is its prototype, Aristocracy may be regarded as symbolizing with its very essence. They are mixed: one can now scarce be distinguished from the other. . . .[178]

When Elizabeth Hitchener expressed a desire to continue in some kind of religious belief, he answered: "But for this purpose, the religion of the Deist, or the worshipper of virtue would suffice, without involving the persecution, battles, bloodshed, which countenancing Christianity countenances."[179] Shelley now was not so much opposed to religious belief per se as to religious belief associated with social reaction.

The essence of Shelley's ethical philosophy in this period, and, indeed, for his life as a whole, we find expressed in a letter to a minor poetess, Janetta Philipps, in whom he had taken some interest: "Why are we here? What does man exist for? Surely not for his own happiness, but as a more perfect instrument of that of others. This even common morality will tell, for *this* we do not want any theological system, not even the belief of a God, the anticipation of his kingdom."[180] A morality based on service to humanity, having its roots not in love of heaven or fear of hell but in human goodwill; such was Shelley's concept.

His views on free love and marriage remained unchanged, even by his own marriage. The legal binding of two people to spend their lives together he regarded (in May) as "detestable." [181] "Read the Marriage Service," he advised Hogg, in their controversy on the subject, "before you think of allowing an amiable, beloved female to submit to such degradation." [182] In November he still considered marriage "an evil." "Marriage is monopolizing, exclusive, jealous. . . . A law to compel you to hear . . . music, in the company of such a particular person, appears to me to parallel that of marriage." [183] He himself had married because the woman has to bear the brunt of the social attack in a free love union and the husband loses his "political rights." [184] The opponent of marriage should not act individually—"how useless to attempt by singular examples to renovate the face of society"—but endeavor to change society as a whole.[185] Two people, he believed, as he later stated in the Notes to *Queen Mab,* should live together only so long as they were in love.[186] And he had informed Harriet of his belief. "While you were at Keswick," Southey recalled some years later, "you told your bride that you regarded marriage as a mere ceremony, and would live with her no longer than you liked her." [187]

As to Shelley's interest in science, there is not much to record. He continued his reading in it, studying Erasmus Darwin in July and in the following February (after he had arrived in Ireland) *Organic Remains,* a geological work by James Parkinson, echoes from which later found their way into *Prometheus Unbound.*[188] His opportunities for experiment were naturally limited in these months but we hear of him almost being evicted at Keswick for making flames with hydrogen gas and alarming the superstitious townsfolk.[189]

The year 1811 was the decisive year of Shelley's life. He entered it as an Oxford student and heir to a great estate, with every prospect, as he informed Hunt, of succeeding his father in a political career; he ended it as an outcast, expelled from his university, married to an ex-tavernkeeper's daughter. "He had only," wrote Hunt, "to become a yea and a nay man in the house of commons, to be one of the richest men in Sussex. . . . Had he now behaved himself pardonably in the eyes of the orthodox, he would have gone to London with the resolution of sowing his wild oats, and becoming a decent member of society; that is to say, he would have seduced a few maid-servants, or at least haunted the lobbies; and then bestowed the remnant of his constitution upon some young lady of his own rank in life, and settled into a proper church-and-king man, perhaps a member of the [Society for the] Suppression of Vice." [190] Shelley, in short, had broken caste; he was, as a consequence, whirled out of the orbit of his class, and, after a brief comet-like career, was to enter a new orbit, that of the city middle class, the class of Hunt and Godwin, of Hookham and Peacock, of Hazlitt and Bentham, a class in the throes of struggle.

In the events of this year the mind and character of Shelley develop and take shape. He emerges essentially as a young man with a purpose, dedicated to the service of humanity. Thornton Hunt, who although only a child when he knew Shelley, remembered him well as he was in 1816–1818. Many years later he took pen to attack the concept of Shelley then emanating from Hogg and Peacock. "The impulsiveness which is ascribed to him," he complained, "is a wrong expression, for it is usually interpreted to mean the action of sudden motives, waywardly, capriciously, or at least intermittently working; whereas the character which Shelley so constantly displayed was an overbearing strength of conviction and feeling. . . ." "Although," he continued, "the general aspect was peculiarly slight, youthful, and delicate, yet, when you looked to 'the points' of the animal, you saw well enough the indications of a masculine vigour, in many respects far above average. . . . a look of active movement, promptitude, vigour and decision. . . ." [191] And these characteristics of the man are clearly visible in the boy of 1811. The boy must, many times, in the course of the events of this year, have felt frightened and alone, but there was a hardness in the core of his character, and a drive, based on conviction, that kept him unswervingly on the path he had charted. We must not overlook, in the maze of events and emotions, that it took unusual courage and determination to make the break with his family, and although one might upbraid him for deceiving them, their attitude had, as he pointed out to his father, left him no choice: "This action (admitting it to be done) in its very nature required dissimulation, much as I may regret that I had descended to employ it." [192] And behind this courage and determination was a central purpose, a purpose whose principles made all else—family position, personal comforts, friendship, and marriage—seem dim and secondary in the comparison. Shelley, once he grasped a principle—as others were to discover later—ordered his life in accordance with it. The wishes of his father, the opinions of his class, seemed but part of a stultifying social cosmos—"this detestable coil of primaeval prejudice"—he had vowed to shatter. The decision was not an easy one; he had a genuine love for his family—"I regard these family differences as a very great evil, and I much lament that I should in any wise have been instrumental in exciting them" [193]—but the break had to be made, and he made it.

If this central core of purposiveness, of "masculine vigor," has been missed by the biographers and the emphasis placed on more spectacular but peripheral characteristics, the blame is not wholly theirs. "He was [wrote Hogg] altogether incapable of rendering an account of any transaction whatsoever, according to the strict and precise truth, and the bare, naked realities of actual life; not through an addiction to falsehood, which he cordially detested, but because he was the creature, the unsuspecting and unresisting victim, of his irresistible imagination." [194] And although he is exaggerating somewhat, Hogg is essentially right. The boyish fancy which conjured up the tales of the tortoise and the alchemist and invented the detailed account of the visit to the village ladies has grown into a pathological love for mystification combined with a limitless capacity for the projection of its owner into semi-fictionalized roles. True, as Hogg says, he "detested falsehood," and in important matters was conscientiously accurate, but in the events of his personal life he often allowed himself considerable scope for romantic dramatization, especially if he had some special motive for so doing. His accounts of his expulsion are, as we have noted, all to some degree suspect, and the events leading to his elopement he distorted and reshuffled in accordance with his emotional reactions to Hogg and Elizabeth Hitchener and the respective pictures of himself which he believed they possessed. In this latter regard especially, he has done himself harm, for his picture of himself as passive victim of his chivalric instincts has easily been exaggerated into that of irresponsible dupe in a plot he had not the good sense to perceive.

"I always go on until I am stopped," Shelley said in later years to his friend Trelawny, "and," he added, "I never am stopped." [195] But sometimes he was stopped. And when he was, he became uncontrollably enraged. The "violent and extremely excitable temper" of the child, and the adolescent's frenzy on the loss of Harriet Grove rose to a new pitch in the wild descent upon Field Place—"Bysshe, Bysshe, Bysshe . . . Aye, Bysshe, until you're deaf"—with its whirling insults and fantastic charges. These rages—"violent fits of passion"—which apparently were as rare as they were violent, Peacock later (1813–18) recognized and talked about in private but omitted from his printed account of Shelley, and Merle records one of them in his picture of Shelley's furious anger when his anti-religious opinions were challenged:

As I proceeded he became angry; indeed almost furious. "Do not," said he, "talk such stuff to me; I hear enough of it at home. There is my father, who, with a painting of that impostor, Christ, hanging up in his library, is some-times vain enough to suppose that he can bring reason prostrate before absurdity. I have too many of these follies before my eyes: they drive me mad!" And mad, indeed, he was. I think I see him still. His eyes flashed fire; his words rolled forth with the impetuosity of a mountain-torrent; and even attitude aided the manifestation of passion. . . . "No more of this, Shelley, or from this moment we become strangers, as we have been friends; nay, if it must be so, enemies, as we have been brothers." "Have your own way, mad fool!" exclaimed Shelley; and, taking his hat, he quitted the room.[196]

Everything that Shelley did he did energetically—the assault with his uncle, Captain Pilfold, on Field Place, the pursuit of Harriet, the repudiation of Hogg, the virulence against his father—and when he was on the move, he was not to be lightly tampered with; even Whitton quailed: "I shall not like to meddle with such a chicken. . . ." Always, out from the main stream of his energies, directed toward whatever purpose he has in mind, there gush those endlessly eddying side streams of self-projection and fantasy, of rages and intrigues, tangential swirlings not entirely subject to conscious control. We have to remem-ber, also, that Shelley was very young, that the intensities and instabil-ities are, in part, the usual intensities and instabilities of youth. The sex urges, the emotional waverings, the moral concepts, of a man of nineteen or twenty are not those of middle age, and, in middle age, men, psychologically blocked on their own youthful thoughts and ac-tions, make out-of-perspective analyses. Shelley has especially suffered in this regard because the documents of his youth have been preserved. We do not see him as he might have chosen in later life to have regarded himself but as he actually was at the time; and few people would hold up well under such scrutiny. His insults against his father, for instance, are not unique. (One remembers Samuel Johnson stand-ing, hat in hand, in the rain at Lichfield.) Ambivalence, we have learned, is inevitably inherent in family relationships. What is unusual about Shelley's remarks—and by December he was regretting them, though too proud fully to retreat—is their intensity. And so, too, with the emotional zig-zagging of the courtship with Harriet. It is more highly charged, more imaginatively visualized in fictional patterns than the average, but its main characteristics are standard. Biographers who presuppose ideals of unsullied filial affection and sexless court-ship must unavoidably resort either to attack or protective apology.

To the material on Shelley's sex life, already noted in this chapter, one more piece of evidence must be taken into account, Thornton Hunt's comments in his article on Shelley:

Again, accident has made me aware of facts which give me to understand, that in passing through the usual curriculum of a college life in all its paths, Shelley did not go scatheless,—but that, in the tampering with venal pleasures, his health was seriously, and not transiently, injured. The effect was far greater on his mind than on his body; and the intellectual being greater than the physical power, the healthy reaction was greater. But that reaction was also, especially in early youth, principally marked by horror and antagonism. Conscientious, far beyond even the ordinary maximum amongst ordinary men, he felt bound to denounce the mischief from which he saw others suffer more severely than himself, since in them there was no such reaction. I have no doubt that he himself would have spoken even plainer language, though to me his language is perfectly transparent, if he had not been restrained by a superstitious notion of his own, that the true escape from the pestilent and abhorrent brutalities which he detected around him in "real" life is found in "the ideal" form of thought and language. Ardent and romantic, he was eager to discover beauty "beneath" every natural aspect.[197]

In support of these comments Hunt quotes the following passage from *Epipsychidion,* remarking, "This is a plain and only too intelligible reference to the college experience to which I have alluded":

> There,—One, whose voice was venomed melody
> Sate by a well, under blue nightshade bowers;
> The breath of her false mouth was like faint flowers,
> Her touch was as electric poison,—flame
> Out of her looks into my vitals came,
> And from her living cheeks and bosom flew
> A killing air, which pierced like honey-dew
> Into the core of my green heart, and lay
> Upon its leaves; until, as hair grown gray
> O'er a young brow, they hid its unblown prime
> With ruins of unseasonable time.[198]

This material of Hunt's has been generally omitted or rejected by the biographers,[199] but it is more likely to contain truth than not. Hunt was a reputable Victorian publicist and essayist, an intimate friend of G. H. Lewes and editor of *The Leader,* a liberal periodical with advanced views on politics and religion. He was "favorably known" to

Queen Victoria who sent him "a good deal of confidential information" as a result of his writings on the Prince Consort. He was well liked by Gladstone and had literary dealings with Dickens, Kingsley, Arnold, and Thackeray, all of whom seem to have regarded him highly.[200] Further, his article on Shelley is a serious analysis, avoiding all sensation-mongering, and reveals a deep love and respect for its subject. Hunt, therefore, would not have made such a speculation if he had not believed that he had good grounds for it. On the other hand, if he had had such grounds, he would not have omitted it, for he was in rebellion against Victorian morality.

His deduction from the *Epipsychidion* passage is clearly justified. *Epipsychidion* is a sketch of Shelley's love life and love philosophy;[201] the passage in question occurs in a section which would correspond to Shelley's Oxford period. It is, indeed, "a plain and only too intelligible reference," especially so if we note the comment on graying hair, for it was a commonly accepted belief that venereal disease turned hair gray prematurely, and Shelley's hair, like that of the poet in *Alastor,* was prematurely graying, as Medwin noted and as is clear from Williams' portrait.[202]

That a youth so aware of his sexual instincts as was Shelley should seek out one of the prostitutes who formed so conspicuous a part of the social scene of Regency England is hardly surprising. (London, in 1812, according to a shocked letter in *The Examiner,* harbored 50,000 "public prostitutes" and four to five thousand "receptacles of infamy.")[203] And, if he did seek one out, naive as he was, it is likely that he would contract a venereal infection. His attack, a year or so later, on prostitution is unusually heated:

Thus is formed one-tenth of the population of London: meanwhile the evil is twofold. Young men, excluded by the fanatical idea of chastity from the society of modest and accomplished women, associate with these vicious and miserable beings, destroying thereby all those exquisite and delicate sensibilities whose existence cold-hearted worldlings have denied; annihilating all genuine passion, and debasing that to a selfish feeling which is the excess of generosity and devotedness. Their body and mind alike crumble into a hideous wreck of humanity; idiocy and disease become perpetuated in their miserable offspring, and distant generations suffer for the bigoted morality of their forefathers.[204]

In Shelley's intellectual development during these months following his expulsion, the main phenomenon has been the sharpening of half-formed theories into definite shape; deism becomes atheism, abstract social radicalism becomes revolutionary egalitarianism. And this development was due, not to further reading but to experience: expulsion, family conflict, economic need, marital responsibility. The views, which had resulted in these experiences were, in turn, re-formed by them.

IV THE IRISH QUESTION

Address to the Irish People
Proposal for an Association
Declaration of Rights

THE IRISH SCENE 1780-1811

We first hear of Shelley's decision to go to Ireland in a letter of December 11, 1811.[1] The reason for this decision was doubtless the popularity then being achieved by the great, new movement for Catholic emancipation led by Daniel O'Connell. Shelley had long been interested in Ireland—*vide* his early "Irishman's Song," *The Devil's Walk* and his efforts on behalf of Finnerty—and the rise of such a movement as this would certainly capture his imagination. It is, however, possible that the initial suggestion for such a trip came from the Duke of Norfolk. The Duke, as we have seen, had for many years been an outstanding champion of Catholic emancipation and Irish rights. In February, 1812—the very month in which Shelley left for Ireland—he attacked the Prince Regent for his turncoat tactics on Ireland and refused the Order of the Garter.[2] And he spoke several times in Parliament in these years in favor of Catholic emancipation. The Duke must, therefore, have been well acquainted with the O'Connell movement, and it may be that he either suggested the trip or his comments on the Irish situation put the idea in Shelley's mind, for it was immediately after his return from Greystoke that Shelley first mentioned plans for such an expedition, and asked the Duke to advance him £100.[3]

The significance of Shelley's works on the Irish question and his activities in Ireland can be understood only in the perspective of the contemporary Irish scene and its background. The root of that question lay in the seizure of the land of Ireland by the English ruling class:

The superficial contents of the island [declared Lord Clare in 1800] are calculated at 11,042,682 acres. The state of the forfeitures [i.e. English seizures of land] was as follows—In the reign of James I, the whole province of Ulster, 2,836,837 acres; set out by the Court of Claims at the Restoration, 7,800,000; Forfeitures of 1688, 1,060,792 acres; total number of acres forfeited, 11,697,629. So that the whole of your island has been confiscated, with the exception of the estates of five or six families of English blood . . . and no inconsiderable portion of the island has been confiscated twice, or perhaps thrice in the course of a century.[4]

To hold these economic seizures, the English established a political dictatorship based on the ancient principle of "divide and conquer." In this they were assisted not only by the religious division of the Irish into Catholics (four fifths of the population) and Protestants, but by the economic division of the Irish upper class into two groups: the landed aristocracy, and the city merchants and professional men. "Generally speaking," writes a modern historian, "the idea was that England should control the Protestants and the Protestants the Catholics in the island."[5] Upper-class Catholics were allowed (after 1793) to vote but could vote only for Protestants; Catholics could not sit in Parliament or become judges or king's counselors. As for the great mass of the population, the working people of town and country, they had no voting or other political rights whatsoever. Those in the country lived in virtual serfdom on estates often owned by Englishmen; those in the cities lived largely in slums.[6]

Throughout the centuries various attempts had been made by the Irish to alleviate their condition, sometimes by open rebellion, sometimes by political pressure. During the period in which we are interested their struggle had passed through three phases: that of Henry Grattan and his volunteer army (1779–83); that of Wolfe Tone and the United Irishmen (1791–98); and, finally, that of Daniel O'Connell and the Catholic Committee, just getting into full swing at the time of Shelley's contemplated visit.

When, in the year 1778, there appeared some danger of a French invasion of Ireland, the Irish Protestant aristocrats formed a volunteer army, which, the following year, had reached the total of 42,000 men. Henry Grattan, a member of the Irish Parliament, emerged as the leader of the movement, demanded political rights for the Irish upper classes, and used this armed force as a bargaining power with the English authorities. The English, harassed by their war with America, were in no position to refuse, and Grattan wrested certain concessions

from them, the most important of which were the granting of the vote
to the upper-class Catholics and the declaration that the Irish Parliament could pass laws without interference from England. Flushed
with the success of his movement, however, Grattan dissolved the
volunteer army and so lost whatever power of persuasion he had
held.[7]

The United Irishmen, built up by Wolfe Tone and his followers in
1791, was a very different kind of movement. Tone was not, like
Grattan, interested in securing political rights for the upper-class Irish,
but in alleviating the conditions of the Irish lower classes even if this
meant a battle against the Irish upper class as well as the English.
Thus, of the right of the Irish Parliament to pass its own laws—hailed
by Grattan with enthusiasm, "Ireland is a nation . . . esto perpetua" [8]
—Tone acidly remarked: "formerly we had our distresses, our injuries
and our insults *gratis* at the hands of England, but now we pay very
dearly to receive the same with aggravation through the hands of
Irishmen." [9] The essence of Tone's program was that of uniting all
Irishmen, Catholics and Protestants, for breaking ties with England—
"separation and a republic"—and for reforming their own Irish Parliament along democratic lines: "the abolition of distinctions between
Irishmen." Grattan was a Whig, Tone a revolutionary Republican,
regarding Paine's *Rights of Man* as his Koran.[10] Although he vigorously supported Catholic emancipation he abhorred Catholicism as a
religion, declaring his abhorrence in words which show that Shelley's
injudicious remarks on the subject were not without precedent:

The emancipated and liberal Irishman, like the emancipated and liberal
Frenchman, may go to Mass, may tell his beads, or sprinkle his mistress
with Holy Water; but neither the one nor the other will attend to the rusty
and extinguished thunderbolts of the Vatican or the idle anathemas which,
indeed, His Holiness is nowadays too prudent and cautious to issue.[11]

Two other leaders of the United Irishmen we might note, as Shelley
later evidenced interest in them. In 1791, the United Irishmen were
astonished to find their ranks joined by a wealthy and prominent Whig,
Archibald Hamilton Rowan.[12] Tone apparently did not entirely trust
Rowan, feeling that his family position would prevent him from going
the whole way with the radical aspirations of the organization, but
Rowan, for a time, was among the most extreme of its members,
standing up and shouting for the playing of the "Volunteer March"
in the midst of "God Save the King" and defiantly parading the

streets of Dublin in his green uniform.[13] In 1794, he was put on trial for allegedly passing out seditious leaflets, and in spite of a most eloquent defense by the famous liberal lawyer, John Philpot Curran, was sentenced to two years in prison.

One of the most radical of the United Irishmen was Arthur O'Connor, who, like Tone, was a Republican in politics and a free thinker in religion. O'Connor joined the organization in 1796 and in 1798 was arrested in England. At his trial, Fox and the Duke of Norfolk appeared as witnesses in his favor. In 1803 he went to France and became a general in Napoleon's army, and, in 1807, married the daughter of Condorcet.[14]

Unfortunately for the cause of the United Irishmen, they allowed themselves to be goaded into armed rebellion in 1798,[15] and, assistance from the French failing to be effective, they were crushed. Tone, captured on board a French warship, committed suicide in a Dublin prison. This rebellion was put down with extreme brutality by Lord Castlereagh—"dabbling its sleek young hands in Erin's gore"—who was then occupying his first important government post as acting Chief Secretary for Ireland. His feats in this suppression were never forgotten by the Irish or by the English liberals.[16]

In 1803, a recrudescence of the United Irish movement took place when Robert Emmet attempted an armed uprising which failed. Emmet, like Tone, had relied on French help which did not arrive. He could himself have escaped, but was in love with Sarah Curran, daughter of John Philpot Curran (and sister of the artist of the best known portrait of Shelley); delaying to get her answer to his proposal before leaving for America, he was captured and executed, an episode which inspired Moore's "She is far from the land," and "Oh breathe not his name."

Fast upon the failure of the 1798 rebellion, the British government moved for the abolition of the Irish Parliament and the transference of its members to the English Parliament. By the use of wholesale bribery, the Irish Parliament was persuaded to vote itself out of existence, thus negating at one blow Grattan's proud cry, "Ireland is a nation," and in 1800, the Act of Union between Great Britain and Ireland was passed, whereby the British House of Lords received a gift of thirty-two Irish peers and prelates and the British House of Commons one hundred Irish members.[17]

From this time on the repeal of the Act of Union became a focal point of Irish agitation. The Irish had been led to believe that this

Act would bring Catholic emancipation and other concessions with it, but found that it brought nothing but a decrease in trade and an increase in the national debt. For some years after 1800, however, and especially following the abortive rebellion of Emmet in 1803, no effective organizational action was taken on either Catholic emancipation or the repeal of the Union Act, and republican programs were forgotten entirely.

By the year 1810, however, a movement that was destined to become the most powerful in Irish history in the nineteenth century was getting under way. This was the Catholic Committee (later the Catholic Association) led by Daniel O'Connell. This Committee, established in 1806 on the basis of an older Catholic organization, was originally designed to express the demands of the Catholic aristocracy; but a struggle for power took place within its ranks as the leadership of the aristocracy was challenged by the Irish merchant and professional classes. "The question had now become acute," writes Denis Gwynn in his life of O'Connell, "whether the influence of the Catholic peers, who deplored any policy that might embarrass the English Whigs, or the more adventurous policy of the young Catholic barristers, was to prevail." [18] The essence of the conflict was that the peers, led by Lord Fingall and Lord Ffrench, dreading the rise of a popular organization, urged leaving the question of Catholic emancipation to the Whigs, the Irish members of the English Parliament—led by Grattan and, of course, hopelessly outvoted by the Tories and conservative Whigs—and the Prince Regent. The Prince Regent, as Prince of Wales, had supported Catholic emancipation, and the Catholic peers naïvely believed that once he had assumed power as Regent he would grant their request.[19] O'Connell, on the other hand, while not at first attacking the Prince Regent or the Whigs, claimed that only by building a powerful native organization as a pressure group could concessions be gained. In the end O'Connell won, the aristocrats under Lord Fingall were pushed into second place, and the Catholic Committee became chiefly the organ of the city professional and business classes. O'Connell, however, in spite of his opposition to the aristocracy, was not at all a republican radical of the Wolfe Tone variety, but declared his ideal to be only "an Irish King, an Irish House of Lords, and an Irish House of Commons." [20] O'Connell, although less conservative than the peers, was, nevertheless, a representative of Irish upper-class interests and had no perspective beyond the establishment of a capitalist-aristocratic Ireland on the model of contemporary England. Yet, in spite of this lack of perspective, O'Connell had something that previous Irish leaders had lacked—a genius for rallying great masses of people around a simple program. He had one basic point of policy to which he stuck through thick and thin: Catholic emancipation. And on this point he built an enormous movement, which eventually gained its ends in the passage of the Catholic Emancipation Act in 1829. His main task he considered to be the uniting of all sections of the Irish population, the upper class and the lower class, Catholics and Protestants, around this one point. This theme of unity runs through all his speeches. He attacked especially that "religious dissension which the enemies of Ireland have created, and continued, and seek to perpetuate amongst ourselves, telling us off, and separating us into wretched sections and miserable subdivisions." [21]

They separated the Protestant from the Catholic, and the Presbyterian from both; they revived every antiquated cause of domestic animosity, and they invented new pretexts of rancour; but above all, my countrymen, they belied and calumniated us to each other—they falsely declared that we hated each other; . . . and they continued to repeat the assertion until we came to believe it; they succeeded in producing all the madness of party and religious distinctions; and whilst we were lost in the stupour of insanity, they plundered us of our country, and left us to recover at our leisure from the horrid delusion into which we had been so artfully conducted.[22]

At the same time, O'Connell carried on agitation in favor of the repeal of the Union Act of 1800. This, he realized, was a more fundamental problem than that of Catholic emancipation: "I trample under foot the Catholic claims, if they can interfere with the Repeal; I abandon all wish for Emancipation if it delays that Repeal." [23] His organization, however, was built on the Catholic emancipation question, and it was not until after 1829 that he began a serious attempt to break the Union Act, an attempt which failed.

O'Connell's special technique for agitation was the "aggregate meeting." This was an ingenious device to circumvent a government ban on meetings of organizational delegates. Instead of calling a meeting of delegates he simply called a public meeting, known as an "aggregate meeting," at which, of course, all those who would have been delegates were present but merely as members of the public. These aggregate meetings were held regularly in Dublin's famous Fishamble Street Theatre (once graced by Handel's presence and anathematized by Swift).

When Shelley decided, late in 1811, to go to Ireland, this movement of O'Connell's was in the ascendant and the whole country astir as it had not been since the days of Grattan and his Volunteers.

AN ADDRESS TO THE IRISH PEOPLE

An Address to the Irish People was written, it should be noted, not in Ireland, but in England. We first hear of it in a letter from Shelley to Elizabeth Hitchener on January 20, 1812—"I am now writing an 'Address' to the poor Irish Catholics" [24]—in which he quotes a passage from an early section of the essay, and comments: "I consider the state of Ireland as constituting a part of a great crisis in opinion." [25] Some six days later he makes the further comment:

I have the vanity to think that you will be pleased with my "Address to the Irish". It is intended to familiarize to uneducated apprehensions ideas of liberty, benevolence, *peace,* and toleration. It is *secretly* intended also as a preliminary to other pamphlets to shake Catholicism at its basis, and to induce Quakerish and Socinian principles of politics, without objecting to the Christian religion, which would be no good to the vulgar just now, and cast an odium over the other principles which are advanced.[26]

On January 28 he wrote to Godwin:

I shall devote myself with unremitting zeal, as far as an uncertain state of health will permit, towards forwarding the great ends of virtue and happiness in Ireland, regarding as I do the present state of that country's affairs as an opportunity which if I, being thus disengaged, permit to pass unoccupied, I am unworthy of the character which I have assumed.[27]

And a later comment to Godwin:

I have wilfully vulgarized the language of this pamphlet, in order to reduce the remarks it contains to the taste and comprehension of the Irish peasantry, who have been too long brutalized by vice and ignorance.[28]

From these comments, we can draw the following conclusions in regard to the *Address:* (a) Shelley believed Ireland was at the time in the throes of a movement for national regeneration (O'Connell and the Catholic Committee); (b) this movement was part of a European or world movement of liberterian revival; (c) he considered himself a political propagandist with a duty to assist in this movement; (d) he was writing for the "poor Irish Catholics" and deliberately simplifying his style; (e) while he was interested in helping the Irish gain their political demands, he had, at the same time, a secret motive: the ultimate undermining of Catholicism.

Shelley begins the *Address* with a brief introduction in which he attempts to alleviate Irish suspicions of an English advocate, and then launches into the first main section of the work, a discussion of the Catholic and Protestant religions, designed to show the injustice of a denial of political rights on religious grounds, and to indicate, at the same time, some of the evils of Catholicism as a religion. He points out that the Catholic Church committed evils in the past—"in truth, at that time the Priests shamefully imposed upon the people" [29] (all designed for the subtle undermining of Catholicism)—but that Protestants had committed equal evils and so had no moral basis for refusing Catholic emancipation. Much though he opposed Catholicism as a doctrine, the denial of political rights on religious grounds he denounced as tyrannous.[30] The section concludes with a brief plea for the repeal of the Union Act of 1800, which he protests mainly because of the added burdens it has placed on the poor by the withdrawal of wealth from Ireland.[31]

The second section—Shelley has not made formal divisions but the sectioning is clear from the arguments—expounds the program for the alleviation of the injustices exposed in the first section, and opens with the words: "Perhaps you all agree with me on both these subjects, we now come to the method of doing these things" [32] (i.e. securing Catholic emancipation and repeal of the Union Act).

Shelley begins with a warning against the use of violence, a point much stressed by O'Connell, and, in both Shelley and O'Connell, stemming specifically from the failures of Wolfe Tone and Robert Emmet.

He warns the Irish not to place all their trust in the Prince Regent and the Whigs (as Lord Fingall and the right wing of the Catholic Committee urged), and in this regard anticipates O'Connell, who did not challenge the Regent until June, 1812: "whether or no he will consider the promise of a Prince of Wales binding to a king of England, is yet a matter of doubt." [33]

The British *people,* he emphasizes, are not against the Irish; only the English upper class is against them; a class that "employs" the ministers and politicians:

The ministers have now in Parliament a very great majority. . . . These men of course, are against you, because their employers are. But the sense of the country is not against you—They feel warmly for you—in some respects they feel with you. The sense of the English and of their governors is opposite.[34]

He urges that the Irish maintain their political organizations and advocates a device similar to that of the aggregate meeting: the govern-

ment will not let the people assemble for the express purpose of discussing political theory but it cannot prevent their assembling for
general discussion and such discussion could legitimately turn to political science.[35] But he does not suggest what types of organizations
should be established or what their specific aims should be, and he mars
his generally sound advice by pious exhortations to individual study
and reform and the eschewing of violence, exhortations whose number,
repetitiveness, and naïveté are to be explained, in part, as concessions
to Godwin, for whose favor he was eager and whose advice he had
flouted in advocating organization, and, in part, also, to an underestimation of the political comprehension of "poor Irish Catholics."

Up to this point in the *Address,* Shelley has been treating, although
largely by indirection, the immediate problems of Catholic emancipation and the repeal of the Union Act. In the third section, he shifts to
the general economic and political situation in Ireland and its future
perspectives: "The Catholic Emancipation I consider, is certain."
"You will," he continues sarcastically, "be rendered equal to the people
of England in their rights and privileges, and will be in all respects,
so far as concerns the state, as happy. And now Irishmen, another, and
a more wide prospect opens to my view." [36]

If the rather airy dismissal of Catholic emancipation as "certain"
reveals a serious underestimation of the coming conflicts, it was one
that was prevalent at the time. O'Connell himself a few weeks later
used almost the same words: "I hasten to conclude by expressing my
conviction that the emancipation is certain, and will be immediate." [37]
Yet, at the same time, Shelley was under no delusion that either Catholic emancipation or the repeal of the Union Act would solve the basic
problems of the Irish; even if they were achieved, the Irish would but
be in the same "happy" state of servitude as their English brethren, and
would then have to begin the battle for parliamentary reform and a
democratic republic. Shelley did not—any more than Tone would have
done—share O'Connell's naïve belief in "an Irish king, an Irish House
of Lords, and an Irish House of Commons" as "the greatest of political
blessings." [38] The economic basis of the Irish state, as that of England
and all other countries, he pointed out, was inequality and exploitation,
its political basis dictatorship, but these universal evils were aggravated,
in the case of Ireland by tyranny:

It is horrible that the lower classes must waste their lives and liberty to
furnish means for their oppressors to oppress them yet more terribly. . . .
but what words can express the enormity of the abuse that prevents them
from choosing [political] representatives. . . .[39]

Only if one thought, as did O'Connell, almost exclusively of the political oppressions of the Catholic upper class could one believe in Catholic emancipation and repeal of the Union Act as panaceas. The Irish leaders, he is implying, while right in insisting on the removal of these evils, must lift their sights higher, must begin to think—as had the United Irishmen—of the people as a whole.

Unless these more fundamental problems were solved, the masses, in Ireland as everywhere, would still be subject to the horrors of war (as exemplified by Wellington's campaign in Spain), economic exploitation, and imperialist conquest:

Is war necessary to your happiness and safety. The interests of the poor gain nothing from the wealth or extension of a nation's boundaries, they gain nothing from glory, a word that has often served as a cloak to the ambition or avarice of Statesmen. The barren victories of Spain, gained in behalf of a besotted and tyrannical Government, are nothing to them. The conquests of India, by which England has gained glory indeed, but a glory which is not more honourable than that of Buonaparte, are nothing to them. The poor purchase this glory and this wealth at the expense of their blood and labor, and happiness, and virtue. They die in battle for this infernal cause. Their labor supplies money and food for carrying it into effect; their happiness is destroyed by the oppression they undergo, their virtue is rooted out by the depravity and vice that prevail throughout the army and which under the present system, is perfectly unavoidable.[40]

Like O'Connell—"Learn discretion from your enemies . . . they have crushed your country by fomenting religious discord . . . serve her by abandoning it forever"—Shelley emphasizes the importance of Catholics and Protestants uniting their activities, pointing out that, although it is true that Catholics suffer a special oppression, both are subject to certain fundamental injustices which cut across religious divisions: "the Protestants and a certain rank of people, of every persuasion, share with them all else that is terrible, galling and intolerable in the mass of political grievance."[41]

The ferment in Ireland, as Shelley had indicated in his letter to Elizabeth Hitchener on January 20, he believed to be the harbinger of a world-wide evolution to a higher state of society; a second, but, this time, universal and uncheckable sweep, following the patterns of the American and French Revolutions:

I desire Catholic Emancipation but I desire not to stop here. . . . all steps however good and salutary, which may be taken, all reforms consistent with the English constitution that may be effectuated can only be subordinate and preparatory to the great and lasting one which shall bring about the peace, the harmony, and the happiness of Ireland, England, Europe, the World.[42]

The new order, toward which the nations of the world were, he believed, beginning to progress, is, in essence, that of Godwin and Condorcet, a society based on economic equality and political freedom, and hence providing a basis for the elimination of social evils and the transformation of the human personality. The passage is of special interest as being the first of Shelley's pictures of this ultimate society (the last and best coming in *Prometheus Unbound*):

Can you conceive, O Irishmen! A happy state of society—conceive men of every way of thinking living together like brothers. The descendent of the greatest Prince would there, be entitled to no more respect than the son of a peasant. There would be no pomp and no parade, but that which the rich now keep to themselves, would then be distributed among the people. None would be in magnificence, but the superfluities then taken from the rich would be sufficient when spread abroad, to make everyone comfortable.—No lover would then be false to his mistress, no mistress would desert her lover. No friend would play false, no rents, no debts, no taxes, no frauds of any kind would disturb the general happiness: good as they would be, wise as they would be, they would be daily getting better and wiser. No beggars would exist, nor any of those wretched women, who are now reduced to a state of the most horrible misery and vice, by men whose wealth makes them villainous and hardened. No thieves, or murderers, because poverty would never drive men to take away comforts from another, when he had enough for himself. Vice and misery, pomp and poverty, power and obedience, would then be banished altogether.[43]

This new order, however, was something that would take many years to accomplish. It was an ultimate not an immediate goal. The point is worth emphasizing in view of the widespread illusion that Shelley expected the millennium to burst hourly:

I look to these things with hope and pleasure, because I consider that they will certainly happen. . . . But I do not consider that they will or can immediately happen; their arrival will be gradual, and it all depends upon yourself how soon or how late these great changes will happen. . . . I cannot expect a rapid change. Many are obstinate and determined in their vice, whose selfishness makes them think only of their own good . . .[44]

Thus, not even in the earliest period of his radical political thinking did Shelley believe that the egalitarian state was a matter for the immediate future; indeed, he did not even think it a matter for the existing generation at all: "I have also said that we can expect little amendment in our time, and that we must be contented to lay the foundation of liberty and happiness, by virtue and wisdom." [45]

With this section, the main part of the *Address* ends. The rest consists of a vigorous plea for the freedom of the press—"It is really ridiculous to hear people yet boasting of this inestimable blessing, when they daily see it successfully muzzled and outraged by the lawyers of the crown" [46]—a denunciation of the continued imprisonment of Peter Finnerty—"He was imprisoned for persisting in the truth"—and a repetitive summary of ideas previously presented.

The outstanding value of the *Address* lies in its sense of historical evolution and its insistence on transcending a narrow middle-class outlook. Shelley does not, as did most of the Irish leaders of the time, bog down in the issues of the day, but continually, even while treating those issues, insists on perspectives: behind Catholic emancipation is the issue of all political oppression; behind political oppression is economic exploitation; a movement of Catholics to alleviate their own particular grievance is not sufficient, but must be converted into part of a vaster movement of Irish men and women of all classes for the elimination of their common oppressions, and this movement must itself be seen as part of a world movement. Yet, this very sense of historical perspective which enables the *Address* to make a unique contribution to the Irish political thought of the time, is also its weakness, for Shelley gets so absorbed in perspectives that he fails to give adequate treatment to immediate issues. One almost gets the feeling that he is glad to get Catholic emancipation and repeal of the Union Act out of the way so that he can go on to develop his general theory. It is not so much the Irish situation itself that interests him but its implications for humanity. Those underlying motives which, as we learn from his letters, he intended to form the framework of the pamphlet, do in fact, form it. One of them, indeed, the undermining of Catholicism, led him into more serious error, for his anti-Catholic remarks were such that they would have had little effect except to prejudice the main Irish political group against his work and harm the religious concord he advocated. His simplification of style, also, in so far as it becomes oversimplification, detracts from his message and at times gives an impression of political naïveté which is belied by the content. Yet, in spite of his errors in the treatment of immediate issues, Shelley, when dealing with these issues, gives sound tactical advice in emphasizing the need for unity of Catholics and Protestants, the establishment of open organizations using legal means instead of secret ones advocating adventurist violence, the development of friendly relations with the English "people."

In his treatment of more general problems Shelley gives us some new insights into his political philosophy. All the earliest components of this philosophy are present and usually intermixed with later ones. Thus his anti-war and anti-imperialist sentiments have a Whig basis, but the vehemence of his opposition and his passionate feeling for the sufferings of the common people—"the poor purchase this glory and this wealth at the expense of their blood and labor"—pass into a truly republican indignation. His comments on the ruling class, "employers" of the English Parliament and ministry, reveal an insight into the nature of the political structure that had not previously appeared in his writings. From his picture of the egalitarian state, we gather that he had no more concept of an expanding economic foundation as a prerequisite for its accomplishment than did Godwin, but thought of little more than a division of existing wealth. But, though it is thus true that his ultimate society is Utopian, his perspective is not altogether false. He was right in perceiving the Irish crisis as part of a vaster movement. It can now be seen to have been, in fact, the first stirring in Europe against nationalistic oppression and feudal reaction following the defeat of the French Revolution, a stirring which was followed in 1820 and 1821 by revolutions in Spain, Italy, and Greece, the last of which turned into a revolutionary war leading to the threshold of 1830, famed "year of revolutions." It should be emphasized, too, that although he followed Godwin in his concept of the ultimate society he rejected his impractical program of static individual "enlightenment" for one of concerted political action passing through stages: "all steps . . . all reforms . . . preparatory to the great and lasting one." That the change would come he believed to be inevitable; but the speed with which it came depended on the effectiveness of human action: "they will certainly happen . . . but . . . it all depends on yourselves how soon or how late."

The *Address* is significant as Shelley's manifesto of his new faith, his first major work since *St. Irvyne*. The political thinking behind it is not, for all the author's youth, that of a novice, but of a young man who has lived in a political atmosphere since childhood and has read widely among the most advanced thinkers of his age. In its worst passages, it is ingenuous and repetitive, but in its best it is powerful and stirring.

ACTIVITIES IN IRELAND

On February 12, 1912, Shelley, Harriet, and Eliza arrived in Dublin and took rooms at 7 Sackville Street, one of the principal streets of the city. Shelley does not seem to have lost much time in pursuing his objectives, for by February 24, the *Address to the Irish People* was off the press [47] and on the next day was offered to the public via the following advertisement in *The Dublin Evening Post:*

> This day is published, price Fivepence, to be
> had of all the Booksellers,
>
> AN ADDRESS TO THE IRISH PEOPLE
>
> By Percy B. Shelley

Advertisement.—The lowest possible price is set on this publication, because it is the intention of the Author to awaken in the minds of the Irish poor a knowledge of their real state, summarily pointing out the evils of that state, and suggesting rational means of remedy.—Catholic Emancipation, and a Repeal of the Union Act (the latter the most successful engine that England ever wielded over the misery of fallen Ireland) being treated of in the following Address, as grievances which unanimity and resolution may remove, and associations conducted with peaceable firmness, being earnestly recommended as means for embodying that unanimity and firmness which must finally be successful. [48]

This advertisement shows that Shelley had not been long in Dublin before he realized that he would have to emphasize more specifically than in the *Address* the questions of emancipation and repeal and the formation of an organization. It shows also that he had fulfilled his intention, expressed before leaving England, of printing the *Address* "very cheap" for popular circulation even though he would lose money by it. [49]

Some ridicule has been cast on Shelley's distribution of this pamphlet by his statement that he threw some from the balcony of his lodgings at each man who "looked likely" and by Harriet's comment that she and Shelley handed them out in the street. [50] It has been forgotten, however, that this is only a small part of the story. Shelley printed 1,500 copies: 400 had been distributed within two days, some of them mailed out to Irish patriots and publicists; 60 he sent to those important havens of political controversy, the taverns, presumably to be posted up (an intention expressed before leaving England—in emulation, as he said, of Tom Paine). [51] He advertised the pamphlet in the local papers [52] and kept the price low to aid its circulation. He had at least one man selling them throughout the city,[53] and the Dublin *Weekly Messenger* reported that they were circulated with "uncommon industry through the metropolis." [54] By March 18 only a few copies remained.[55] Shelley, in short, seems to have done about all that could be done to secure an adequate distribution of the work.

At the same time as he was dispensing the pamphlet, Shelley attempted to get in touch with various Irish leaders. On February 24, and again on March 8, he wrote to Godwin saying that he had tried to see John Philpot Curran (to whom Godwin had given him a letter of introduction), but without success. Curran later called on him and had Shelley twice at his house for dinner. Shelley, however, found that the Curran of 1812 was not the Curran who had defended with such impassioned vehemence Hamilton Rowan, Wolfe Tone, and Peter Finnerty, and whose speeches he had read with admiration before leaving England (with such admiration, in fact, as to lift, without acknowledgment, some sentences from them for the *Address*).[56] Curran had accepted the position of Master of the Rolls in 1806—an act which Shelley (and others) disliked—and had settled into a comfortable inactivity.

Another Irish leader with whom Shelley tried to get acquainted was Hamilton Rowan, the former wealthy champion of the United Irishmen. On February 25, he sent the following letter to Rowan:

Although I have not the pleasure of being personally known to you, I consider the motives which actuated me in writing the inclosed sufficiently introductory to authorize me in sending you some copies, and waiving ceremonials in a case where public benefit is concerned. Sir, although an Englishman, I feel for Ireland; and I have left the country in which the chance of birth placed me for the sole purpose of adding my little stock of usefulness to the fund which I hope that Ireland possesses to aid me in the unequal yet sacred combat in which she is engaged. In the course of a few days more I shall print another small pamphlet, which shall be sent to you. I have intentionally vulgarized the language of the inclosed. I have printed 1,500 copies, and am now distributing them throughout Dublin.[57]

But Rowan, like Curran, had grown conservative; he did not answer Shelley's letter and he did not assist him in the distribution of the *Address*. There was to be for him "no repetition of the intoxicating days when Tone or Edward Fitzgerald came to dinner and when the language of freedom whirled its fumes around the brain." [58]

That, in addition to these attempts to see Curran and Rowan,

Shelley was getting acquainted with a number of other Irish radicals is evident from a letter to Elizabeth Hitchener on February 27:

O'Connor, brother to the Rebel Arthur, is here: [I have] written to him. —Do not fear what you say in your letters.—I am resolved.—Good principles are scarce here. The public papers are either oppositionists or ministerial: one is as contemptible and narrow as the other. I wish I could change this. I of course am hated by both these parties. The remnant of United Irishmen, whose wrongs make them hate England, I have more hopes of. I have met with no determined Republicans, but I have found some who are *democratifiable*. I have met with some waverers between Christianity and Deism.[59]

This letter makes clear what was implied in the *Address,* that Shelley was not interested in the Irish Whigs—"oppositionists"—who were largely controlled by the Irish Catholic aristocracy. A few days later he commented: "I do not like Lord Fingall, or *any* of the Catholic aristocracy. Their intolerance can be equalled by nothing but the hardy wickedness and falsehood of the Prince." [60] Shelley, that is to say, renounced the aristocratic Catholic movement of Lord Fingall and Lord Ffrench, who formed the right wing opposition to O'Connell in the Catholic Committee and who advocated reliance on the Whigs and the Prince Regent. For his part, he was seeking out "the remnant of United Irishmen," republicans and freethinkers. Roger O'Connor, "brother to the Rebel Arthur" (vouched for by Fox and the Duke of Norfolk), had been one of the leaders of the United Irishmen, and although imprisoned several times, remained unshakably loyal to the cause. He was a personal friend of Sir Francis Burdett, and is said to have declared that Voltaire was his God—both attributes that would endear him to Shelley. His son, Feargus, was later editor of the Chartist paper, *Northern Star.*

Whether Shelley ever met Roger O'Connor, we do not know, but we do know that he struck up a friendship with one Irish radical who had some influence in Dublin. This was John Lawless, later editor of *The Weekly Messenger,* a nationalist Dublin newspaper. Lawless had been intimate with the leaders of the United Irishmen and had been refused admittance to the bar because of his connections with them. He was a member of the Catholic Committee and later of the Irish Association, and hence, an associate of O'Connell. In both organizations, however, he seems to have been to the left of O'Connell, for in 1812, he made a motion in the Catholic Committee "censuring those Catholics who had betrayed their cause by voting for the enemies of Ireland," a motion opposed by O'Connell; [61] in 1824, he attacked O'Connell for making some concessions to the English, accusing him of "selling the people for a silk gown"; [62] in 1828, he worked in an election campaign which O'Connell and other members of the Catholic Association had considered hopeless, built up a following among the peasants, and marched with them, 140,000 strong, into Ballybay and nearly precipitated a riot.[63] Thomas Wyse in his *Historical Sketch of the Late Catholic Association* (1829) dryly remarked: "Mr. Lawless would have made a good commissioner to the Department under the French Republic." [64]

The first mention of Lawless in Shelley's life comes in a letter of March 10, 1812, that Harriet and Eliza are out "walking with a Mr. Lawless (a valuable man)"; [65] by March 14, Shelley and Lawless are concocting schemes for running a radical newspaper together: "I shall soon however have the command of a Newspaper with Mr. Lawless, of whom I shall tell you more: this will be a powerful engine of amelioration, Mr. L., though he regards my ultimate hopes as visionary, is willing to acquiesce in my means. He is a republican." [66] On March 20, Shelley is assisting Lawless "in the publication of a voluminous History of Ireland" (which was published in 1814),[67] and later, after returning from Ireland, continued to write to him.[68]

One other Irish radical with whom Shelley became acquainted was Catherine Nugent, of whom we first hear in a letter by Harriet to Elizabeth Hitchener on March 18:

I have seen her but twice before, and I find her a very agreeable, sensible woman. She has felt most severely the miseries of her country, in which she has been a very active member. She visited all the Prisons in the time of the Rebellion to exhort the people to have courage and hope. She says it was a most dreadful task; but it was her duty, and she would not shrink from the performance of it. This excellent woman, with all her notions of Philanthropy and Justice, is obliged to work for her subsistence—to work in a shop which is a furrier's; there she is every day confined to her needle. Is it not a thousand pities that such a woman should be so dependent upon others? She has visited us this evening for about three hours, and is now returned home. The evening is the only time she can get out in the week; but Sunday is her own, and then we are to see her.[69]

Catherine Nugent was born in 1771. She had been active in the 1798 revolution—so active, indeed, that she used to say that if she had been a man she would certainly have been executed—and she carried on an extensive correspondence with her fellow United Irishmen. Unlike

Shelley's other Irish acquaintances she was of the working class, being employed as a fur worker at the shop of one John Newman at 101 Grafton Street. She later lived with the Newmans and is said to have built up a small literary circle with their home as the center. A friend described her in 1826 as "a wonderful woman—altho' very plain, little and republican looking," and in 1833 commented on her "amazing spring and elasticity of mind . . . her depth of charity and love of mankind—her utter absence of personal selfishness—her quiet un- ostentacious benevolence." A letter of 1827 reveals her a well-educated and intelligent woman.[70] From her Shelley must have derived a more intimate feeling for the United Irishmen and a deeper sense of Irish problems in general.

On February 28, there occurred the climactic action of Shelley's stay in Dublin, his speech at one of O'Connell's aggregate meetings at the Fishamble Street Theatre. In order to understand the significance of this particular meeting, it is necessary to go back a few months and note some of the main events in the history of the Committee.

In July, 1811, the Catholic Committee held an aggregate meeting in the Fishamble Street Theatre on the question of sending a petition to the Prince Regent asking for his support. Following this meeting a number of the participants, including one Thomas Kirwan, were ar- rested. A short time later the government sent a police magistrate to a meeting of the Catholic Committee to declare it unconstitutional. Lord Fingall, who occupied the chair, refused to admit that it was a delegate meeting and under the sharp legal questioning of O'Connell the magistrate withdrew. In December the Committee called another aggregate meeting with O'Connell as the main speaker to protest against this attack upon their rights, and this protest grew into a nationwide movement:

Hitherto, the Catholic Committee in Dublin had been all that mattered. Now county meetings were being summoned all over Ireland, and the Government's blundering attack upon the Committee in Dublin had created a new pretext for holding aggregate meetings of protest everywhere. And linked with the demand for Catholic Emancipation—which it was assumed, in every series of resolutions, that the Prince of Wales must favour—there arose a new agitation for the repeal of the disastrous Union.[71]

The answer of the government to this popular challenge was twofold. It uncovered a faked plot designed to show that the Irish were in favor of civil war, and it declared Thomas Kirwan guilty. This latter act started a storm center in Dublin because the trial of the first of the men arrested with Kirwan, and on the same charge as he, had already taken place and the accused declared not guilty. It was clear, therefore, that the government was using the Kirwan case to hit back at the Catholic Committee for its agitation.

It was on these two counts, the Kirwan case and the fake plot, that the aggregate meeting of February 28 was called. For this meeting the Fishamble Street Theatre was crowded as usual, "brilliantly illuminated"—the *London Chronicle* reported—its boxes adorned with ladies and gentlemen in evening dress,[72] come, in the main, of course, to hear the great O'Connell. O'Connell began his speech with a review of the Kirwan case, bitterly assailing the judge, the Solicitor General and the Attorney General, and then went on to attack the plot as "a scheme to dupe the poor, in order to continue the vassalage of the rich."[73] He touched on the question of Catholic emancipation, declaring, as Shelley had in the *Address,* that it "is certain and will be immediate." On the Prince Regent he was cautious: "On the Prince, I say nothing—uncertainty as to present circumstance—reliance on the past, and the lingering and dutiful affection in a heart devoted to the friend of Ireland, restrain me."[74]

One special feature of this meeting was the presence of two non-Catholic speakers, Lord Glentworth, a Protestant nobleman, and Shelley. Their presence and that of other non-Catholic visitors was considered sufficiently important to warrant the introduction of a special resolution:

RESOLVED, That the grateful thanks of this Meeting are due, and hereby returned to Lord Glentworth, the Right Hon. Maurice Fitzgerald, and the other *Distinguished Protestants* who have this day honoured us with their presence.[75]

It was to this resolution that Shelley spoke. The following account of his speech appeared in *The Dublin Evening Post:*

Mr. Shelley requested a hearing. He was an Englishman, and when he reflected on *the crimes committed by his nation on* Ireland, he could not but blush for his countrymen, did he not know that arbitrary power never failed to corrupt the heart of man. (Loud applause for several minutes.)

He had come to Ireland for the sole purpose of interesting himself in her misfortunes. He was deeply impressed with a sense of the evils which Ireland endured, and he considered them to be truly ascribed to the fatal effects of the legislative union with Great Britain.

He walked through the streets, and he saw the *fane of liberty converted into a temple of Mammon.* (Loud applause.) He beheld beggary and famine in the country, and he could lay his hand on his heart and say that the cause of such sights was the union with Great Britain. (Hear, hear.) He was resolved to do his utmost to promote a Repeal of the Union. Catholic Emancipation would do a great deal towards the amelioration of the condition of the people, but he was convinced that the Repeal of the Union was of more importance. He considered that the victims whose members were vibrating on gibbets were driven to the commission of the crimes which they expiated by their lives by the effects of the Union.[76]

Shelley, apparently, placed the main emphasis in his speech on the repeal of the Union Act, but, in so placing the emphasis, he did not fail to support Catholic emancipation also, and—as we can gather from an account in another Dublin paper, *The Patriot*—pointed to America as a shining example of religious freedom:

He could not imagine that the religious opinion of a man should exclude him from the rights of society. The original founder of our religion taught no such doctrine. Equality in this respect was general in the American States, and why not here? Did a change of place change the nature of man? He would beg those in power to recollect the French Revolution: the suddenness, the violence with which it burst forth, and the causes which gave rise to it.[77]

That, in his remarks on religious freedom, Shelley also brought in some of the anti-Catholic sentiments of the *Address* is apparent from his later comment to Elizabeth Hitchener that there were some hisses when he "spoke of religion." [78] On the other hand, the *Evening Post* account shows that his speech on the whole was well received; and the *Freeman's Journal* noted that "he was received with great kindness." [79] And this is supported by a letter to the editor of *The Dublin Journal* which notes that Shelley's "invectives" against the British government were "hailed by the assembly" with "transport." [80]

It remains to be mentioned only that the government had its spies at the meeting, one of whom made the enlightening notation that a "Mr. Shelley, who stated himself to be a native of England," spoke.[81] A few days after this meeting Shelley issued the second of his Irish pamphlets, *Proposals for an Association*.[82]

PROPOSALS FOR AN ASSOCIATION

Shelley's second pamphlet is a more acutely reasoned and maturely written piece of work than his first. After actual contact with the Irish situation, his understanding of its essential issues and needs had

sharpened; and, furthermore, he wrote in his own "natural style." ("I
send you the first sheet of my first 'Address' as it comes out. The style
of this, as you will perceive, is adapted to the lowest comprehension
that can read. It will be followed by another in my own natural style
though in the same strain.") [83] The two pamphlets were addressed to
different audiences and intended to accomplish different objects. The
Address was directed to the mass of the "poor Catholics" and was designed to point out the nature of the evils afflicting them; the *Proposals*
was directed to the professional classes and designed to create an organization of intellectual liberals and radicals. Shelley maintained the
same duality of political audience in Ireland as he had in England.

The *Proposals* consists of two main sections: (a) Catholic emancipation and repeal of the Union Act; (b) the proposed organization; and
three digressions: on the rights of government; on the French Revolution; on Malthus.

Shelley begins by hinting, in the introductory pages, his thesis that
Ireland represented a specially significant field for the reformer because
the struggle for Irish rights had started a movement which might
presage a new revival of humanity's struggle for liberation (regardless
of the motives of those who had begun the movement). [84]

His treatment, in the first part, of Catholic emancipation and the
repeal of the Union Act shows the same relative emphasis as in his
speech on February 28 and reveals that he had thought through these
problems in more detail than he had in the *Address*. He repeats, but
now more clearly and specifically, what he considered to be the essence
of the situation: Emancipation means that the upper-class Catholics
will gain some legal rights; it is not therefore a question that will effect
the well-being of the majority; nevertheless one should support it as a
relatively progressive measure:

> It is my opinion that the claims of the Catholic inhabitants of Ireland, if
> gained tomorrow, would in a very small degree, aggrandize their liberty and
> happiness. The disqualifications principally affect the higher orders of the
> Catholic persuasion. . . . I am happy however, at the near approach of
> this emancipation, because I am inimical to all disqualifications for opin-
> ion. . . . It is a sign of benefits approaching. . . . [85]

The repeal of the Union Act is a different kind of question; unlike
Catholic emancipation it is a measure which will directly benefit the
mass of the people and so should be given unqualified support:

I will not pass unreflected on the Legislative Union of Great Britain and Ireland, nor will I speak of it as a grievance so tolerable or unimportant in its own nature as that of Catholic Disqualification. The latter affects few, the former thousands. The one disqualifies the rich from power, the other impoverishes the peasant, adds beggary to the city, famine to the country, multiplies abjectedness, whilst misery and crime play into each other's hands, under its withering auspices. I esteem then, the annihilation of this second grievance to be something more than a mere sign of coming good. I esteem it to be in itself a substantial benefit.[86]

(Reading these passages some thirty-four years later, O'Connell's son commented: "The allusion to the effect on the 'higher orders' of Catholics was, so far as those of them who have benefited by the Emancipation Act, truly prophetic. 'Power and wealth' have sadly injured, with them, 'the cause of freedom and virtue' . . . . In the remarks upon Repeal there is the same singular appositeness to the present day . . .")[87]

These and other objectives can be secured only by organization. "I think that individuals acting singly, with whatever energy can never effect so much as a society": [88]

I conclude these remarks which I have indited principally with a view of unveiling my principles, with a proposal for an Association for the purposes of Catholic emancipation, a repeal of the union act, and grounding upon the attainment of these objects a reform of whatever moral or political evil may be within its compass of human power to remedy.[89]

This organization, as we should expect, was not to be secret but open; it would be opposed by the aristocrats "because its ultimate views look to a subversion of all factitious distinctions, although from its immediate intentions I fear that aristocracy can have nothing to dread"; [90] the priesthood would attack it because it would advocate a severance of church and state; it should diffuse "knowledge and virtue throughout the poor classes of society in Ireland" and it should cooperate with "any enlightened system of education"; it is not only to discuss problems but also to act: "I propose to these to form an association for the purposes, first, of debating on the propriety of whatever measures may be agitated, and secondly, for carrying, by limited or individual exertion such measures into effect when determined on." [91]

Shelley, then, is proposing an organization which will have, for its immediate aims, Catholic emancipation and repeal of the Union Act, and, for its later aims, a republican and egalitarian form of society (for this latter is clearly what he is burying in the discreet phrases on the "reform of moral and political evil"). Its members are both to educate themselves and to go out among the people with its message and program. This concept is clearly close to a revival of some of the methods and ideas of the United Irishmen; like the United Irishmen it was to have more than immediate objectives and to aim at an eventual republican state; like the United Irishmen—at least after the ascendency of Tone—it was to renounce secrecy and violence. It was, in short, the same kind of organization for Ireland as he had advocated for England in his letter to Leigh Hunt from Oxford almost exactly one year previously. And he was right in thinking that there was a need for such a group in Ireland, a group to transcend the narrower view of the O'Connell movement and yet to cooperate with that movement.

As one of the functions of such an organization would be to discuss the nature of government, Shelley informs us that he will digress briefly with some comments on this topic, and the pamphlet moves into the first of the three digressions with which it concludes. In this first digression, he argues the legal point that as Great Britain has no written constitution it is impossible that the proposed organization should run counter to it. As for the Tory argument that to break the traditional forms of the constitution would be like destroying an aged oak, he answers with typically republican invective:

I call expressions similar to these political cant, which, like the songs of Rule Britannia and God Save the King, are but abstracts of the caterpillar creed of courtiers, cut down to the taste and comprehension of a mob; the one to disguise to an alehouse politician the evils of that devilish practice of war, and the other to inspire among clubs of all description a certain feeling which some call loyalty and others servility.[92]

The digression on the French Revolution, which follows, has a special interest as Shelley's earliest extant treatment of a theory which became fundamental to many of his works (including *The Revolt of Islam* and *Prometheus Unbound*).

To Shelley, as to other liberal thinkers, the defeat of the French Revolution was the major historical tragedy of the age. Instead of the period of democratic progress that seemed about to be ushered in— "the budding rose above the rose full blown"—came the smothering tyranny of Napoleon and the slaughter of European war. To seek the explanation for this shattering reversal and to discover methods for avoiding similar defeats in the future became a ruling passion with Shelley.

The essence of the problem, as he had worked it out, at least by February, 1812, and probably by the fall of 1811—when it likely formed the central lesson of *Hubert Cauvin*—was that there had been insufficient men of enlightened minds and unselfish spirits to guide the French masses into more constructive paths; it was violence which evoked the counter-despotism of Napoleon and the militarists.

The French nation was bowed to the dust by ages of uninterrupted despotism. They were plundered and insulted by a succession of oligarchies, each more blood-thirsty and unrelenting than the foregoing. In a state like this, her soldiers learned to fight for freedom on the plains of America, whilst at this very conjuncture, a ray of science burst through the clouds of bigotry that obscured the moral day of Europe. The French were in the lowest state of human degradation, and when the truth, unaccustomed to their ears, that they were men and equals was promulgated, they were the first to vent their indignation on the monopolizers of earth, because they were most glaringly defrauded of the immunities of nature. . . . In the revolution of France, were engaged men, whose names are inerasible from the records of Liberty. Their genius penetrated with a glance the gloom and glare which Church-craft and State-craft had spread before the imposture and villainy of their establishments. They saw the world—, were they men? Yes! They felt for it! they risked their lives and happiness for its benefit!—Had there been more of these men France would not now be a beacon to warn us of the hazard and horror of Revolutions, but a pattern of society, rapidly advancing to a state of perfection, and holding out an example for the gradual and peaceful regeneration of the world.[93]

How could this tragedy again be averted? Only by insuring that in future revolutions there would be sufficient of these intellectual leaders to guide the masses. Hence, the need for such organizations as he was proposing: "I consider it to be one of the effects of a Philanthropic Association, to assist in the production of such men as these, in an extensive development of these germs of excellence, whose favourite soil is the cultured garden of the human mind." [94] For the present, the unique situation in Ireland provided the most favorable ground for the establishment of such organization but later—as he hints in this pamphlet and states in a letter to Elizabeth Hitchener—they should be set up in England and other countries.[95] To the dream of the world republic of the *Address* is now added that of a world organization to accomplish it.

The third digression, that on Malthus, reflects the liberal view of the day of Malthus as an apologist for upper-class oppression. His arguments in favor of poverty and war as valuable checks to population growth were as severely attacked by Godwin, Hazlitt, Cobbett, and others as by Shelley:

War, vice, and misery are undeniably bad, they embrace all that we can conceive of temporal and eternal evil. Are we to be told that these are remedyless, because the earth would, in case of their remedy, be over-stocked? That the rich are still to glut, that the ambitious are still to plan, that the fools whom these knaves mould, are still to murder their brethren and call it glory, and the poor are to pay with their blood, their labor, their happiness, and their innocence, for the crimes and mistakes which the hereditary monopolists of earth commit? Rare Sophism! [96]

The passage is of interest, too, as foreshadowing future attacks on Malthus in the Prefaces to *The Revolt of Islam* and *Prometheus Unbound* and in *Swellfoot the Tyrant*. When Godwin's book against Malthus was published in 1820, Shelley received it enthusiastically.

In addition to his two pamphlets, Shelley produced four minor works in Dublin: the *Declaration of Rights* and three poems, one on Mexico, one on Ireland, and one on the grave of Robert Emmet. Of these, only the first was printed in Dublin.

The *Declaration of Rights* is a summation of the republican creed, indebted, as W. M. Rossetti has pointed out, to two French Declarations of Rights, that adopted by the Constituent Assembly in August, 1789, and that proposed by Robespierre in April, 1793.[97] It is generally indebted also to Paine, and in at least two clauses the influence of Godwin is discernible: "Politics are only sound when conducted on principles of morality. They are, in fact, the morals of nations"; "No man has a right to monopolize more than he can enjoy; what the rich give to the poor, whilst millions are starving, is not a perfect favour, but an imperfect right." [98]

The *Declaration* was printed on one sheet and—like *The Devil's Walk*, which was similarly printed—intended for mass distribution.

The poem on Mexico and part of that on Ireland appear in a letter to Elizabeth Hitchener on February 14, that on Mexico being prefaced by the words: "Have you heard [that] a new republic is set up in Mexico? I have just written the following short tribute to its success." [99] The reference is to the revolution against the Spanish authorities led by the priest Marelos.[100] Shelley is a little premature in his rejoicing as the constitution was not actually proclaimed until October, 1812, but the poem reveals his early interest in liberationist and republican movements (later to form the substance of the first chapter of *A Philo-*

sophical View of Reform), and his awareness of the international anarchy around him:

> Can the daystar dawn of love,
> Where the flag of war unfurled
> Floats with crimson stain above
> The fabric of a ruined world?

The poem on Ireland is fragmentary; that on Emmet, perhaps inspired by Moore's and Southey's poems on Emmet,[101] reveals rather more technical smoothness than had previously marked his versification. (Shelley's early verse is notably inferior to his prose.)

> No trump tells thy virtues—the grave where they rest
> With thy dust shall remain unpolluted by fame,
> Till thy foes, by the world and by fortune caressed,
> Shall pass like a mist from the light of thy name.

LAST DAYS IN IRELAND

Following the publication of the *Proposals* early in March, a revealing correspondence between Shelley and Godwin took place. Shelley, in a letter of February 24, had enclosed a copy of the *Address* intimating that its influence would be "benevolent." [102] To this Godwin replied on March 4:

In the pamphlet you have just sent me, your views and mine as to the improvement of mankind are decisively at issue. You profess the immediate object of your efforts to be "the organization of a society, whose institution shall serve as a bond to its members." If I may be allowed to understand my book on "Political Justice," its pervading principle is, that association is a most ill-chosen and ill-qualified mode of endeavouring to promote the political happiness of mankind. . . . Discussion, reading, inquiry, perpetual communication, these are my favourite methods for the improvement of mankind: but associations, organized societies, I firmly condemn; you may as well tell the adder not to sting . . . as tell organized societies of men, associated to obtain their rights and to extinguish oppression, prompted by a deep aversion to inequality, luxury, enormous taxes and the evils of war, to be innocent, to employ no violence, and calmly to await the progress of truth.[103]

This Shelley answered rather sharply:

I am not forgetful or unheeding of what you said of associations. But "Political Justice" was first published in 1793; nearly twenty years have elapsed since the general diffusion of its doctrines. What has followed? Have men ceased to fight. Have vice and misery vanished from the earth? Have the fireside communications which it recommends taken place? Out of the many who have read that inestimable book, how many have been blinded by prejudice; how many, in short, have taken it up to gratify an ephemeral vanity, and when the hour of its novelty had passed, threw it aside, and yielded with fashion to the arguments of Mr. Malthus?

I have at length proposed a Philanthropic Association, which I conceive not to be contradictory, but strictly compatible with the principle of "Political Justice." [104]

This response reduced Godwin to panic:

I take up the pen again immediately on the receipt of yours, because I am desirous of making one more effort to save yourself and the Irish people from the calamities with which, I see, your mode of proceeding to be fraught. . . . Shelley, you are preparing a scene of blood! If your associations take effect to any extensive degree, tremendous consequences will follow, and hundreds, by their calamities and premature fate, will expiate your error. . . . Do not be restrained by a false shame from retracting your steps; you cannot say, like Macbeth, "I am in blood stepp'd in so far that should I wade no more, returning were as tedious as go o'er."

I wish to my heart you would come immediately to London.[105]

It has frequently been assumed that in this exchange Godwin was right and Shelley wrong. But this is not so. The Godwin of 1812 was not the Godwin of the halcyon days of *Political Justice,* but a retired scholar out of touch with the new political movement. His argument that organization would lead to violence was being disproved by the reform organizations of Burdett, Cobbett, and Cartwright at the very time he was writing and was to be further disproved in the succeeding decade both in England and Ireland. If the reformers had followed his injunctions there would have been no reform movement and the Tory domination of Parliament would have remained unbroken. Nor was there any special factor in the Irish situation which made his views more valid there. If a vast organization such as O'Connell's could grow and exist without any tendency to violence, it is clear that such a small organization of professional men and thinkers as Shelley proposed could have had no harmful effects.

The final letter in this exchange came from Shelley on March 18:

I have said that I acquiesce in your decision, nor has my conduct militated with the assertion. I have withdrawn from circulation the publication wherein I erred, and am preparing to quit Dublin. It is not because I think that *such* associations as I conceived, would be deleterious, that I have withdrawn them. It is possible to festinate, or retard, the progress of human perfectibility; such associations as I would have recommended would be calculated to produce the former effect. . . . My schemes of organizing the ignorant I confess to be ill-timed. I cannot conceive that they were dangerous. . . . It is undescribably painful to contemplate beings capable of soaring to the heights of science, with Newton and Locke, without attempting to awaken them from a state of lethargy so opposite. . . . But I submit; I shall address myself no more to the illiterate. I will look to events in which it will be impossible that I can share, and make myself the cause of an effect which will take place ages after I have mouldered in the dust. . . .[106]

That Shelley should have become discouraged is not surprising. The only progressive movement of any influence in Ireland, the Catholic Committee, was, as we have seen, in the hands of business and professional men who were interested mainly in securing the right to sit in Parliament and hold judgeships. Shelley, however, thinking not in terms of upper-class privilege but of the welfare of the people, wished to emphasize more fundamental issues: repeal of the Act of Union; the class nature of the British government; the extension of the franchise; the redress of economic exploitation; the ultimate advances to republican and egalitarian states. The only people to whom he found he could appeal on these issues were the "remnant of united Irishmen," and these remnants were too small to be of any practical value in setting up an organization.

But, although it is true that Shelley was disappointed, his letter to Godwin gives something of a false picture. It was most important to Shelley, then an unknown but ambitious young radical, to keep in the good graces of Godwin. His consciousness of his role as reproved disciple causes him to exaggerate his disappointment and overemphasize his realization of error. A month or so later he commented to Elizabeth Hitchener, more scantily but more accurately:

We left Dublin because I had done all that I could do; if its effects were beneficial, they were not greatly so. I am dissatisfied with my success, but not with the attempt. . . .[107]

Shelley had not come to Ireland—as one would gather from some commentators—with the intention of single-handedly overturning the country in a night. He had intended to go there for a brief period only, to publish some pamphlets, to make contact with the Irish leaders, to attempt to set up an organization, and to contribute his "own little stock of usefulness," as he told Rowan, to the movements already under

way. Before leaving England he had made plans to go to Wales after
a few months in Ireland.[108] His disappointment was not a general disillusionment but a specific disappointment on discovering the impossibility of setting up the type of organization he felt to be needed. As
early as March 10 he wrote to Elizabeth Hitchener: "I have at least
made a stir here, and set some men's minds afloat. I *may* succeed; but
I fear I shall not, in the main object of Association." [109] And on March
18 Harriet wrote: "All thoughts of an association are given up as
impracticable." [110]

But although he was realizing the impossibilities of establishing the
type of organization he wished, his final weeks in Dublin show that
he had by no means abandoned his activities, or, as he had informed
Godwin, set his sights exclusively on the remote future. By March 10
he had at least three projects under way: he was trying to free an Irish
soldier who had been seized for service by the British army in Portugal
and he was apparently in communication with Sir Francis Burdett on
this question; he was about to tutor "a poor boy, whom I found starving
with his mother in a hiding place of unutterable filth and misery"; he
had rescued from the police "a widow woman with three infants" who
had stolen a penny loaf, and commented with bitterness: "The rich
grind the poor into abjectness, and then complain that they are abject.
They goad them to famine, and hang them if they steal a loaf." [111] On
March 14, he was considering the establishment of the newspaper in
conjunction with Lawless; on or before March 18, he sent copies of the
Address and the *Declaration of Rights* to Elizabeth Hitchener for
distribution; [112] on March 20, he wrote asking Mr. Medwin for a loan
to assist in the publication of Lawless's history of Ireland on which he
was collaborating.[113] He intended, on leaving Ireland, to set up "associations" in Wales and England.[114]

It may, on the surface, seem strange that Shelley ever thought that
he might be able to set up an organization or have any influence on
the Irish scene. We have to remember, however, that he was the son
of a Member of the English Parliament and the heir to a baronetcy.
The presence of any Protestant Englishman in Ireland was of great
importance to the Irish leaders—as the special resolution at the aggregate meeting shows—to demonstrate that the Irish movement had
English allies, and the presence of one with such unusual qualifications
was especially significant. If Shelley had remained in Ireland and had
been content to enlist himself under the banner of O'Connell, he could
have become prominent in the movement. That he failed to make any

appreciable contribution to the cause at the time was due to his youth —"my youth is much against me here" [115]—his impatience—he had intended to stay but a brief period in Dublin—and his relatively too-advanced views. But his trip was not in vain, for Irishmen later looked back with pride to the fact that one of the great English poets had joined in their cause, and were surprised at his insight; [116] and the Irish at the time, while aware of his errors and limitations, regarded him with sympathy. The audience at the aggregate meeting applauded him. In the Dublin *Weekly Messenger* for March 7, 1812, there appeared an extended article on him:

The highly interesting appearance of this young gentleman at the late Aggregate Meeting of the Catholics of Ireland, has naturally excited a spirit of enquiry, as to his objects and views, in coming forward at *such* a meeting; and the publications which he has circulated with such uncommon industry, through the Metropolis, has set curiosity on the wing to ascertain who he is, from whence he comes, and what his pretensions are to the confidence he solicits, and the character he assumes. . . . To this gentleman Ireland is much indebted, for selecting her as the theatre of his first attempts in this holy work of human regeneration; the Catholics of Ireland should listen to him with respect, because they will find that an enlightened Englishman has interposed between the treason of their own countrymen and the almost conquered spirit of their country; that Mr. Shelley has come to Ireland to demonstrate in his person that there are hearts in his own country not rendered callous by six hundred years of injustice; and that the genius of freedom, which had communicated comfort and content to the cottage of the Englishman, has found its way to the humble roof of the Irish peasant, and promises by its presence to dissipate the sorrows of past ages, to obliterate the remembrance of persecution, and close the long and wearisome scene of centuries of human depression.[117]

V SEEDS OF REVOLUTION

A Letter to Lord Ellenborough

The theoretical foundations of Shelley's social philosophy, acquired from the Whig background of his family and from reading in radical literature, had, as we have seen, been given a new reality by personal experience. The expulsion from Oxford and the elopement, throwing him out of the bounds of his family and his class, brought him face to face with economic hardship and social ostracism. Ireland took the process a step further. Experience once more gave life to abstraction, but, this time, not so much personal experience as social experience. In Dublin, Shelley first had contact with a political movement, and a political movement in the midst of a national struggle. There, too, he saw poverty, exploitation, and brutalized tyranny on a scale that he had never envisaged: "I had no conception of the depth of human misery until now." And the sight not only gave flesh and blood to his theories but incited him to action: "With what eagerness do such scenes as these inspire me." [1] When he returned to England he saw his country with new eyes, a country of social conflict and predatory war, of cynical dictatorship and rising protest, of arrogant suppression and courageous resistance. Out of living contact with this England of 1812–1817 there grew the final flowering of Shelley's radical doctrine. Without this contact, the writings of Paine and Godwin, of Condorcet and Volney would have remained so much museum lumber. Shelley—and the point is worth re-emphasis in view of the current history-of-ideas-in-a-vacuum vogue—became what he was, not so much because he read as because he lived.

The England of these years was an England in turmoil. At the root of the turmoil, although the thinkers of the day were only imperfectly aware of it, lay the industrial revolution. That revolution which brought about so startling a rise in iron and coal and cotton, in machinery and transportation, brought with it, also, two new classes, a class of industrial capitalists who owned the new machinery of production, and a class of industrial workers who operated it. The old eighteenth century England of mercantile capitalists and artisans, of landed gentry and tenants, began to be metamorphosed into the nineteenth century England of class struggle and trade unionism, of factory towns and Chartism, of that Niagara of "democratic ascendency" which Bentham welcomed and Carlyle anathematized. The first thought of the ruling oligarchy of mercantile capitalists and great landowners, represented, in the main, by the Tory party, when confronted with the new classes was that of suppression. Both classes were barred from political power by the restriction of the franchise and the rotten borough system. Old Sarum, with seven voters, had two members in Parliament, the new industrial towns of Manchester, Birmingham, Leeds, and Sheffield had none. The situation had not changed much since 1793 when "more than 300 out of the 513 representatives for England and Wales owed their return to individual 'proprietors'" [2] (seats were advertised for sale in the newspapers), and 257 members were returned by 11,075 voters (in a country of about 11,000,000 population).[3] This monopoly of political power the oligarchy had no intention of either forfeiting or sharing. The new capitalists and their middle-class supporters were thus unfranchised; the new working class was not only unfranchised but was suppressed by force. A network of military barracks was set up in the industrial centers:

. . . at the beginning of the French War the government had barrack accommodation for some 21,000 troops in forty-three garrison towns; by 1815 a hundred and fifty-five barracks had been built to contain 17,000 cavalry and 138,000 infantry. Troops were distributed all over the country, and the north and Midlands and the manufacturing region in the south-west came to resemble a country under military occupation. The officers commanding in the different districts reported on the temper and circumstances of their districts, just as if they were in a hostile or lately conquered country; soldiers were moved about in accordance with fluctuations in wages or employment, and the daily life of the large towns was watched anxiously and suspiciously by magistrates and generals.[4]

Trade unionism was forbidden by the Combination Acts of 1799 and 1800; political demonstrations were broken up by the military; the punishment for food rioting or machine breaking was death or exile; a bill to limit the daily working span of children in the mines and mills to twelve and a half hours and set the beginning age at ten aroused a fury of denunciation.[5] Those who voiced opposition to the system were jailed. In 1810, Peter Finnerty, as we have seen, was imprisoned for attacking the government policy on the Walcheren expedition, and Sir Francis Burdett was committed to the Tower for continuing the agitation. In 1810, William Cobbett, the outstanding leader of the popular movement for parliamentary reform, was sentenced to two years imprisonment for protesting the use of flogging in the army. In 1813, the Hunts were similarly sentenced for an attack on the Prince Regent. In 1812, a radical bookseller, Daniel Isaac Eaton, was jailed and put in the pillory for publishing part three of Paine's *The Age of Reason.* In 1817, two men were flogged at the public whipping post for distributing one of Cobbett's pamphlets.[6] In 1817, two anti-government editors, William Hone and Thomas Jonathan Wooler, were tried for "seditious blasphemy." In the same year a magistrate seeing the name Paine on a pamphlet sentenced the distributor to prison, where he would have remained had not a protest to the Home Office disclosed that the pamphlet was not for Paine but against him.[7]

At the pyramidal top of this vast machinery of "order" stood the Home Office; and the directing force behind the Home Office was Lord Sidmouth, Secretary of State. Sidmouth, through the Lord Lieutenants, directed the maneuvers of the army against the workers; through the magistrates, he controlled the implementation of "justice"; through an elaborate spy and police system, he kept his fingers on developments in every county. When the situation seemed threatening, he ordered suspension of habeas corpus and introduced the infamous "Six Acts," gagging the press and illegalizing reform agitation.

In spite of the repression, however, opposition grew. The city middle classes began to agitate for parliamentary reform, a type of reform especially designed to give them control of the Commons without at the same time turning it over to the mass of the population: the extension of the franchise only to those with property qualifications. By the year 1817, eight years after Burdett made his historic motion, this movement of the "moderate" reformers, as they were called, had developed into a powerful political group with a press of its own (its intellectual wing represented by *The Examiner*), and in 1832 finally gained its ends in the Reform Act.

The reaction of the workers was somewhat different. At first they simply met force by force, and Luddite riots swept the industrial north and midlands. But later they, too, under the guidance of Cobbett and Major Cartwright began to turn to parliamentary reform, and, when they did, they developed leaders and demands different from those of the "moderates." Not being property owners, they naturally rejected the moderate platform of restricting the vote and demanded instead the vote for all adult males regardless of property qualifications ("radical" reform). And they, too, developed a powerful movement, whose main organ was *Cobbett's Political Register,* and whose leaders were Cobbett and Henry ("Orator") Hunt. This movement, following its betrayal by the Whigs in 1832, moved on to Chartism, and finally it, too, achieved its aims.

The year in which Shelley returned to his native island, 1812, was of special significance both in the unfolding of this struggle and in his own development. Out of its stirring events—which he watched with unflagging interest day by day—his old radical philosophy acquired new meaning and his first major poem, *Queen Mab,* took form.

ENGLAND, 1812

In November, 1811, the first important Luddite riots had broken out in one of the "new towns" of the industrial midlands, Nottingham. These riots were not caused, as is popularly supposed, by the opposition of the workers to the introduction of machinery, but were a protest measure against unemployment, low wages, and inflationary prices.[8] The Orders in Council, forbidding trade with countries controlled by Napoleon, had ruined the British cotton and woolen industries and precipitated a serious depression. Between November 15 and December 15, nine troops of cavalry and two regiments of infantry moved into the area;[9] and Shelley, as we have seen, took note of their presence in a letter: "The manufacturers [workers] are reduced to starvation. My friends the military are gone to Nottingham . . . Curses light on them for their motives, if they destroy one of its famine-wasted inhabitants."[10]

The year 1812 opened quietly, but on January 7, with the assembling of Parliament, an action took place that was symptomatic of a spreading protest. The Commons was preparing, as usual, to open with an Address to the Prince Regent, surveying, in flattering terms, the condition of the realm. Before the official presenter of the Address, Lord Jocelyn, could arise, Sir Francis Burdett demanded the floor. The speaker, presuming that he wished it merely on a point of order, recognized him; whereupon the radical baronet took it upon himself to deliver the Address to the Regent, and had it so registered in the parliamentary records, the strangest Address ever presented to a British ruler. He began with a bitter tirade against the war with Napoleon as involving an alliance with decadent aristocracies—"having stirred up, in hostility to freedom, almost every sovereign on the continent of Europe"—and moved into a denunciation of dictatorship at home:

To counteract the effect of opinions so obviously just, a system of terror was resorted to; false alarms were excited; spies and informers were hired . . . fortresses in the name of barracks, were established throughout the land; and the fame and person of every man were placed at the absolute disposal of those, who, calling themselves the servants of the king, were, in fact, the agents of that rapacious and haughty oligarchy, who had long fattened on the miseries of the country, and who, in the progress of the principles of liberty, saw the seeds of a destruction of their ill-gotten power.[11]

Burdett's address, printed as a pamphlet, went through 15 editions and sold 30,000 copies.[12]

On February 23, the House rebelled against a request from the Regent that a favorite of his, Colonel McMahon, be given the job of Paymaster of Widow's Pensions, a sinecure paying £2000 a year for work farmed out to subordinates. Ever since the proposal had first been made on January 9, the McMahon case had been a national scandal, featured in cartoons by Cruikshank and broadsides by Peter Pindar. The Regent's request was denied, but he defiantly appointed McMahon Keeper of the Privy Purse.[13]

On February 27, the Frame Work Bill, making the destruction of machinery a capital offense, was introduced into the Lords, and received an excoriating attack from a new peer in his maiden speech:

Is there not blood enough upon your penal code, that more must be poured forth to ascend to Heaven and testify against you? How will you carry the Bill into effect? Can you commit a whole county to their own prisons? Will you erect a gibbet in every field and hang up men like scarecrows? . . . Are these the remedies for a starving and desperate populace? Will the famished wretch who has braved your bayonets, be appalled by your gibbets . . . ? suppose one of these men, as I have seen them, meagre with famine, sullen with despair, careless of a life which your lordships are perhaps to value at something less than the price of a stock-frame—suppose this man . . . dragged into court, to be tried for this new offence, by this new law; still there are two things wanting to convict and condemn him; and these are, in my opinion,—Twelve Butchers for a Jury, and a Jeffries for a Judge!

Lord Byron was supported by Lord Holland and assailed by Lord Eldon, the Lord High Chancellor: "The prevention of offences was the legitimate object of enacting the punishment of death." [14]

In March, the Commons was concerned with a debate on the legitimacy of flogging in the army, with Burdett leading the opposition, a "Petition from the Frame Work Knitters against the Orders in Council," and a bill to raise the annual allowance of the Royal Princesses from £30,000 to £36,000.[15]

In April rioting broke out again with increased violence and in widespread localities: Manchester, Bolton, Carlisle, Bristol, Truro, and Barnstaple. Again the military moved in and Parliament debated. Two of Cobbett's most significant issues of the *Political Register* (April 18 and 25) were devoted to these events, for Cobbett was now beginning his campaign to turn the workers from rioting and machine breaking to political action.[16] Rumors of a national revolution reached the Home Office. "There was talk of a general rising, the disaffected of Manchester and district rising in concert with their fellows in the midlands, in London, in Scotland, and in Ireland. So early as the 19th of April reports were reaching the Home Office that such a rising was intended for May 1. It was widely believed that the first few days of May would see a general, national outbreak verging upon revolution."[17] The liberal *Examiner* found its sympathy for the workers under a strain: "Violences of this nature, however, are always to be deprecated as much by the opposer as by the friend of abuses."[18]

On April 20, blending with Cobbett's mass agitation, a group of upper- and middle-class reformers founded the first Hampden Club, devoted to parliamentary reform. Among its members it numbered the Duke of Norfolk, Lord Byron, Sir Francis Burdett, and William Madocks.[19] On April 21 the Duke of Norfolk presented the Lords with a "Petition from certain manufacturers [workers], traders, and others, of the town of Birmingham, against the continuation of the Orders in Council."[20] On the same day Lord Byron arose, in a debate on Catholic emancipation, to make his second speech, a vigorous denunciation of British policy in Ireland, in the course of which he linked, as Shelley had done previously, the cause of Catholic emancipation with the repeal of the Act of Union: "If it must be called an Union, it is the union of the shark with his prey."[21]

May opened with a violent debate in the Commons on the barracks system and the use of the troops against the people. Sir Francis Burdett was, as usual, the spearpoint of the opposition: "Were not the soldiers on the slightest occasions called in to keep down the people? Did they not commit murders upon the people? [Order! order! order!] This was indeed a new, and an auspicious aera. [Order!] Gentlemen might make what exclamations they pleased, but they should not drown his voice, which was only uttering the truth." [22] *The Examiner,* now in full flight, "could not but deprecate and lament" Burdett's speech: "there are times and occasions in which . . . a recourse to military interference is . . . necessary for the commonest security of property and life." [23] Burdett's attack, indeed, was considered serious enough to warrant a reply from the Prime Minister and Chancellor of the Exchequer, Spencer Perceval:

. . . this mob of rioters and incendiaries were called by him, the people; and government was charged with making war upon the liberties of the people, because they would not allow a turbulent populace to destroy all the valuable accumulations of wealth, property and ingenuity in the realm. To preserve the peace of the districts so disturbed, government had been obliged to draw troops from different parts of the kingdom. . . .[24]

Ten days later Perceval lay dead with a bullet in his heart. His assassin, John Bellingham, claimed that the government was responsible for his financial failure. For three years he had sought redress, finally sending Perceval a petition to present to the House, which Perceval refused to do. On May 11, he hid behind the folding doors of the House of Commons lobby, a pistol concealed in a special pocket in his coat, and, when Perceval passed, stepped out and shot him dead. It was a desperate deed of a desperate man, yet a deed symptomatic of the charged atmosphere of hatreds and bitterness that everywhere prevailed. Its aftermath was symptomatic also. "When the news of his murder reached Nottingham, a numerous crowd publicly testified their joy by shouts, huzzas, drums beating, flags flying, bells ringing, and bonfires blazing. The Military being called out, and the Riot Act read, peace was restored." [25] And the crowd at the execution of Bellingham, cried, as the black cap was pulled over his face: "God bless you! God bless you! God Almighty bless you!" [26]

In June, the United States of America declared war on Great Britain. Some ten days before this event the Duke of Norfolk had arisen in the Lords to urge the rescinding of the Orders in Council (barring trade with the Continent) and to urge the government to open negotiations with the United States: ". . . hostility might be prevented by timely acts on the part of this government." [27]

June marked an important turning point, for in June the Orders in Council were finally repealed and much of the economic distress began to lift. But the effects of this act were not immediate. On June 27, the Prince Regent sent to both Houses a message on the "Disturbed State of Certain Counties," and "Committees of Secrecy" were set up to investigate.[28] On July 1, the Lords were shaken by a new debate on Catholic emancipation. The Duke of Norfolk urged that it go the way of the Orders in Council; Sidmouth stated that, in his opinion, "the temper of the Catholics of Ireland rendered it unworthy of the dignity of the House to grant their claims." [29] On July 9 Cobbett was released from jail after two years imprisonment, and a great celebration banquet was held with Sir Francis Burdett in the chair.[30] The rest of the summer passed quietly, but October and November witnessed one of the most hard-fought election campaigns of the day as Burdett and Cochrane ran again in Westminster, and, in spite of the strength of the opposition, were triumphantly re-elected. In November, the news of Napoleon's defeat at Moscow began to trickle back to London and the magnitude and significance of it to dawn on the British Cabinet. On December 9, John and Leigh Hunt were put on trial; in January, the mass trial of the Yorkshire Luddites began; and on February 4, the Hunts were sentenced to two years imprisonment.

SHELLEY, 1812

"Shelley's Irish campaign," as White correctly remarked, "had been thought of from the first as only one phase of a general campaign against oppression. . . . The departure from Ireland, therefore, was more a shift of base than a surrender." [31] Before leaving Ireland, Shelley had informed Elizabeth Hitchener that he was considering setting up associations of advanced liberals in Wales and Sussex similar to that he had attempted in Dublin.[32] After arriving in Wales, however, and surveying the situation there and in England, he apparently decided that the best use of his talents lay not in organization but in propaganda: propaganda of a general nature designed to reveal fundamental flaws and fundamental solutions, and propaganda on particular issues. The first of these aims he fulfilled in *Queen Mab,* the second in *A Letter to Lord Ellenborough.*

Accompanied by Harriet and Eliza, he arrived at Holyhead in north Wales on April 6, and by the middle of the month was established in a large farmhouse near his cousins, the Groves, in the neighborhood of Rhayader, where he had lived the previous summer before making his historic journey to London and Harriet. There he intended to make his living from the farm—heir to a large farming estate, he had listed his occupation on his marriage certificate as "farmer"—to hire an overseer, and to settle down to his political writing.[33] He wrote requesting his father to advance £500 for the project (a request which exceeded

Timothy's confidence in his son's agricultural abilities).[34] He felt that Elizabeth Hitchener would prove a useful collaborator, and suggested to her that her father might be interested in the job of overseer,[35] an offer, which, if it was conveyed to him, he was wise in turning down, for, by June 6, the members of the menage had been rudely dispossessed and were boarding with the Groves.

Nothing of biographical importance took place during this time, but Shelley's and Harriet's letters are interesting in revealing the interest with which they were following the troubled political scene. Shortly after settling in his intended estate, Shelley commented to Elizabeth Hitchener on the main events of the preceding weeks: the Luddite and food riots in Manchester, Bristol, and Carlisle; the debate on increasing the allowances of the princesses; the McMahon scandal:

Manchester, Carlisle, Bristol, and other great towns, are in a state of disturbance. That infernal wretch the P[rince] of Wales demands more money, the Princesses must have more; Mr. McMahon must have more. And for what? For supplying the Augean stable of the Prince with filth which no second Hercules can cleanse. The question becomes one in the rule of three. If the murderer of Marr's family, containing six persons, deserves a gibbet, how much more does a Prince whose conduct destroy[s] millions deserve it? [36]

To Catherine Nugent, on May 7, he made further comment on the riots, and was alarmed at the prospect of war with the United States:

I fear that hunger is the only excitement of our English riotings; any change which they may produce appears to me likely to be devoid of principle and method. I sincerely hope that a just indignation against that crowned coward and villain the Prince does prevail, but I do not think that it has gained any strength. The local Militia, that body of soldiery nearest approaching, and immediately mingling with the character of citizen, have been called out near Carlisle and other great towns to quell the populace. That the Government has dared to call the local [forces] into action appears to be an evidence that at least they do not think that disaffection to Government (except so far as directly connected with starvation) has any share in these tumults. War with America appears in a manner now inevitable. Ministers have been at some *ministerial* work in that country, viz., Capt. Henry and Sir [James Henry] Craig.[37]

The same letter shows Shelley following the Commons debate on barracks, for across the writing on the first page, he scrawled: "Did you see Sir F. Burdett's speech on the Marylebone Barracks?" [38] The letter reveals also that Shelley was continuing to work on behalf of the Irish soldier, Redfern, who had been seized by the British army authorities in Portugal. A copy of a letter by Redfern had been printed and Shelley now wished to distribute it. What method of distribution he followed we do not know, but presumably he mailed copies to prominent individuals (doubtless including Sir Francis Burdett, whom he had earlier intended to get in touch with on the case). One of these letters (along with the *Address to the Irish People*) seems to have been sent to a Lewes (Sussex) newspaper, presumably by Elizabeth Hitchener, from nearby Hurstpierpoint, and was cautiously commented upon by the editor:

We have been favoured with the address of P.B.S., Esq., and entertain no doubt of his benevolent and humane intentions, Nevertheless, after due consideration, we are of opinion that any especial notice of the accompanying letter would have a tendency to defeat the ends he has in view, as a public exposure of the accused parties, however just, might irritate their minds and lead them to direct, with greater severity, the lash of tyranny and oppression against the object of his commiseration, who appears to be completely within their power.[39]

On June 7, Harriet, in a letter to Catherine Nugent, noted the assassination of Perceval by Bellingham, apparently an event which had excited considerable discussion in the household:

What have you thought upon the murder of the Prime Minister? Undoubtedly it was very distressing, but the man's composure is astonishing. I think he was a Methodist from his behaviour. I am sorry for his family. It had been better if they had killed Lord Castlereagh. He really deserved it; but this poor Mr. P[erceval] I believe was a very good private character. Do you not think it nonsense for all the little towns and villages to send petitions to the Prince upon the occasion.[40]

Harriet's trenchant gloss upon the event—"it had been better if they had killed Lord Castlereagh"—was doubtless called forth because Castlereagh, as foreign minister, was considered mainly responsible for the government's war policy and was especially remembered in Ireland for his suppression of the 1798 rebellion. Then, finally, on June 11, we have Shelley's indignant comments on the conviction of Daniel Isaac Eaton, and a few days later he began *A Letter to Lord Ellenborough*.

If nothing of biographical importance happened during Shelley's stay in Wales, events of some interest to him and of which he knew nothing were taking place elsewhere. Shelley had sent to Elizabeth Hitchener from Dublin a box containing his *Address to the Irish*

People, the *Declaration of Rights,* and a letter from Harriet.[41] This box Shelley, perhaps being short of funds, dispatched only as far as the Welsh port of Holyhead, hoping that it would be forwarded from there to Miss Hitchener in Sussex. The box, however, reposed in the customs at Holyhead, and, not being claimed, was opened by the Surveyor of Customs, one Pierce Thomas, on about March 27 to see if it contained any dutiable articles. Finding himself confronted, instead, with sedition, he shakily rushed to consultation with one William D. Fellowes, an agent of the Post Office. On the urgings of Fellowes, he penned a rather breathless letter to the Secretary of State:

Confidential.   Holyhead, March 30th, 1812

Sir,—The important contents of the enclosed letter, with a Pamphlet and a Declaration of rights (forming part of the contents of a box detained by me), which I feel it my duty to transmit to you, will, I trust, be a sufficient apology for addressing myself to you in the first instance. Holding as I do an official situation under the Board of Customs, it would perhaps have been more strictly regular to have first communicated them to my own Board, and if the not having done it should appear to you to be informal, I must trust to your candour in not implicating me for my zealous intentions. Some days since a large deal box, directed to Miss Hitchener, Hurst-pierpoint, Brighton, England, was landed from on board one of the Holyhead Packets, and brought to the Custom House, where, as Surveyor and Searcher of the Customs, I opened it, and found the enclosed open letter— the tendency of which at this moment I need not point out; and it still remains in my custody. If it should be your desire to have them transmitted to London, and withheld from the person to whom they are addressed, I should be glad to be honoured with your confidential opinion and commands in what way I ought to forward it, consistent with my public duty as an officer of the Customs, and the respect due to my Board.

I have the honour to be

Your very obedient servant,

PIERCE THOMAS

Private

The Right Honble. R. Ryder, Secretary.[42]

The following day (March 31) Fellowes also wrote a letter, this one to Francis (later Sir Francis) Freeling, the secretary of the Post Office, headed "Most Private."

The Surveyor of the Customs consulted me yesterday on having discovered in the Custom House, a few days since, a Large deal box, directed to a "Miss Hitchener, Hurst per pier, Brighton, Sussex, England," which had been landed from one of the Packets from Ireland. It contained, besides a great quantity of Pamphlets and printed papers, an open letter, of a tendency so dangerous to Government, that I urged him to write without further loss of time, a confidential letter, either to the Secretary of State, or to Mr. Percival, and enclose the letter, and one of each of the Pamphlets and printed Declarations (as they are styled), which he accordingly did by yesterday's Post, to Mr. Percival.[43]

But even Freeling felt that the matter was too big for him and sent the letter on to the Earl of Chichester, the postmaster general, from whom, on April 5, he received the following reply:

Dear Freeling,—I return the Pamphlet and Declaration, the writer of the first is son of Mr. Shelley, member for the Rape of Bramber, and is by all accounts a most extraordinary man. I hear that he has married a Servant, or some person of very low birth; he had been in Ireland some time, and I heard of his speaking at the Catholic Convention.

Miss Hichener, of Hurstperpoint, keeps a school there, and is well spoken of; her Father keeps a Publick House in the neighbourhood, he was originally a smugler [sic], and changed his name from Yorke to Tichener [Hitchener], before he took the public House.

I shall have a watch upon the Daughter, and discover whether there is any connexion between her and Shelley.

I shall come to Town on Wednesday.

As I am to see Mr. Scott tomorrow, I shall keep the Brighton Papers untill I have seen him.

> Yours most sincerely,
> CHICHESTER [44]

This letter Freeling endorsed and filed: "5th April, 1812. Stanmer. Earl of Chichester. 'Inflammatory Irish Papers addressed to Hurst Perpoint, seized at Holyhead.'" In the meantime, the Secretary of State had passed the material unearthed by Pierce Thomas on to Wellesley-Pole, the Chief Secretary for Ireland, in Dublin, and it was returned to him on April 8.[45] With this the incident closed. The name of Percy Bysshe Shelley had been added to the Home Office files.

Unable either to raise the funds to purchase the farm they desired or to stay indefinitely with the Groves, the Shelleys moved south to Devon, attracted by the prospects of obtaining cheaper accommodations and, perhaps, by the political unrest which had spread thence in April and May. There they settled in the little village of Lynmouth, not far from Barnstaple, the industrial and political center of north Devon, and stayed throughout July and August. Shelley continued his political writing, completing the *Letter to Lord Ellenborough* and *The Voyage,* a poem commenting on brutality in the navy—a subject frequently agitated in Parliament—and working on *Queen Mab*. About the middle of July, they were joined by Elizabeth Hitchener.

Elizabeth Hitchener has been the subject of a good deal of ridicule since Hogg painted his typically Dickensian portrait of her, but although it is true that she was not so talented as Shelley in his first enthusiasms considered her, she was an unusual woman to emerge from the country districts of Sussex in an age when even advanced political thinkers laughed out of court the concept of votes for women.[46] Merle, who knew her slightly, informs us that she "had received a superior education; and had turned it to profit, for she had a boarding school at Hurstpierpoint, and was rather successful in the speculation . . . . This lady was also a disciple of infidelity, although prudence taught her to conceal the fact from the world. The open profession of such doctrines was not calculated to increase the number of her pupils. . . ."[47] Shelley's picture of her is similar, although he was under the impression that she was more open in her expression of radical dissent:

. . . her mind naturally inquisitive and penetrating overstepped the bounds of prejudice. She formed for herself an unbeaten path of life.

By the patronage of a lady, whose liberality of mind is singular, this woman at the age of twenty was enabled to commence the conduct of a school. She concealed not the uncommon modes of thinking which she had adopted, and publickly instructed youth as a Deist and a Republican. When I first knew her she had not read "Political Justice," yet her life appeared to me in a great degree modelled upon its precepts.[48]

In addition to her liberal tendencies in religious and political thinking, Miss Hitchener was an advocate of the rights of women, and even through Hogg's caricatured picture something of her fervor is evident:

There being little conversation during tea, I ventured to inquire again about the Rights of Women. The Goddess of Reason began incontinently to lecture with fluency and animation. Presently Bysshe quitted his chair, and came and stood before her, listening with attention, and looking enthusiastic . . .[49]

We get an interesting picture of her, too, in a letter by Harriet to Catherine Nugent, shortly after her arrival in Devon, reading Shelley's exposé of anti-Irish politicians, "Pieces of Irish History," intended originally to form part of Lawless's history of Ireland:

Your friend and our friend, *Bessy,* has been reading "Pieces of Irish History," and is so much enraged with the characters there mentioned that nothing will satisfy her desire of revenge but the printing and publishing of them to exhibit to the world those characters which are (shameful to say) held up as beings possessing every amiable quality, whilst their hearts are as bad as it is possible to be. They will be shown to the world in a new light, and it will remain to be seen if that world does not repay them as they so eminently deserve.[50]

From her letters she seems an earnest and sincere woman, striving, at first on her own—"I so rarely meet with any one possesing the requisites for intellectual pleasures"—and, later, with Shelley's help, to come to grips with religious and philosophical problems, e.g.: "I have just been reading Locke and am not pleased with his mere affirmation of a Deity tho' this you had prepar'd me to meet; yet I had hop'd to have found some clue to reason on. . . ." She owes the beginning of her liberal development to a Miss Adams, a schoolmistress: "My Mother condemns her because she did not treat me as she had done, and for *allowing a girl* to have an *opinion*. . . ."[51] She produced two books of verse, *The Fireside Bagatelle* (1818) and *The Weald of Sussex* (1822), the latter of which, Dowden commented, "proves that its author, though not a poet, was a woman of some culture and vigor of mind."[52]

Shelley, as we have seen, had met her through his uncle Captain Pilfold, and had continued a correspondence with her since the summer of 1811 on political and philosophical questions. He had long looked upon her as a potential collaborator—Harriet and he had urged her to join them in Ireland—[53] and now that he had settled down for his campaign in England, he felt that her cooperation would be helpful.

Shortly after his arrival in Devon, Shelley took the manuscript of the first important blast in his campaign against oppression, the *Letter to Lord Ellenborough,* to the printing shop of a Mr. Syle at Barnstaple. He had hoped, also, to get a publisher for the work in the person of Thomas Hookham, a liberal publisher in the Unitarian radical tradition, whose establishment "The Library," in Old Bond Street, was well known as "the habitual resort of the *litterateurs* of the day."[54] How Shelley became acquainted with him we do not know, but, as "The Library" was situated not far from the Westbrooks home in Chapel Street, he had probably visited it during his peregrinations in the region in the spring and summer of 1811. On July 29, he wrote to Hookham as follows:

I delayed to answer your very flattering letter until the Printer sent me complete copies of the little work, 25 of which I send you. I beg you to accept of them that you may shew them to any friends who *are not in-*

formers. I shall not persist in my intention of procuring a publisher. Possesing the knowledge I now posess, it would be unjust in me to attempt to draw upon any one the indignation of bigotry and despotism. I have changed, therefore, my former plan to that of gratuitous distribution. In case you could dispose of more than those which I now send, I beg that you will not hesitate a moment in informing me. I have several works, some unfinished, some yet only in contemplation. They are principally in the form of poems or essays. As soon as any one of them is completed I will send it to you, and shall take it as an additional favour if you can, consistently with safety, publish it.

I have received the parcel safe.[55]

It would appear from this letter that Shelley had sent Hookham either the manuscript of the *Letter* or an outline of it, for Hookham seems to have refused publication, something he could hardly have done without some knowledge of it, and, indeed, seems to have gone further and advised against publishing at all. This refusal Shelley is attempting to circumvent by making Hookham a distributing agent. It was perhaps as a result of Hookham's representations that he felt that the printer should be protected also.

In 1871 old Mrs. Blackmore, niece to Shelley's Lynmouth landlady, remembered that the young gentleman had a number of papers printed at Barnstaple and "when they came home," said she, "he had me to cut the printer's name off," for why should Mr. Syle suffer on his account? [56]

These copies, dutifully clipped by Mrs. Blackmore, then a girl of twelve or thirteen, were probably those sent to Hookham on July 29 and again on August 18; one was also sent to Catherine Nugent on, or shortly before, August 4,[57] and Shelley perhaps had plans for further consignments. On the next day, August 18, however, his plans were interrupted by the arrest of his servant, Daniel Healey, in Barnstaple for posting up copies of the broadside *Declaration of Rights,* previously printed in Dublin. The facts of this arrest and its aftermath were first published in *Sketches of the Literary History of Barnstaple* (1866) by John Roberts Chanter, who learned of them from one of Syle's printers:

During this period Shelley came into Barnstaple, and called at Mr. Syle's printing-office, bringing with him a bundle of MSS., of which he desired Mr. Syle to have one thousand copies printed. This was done, Shelley coming in from time to time to read the copy and correct the press. . . . Shelley had about fifty copies as they were printed; but before publication a strange circumstance occurred. A poor labouring man of the neighbourhood was taken up for posting bills about the town and neighbourhood, headed

"Government has no Rights." It being seditious, he was tried and sentenced to three months' imprisonment. His defence was, that a gentleman between Lynton and Barnstaple had given him the bills to post, and paid him 2s. 6d. for doing the job. . . . This circumstance naturally alarmed Mr. Syle, as the pamphlet was quite as seditious in its tone and contents. He at once suppressed and destroyed the remaining sheets, and had several interviews with Shelley to endeavour to get back the ones previously delivered, but unsuccessfully, as they had been mostly distributed.[58]

Thus, the first major document of Shelley's projected campaign reached an impasse in the panic of his printer and the reluctance of his publisher. That Shelley, himself, pressed the matter no further, and did not—in contradistinction to his practice in regard to the Irish pamphlets —allow his name to be placed on the title page, was doubtless due to his own fear of prosecution. Nor, in view of the persecution of Finnerty, Burdett, Cobbett, Eaton, and the Hunts, can it be said that this fear, either on his part or that of Syle and Hookham, was without basis.

Dan was arrested on August 19. On the following day, Shelley visited him in the jail at Barnstaple. "Mr. Shelley," Mrs. Blackmore recalled, "asked him how he came to be so foolish, and gave him one of the papers to read, and he held it upside down." [59] On the same day, one Henry Drake, town clerk of Barnstaple, wrote to Lord Sidmouth:

My Lord,

I am directed by the Worshipful the Mayor of this Town to address your Lordship on the following circumstances.

Last evening a Man was observed distributing and posting some Papers about this Town intituled "Declaration of Rights," and on being apprehended and brought before the Mayor, stated his name to be Daniel Hill, and that he is a Servant to P.B. Shelley, Esq. now residing at Hooper's Lodgings at Lymouth near Linton a small village bordering on the Bristol Channel and about 17 miles from Barnstaple. On being asked how he became possessed of these Papers, he said, on his road from Linton to Barnstaple yesterday, he met a Gentleman dressed in black, whom he had never seen before, who asked him to take the Papers to Barnstaple and post and distribute them, and on Hill's consenting, the Gentleman gave him 5 Shillings for his Trouble—On interrogating Hill more particularly respecting his Master, he said he principally lived in London but in what Part of it he did not know, but that he had lived with him in Sackville Street— that he married a Miss Westbrooke or Westbrooks a Daughter of Mr. Westbrooke of Chapel Street Grosvenor Square and that two sisters of Mrs. Shelley are now with her at Lymouth, and Mr. Shelley his Master's Father is a member of Parliament.—This is all the Information the Mayor could get from Hill, but he has been informed that Mr. Shelley has been regarded with a suspicious eye since he has been at Lymouth, from the Circumstances of his very extensive correspondence, and many of his Packages and Letters being addressed to Sir Francis Burdett—and it is also said that Mr. Shelley has sent off so many as 16 Letters by the same Post—The Mayor has also been informed that Mr. Shelley has been seen frequently to go out in a Boat a short distance from Land and drop some Bottles into the Sea, and that at one time he was observed to wade into the Water and drop a Bottle which afterwards drifting ashore was picked up, and on being broken was found to contain a seditious Paper, the Contents of which the Mayor has not yet been able to ascertain but will apprize your Lordship immediately on learning further particulars.

Daniel Hill has been convicted by the Mayor in 10 Penalties of 20 £ each for Publishing and dispersing Printed Papers without the Printer's name being on them under the Act of 39 Geo. 3 c. 79. and is now committed to the Common Gaol of this Borough for not paying the Penalties, and having no Goods on which they could be levied.

I have taken the liberty of transmitting to your Lordship a Copy of the Paper intituled "Declaration of Rights" and also another intituled "The Devil's Walk" which was also found in Daniel Hill's Possession.

I have the Honour to be
My Lord
Your Lordship's very obedt.
humble Servant
HENRY DRAKE
Town Clerk.

Barnstaple
Aug. 20, 1812.[60]

This letter Sidmouth endorsed as follows:

Acknowledge receipt, with Lord Sidmouth's thanks. Recommend that Mr. Shelley's proceedings be watched if he is still at Linton. It would also be desirable to procure the address of his different correspondents, to whom he writes, from the post-office. Lord S. will be obliged by any further information respecting Mr. S., and, in the meantime, inquiries will be made about him here. Lord S. quite approves of the steps that have been taken respecting Daniel Hill.—August 22.[61]

The town clerk, however, was not the only official taking an interest in Shelley's doings. On Aug. 22, Richard Jones, postmaster of Barnstaple, addressed an epistle to Francis Freeling, secretary of the General Post Office, at London, who, as he had done before, sent it on to his superior, the Postmaster General, the Earl of Chichester, with the following memo:

For Lord Chichester—who will recollect the newspapers he [Shelley]
sent to Miss Hitchener some time since, one of which contained a copy of
the enclosed paper.

Might it not be advisable to communicate with the Secretary of State.
Mr. Shelley is so active in disseminating his principles?—24 August, 1812.[62]

To this the Earl of Chichester appended the note:

I think it right to communicate the circumstances to the Secretary of
State. It will have no effect to speak to Mr. Shelley's family, they suffer
enough already for his conduct.

On September 9, Henry Drake entered the picture once more with
a second letter to Sidmouth. Mr. Drake had made a special trip to
Lynmouth to pursue his investigations on the scene. He had now ascertained the following facts: Shelley had visited Hill in jail the day
after his arrest but had not reproved him ("which," comments Drake,
"appears rather extraordinary"); the seditious paper contained in the
previously mentioned bottle had been *The Devil's Walk;* Shelley had
not only sent bottles but also boxes out to sea, their launchings often
witnessed by "a female servant (supposedly a foreigner)"—doubtless
Elizabeth Hitchener, who was rather dark complexioned; "Mr. Shelley
had with him large chests, which were so heavy that scarcely three men
could lift them, which were supposed to contain papers." [63]

This second letter Sidmouth passed on to a Mr. Litchfield, apparently
a legal advisor to the Home Office, who replied that "it would be proper
to instruct some person to observe his future behaviour, and to transmit
any information which might be obtained concerning him." This
espionage function was then entrusted to the Mayor of Barnstaple, and
with this somewhat inept procedure—for Shelley was by then miles
away from the scene of the crime—the incident closed.

As with the episode of the box to Elizabeth Hitchener, we may again
note the seriousness with which Shelley's activities were taken. The
town clerk considered the matter important enough to write directly
to Sidmouth; once again the Post Office Department and Freeling
enter the picture; Freeling was sufficiently disturbed to send the letter
on to the Earl of Chichester, who, in turn, considered that it warranted
the attention of the Home Secretary; Sidmouth passed it on to one of
his specialists in such problems, whose advice was to set a spy on
Shelley's trail, just as previously Chichester had advised in regard to
Elizabeth Hitchener. We can once more see a reflection of what the
authorities elegantly referred to as "the disturbed state" of the country;

but in this instance the authorities had a special motive for alarm, for in the months immediately preceding Shelley's arrival in Lynmouth, the "disturbances" which had until then threatened only the midlands and the north had spread south into the adjoining counties of Devon and Cornwall. Cobbett, in his *Political Register* for April 18, noted this phenomenon, and reported a riot at the Cornish mining town of Truro. The miners went on strike against the lack of food and "assembled in groups of considerable numbers, in the quarter between Redruth and Truro, and then dispersed themselves over the country with their empty sacks, to purchase corn among the farmers." [64] "The next duty of Magistry," runs the newspaper account Cobbett is quoting, "was to protect property and preserve the public peace . . . With this in view, our worthy high Sheriff signed an order for the march of a part of the Monmouth and Brecon regiment . . . from Falmouth to Redruth." The movement next spread into Devon: "At Barnstaple, Falmouth and Plymouth a similar disorderly disposition of the people was reported. The authorities tried to secure stocks of grain from vessels in port at Falmouth, while at Plymouth the Mayor ordered the constables to maintain order in the market and prevent regrating." [65] Cobbett in the April 25 issue of his *Register* inserts the following item under the heading, "Barnstaple, Devonshire": "We are sorry to hear, that the sudden rise in the price of grain and potatoes, has had a mischievous effect on the north-east of Cornwall and its neighbouring quarter of Devonshire. About Barnstaple, some threatening letters of rather a serious style have been sent to persons supposed to be in possession of corn etc." In May, when the news of Perceval's assassination was reported, there were celebrations among the miners at Truro.[66]

It is little wonder, then, that the town clerk of Barnstaple should write directly to the Home Secretary. His action and its consequences give us an interesting glimpse of one small corner of Sidmouth's information system, one of the most extensive ever to be organized. "Bills for spies are for many years a regular feature of the Home Office papers. Spies were employed by the Home Office itself, by some of the officers commanding in the industrial districts, and by several of the more active magistrates or their clerks . . ." [67] "The spies and informers of Ryder and Sidmouth," writes another authority, "were the detective department of the government." [68] Some spies were professionals, a few of them, like the notorious Oliver, achieving a kind of ghoulish stardom, others were simply informers, like the town clerk of Nottingham—or Barnstaple.[69]

As Shelley was unable to pay Dan's fine (£200), Dan was sent to prison for six months [70]—for the crime of posting a list of elementary political rights. Dan, like most of Sidmouth's victims, took his punishment with his lips sealed.[71] When arrested, he invented the red herring story of the "gentleman in black"; when visited by his master in prison he feigned ignorance of the nature of the material he had been distributing.[72] It was not for Daniel Healey to betray to English officials the author of the *Address to the Irish People.*

Drake's letter informs us that Shelley was observed to "go out in a Boat a short distance from Land and drop some Bottles into the Sea" (an incident also recorded, in sonnets, by its author, along with the similar dispatching of a balloon). Two of these bottles were picked up, and were the subject of further communication to Sidmouth:

On 14 September, from the *Speedwell* Revenue Cutter off St. Ives, John Hopkins, Inspecting Commander of Revenue Cruisers, Western District, sent up to Lord Sidmouth a paper (the *Declaration*) with its envelope—paper tattered owing to dampness—"having found the same in a Sealed Wine Bottle, floating near the Entrance of Milford Haven on the 10th Inst." The Inspector had heard that a similar paper was taken up in a similar manner a few weeks before near Lynmouth by a Preventive Revenue Boat at Porlock, envelope pointing to "a person of the name of Shelley living thereat." So, if thought of sufficient importance, it might lead to "a discovery of the Parties concerned in this novel mode of disseminating their pernicious opinions, and which appear to me intended to fall into the hands of the Sea-faring part of the People, many hundreds of which may thus reach that Class and do incalculable mischief among them." [73]

The humor in these bottle launching episodes has been more apparent to later commentators than it was to the naval authorities of 1812, and one sometimes gets the impression that Shelley spent most of his time in Devon putting bottles into the sea and balloons into the air in the hope of hourly evoking the millennium. These, however, were but diversions from his main political tasks, the *Letter to Lord Ellenborough,* the "very extensive correspondence" with Burdett and others (which made town clerk Drake, and not him alone, regard him "with a suspicious eye"), and the distribution of *A Declaration of Rights* in the volatile Barnstaple district. That he would indulge in such diversions at all is, it is true, symptomatic of an individualistic, free-lance radicalism, divorced, as yet, from the main stream of English reformism, and in this lies the weakness of Shelley's activities in this period, but the episodes are symptomatic also of an overwhelming

feeling of humanitarian urgency in a time of war and starvation, a
hope of somehow giving a "ray of courage to the oppressed and poor"
(as he wrote in the sonnet on the balloon), some "beacon" however
faint, "in the darkness of the Earth."

The correspondence with Burdett (which has apparently not been
preserved) [74] was, doubtless, largely directed towards getting the reformist leader to raise his voice in Parliament on some special issues,
perhaps the Redfern case and the persecution of Eaton. We learn from
a letter of Harriet's that he sent Burdett a copy of the *Letter to Lord
Ellenborough:*

What do you think of Cobbett? A man that can change his opinions so
quickly I do not admire, and particularly when he could write of Sir F.
Burdett in such an abusive and contradictory a way. It seems to me that
Cobbett merely changes his sentiments as occasion requires as best suits his
interests. I hope I am mistaken, tho' his behaviour looks very like it. Percy
has sent you a defense of D.I. Eaton. It must not be published, but you
[will] give us your opinion of it. What think you of Lord Stanhope?—
divine being, how beautifully he speaks. We have sent him one as well as
Sir F. Burdett.[75]

(Lord Stanhope, one of the leaders of the radical opposition within
the House of Lords, had spoken in favor of religious freedom in the
"Toleration Bill" debate, a subject which would be especially interesting
to the Irish Miss Nugent.) [76] A few days previously Shelley had written
to Godwin: "I have as great a contempt for Cobbett as you have, but
it is because he is a dastard and a time server; he has no refinement . . ." [77] Shelley and Harriet are, in these comments, echoing a
series of attacks on Cobbett appearing in the press at the time, perhaps
those in the current *Examiners*. Cobbett, at the celebration banquet
for his release on July 9, had denied *The Times'* charge that he had
offered to give up his *Register* two years previously if the government
would drop proceedings against him, but later had admitted that it
was partly true.[78] At the same time, an old political attack of his against
Burdett, who was in the chair at the banquet, was dug up and secretly
placed under the plates of the guests. Three days later, *The Examiner*
(representing the more genteel reformers) assailed him as "a man of
petty habits and shuffling mode of talking . . . who betrays his small
passions and prejudices at every movement. . . ." [79] In the July 26 issue,
the attack was renewed. He was attacked as "vulgar, turbulent, weak
. . . a poor demagogue":

We think it possible for the most upright men, though not possible for the most cool headed, to go directly from one side of an opinion to another; and all that we ever advanced against him on this head is, that he should have been in such an extreme in both instances, first calling Sir Francis all that was diabolical, and then representing him as all that was angelic.[80]

Shelley, a few years later, exhibited a sympathetic interest in Cobbett and his economic reform theories. And here he and Harriet are not so much expressing disagreement with Cobbett's doctrines as—under the influence of the (largely unjustified) attacks on him—assailing what they believed to be examples of double-dealing and inconsistency. Be this as it may, however, Shelley clearly displays an admiration for Burdett, the aristocratic radical, in these years, that he does not for Cobbett, the democratic political agitator and organizer. Much though he wished to see the overthrow of the aristocratic state, he feared that the masses, unless influenced by intellectual leaders, would fail to achieve a constructive solution (a "change . . . devoid of principle and method"). Although excoriating aristocratic arrogance as fit only for "an age of Vandalism and brutality" and opposing aristocratic equally with commercial "monopoly," he felt that something of the cultured aristocratic way of life should be carried over into the new order as an antidote to the gray hurly-burly of the city middle class. He preferred, he told Hogg, "chivalry and refinement" to "commerce and vulgarity." [81] But in spite of this preference, and a certain snobbish disdain—exaggerated for Hogg's benefit—for "pot house democracy," it is notable that he did not waver, as did Leigh Hunt and *The Examiner,* when confronted with the threat of popular revolution. Like Burdett, his sympathies are completely with the workers, his antagonism directed solely against the military and the government. ("If such things must be, I will take the side of the people.")

Some ten days after Dan Healey's arrest, Shelley, realizing, as he later told Medwin,[82] that government spies were watching him, left Lynmouth and returned once more to Wales, where, early in September, he settled in the little town of Tremadoc.

A LETTER TO LORD ELLENBOROUGH

During the period under discussion in this and the following chapter—April, 1812, to the winter of 1813–1814—Shelley produced eight works: a group of minor poems, including *The Voyage* and *Retrospect of Times of Old,* still mainly unpublished although existing in manuscript; [83] *A Letter to Lord Ellenborough;* two tracts on vege-

tarianism and abstinence from alcohol, *A Vindication of Natural Diet*
and *On the Vegetable System of Diet; Queen Mab* and its Notes; a
philosophical, anti-religious treatise, *A Refutation of Deism;* a minor
anti-religious work now lost, *Biblical Extracts.* Some overlapping takes
place between the prose works and the Notes to *Queen Mab: The
Necessity of Atheism* and *A Vindication of Natural Diet* are there reprinted; some passages from *A Letter to Lord Ellenborough* are
incorporated; some of the anti-religious material in the Notes appears
in *A Refutation of Deism.* These works, taken together, in spite of
their divergence in style and content, are essentially a unity, centering
around the expression of Shelley's radical philosophy in politics, ethics,
and religion.

The central work of the group is *Queen Mab,* which was intended
by Shelley as an epitome of his message to mankind, but the most
mature is the *Refutation of Deism. The Vindication of Natural Diet*
and *The Vegetable System of Diet* are minor works but not without
interest as revealing some aspects of the development of his thinking.
A Letter to Lord Ellenborough is his first prose work of consistent
power and insight.

The victim of the injustice which produced this latter work, Daniel
Isaac Eaton, is one of the great forgotten figures in the history of English radical journalism. Eaton was a staunch republican and forwarded his political radicalism for a time in his paper *Politics for the
People or A Salmagundy for Swine* (an ironical derivative from Burke's
comments on the "swinish multitude"—used also by Thomas Spence
in his *Pig's Meat*); and a militant deist who published several anti-
Christian works including two by Holbach, *Le Système de la Nature*
and *Histoire Critique de Jésus-Christ,* issued under its sub-title, *Ecce
Homo.* On March 6, 1812, he was put on trial for publishing "a blasphemous and profane libel on the Holy Scriptures, entitled 'The Age
of Reason: Part the Third,' by Thomas Paine." [84] The presiding judge
was Lord Chief Justice Ellenborough, well described as a man "of
feudal sentiments and traditional faith," [85] whose record as a suppressor
of liberties was rivaled only by that of Lord Eldon, the Lord Chancellor, himself.

The trial was a travesty on justice, symptomatic of the prevailing
Tory panic and vindictiveness against everything smacking of radicalism. The Attorney General, in his initial speech, set the stage by
openly working to prejudice the jury against the defendant through
an emotional appeal to their religious beliefs: "He states, that the holy

scriptures are, from beginning to end, mere fables, he tells you, that the authors of that work are liars and deceivers; he denies the miracles, the divinity, the resurrection, and the ascension of our Saviour . . ." [86] If, the Attorney General continued, such blasphemy were allowed to be propagated, all morality would be undermined, for only men's religious belief in reward or punishment after death kept them from excesses in this life. Furthermore, and this was the main point, such doctrines were politically dangerous: "Our civil and religious constitutions are so closely interwoven together, that they cannot be separated—the attempt to destroy either is fraught with ruin to the state."

Lord Chief Justice Ellenborough, far from preventing such emotional tirades, joined in them and when Eaton arose to make his defense continually interrupted him:

Lord Ellenborough.—You are evidently coming to something reprehensible, and it is necessary you should be checked.

Defendant.—My Lord, I have only two or three more sheets to read.

Lord Ellenborough.—It is not the length of the address which constitutes the offence, but the matter of which it is composed. It is shocking to every Christian present.

Defendent.—When the address is heard out, it will be found relevant to my defense.

Lord Ellenborough.—You must omit those passages which cast any reflection on the Scriptures.[87]

Eaton, in his defense, showed clearly enough that he was a deist and not an atheist, and rested his argument mainly on two points: the Jehovah of the Old Testament was a revengeful and primitive deity who had no connection with Christ; Christ himself was "an exceedingly virtuous, good man, but nothing supernatural or divine." [88]

These arguments, however, produced no effect on Ellenborough, who declared, in his summing up, that Eaton's defense "from the beginning to the end, was the most opprobrious invective against what we have always been accustomed to regard as holy and sacred—the religion of our country." [89] On May 15, judgment was passed; Eaton was condemned to "be imprisoned EIGHTEEN MONTHS in His Majesty's gaol of Newgate, and to stand in the PILLORY between the hours of twelve and two, once within a month." [90]

This trial, with its palpable unfairness and its savage sentence, aroused widespread liberal protest. Cobbett wrote an impassioned defense of Eaton, sarcastically noting that the church was a £5,000,000 concern, and challenging clergymen to answer the arguments of Paine.[91] *The Examiner* commented:

On Tuesday, at twelve o'clock, Mr. Eaton was placed in the pillory, opposite Newgate, it being part of the sentence imposed on him for having published the Third Part of Paine's *Age of Reason.*—If Government possesses a common portion of common sense,—to say nothing of humanity or justice,—this will be the last time they will have recourse to such an infliction for *such* an act.—No sooner was Mr. Eaton brought out from prison, than he was greeted by a distinct cheer of approbation, which was repeated every ten minutes during the scene; and when he had been exhibited an hour, he was reconducted to prison amidst the waving of hats and cheerings of the assembly! . . . This is the last remnant of the faggot and fine system." [92]

The first reference to the case by Shelley comes in a letter to Godwin on June 11:

What do you think of Eaton's trial and sentence? I mean not to insinuate that this poor bookseller has any characteristics in common with Socrates, or Jesus Christ, still the spirit which pillories and imprisons him is the same which brought them to an untimely end—still, even in this enlightened age, the moralist and reformer may expect coercion analogous to that used with the humble yet zealous imitator of their endeavours. I have thought of addressing the public on the subject, and indeed have begun an outline of the address. May I be favoured with your remarks on it before I send it to the world? [93]

And a few days later his comment to Elizabeth Hitchener shows how strongly he felt about the case: "I have been writing a defense of Eaton. Today I have not coolness enough to go on." [94] By August 4, the work had been printed,[95] and appeared as a small book of twenty-three pages of text, carrying the following quotation on the title page: "It is contrary to the mild spirit of the Christian Religion, for no sanction can be found under that dispensation which will warrant a Government to impose disabilities and penalties upon any man, on account of his religious opinions. (Hear, Hear.) Marquis Wellesley's Speech. Globe, July 2." The Marquis of Wellesley, brother of the Duke of Wellington, was noted for his championing of the cause of Catholic emancipation and had been asked by the Regent in May, 1812, following the assassination of Perceval, to form a cabinet on the twin platforms of Catholic emancipation and prosecution of the war against Napoleon. On July 1, he made the speech in the House of Lords [96] from which Shelley quotes this excerpt. Its use on the title page was probably to show that Ellenborough's action was contrary to the announced principles of a leading political figure and not a matter for attack by the radicals only.

Shelley's first argument in his *Letter* was that Ellenborough had acted contrary to accepted juridical practice in allowing the Attorney General to prejudice the jury against Eaton on purely emotional theological grounds:

When the prejudices of the jury as Christians, were strongly and unfairly inflamed against this injured man, as a Deist, wherefore did not you, my Lord, check such unconstitutional pleading, and desire the jury to pronounce the accused innocent or criminal without reference to the particular faith which he professed? [97]

To this Shelley adds two footnotes, showing that he had followed the trial and its implications with some care: "See the Attorney General's speech" (i.e. at the trial), and "By Mr. Fox's bill (1791) juries are, in cases of libel, judges both of the law and the fact."

The real reason for the persecution of Eaton, Shelley argues, is that he is a deist. This amounts to a punishment of a man for his belief and proceeds on the ground that belief is a matter of volition, a recapitulation of the argument that he had contributed to *The Necessity of Atheism* the previous year and which was to reappear in the Notes to *Queen Mab* and *A Refutation of Deism*. The whole procedure, he argues, boils down to a question of difference of opinion:

Mr. Eaton asserted that the scriptures were, from beginning to end, a fable and imposture, that the Apostles were liars and deceivers. He denied the miracles, the resurrection, and ascension of Jesus Christ. He did so; and the Attorney-General denied the proposition which he asserted, and asserted that which he denied. What singular conclusion is deducible from this fact? None, but that the Attorney-General and Mr. Eaton sustained two opposite opinions. The Attorney-General puts some obsolete and tyrannical laws in force against Mr. Eaton, because he publishes a book tending to prove that certain supernatural events, which are supposed to have taken place eighteen centuries ago, in a remote corner of the world, did not actually take place. But how is the truth or falsehood of the facts in dispute relevant to the merit or demerit attachable to the advocates of the two opinions? [98]

The legal charge against Eaton was that of "blasphemous libel"; [99] hence it had been his main task at the trial to show that the work he had published was not blasphemous. But he failed, at the same time, to analyze the law itself and point out its basic absurdity and injustice.

Shelley next attacks the Attorney-General's contention that the subverting of religious principles would adversely affect morality. As this was one of the Attorney-General's main points, he answers it in some detail. He asserts, as his first premise, that morality has no connection with religious belief. It is the product of society and is governed only by the laws of social development. And these laws are no more subject to supernatural change than are the laws of the physical sciences:

It is plain that the utmost exertion of Omnipotence could not cause that to be virtuous which actually is vicious. An all-powerful Demon might, indubitably, annex punishments to virtue and rewards to vice, but could not by these means effect the slightest change in their abstract and immutable natures.[100]

Having thus asserted his general premises that belief is not a matter of will, that the trial is based on a mere difference of opinion, and that morality is a socially determined phenomenon, Shelley proceeds, in the second part, to examine the nature of the truths of Christianity.

The only kind of belief that can exist permanently, he argues, is one based on self-evident truths and propagated by reason. A belief based on persecution and violence cannot long exist, and a Christianity utilizing such means will become obsolete: "men will then laugh as heartily at grace, faith, redemption, and original sin, as they now do at the metamorphoses of Jupiter . . ." [101] On the other hand:

Had the Christian Religion commenced and continued by the mere force of reasoning and persuasion, by its self-evidence, excellence and fitness, the preceding analogy would be inadmissible. We should never speculate on the future obsoleteness of a system perfectly conformable to nature and reason: it would endure so long as they endured; it would be a truth as indisputable as the light of the sun . . .

Eaton, in short, was being tried for disputing the truths of Christianity, as though those truths were not disputable. But these are not truths of the same nature as those of science, "the principles which have been established concerning matter and mind, by Locke and Newton." [102] That they are not truths of this nature is shown by the fact that there is constant debate about them (an argument, and its concluding sentence, borrowed from Holbach):

If the truth of Christianity is not disputable, for what purpose are these books written? If they are sufficient to prove it, what further need of controversy? *If God has spoken, why is the universe not convinced?* [103]

The truths of Christianity, then, are disputable; but even if we assume that they are correct and that Eaton is wrong, this does not justify persecuting him:

Let us suppose that some half-witted philosopher should assert that the earth was the centre of the universe, or that idea could enter the human mind independently of sensation or reflexion. This man would assert what is demonstratably incorrect; he would promulgate a false opinion. Yet, would he therefore deserve pillory and imprisonment?

Why then was Eaton persecuted? Shelley indicates, as had Cobbett, one of the main reasons a few sentences further on: "A very large portion of society, and that powerfully and extensively connected, derives its sole emolument from the belief of Christianity, as a popular faith." Eaton was not being tried because of a difference in belief, or a subverting of morality, but because the propagation of his views was endangering the livelihood of the clergy.

Following this final barb Shelley moves on to his climactic and powerful conclusion:

The time is rapidly approaching, I hope that you, my Lord, may live to behold its arrival, when the Mahometan, the Jew, the Christian, the Deist, and the Atheist, will live together in one community, equally sharing the benefits which arise from its association, and united in the bonds of charity and brotherly love. My Lord, you have condemned an innocent man: no crime was imputed to him—and you sentenced him to torture and imprisonment. I have not addressed this letter to you with the hope of convincing you that you have acted wrong. The most unprincipled and barbarous of men are not unprepared with sophisms to prove that they would have acted in no other manner, and to show that vice is virtue. But I raise my solitary voice to express my disapprobation, so far as it goes, of the cruel and unjust sentence you passed upon Mr. Eaton—to assert, so far as I am capable of influencing, those rights of humanity which you have wantonly and unlawfully infringed.

A Letter to Lord Ellenborough is a product of the England and the Shelley of 1812. Its language is the language of *The Examiner* and the *Political Register,* its violence of protest typical of Hunt and Cobbett and Burdett and Byron. How deep the fires of Dublin had burned, how sharp was the response to the turmoil of England, is revealed in its new intensity of insight, its new humanitarianism, its new sense of man's fate and man's destiny. For it is within these perspectives that the case of Eaton is viewed. And the perspectives do not blunt the realism of vision. The subterfuges solemnly set up by the law are remorselessly swept aside. This is no trial; it is persecution. The issue is not "blasphemy" but oppression. Attacks on religion endanger the economic position of the church and threaten the state. As in his Irish pamphlets, Shelley refuses to accept the appearances, and penetrates to the reality, examines not the superstructure but the foundation. And the foundation is not the law but the social forces of which the law is an expression. "A superficial observer," he wrote in a later essay, "considers the laws of his own society universal." [104] But the political theorist must look deeper. The law of blasphemy, viewed, as it must be, in the broader light of human justice, is seen to rest, ideologically, on mere difference of opinion, and, socially, on the defense of entrenched privilege. And once this overall framework is established, the logical demolition of the arguments of Ellenborough and the Attorney General proceeds within it systematically and with a frankness that gives one to understand why Syle panicked and Hookham warned.

A Letter to Lord Ellenborough is Shelley's first important work of literature, a work to be ranked among the classics of the struggle for freedom of speech. It succeeds in transcending—as the Irish pamphlets do only partially—the issues of the day into a universal application. In it, too, we see manifested unmistakably for the first time that unique blending of passion, perspective and reason which was to characterize, although in a higher creative medium, the Shelley of *Adonais* and *Prometheus Unbound*.

It remains only to be noted that the *Letter* has twice been reprinted in protest against sentences for blasphemy; once, in 1879, in New York, when D. M. Bennett, editor of *The Truth Seeker* and friend of Robert Ingersoll, was sentenced to thirteen months imprisonment, and once, in 1883, in London, when George William Foote, editor of *The Freethinker,* and his associates, were given sentences of from one year to three months.[105] On this latter occasion the work was prefaced by a militant Introduction: "Now that the Blasphemy Laws, which have slumbered for fifty years, are once more invoked by the agents of political and spiritual oppression, it is well that Shelley's noble appeal should go forth in a cheap form to the English people, who are the final judges of judges, and the unmakers as well as the makers of law." [106]

VI MEN AND VEGETABLES

A Vindication of Natural Diet
On the Vegetable System of Diet

WILLIAM MADOCKS

Tremadoc was an unusual town, named after and created by William Alexander Madocks, M.P., and engaged, at the moment of Shelley's arrival, in a nationally famed project for salvaging land from the sea. Shelley must long have been acquainted with Madocks's activities, not only for his salvaging project but as one of the most ardent of Sir Francis Burdett's little band of parliamentary reformers.

Madocks came to national prominence with dramatic suddenness in May, 1809, when he proposed the impeachment of the Prime Minister, Lord Perceval, and the Foreign Secretary, Lord Castlereagh, for "corrupt practices." Madocks made his motion to a startled House on May 5 and was supported by Burdett. The debate continued on May 11, and it was then that Madocks made his main speech. Both Perceval and Castlereagh, he asserted, had been privy to a deal whereby a Mr. Dick had bought a seat in Parliament for £5000; but when Dick refused to vote with the government in the celebrated debate on the Duke of York's mistress, Mrs. Clarke (who was charged with taking bribes in order to procure army commissions and promotions), he had been summarily told to vacate his seat by the very men from whom he had purchased it. Madocks, however, was interested not only in exposing Perceval and Castlereagh, but in using their chicanery as an excuse for precipitating a general debate on parliamentary reform (which had been a dead issue since the famed debate of 1797): "Serious as the charges were which had been brought in both the instances he had alluded to, they were comparatively trifling, when considered in relation to that most flagitious of all abuses, by which the influence of the Treasury was exerted in returning members to that house. In the good old times of the country, the crime was looked upon in its proper light . . ."[1] He gave a list of famed pocket boroughs: Hastings, with fifteen voters, owned by a government official on a sinecure of £1425 a year; Rye, with six voters, owned by an "agent for the Treasury"; Cambridge owned by a banker whose salary and whose deputy's salary were both paid by the government; Queensborough, owned by the "ordnance and the navy boards, at a cost of £2368 a year"; Westbury and New Romney, which were "openly sold for money."[2]

Madocks's charges (ably supported by Burdett and Cochrane) created a national sensation. The ministerial supporters were shaken, the reform press rejoiced. Cobbett reprinted the whole debate: "Mr. Madocks has brought the thing to a point; indeed to an issue. . . . This debate, therefore, is beyond all comparison, the most important that I have ever had any knowledge of. It will, I hope, be read by every man that can read, in this whole kingdom."[3]

In the following month, when Burdett brought forward his celebrated reform plan (noted by those macabre poetasters, Victor and Cazire), he was seconded by Madocks, who used the occasion to direct further attacks against the rotten borough system: "How monstrous that the few private fortunes that possessed them can send three times as many votes to tax the people, as all the landed property of Yorkshire."[4]

Following these historic debates Madocks was not prominent in the Commons. He was not, as was Burdett, a general radical, interested in all humanitarian issues, but strictly a parliamentary reformer. In 1811, he joined Burdett and Cartwright in their attempts to unite the left Whigs with the reformers, and, when the Whigs backed out, Madocks stuck by his guns,[5] and, later, as we have noted, joined the Hampden Club. But, even though Madocks did not play a prominent role in the stormy parliamentary battles of 1812, he had become a heroic symbol in the reform ranks. Cobbett, for instance, refers to his historic motion of May, 1809, in issue after issue of the *Register*.

The first of Madocks's land salvaging projects had occurred in 1800 when he salvaged two thousand acres from the sea in Carnarvonshire and began to build a model town, Tremadoc, on the reclaimed land. In 1807, by a special grant of Parliament, he received in perpetuity, for himself and his heirs, "all the sands known as Traeth Mawr" in a nearby estuary and began an even vaster project.[6] In the September, 1811, issue of the *Gentleman's Magazine* we read of the completion of this enterprise:

The embankment across the Traeth Mawr, near *Tre-Madoc,* has at length been closed, and this stupendous work is thus far executed. . . . The embankment is 1500 yards in length, and eight or nine feet wide at the top. The extent of the land gained from the sea is not correctly ascertained, but it is supposed that it will be from 4 to 5000 acres. This great work has been accomplished by W.A. Madocks, esq., M.P. for Boston.[7]

But in the April, 1812, issue, another item informs us of misfortune: "Mr. Madocks's new embankment, at *Tre Madoc,* was greatly injured by a high wind and tide. In the second week after the accident, 400 men, with 222 horses, and 67 carts, were employed in repairing the breach." [8]

When Shelley arrived in September, however, the breach had still not been repaired and the sea rushed through a hundred foot gap in the middle with such force as to jeopardize the whole project. Madocks had run into financial difficulties—the project was estimated to have cost £100,000—and he and his overseer, John Williams, were attempting to raise money. Shelley contacted Williams and offered to assist in this campaign, an offer that was relayed to Madocks, then in London for the current session of Parliament. Madocks's reply to Williams has been preserved among his papers:

The interest Mr. Shelley takes in the Embankment and his proposals on the subject are very handsome. When I have considered the matter more fully *in London* I shall be better able to express my feelings on the subject and on his handsome conduct.[9]

In the early 1820's, Madocks's financial plight became so serious that he had to retire to the continent (he died in Paris in 1828). In Florence, he ran into Thomas Medwin, and, finding that they both had known Shelley, they fell to reminiscing:

Mr. Maddocks, like all who really knew Shelley, perfectly idolised him. I have often heard him dilate on his numerous acts of benevolence, his relieving the distresses of the poor, visiting them in their humble abodes, and supplying them with food and raiment and fuel during the winter, which on that bleak coast, exposed to the north, is particularly severe. But he laid Mr. Maddocks under a debt of gratitude that could never be repaid.

During his temporary absence in a distant county in England, an extraordinary high tide menaced that truly Dutch work, his embankment against the sea, by which he had rescued from it many thousand acres. Shelley, always ready to be of service to his friends, and anxious to save the dyke from destruction, which would have involved his landlord and hundreds in ruin, heading a paper with a subscription of £500, took it himself all round the neighbourhood, and raised a considerable sum, which enabling him to employ hundreds of workmen, stopped the progress of the waves.[10]

Medwin (or Madocks) is exaggerating somewhat. Shelley's offered subscription was £100 and not £500, and his fund raising activities alone were not responsible for saving the embankment. Nevertheless he did play an important part in the project. A meeting of Welsh dignitaries on the problems of the embankment held at Beaumaris (some twenty miles north of Tremadoc) was reported in the *North Wales Gazette,* October 1, 1812:

Last Monday [September 28] there was a well-attended meeting of the Corporation at Beaumaris; Lord Bulkeley and many gentlemen of respectability were present. Sir Robert Williams, Bart, M.P., Mayor, in the Chair. . . . Mr. John Williams expressed his sincere acknowledgment of this public testimony of regard, and assured the meeting that the Embankment of Tremadoc was proceeding with renovated activity and spirit; that from the providential interference of a friend, he had been enabled to put in employ so many men as, in the event of his meeting with public encouragement, would fortify the Embankment against any apprehended damage. He referred the meeting to his friend Mr. Shelley, who would explain their mutual sentiments at large.

Mr. Shelley requested the indulgence of the meeting; though a stranger he knew that he carried with him a legal passport to their indulgence—the desire of benefiting their country. Mr. J. Williams, who had just sat down, would testify to them the sincerity and disinterestedness of his intentions. That man he was proud to call friend—he was proud that Mr. Williams permitted him to place himself on an equality with him; inasmuch as one yet a novice in the great drama of life, whose integrity was untried, whose strength was unascertained, must consider himself honoured when admitted on an equal footing with one who had struggled for twelve years with incessant and unparalleled difficulties, in honesty, faithfulness, and fortitude. As to Mr. Madocks, he had never seen him—but if unshaken public spirit and patriotism, if zeal to accomplish a work of national benefit, be a claim, then was *he* the strongest. The Embankment at Tremadoc is one of the noblest works of human power—it is an exhibition of human nature as it appears in its noblest and most natural shape—benevolence—it saves, it does not destroy. Yes! the unfruitful sea once rolled where human beings now live and earn their honest livelihood. Cast a look round these islands, through the perspective of these times—behold famine driving millions even to madness; and own how excellent, how glorious, is the work which will give no less than three thousand souls the means of competence. How can anyone look upon that work and hesitate to join me when I here publicly pledge myself to spend the last shillings of my fortune, and devote the last breath of my life, to this great, this glorious Cause.

Sir R. Williams then rose, and returning Mr. Shelley thanks in the name of the meeting, for his honourable and liberal exertions, proposed his health. Mr. Shelley expressed his thanks for the indulgence and liberality of the meeting, and said that he now took the opportunity of remarking what before he had through inadvertence omitted, that it was no little argument in his favour, that Lord Bulkeley and Sir R. Williams had given the Tremadoc Embankment their generous and praiseworthy support.[11]

In the subscription list appended to this account we find the name of Shelley down for £100.

That the completion of the project was considered of national importance is clear from the presence at the meeting of Lord Bulkeley, Lord Lieutenant of Wales. The regard with which it was held by the people is shown by the *North Wales Gazette* account of their response to the damage wrought in the spring:

. . . immediately as it was known, the tenantry of the neighbourhood, with alacrity and generosity, stepped forward to assist by man and teams to close the breach night and day; as the news reached them the men of fortune, for 40 miles around and upwards, their tenantry, servants and horses, all steered one course like the compass to the point to give their assistance.[12]

Shelley's interest in this important project, as is clear from his speech, was not engineering but humanitarian. In an age of war (the anti-war touch of "it saves, it does not destroy" would not be missed by the audience), of Luddites and food riots—"famine driving millions even to madness"—a project of this type assumed special significance. He had succeeded, as Williams testified, in supplying both men and money at a critical moment in the history of the undertaking.

But even these efforts proved insufficient. Shelley himself was arrested in nearby Carnarvon for debt and was released only when Williams and a local physician went bail for him.[13] His only hope of raising adequate funds lay in London or Sussex. Hence, shortly after the September 28 meeting he left Tremadoc for London.

WILLIAM GODWIN

Shelley arrived in London on October 4 and on the same day paid his long anticipated first visit to William Godwin.[14] For the next six weeks Godwin's journal records conferences every two or three days.[15] Godwin, talking to Shelley, must have felt, as Southey had, that he was encountering the ghost of his own youth; Shelley, that he was privileged to meet one of the great spirits of the past, as if Tom Paine or Mary Wollstonecraft or Rousseau had come alive again.[16]

William Godwin had been born on March 3, 1756, and so was fifty-six when Shelley (aged twenty) met him. He had begun life as a dissenting minister but at the early age of twenty-six, after falling out with his congregation, came to London to make fame and fortune as a writer. He had begun, as Shelley had, with romantic novels, but turning to politics fell in among Whigs, "left" Whigs under Sheridan and Fox, and was asked to edit their *Political Herald.*[17] He went through the successive stages of deism and atheism, influenced by Holbach's *System of Nature.*[18] With the outbreak of the French Revolution he became an enthusiastic supporter of its principles: "My heart beat high with great swelling sentiments of Liberty." [19] He joined a revolutionary organization headed by Lord Stanhope (whose speech in favor of religious liberty Harriet admired), and wrote an official letter of greetings to his brother French revolutionists. He achieved no particular fame, however, until the publication of *Enquiry Concerning Political Justice* in 1793, a work which, as we have seen, startled the English radical intelligentsia by going beyond Paine's proclamation of political freedom into a condemnation of economic inequality. At one stroke Godwin became the recognized intellectual leader of English radicalism, the idol of writers and political thinkers alike. Nor was he, in these years, as he later liked to claim, a purely academic radical. In 1794, three leading reformers, Horne Tooke, the philologist, Thomas Hardy, a shoemaker, and Thomas Holcroft, the dramatist, were arrested and charged with high treason. The liberals, realizing that if Pitt succeeded in this case, a general proscription would follow—Lord Grey, for instance, was prepared to leave the country—rallied to fight. Godwin provided them with a powerful weapon in an open letter in *The Morning Chronicle,* a letter whose combination of incisive irony and indignant exposé of motive was, some observers believed, instrumental in turning the case against the government: "An association for Parliamentary Reform may desert its object, and be guilty of High Treason. True: so may a card club, a bench of justices, or even a cabinet council . . . . But the authors of the present prosecution probably hope that the mere names of Jacobin and Republican will answer their purposes; and that a Jury of Englishmen can be found who will send every man to the gallows without examination, to whom these appellations shall once be attributed!" [20]

In 1797, London radical circles were agog with the news that Godwin had married Mary Wollstonecraft. He had met her briefly in 1791 with Paine, but the following year she left for Paris, where she was already known for her defense of the Revolution (in answer to Burke), there to write her *History and Moral View of the French Revolution,* and there, too, to fall in love with a young veteran of the American Revolutionary War, Gilbert Imlay. On May 14, 1794, their child, Fanny, was born at Le Havre, and Imlay left for London a few months later on business. When Mary followed, in April, 1795, Imlay had broken away from her. In 1796, she again met Godwin and the two soon fell in love.

"We did not marry," Godwin wrote later in his *Memoirs of the Author of A Vindication of the Rights of Woman,* ". . . nothing can be so ridiculous upon the face of it, or so contrary to the genuine march of sentiment, as to require the overflowing of the soul to wait upon a ceremony . . ." [21] And when they finally did marry in April, 1797, Godwin's self-conscious apologetics are the more interesting as they have, for the Shelley scholar, a familiar ring: "Nothing but a regard for the happiness of the individual, which I had no right to injure, could have induced me to submit to an institution which I wish to see abolished . . ." [22] On August 30, 1797, Mary gave birth to a girl named after her,[23] and died tragically of an infection some ten days later.

Shortly after these events, the eclipse of Godwin as a public figure began. This was in part due to financial difficulties, which in time brought about some moral deterioration, but essentially it was the result of Godwin's political retreat. Not that he became, along with his erstwhile disciples, Wordsworth, Southey, and Coleridge, a Tory apologist. On the contrary, he retained the theoretical political principles of *Political Justice,* his modifications (usually ethical or metaphysical) of his doctrine being of a secondary nature.[24] But he lost the revolutionary fervor that had animated this work, and kept aloof from the struggles of the day: "I am the adherent of no party; I have passed the greater part of my life in solitude and retirement." [25] He did not lift his pen in 1812 to defend Eaton; he raised no voice against the imprisonment of Finnerty or Burdett or Cobbett or the Hunts or Richard Carlile. The great battles for parliamentary reform, for the repeal of the child labor laws, for the abolition of the slave trade, for the legalization of trade unionism, all passed unheeded like so many storms beyond the windows of a greenhouse.

In 1801, he married again, this time a Mrs. Clairmont, a widow with two children, Charles, and Mary Jane (later calling herself "Claire"), born April 27, 1798. On March 28, 1803, a child, William, was born to them. Godwin, thus, from this date on, was faced with the severe financial burden of caring for a wife and five children (including Mary and

Fanny), for which his profession heretofore of free-lance radical writer was inadequate. In 1805, he and his wife entered the publishing business —but not under his own name for fear of Tory reprisals—and in 1808, he received a substantial subsidy from a group of Whig politicians, including Grey, Holland, Kinnaird, and the Irish moderates, Curran and Grattan. (The Duke of Norfolk apparently turned him down.) [26] In 1806, on the occasion of the death of Fox, he had penned an obituary: "Fox is the most illustrious model of a Parliamentary Leader, on the side of liberty, that this country has produced." [27] Thus we have the peculiar phenomenon of Godwin, advocate of the most radical theoretical doctrine of the age, being in his everyday political beliefs a Whig; and a Whig he remained to the end of his life.

When the Shelleys visited Godwin in October, 1812, he was living in the house in Skinner Street which served as headquarters for his book business. There they met Mrs. Godwin, Fanny (19 years of age), and little William. Fanny, Harriet thought, "very plain but very sensible," and Fanny thought Harriet too much of a "fine lady." [28] "There is," Harriet continued, "another daughter of hers [Mary Wollstonecraft], who is now in Scotland. She is very much like her mother, whose picture hangs up in his study. She must have been a most lovely woman." [29]

It is often forgotten that Shelley did not acquire his knowledge of Godwin's doctrines from reading alone but from close personal acquaintance. And this first series of meetings, in 1812, were doubtless the most consequential. What Shelley and Godwin discussed during their frequent talks during these six weeks, we do not know in detail, but the following topics recorded in Godwin's journal show the main drift: "matter and spirit, atheism, utility and truth, the clergy, Church government," and "the characteristics of German thought and literature." [30] On the first topic, Godwin no doubt shocked his disciple by pronouncing sympathy for Berkeley. "I am," he had written in 1809, "more inclined to the opinion of the immaterialists, than of the materialists." [31] And later in his essay "Of the Material Universe," he developed his views further. He did not completely agree with Berkeley but he admitted that Berkeley and Newton (with his view of matter as mainly "porous") had made it very probable that matter was not a simple material substance; but whether this was so or not did not affect the operations of the laws of nature or the validity of the theory of necessity. "The belief in the reality of matter explains nothing . . . the material world goes on for ever according to certain laws that admit of no discrimination. They proceed upon a first principle, an impulse given them from the beginning of things." [32]

On atheism and kindred subjects the two would find little disagreement. Godwin was as violently opposed, at this date, to church doctrines and the emphasis upon faith as was Shelley: "There is nothing that has contributed more to the introduction and perpetuation of bigotry in the world, than the doctrines of the Christian religion. It caused the spirit of intolerance to strike deep roots . . . It is the characteristic of this religion, to lay the utmost stress upon faith." [33] Godwin, as he himself records, first became a deist, then an atheist, and, finally, seven years after the publication of *Political Justice,* a theist:

In my forty-fourth year I ceased to regard the name of Atheist with the same complacency I had done for several preceding years, at the same time retaining the utmost repugnance of understanding for the idea of an intelligent Creator and Governor of the universe, which strikes my mind as the most irrational and ridiculous anthropomorphism. My theism, if such I may be permitted to call it, consists in a reverent and soothing contemplation of all that is beautiful, grand, or mysterious in the system of the universe, and in a certain conscious intercourse and correspondence with the principles of these attributes, without attempting the idle task of developing and defining it—into this train of thinking I was first led by the conversations of S. T. Coleridge.[34]

No doubt the young disciple listened with interest to these modifications of the rigid materialism of *Political Justice,* and no doubt they had an effect upon him.

The argument on utility centered around morality. Godwin, along with Bentham, argued against the derivation of ethical theory from abstract principle or religious dogma. Conduct must be based solely on the interests of the social community, i.e. on its practical usefulness in promoting happiness, "the greatest good of the greatest number." The theory found its way into the Notes to *Queen Mab:* "Utility is morality; that which is incapable of producing happiness is useless." [35]

On the "clergy and self-government," there would have been no disagreement. Godwin was certainly as bitterly opposed to the clergy as was Shelley.[36] "Self-government" doubtless refers to the view—combatted in *A Letter to Lord Ellenborough*—that religion is the basis of morality.

Not only on German literature—an interest to which Shelley had already turned but which may have been aided by Godwin's comments —but on literature in general Godwin must have held forth at some length. His final essay in *The Enquirer,* "Of English Style," is a rather lengthy historical sketch of English literature. The general nature of his advice to Shelley can be found in it and, more especially, in his "Letter of Advice to a Young American" (1818), for the reading that he urges on the young American is largely duplicated in two book lists drawn up by Shelley following these talks. The "young American" is advised to read "the histories of Greece and Rome," Sidney's *Defence of Poetry,* Schlegel's *Lectures on Dramatic Literature* (both of which were later to play their part in another *Defence of Poetry*), Bacon, "one of the first writers that has appeared in the catalogue of human creatures," an estimate later shared by Shelley. Of French literature, except Montaigne, he had a low opinion and his views may well have influenced his disciple, who repeated them almost verbatim seven years later.[37] The young American, we might note, is advised also to read Berkeley, Hume, and Hartley.

One topic that must have taken up a good deal of the discussions was contemporary affairs. October was a month of important happenings at home and abroad. On October 3, the day before that on which Shelley paid his first visit to Godwin, *The Courier* announced the defeat of the Russians at Borodino. (Godwin, on September 14 made the journal entry: "French enter Moscow.") [38] On October 7, *The Courier* printed a false Russian dispatch claiming victory (a device, according to *The Examiner,* to assist in the re-election of the Tory administration); on October 13, came the British declaration of war against the United States of America, and on October 15, the burning of Moscow (which was to appear in *Queen Mab*). On these questions Shelley and Godwin would differ little; both opposed the war with Napoleon and both would certainly oppose that against the United States, then regarded by English liberals as the last haven of liberty in a world of dictatorship and war. Although opposed to the war with France—and Godwin wrote two vigorous letters to the *Morning Chronicle* in 1815 urging the allies to make peace with Napoleon after his escape from Elba—they agreed on condemning Napoleon as a dictator, Shelley perhaps more vigorously than Godwin, who apparently still retained some of his early admiration for him.[39] Shelley, like Godwin, was interested mainly in the establishment of peace.

Excepting Lord Castlereagh [he wrote to Hogg] you could not have mentioned any character but Buonaparte whom I contemn and abhor more vehemently. With respect to those victories in the North; if they tend towards peace, they are good; if otherwise, they are bad. This is the standard by which I shall ultimately measure my approbation of them. At the same time, I cannot but say that the first impression which they made on me was one of horror and regret.[40]

October, too, was the month of the British general election, the first for five years, and the country was getting some touch of the great reform battles soon to come in the campaigns of Burdett and Cochrane in Westminster and "Orator" Hunt in Bristol.[41] The full power of the Tory machine was turned on in an attempt to defeat Burdett, and *The Courier* published long radical-baiting articles against the Whigs for allowing such a monster in their midst, but when he was elected, it chose to note the fact in three lines on the back page of its October 9 issue. On October 11, *The Examiner* printed Burdett's Election Address (some aspects of which perhaps later found an echo in a sonnet on England in the year 1819): "an army of spies and informers . . . a Phantom for a king; a degraded aristocracy; an oppressed People . . . a corrupt and intimidated press . . . vague and sanguinary Laws . . . ."[42] On October 30, the press noted the re-election of the Honorable Member for New Shoreham. In this field, disagreement between master and prospective disciple apparently flared. Godwin, wrote Harriet, some weeks later, to Catherine Nugent, "wanted Mr. Shelley to join the Wig [sic] party and do just as they pleased, which made me very angry, as we know what men the Wigs [sic] are, now. He is grown old and unimpassioned, therefore, is not in the least calculated for such enthusiasts as we are."[43]

That Godwin should advise Shelley, as the Duke of Norfolk had previously, to join the Whigs is not surprising, for Godwin, as we have seen, had, in spite of his theoretical radicalism, long been a Whig in his practical politics. Yet, to advise a young radical in the year 1812 to join the Whigs was hardly sagacious, for the Whigs had long ceased even to make gestures of liberalism, many of them actually boycotting parliamentary sessions. Godwin had, in truth, grown "old and unimpassioned." It is little wonder, then, that while Shelley should at first have been fascinated by his theoretical pronouncements he should have become disgusted by his inactivity and pathetic allegiance to the Whigs. Godwin, moreover, attempted to modify Shelley's views through his recommended reading list, heavily featuring historical and chivalric works.[44] It was doubtless in reaction to these conservative pressures that Shelley left London precipitously on November 13 (after having

invited Godwin to dinner).[45] Yet, it is probably true also that Shelley
would not have remained so long in London, neglecting his projected
work on the Tremadoc embankment, had it not been for Godwin.

The visits to Godwin must have taken up much of Shelley's time in
London, but they did not take up all of it. Shelley had not forgotten
the embankment project, but "his being a minor" Harriet noted, made
the raising of funds difficult.[46] He had visited Sussex early in November,[47] but found his friends and relatives there uniformly uninterested
in the building of an embankment in Wales—"a parcel of cold, selfish
and calculating animals" [48]—and the Duke of Norfolk, later approached
in London, also saw fit to decline the honor of being enrolled among
Mr. Madocks's saviors.[49] (Mr. Madocks, lamented Harriet, perhaps
with the Duke in mind, unfortunately possessed "only a small fortune,
when compared to the immense sums that others possess.") [50]

Shelley was occupied also with the composition of *Queen Mab,* which
he showed to Godwin in manuscript, and met his intended publisher,
Thomas Hookham, now perhaps twice shy after the untimely fate of
the *Letter to Lord Ellenborough,*[51] and one of Hookham's young
authors, Thomas Love Peacock.[52] He made another new friend in John
Frank Newton, a vegetarian advocate, and renewed his old friendship
with Hogg, now a law student in London. Shelley, himself already a
vegetarian, had perhaps read Newton's book, *The Return to Nature,*
and when young William Godwin went on Guy Fawkes Day (November 5) to set off firecrackers with the Newton children, Shelley accompanied him, and later went into the Newton's house. One of the children later remembered the occasion: "My father easily discovered that
the young visitor who had so agreeably surprised them was well read.
I recollect his saying that he never met with so young a man who had
acquired so much real knowledge of numerous authors." [53]

Shelley sought Hogg out late in October, after he returned from a
vacation in York, and a few days later Hogg visited the Shelleys—in
their rooms in Lewis's Hotel—for the first time since the rupture at
York twelve months previously. There he noted "a few shabby, ill-
printed books, productions of the Irish press . . . which treated of the
history of Ireland and the affairs of that country," and was shown by
Harriet a broadside sheet of Robert Emmet's trial,[54] both items testify-
ing to Shelley's continuing interest in Ireland. On both, Hogg waxed
humorous, and it is significant that (as he noted) Shelley did not speak
to him of Ireland; nor did he tell him of his activities at Lynmouth and

Barnstaple. Hogg's growing conservatism had erected a barrier which prevented the re-establishment of the friendship on the old basis. Hogg himself had become sensitive to this and protested it to Shelley, who replied, at first, evasively, and, finally, when Hogg apparently pushed the issue, with some sharpness:

I need not say that your letters delight me, but all your principles do not. The species of pride which you love appears to me incapable of bearing the test of reason. . . . This chivalric pride, although of excellent use in an age of Vandalism and brutality, is unworthy of the nineteenth century. A more elevated spirit has begun to diffuse itself, which, without deducting from the warmth of love, or the constancy of friendship, reconciles all private feelings to public utility . . .[55]

From this time on, he avoided fruitless discussions with Hogg on political matters, thus very largely cutting Hogg off from an observation of his intellectual life.

One final and painful act concluded the visit to London, the departure of Elizabeth Hitchener on November 8 for her native Sussex. Hogg who witnessed the departure found it amiable enough,[56] but under the surface tensions had mounted. A few days later, as the now depleted party passed through Stratford—where they had perhaps lingered to view the Shakespeare relics—on the way back to Wales, Harriet gave her account of things to Catherine Nugent:

The lady I have so often mentioned to you, of the name of Hitchener, has to our very great happiness left us. We were entirely deceived in her character as to her republicanism, and in short everything else which she pretended to be. We were not long in finding out our great disappointment in her. As to any noble disinterested views, it is utterly impossible for a selfish character to feel them. She built all her hopes on being able to separate me from my dearly loved Percy, and had the artfulness to say that Percy was really in love with her, and was only his being married that could keep her within bounds now. Percy had seen her once before his marriage. He thought her sensible but nothing more. She wrote continually, and at last I wrote to her, and was very much charmed with her letters. We thought it a thousand pities that such a mind as hers appeared to be should be left in a place like that she inhabited. We therefore were very urgent for her to come and live with us; which was no sooner done than we found out our mistake. It was a long time ere we could possibly get her away, till at last Percy said he would give her £100 per annum. And now, thank God, she has left us never more to return. We are much happier now than all the time she was with us.[57]

Elizabeth Hitchener, returning jobless to her small home town in Sussex, found herself surrounded by a wall of gossip. The story was, as Merle picked it up, that she "had abandoned her school and eloped with him [Shelley] to Wales. They remained there together, I believe, for several months; but if they were to be credited, their union was purely platonic. This might be true, but worldly people did not believe it; and when the lady returned, and endeavoured again to set up a school, she could not obtain a single pupil." [58] To this she retaliated with scandalous stories about the Shelleys and threatened to inform the government of his radical activities.[59] Merle, meeting her at this time, felt she was "evidently labouring under the effects of a disordered imagination," and would not have been surprised to "learn that her wanderings had ended in insanity." [60] (As a matter of fact, they led her to the continent where she married an Austrian officer.) [61]

Shelley's reaction we can gather from his rambunctious comments to Hogg on December 3:

The Brown Demon, as we call our late tormentor and schoolmistress, must receive her stipend. I pay it with a heavy heart and an unwilling hand; but it must be so. She was deprived by our misjudging haste of a situation, where she was going on smoothly: and now she says that her reputation is gone, her health ruined, her peace of mind destroyed by my barbarity; a complete victim to all the woes mental and bodily, that heroine ever suffered! This is not all fact; but certainly she is embarrassed and poor, and we being in some degree the cause, we ought to obviate it. She is an artful, superficial, ugly, hermaphroditical beast of a woman, and my astonishment at my fatuity, inconsistency, and bad taste was never so great, as after living four months with her as an inmate. What would Hell be, were such a woman in Heaven? [62]

Hogg, a shrewd observer of people in their personal relationships, had, however, long been aware of the essence of the situation:

At first she possessed some influence over the young couple; but the charming Eliza would not tolerate any influence but her own. She had worked upon Harriet's feelings, and the good Harriet had succeeded in making his former favourite odious to Bysshe.[63]

The root of the problem was not, as one would often gather, Shelley's disillusionment with Elizabeth Hitchener, but a domestic quarrel between Eliza Westbrook and Elizabeth Hitchener, two incompatible women in the same household. Whether the man in the household had been Shelley or another, whether he had previously over-idealized the woman in question or not, the battle lines would have been drawn and he would have been involved, if not at that time, then later, if not on one excuse, then on another; and when the explosion came, it would have been accompanied by the general abuse of which Shelley's letter to Hogg is symptomatic. That Eliza should have been able to secure Harriet as an ally—and the story of Elizabeth Hitchener's designs on "Percy" perhaps came from her—is not surprising. Harriet must have harbored some jealousy of the newcomer, who, doubtless, shared Shelley's intellectual life more completely than she could. (Harriet noted shortly after her arrival, with dismay, that she was a "great talker.") [64] That Eliza should also have recruited Shelley under her banner is not surprising either. When he had first met and corresponded with Elizabeth Hitchener, he had been a lonely boy of nineteen breaking with his family. The correspondence filled a need for sympathetic understanding, both emotional and intellectual, and, like most such post-adolescent effusions, was often extravagant and idealistic. But he had probably not lived long in the same household with her before he realized that he had over-estimated her and that her presence was producing an uncomfortable domestic situation. That, when he did enter the alliance, he entered it with apparent relish may appear surprising at first, but the fact is that Shelley had a penchant for mild gossip and intrigue, early acquired, perhaps, as I have suggested, in the little sisterdom of Field Place. In this particular instance, the excess of abuse is the result, once more, of self-dramatization and projection, with Harriet, Hogg, and Elizabeth as audience (Harriet and Eliza were shown his letters). But underlying the euphoric and semi-fictional flights—e.g. "a woman of desperate views and dreadful passions" [65]—is a genuine regret and a desire to make amends. As for Elizabeth Hitchener, she must still be recorded as a woman of courage and talent, even though she fell below Shelley's initial concept. Her threats to expose Shelley to governmental investigation were certainly opprobrious enough, but she was, we must remember, placed in a situation calculated to bring out the worst in anyone. She apparently never carried out her threats, and when the smoke of battle cleared, she was able to look back on Shelley in later years as the one really inspiring force in a rather lonely life:

> Yet once,—a vision waked thy slumbering lyre,
>   Which fancy whispered wise and great and fair;
> One which could loftiest, noblest strains inspire,
>   And to sweet cadence tune thy wildest air.[66]

TREMADOC ONCE MORE

On Shelley's first brief stay at Tremadoc, he probably spent little more than a week in his efforts on behalf of the embankment before he left for London. Returning now in the middle of November, he remained for three and a half months, renting Madocks's house "Tanyrallt," high on a lonely mountain side beyond the town; it was during this period that his main work on that project took place. "He helped my husband to write letters," Mrs. Williams, wife of Madocks's overseer, commented later in the century, "and was in the office from morning to night using every means in his power to show his kind interest." [67] Two of his letters on this business have survived, both of them to a John Evans of Carnarvon and both displaying a noted lack of tact, the second one running:

In reply to a message which I sent you by Mr. John Williams, you asserted that you had never received my letter. To obviate the repetition of so singular an occurrence I sent this by a personal messenger.

The substance of my former letter was to remind you, by right of being a fellow subscriber, of your debt to the Tremadoc Embankment, which, being a debt of honor, ought to be of all others the most imperious and to press the necessity of its immediate payment, to lament also the apathy and backwardness of defaulters in such a cause.[68]

Such letters, coming especially from one who had a few weeks previously been arrested for debt in Mr. Evans's town, could hardly be calculated to bring the funds rolling in to a project which, after all, was a private investment of Madocks.

But not all of Shelley's time was taken up by embankment affairs. He informed Hookham on January 26 that he expected to finish *Queen Mab* by March, and that he had other poems in preparation to a total of about 2,800 lines which he intended to publish as a separate volume, all of them, he declared "breathing hatred to government and religion, but," he discreetly added, with Hookham as possible publisher in mind, "I think not too openly for publication." [69]

In addition to his writing and work on the embankment, Shelley was stirred by the two famous political trials of the year, that of the Yorkshire Luddites and that of John and Leigh Hunt. The Luddite riots and counteraction by the mill owners and militia had been especially violent in Yorkshire, reaching a climax in April in a pitched battle at a mill owned by William Cartwright. In January, the trials of the Luddites began at York, the celebrated liberal attorney, Henry

Brougham (later Lord Brougham), appearing for the defense. Sixty-four workers had originally been arrested; of these thirty were discharged before the trials opened, leaving thirty-four to go on trial.[70] Of these, seventeen were hanged, six sentenced to transportation for seven years, and the rest discharged; three were hanged on January 8, fourteen on January 16, seven at 11 a.m., seven more at 1:30 p.m. "The bodies," *The Courier* reported, "were cut down at half past two o'clock, and delivered to their respective relations." *The Courier* noted with satisfaction that the men seemed contrite and ran an editorial praising the Home Office for its efficiency.

On January 31, Harriet Shelley wrote to Hookham:

I see by the Papers that those poor men who were executed at York have left a great many children. Do you think a subscription would be attended to for their relief? If you think it would, pray put down our names and advertise it in the Papers. Put down my Sister's name, Mr. Shelley's and mine for two guineas each; if this meets with your approbation we will enclose the sum.[71]

Before the assumption of the title of Prince Regent by the Prince of Wales, his Whig supporters had hoped that he would fulfill his promises of liberal policies; but as the ensuing months revealed that he intended to work hand in glove with the Tory administration and desert his former friends, the reaction against him mounted. (We have already noted Shelley's and O'Connell's comments in February.) Some of the most outspoken attacks upon him appeared in *The Examiner* of John and Leigh Hunt; in fact, hardly an issue passed without an excoriation of the royal renegade. An amusing squib in the March 22 issue—

> Some wind has blown the Wig away
> And left the Hair Apparent—

was counterbalanced by a violent attack. Outraged by an adulation of the Regent in the *Morning Post,* the editors replied, taking the words of the *Post* as their text:

What person, unacquainted with the true state of the case, would imagine, in reading these astounding eulogies, that this *Glory of the People* was the subject of millions of shrugs and reproaches! That this *Protector of the Arts* had named a wretched Foreigner his Historical Painter in disparagement or in ignorance of the merits of his own countrymen! That this *Mecaenas of the Age* patronized not a single deserving writer! That this *Breather of Eloquence* could not say a few decent extempore words,—if we are to judge at least from what he said to his regiment on its embarkation for

Portugal! That this *Conqueror of Hearts* was the disappointer of hopes! That this *Exciter of Desire* (bravo, Messieurs of the *Post*!) this *Adonis in Loveliness,* was a corpulent gentleman of fifty! In short, that this *delightful, blissful, wise, pleasurable, honourable, virtuous, true,* and *immortal* PRINCE, was a violator of his word, a libertine over head and ears in debt and disgrace, a despiser of domestic ties, the companion of gamblers and demireps, a man who has just closed half a century without one single claim on the gratitude of his country or the respect of posterity! [72]

On December 9, following a postponement of more than five months, the editors were put on trial for libel, Lord Chief Justice Ellenborough presiding. Brougham, for the defense, was handicapped from the start by his Lordship's obstructionist methods, Ellenborough blandly forbidding him either to produce proof of the charge or to read the original article in the *Post* which had provoked the attack:

Lord Ellenborough.—I understand you, now, to say that you mean to produce a publication, to which the libel in question may refer, for an explanation of it.
Mr. Brougham.—Undoubtedly, my Lord.
Lord Ellenborough.—No; that you cannot do.
Mr. Brougham.—I may read it, as part of my speech.
Lord Ellenborough.—There is no reading of anything, as part of a speech, in *this* place,—except evidence.[73]

In his (presumably impartial) summing up, his Lordship instructed the jury to "pronounce this publication, as I feel it my duty to pronounce it, a foul, atrocious and malignant libel." [74]

Shelley had probably read the full account of the trial in *The Examiner* for December 13 and December 20, and on December 27 he wrote to that promising young law student, Thomas Jefferson Hogg, who had apparently commented upon Brougham's defense adversely (and doubtless with his usual flavoring of Tory wit):

Brougham's defence was certainly not so good as it might have been; it was fettered by the place wherein he stood. Entire liberty of speech was denied. He could not speak treason; he could not commit a libel; and therefore his client was not to be defended on the basis of moral truth. He was compelled to hesitate when truth was rising to his lips; he could utter that which he did utter only by circumlocution and irony. The speech of the Solicitor-General appeared to me the consummation of all shameless insolence, and the address of Lord Ellenborough so barefaced a piece of time-servingness, that I am sure his heart must have laughed at his lips as he pronounced it.[75]

On February 4, Ellenborough passed sentence: two years imprisonment, plus a joint fine of £1000, plus a security of £1500 on release from prison for good behavior for the succeeding five years. Shelley wrote to Hunt, making, according to Hunt, a "princely offer," [76] and on February 18, wrote to Hookham:

I am boiling with indignation at the horrible injustice and tyranny of the sentence pronounced on Hunt and his brother, and it is on this subject that I write to you. Surely the seal of abjectness and slavery is indelibly stamped upon the character of England.

Although I do not retract in the slightest degree my wish for a subscription for the widows and children of those poor men hung at York, yet this £1,000 which the Hunts are sentenced to pay is an affair of more consequence. Hunt is a brave, a good, and an enlightened man. Surely the public for whom Hunt has done so much will repay in part the great debt of obligation which they owe the champion of their liberties and virtues. . . . Well I am rather poor at present but I have £20 which is not immediately wanted. Pray begin a subscription for the Hunts. . . . If no other way can be devised for this subscription, will you take the trouble on yourself of writing an appropriate advertisement for the paper, inserting by way of stimulant, my subscription. On second thoughts, I enclose the £20.[77]

On February 26, however, a strange circumstance made him write asking Hookham to return the £20: "I have just escaped an atrocious assassination. Oh send me the £20 if you have it—you will perhaps hear of me no more." [78] To this note Harriet added a postscript

Mr. Shelley is so dreadfully nervous today from having been up all night that I am afraid what he has written will alarm you very much. We intend to leave this place as soon as possible as our lives are not safe so long as we remain. It is no common robber we dread but a person who is actuated by revenge and who threatens my life & my sisters as well. If you can send us the money it will greatly add to our comfort.

This is our first intimation of an event which has become one of the major cruxes of Shelley biography. In addition to this brief note, Shelley himself has left only two recorded comments on the occurrence. A day or so later he wrote to Williams:

I am surprised that the wretch who attacked me has not been heard of. Surely the inquiries have not been sufficiently general, or particular?

Mr. Nanney requests that you will order that some boards should be nailed against the broken window of Tanyrallt. We are in immediate want of money.[79]

And on March 6 to Hookham:

We expect to be there [i.e. in Dublin] on the 8th. You shall then hear the detail of our distresses. The ball of the assassins pistol (he fired at me twice) penetrated my night gown and pierced the wainscot. He is yet undiscovered though not unsuspected as you will learn from my next.[80]

The "next," however, was not written by Shelley but by Harriet on March 12. In this letter we have what we might call the basic account, an account repeated earlier in a letter to Hogg now lost.

Mr. S. promised you a recital of the horrible events that caused us to leave Wales. I have undertaken the task, as I wish to spare him, in the present nervous state of his health, every thing that can recall to his mind the horrors of that night, which I will relate.

On Friday night, the 26th of February, we retired to bed between ten and eleven o'clock. We had been in bed about half an hour, when Mr. S. heard a noise proceeding from one of the parlours. He immediately went downstairs with two pistols, which he had loaded that night, expecting to have occasion for them. He went into the billiard room, where he heard footsteps retreating. He followed into an other little room, which was called an office. He there saw a man in the act of quitting the room through a glass window which opens into the shrubbery. The man fired at Mr. S., which he avoided. Bysshe then fired, but it flashed in the pan. The man then knocked Bysshe down, and they struggled on the ground. Bysshe then fired his second pistol, which he thought wounded him in the shoulder, as he uttered a shriek and got up, when he said these words: By God. I will be revenged! I will murder your wife. I will ravish your sister. By God. I will be revenged. He then fled—as we hoped for the night. Our servants were not gone to bed, but were just going, when this horrible affair happened. This was about eleven o'clock. We all assembled in the parlour, where we remained for two hours. Mr. S. then advised us to retire, thinking it impossible he would make a second attack. We left Bysshe and our manservant, who had only arrived that day, and who knew nothing of the house, to sit up. I had been in bed three hours, when I heard a pistol go off. I immediately ran down stairs, when I perceived that Bysshe's flannel gown had been shot through, and the window curtain. Bysshe had sent Daniel to see what hour it was, when he heard a noise at the window. He went there, and a man thrust his arm through the glass and fired at him. Thank Heaven! the ball went through his gown and he remained unhurt, Mr. S. happened to stand sideways; had he stood fronting, the ball must have killed him. Bysshe fired his pistol, but it would not go off. He then aimed a blow at him with an old sword which we found in the house. The assassin attempted to get the sword from him, and just as he was pulling it away Dan rushed into the room, when he made his escape.

This was at four in the morning. It had been a most dreadful night; the wind was as loud as thunder, and the rain descended in torrents. Nothing has been heard of him; and we have reason to believe it was no stranger, as there is a man of the name of Leeson, who the next morning that it happened went and told the shopkeepers of Tremadoc that it was a tale of Mr. Shelley's to impose upon them, that he might leave the country without paying his bills. This they believed, and none of them attempted to do anything towards his discovery.

We left Tanyrallt on Saturday, and staid till every thing was ready for our leaving the place, at the Sol[icitor] General of the county's house, who lived seven miles from us. This Mr. Leeson had been heard to say that he was determined to drive us out of the country. He once happened to get hold of a little pamphlet which Mr. S. had printed in Dublin; this he sent up to Government. In fact, he was for ever saying something against us, and that because we were determined not to admit him to our house, because we had heard his character and from many acts of his we found that he was malignant and cruel to the greatest degree.[81]

In addition to this we have two other accounts. On the morning of February 27, Williams called at the house, and in later years his widow remembered his reactions as follows:

My husband has often talked to me about "Shelley's ghost," as it used at the time I married, in 1820, to be the topic of conversation among strangers who used to visit this place. They were seldom satisfied, as my kind husband never used to talk of Mr. Shelley to people who only wished to gratify their curiosity. His answer was, "He was my friend": but to me he often said he believed that there was no attempt at burglary, or was there anything like an apparition at Tanyrallt at the time alluded to; it was all produced by heated imagination. . . . Mr. Williams was sent for, and found Mr. Shelley in a sad state of distress and excitement; he had fancied that he saw a man's face on the drawing-room window; he took his pistol and shot the glass to shivers, and then bounced out on the grass, and there he saw leaning against a tree the ghost, or, as he said, the devil; and to show Mr. Williams what he had seen, he took his pen and ink and sketched the figure on the screen, where it *is* at this moment, showing plainly that his mind was astray . . . When I add that Mr. Shelley set fire to the wood to burn the apparition (with some trouble they were saved), you may suppose it was not all right with him.[82]

On February 27, Shelley made a deposition to the local authorities on the events. This deposition is unfortunately no longer extant, but, some ten years later, Medwin in his meeting with Madocks received the following version of it which he printed in 1832:

I had a long conversation with Mr. Maddocks, whose tenant he was, in Carnarvonshire, as to what occurred, or Shelley supposed to occur, there. The scene at the inn in "Count Fathom," was hardly surpassed in horror by the recital Shelley used to make of the circumstance. The story was this: At midnight, sitting in his study, he heard a noise at the window, saw one of the shutters gradually unclosed, and a hand advanced into the room, armed with a pistol. The muzzle was directed towards him, the aim taken, and the trigger drawn. The weapon flashed in the pan. Shelley, with that personal courage which particularly distinguished him, rushed out to discover and endeavour to seize the assassin. In his way towards the outer door, at the end of a long passage leading to the garden, he meets the ruffian, whose pistol misses fire a second time. A struggle now ensues.—This opponent he described as a short powerful man. Shelley, though slightly built, was tall, and at that time strong and muscular. They were no unequal match. It was a contest between mind and matter.—After long and painful exertion the victory was fast declaring itself for Shelley, which his antagonist finding, extricated himself from his grasp, rushed into the grounds, and disappeared among the shrubbery. Shelley made a deposition before Maddocks the next day to these facts. An attempt at murder caused a great sensation in the principality, where not even a robbery had taken place for twenty years. No clue could be found to unravel the mystery; and the opinion generally was, that the whole scene was the effect of imagination.[83]

To these accounts should be added the comments of Hogg and Peacock:

Persons acquainted with the localities and with the circumstances, and who had carefully investigated the matter, were unanimous in the opinion, that no such attempt was ever made.[84]

I may state more particularly the result of the investigation to which Mr. Hogg alludes. I was in North Wales in the summer of 1813, and heard the matter much talked of. Persons who had examined the premises on the following morning had found that the grass on the lawn appeared to have been much trampled and rolled on, but there were no footmarks on the wet ground, except between the beaten spot and the window; and the impression of the ball on the wainscot showed that the pistol had been fired towards the window, and not from it. This appeared conclusive as to the whole series of operations having taken place from within. The mental phenomena in which this sort of semi-delusion originated . . .[85]

Peacock's skepticism he later passed on to Harriet who told Mrs. Godwin of it in 1814:

Mrs. Godwin adds that Harriet was always angry when Leeson was named, and used to say that her husband wanted to frighten her, and for long she was frightened; but Peacock told her it was untrue.[86]

To account for these events, three theories have been proposed. First, there is Shelley's own story, at first believed by Harriet, that an actual attempt at assassination took place (followed by Dowden, Blunden, and others),[87] with the suggestion that the culprit was Leeson (which is doubtless also what Shelley is hinting to Hookham in his March 6 letter). Second, there is the belief of Williams, Madocks, Newton,[88] and Peacock (followed by White) [89] that it was a kind of delusion.[90] And, finally, there is Leeson's story (followed by Jeaffreson) [91] that Shelley invented the episode to escape from Tremadoc in order to avoid paying his debts. The evidence against any actual attempt at assassination having taken place is, it seems to me, cumulatively conclusive. The three versions of the story—Harriet's, Mrs. Williams's, Medwin's—all emanating from Shelley, all differ materially. Harriet's version contains two episodes—the man in the office and the arm at the window—the Williams and Madocks versions contain the second episode only. The Williams version is essentially a ghost story: (1) Shelley sees a man's face at the window; (2) he shoots at the face through the glass; (3) he rushes out on the grass; (4) he sees the devil leaning against the tree. In the Madocks version, the episode is transformed from a ghost story into an attempted assassination: (1) Shelley sees the window shutter slowly open; (2) a hand holding a pistol appears, the muzzle aimed at Shelley, the trigger drawn; (3) the pistol flashes in the pan; (4) he rushes down a long passage to the garden, at the end of which he finds a short, powerful man; (5) the man fires but again his pistol fails; (6) Shelley and the man fight in the passage; (7) the man rushes into the garden and disappears through the shrubbery. Harriet's version differs from both: (1) an arm and pistol are thrust through the glass of the window; (2) the pistol goes off; (3) Shelley is standing sideways and the ball passes through his nightgown; (4) Shelley fires but his pistol fails to go off; (5) Shelley strikes at the man with a sword (apparently through the broken window); (6) the man (presumably still outside the window) grasps the sword; (7) Dan arrives in the room just as the man is pulling the sword through the hole in the window and the man runs away. To these inconsistencies we must add the following salient pieces of evidence: (a) the bullet was fired not inward from the window but outward from the inside of the room; (b) there were no footsteps leading away from the garden; (c) only Shelley saw the man either in the first or second episode (all Dan saw apparently was a sword in the broken window with Shelley holding one end of it); (d) the visibility on a dark, rainy, moonless [92] night would not have enabled Shelley to see a man leaving the billiard room; (e) the general tenor of events—the arm thrust through the glass, the cry of the villain, "I will murder your wife, I will ravish your sister," the ball passing through the nightshirt—is that of the novel of terror rather than of reality; (f) the investigators, presumably including the Solicitor General and others acquainted with the nature of evidence, disbelieved the story; (g) Leeson was apparently unwounded or otherwise injured; (h) a similar incident, equally suspect, had been related by Shelley the previous year at Keswick:

About seven o'clock on the night of Sunday, January 19, Shelley, alarmed by an unusual noise, went to the door of his cottage, opened it, and instantly received a blow which struck him to the ground, where he remained for a time senseless. Mr. Dare, his landlord, who was at hand, hearing the disturbance, rushed into the house, and the assailants, perceiving that he was armed, fled immediately.[93]

Such was the story as Shelley gave it to the local newspapers, but, as with the Tanyrallt attack, the inhabitants were skeptical: "Mr. Calvert's daughter, Mrs. Stranger, states that the residents in Keswick supposed that Shelley was laboring under an illusion as to the attack."

The second theory, that Shelley was the victim of a delusion or "semi-delusion," has been most elaborately stated by White:

It is of little actual importance that the assault upon Shelley almost certainly never happened. The essential reality was mental rather than physical. . . . The devil Shelley saw was certainly not real, but he was so real to Shelley that he sketched a picture of him and then sought to destroy him by destroying the picture. . . . The after-effects were also much too real for anyone to suppose that Shelley deliberately fabricated the story, as an escape from creditors or for any other motive. In Mr. Williams's opinion he was actually out of his right mind immediately after the experience.[94]

Let us consider what this theory entails. It means that Shelley imagined that he was wrestling with a man when there was no man there; saw an arm and pistol thrust through a window, smashing the pane, when there was neither arm nor pistol; heard a voice speak when there was no voice; shot a pistol at the non-existent man; and saw a devil leaning against a tree. A psychological phenomenon of this type can only be explained on two grounds; it is either invented or it is a psychotic hallucination. A dark house on a stormy night might produce fears and fancies but not a sustained drama (in two acts) played through by phantasms and accompanied by pistol shooting, sword play, and wrestling matches. If, therefore, we consider the phenomenon as psychological, we cannot consider it as a simple evocation of the imagination. On the other hand, it cannot be a hallucination. A normal person, no matter how well developed his imagination, cannot produce a hallucination, any more than a non-tubercular person can produce a tubercular cough; a hallucination is a symptom of a deep mental derangement not subject to conscious control, and is generally the product either of a chronic psychosis or a lifelong drug addiction. But if Shelley had been a hallucinating psychotic or a chronic drug addict, the symptoms, in either case, would have been continuous and obvious. (He took laudanum occasionally but laudanum is a mild narcotic and would have done no more than put him to sleep.) [95]

In the whole welter of conflicting evidence and theories, four physical facts stand out: (a) the glass in the window was broken; (b) the ground was rolled on by someone coming from inside the house and returning to the house; (c) there was a bullet hole through Shelley's gown and through the curtain; (d) there was a bullet in the wainscot that had come from inside the room. Once we discard the theory of an actual assassin, these facts can be accounted for only on one assumption: Shelley broke the glass, trampled up the ground, held out his gown with one hand and fired through it with the other, the bullet then piercing the curtain and the wainscot. This series of actions, we may note, imply a deliberateness of procedure that further discounts the "mental reality" theory.

Shelley, in brief, was acting out a typical novel-of-terror scene. The objective, external causes that drove him to this action—essentially an escape mechanism produced by frustration—are visible enough in the developing situation at Tremadoc if one examines it. In the first place he had, within a few months, run up £400 in debts, twice the annual allowance given him by Timothy. He had not, however, done this, as Leeson intimated and Jeaffreson chose to believe, with the intention of not paying his creditors, nor was it the result of personal extravagance. For Shelley, himself, lived very plainly. Harriet, however, had not been trained to do housework and did none (nor, apparently, did Eliza); the menage possessed at this time, and had to pay wages for, three maidservants in addition to Dan, who, although not in the household in these months, was receiving his fifteen shillings a week in the Barnstaple jail.[96] And Shelley, with typical generosity, was sending money to the collection fund for the Luddites and the Hunts, and doubtless putting some of his own money into the embankment project.

Whenever he was financially able to repay debts, especially to those in poor circumstances, he did so. His landlady at Devon, he attempted to pay, difficult though his situation was, and he repaid the debt for which he was arrested at Carnarvon.[97] And the Tremadoc debts he expected to be able to pay in August when he came of age.[98] He had begun to hate the exploitation and narrowness of outlook he found around him— "it is the last stronghold of the most vulgar and commonplace prejudices of aristocracy . . . the peasants are mere serfs and are fed and lodged worse than pigs, the gentry have all the ferocity and despotism of the ancient barons."[99] The embankment project had become an intolerable burden. "I have," he wrote on February 7, to Hogg, "been teased [i.e. tormented] to death for the last fortnight. Had you known the variety of the discomfitures I have undergone, you would attribute my silence to anything but unkindness and neglect. I allude to the embankment affairs, in which I thoughtlessly engaged . . . 'Mab' has gone on but slowly, although she is nearly finished. They have teased me out of all poetry."[100] He had to put up with anti-radical gossip and personal slander such as Leeson's; his own occasionally imperious attitude—if we may judge by the letters to Evans—had doubtless engendered other resentments. The prospect of being chained down indefinitely at Tremadoc was unbearable. (And this was indeed the prospect. When he finally left Tremadoc it was understood that he would be gone for a brief period only; he was expected back to stay and work until the embankment was completed.)[101] Queen Mab was not being written; all creative writing, in fact, was being hampered by the drudgery of an office routine which he had begun to hate.

In addition to these problems, another matter was preying on his mind. In Dublin, he had taken a volume of poems (totaling some 2,000 lines) and "other pieces," to a printer named Stockdale, who had agreed to print them and collect his money in part from the sales. Once Shelley returned to England, however, Stockdale refused either to go on with the printing or to return the manuscripts until he had been paid. Continuous efforts, from June to January, failed to recover them. Yet he had promised Hookham to deliver the poems to him in March along with Queen Mab and its Notes—and the "other pieces" contained material for these Notes—all to come out as one large volume, the volume that was to launch him as a poet.[102] The only way to obtain these poems was to go to Dublin. This situation, combined with the debts and the "embankment affair," could, given Shelley's temperament and interests, produce a state of trapped desperation; and this state is implicit in his letter to Hogg. The final straw must have been the return of Dan, for it cannot be coincidental that the day of Dan's return was the day of the episode. Dan would have told Shelley more of the government's investigations in Devon, specifically perhaps, of the spy that had been put on his trail. Yet, escape was not easy. He had already been arrested for debt, and the Tremadoc tradesmen might well have him arrested again if he left town on any normal excuse. He might, perhaps, have been able to get Williams to soothe things down for him and to make arrangements for future payments if he had told him that he was weary of the whole project. But this meant admitting defeat, and admitting defeat was always difficult for Shelley. In this instance it was especially so, for he had been honored at a public banquet as a leading disciple, and he had poured scorn on those who, like Evans, had weakened in the fight. He could not now, in his turn, bear the opprobrium of the remaining faithful. The only way out seemed to be to devise an excuse of a nature that would make a brief vacation seem reasonable and desirable without indicating a retreat from the cause. An alleged murderous attack producing a state apparently verging on mental derangement would provide such an excuse. He first laid the basis for the scene by mysteriously taking his pistols to bed with him; he then acted out the first episode, apparently convincingly; he next dismissed the assembled company with the exception of Dan, waited for a time with Dan, and, then, sending him out of the room, staged the second episode. The deliberateness of these procedures indicates, as I have suggested, that he was conscious of what he was doing, but he was, doubtless, at the same time entering into the mood of his own fantasies. His excitement a few hours later, when Williams called, was due, essentially to the necessity for convincingly continuing the fiction once he had begun it (continued, too, in his letters) and for giving an impression of mental derangement, but it was also a reflection of an actual overwrought condition.

These psychological phenomena, strange though they may at first appear, do not, it should be noted, represent an aberration from previously observed patterns of behavior but an extension of them. The fictionalizing imagination and capacity for self-projection which lie at the root of this episode had been many times demonstrated before: the childhood story, in detail, of the visit to the village ladies; the distortions of the courtship with Harriet to Hogg and Elizabeth Hitchener; the fantasies on his mother and Graham; the elaborate fiction on the finding of the Wandering Jew fragment. The supercharged emotionalism present in the episode was present also in the letters on the break with Hogg. The unusually strong reaction to frustration was present in the rejection by Harriet Grove, the "rage" at Merle on religious disagreement; and the strange forms it could assume were well demonstrated in the "raid" on Field Place. This raid demonstrated, too, the acting through of a fantasy, acting so violent as also to give the impression of insanity; and a later attempt to bluff the fantasy out was illustrated in his letters on his mother and Graham to the Groves and Elizabeth Hitchener, following that raid, just as it had been shown earlier when Stockdale had detected the Victor and Cazire plagiarisms. The "Tanyrallt" episode differs from any previous similar episode not in kind but in its extravagance of fictionalization, its sustained acting and its clearly defined paranoid pattern, a pattern perhaps having its roots in the persecution at Syon House and apparent also in the alleged Keswick attack.[103] And these characteristics continued into later life although in modified form: the story to Peacock of a visit by Williams of Tremadoc; the attack in the Post Office at Pisa.[104] A desperate situation had produced a desperate solution; that it was not a mature solution is true; but Shelley, at the time, although unusually mature intellectually, was, in some of his emotional reactions, essentially adolescent.

NEWTON, MRS. BOINVILLE, PEACOCK

From Tremadoc, Shelley, Harriet, and Eliza went to Dublin, arriving there on March 9. He probably soon visited Stockdale for it was shortly before March 22 that he sent *Queen Mab* to Hookham for publication, informing him that the Notes and other poems would follow.[105] While in Dublin he stayed at the home of his Irish radical friend, John Lawless, perhaps talking over with him again the projected newspaper and history of Ireland. Hogg, arriving in Dublin shortly afterwards for a visit, found Lawless loud in Shelley's praise:

He spoke frequently of Bysshe, and with uniform, unvarying kindness and respect; and so spoke all in Dublin, who had ever seen him, in a handsome, liberal, and gentlemanlike manner.[106]

On about March 21, Eliza wrote to John Williams that "Mr. Shelley and myself have determined against our residing again at Tanyrallt. . . . We are going to tour the South of Ireland . . ."[107] After staying some five days at Killarney, surrounded with books, presumably for the Notes to *Queen Mab,* Shelley learned of Hogg's presence in Dublin and returned there with Harriet. On finding that Hogg had already departed, they decided to proceed to London, Eliza being left at Killarney with the books. One reason for this decision was perhaps that Shelley may have heard adversely from Hookham on publishing *Queen Mab*.[108] Another was that Harriet was six months pregnant. Shelley had commented on her courage in making a 240 mile coach trip to Dublin—"two days and nights of hard traveling" [109]—and may have hesitated in considering a return journey, especially to a spot so removed from adequate medical aid. But perhaps the strongest motive was to escape from Eliza. "He was," wrote Hogg, seeing him shortly afterwards in London, "evidently weary of angelic guardianship, and exulted with malicious pleasure that he had fairly planted her at last." [110] Harriet, Hogg continued, "smiled in silence and looked sly." But whatever ambivalence there might have been in her attitude, her preponderant emotion was still that of dependence. "My sister has joined me some time," she wrote later to Catherine Nugent, "You may suppose I was not a little pleased to see her again." [111] And although for a brief period Eliza was in the household only part of the time [112]— Shelley and Harriet took rooms just around the corner from the Westbrooks—she was soon a regular member once more, and when the young couple left for Edinburgh in the fall, she accompanied them.

In the first weeks following his arrival in London, Shelley was engaged in seeing *Queen Mab* through the press and in renewed negotiations with his father. He had long believed that he would be the heir to a considerable fortune on his twenty-first birthday. The story was, as he had but recently told it to John Williams at Tremadoc, that there existed "a copy of a deed in Doctors' Commons" which would prove that when he came of age he would "come into possession of a large property." [113] There was no basis for this belief, but there was a basis for thinking that Timothy would make some arrangement when his son came of age for the simple reason that his son could then raise money by *post obit* bonds which could seriously deplete the estate, for these bonds—carrying a guarantee of payment solely on the deaths of his father and grandfather—were obtainable only at ruinous interest rates. And Shelley was now approaching his twenty-first birthday. "It was confidently asserted," writes Hogg, who was with him in these weeks, "and generally believed, that his father would then come to a satisfactory and proper arrangement. . . . His father, it was said, would pay his debts . . . and make him a moderate, permanent, and suitable allowance." [114] These prospects raised high hopes in the hearts of

Shelley and Harriet (and doubtless Eliza). "Mr. Shelley's family," wrote Harriet, on May 21, "are very eager to be reconciled to him, and I should not in the least wonder if my next letter were not sent from his Paternal roof, as we expect to be there in a week or two."[115] Shelley took the initiative by writing to the Duke of Norfolk informing him that he wished reconciliation, and was "agreeably surprised" to find that his Grace had taken the trouble to visit him on receipt of his letter,[116] an act which showed that the Duke was still seriously interested in him. On May 18 he happily wrote to Timothy of his "willingness to make any Concessions that may be judg'd for the Interest of my Family."[117] But Timothy's reply must have constituted a shock, for he demanded—on Whitton's advice—that Shelley "write to the people at Oxford, and declare his return to Christianity."[118] This Shelley refused, and Timothy bluntly replied that no further communication or interview could take place until his son yielded.[119] On May 28, Shelley gave his point of view to the Duke: "I was prepared to make my father every reasonable concession, but am not so degraded and miserable a slave as publicly to disavow an opinion which I believe to be true."[120] This inflexible attitude on the part of his father apparently made him fear that it might be possible to deprive him of his inheritance entirely, and on June 16, he wrote to Thomas Charles Medwin, that "expert on Manorial Law and Custom,"[121] in some anxiety: "I know I am heir to large property. How are the papers to be seen? Have you the least doubt but that I am safe heir to a large landed property? Have you any certain knowledge on the subject?"[122] On July 7 and 9, Mr. Medwin, on a visit to London, had dinner with Shelley and was not too encouraging, apparently intimating that disinheritance was not impossible and perhaps giving Shelley the impression that the Duke of Norfolk was privy to the plot.[123] As it turned out, such a measure was impossible (as Whitton had informed Timothy the previous year), but the failure to make a financial settlement must have been one of the major shocks in Shelley's life. He had in the preceding three years run up debts totaling more than £2000,[124] presumably with the intention of clearing them up on his coming of age. He had, indeed, but recently bought a carriage for Harriet.[125] Now, he was not only saddled with an immense debt but seemed to have no future financial prospects until the deaths of both Sir Bysshe and Timothy, and even of this he was uncertain. The severity of the blow not only to Shelley but to Harriet is clear from a letter of Harriet's on August 8 (from

Bracknell in Berkshire, where they had moved about the middle of July):

Mr. S. is of age, but no longer heir to the immense property of his sires. They are trying to take it away, and will I am afraid succeed, as it appears there is a flaw in the drawing up of the settlement, by which they can deprive him of everything. This is a beautiful idea, and well worthy the noble men who have formed it, among whom I suspect a certain *great personage*. They have put it into Chancery, though I fancy it can and will be kept an entire secret. You may suppose that we will do everything to prevent this shameful abuse of property, as we are convinced that more good would be effected if we have it, than if they regain it. We are now in a house 30 miles from London, merely for convenience. How long we remain is uncertain, as I fear our necessities will oblige us to remove to a greater distance. Our friends the Newtons are trying to do everything in their power to serve us; but our doom is decided. You who know us may well judge of our feelings. To have all our plans set aside in this manner is a miserable thing. Not that I regret the loss, but for the sake of those I intended to benefit.[126]

Gone now was the rosy prospect of happy reunion under the "Paternal roof" and even that of ultimately becoming lady of Field Place seemed dubious. Instead there loomed the reality of living in a small Berkshire village "for convenience" and the prospect of remoter flights to escape the clutches of creditors and bailiffs, the latter of which gentry were hot on Shelley's trail for payment on the carriage.[127] It was indeed a "miserable thing," and even though Harriet's interest in the vanishing property was correctly Shelleyian—a means to philanthropic benevolence—it may perhaps not have escaped Mr. John Westbrook that the misery could be reversed if his son-in-law would simply write a letter to Oxford.

During this period in London and in Bracknell, Shelley, for the first time in his life, found himself part of a social and radical circle of congenial spirits. At Oxford he had had a close friend in Hogg, but with others, apparently only slight acquaintance. In the succeeding months in London, Field Place, and Wales, his life was essentially lonely, his main contacts being with his relatives, Hogg, and the Westbrooks. And so, too, during the early months of his marriage at Edinburgh, York, and Keswick. In Ireland he had become acquainted with Lawless and other Irish radicals but was not intimately part of any group. In Wales and Devon the story was the same, and it was not until his visit to London in October and November, 1812, that he laid the foundations for future friendships by making the acquaintance of Hookham, Peacock, Godwin, and the Newtons. Shelley, in short, had seen little of normal group life and had had almost no experience with people who had knowledge of the social world and its ways. His injection during these months into the circle surrounding the Newtons and Mrs. Newton's sister, Mrs. Boinville, was an important and enlarging experience for him.

John Frank Newton was a follower of the school of millennialism and back-to-naturism popular in the late eighteenth century, a school which found its most authoritative expression in the twelve bulky volumes of Lord Monboddo's *Antient Metaphysics* and his *On the Origin and Progress of Language*. The school rested upon two tenets: (a) man in the "natural" state of early society was healthy, happy, and well-adjusted, but in civilized society was beset by numerous physical and moral ills—including war and poverty—arising from such "unnatural" elements as the eating of meat and the drinking of liquor, wearing clothes, and living in cities; [128] (b) as a result of these evils the human race had deteriorated and would continue to deteriorate, until God, taking mercy upon mankind, would bring about the millennium.[129] Newton, like Monboddo, advocated a return to the natural life, vegetarianism, nudism—Hogg tells us of the Newton children running naked to the door to greet Shelley [130]—temperance, etc. Like Monboddo, too, he believed that the species had deteriorated—and Peacock makes riotous fun of these doctrines and of Newton in *Headlong Hall* (Mr. Escot, the "deteriorationist") and *Nightmare Abbey* (Mr. Toobad)—but Newton added to Monboddo's millennialism an astrological slant: the period of deterioration was, in accordance with Zoroastrian doctrines, under the black realm of the evil spirit Oromazes; the new age would come only when the good spirit Ahrimanes rose to the ascendancy. These views he put forward in *The Return to Nature* (1811), four letters in *The Monthly Magazine* (1812), and *Three Enigmas Attempted to be Explained* (1821).[131] His influence on Shelley lay not so much in his own peculiar contributions to the school—for Shelley was a vegetarian before he met Newton, his theories were differently based, and he had no serious belief in Zoroastrianism—but in introducing him to its general lines of thought. It was after his first acquaintance with Newton that Shelley ordered Monboddo's *Origin and Progress of Language*.[132]

Through Mrs. Boinville and the circle centered around her, Shelley made his first living contact with the traditions of the French Revolution. Her husband, Jean Baptiste Chastel de Boinville, a friend of André Chénier, had been aide-de-camp to Lafayette. He had been with Lafayette on the wild night of the abduction of the royal family from Versailles, and his continued close relationship with him indicates that he shared Lafayette's liberal program in the Constituent Assembly (where Lafayette pleaded for religious tolerance, the extension of the franchise, the abolition of titles, the emancipation of slaves, and the freedom of the press). In 1789, Lafayette, fearing an aristocratic reaction, sent the powerful Duke d'Orléans to England, and when he needed a confidential messenger to convey a warning to him to stay there, he chose De Boinville for the task. Among Lafayette's papers we find the "Instructions pour M. de Boinville, mon aide-de-camp" drawn up for this occasion.[133] Boinville, however, was more than a messenger. From him Lafayette hoped to discover more of the "projets aristocratiques et orléanistes" in London. ("Londres," he wrote, "est un foyer d'aristocratie française; il y a de grandes connaissances à tirer de ce côté, et comme M. de Boinville en fera son occupation unique, je ne doute pas qu'il ne me donne des avis très utiles." [134]) Later, when he refused to go along with the more advanced revolutionary parties, Lafayette was imprisoned; De Boinville's property in France was confiscated and he remained in England as an émigré.[135] There he married the daughter of an ex-planter from the West Indies, Collins, a man of liberal sentiments whose house "was the resort of many of the constitutional emigrants," and who was probably the author of a book on the treatment of slaves which became a document in the abolitionist movement and was commended by Wilberforce.[136] Boinville and his wife attempted to secure Lafayette's freedom and Lafayette mentions him as a likely source of aid in a letter from prison in 1793.[137] In 1797, Lafayette was released by Napoleon and it was probably shortly afterwards that De Boinville returned to France, accompanied by his wife, who was presented to the now aging veteran of two revolutions. In 1812, De Boinville went on the disastrous Russian campaign with Napoleon as "Directeur de Vivres," and died, on February 7, 1813, in the retreat from Moscow. When Shelley was introduced to Mrs. Boinville (doubtless by her sister, Mrs. Newton) in the summer of the same year, she had but shortly returned from France and was living in lodgings in the Pimlico district of London, her hair prematurely white from the recent news of her husband's death. Later, she too moved to Bracknell.

"Round her slight figure," writes her grandson, later a Presbyterian minister in Paris, "she wore the badge of republicanism—a wide red band—and I have often heard her call herself *une enfant de la Révolution*. With this she had also unfortunately accepted the principles of the false philosophers of the age. . . ."[138] Mrs. Boinville, in other words, was an advanced radical in her political views and a free-thinker in religion. Around her she had gathered a group of associates of whom Hogg gives the following burlesque picture:

I generally found there two or three sentimental young butchers, an eminently philosophical tinker, and several very unsophisticated medical practitioners, or medical students, all of low origin, and vulgar and offensive manners. They sighed, turned up their eyes, retailed philosophy, such as it was, and swore by William Godwin and Political Justice . . .[139]

Peacock's account is similar:

At Bracknell, Shelley was surrounded by a numerous society, all in a great measure of his own opinions in relation to religion and politics, and the larger portion of them in relation to vegetable diet. But they wore their rue with a difference. Every one of them adopting some of the articles of the faith of their general church, had each nevertheless some predominant crochet of his or her own, which left a number of open questions for earnest and not always temperate discussion. I was sometimes irreverent enough to laugh at the fervour with which opinions utterly unconducive to any practical result were battled for as matters of the highest importance to the well-being of mankind; Harriet Shelley was always ready to laugh with me, and we thereby both lost caste with some of the more hot-headed of the party.[140]

Putting these two accounts together, and reading between the lines, it appears that the group consisted of radicals of a predominantly theoretical character, interested in discussing the general principles of republicanism and egalitarianism rather than the immediate problems of English parliamentary reform (toward which Peacock was sympathetic). They appear to have been largely French republican émigrés, of which there was quite a large colony in London at the time. These émigrés, according to a letter in *The Examiner* in January, 1812, consisted of two classes: "respectable gentlemen and whole families" living "either on a scanty allowance, or by means of honest industry"; and "mechanics, tradesmen and artists."[141] Mrs. Boinville had brought people from both groups together in her circle, and it was this mixture of middle class and working class that upset Hogg. But, be Hogg's attitude what it may, there can be no doubt that the Boinville circle opened a new world to Shelley. Seven years later, the memory of it was still strong upon him:

I could not help considering Mrs. B., when I knew her, as the most admirable specimen of human being I had ever seen. Nothing earthly ever appeared to be more perfect than her character and manners. It is improbable that I shall ever meet again the person whom I so much esteemed, and still admire. I wish however that when you see her, you would tell her that I have not forgotten her, or any of the amiable circle once assembled round her.[142]

There was nothing ridiculous about the Boinville circle to Shelley. It was his first introduction to a society of intellectual radicalism, a society presided over by a lady of intelligence and charm. (Nor did the years rob her of attraction. Thirty years later, Shelley's widow wrote to Claire Clairmont, then living in the same street in Paris as the De Boinvilles: "I like the society of Mme de Boinville and it is privation to me not to see her when in Paris . . . there is something in her society and conversation that animates and pleases me—& I find this so seldom among my fellow creatures—& finding it enjoy it so seldom, that it is a privation not to get it when I can.") [143]

It was during his acquaintance with the Boinville circle that Shelley first grew to know the third of his biographical sons of light, Thomas Love Peacock. Peacock in 1813—thirty-seven years before he became the "jolly old worldling" that Thackeray remembered—was a young liberal intellectual. He was a bitter foe to all political corruption—which he satirized in *Melincourt* with acid burlesque in the election of Sir Oran Haut-ton to Parliament for the borough of Onevote—and to those literary men who, like Wordsworth (Mr. Paperstamp), Southey (Mr. Feathernest), and Coleridge (Mr. Mystic) supported it, either openly or tacitly. He had read *Political Justice* and penned two poems on Necessity. He was an atheist (much to the horror of the good people of Wales, as Shelley discovered),[144] scorning belief in immortality. He was also, doubtless, then, as he was later, a staunch admirer of Thomas Jefferson—"the greatest public benefactor that has yet appeared in the nineteenth century" [145]—and the American democratic system. His general learning, especially in the classics, was considerable (even extending to an interest in Zoroastrian lore, for which he later satirized Newton).[146] He was, moreover, a poet of promise, with three books safely behind him. Peacock's views and interests, in short, were not so far out of line with those of the Boinville circle as he later chose to intimate, and it is clear why Shelley took him up with enthusiasm and the two became such fast friends. In one respect, however, Peacock differed sharply from Shelley. Shelley was an enthusiastic revolutionary, convinced that mankind was moving into a new order fundamentally different from any that had existed previously. Peacock had no such belief. Mankind, he felt, would remain essentially as it had been and one could expect no more than an alleviation of evils within a set framework. He was, moreover, although opposed to war in general, a champion of British commerce and as such was assailed by Shelley:

Mr. Peacock conceives that commerce is prosperity; that the glory of the British Flag, is the happiness of the British people; that George III. so far from having been a warrior and a Tyrant, has been a Patriot. To me it appears otherwise; and I have rigidly accustomed myself, not to be seduced by the loveliest eloquence or the sweetest strains to regard with intellectual toleration [that] which ought not to be tolerated by those who love Liberty, Truth, and Virtue.[147]

Peacock considered himself as a "practical" reformer to whom (as to Hazlitt) the excesses of left-wing enthusiasts were as "crotchety" as the eccentricities of vegetarianism and natural ameliorationism. Hence, in his satirical novels, the ideas of Shelley, in the person of Forester, Foster, and Scythrop, are ridiculed equally with the "mysticism" of Coleridge or the naturism of Monboddo. These attitudes determine the framework of his *Memoirs of Shelley*. Peacock does not regard Shelley as a thinker or poet of the highest order; and it is significant that he is content to view him within a biographical perspective and to let his collection of anecdotes and comments remain as his last word on him. Within his limits, however, Peacock is a perceptive guide, for he is a man of insight and integrity, and although his wit—like Dr. Johnson's would-be-philosopher friend's cheerfulness—keeps breaking through, he does not allow it, as does Hogg, to distort what he considered to be the essential picture.

Shelley must have found Peacock a stimulating and delightful companion—even though some of the Boinville circle understandably thought him "cold" [148]—and Peacock's influence must have been, on the whole, a healthy one. Peacock was never able to shake any of Shelley's fundamental beliefs or to add to them, but he probably performed the important service of lopping off unneeded and harmful excrescences. It is, I suspect, to Peacock's penetrating witticisms—and how devastating these could be, *Melincourt* bears ample testimony—

that we owe the elimination from Shelley's thinking of some of the more extreme doctrines of the naturist school which found their way into *Queen Mab* and its Notes. He perhaps helped also in focusing Shelley's mind more specifically upon questions of reform, particularly economic reform.[149] And it was certainly Peacock who gave Shelley his first insight into the greatness of classical literature, an insight which immeasurably enriched his later poetry.[150] How great was Shelley's enthusiasm for Peacock—although he played this down in his comments to Hogg, who might have been jealous of the new friend—is shown by his choice of him as a companion, when, in the fall, the "necessities" hinted at by Harriet became pressing and he decided to escape his creditors by a trip to the Lake District. On October 5, Shelley, Harriet, with their baby girl Eliza Ianthe, born late in June in London,[151] Eliza, and Peacock entered Harriet's new carriage and set off for the north. In the Lake District, however, they were unable to secure a house and moved on to Edinburgh. "A little more than two years has passed," wrote Harriet to Catherine Nugent, "since I made my first visit here to be united to Mr. Shelley. To me they have been the happiest and longest years of my life." [152] But financial difficulties pursued them even there,[153] and by December 10 they were back in London. The year closed with Shelley again engaged in attempting to raise money (now for Godwin as well as himself) by *post obits*.

During his months in London and Bracknell, Shelley had not relaxed his literary efforts. Hogg tells us that he completed a translation of a French work "on the Perfectibility of the Human Species," and if this was the bulky two-volume *System of Nature* he had been engaged on in Devon,[154] it was a task of some magnitude. But his main efforts must have been devoted to his atheistical treatise (101 pages in length), *A Refutation of Deism,* which, according to Hogg, was published early in 1814.

A VINDICATION OF NATURAL DIET
ON THE VEGETABLE SYSTEM OF DIET

Although Shelley's interest in vegetarianism may have begun at Oxford, where, Hogg informs us, he was "temperate" in his diet, he did not begin an actual vegetarian regimen until about the first of March, 1812, when he was residing in Dublin.[155] What first influenced him to adopt this diet, we do not know. He did not meet Newton until the fall, and we know of no Irish acquaintances who were vegetarians. It is possible that his thoughts were first turned in this direction by Plutarch's two essays on flesh-eating which may have been included in his classical reading at Eton or Oxford. On November 26, 1813, he informed Hogg that he had translated these essays, "which we read together," [156] but whether this reading together took place at Oxford or later we cannot tell. And he could have picked up vegetarian ideas from various other writers with whom he was early acquainted: Paley, Rousseau, Thomson (in *The Seasons*), Pope (*Essay on Man*), and Plato.[157] The transformation of this personal adherence to vegetarianism into proselytizing activity was almost certainly the result of his acquaintance with Newton, who introduced him not only to his own book, *The Return to Nature or A Defence of the Vegetable Regimen* (1811), but, in all probability, also to Monboddo, to Joseph Ritson's *An Essay on Abstinence from Animal Food as a Moral Duty* (1802), and to Thomas Trotter's *A View of the Nervous Temperament* (1808).

The overall philosophy of the school is, as I have noted, that of Monboddo, namely that all the ills of man and society are due to "unnatural" living, under which Monboddo included not only meat and alcohol but clothes, smoky air, narcotics, homosexuality, masturbation, marriage, tobacco, and money.[158] In contrast to the feeble and immoral "animal of prey" that is modern man, stands the noble "Oran Outang of Angola," vegetarian, teetotaler, nudist, representing "the first stage of human progression," a creature of "human intelligence" (or, at least, the philosopher qualifies, "as much as can be expected in an animal living without civility or arts"), and unlike man, possessing "the sense of modesty, of honour, and of justice," a concept delightfully satirized in Peacock's Sir Oran Haut-ton.[159] Newton, Ritson, and Trotter, while rejecting some of Monboddo's more extreme crochets, accepted his general naturist point of view, and each placed the emphasis on one or another aspect of the theory, Newton and Ritson on vegetarianism (although each from a different point of view), and Trotter on general simplicity of diet and abstention from alcohol (he was also the author of *An Essay, Medical, Philosophical, and Chemical on Drunkenness*).

The fountainhead of the vegetarian creed was Plutarch, his arguments becoming its articles of foundation: (a) the human body is constructed for vegetable eating and not meat eating—"it hath no hawk's bill, no sharp talons, no roughness of teeth"—and, hence, meat eating is unnatural for man; (b) cruelty is involved in the slaughter of animals; (c) overindulgence in food and acceptance of animal slaughter respectively bring about, in the human being, "all sorts of luxury and expensiveness" and hardness of heart towards his fellows. "Is not," he asks, "accustoming one's self to mildness and a humane temper of mind an admirable thing?" [160]

Newton, specifically influenced by the work of a prominent London physician, Dr. William Lambe, who advocated a diet of vegetables and distilled water as the pathway to health and long life, based his plea for vegetarianism mainly on the grounds of physical well-being.[161]

John Ritson, celebrated not only for his scholarship but for his radical political views (especially following an enthusiastic trip to Paris in 1791), which for a time made him an associate of Godwin and Holcroft, developed Plutarch's humanitarian argument and placed the emphasis on moral benefits, his vegetarianism, apparently, being an offshoot of his social philosophy.

His *Essay* begins with a naturist introduction on the history of man in his primitive state, then presents, in part two, the medical argument that animal food is not natural to man nor necessary to health, and, in part three, develops the author's own socio-moral approach. Cruelty to animals, he argues, leads to cruelty to man and thus forms one of the bases of political oppression: "In the same manner oppressors and tyrants began to shed blood." Not only this, but the mere eating of animal flesh produces ferocity: "The fierce and cruel disposition of the wild Arabs is suppose'd, chiefly, if not solely, to proceed from their feeding upon the flesh of camels." [162] And for these views he had the sanction of no less renowned a thinker than Rousseau: "For, however the experience may be explained, it is certain that great eaters of flesh are, in general, more cruel and ferocious than other men. . . . All savages are cruel, and it is not their morals that urge them to be so; their cruelty proceeds from their food." [163] Ritson takes the argument a step further: "As the use of animal food makes man cruel and barbarous, and to take delight in pains and torture . . . so the abstinence from that habit has an immediate tendency to soften the manners, and dispose the mind to receive uncommon satisfaction from the exercise of gentleness and humanity towards the minutest objects of creation." [164]

It has not been sufficiently noted that Shelley is as much against liquor drinking as meat eating. And here one of his guides was Thomas Trotter, M.D., both of whose works are on his book list of December 24, 1812, immediately following his first acquaintance with Newton.[165] "Sudden death, apoplexy, palsy, dropsy, madness, and a hideous list of mental disquietudes and nervous failings," Trotter warns, "prey upon the shattered frame of the inebriate, and prove fatal in the end." [166] The drunkard can only be cured, he contends (and Shelley notes approval), by "leaving off the bottle at once." [167] Tapering off is useless.

But more interesting than Trotter's theories on alcoholism is his picture of the "nervous temperament," a kind of crude foreshadowing of the modern concept of neurosis. Literary men, Trotter contends, living inactive, indoor lives, are especially prone to "nervous diseases." "The *pathology* of these diseases," he writes, "is to be sought in the deranged sensations, and inverted sympathies of the GREAT SYMPATHETIC NERVE; and in the irregular action of all those organs to which it is distributed." The "remote causes" of the disease are to be found in the fact of living in "populous towns." Its physical symptoms are "cramps and spasms, which particularly affect the stomach, bowels, kidneys, ureters and bladder." Its psychological symptoms are lowness of spirits and unbased anxieties:

The person who is subject to nervous affections, can seldom promise himself long equality of health or spirits; these vicissitudes must often happen, from causes which neither can be foreseen nor prevented, and sometimes when least to be expected. The mind however is not always prepared to combat sensations which impress it with the ideas of dissolution, otherwise it could not so fully believe in imaginary horrors. It is a singular fact, that even men whom I have known, renowned for valour and personal courage, and who have been familiar with danger, should sometimes be found among those who conceive such dread from indescribable feelings, and torture themselves with a fantom. When these hallucinations come to be removed, they can condemn the imbecility that created their fears; yet nevertheless on a next attack their apprehensions are renewed as strong as ever.[168]

The best treatment is "low diet, with entire abstinence from spiritous and fermented liquor," and "change of scene." "Nervous persons," he warns, "do best to dine off few dishes; and those of the simplest kind." They should avoid "tea, coffee, opium and all other narcotics."

Change of climate is one of those means of relief in nervous cases, that may sometimes be resorted to with great advantage. There are nervous persons who are most sensibly affected by variable weather; where the transitions are quick, particularly from settled and clear, to damp and foggy. The human nerves in such patients are like barometers; it is thus the fall of the year, in November and December, is proverbial for lowness in spirits and melancholy. A residence in Italy or the south of France, for some time, may therefore be useful to such as can afford it.

A "predisposition" to nervous temperament can be acquired from human milk. "This predisposition may take root, even during the earliest stages of infancy, in children born of the healthiest parents. The effects of the milk of an unwholesome nurse often lay this foundation." A mother should nurse her own child. "It is the duty of the husband to encourage the wife in the exercise of this amiable duty to the infant; and if he prevents it, he rends asunder one of the strongest ties of human affection." [169]

It is difficult to believe that Shelley's vegetarianism, "low diet," abstinence from alcohol and tea, sudden shifts of scene and climate, and horror when Harriet did not nurse their child [170] did not have some of their basis in this type of medical lore. Even though his purposeful energy and usually good spirits made the analogy only partially applicable, he could hardly avoid seeing something of himself and his "nervous attacks" [171] in Trotter's pictures of ragged nerves, unevenness of spirits, tendency to "imaginary horrors," and "cramps and spasms." [172]

Of Shelley's two tracts, the first, *A Vindication of Natural Diet,* probably written in November, 1812, and published early in 1813,[173] is the better known, and expositions of Shelley's vegetarianism have commonly been based on it alone. The second, *On the Vegetable System of Diet,* however, written apparently about a year later,[174] gives a more perceptive treatment.

A Vindication of Natural Diet begins with the Monboddoish pronouncement, "I hold that the depravity of the moral nature of man originated in his unnatural habits of life . . . at some distant period man forsook the path of nature, and sacrificed the purity and happiness of his being to unnatural appetites." In Christian mythology this catastrophe was reflected, as Milton was well aware, in the story of the fall of man; in Greek mythology, in the story of Prometheus—all of which is a condensation from Ritson (even to use of the same quotation from *Paradise Lost*) and Newton.[175] The nature of the "event" which produced this catastrophe was the shift from a vegetable diet to meat eating and "spiritous liquors"; this diet—*vide* Plutarch, Rousseau, Monboddo, and Ritson—brought about a coarsening of the moral fiber which resulted in social evil. (In the *Queen Mab* Note a paragraph is interpolated on other "unnatural" evils: sexual distortions—"the miseries and diseases of unsatisfied celibacy, unenjoying prostitution"—"the putrid atmosphere of crowded cities," superfluous clothes.[176] Shelley had perhaps studied Monboddo, whose *Origin and Progress of*

Language he had ordered in December, 1812, between the writing of the *Vindication* and the Note.) Plutarch and Monboddo blend—with a touch of Cuvier, the note informs us—to give the argument that man is not "naturally" carnivorous, having "neither claws to seize his prey, nor distinct and pointed teeth." "The orang-outang perfectly resembles man both in the order and number of his teeth," yet the orang-utan is "strictly frugivorous." (And this anatomical argument is all we hear of the noble beast, Shelley, apparently, like Newton, rejecting Monboddo's and Ritson's [177] extravaganzas on the theme.) The argument next switches, in a recounting of the diseases and other horrors of modern society, to absurdities on meat eating being responsible for the dictatorial and militarist character, absurdities which have been rightly ridiculed, but usually without noting that they were common also to Rousseau and Ritson.

In the concluding section of the essay, Shelley shifts from Newton and Ritson to bring in a new type of argument, namely that the use of land for pasturage instead of agriculture is both wasteful and socially evil, producing poverty, imperialism, and war. For these arguments, he was almost certainly indebted to Paley and Plato,[178] that from Paley (favored of Timothy) perhaps, being general gospel at Field Place:

> *A great part of the richest lands of the country are converted to pasturage.* Much also of the corn bread, which went directly to the nourishment of human bodies, now only contributes to it by fattening the flesh of sheep and oxen. *The mass and volume of provisions are hereby diminished,* and what is gained in the amelioration of the soil is lost in the quality of the produce. . . . Tillage is also recommended by the additional advantage— that it affords employment to a much more numerous peasantry.

Paley had doubtless taken the argument from a well-known passage in *The Republic;* but Plato had gone a step further:

> "The country, too, I presume, which was formerly adequate to the support of its then inhabitants, will be now too small, and adequate no longer, Shall we say so?"
> "Certainly."
> "Then we must cut ourselves a slice of our neighbour's territory if we want to have land both for pasture and tillage? . . . Will our next step be to go to war, Glaukon, or how will it be?"
> "As you say."

These arguments Shelley develops in accordance with the conditions of the day and in the terms of his own general social philosophy:

The quantity of nutritious vegetable matter, consumed in fattening the carcase of an ox, would afford ten times the sustenance, undepraving indeed, and incapable of generating disease, if gathered immediately from the bosom of the earth. . . . It is only the wealthy that can, to any great degree, even now, indulge the unnatural craving for dead flesh. . . . On a natural system of diet, we should require no spices from India; no wines from Portugal, Spain, France, or Madeira; none of those multitudinous articles of luxury, for which every corner of the globe is rifled, and which are the causes of so much individual rivalship, such calamitous and sanguinary national disputes.[179]

One of the causes for war and colonial conquest—denounced in the *Address to the Irish People*—lies in the rich meat and liquor diet of the upper class (of which the Regent's paunch became a Shelleyan symbol). And not of war and colonial conquest only, but of exploitation at home:

The labour requisite to support a family is far lighter than is usually supposed. The peasantry work, not only for themselves, but for the aristocracy, the army, and the manufacturers.

The agricultural base of Shelley's radicalism is nowhere so well revealed as in these passages, not only in his comments on the existing situation but in his implications for the future state:

Again, the spirit of the nation, that should take the lead in this great reform, would insensibly become agricultural; commerce, with all its vices, selfishness, and corruption, would gradually decline; more natural habits would produce gentler manners, and the excessive complication of political relations would be so far simplified, that every individual might feel and understand why he loved his country, and took a personal interest in its welfare. . . . Is it impossible to realise a state of society, where all the energies of man shall be directed to the production of his solid happiness? Certainly if this advantage (the object of all political speculation) be in any degree attainable, it is attainable only by a community, which holds no factitious incentives to the avarice and ambition of the few, and which is internally organised for the liberty, security and comfort of the many. None must be entrusted with power (and money is the completest species of power) who do not stand pledged to use it exclusively for the general benefit. But the use of animal flesh and fermented liquors, directly militates with this equality of the rights of man.

Shelley's egalitarian state was, it is clear, to be economically based on agriculture rather than commerce. The rise of industry, bringing with it enclosure and the impoverishment of the rural masses, he regarded with apprehension. This is made even clearer by his acquiescing references in a footnote to Samuel Jackson Pratt's *Cottage Pictures, or the Poor,* for Pratt's poem is essentially a protest against these evils.

The *Vindication* concludes with a list of the illustrious aged (due to a vegetable diet) taken, in part, from Ritson.[180]

On the Vegetable System of Diet covers the same ground as the *Vindication,* but in it we are treated to no elaborate panegyrics on a vegetarian age of innocence, of Adam, or Prometheus. The theory of the transmission of diseased characters from body to mind and their subsequent inheritance is now clearly recognized as the fundamental point at issue, and a more developed concept of it presented:

Man is an whole the complicated parts of which are so interwoven with each other, that the most remote and subtle springs of his machine are connected with those which are more gross and obvious, and reciprocally act and react upon each other. . . . The vital principle, by some inexplicable process, influences and is influenced by, the nerves and muscles of the body. The flesh is wasted by an excess of grief and passion. Thought is suspended by the languor of a lethargy, and deranged by the excitement of a fever.[181]

As a result of "unnatural habits," and the definition is exact—"by an unnatural habit is to be understood such an habit as is manifestly inconsistent with the conformation of any animal"—physical disease has arisen, and, "in the silence of innumerable ages," has been inherited.[182] And this universal disease has penetrated from the physiological to the psychological until mankind has become one diseased mass both in body and mind. Out of this universal morbidity arises "much of that spirit in which human beings persecute and destroy each other." That such consequences could arise from "a mere question of dietetics" seems at first unlikely, but, once the principle of the interaction of body and mind is grasped, it becomes intelligible.

Shelley's acceptance of vegetarian doctrines had placed him in something of a dilemma. In the *Vindication*—written in the first flush of inspiration from Newton—he bluntly stated:

The advantage of a reform in diet, is obviously greater than that of any other. It strikes at the root of the evil. To remedy the abuses of legislation, before we annihilate the propensities by which they are produced, is to suppose, that by taking away the effect, the cause will cease to operate.[183]

But, if this were so, why engage in political action at all? Why write the *Letter to Lord Ellenborough*? Why attempt to set up organizations? The logical thing to do would be to convert the Irish and Lord Ellenborough to vegetarianism. In the *Vegetable System,* Shelley modifies the concept by arguing that social evil does not originate from "unnatural habits" alone but from a combination of these habits with a deficient social structure:

The source of the errors of mankind is to be found not only in the external circumstances of his situation, but in these peculiarities of internal organization which modify the operation.[184]

"Much" of the spirit of destruction and persecution arises from unnatural habits, not "all" of it. "Here," he adds, "lies exposed *one* of the most important sources of the wretchedness of man." "Let not however," he warns, "the expectations which may reasonably be indulged from the dereliction of a destructive custom be exaggerated. Disease is hereditary . . ." and the adoption of natural habits would only "diminish" it "in some degree." Yet, at the same time, he adds: "Before the human race shall be capable of any considerable advance towards that happiness which is the ultimate object of all human exertion, habits demonstrably unnatural must be unsparingly discarded."[185]

The main emphasis for present action is, by implication, political. Even the existing population is capable of making important advances and one should push these to their limits. Mankind, however, will not be able to advance to the ultimate egalitarian society until this social progress is balanced with the moral progress to be derived from the eradication of disease both physical and mental through the adoption of "natural" modes of life.

That vegetarianism is scientifically unsound is true, and it is true also, that parts of the *Vindication* deserved nothing except the riotous parody that a contemporary wit (probably Peacock) obligingly provided:

The depravity of man is undoubtedly to be sought for in the indulgence of carnivorous propensities. This has been the persuasion of the enlightened of all ages. This fact has been darkly hinted at in the mythology of all religions. The biblical allegory of the forbidden fruit admits of no explanation but this:—The apple of the fatal tree was nothing, gentlemen, but a well-dressed beefsteak, whether plain or with oyster-sauce is doubtful. . . . The fable of Prometheus may be similarly explained . . .[186]

On the other hand, however, we have to remember that these excesses were not personal eccentricities of Shelley's but were to be found in such then distinguished scholars as Ritson and Monboddo, or recognized physicians such as Lambe and Trotter, and that while Peacock might parody the theory he could not disprove it. Shelley's vegetarianism was not out of line with the scientific knowledge of his time; his tract was, it should be emphasized, brought out by a recognized publisher of medical and scientific works ("J. Callow, Medical Bookseller").[187] That he should consider all disease as arising from faulty diet is not surprising for the bacterial basis of disease had not then been discovered. Pasteur was not born until ten years after the composition of the *Vindication*. And little was then known of the complexities of the processes of metabolism and heredity. It seemed reasonable enough to the men of the early nineteenth century to think of all or most disease as being somehow associated with a departure from "natural" living and to be completely inheritable. Nor, although the theory is built on faulty and often eccentric general premises, were all of its contentions incorrect. Some disease is due to diet and some disease is inheritable, and, as the new science of psychosomatic medicine is revealing, the interconnection of mind and body in disease is greater than we had believed.

Nor does Shelley simply restate the general views of the school. His acquaintance with the most advanced political thought of his age gives him a perspective not to be found in Ritson, Newton, and the others. Whereas to them, the spreading of the doctrine was seen as a process of personal indoctrination within a static framework, Shelley viewed it in relation to the general social advance of mankind. His naturism was subordinated to the Godwinian vista. It arises, as a natural consequence, from his social philosophy, but has minor roots also in that sympathy for animals which was part of the radical movement of the day (for example in Coleridge's "young ass" and water snakes), and which is conspicuous in Shelley's fragmentary essay on the English game laws, e.g.: "Persons of great property nurture animals on their estates for the sake of destroying them." [188] Nor is it only in his viewing of naturist doctrines in the broader social perspectives that Shelley is able to make an original contribution. His early interest in science is evident in his clear generalized statement of theory in the *Vegetable Diet*, and his concept of the vital interaction of mind and body in the same work is much in advance of similar concepts in Monboddo, Ritson, or Newton.

VII POET AND PROPAGANDIST

Queen Mab and *A Refutation of Deism*

MINOR POEMS

As early as December, 1811, Shelley informed Elizabeth Hitchener that he intended to "make a selection of my younger poems for publication." [1] These poems he took with him when he left for Ireland in February and there, as we have noted, they languished in Stockdale's printing establishment, and were probably not retrieved until Shelley's second visit to Dublin in March, 1813. [2] Hookham, sounded out as a possible publisher, evidently fought shy, and by May, 1813, Shelley himself had decided not to proceed further. [3] With a few exceptions the poems remained in manuscript until 1886 when Dowden published the ones he considered of biographical interest. [4] The bulk of the volume still remains unpublished, and is today in the possession of Shelley's great-grandson. It is, however, possible through an examination of the available poems, Shelley's comments on the nature of the work as a whole, and Dowden's comments on the unpublished poems to get a fairly complete picture of the volume as Shelley projected it.

"My poems will, I fear," Shelley informed Hookham, "little stand the criticism even of friendship. Some of the later ones have the merit of conveying a meaning in every word, and these all are faithful pictures of my feelings at the time of writing them. But they are, in a great measure, abrupt and obscure—all breathing hatred of government and religion, but I think not too openly for publication. One fault they are indisputably exempt from, that of being a volume of *fashionable literature*." [5] They would, he further informed him, total about 2,800 lines (which is, according to Dowden, approximately the length of the manuscript volume). [6] Of their literary merits Shelley clearly had qualms—which he expressed also to Elizabeth Hitchener—and it was probably these that decided him against further publishing efforts. (It was perhaps his restraint in this instance that emboldened him later to give advice to Keats against publishing "first blights.") [7]

The volume was to consist of about thirty to thirty-five poems, falling into three groups: narratives; political or anti-religious poems; personal poems (mainly on Harriet). As the narratives and some of the personal poems contain a social message, the overall tone would be, as Shelley stated, radical and propagandistic; and this, clearly, was his main object in the work.

The narratives were four in number: *Zeinab and Kathema, Henry and Louisa, The Voyage,* and *A Tale of Society as it is.* Of these only the last has been published—and that incompletely—and for the others we have to rely on Dowden's comments. *Zeinab and Kathema* appears to be a kind of weak foreshadowing of *The Revolt of Islam,* in that it deals with the adventures of a pair of lovers (from Cashmire), who are separated by "Christian guile" and, in the end, perish melodramatically; the poem emphasizes "the vengeance of indiscriminating and pitiless laws." *Henry and Louisa* is similarly the tale of two lovers but with the emphasis apparently on anti-war propaganda, Henry being "borne from his lover's arms by the insane lust of conquest and of glory" only to die "on the bloody sands" of Egypt [8] (in reference, perhaps, to Napoleon's Egyptian campaign). Both of these poems appear to have been written in 1811 and were doubtless among the batch of "younger poems" taken to Ireland. *The Voyage,* which Dowden dates August, 1812, deals, in part, as we have already noted, with the depredations of the press gang. *A Tale of Society as it is,* Shelley enclosed in a letter to Elizabeth Hitchener on January 7, 1812, with the notation that he had written it that morning. It tells the story of a son forced into the army—to "become a thing more senseless than the sword of battlefield"—ultimately returning to his mother, but corrupted in body and mind, and left by an ungrateful country to the humiliations of poverty and charity:

> And now cold charity's unwelcome dole
> Was insufficient to support the pair;
> And they would perish rather than would bear
> The law's stern slavery, and the insolent stare
> With which law loves to rend the poor man's soul. [9]

The political and anti-religious poems intended for the volume can most simply be classified as general and specific. The specific poems, i.e. those arising from some specific event or occasion, we have already noted: *To the Republicans of North America* (enclosed in a letter to Elizabeth Hitchener from Dublin on February 14, 1812); *On Robert Emmet's Tomb;* and the two sonnets on launching the bottles and balloon in Devon.[10] The poems developing these themes in their more general aspects are eight in number: (a) *Falsehood and Vice:* a dialogue in which Falsehood and Vice argue, in a heightened, immature style reminiscent of the poem *War* in the *Margaret Nicholson* volume, as to which has brought the more misery to the age; (inserted in the Notes to *Queen Mab*); (b) *The Tombs:* known only by Dowden's description; apparently dealing with the theme, treated also in *On Robert Emmet's Tomb,* of the immortality of the "courage and charity and truth" of dead revolutionists; (c) *A Sabbath Walk:* apparently, from Dowden's brief comment, mainly anti-religious; the poet walks away "from the church and church-goers" to speculate, in contrast, on "the man sincerely good" devoted every day to "deeds of living love"; (d) a translation of *The Marseillaise:* one stanza of which was included in a letter to Graham in the summer of 1811; (e) *To Liberty:* a lyric apparently centering around the theme common in Shelley's poetry from *The Revolt of Islam* to *Hellas,* of the American republic as the beacon of revolutionary hope in the world; (f) *The Wandering Jew's Soliloquy:* a restatement of the Eternal Venger theme of the early poem but in more mature verse; (g) *A Retrospect of Times of Old:* "a rhymed piece . . . which pictures the fall of empires, and celebrates the oblivion that has overtaken the old rulers of men and lords of the earth"; (h) *The Crisis:* the poet gazes into the future expecting in the darkest midnight of doubt and fear a sudden dayspring:

> Then may we hope the consummating hour,
> Dreadfully, sweetly, swiftly is arriving,
> When light from darkness, peace from desolation,
>   Bursts unresisted.

These last three pieces, we may note, treat themes also treated in *Queen Mab,* the first of them probably indebted to Peacock's *Palmyra* and Volney's *Ruins.*[11]

The personal poems may most conveniently be divided into those dealing either in whole or in part, with Harriet, and those on other topics. Of the latter, the best is a lyric on death—untitled—which Shelley later included in the *Alastor* volume. It shows a depth of personalized emotion and a technical smoothness above any that had yet appeared in his verse, a genuine foreshadowing of future greatness in the lyric:

> This world is the nurse of all we know,
>   This world is the mother of all we feel,
> And the coming of death is a fearful blow
>   To a brain unencompassed with nerves of steel;
> When all that we know, or feel, or see,
> Shall pass like an unreal mystery.[12]

In addition to this lyric we have a sonnet written on the occasion of going from Devon to Wales (a few lines of which Dowden printed), and a longer poem *On Leaving London for Wales,* probably written in November, 1812, after personal contact with Godwin and his pacifistic radicalism:

> I am the friend of the unfriended poor,—
> Let me not madly stain their righteous cause in gore.[13]

In July, 1811, Shelley, we remember, had stayed with his relatives, the Groves at Cwm Elan, Rhayader in Wales. On his return there with Harriet in June, 1812, following his Irish trip, he composed a narrative poem, 154 lines in length, *The Retrospect: Cwm Elan,* in which he contrasted the unhappiness of his previous visit without Harriet to the happiness of his present one with her. On the previous visit—and the anticipation of the *Alastor* hero is unmistakable—[14] a "ceaseless flame" "preyed" on his "withered vitals" and he used to stretch his "languid frame" "Beneath the wild-woods' gloomiest shade." He was still brooding melodramatically over his rejection by Harriet Grove:

> Yes! whilst the faithful bosom swelled,
> Then the envenomed arrow came.

His family and friends were cold and unresponsive either emotionally or intellectually, absorbed in the artificial values of a governing social caste:

> But they might shine in courtly glare,
> Attract the rabble's cheapest stare,
> And might command where'er they move
> A thing that bears the name of love.

But now, with Harriet by his side, "how changed" (l. 118 ff.) is his situation:

> Thou fair in form, and pure in mind,
> Whose ardent friendship rivets fast
> The flowery band our fates that bind.

The poem, in spite of occasional awkwardness, as in the inversion in the final line above, exhibits a sustained technical proficiency that he had not previously exhibited. Traces of the younger Milton and of Wordsworth are present, but the blatant echoing, in the early verse, from Moore, Monk Lewis, and Scott has disappeared, and one can see the beginnings of that personalized narrative style that later grew to perfection in *Julian and Maddalo* or the *Letter to Maria Gisborne*. One can see also the germs of that penchant for morbid self-dramatization that became an inevitable accompaniment of the personal poems, and, in the final years, was to mark (and mar) *Adonais* and *Epipsychidion*.

It was probably a few months later, in Lynmouth, that Shelley penned his most extended tribute to Harriet, a poem of seventy-two lines:

>   Oh thou
> Whose dear love gleamed upon the gloomy path
> Which this lone spirit travelled, drear and cold . . .
>   I would give
> The longest and the happiest day that fate
> Has marked on my existence but to feel
> *One* soul-reviving kiss . . .
>
> Nor when some years have added judgement's store
> To all thy woman's sweetness, all the fire
> Which throbs in thine enthusiast heart; not then
> Shall holy friendship (for what other name
> May love like ours assume?) not even then
> Shall custom so corrupt, or the cold forms
> Of this desolate world so harden us,
> As when we think of the dear love that binds
> Our souls in soft communion . . .

At Lynmouth, too, on August 1 (1812), he penned the sonnet *To Harriet on her Birthday,* which, from Dowden's comments and the four lines of it he prints, deals with a similar theme:

> Still may thine heart with those pure thoughts o'erflow
> Which force from mine such quick and warm return.

The tribute, in both poems, is sincere and heart-felt, but it is not the expression of a passionate love or a love between equals. The emphasis upon "soft communion," "holy friendship," "pure thoughts"—as on the "pure in mind" in *The Retrospect*—indicates a union on a level of intellectual sentimentality; and the hope that the "woman's sweetness" may yet develop "wisdom's store" echoes the romantic condescension of the earlier plea to Elizabeth Hitchener to "assist me to mould a really noble soul into all that can make its nobleness useful and lovely." [15] But if Harriet is incapable of real intellectual companionship or a deeply passionate emotional response, Shelley is, for the male, peculiarly passive: "to feel *One* soul-reviving kiss"; or, again:

> will not thy glowing cheek,
> Glowing with soft suffusion, rest on mine,
> And breathe magnetic sweetness thro' the frame
> Of my corporeal nature . . .

Here, in 1812, is the attitude of *The Indian Serenade* or *Epipsychidion*. The parallel with *Epipsychidion*, indeed, is even more extensive (and ironic). Harriet, we learn from this poem of 1812, rescued Shelley from a "cold" and "gloomy path" to give him solace in "sweetness" and "soft communion"; from *Epipsychidion* and the Dedication to *The Revolt of Islam*, we learn that he was similarly later rescued from "hard hearts and cold" (Harriet and Eliza) by a wise Moon-lady (Mary), who gave him intellectual companionship, but who, in turn, was found to be "cold" and his life with her "a wintry wilderness of thorns." [16] The search for a woman who would bring passionate warmth to him (never, primarily, him to her) continued throughout his life.

Three final poems to Harriet were to be included in the volume, a sonnet, dated July 31, 1813, and, hence, written at Bracknell, a sonnet to Ianthe, dated September, 1813, and some dedicatory verses. The Bracknell sonnet hints at some minor domestic discord; Harriet is compared to the sun whose "spots" are present but of little significance compared to its overall beauty; one should no more single them out than attempt to "Pick flaws in our close-woven happiness." *To Ianthe* is a sentimental tribute, not so much to Ianthe as to Harriet; he loves the child most when she reminds him "of her Who bore thy weight beneath her spotless bosom." The Dedication, originally intended for this volume, was transferred to *Queen Mab*, even to the retention of a reference to "these early wilding flowers," which fits the intended volume but not *Queen Mab*. [17]

QUEEN MAB

On December 11, 1811, Shelley wrote to Elizabeth Hitchener, that he had "last night" got an idea for a major poem: "I intend it to be by anticipation a picture of the manners, simplicity, and delights of a perfect state of society, tho' still earthly."[18] At the same time he was working on his intended volume of "minor poems"[19] and this work pushed the larger project to one side. "My poems," he wrote again, in answer to Elizabeth Hitchener's queries, on January 2, 1812, "will make their appearance as soon as I can find a printer. As to *the* poem, I have for the present postponed its execution."[20] In Ireland it was apparently pushed aside again, this time by the press of political activities, for he tells Elizabeth Hitchener no more of "*the* poem" in his letters from there, as he almost certainly would had he been engaged on it. We next hear of it in a letter from Devon to Thomas Hookham on August 17, 1812:

I enclose also by way of specimen all that I have written of a little poem begun since my arrival in England. I conceive I have matter enough for 6 more cantos. You will perceive that I have not attempted to temper my constitutional enthusiasm in that Poem. Indeed, a Poem is safe: the iron-souled Attorney general would scarcely dare to attack

"genus irritabile vatum."

The Past, the Present, and the Future are the grand and comprehensive topics of this Poem. I have not yet half exhausted the second of them.[21]

In October, when he went from Wales to London, Shelley took a manuscript of the poem with him and consulted with Godwin on it, Godwin noting, with typical exactitude, on October 31, that he had read forty-four pages.[22] On February 19, 1813, Shelley informed Hookham that "Queen Mab is finished and transcribed," but he did not actually send it to him until the middle of March, and it was not in the press until May.[23]

Thus *Queen Mab* was not begun, as Medwin absurdly stated, in 1809;[24] nor was it written, as Shelley himself later claimed, "at the age of eighteen,"[25] nor is there any evidence for the suggestion that it embodied extensive earlier material (the evidence, in fact, is in the opposite direction).[26] Shelley did not even conceive of the idea for *Queen Mab* until December 10, 1811, and his statement that he did not begin it until after his return to England in April, 1812, is supported by the lack of reference to it in Ireland; by the middle of August he had four or five cantos completed and there is indication that these were later revised; [27] general revision, in fact, was possible as late as May, 1813. The conclusion indicated by all available facts is that Shelley did not, as he truthfully informed Hookham, begin *Queen Mab* until after his arrival in England (in April), that he did not insert earlier material in it, and that he worked hard on it, revising and polishing it over a period of many months. *Queen Mab,* therefore, was not, contrary to the widely circulated belief, a post-adolescent product, either in whole or in part. Shelley, when he wrote it, had considerable political and literary experience behind him. He had published two novels and two books of poems, a tract on atheism, a tract on vegetarianism, two political pamphlets, and the *Letter to Lord Ellenborough,* and had written, but not published, a third volume of poems, a series of "moral and metaphysical essays" and a political novel.[28] He had read widely in many fields and had had contact with a political movement for national emancipation. *Queen Mab* is the summation of this development. In his previous works of a socio-literary character, he had always had some specific purpose in mind: dietary reform; freedom of speech; the repeal of the Act of Union; Catholic emancipation; the establishment of an organization of Irish radical intellectuals; and in treating these subjects he had perforce developed something of his more general view but this had, in no case, been his main object. In *Queen Mab,* it was his main object, for *Queen Mab* he intended as the embodiment of his world view, his concept of the relation of man to society and society to nature, an object which he later attempted also in *The Revolt of Islam* and *Prometheus Unbound.*

The materials that went into the making of *Queen Mab* were many and varied. It was, in its essence, a poem of the England of 1812, as typical as the speeches of Burdett or the articles of Cobbett. Its overall political theory drew upon Godwin, Paine, Condorcet, and Volney; its metaphysics combined concepts from the skepticism of Hume, the materialism of Holbach, the dualism of Pope, the idealism of William Drummond; its science was compounded from many sources including (in verse) Pope and Erasmus Darwin; its literary style was influenced by Southey, Campbell, and Milton. Yet the influence is never simple or mechanical. Shelley nowhere follows blindly, but accepts and rejects in accordance with his own general view. He accepts (in the Notes) Hume's illustrations of Necessity but rejects his nihilistic skepticism; he accepts Monboddo's concept of a new age but rejects the deteriorationist theory on which the coming of this age was based; he accepts Pope's picture of the Newtonian universe but rejects his religious interpretation of it. Only occasionally can one pin down a definite influence on a passage; for although certain main lines of thought can be traced, the end product, as it appears in the poem, is usually a blend from many sources, encyclopedia articles on "light" or "man" mixing with Cabanis and Laplace,[29] political views rising as easily from a reaction to a current *Examiner* as to *Political Justice*.

"*Queen Mab*," Bernard Shaw once remarked, "is a perfectly original poem on a great subject. Throughout the whole poem Shelley shows a remarkable grasp of facts, anticipating the modern view that sociological problems are being slowly worked out independently of the conscious interference of man."[30] And, in the deepest sense, *Queen Mab* is original. In spite of the wide reading behind it, it is not a bookish poem but a poem arising from life, the reaction of a mind sharpened by shattering experience to the social realities of the world around it, and transmitting material in the crucible of this experience. It is the bitter and angry cry of a young revolutionary, its visionary penetration that of a man rising on the wave of a titanic historical struggle to see deep and far, farther and deeper in essentials than many later and more particularized thinkers.

The detractors of the poem have complained that its ideas are outmoded and its style immature.[31] Some of its ideas—especially those emanating from the naturist theory—are certainly absurd, but, on the whole, it is representative of the most advanced school of social thought of the age, and, many of the attacks on it, although the attackers seem unaware of this, are not so much attacks on Shelley as on this school (deriving from the French and American Revolutions and the English radical movement). Many of the views of its leading thinkers, Paine and Jefferson, Diderot and Holbach, Godwin and Cobbett, are, it is true, outmoded today, for they were the product of the conflict of a revolutionary commercial capitalism against a feudal reaction (a conflict whose roots, we might note, were recognized at the time: "There has been a continued war in the constitution of *England* between two jarring principles; the evil principle of the feudal system with his dark auxiliaries, ignorance and false philosophy; and the good principle of increasing commerce, with her liberal allies, true learning and sound reason.")[32] And this conflict has long passed into history. But many of the aspects of its evils—economic exploitation, religious intolerance, prostitution, political dictatorship, war—are still very much with us, albeit not always in exactly the same forms; and the views of these thinkers have a greater relevance—even though re-evaluations in terms of modern perspectives are frequently necessary—to many of these questions today than is often recognized. And Shelley was essentially part of this school, for even though, like Byron and Burdett, he feared the cultural crudity of the middle class, and thought of his ultimate society largely in rural Utopian terms, he hated feudalism from its foundations, and the wellsprings of his thinking arose from the social forces which this class had stirred up in its massive struggle for power.

That the style of the poem has some weaknesses of immaturity is undeniable and inevitable. Shelley is, at times, unable to sustain a passage when sustained power is needed, and the emotion, starting with vigor, sometimes thins to brittleness. Other passages lose the effect of suggestion through prosaic directness and over-elaboration. But the degree of one's sensitivity to these faults depends largely on one's reaction to the content. The unsympathetic reader, failing to enter into the spirit of the poem, will see mainly faults; the sympathetic reader, catching something of its impassioned flow—"horror and scorn and hate and fear and indignation"—will find passage after passage of power and beauty. *Queen Mab* is a revolutionary poem, not a parlor poem, and must be evaluated in terms of its own genre and not of some other. Those looking in it for the ironic gentility or super-sensory insinuation elevated in some critical circles today to the status of absolutes, will look in vain.

Shelley's general plan for the poem, stated in the letter to Hookham already quoted, is to give a picture of past historical development and a survey of the present, and, on the basis of the social analysis contained in them, to predict the future. These objectives are repeated in the poem itself. Canto I and the first ninety-six lines of Canto II are introductory and relate the descent of Queen Mab, queen of the fairies, in a magic car drawn by "celestial coursers," to the bedside of a sleeping girl, Ianthe, whose spirit she transports through space to receive the vision of the world in its development:

> Spirit, come!
> This is thine high reward:—the past shall rise;
> Thou shalt behold the present; I will teach
> The secrets of the future.

The remaining 161 lines of Canto II contain a brief picture of the past—emphasizing dead civilizations—and the poem hastens on to its main section, the present, Cantos III–VII; III, dealing with the evils of monarchy; IV, with political tyranny; V, with economic corruption;

VI and VII, with religion. The final cantos, VIII and IX, present the vision of the future, and Ianthe's spirit is returned to earth with the adjuration to work in the present to help to secure the perfectibilian future she has beheld. For this plan Shelley was indebted to Condorcet and Volney. Condorcet summarized the purpose of his *Historical View of the Progress of the Human Mind,* as follows: "From these observations on what man has hitherto been, and what he is at present, we shall be led to the means of securing and accelerating the still further progress, of which, from his nature, we may indulge the hope . . . the progress of this perfectibility, henceforth above the control of every power that would impede it, has no other limit than the duration of the globe upon which nature has placed us." [33] And the various chapters of the book depict the advance of man through the past, in the present, and into the future.

The indebtedness to Volney is more specific. *The Ruins* of Count Constantin François Volney (like Condorcet, an intellectual leader in the French Revolution) [34] became one of the revolutionary handbooks of the age. Medwin informs us that Shelley became acquainted with the work shortly after his expulsion from Oxford, and Hogg relates that it was a favorite of Harriet's on the honeymoon trip in Edinburgh a few months later.[35] In 1817 Shelley derived from it the main political concept of *The Revolt of Islam* and based many scenes and passages upon it.[36]

At the opening of *The Ruins,* the narrator is standing in gloom amid the ruins of Palmyra when a Genius in flowing white robes appears and "wafts" him "to the regions above." "Thence, from the aerial heights, looking down on the earth, I perceived a scene altogether new. Under my feet, floating in the void, a globe like that of the moon, but less large and less luminous, presented to me one of its phases . . . He touched my eyes; and immediately they became piercing as those of an eagle . . ." [37] He is then granted a vision of past civilizations and the ascent of mankind; and, next, a view of the present, with its injustice, oppression, and wars (whose armies look like "swarms of moving creatures, which like ants or grasshoppers disturbed by the foot of a passenger, agitated themselves with vivacity").[38] This vision reduces the narrator to despair: "Since there is no choice but to be the accomplice or the victim of oppression, what remains to the man of virtue but to mingle his ashes with those of the tomb?" The Genius decides to cheer him up by showing him the future: "The past is perhaps too discouraging; let us then disclose to the eye of virtue the astonishing age that is ready to begin; that on viewing the object she desires, she may be animated with a new ardour, and redouble her efforts to attain it." [39] The Genius then discloses to him a great revolution "in one of the nations of Europe," followed by a General Assembly of all the nations of the world. At this assembly—presided over by a wise Lawgiver—all religions are called to present their arguments; all are attacked and allowed noisily to cancel each other out; at the conclusion, mankind, freed from superstition, prepares to usher in a great new age.

Shelley, although adopting Volney's general plan and taking over suggestions from the attack on religion, omits the vision of the revolution—to use it five years later in *The Revolt of Islam*—and of the concourse of nations; and he rejects the concept of the Genius and the narrator for that of the fairy queen and Ianthe. For this he was indebted to the opening of Sir William Jones's *Palace of Fortune,* in which the girl Maia sees "a goddess gliding in a golden car. . . . By two fair yokes of starry peacocks drawn." The goddess is Fortune, who shows to Maia a vision of the world—"At distance hung the dusky globe surveyed." The goddess informs her:

> To me has fate the pleasing task assign'd
> To rule the various thoughts of humankind.[40]

Queen Mab similarly tells Ianthe:

> to me is given
> The wonders of the human world to keep,
> And Fancy's thin creations to endow
> With manner, being, and reality

The framework of *Queen Mab* clearly came from a blending of Volney and Jones (with minor suggestions from other sources).[41] The stylistic form is derived from the free blank verse technique of Southey's long narrative poems, especially *Thalaba,* as can be seen at a glance by comparing the opening of *Thalaba*—

> How beautiful is night!
> A dewy freshness fills the silent air;
> No mist obscures, nor cloud, nor speck, nor stain
> Breaks the serene of heaven:
> In full-orbed glory yonder Moon divine
> Rolls through the dark blue depths—

with the opening of *Queen Mab*—

> How wonderful is Death,
> Death and his brother Sleep!
> One, pale as yonder waning moon
> With lips of lurid blue.

"The didactic," Shelley informed Hogg as he was writing the poem, "is in blank heroic verse, and the descriptive in blank lyrical measure. If an authority is of any weight in support of this singularity, Milton's 'Samson Agonistes,' the Greek Choruses, and (you will laugh) Southey's 'Thalaba' may be adduced." [42] (It is interesting to note in passing that three of the main influences on *Queen Mab* came from three men with whom Shelley had had personal contact in 1812, Southey, Godwin, and Newton.) One of Shelley's objects in thus using the measure that Southey had made famous and in beginning his poem as though it were to be a typical Southey narrative—complete with the magic element of a fairy queen, a spirit, and a trip through the stars in a celestial chariot—was, doubtless, to ease his readers by degrees into the radical propaganda which forms the core of the poem.

The main interest of this early section is in the scientific and pseudo-scientific concepts which it presents. The journey through space, although at times censurable for the false "sparkle and glittering" that Godwin complained of in the style,[43] shows a more scientific and imaginative comprehension of the universe than do most such accounts (for instance, in Jones or Volney), and reveals, too, a sense of the universe as flow and beauty absent from the usual Newtonian picture (as in Pope's *Essay on Man,* or Darwin's *Temple of Nature,* or such standard accounts of the time as those in Rees' *Cyclopædia*).[44] The degree to which Shelley rises above his sources cannot be better illustrated than by comparing Darwin's mechanical representation of the Temple of Nature [45] (which was doubtless Shelley's direct model)—

> Here, high in the air, unconscious of the storm
> Thy temple, NATURE, rears its mystic form;
> From earth to heav'n, unwrought by mortal toil,
> Towers the vast fabric on the desert soil—

with Shelley's sense of cosmic grandeur—

> Spirit of Nature! here!
> In this interminable wilderness
> Of worlds, at whose immensity

> Even soaring fancy staggers,
> Here is thy fitting temple. . . .
> The flood of ages combatting below,
> The depth of the unbounded universe
> Above, and all around
> Nature's unchanging harmony.

Shelley did not conceive of this vast universe of suns and constellations as separate from man and the earth. The early nineteenth-century thinkers, taking over the "vast chain of being" concept from the eighteenth—where it received its most influential literary expression in Pope—looked on all matter, animate and inanimate, as a unity, from the smallest atoms to the remotest stars, from microbes to man, a unity, however, animated by Divine Spirit. Shelley took over the chain-of-being concept but rejected the Divine Spirit. From the "countless and unending orbs" of the universe to "those living things, To whom the fragile blade of grass . . . is an unbounded world" to man, all is part of nature and pervaded by her spirit:

> Man, like these passive things,
> Thy will unconsciously fulfilleth.

The concept of microbes, as Marjorie Nicolson has shown us, was extremely popular throughout the eighteenth century, the poets taking over where Leeuwenhoek and Spallanzani (whose works Shelley sent for) [46] left off. Shelley here is directly indebted to Pope—

> Mark how it mounts, to Man's imperial race,
> From the green myriads in the peopled grass—

and perhaps to Thomson, with whose *Seasons* he was acquainted.[47] It was perhaps in Pope, also, that he first found the concept so dominant in his poem of the all-pervading quality of life—"All matter quick and bursting into birth" [48]—and he would have found it more scientifically presented in Monboddo and Sir William Drummond, whose *Academical Questions* had so deep an influence upon him.[49] The concept is then elaborated into the eccentric theory of both microbes and atoms as part of a highly organized living matter:

> I tell thee that those viewless beings,
> Whose mansion is the smallest particle
> Of the impassive atmosphere,
> Think, feel and live like man.

> Every grain
> Is sentient both in unity and part,
> And the minutest atom comprehends
> A world of love and hatreds.

This view, as applied to microbes, was current in the eighteenth century. "The microscope," wrote Henry Baker, "discovers almost every Drop of Water, every Blade of Grass, every Leaf, Flower, and Grain swarming with Inhabitants; all of which enjoy not only life but happiness. . . ." [50] The extension of the concept to include atoms can be found in Monboddo, [51] and it was perhaps from a combination of Monboddo and Drummond that Shelley developed the animated universe theory. "Monads," Drummond explains, in his account of Leibnitz, "are the atoms of nature, and the elements of things." Each one is a "living mirror" of the universe. In a mass of monads, one becomes central and this "central monad becomes a soul, and makes with its surrounding monads, an individual organized body, or living animal." [52]

In this introductory section Shelley is setting his perspective. "Man," wrote Laplace, summarizing the most advanced scientific view of the time, "now appears, upon his small planet almost imperceptible in the vast extent of the solar system, itself only an insensible point in the immensity of space." [53] And it is in the light of this mighty vista that Shelley views the drama of the development and fate of man. His stage is the universe. Man is viewed, not metaphysically (as in Goethe), or theologically (as in Milton), but in relation to the realities of existence as science has disclosed them. Nor do these realities make man seem to him, as they do to Laplace, less significant. The universe may be immense but the power of man is limitless; its vastness is not alien to man, for both are part of the same life force, each responsive to the other. Throughout the action Shelley is aware of his setting, and the concluding cantos swing the cycle back to it once more.

When the scene descends next to the earth itself and to man's history upon it, Shelley's view is that of the catastrophic evolution of Erasmus, Darwin, Cuvier, and James Parkinson. "The formation of the exterior part of the globe and the creation of its various inhabitants," wrote Parkinson, "must have been the work of a vast length of time, and must have been effected at several distant periods." At one of these periods had come a great upheaval, corresponding to the Biblical flood, which was the cause of many geological phenomena (for example, the formation of coal from uprooted forests). The world, once an "Elysium," had been "desolated, and rendered one vast mass of seeming ruin . . . torn up and carried away by the force of the tremendous torrent, the trees of the mountains . . . laid on those of the valleys, and . . . together buried by the subsequent subversion of the mountains themselves." [54] In Darwin, Shelley doubtless had encountered the theory—in which Erasmus anticipates to some degree, as Samuel Butler argues, his illustrious grandson—that "all vegetables and animals now existing were originally derived from the smallest microscopic ones, formed by spontaneous vitality," and these by "innumerable reproductions, during innumerable centuries of time, gradually acquired the size, strength and excellence of form and faculties, which they now possess." [55] But one must not make the mistake of thinking—and in the face of the brilliance of their speculations, it is deceptively easy to do so—that these early evolutionists had the perspectives of present-day science on relative geological and historical time sequences or that they had a truly developmental theory of evolution. And so, too, with Shelley. It is often surprising to see the degree to which he anticipates modern scientific theory; but it is often startling also to see how radically different some of his concepts were. He had no concept of man having evolved from lesser species—perhaps, indeed, believing with Holbach, that man had, like the universe, existed from eternity—and he completely confuses geological and historical events, considering, for instance, the rise and fall of civilizations as concomitant with major changes in the earth's climate:

> And from the burning plains
> Where Libian monsters yell,
> From the most gloomy glens
> Of Greenland's sunless clime,
> To where the golden fields
> Of fertile England spread
> Their harvest to the day,
> Thou canst not find one spot
> Whereon no city stood.[56]

Or, as he wrote to Elizabeth Hitchener from Keswick:

Imagination is resistlessly compelled to look back upon the myriad ages whose silent change placed them [mountains] here; to look back when perhaps this retirement of peace and mountain-simplicity was the Pandemonium of druidical imposture, the scene of Roman Pollution, the resting-place of the savage denizen of these solitudes with the wolf.—Still, still further. Strain thy reverted Fancy when no rocks, no lakes, no cloud-soaring mountains, were here; but a vast, populous and licentious city stood in the midst of an immense plain, myriads flocked toward it, London itself scarcely exceeds it in the variety, the extensiveness of consummateness of its corruption! [57]

Within the range of known history, however, one can trace the rise and decline of many civilizations:

> Behold, the Fairy cried
> Palmyra's ruined palaces! . . .
>
> There once old Salem's haughty fane
> Reared high to Heaven its thousand golden domes,
> And in the blushing face of day
> Exposed its shameful glory.
> Oh! many a widow, many an orphan cursed
> The building of that fane; and many a father,
> Worn out with toil and slavery, implored
> The poor man's God to sweep it from the earth,
> And spare his children the detested task
> Of piling stone on stone, and poisoning
> The choicest days of life,
> To soothe a dotard's vanity.
> There an inhuman and uncultured race
> Howled hideous praises to their Demon-God.

The influence of Volney (and Peacock, whose *Palmyra* Shelley admired) [58] is obvious; but while Volney and Peacock place the emphasis nostalgically on the moldering of ruins, Shelley places it upon the exploitation of man. Nor does he miss an opportunity to stress his favorite theme of the barbarity of the ancient Jews ("Salem's haughty fane" is Solomon's temple) from whom sprang the Jehovah concept of God.

Having thus briefly dismissed the Past as a period of exploitation and primitive superstition, Shelley moves into the central section of the poem, the Present, Cantos III–VII. The section opens with a vigorous denunciation of the first of the quadruple evils of the age—monarchy:

> The King, the wearer of a gilded chain
> That binds his soul to abjectness, the fool
> Whom courtiers nickname monarch.

And, along with monarchy, the twin evil of aristocracy:

> Those gilded flies
> That, basking in the sunshine of a court,
> Fatten on its corruption! What are they?
> —The drones of the community; they feed
> On the mechanic's labour: the starved hind
> For them compels the stubborn glebe to yield
> Its unshared harvests; and yon squalid form,
> Leaner than fleshless misery, that wastes
> A sunless life in the unwholesome mine,
> Drags out in labour a protracted death,
> To glut their grandeur; many faint with toil,
> That few may know the cares and woe of sloth.

From these have arisen the desolating horrors of war and domestic oppression:

> Stern is the tyrant's mandate, red the gaze
> That flashes desolation, strong the arm
> That scatters multitudes.

In opposition is, as in Volney,[59] "the virtuous man"—and Shelley is doubtless thinking of Eaton and the Hunts—who

> stands amid the silent dungeon-depths
> More free and fearless than the trembling judge.

All this, we may note, was extremely dangerous material, for, in spite of its protective coloring of generalization, its specific and seditious application to the Regent and the Lords would be unmistakable. The ultimate literary influence is that of Paine's militant republicanism (excerpts from whose works Shelley had intended to publish in Ireland and in whom he expressed a special interest while writing *Queen Mab*),[60] but the real spirit of the passage comes from the life-struggles of the day—the castigation of the exploitation of the worker, for instance, doubtless arising from Shelley's indignation at the oppression of the Luddites (which he perhaps has specifically in mind in "the arm That scatters multitudes"). Those who have criticized the sentiments in such passages as excessive, with the implication that they were unique to Shelley, forget that in an age of war and revolution they were common enough, not only in the political battlers, such as Paine and Cobbett, but in the writers as well, Byron, Hazlitt, Hunt, Coleridge, and Southey, the latter two equally polemical on both sides. Here, we might recall *Wat Tyler,* that drama of Southey's youth which he had probably shown to Shelley at Keswick:

> who should pay for
> the luxuries and riots of the court?
> Who should support the flaunting courtier's pride,
> Pay for their midnight revels, their rich garments,
> Did not the state enforce? [61]

The Canto develops also a favorite theme of the age, the antithesis of society and nature—

> Yon sun
> Lights it the great alone? . . .
>
> - Is mother earth
> A step-dame to her numerous sons, who earn
> Her unshared gifts with unremitting toil?

In poetry the thought may be paralleled in Campbell—

> Nature stamped us in a heavenly mould!
> She bade no wretch his thankless labour urge—

or, again, in *Wat Tyler*—

> They sell you with their land, claim all the fruits
> Which the kindly earth produces, as their own—

and, in its broader implications, it is inherent in the nature philosophy of Wordsworth and the religious humanitarianism of Coleridge.[62]

Canto IV opens with a vivid depiction of the burning of Moscow, (the first news of the Russian disaster, as we noted, reached London during Shelley's stay there in the late fall of 1812)—"Black ashes note where their proud city stood"—and Napoleon's subsequent decimating retreat.[63] The spirit, seeing the horror of death and wide-spread desolation, trembles for the iniquity of man; but the Fairy answers—as would Rousseau or Paine or Godwin—that not man but the dictatorial state which has perverted man is responsible:

> Man's evil nature, that apology
> Which kings who rule, and cowards who crouch, set up
> For their unnumbered crimes, sheds not the blood
> Which desolates the discord-wasted land.
> From kings, and priests and statesmen, war arose,
> Whose safety is man's deep unbettered woe,
> Whose grandeur his debasement.

The dictatorial state does not rule by simple force; it corrupts human
nature from childhood on (a favorite theme with Mary Wollstonecraft
and Godwin), breeding militaristic and brutal patterns of behavior:

> The child
> Ere he can lisp his mother's sacred name,
> Swells with unnatural pride of crime, and lifts
> His baby-sword even in a hero's mood.[64]

When the child grows to be a man he is "cajoled with gold, And
promises of fame" into the army (the theme of *A Tale of Society as
it is*). To protect this infamous system, the ruling caste employs special
bands of armed men—"the hired bravos who defend The tyrant's
throne—the bullies of his fear"—and the whole state structure is preserved by befuddling the minds of the people, from infancy on, with
the lulling perversions of religious superstition. The Canto concludes
with what is in effect an excoriation of the Prince Regent—"Look to
thyself, priest, conqueror, or prince!"—as violent, even though less
direct, as that of Hunt, which, in part, it seems to echo—

> thy lusts
> Deep wallow in the earnings of the poor. . . .
> thou dost load
> With cowardice and crime the groaning land.

In a letter to Elizabeth Hitchener in August, 1811, Shelley had given
his views on the relationship of aristocratic dictatorship to commercial
monopoly: both control wealth and use it for exploitation; "both are
flagrant encroachments on liberty"; both must be eliminated before
progress is possible; "neither can be used as an antidote for the poison
of the other." [65] Having treated the former in Canto IV he proceeds
to the latter in Canto V:

> Hence commerce springs, the venal interchange
> Of all that human art or nature yield.

The attack, which follows, on commercial wealth as the source of economic inequality and exploitation, imperialism and war, and the psychological distortion of the individual is one of the most powerful in
the poem. Vast wealth in the hands of a few, poverty for the many, is
the law of the existing system, and its curse lights not only on the many
but on the few also. Both are "poisoned body and soul," the wealthy
suffer from "full-fed disease" (*A Vindication of Natural Diet*), the

poor from "pining famine" (a favorite theme in Pratt's *Cottage Pictures*);[66] both are psychologically corrupted, and the whole given theoretical justification by the prevailing Adam Smith doctrines of benign imperialism:

> The harmony and happiness of man
> Yields to the wealth of nations . . .
> The weight that drags to earth his towering hopes,
> Blighting all prospects but of selfish gain,
> Withering all passion but of slavish fear.

The middle class, too, suffers from this general corruption of society; their sons, too, can be dragged off to war, their wives driven insane; but they do not see the full horror of the system; they can be confused by the "cold sophistry" of the ruling class. The "poor man," on the other hand, does not suffer intermittently but continuously; the hunger of his children is ever with him and their "pale mother's uncomplaining gaze"; he "wakens but to fruitless toil" and "the heart-breaking scene of thousands like himself," poverty and misery akin to that which Shelley had witnessed in Ireland and Wales and, doubtless, in Edinburgh and in London also. The worker, unlike the middle class "man of ease," is not deceived by "the vain and bitter mockery of words":

> Feeling the horror of the tyrant's deeds,
> And unrestrained but by the arm of power,
> That knows and dreads his enmity.

The new industrialism had brought with it the class war of Luddite riots and the barrack system. But even more tragic is the stifling of the creative potential of the mass, both of country and town:

> How many a vulgar Cato has compelled
> His energies, no longer tameless then,
> To mould a pin or fabricate a nail!

"It is indescribably painful to contemplate beings capable of soaring to the heights of science, with Newton and Locke," Shelley had written to Godwin from Dublin, "without attempting to waken them from a state of lethargy so opposite."[67] The system has corrupted society from top to bottom, breeding hypocrisy, perverting every human instinct by the power of wealth, until the intellectual and moral world has degenerated to the status of a market:

> All things are sold . . . even life itself
> And the poor pittance which the law allows
> Of liberty, the fellowship of man,
> Those duties which his heart of human love
> Should urge him to perform instinctively,
> Are bought and sold as in a public mart
> Of undisguising selfishness, that sets
> On each its price, the stamp-mark of her reign.
> Even love is sold; the solace of all woe
> Is turned to deadliest agony . . .

An age of war and dictatorship, of exploitation and corruption, of crime and vice and prostitution, of the warping of the human spirit, of slums and poverty, cold hypocrisy and violent hatreds, such is the picture in these cantos, and, in its essence, it is a true picture. If at times the language, in its revolutionary bluntness, short-circuits finer aesthetic transmutations, its cascading sincerity gives it a rugged intensity of power unique in English poetry. In spite of the higher harmonies and soaring visionariness of *Prometheus Unbound, Queen Mab,* dealing with the same theme, cannot simply be regarded as a juvenile precursor. It is a great poem in its own right.

Shelley's twin objects in the "present" section of the poem, as he implied to Hogg, were "cosmopolitical" and "anti-Christian." [68] Cantos III–V are the "cosmopolitical" cantos, VI and VII the "anti-Christian," the central attack on Christianity occurring in Canto VII. Canto VI, mainly devoted to an exposition of the doctrine of Necessity, contains some of the best philosophical poetry since the *Essay on Man,* and, is, at times, worthy to rank with its ultimate model, the *De Rerum Natura.* The main ideological influence is not, as is frequently supposed, Godwin, but—as a glance at Shelley's notes to line 171 will suffice to show—Holbach's *Le Système de la Nature,* even the key phrase "Necessity! thou mother of the world," coming directly from a footnote in Holbach's book. [69] Shelley, however, differs from Holbach—whose theories I shall discuss further in connection with *A Refutation of Deism*—in one major respect. To Holbach the laws of Necessity are the same as the laws of nature, and arise from the very fact of motion, which is itself a quality of matter. Shelley, however, departs from this strict materialism in his dualistic conception of Necessity as a spiritual force pervading matter but not identical with it. But he does not conceive of this force as creative and hence denies that it can be considered a Deity; in fact he is always at pains to deny creation and to insist on the eternity of all things, both spirit and matter.[70] As he succinctly expressed it in his Notes: "*'There is no God!'* This negation must be understood solely to affect a creative Deity. The hypothesis of a pervading spirit coeternal with the universe, remains unshaken." [71] The origin of this dualistic concept was perhaps that passage in the *Essay on Man* that Shelley so greatly and so early admired ("something more than Poetry; it has ever been my favourite theory"):

> All are but parts of one stupendous whole
> Whose body Nature is, and God the soul;
> That, changed thro' all, and yet in all the same;
> Great in the earth as in th' ethereal frame;
> Warms in the sun, refreshes in the breeze,
> Glows in the stars, and blossoms in the trees,
> Lives thro' all life, extends through all extent,
> Spreads undivided, operates unspent;
> Breathes in our soul, informs our mortal part,
> As full, as perfect, in a hair as heart.[72]

Thus, though Shelley follows, in fact (as his Note reveals), almost paraphrases Holbach in his insistence on the rigid mechanism of natural law, both in nature—

> No atom of this turbulence fulfills
> A vague and unnecessitated task
> Or acts but as it must and ought to act—

and in society—

>   nor less
> When merciless ambition, or mad zeal,
> Has led two hosts of dupes to battle-field—

he conceives of this law as acting through spirit upon matter and upon the human mind. It is not, however, a spirit that can in any way be appealed to by man, for it is not a sentient spirit, but—like the God of Spinoza—a blind, ineluctable force:

> all that the wide world contains
> Are but thy passive instruments, and thou
> Regardst them with an impartial eye
> Whose joy or pain thy nature cannot feel,
>   Because thou art not human sense,
>   Because thou art not human mind.

And in the Notes he adds a long, sarcastic passage on the inefficacy of prayer.[73] Of the two substances, the spiritual and the material, however, Shelley clearly considers the spiritual as predominant. In fact, as we have seen, he refuses to admit the existence of dead matter at all, accepting the monadic rather than the atomic theory. And this is what he has in mind in the following passage:

> Throughout this varied and eternal world
> Soul is the only element: the block
> That for uncounted ages has remained
> The moveless pillar of a mountain's weight
> Is active, living spirit.

The passage is not, as it is frequently taken to be, an exposition of Berkeleian idealism, for Shelley like Pope, or Leibnitz, is positing the existence of both matter and spirit, albeit a matter permeated with and responsive to spirit. "Immateriality," he had written to Godwin in July, 1812, "seems to me nothing but a simple denial of the presence of matter, of the presence of all the forms of being with which our senses are acquainted, and it is surely somewhat inconsistent to assign real existence to what is a mere negation of all that actual world to which our senses introduce us." [74] And he agreed with Godwin—as critics of his later poems have not always noted—that the question of materialism, idealism, or dualism is irrelevant to the workings of Necessity.[75] The laws of Necessity operate no matter in what medium one conceives of them as existing. There is no inconsistency in his reasoning on these points. The following passage, however, is undeniably inconsistent:

> Hath Nature's soul,
> That formed this world so beautiful, that spread
> Earth's lap with plenty . . .

"Nature's soul," is identical with Necessity—"Soul of the Universe!"—and identical also with the non-creative, coeternal spirit. But it is clear that a non-creative spirit cannot have "formed" the world. The unconscious lapse into the attractive images of Platonic idealism is interesting as showing that Shelley's mind was already (perhaps under Godwin's influence) moving in this direction, but he was not at this period a Platonist.

The Canto closes with a powerful image of the life-force omnipresent and resurgent:

> And life, in multitudinous shapes,
> Still pressing forward where no term can be,
> Like hungry and unresting flame
> Curls round the eternal columns of its strength.

Shelley may have been indebted to the materialism of Holbach and the dualism of Pope but both are transcended by and blended into his own deep vision of life as development and eternal power.

Canto VII opens with a scene of the burning of an atheist, for which Shelley was probably indebted to a similar scene in Volney,[76] and then goes on to the further development of the argument inherent in the treatment of Necessity that "infinity within, infinity without, belie creation," i.e. no final cause can be found either in space or within matter:

> Let every part depending on the chain
> That links it to the whole, point to the hand
> That grasps its term!

(Again, we might note the dependence on Pope—"Vast chain of Being . . . from infinite to thee, From thee to Nothing"—with the typical omission of Pope's [contradictory] "which from God began.") [77] Shelley's reasoning—both here and in the preceding arguments—is made clearer in a passage to Elizabeth Hitchener on his theological discussions with Southey at Keswick:

I have lately had some conversation with Southey which has elicited my true opinions of God. He says I ought not to call myself an atheist, since in reality I believe that the universe is God. I tell him I believe that God is another signification of the Universe. I then explain:—I think reason and analogy seem to countenance the opinion that life is infinite; that as the soul which now animates this frame was once the vivifying principle of the *infinitely* lowest link in the Chain of existence, so is it ultimately destined to attain the highest . . . that everything is animation (as explained in my last letter); and in consequence being infinite we can never arrive at its termination. How, on this hypothesis, are we to arrive at a first cause?— Southey admits and believes this.—Can he be a Christian? Can God be Three? Southey agrees in my idea of Deity, the mass of infinite *intelligence* . . . I, you, and he, are constituent parts of this immeasurable whole. What is now to be thought of Jesus Christ's divinity? To me it appears clear as day that it is the falsehood of human-kind.[78]

The theological doctrines of Christianity, he is arguing in the conclusion, if seen in the perspectives of an infinite and eternal universe, dwindle to absurdity. "The indefinite immensity of the universe," he comments in a Note, "is a most awful subject of contemplation. . . . It is impossible to believe that the Spirit that pervades this infinite machine begat a son upon the body of a Jewish woman." [79] So, too, in the poem:

> The exterminable spirit it [the universe] contains
> Is nature's only God; but human pride
> Is skilful to invent most serious names
> To hide its ignorance.

If this were all, however, Shelley would—as he once told Elizabeth Hitchener [80]—have little objection. The trouble is not that man has invented God but that he has used the invention as an excuse for bigotry, persecution, crime, and war: "The name of God has fenced about all crime with holiness." And the attack that follows on the history of religion—"Seeva, Buddh, Foh, Jehovah, God, or Lord"—is a condensation from Volney's similar but extended treatment.[81] Shelley, however, is not aroused mainly by a contemplation of the religious atrocities of the past but of the present:

> And priests dare babble of a God of peace,
> Even whilst their hands are red with guiltless blood,
> Murdering the while, uprooting every germ
> Of truth, exterminating, spoiling all,
> Making the earth a slaughter-house! [82]

It is a contemplation of twenty years of war and oppression being sanctified by the church that stirs him to a fury of indignation as it had previously stirred Campbell:

> Trade, wealth, and fashion, ask you still to bleed,
> And holy men give Scripture for the deed.[83]

Following the excoriation of religion, Mab calls up the spirit of Ahasuerus, the Wandering Jew, to deliver a special broadside on Christian history and doctrine. The only point we need note at present—for the subject is better handled in *A Refutation of Deism*—is the attitude to Christ. In *A Letter to Lord Ellenborough,* Christ is presented as a "meek reformer . . . immolated to the sanguinary Deity of the Jews." [84] And in the Notes to *Queen Mab* the same attitude— essentially that of Paine—is present. Shelley, however, adds a footnote to the Note: "Since writing this note, I have some reason to suspect that Jesus was an ambitious man, who aspired to the throne of Judea." [85]

And the attitude in the poem, contrasting both with Shelley's attitude in the immediate past and in the future (e.g. *An Essay on Christianity, Prometheus Unbound, Hellas*), is sardonic and hostile. Christ is not a "meek reformer" but a "parish demagogue" followed by the "rabble of his native town." He, himself, and not later churchmen perverting his doctrine, as Shelley usually contended, inculcated ideas of bloodshed and persecution; his soul is "malignant." The reason for this reversion to the anti-Christ violences of the early letters to Hogg—"Let this horrid Galilean rule the canaille" [86]—is not clear, but it may be that Shelley had been recently reading, or re-reading, the most famous work of this character, Holbach's *Histoire Critique de Jésus-Christ*.[87] Holbach hints that Christ had ambitions to the throne, and in general treats him in a spirit of debunking cynicism, as "a juggler, a charlatan, a dangerous impostor" from the lower classes: "a company so numerous as that of the idlers he dragged in his suite." [88]

The final movement of the poem, the society of the future and its development, begins with Canto VIII:

> The present and the past thou hast beheld:
> It was a desolate sight. Now Spirit, learn
> The secrets of the future.

The state of society depicted is that of Godwin's ultimate egalitarian state in which mind had achieved "omnipotence" over matter and man has become immortal (a concept to be found also in Condorcet):

The sum of the arguments which have been here offered, amounts to a species of presumption, that the term of human life may be prolonged and that by the immediate operation of intellect, beyond any limits which we are able to assign.[89]

> And man, once fleeting o'er the transient scene
> Swift as an unremembered vision, stands
> Immortal upon earth . . .

> While every shape and mode of matter lends
> Its force to the omnipotence of mind.

This change has come about as a result of the workings of Necessity in the social realm, workings whose first stages Shelley elucidated in a fragmentary essay on parliamentary reform:

The distribution of wealth, no less than the spirit by which it is upheld and that by which it is assailed, render the event inevitable. Call it reform or revolution, as you will, a change must take place; one of the consequences of which will be, the wresting of political power from those who are at present the depositories of it.

The progress of this Necessitarian advance through successive stages to egalitarianism he latter developed in *A Philosophical View of Reform:* "Equality of possessions must be the last result of the utmost refinement of civilization." [90] On this egalitarian economic structure would rest a libertarian, indeed, anarchist state, and in the resulting high social order, man, aided by science—"happiness and science dawn, though late upon the earth"—would become psychologically and morally transformed.

The vision is similar to that in *An Address to the Irish People,* with, however, one important exception: not only is society changed, nature is changed also:

> The habitable earth is full of bliss;
> Those wastes of frozen billows that were hurled
> By everlasting snow-storm round the poles . . .
>   are unloosed;
> And the fragrant zephyrs there from spicy isles
> Ruffle the placid ocean deep.

The "deserts of immeasurable sands" have been converted into fertile land; the oceans have been spangled with islands; storms have disappeared from the face of the earth; "fruits are ever ripe, flowers ever fair." Shelley is here, in part, thinking of that transformation of the world by the aid of a highly developed science on which he had expatiated to Hogg at Oxford: "by chemical agency the philosopher . . . may transmute an unfruitful region into a land of exuberant plenty." Further transformation would come about through the control of electricity (then in its infancy): "how many of the secrets of nature would such a stupendous force unlock." [91]

That in these concepts Shelley was on sound ground has been revealed by the direction of science since his time; but this transformation made by man he conceived of as being assisted by a strange natural phenomenon:

> How sweet a scene will earth become!
> Of purest spirits a pure dwelling-place,
> Symphonious with the planetary spheres;
> When man, with changeless Nature coalescing,
> Will undertake regeneration's work,
> When its ungenial poles no longer point
>   To the red and baleful sun
>   That faintly twinkles there.

To this he adds in a note:

The north polar star, to which the axis of the earth, in its present state of obliquity, points. It is exceedingly probable, from many considerations, that this obliquity will gradually diminish, until the equator coincides with the ecliptic: the nights and days will then become equal on the earth throughout the year, and probably the seasons also.

I find the theory noted in Robert Grant's *History of Physical Astronomy:* "An interesting question arises: will the obliquity continually diminish until the equator and ecliptic coincide? If this should happen, the sun will daily attain the same meridional altitude as at the equinoxes, and an eternal spring reign over the whole earth." [92] The belief that such a condition had previously existed apparently went back at least to Herodotus, and Shelley may have encountered it in *Paradise Lost:*

> Some say he bid his Angels turne ascanse
> The Poles of the Earth twice ten degrees and more
> From the Suns Axle.

The further theory that such a condition would prevail in the future he had doubtless early encountered in the lectures of Adam Walker:

Must not the solar impulse [i.e. light particles], therefore, be greater in summer on the northern hemisphere, than on the southern? and, in winter, greater on the southern, than on the northern hemisphere? and thus force the earth's axis progressively more and more towards a perpendicular (as is well known to be the case), and produce the precession of the equinoxes? . . . Must not these irregularities alter the position of the earth's axis, and make it recede farther and farther from its direction to the polar star . . . ? [93]

The decision to champion the theory in *Queen Mab,* however, perhaps came from his talks with Newton in London in the fall of 1812. Newton presents it in *The Return to Nature:*

It is an astronomical fact that which can not be easily disputed, that the poles of the earth were at some distant period perpendicular to its orbit, as those of the planet Jupiter are now, whose inhabitants must therefore enjoy a perpetual spring.

It was a tenet of the most ancient priests of whom we have any knowledge, the Brachmans, that still, by some portentous bursting forth of the Earth's bowels, a second change will be accomplished, which shall bring back equal seasons and perpetual spring. [94]

It was after his return from London to Wales in 1812 that Shelley
added a note to a letter to Hookham: "You would very much oblige
me if you would collect all possible documents on the Precession of the
Equinoxes, as also anything that may throw light upon the question
of whether or no the Position of the Earth on its poles is not yearly
becoming less oblique?" [95] One of the volumes that Hookham probably sent was Laplace's *Le Système du Monde* with its chapter "Of the
Precession of the Equinoxes, and of the Mutation of the Axis of the
Earth," in which Laplace demonstrates conclusively that there is no
constant diminution of obliquity but merely an oscillation, which
before perpendicularity (the earth weaving back and forth like a
large spinning top) could possibly be reached, would begin a return
movement (a process occupying about 26,000 years). This view Shelley
repudiates in the Notes, arguing that geological discoveries indicate
past periods of very different climatic conditions (which, in a limited
sense, is true, but which is no repudiation, as such conditions, i.e. the
ice age, could be accounted for equally well on the basis of oscillation). [96] The view put forward by Laplace was, moreover, by Shelley's
time generally accepted (see, for instance, Nicholson's *British Encyclopedia,* "Equinox") and the older view was clearly exposed as un-
scientific. Shelley is therefore, in this instance, running counter to the
science of his time in order to support a theory which he finds aesthet-
ically and politically attractive.

In Canto VIII, we are given the picture of a society already transformed; in IX, Shelley represents the development of society towards
that transformation. He is not, in this picture, any more than he is in
Prometheus Unbound, either making an expository analysis of social
stages—for this the reader may turn to his political pamphlets—or,
some commentators to the contrary, depicting a miracle. Behind the
impressionistic picture lies the theories of social development which
we have already examined, but the treatment, in a creative medium,
is necessarily impressionistic and symbolic. Let us take, for instance,
the following passage on the beginning of the change:

> First, Crime triumphant o'er all hope careered
> Unblushing, undisguising, bold and strong;
> Whilst Falsehood, tricked in Virtue's attributes,
> Long sanctified all deeds of vice and woe,
> Till done by her own venomous sting to death,
> She left the moral world without a law,
> No longer fettering Passion's fearless wing,

Nor searing Reason with the brand of God.
Then steadily the happy ferment worked;
Reason was free; and wild though Passion went
Through tangled glens and wood-embosomed meads,
Gathering a garland of the strangest flowers,
Yet like the bee returning to her queen,
She bound the sweetest on her sister's brow,
Who meek and sober kissed the sportive child,
No longer trembling at the broken rod.

In the first lines Shelley is giving an impressionistic picture of his own age, an age marked by such "crime" as war and oppression, and ideologically dominated by the "falsehood" which justifies them (especially in the name of religion; the theme is duplicated in "Vice and Falsehood"). The "steady" working of the "happy ferment" which finally set "reason" free must be taken to embrace a long period of social upheavals and advances. The conclusion is a symbolic representation of the blending of reason and emotion (especially love) as the new society develops; all harmful repressions vanish with the psychological transformation of man.

In the early stages of the new order, man is not "immortal upon earth" but "the slow necessity of death" has become "mild," and the "human frame" free from "The deadly germs of languor and disease" (both "naturist" conceptions perhaps emanating from Monboddo, who informs us that in a state of Nature death is "rather sleep than death" and disease and idleness non-existent).[97] The great mass of disease, which Shelley considered as resulting from unnatural diet and living conditions and believed to be inheritable, slowly vanishes; and along with it prostitution and venereal disease:

No longer prostitution's venomed bane
Poisoned the springs of happiness and life.

Along with the physical and moral change goes social change. Palaces, prisons, and churches are abandoned:

The ponderous chains, and gratings of strong iron,
There rusted amid heaps of broken stone
That mingled slowly with their native earth.

Shelley, however, does not, as we have noted, end his poem with this vision of the future. His object in writing it was not aesthetic but agitational; not simply to impress with the horrors of the present or the beauties of the future, but—as with Volney or Condorcet also—to

inspire men to act. Hence in the conclusion he moves the scene back
through time again and strikes, as a final note, the urgency of social
struggle in the present:

> My spells are passed: the present now recurs.
> Ah me! a pathless wilderness remains
> Yet unsubdued by man's reclaiming hand.

> Yet, human Spirit, bravely hold thy course,
> Let virtue teach thee firmly to pursue
> The gradual paths of an aspiring change.[98]

> . . . bravely bearing on, thy will
> Is destined an eternal war to wage
> With tyranny and falsehood, and uproot
> The germs of misery from the human heart.

THE NOTES TO *QUEEN MAB*

To consider the Notes to *Queen Mab* as a mere adjunct to the poem
is to underestimate their significance, for although they express the
same philosophy as the poem, they constitute a separate expression of
it. The poem gives a predominately creative expression, the Notes an
expository one, and the two, supplementing and blending with one
another, are intended to form a unity.

The Notes are seventeen in number, eleven of them fairly short and
usually presenting explanatory material for the text, six of them longer
and rather separate essays than genuine notes: one on the labor theory
of value; one on free love and marriage; one on Necessity; two on
anti-religious subjects, and one on vegetarianism. The first of the anti-
religious notes consists mainly of a reprint of *The Necessity of Atheism,*
and a long quotation from Holbach; the material in the second is
largely duplicated in the *Necessity, A Letter to Lord Ellenborough,* and
A Refutation of Deism. The note on vegetarianism is, I have already
indicated, a reprint of *A Vindication of Natural Diet.*[99] In these six
notes Shelley presents the core of his radical philosophy, in economics,
politics, religion, and morals. They are, however, more directly derivative than is the poem—owing especially to Godwin and Holbach—
and even some of those not previously printed were, almost certainly,
in part, of earlier origin, three of them probably containing material
from the original "moral and metaphysical essays." The material in the
note on vegetarianism and the first anti-religious note, we have already
treated; most of the arguments in the second anti-religious note not
yet encountered will appear in *A Refutation of Deism.* We are thus

left with three of the main notes: on the labor theory of value; on free love and marriage; on Necessity.[100]

The central arguments of the note on the labor theory of value (in its pre-Marxian form, deriving ultimately from Adam Smith) are to be found in Godwin, partly in *Political Justice* and partly in *The Enquirer*. The opening paragraph is based on *The Enquirer* essay "Of Avarice and Profusion":

There is no wealth in the world except this, the labour of man. What is misnamed wealth, is merely a power vested in certain individuals by the institutions of society, to compel others to labour for their benefit. . . . Every new luxury is a new weight thrown into the scale. The poor are scarcely ever benefited by this. It adds a certain portion to the mass of their labour; but it adds nothing to their conveniences. Their wages are not changed. They are paid no more for the work of ten hours, than before for the work of eight. They support the burden but they come in for no share of the fruit.[101]

So, too, in Shelley:

There is no real wealth but the labour of man. Were the mountains of gold and the valleys of silver, the world would not be one grain of corn the richer; no one comfort would be added to the human race. . . . The poor are set to labour,—for what? Not for the food for which they famish; not for the blankets for want of which their babes are frozen by the cold of their miserable hovels . . . no . . . for the false pleasures of the hundredth part of society . . . employments are lucrative in an inverse ratio to their usefulness . . .

"I will not," he continues, echoing the sentiments of his letters to Elizabeth Hitchener in the summer of 1811, "insult common sense by insisting on the doctrine of the natural equality of man. The question is not concerning its desirableness but its practicability; so far as it is practicable it is desirable. That state of human society which approaches nearer to an equal partition of its benefits should, *caeteris paribus,* be preferred." [102] Again the source is in Godwin's comments on "a state of cultivated equality": "Without entering into the question whether such a state can be realized to its utmost extent, we may venture to pronounce that mode of society best, which most nearly approaches this state." [103] Shelley concludes that only in such a state can all people have sufficient leisure for the development of the mind and personality; so too in Godwin (this time in *Political Justice*).[104] Shelley's essay gives the impression of being an attempt to restate Godwin, perhaps made in the first flush of enthusiastic awakening to the significance of his doctrine in 1811; [105] but his language is more vigorous than that of his model, and his feeling deeper for the miseries of the poor.

The note, or, rather, essay on marriage derives from the free love and feminist literature which was then popular in advanced intellectual circles and which laid the basis for that freer expression of sexual problems that later came to fruition in the works of such writers as Edward Carpenter and Havelock Ellis. Its direct sources are three: Godwin, Mary Wollstonecraft, and Sir James Lawrence, with overtures on chastity and Christianity from Gibbon.

Shelley opens with a recapitulation of his 1811 arguments to Hogg and Elizabeth Hitchener and (on Harriet) to Southey concerning the anomaly of setting legal restraints on what is essentially a personal relationship: "A husband and wife ought to continue so long united as they love each other; any law which should bind them to cohabitation for one moment after the decay of their affection, would be a most intolerable tyranny, and the most unworthy of toleration." [106] The next paragraph, as a note informs us, is partly indebted to Gibbon's masterly satire on the celibacy of the early church fathers: "The narrow and unenlightened morality of the Christian religion is an aggravation of these evils." [107] "Love," Shelley continues, again echoing his comments of the previous year, "is free: to promise for ever to love the same woman, is not less absurd than to promise to believe the same creed." A union continuing longer than love results in "a state of incurable bickering and hostility"; worse, it ruins the lives of the children: "The early education of the children takes its colour from the squabbles of the parents: they are nursed in a systematic school of ill humour, violence and falsehood." One further result of this system, whereby a man is tied to a woman for whom he no longer has affection, is prostitution: "Prostitution is the legitimate offspring of marriage and its accompanying errors." Prostitution is, thus, the product of the social system; instead, however, of condemning the system, society condemns the prostitute: "Society declares war against her, pitiless and eternal war; she must be the tame slave, she must make no reprisals; theirs is the right of persecution, hers the duty of endurance." Another reason for the existence of prostitution is the enforcing of chastity on women before marriage, and this in turn—by sending men to prostitutes—coarsens the male sensibilities and spreads venereal disease (to successive generations). [108]

Such, then, are the evils which spring from the existing system of rigid chastity before marriage and an unbreakable legal union after marriage. If this system were abolished what would result? Would people immediately turn to an orgy of unabated promiscuity? Shelley does not believe so:

I conceive that from the abolition of marriage the fit and natural arrangement of sexual connection would result. I by no means assert that the intercourse would be promiscuous; on the contrary it appears from the relation of parent to child that this union is generally of long duration, and marked above all others with generosity and self-devotion.

Again a main source is in Godwin, the celebrated free love passage in the first edition of *Political Justice* (the argument is subdued in the later editions):

It is absurd to expect that the inclinations and wishes of two human beings should coincide through any long period of time. To oblige them to act and to live together, is to subject them to some inevitable portion of thwarting, bickering and unhappiness. . . . The institution of marriage is a system of fraud. . . . We ought to dismiss our mistake as soon as it is detected; but we are taught to cherish it. We ought to be incessant in our search after virtue and worth; but we are taught to check our inquiry, and shut our eyes upon the most attractive and admirable objects. Marriage is law, and the worst of all laws . . . an affair of property and the worst of all properties. . . . So long as I seek to engross one woman to myself, and to prohibit my neighbour from proving his superior desert and reaping the fruits of it, I am guilty of the most odious of all monopolies. . . . The abolition of marriage will be attended with no evils. We are apt to represent it to ourselves, as the harbinger of brutal lust and depravity. But it really happens, in this, as in other cases that the positive laws which are made to restrain our vices, irritate and multiply them . . .

And in the second edition he added:

It is a question of some moment whether the intercourse of the sexes in a reasonable state of society will be wholly promiscuous, or whether each man will select for himself a partner, to whom he will adhere, as long as that adherence shall continue to be the choice of both parties. The general probability seems to be in favour of the latter . . . inconstancy, like any other temporary dereliction, would not be found incompatible with a character of uncommon excellence. What at present renders it in many instances peculiarly loathsome, is its being practiced in a clandestine manner.[109]

Shelley's debt to Lawrence and Mary Wollstonecraft he acknowledges in a letter to Lawrence on August 17, 1812:

Your "Empire of the Nairs," which I read this Spring, succeeded in making me a perfect convert to its doctrines. I then retained no doubts of the evils of marriage,—Mrs. Wollstonecraft reasons too well for that; but I had been dull enough not to perceive the greatest argument against it, until developed in the "Nairs," viz., prostitution both *legal* and *illegal*. . . . I need not say how much I admire *"Love"*. . . .[110]

Mary Wollstonecraft's attitude is very different from Godwin's (or Lawrence's). She sees sexual and marriage questions in the perspectives of a general republican philosophy: "From the respect paid to property flow, as from a poisoned fountain, most of the evils and vices which render this world such a dreary scene. . . . One class presses on another . . ."[111] In a society thus based on competition and domination, it is but to be expected that these characteristics should control also the relations of the sexes. Men refuse to give women political or social rights, and treat them with the artificial and insulting condescensions of "chivalry," while in practice regarding them essentially as sexual instruments:

Riches and hereditary honours have made cyphers of women to give consequence to the numerical figure; and idleness has produced a mixture of gallantry and despotism in society, which leads the very men who are the slaves of their mistresses to tyrannize over their sisters, wives and daughters. Strengthen the female mind by enlarging it, and there will be an end to blind obedience; but as blind obedience is ever fought for by power, tyrants and sensualists are in the right when they endeavour to keep women in the dark, because the former only want slaves and the latter a plaything. The sensualist, indeed has been the most dangerous of tyrants . . .[112]

As a result, a "state of warfare . . . subsists between the sexes." In this war some women are driven to clandestine affairs, others to prostitution:

Still, highly as I respect marriage, as the foundation of almost every social virtue, I cannot avoid feeling the most lively compassion for those unfortunate females who are broken off from society, and by one error torn from all those affections and relationships that improve the heart and mind. It does not frequently even deserve the name of error; for many innocent girls become the dupes of a sincere, affectionate heart, and still more are, as it may emphatically be termed, *ruined* before they know the difference between virtue and vice:—and thus prepared by their education for infamy, they become infamous.

"When a man seduces a woman . . . the man should be *legally* obliged to maintain the woman and her children."[113]

Mary Wollstonecraft, although attacking the evils of marriage and protesting against the suppression of women, is not an advocate of free love, and is strong in her denunciations of sensuality. If one feels at times that this latter implies also an aversion to physical passion in love, this is more than compensated for by her healthy insistence on the primacy of reproduction and responsibility for off-spring.

Sir James Lawrence published in 1811 a free love novel called *The Empire of the Nairs,* based on the customs of the Nayars in southern India (which the curious may find detailed in Westermarck).[114] The book opens with an essay on free love, which contains a vigorous attack on marriage and an equally vigorous advocacy of co-education and the rights of women. The novel itself is a long, rambling affair—told with interminable flash-backs—dealing in the main with the adventures of an Englishman called De Grey. Early in the book De Grey meets a Nair lady, the Countess of Malabar, whose daughter shocks him by unconcernedly skimming off her garments in his presence and diving into the water to swim in the nude.[115] Later he is surprised at a dance to see that each man and woman goes off to bed with whoever happens to be his or her dancing partner of the moment.[116] Lawrence is trying to shock by developing an atmosphere of lurid sensuousness. His view of women—in contrast to Mary Wollstonecraft's women-are-human-beings attitude—is that of romantic idealization; and something of this Shelley shared and—*vide Epipsychidion*—never quite lost even though he merged it with his larger social view.

The second work of Lawrence to which Shelley refers, "Love: an Allegory," is a narrative poem attacking religion for having engendered false notions of chastity and advocating free love. In Part One, named "Paradise," Love rules on the earth (the primitive Rousseauistic state); Jupiter decides to send Religion to earth as his Regent with Reason as her assistant. In Part Two, "Paradise Lost," Superstition joins Religion, banishes Reason, and makes Love "a prisoner of State" under the charge of Hymen (marriage). Love "contrived to break her chain" and escaped, but not "knowing where to hide her head" she is forced to join the vices (i.e. physical love is regarded with moral disapprobation). Hymen, in the meantime, reluctant to admit that Love is no longer under his care, displays a number of evils and calls them Love (marriage today subsists on hypocrisy and falsehood). In Part Three, "Paradise Regained," the ultimate defeat of "False Chastity and Superstition" is foretold. Then Hymen—

> . . . would fling away his lock and key
> And keep an Inn, but not a jail.

Love would return and "False Chastity would feel her glory at an end."[117]

Such are the elements out of which Shelley's essay is compounded. The attack on marriage in the first paragraph and the conclusion that its abolition would result in a new monogamy based on free choice, derive from Godwin, with overtones from Lawrence; the analysis of prostitution as a social evil, the emphasis on the warping of the child, and the abhorrence of sensualism and gallantry, owe to Mary Wollstonecraft; the diatribe on chastity, the linking of religion with repression and marriage with prostitution, have direct roots in Lawrence. Shelley, weaving all three into a consistent position and writing with the vigor of personal conviction, has produced the most incisive free love argument of his time. And, let us note, it is a genuine free love argument (as was Godwin's and Lawrence's), not, as some critics have stated, simply a plea for the modification of existing marriage and divorce laws (which is what Godwin's later arguments tend to become).[118] It is not, on the other hand, an advocacy of promiscuity. Shelley's abhorrence of sexual relations without love is as vigorous as anything in Mary Wollstonecraft, and, was, as we have previously noted, a life-long conviction. His statement of the free love creed is also happily free of the graceless innuendoes and stolid unpassion of Godwin. In spite of his overall theoretical view, however, he still maintained the position he had previously stated to Elizabeth Hitchener— that individual defiance of law was ineffective.[119] Thus, in his letter to Lawrence (in reference to Lawrence's allegory of Love in jail), he mentions that although he has been married for a year, "Love seems inclined to stay in the prison, and my only reason for putting him in chains, whilst convinced of the unholiness of the act, was a knowledge that in the present state of society, if love is not thus villainously treated, she, who is most loved, will be treated worse by a misjudging world."[120] But while he was ready to make this concession to society, he was prepared to go no further, and was deeply convinced of the immorality of two people continuing to live together without mutual love.

The note on Necessity is essentially a re-statement from Godwin and Hume, the influence from Hume doubtless stemming from Shelley's reading at Oxford, where, Hogg informed us, Hume was one of his favorite authors.[121] Although Shelley is, in some passages, directly indebted to Hume, sometimes quoting him, sometimes paraphrasing, in others the indebtedness is mixed, for Godwin himself was greatly influenced by Hume (the section "Of Liberty and Necessity" in the *Enquiry Concerning Human Understanding*).[122]

Shelley begins by insisting that Necessity is a force acting not only in the physical universe but in society and the human mind: "Whilst none have scrupled to admit necessity as influencing matter, many have disputed its dominion over mind," a point emphasized by Godwin.[123] The influence over matter he had exemplified in the preceding note in an excerpt from Holbach; this note he devotes almost entirely to its effect on human action:

He who asserts the doctrine of Necessity means that, contemplating the events which compose the moral and material universe, he beholds only an immense and uninterrupted chain of causes and effects, no one of which could occupy any other place than it does occupy, or act in any other place than it does act.

The contrary of this doctrine—i.e. the doctrine of the freedom of the will—is manifestly incorrect, for, unless we posit necessity as underlying action, psychology, history, and everyday life become an unintelligible chaos:

Were the doctrine of Necessity false, the human mind would no longer be a legitimate object of science; from like causes it would be in vain that we should expect like effects; the strongest motive would no longer be paramount over the conduct; all knowledge would be vague and undeterminate; we could not predict with any certainty that we might not meet as an enemy to-morrow him with whom we have parted in friendship to-night.

"The advocates of free-will," he continues, "assert that the will has the power of refusing to be determined by the strongest motives . . . But it is equally certain that a man cannot resist the strongest motive, as that he cannot overcome a physical impossibility." Godwin develops the point further, arguing that while it is true that one has a feeling that each individual act is self-determined, one has only to realize that each act is itself part of a chain of preceding acts to realize that the feeling is a delusion:

The ultimate act resulted completely from the determination that was its precursor. It was itself necessary; and, if we look for freedom, it must be to that preceding act. But in that preceding act also, if the mind were free, it was self-determined, that is, this volition was chosen by a preceding volition, and, by the same reasoning, this also by another antecedent to itself. . . . Trace back the chain as far as you please, every act at which you arrive is necessary.[124]

The application of the doctrine of Necessity to society will, Shelley next argues, "introduce a great change into the established notion of morals." The essence of his argument here is that once one realizes that crime arises from sociological necessity it is vain to pass moral judgments on the criminal or to inflict punishment aggravated by moral indignation beyond the point needed for correction. The argument is summarized from Godwin's long and careful analysis of the nature of punishment, e.g.:

Punishment is also often used to signify, the voluntary infliction of evil upon a vicious being, not merely because the public advantage demands it, but because there is apprehended to be a certain fitness and propriety in the nature of things, that render suffering, abstractedly from the benefit to result, the suitable concomitant of vice.

The justice of punishment however, in this import of the word, can only be a deduction from the hypothesis of free-will, if indeed that hypothesis will sufficiently support it; and must be false, if human actions are necessary. Mind, as was sufficiently apparent when we treated of that subject, is an agent, in no other sense than matter is an agent. It operates and is operated upon, and the nature, the force and line of direction of the first, is exactly in proportion to the nature, force and line of direction of the second . . . the only measure of equity is utility, and whatever is not attended with any beneficial purpose, is not just.[125]

The doctrine of Necessity, Shelley continues, not only modifies our concepts of justice and morality, it also "destroys religion," for it explains all the phenomena of the "moral and material universe" in rationalistic terms: "The doctrine of Necessity teaches us, that in no case could any event have happened otherwise than it did happen, and that, if God is the author of good, he is also the author of evil." In this final section—which foreshadows Asia's questioning of Demogorgon— Shelley breaks away from Godwin, who is careful not to disclose the anti-religious implications of his doctrines in *Political Justice*.[126]

The ridiculing of the doctrine of Necessity has been so long practiced by Shelley's critics that the fact of its "absurdity" has by now become sanctified into a kind of dogma. It is time, therefore, to point out that the doctrine of Necessity was fundamental in establishing man's approach to the problems of social development on a scientific basis. As the late eighteenth-century thinkers saw it, there were two alternatives; either social and historical change took place simply because men willed it or took place in accordance with certain laws arising from the structural patterns of society, just as development in the physical world took place in accordance with certain laws arising out of its patterns. It is true that, in breaking with the free-will concept, the Necessitarians developed too-rigidly mechanistic a view and that they did not sufficiently perceive the essential difference between the nature of the laws of living and of dead matter (which is hardly surprising, in view of the low development of the biological and psychological sciences at the time); but the usual attack on them, namely that, if they conceived of future social change as inevitable, they were contravening their doctrine by at the same time advocating it, is irrelevant. They did not conceive of the laws of social development as automatically and directly producing change in society as the laws of nature did in nature, but as first, influencing human beings, who, in turn, would produce further change in the social system. The answer to the objection is inherent in Shelley's and Godwin's attack on the freedom of the will, namely, that they themselves, existing in society, were compelled to act in accordance with the "strongest motive" and that this motive was the renovation of society. "These great changes," Shelley told the Irish people, ". . . will certainly happen . . . but . . . it all depends upon yourselves how soon or how late."

Queen Mab, taken together with the Notes, constitutes the most revolutionary document of the age in England. Its forthright attacks on the existing systems of morality, religion, economics, and politics and its advocacy of fundamental change in every sphere is unmatched in any other single work even though one will find similar doctrines, in whole or in part, in Godwin, Robert Owen, Byron, Richard Carlile, and others. Nor was Shelley himself, although he was to write greater works, ever again to match its concentrated iconoclastic sweep. Indeed, in later years, he felt some doubt—although he never deviated from any of its social doctrines—as whether its directness of attack might not be used against the reform movement, and when in 1821 a pirated edition was planned he attempted to prevent it.[127] But *Queen Mab* could not be held back even by its author. Sponsored by such radicals as John Jacob Holyoake and Richard Carlile, enthusiastically circulated by the Owenites and the Chartists, it survived prosecution by the Society for the Suppression of Vice and a series of lawsuits, to emerge as one of the standard pieces of radical literature of the nineteenth century. As White summarizes:

From this moment [1821] Shelley's *Queen Mab* became an important weapon in the arsenal of British working-class radicalism. *John Bull's British Journal,* a radical weekly published by William Benbow, gave it a sympathetic review on March 11. *The London Magazine and Theatrical Inquisitor,* though only mildly radical, and not a working-man's magazine, reviewed it favourably in the March issue and prophesied that the author was meant to fulfil a high destiny. Within twenty years fourteen or more separate editions were issued by piratical radical publishers. The book took an honoured place with Volney's *Ruins of Empire,* Palmer's *Principles of Nature,* Byron's *Cain,* and works of Tom Paine in the radical "libraries" constantly offered for sale.

Between 1823 and 1841, White counted 140 items on Shelley (mainly on *Queen Mab*) in working-class or radical periodicals. In 1892, George Bernard Shaw was informed by an old Chartist that "Queen Mab was known as The Chartist's Bible," a sphere of influence commented upon also, he found, by Karl Marx; and it was similarly regarded by Robert Owen and his followers.[128]

A REFUTATION OF DEISM

A Refutation of Deism was published in 1814, Hogg thought at the "beginning of the year," and it was most probably written in the final months of 1813.[129] It has not been recognized as one of Shelley's major prose works because of its anti-religious subject matter; and Shelley's critics do not seem to know what to do about his anti-religious works except to apologize for them as evidence of youthful metaphysical dissipation.[130] It does not seem to have been recognized that anti-religious literature is a genre and that the evaluation of Shelley's anti-religious works is a legitimate problem. This evaluation can obviously be attempted only on the basis of some acquaintance with the genre and Shelley's relationship to it.

Following the classical skepticism of Lucretius and Pliny, the earliest writing to influence Shelley's religious thinking was that of Spinoza. Shelley's interest in Spinoza was lifelong, and he worked, off and on, for some years on a translation of the *Tractatus Theologico-Politicus.*[131] Spinoza opens, in his preface, with a vigorous attack on superstition as a tool of statecraft, an argument popular with most later freethinkers and early exhibited in Shelley:

But if, in despotic statecraft, the supreme and essential mystery be to hoodwink the subjects, and to mask the fear, which keeps them down, with the specious garb of religion, so that men may fight as bravely for slavery as for safety, and count it not shame but highest honour to risk their blood and their lives for the vainglory of a tyrant; yet in a free state no more mischievous expedient could be planned or attempted.[132]

He next goes on to attack, in turn, prophecy and miracles. Prophecy is summarily dismissed as the product of a vivid imagination. The repudiation of miracles grows inevitably from his concept of God and the universe as identical. In the *Tractatus,* this is expressed in a passage which was a favorite of Shelley's (for he quoted it in the Notes to *Queen Mab* and *A Refutation of Deism*): "Everything takes place by the power of God. Nature herself is the power of God under another name, and our ignorance of the power of God is co-extensive with our ignorance of Nature." [133] A miracle, then, would mean that God was acting "in contravention to the laws of nature," and, as the laws of nature and God are identical, one "would be compelled to assert that God acted against His own nature—an evident absurdity."

A second anti-religious philosopher who, as we have seen, had early been a favorite of Shelley, was David Hume. From Hume, Shelley took three main arguments. The first was that on causation (used in the *Queen Mab* Note on Necessity): [134] we cannot say that one event "causes" another, but only that we see two events succeeding each other in time; the concept of causation is purely subjective. This argument was used to refute the idea that there was a "first cause" for the universe. Hume's second argument was that the concept of a creator for the universe necessitated the assumption of a creator for the creator and, hence, an infinite regression. The third argument we have already noted, that in the *Essay on Miracles,* on the deception or self-deception of the beholders (used in *The Necessity of Atheism*).[135]

From Spinoza and Hume the freethought movement passed, via the English Deists [136]—especially the anti-Christian Thomas Woolston— to Voltaire and Montesquieu, the leaders of the French deistic movement, a movement which took on a strong anti-clerical tinge because of the political conservatism of the Church in France. Voltaire, however, in spite of the vigor of his attacks on Christianity, still held to a belief in a creative deity, a position ridiculed by the atheists, Diderot, D'Alembert, and Holbach, who formed the first important group of materialistic thinkers in modern history, carrying the Lucretian position to a new advance by utilizing the findings of the physical sciences for philosophical argumentation. Of the three, the role of leading propagandist was filled by Holbach, and it was mainly through Holbach that Shelley became acquainted with the thinking of the group.

Holbach produced, apparently in a kind of informal, verbal collaboration with Diderot, Naigeon and others, a series of vigorous, anti-religious works under various pseudonyms (Mirabaud, Boulanger, etc.): *Le Système de la Nature, Histoire Critique de Jésus-Christ, Le Bon Sens, Le Christianisme Dévoilé.* Of these the central work was *Le Système de la Nature,* a translation of which Shelley began in Devon in the summer of 1812.[137]

Le Système de la Nature is the most comprehensive exposition of the materialist creed of the eighteenth century. It falls into two parts, the first expounding a materialist philosophy of man and nature, the second attacking religion. In the first part Holbach presents four main premises: (a) "Man is the work of nature: he is submitted to her laws; he can not deliver himself from them; nor can he step beyond them even in thought"; (b) "The moral man is nothing more than this physical being considered under a certain point of view"; (c) "The only test of truth is experience"; (d) "The universe, that vast assemblage of everything that exists presents only matter and motion." [138]

Taking up the last of these ideas he states that there are two types of motion, visible motion, the motion of physical objects, and invisible motion, the motion of invisible units, as in fermentation and growth. One of these invisible, but nevertheless material, types of motion is thought. Mind is but a form of matter. Thus, all the phenomena in the universe, material and psychological, ultimately reduce to matter in motion. Furthermore, it is the nature of matter to be in motion; matter is not an inert substance needing the breath of God to set it in motion; the concept matter implies motion. The only power in the universe is the power of Necessity, and this is not a supernatural power but arises from the very nature of matter in motion:

This irresistible power, this universal necessity, this general energy, is then only a consequence of the nature of things, by virtue of which everything acts, without intermission of constant and immutable laws. . . . Nature is an active living whole, whose parts necessarily concur, and that without their own knowledge, to maintain activity, life and existence.[139]

The depth of Shelley's interest in this iron, materialist creed—even though he did not completely share it—is revealed by the lengthy quotations from *Le Système* in the Notes to *Queen Mab* and by his undertaking its translation. In *A Refutation of Deism,* he comments: "This book is one of the most eloquent vindications of Atheism." [140] He was, however, also acquainted with at least one other work by Holbach, *Le Bon Sens,* to which he refers in *A Refutation of Deism,*[141] and probably, also, as we have noted, with the *Histoire Critique de Jésus-Christ. Le Bon Sens* is mainly an attack on religion and duplicates to some extent the second part of *Le Système de la Nature.* A typical passage is that which Shelley paraphrases in *A Refutation of Deism:*

In all parts of the globe, intoxicated fanatics have been seen cutting each other's throats, lighting funeral piles . . . to give validity to the cheats of some impostors, in the name and behalf of a being, who exists only in their imagination, and who has made himself known only by the ravages, disputes, and follies he has caused upon earth.[142]

Holbach, as a political radical, does not fail to make one of the central points of his attack the tie-up of the church with political reaction, placing the argument more vigorously than Spinoza:

Tyranny ever was, and ever will be, the true cause of the corruption of morals, and the habitual calamities of men; who always fascinated with religious notions, and metaphysical fictions, instead of turning their eyes to the natural and obvious causes of their misery, attribute their vices to the imperfection of their nature, and their unhappiness to the anger of the gods.[143]

Following Holbach (and his disciple Volney, whose influence we have already noted), the anti-religious movement returned to England where its leading propagandist was Tom Paine whose *Age of Reason* became as much a Bible for freethinkers as his *Rights of Man* had become for political radicals. Among his most prominent followers in England were Daniel Isaac Eaton, Richard Carlile, editor of *The Republican,* and William Hone.[144] It is as part of this English freethought movement, stemming from Paine and the French materialists, that we have to view Shelley's atheism.

The chief merit of Paine's *Age of Reason* is, as always with Paine, its incisiveness and clarity. Paine is not a philosopher and was not much interested in the subtleties of metaphysical discussion. His main motive was a bitter opposition to the church as a conservative political instrument, and he directed his fire almost wholly at an exposition of the contradictions and fallacies of its doctrines. His function, therefore, was essentially a negative one; he did not feel, as did Holbach, any compulsion to set up a consistent materialist system to take the place of that he was attempting to destroy, but contented himself with reiterating the general creed of the deists.

Early in his work Paine launches into a witty attack on the contradictions of the general concept of Christian theology as based on the Bible, of which the following (probably early influencing Shelley) may be taken as typical:

The Christian Mythologists, after having confined Satan in a pit, were obliged to let him out again to bring on the sequel of the fable. He is then introduced into the Garden of Eden, in the shape of a snake or a serpent, and in that shape he enters into familiar conversation with Eve, who is no way surprised to hear a snake talk; and the issue of this tête à tête is that he persuades her to eat an apple, and the eating of that apple damns all mankind.

After giving Satan this triumph over the whole creation, one would have supposed that the Church Mythologists would have been kind enough to send him back again to the pit; or, if they had not done this, that they would have put a mountain upon him (for they say that their faith can remove a mountain), or have put him under a mountain, as the former mythologists had done, to prevent his getting again among the women and doing more mischief. But instead of this they leave him at large, without even obliging him to give his parole—the secret of which is that they could not do without him; and after being at the trouble of making him, they bribed him to stay. They promised him ALL the Jews, ALL the Turks by anticipation, nine-tenths of the world beside and Mahomet into the bargain. After this, who can doubt the bountifulness of the Christian Mythology? [145]

Satirical summaries, such as this, of the Adam and Eve story in conjunction with the New Testament were extremely popular in anti-religious literature. Holbach has one in *Le Christianisme Dévoilée*,[146] Volney has one [147]—more sophisticated than Paine's—and Shelley has four: in *Queen Mab;* in the Notes to *Queen Mab,* in *A Refutation of Deism,* and in his later (1821) essay *On the Devil, and Devils.*

In spite of this scoffing, however, Paine regarded Christ with veneration as a "virtuous reformer and revolutionist," a concept, as we have noted, taken over by Shelley,[148] and makes a distinction between this good founder of Christianity and the subsequent evils of the church. He makes fun of prophecies and miracles, using, in this latter connection, an example followed by Shelley in the *Mab* Notes:

The restoring of persons to life who are to appearance dead, as is practised upon drowned persons, would also be a miracle if it were not known that animation is capable of being suspended without being extinct.[149]

He feels, as did most deists, that the Bible stories of miracles were slanders upon the divine spirit of the universe: "It is degrading the Almighty into the character of a showman, playing tricks to amuse and make the people stare and wonder." [150] Some of the Bible stories, indeed, are not only degrading but obscene (a point also complained of by Shelley).[151]

But, with all his attacks on religion, Paine asserts his own belief in God and immortality: "I believe in one God and no more; and I hope for a happiness beyond this life." [152] He believes in "the pure and simple profession of Deism." [153] This faith, however, he does not attempt to prove in any detail but rests his belief in it on two points; (a) the necessity of there having been a "first cause"; (b) the fact that all the nations in the earth believe in the existence of God shows there must be a God.[154]

It was this apparent contradiction in the deist creed, this "damnable heresy from reason" which shocked Shelley on his first encounter with Leigh Hunt in the spring of 1811,[155] that inspired him to the composition of a work designed to show that if the deists pursued their arguments to logical conclusions they would inevitably arrive at atheism. "The object of the following dialogue" he states in his Preface, "is to prove that the system of Deism is untenable. It is attempted to show that there is no alternative between atheism and Christianity; that the evidences of the Being of a God are to be deducted from no other principles than those of Divine Revelation." [156] Neither deism nor Christian theology, he is going to demonstrate, can rest upon reason. And this he proceeds to do by the highly ingenious method of a dialogue in which one speaker, a deist, annihilates the arguments of Christian theology, while another, a Christian, annihilates those of deism (a device similar to that in Hume's *Dialogues Concerning Natural Religion*), his immediate inspiration perhaps coming from Drummond's deistical attack on atheism in *Academical Questions* which he assails in the Notes to *Queen Mab*.[157] The two thus cancel each other out and nothing is left but atheism or a Christianity based solely on faith and revelation. Although, Shelley, having in mind the possibilities of prosecution for blasphemy,[158] does not openly state as much, the obvious conclusion is that the only philosophy possible for a rational man is atheism.

As a result of this plan of presentation, the work falls into two distinct parts: the attack on Christianity by Theosophus, the deist, and the attack on deism by Eusebes, the Christian. These two parts are some-

what different in method and style and have different values. The first
is a typical, witty attack, using all the weapons traditionally sanctified
for the job of casting ridicule on the grosser forms of theological belief;
the second is a seriously reasoned, philosophical analysis of the weakness of the deistic position.

Before these main dialogues begin, Eusebes opens with what pur-
ports to be a defense of the Christian faith, but which, in reality, is
an ironical attack upon it (the style is reminiscent of Gibbon):

> I dare not think that the God in whom I trust for salvation would terrify
> his creatures with menaces of punishment, which he does not intend to
> inflict. The ingratitude of incredulity is, perhaps, the only sin to which the
> Almighty cannot extend his mercy without compromising his justice.[159]

Theosophus, in reply, launches into his anti-Christian speech. He
begins by stating two general premises, the first, Shelley's old favorite
of *The Necessity of Atheism,* that "our opinions depend not on the will,
but on the understanding," the second that God cannot punish him "for
the conclusions of that reason by which he has thought to distinguish
me from the beasts that perish." [160]

Theosophus then gives one of those sarcastic sketches of the Adam
and Eve and redemption sequence, which, as we have seen, constituted
an inevitable part of anti-clerical literature. Shelley's sketch is certainly
not less effectively satirical than those of Holbach, Volney, or Paine:

> According to this book, God created Satan, who instigated by the im-
> pulses of his nature, contended with the Omnipotent for the throne of
> Heaven. After a contest for the empire, in which God was victorious, Satan
> was thrust into a pit of burning sulfur. On man's creation God placed
> within his reach a tree whose fruit he forebade him to taste, on pain of
> death; permitting Satan at the same time, to employ all his artifice to per-
> suade this innocent and wondering creature to transgress the fatal pro-
> hibition.
>
> The first man yielded to this temptation; and to satisfy Divine Justice
> the whole of his posterity must have been eternally burned in hell, if God
> had not sent his only Son on earth, to save those few whose salvation had
> been foreseen and determined before the creation of the world.
>
> God is here represented as creating man with certain passions and powers,
> surrounding him with certain circumstances, and then condemning him to
> everlasting torments because he acted as omniscience had foreseen, and
> was such as omnipotence had made him. . . . You assert that the human
> race merited eternal reprobation because their common father had trans-
> gressed the divine command, and that the crucifixion of the Son of God

was the only sacrifice of sufficient efficacy to satisfy eternal justice. But it is no less inconsistent with justice and subversive of morality that millions should be responsible for a crime which they had no share in committing; than that, if they had really committed it, the crucifixion of an innocent being could absolve them from moral turpitude.[161]

Theosophus (again following the usual pattern), after having thus attacked the Bible story, goes on to an account of the evils done by the Church. He begins with an ingenious argument (once more, the hand of Gibbon is evident) to show that Christianity cannot have been divine in origin:

It is sufficiently evident that an omniscient being never conceived the design of reforming the world by Christianity. Omniscience would surely have foreseen the inefficacy of that system, which experience demonstrates not only to have been utterly impotent in restraining, but to have been most active in exhaling the malevolent propensities of men. During the period which elapsed between the removal of the seat of empire to Constantinople in 328, and its capture by the Turks in 1453, what salutory influence did Christianity exercise upon the world which it was intended to enlighten? Never before was Europe the theatre of such ceaseless and sanguinary wars, never were the people so brutalized by ignorance and debased by slavery.[162]

Not only was Christianity unable to prevent the spread of such social evils as these; it actually caused a great many of them. It carried on religious wars and massacred and tortured disbelievers. If it be claimed that these things resulted not from Christianity but from the abuse of it, then Christianity cannot have been of divine origin for "Omniscience is naturally chargeable with all the consequences of its conduct."[163]

In addition to spreading wars and massacres, the Church has played a reactionary political role throughout history by building up subservience to existing despotisms (Spinoza, Holbach, Paine):

The doctrine of acquiescing in the most insolent despotism; of praying for and loving our enemies; of faith and humility, appears to fix the perfection of the human character in that abjectness and credulity which priests and tyrants of all ages have found sufficiently convenient for their purposes. It is evident that a whole nation of Christians (could such an anomaly maintain itself a day) would become, like cattle, the property of the first occupier. It is evident that ten highwaymen would suffice to subjugate the world if it were composed of slaves who dared not to resist oppression.[164]

The Church's creed of asceticism with its advocacy of "a total abstinence from sexual intercourse," he argues (with Gibbon and Law-

rence), builds up misanthropic characters apathetic to "love and friendship." Its system of morality cannot be regarded as sound because "Belief
is set up as the criterion of merit or demerit; a man is to be judged not
by the purity of his intentions but by the orthodoxy of his creed."

Following this attack on the Church and its doctrines, Theosophus
shifts to the popular subject of miracles and prophecies by which many
theologians—Paley for instance—tried to prove the validity of Christianity. On miracles he restates the Humean argument: "The actual
appearance of a departed spirit would be a circumstance truly unusual
and portentous; but the accumulated testimony of twelve old women
that a spirit had appeared is neither unprecedented nor miraculous."
As to prophecies, they either did not really precede the events foretold
or are lucky guesses; and, besides, the Bible prophecies are "so unintelligible and obscure" that even Christians argue on their meaning.[165]

With these arguments against miracles and prophecies, Theosophus
relinquishes the floor to Eusebes, and the second part begins.

After some preliminary argumentation, Theosophus is asked by
Eusebes to state the reasons for his belief in the God of Deism, whereupon he gives three standard deistical arguments. The first of them,
interestingly enough, is the central theme of a book by Paley, referred
to in the notes to another passage in *A Refutation of Deism,* his *Natural
Theology.*[166] Paley begins his book by supposing that a man found a
watch lying on a heath and did not know what it was; he would, by
examining it, decide that it had design and therefore must have had
a designer.[167] For the rest of his book he extends this analogy to the
phenomena of the universe—the eye, the ear, etc.—showing that they
too reveal a design and hence imply a designer. Theosophus argues:
"If we examine the structure of a watch, we shall readily confess the
existence of a watch-maker."[168] So, too, with the world: "But design
is sufficiently apparent. The wonderful adaption of substances which
act to those which are acted upon; of the eye to light, and of light
to the eye; of the ear to sound, and of sound to the ear."

His second argument is Paine's, that universal belief indicates the
existence of God; his third argument is that motion itself implies a
God: "The power of beginning motion is no less an attribute of mind
than sensation or thought."

Eusebes then proceeds, using an arsenal of arguments well beyond
anything legitimate in Christian theology, to demolish these points and
to attack all the other major tenets of deism. In regard to the argument
from design he declares bluntly that "Design must be proved before

a designer can be inferred," and that "if, having no previous knowledge of any artificial contrivance, we had accidentally found a watch on the ground, we should have been justified in concluding that it was a thing of nature, that it was a combination of matter with whose cause we were unacquainted." He concludes: "We attribute these effects to human intelligence, because we know beforehand that human intelligence is capable of producing them." (The argument is an extension of Hume's skeptical empiricism, and Shelley may have developed it from the passage in Hume's *Dialogues Concerning Natural Religion,* in which Cleanthes presents the argument from design, and Philo answers that only through "experience" can one recognize "the true cause of any phenomenon," abstract reasoning of itself shows nothing.) [169]

Eusebes then goes on to say that even if we do grant the existence of a creator, where are we then? For we must assume a creator for the creator, and a creator for that creator: "an infinity of creative and created Gods," (Hume's well-known argument, which Shelley could find effectively repeated in Volney).[170] Surely, then, "it is easier to suppose that the Universe has existed, from all eternity, than to conceive an eternal being capable of creating it" (Hume, Holbach; Paine to the contrary). The same is true of man. There must have been a cause for his existence but it is simpler to conceive of a non-divine than a divine cause: "We admit that the generative power is incomprehensible, but to suppose that the same effects are produced by an eternal Omnipotent and Omniscient Being leaves the cause in the same obscurity, but renders it more incomprehensible."

In order to suppose the existence of a God one must premise the existence of a unified, single cause behind the phenomena of the world, but we have no reason to suppose any such unity (Hume):

We can only infer from effects causes exactly adequate to those effects. An infinite number of effects demand an infinite number of causes, nor is the philosopher justified in supposing a greater connection or unity in the latter, than is perceptible in the former.[171]

This series of arguments is then summed up in the following succinct statement of the materialist creed:

The greatest, equally with the smallest motions of the Universe, are subjected to the rigid necessity of inevitable laws. These laws are the unknown causes of the known effects perceivable in the Universe. Their effects are the boundaries of our knowledge, their names the expressions of our ignorance. To suppose some existence beyond, or above them, is to invent a second and superfluous hypothesis to account for what has already been accounted for by the laws of motion and the properties of matter. I admit that the nature of these laws is incomprehensible, but the hypothesis of a Deity adds a gratuitous difficulty, which so far from alleviating those which it is adduced to explain, requires new hypotheses for the elucidation of its own inherent contradictions.

The laws of attraction and repulsion, desire and aversion, suffice to account for every phenomenon of the moral and physical world.

Following this, Eusebes takes up Theosophus's second argument, that the existence of motion indicates the presence of divine mind. His answer, while basically that of Holbach, namely that motion is simply a characteristic of matter—matter without motion cannot exist—is a brilliant development of the concept, showing an extraordinary realization of that interactive fluidity of matter which science is today demonstrating:

Matter, such as we behold it is not inert. It is infinitely active and subtle. Light, electricity and magnetism are fluids not surpassed by thought itself in tenuity and activity; like thought they are sometimes the cause and sometimes the effect of motion; and, distinct as they are from every other class of substances, with which we are acquainted, seem to possess equal claims with thought to the unmeaning distinction of immateriality.[172]

The proposition that because there is "order" in the physical universe there must, therefore, be a God, he opposed once again with the arguments of Holbach: there is no such thing as either order or disorder in the physical world; and to think that there is implies an imaginative extension of our own subjective moral states to a realm where such concepts do not apply.

Eusebes then moves on to the third and last of Theosophus's (and Paine's) arguments, that as all people believe in God there must be a God. To this he counters that there is no such universality of belief; there is only frequency of belief and from mere frequency one can deduce nothing. And even if one accepts this frequency of belief, it is belief in so many diverse phenomena all called God that it does not form any kind of unity: "The word God cannot mean at the same time an ape, a snake, a bone, a calabash, a Trinity and a unity."[173]

As his final point, Eusebes takes up the favorite deist argument—not, however, advanced by Theosophus—from causation. This he answers by Hume's contention that there is really no causation but merely sequence: "Hence it would be inadmissible to deduce the being of a God from the existence of the Universe." [174] Pursuing this point further, he proposes one of Shelley's favorite arguments. It was shown by Locke that the human mind cannot create but can merely supply combinations of what it has perceived: hence if there was a creator of the universe he could not be of the nature of mind.[175] Indeed we cannot conceive of mind as separate from body, and as we do not grant God body we cannot grant him mind. Hence, there is no God: "The distinction therefore between the universe and that by which the universe is upheld, is manifestly erroneous." "In the language of reason," he concludes, echoing Spinoza, "the words God and Universe are synonymous." [176]

After this barrage of materialistic dialectics from his Christian friend, Theosophus finds himself overwhelmed, and can only feebly declare that he will "endeavour to adopt as much of the Christian scheme as is consistent with my persuasion of the goodness, unity and majesty of God." [178] As he had already shown that, according to Christian concepts, God had neither goodness, unity, nor majesty, the obvious conclusion is that both deism and Christianity are untenable. Shelley has allowed them mutually to blot each other out.

Shelley, as a boy, even although receiving little religious instruction, had accepted the elementary tenet of the existence of a God who had created the world and who was responsive to prayer. By 1809, as we can tell from *Zastrozzi,* he had begun to have some religious doubts, and, by 1810, considered himself a deist, i.e. he still believed in a creative God but denied the possibility of determining his attributes. By the spring of 1811, partly as a result of Hogg's influence, he considered himself an atheist. The essence of this change, as it appeared to him, was a denial of the existence of a creative God—accepting Hume's arguments on causation and an infinite regress—and the adoption of the view that the world (and perhaps man also) must have existed from the beginning of time. Yet he did not accept the materialist argument that mind was but a form of matter, but regarded both as separate substances, one material and one spiritual, and retained a belief in the immortality of the soul (mind). By the time of the composition of *Queen Mab* he had begun to wonder about the nature of matter, and, probably mainly as a result of his reading in Drummond, began to feel that it was perhaps, in its apparently infinite fluidity and activity, not so different from mind. Later he accepted the Berkeleian view that it was in fact a spiritual essence, but he had not accepted it when he wrote *Queen Mab.* The belief in *Queen Mab,* as we have seen, was in the eternity of a universe divided into matter and mind, separate substances but both subject to the laws of Necessity (and even when he later accepted the Berkeleian position he still held to the doctrine of an immutable Necessity).

In *A Refutation of Deism* there is no exposition of this dualism; the "coeternal Spirit" of universal mind has disappeared. That this represents the rejection of dualism and the acceptance of a complete materialism between the composition of the two works is possible, but my own feeling is that it does not. Shelley's arguments, in the final section of the work, which often seem to be a refutation of the existence of both a creative deity and the "coeternal Spirit," are, if examined carefully, seen to be directed against the first of these only. For instance, the passage in which he says that "we are incapacitated only by our ignorance from referring every phenomenon . . . to the laws of motion and the properties of matter," sounds at first like a restatement of the Holbachian creed; and so, too, does: "The laws of attraction and repulsion, desire and aversion, suffice to account for every phenomenon of the moral and physical world." But Shelley nowhere states his belief in the fundamental tenet of Holbach's that mind is but an attribute of matter. The concept inherent in both the above statements is, in my opinion, the same as that in *Queen Mab,* namely the Godwinian belief in mind and matter as separate entities both subject to the laws of Necessity. Matter, in accordance with its nature, is responsive to the phenomenon of "attraction and repulsion"; mind, too, is subject to the same basic kind of law, but as its substance differs, this law is, in it, manifested in the phenomenon of "desire and aversion." In the first passage he is speaking only of material phenomena, not of mind and its attributes, and, as the context shows, directing his argument essentially against the existence of a creative Deity.[178]

There are, it seems to me, two reasons for the difference in emphasis between the position as stated in *Queen Mab* and in *A Refutation of Deism.* In *Queen Mab* Shelley is giving a positive statement of his own belief, whereas in *A Refutation of Deism* he is simply examining a position he does not agree with. He felt under no compulsion to state his disagreements with the materialists while refuting the deists. In the second place, *Queen Mab* is a poem, and in a poem personification inevitably gives an emphasis and vividness to abstract concepts that expository prose does not. The roots of Shelley's future partial acceptance of Berkeleian idealism, then, are, in my opinion, present not only in *Queen Mab* but by implication in *A Refutation of Deism* also, and it is wrong to consider him as having passed through an intermediary state of consistent Holbachian materialism.

A Refutation of Deism must be recognized as one of the outstanding works of English free-thought literature. Shelley has not gone into the subject flippantly or superficially, but has read widely and thought deeply, culling arguments from many different sources. He had read in the deist and Christian opposition (Paine and Paley), considered their arguments carefully and refuted them skillfully, extraordinarily so, in fact, for a young man of twenty-one. In the first part (Theosophus on Christian theology) he exhibits that combination of logic and wit characteristic of the best French works. In the second (Eusebes on deism) he reveals an understanding of the deeper philosophical issues involved, that is lacking, for instance, in such a brilliant but essentially negativistic work as Paine's. Nor, in spite of its dependence for so many of its concepts on previous thinkers, can the essay be classed as un-original. In each of the works in the genre there is considerable over-lapping. Only occasionally, as in Hume or Holbach, does one find a really significant advance. Shelley's contribution compared to theirs is small, but its penetrative selection and recombination of ideas places it well above the English average for the time.

With the composition and publication of *A Refutation of Deism* in the winter of 1813–1814, a period in Shelley's life closed. Six years later, in Italy, oppressed by the death of two loved children and by a sense of failure and isolation, he looked back with longing to this period as one in which, like the West Wind, he had been "tameless and swift and proud." It was the period of unwavering defiance of his family, of the crusade to Ireland, of high hopes of speedy fame and of becoming a major force in his age. It was the period of happiness with Harriet. Within a few months all was to change. His marriage was to disintegrate and he was to be in the toils of a shattering moral crisis. His writing was to be interrupted for nearly two years by poverty, social ostracism, and psychological trauma. And when he wrote again, his first work was the subjective, tormented history of the young poet of *Alastor*.

NOTES

Abbreviations Used in the Notes
BOOKS

(Whenever a second or other work by one of the authors in the following list is referred to, the full title for that work is used, and subsequent references may be by short title or *op. cit.* to distinguish it from the primary work. *Op. cit.,* however, is seldom used otherwise. Subsequent references are usually given by name of author only.)

Athenians, The:—*The Athenians, Being Correspondence Between Thomas Jefferson Hogg and His Friends* . . . ed. by Walter Sidney Scott. London: Golden Cockerel Press, 1943.

BAKER:—Carlos Baker, *Shelley's Major Poetry: The Fabric of a Vision.* Princeton Univ. Press, 1948.

BLUNDEN:—Edmund Blunden, *Shelley: A Life Story.* London: Collins, 1946.

DE RICCI:—Seymour de Ricci, *A Bibliography of Shelley's Letters.* Privately printed, 1927.

DOWDEN:—Edward Dowden, *The Life of Percy Bysshe Shelley.* 2 vols. London: Kegan Paul, 1886.

FORMAN:—*The Works of Percy Bysshe Shelley in Verse and Prose,* ed. by Harry Buxton Forman. 8 vols. London: Reeves & Turner, 1880.

GRABO:—Carl Grabo, *The Magic Plant: The Growth of Shelley's Thought.* Univ. of North Carolina Press, 1936.

Harriet and Mary:—*Harriet and Mary, Being the Relations Between Percy Bysshe Shelley, Harriet Shelley, Mary Shelley, and Thomas Jefferson Hogg,* ed. by Walter Sidney Scott. London: Golden Cockerel Press, 1944.

HOGG:—Thomas Jefferson Hogg, "The Life of Percy Bysshe Shelley," in Humbert Wolfe, ed., *The Life of Percy Bysshe Shelley* . . . , Vol. I, p. 1, to Vol. II, p. 158. London: Dent, 1933. (First published, 1858; chapters on Shelley at Oxford reprinted from *New Monthly Magazine,* 1832).

HUGHES:—A. M. D. Hughes, *The Nascent Mind of Shelley.* Oxford Univ. Press, 1947.

INGPEN:—Roger Ingpen, *Shelley in England: New Facts and Letters from the Shelley-Whitton Papers.* London: Kegan Paul, 1917.

JEAFFRESON:—John Cordy Jeaffreson, *The Real Shelley.* 2 vols. London: Hurst & Blackett, 1885.

Journal:—*Mary Shelley's Journal,* ed. by Frederick L. Jones. Univ. of Oklahoma Press, 1947. (Some entries, in the early years, by Shelley.)

Koszul:—A. H. Koszul, *La Jeunesse de Shelley.* Paris: Librairie Bloud, 1910.

Letters About Shelley:—*Letters About Shelley,* ed. by R. S. Garnett. London: Hodder & Stoughton, 1917.

Letters of Mary Shelley:—*The Letters of Mary W. Shelley,* ed. by Frederick L. Jones. 2 vols. Univ. of Oklahoma Press, 1946.

MacCarthy:—Denis Florence MacCarthy, *Shelley's Early Life.* London: John Camden Hotten, 1872.

Medwin:—Thomas Medwin, *The Life of Percy Bysshe Shelley,* rev. ed., ed by H. Buxton Forman. Oxford Univ. Press, 1913. (First published, without revisions—essentially minor—1847.)

Merle: [Joseph Gibbons Merle], "A Newspaper Editor's Reminiscences," *Fraser's Magazine,* XXIII (June, 1841), 699–710.

Peacock:—Thomas Love Peacock, "Memoirs of Percy Bysshe Shelley," in Humbert Wolfe, ed., *The Life of Percy Bysshe Shelley . . . ,* Vol. II, pp. 303–365. London: Dent, 1933. (First published in *Fraser's Magazine,* June, 1858, Jan., 1860.)

Peck:—Walter Edwin Peck, *Shelley: His Life and Work.* 2 vols. London: Ernest Benn, 1927.

Shelley at Oxford:—*Shelley at Oxford: The Early Correspondence of P. B. Shelley with His Friend T. J. Hogg . . .* ed. by Walter Sidney Scott. London: Golden Cockerel Press, 1947.

Trelawny:—Edward John Trelawny, "Recollections of the Last Days of Shelley and Byron," in Humbert Wolfe, ed., *The Life of Percy Bysshe Shelley . . . ,* Vol. II, pp. 159–301. London: Dent, 1933. (First published, 1858.)

White:—Newman I. White, *Shelley.* 2 vols. New York: Knopf, 1940.

Works:—*The Complete Works of Percy Bysshe Shelley* (Julian ed.), ed. by Roger Ingpen and Walter E. Peck. 10 vols. New York: Scribner, 1926–1930.

PERIODICALS AND REFERENCE WORKS

(Abbreviations for periodicals as in *PMLA* annual American Bibliography.)

DNB:—*Dictionary of National Biography.*
ESt:—*Englische Studien.*
JEGP:—*Journal of English and Germanic Philology.*
LTLS:—(London) *Times Literary Supplement.*
MLN:—*Modern Language Notes.*
MLQ:—*Modern Language Quarterly.*
MLR:—*Modern Language Review.*
MP:—*Modern Philology.*
OED:—*Oxford English Dictionary.*
PMLA:—*Publications of the Modern Language Association.*
SP:—*Studies in Philology.*
SR:—*Sewanee Review.*

CHAPTER I

1. For this account I am indebted to: Jeaffreson, I, 13–26; Ingpen, pp. 1–18; White, I, 3–15. Jeaffreson, who had legal training, was the first to point out that the concept of the Shelley family as of old, aristocratic stock was based on the confusing of the two branches. When Sir Bysshe was elevated to the baronetcy in 1806, the family began to feel the advisability of procuring a pedigree. Timothy started to search the records and to call in assistance from the College of Heralds. Within a year, one William Radcliffe of the College had produced the required document, duly tracing the descent of Sir Bysshe to William the Conqueror, a document which he passed on to an assistant with the dry comment: "Transpose the position of this long story as you think proper to make it appear to advantage." (Huntington Library MS, Shelley Family, SH 1–55.) The genealogical tree thus constructed by Radcliffe will be found in: Dowden, 539 f., Forman, V, xxxiv–xl, and at the conclusion of Ingpen.

2. George Santayana, "Shelley: or the Poetic Value of Revolutionary Principles," *Winds of Doctrine* (New York, 1926), p. 159.

3. Hogg, II, 106. On Aug. 13, 1806, Timothy wrote to Whitton informing him that he had "recovered from the gout"—apparently a serious attack and perhaps the same as that remembered by his daughters. (Huntington Library MS, Shelley Family, SH 1–55.)

4. Timothy Shelley to William Whitton, Apr. 18, 1811, quoted in: Ingpen, p. 242. Hogg (I, 189) tells us also that in his letters and conversations with his son, Timothy urged him to "acquire knowledge, to read hard, and particularly to distinguish himself at the university." (His disenchanted advice to his younger son, some years later, however, indicates frailty in Timothy's cultural faith: "Never read a book, Johnnie, and you will be a rich man." White, I, 12, quoting: Maud Rolleston, *Talks with Lady Shelley.* See also: Medwin, p. 105.)

5. Henry Slatter to Robert Montgomery, Dec. 18, 1833, quoted in: Robert Montgomery, "Oxford: or Alma Mater," *Poetical Works* (London, 1854), p. 442. The letter was first quoted in the third (1833) and succeeding editions of *Oxford,* issued as a separate poem.

6. Jan. 10, 16, 28, *Works,* VIII, 239, 243, 259. To these we must add the opinion of J. J. Stockdale, publisher of Shelley's juvenile effusions, 1810–1811, that Timothy was "inclined to exercise parental authority, with most injudicious despotism," and that he "kept his son short of money." (*Stockdale's Budget of "All that is Good, and Noble, and Amiable, in the Country,"* Dec. 20, 1826, p. 9.) But Stockdale had cause to exaggerate, for he came into conflict with Timothy; and his comments on him are consistently derogatory. Shelley in a letter of *ca.* Oct. 15, 1811, to his father implies that Timothy had been in danger of a libel suit by Stockdale. (*Works,* VIII, 156.) (In 1826, Stockdale published the scandalous *Memoirs of Harriet Wilson,* which gave details of her love affairs with men high in English public life. When he was prosecuted, he defended himself by

bringing out a weekly mazagine, the above-mentioned *Budget,* in which he presented juicy bits of scandal from English upper-class society to prove that *Harriet Wilson* was not exaggerated. As part of this material he printed letters he had received from Shelley in 1810–1811 with comments on their relationship, his object being to depict himself as a Christian gentleman attempting to rescue a young atheist. The *Budget* is now a rare item, apparently existing only in the British Museum and Huntington Library copies, but some account of it and Stockdale will be found in: Richard Garnett, "Shelley in Pall Mall," *Macmillan's Magazine,* II [1860], 100–110. See also: *DNB* under Harriette Wilson.)

7. Timothy Shelley to William Whitton, Oct. 25, 1811, Ingpen, p. 347; Shelley to J. T. T. Tisdall, Jan. 1, 1809, *Works,* VII, 290.

8. See, for instance, Shelley's letter to his father, *ca.* Oct. 16, 1811, *Works,* VIII, 155–156, with its violence of insult, or his (*ca.* May, 1811) verse "Letter to Edward Fergus Graham," *Works,* III, 92–94, in which his father is rambunctiously apostrophized as "old Killjoy." This verse letter was probably written shortly before one to Hogg on May 26, 1811 (*Works,* VIII, 97), and at the same time as an undated prose letter to Graham apparently of the same period. (*Works,* X, 416; De Ricci, p. 93.) The MS of this verse letter is at present in the Berg Collection of the New York Public Library. It bears neither date nor stamp, but part of a seal adhering to it probably indicates that it went through the mails folded in a regular letter.

9. See the *Gentleman's Magazine* obituary notice, quoted in: White, I, 14. Hogg's portrait of him (I, 181–186) is, as usual with Hogg, heightened to the point of caricature.

10. Quoted in Medwin, p. 104. Medwin does not name the "popular writer."

11. Blunden, p. 17.

12. Shelley to Hogg, May 15, 1811, *Works,* VIII, 87. Hogg prints "philosopher" for "atheist" regularly; Ingpen (*ibid.*) conjectures that he has done so here also; in view of more recent revelations of Hogg's mutilations along these lines—in the letters edited by Walter Sidney Scott—we may take the conjecture to be certain, and I have made the change accordingly.

13. To Edward Fergus Graham, Nov. 30, 1810, *Works,* VIII, 20. On Graham, a young musician educated at Timothy Shelley's expense, see: *ibid.,* pp. xxiii–xxv. Why Timothy was thus interested in Graham, we do not know.

14. Hogg, I, 179. Hogg is writing specifically of the spring of 1811; as he had been Shelley's intimate friend from the preceding autumn, the inference is that during this period Shelley had expressed warm love for his mother.

15. Dowden, I, 139. When, during this crisis, Timothy sent his brother-in-law, Robert Parker, to see Shelley, Shelley expressed "affection towards his mother and sister." (Robert Parker to Timothy Shelley, Apr. 12, 1811, Ingpen, p. 229. See also: to Mrs. Elizabeth Shelley, Nov. 7, 1812, *Works,* IX, 21.)

16. Dowden, I, 364; Ingpen, p. 405. In a letter to his father on Sept.

15, 1811, Shelley implied that his mother and sisters would welcome him back to Field Place. (*Works,* VIII, 148).

17. Recollection of a "young officer," a Capt. Kennedy, who visited the Shelleys in the summer of 1814; quoted in Hogg, II, 151–152. On the dating of this visit, see: to Hogg, Oct. 3, 1814, *Harriet and Mary,* p. 40. *Shelley Memorials* (pp. 61, 64 n.). Dowden (I, 388) and Blunden (p. 107) incorrectly date the visit 1813. White (I, 311, 333) follows Hogg (*loc. cit.*) in correctly dating it "early summer of 1814," or "about the first week in June."

18. Dowden (I, 5) states that she "had a special grievance" against her son because he did not enjoy field sports (a statement the source of which I have not been able to trace) and leaves it at that. White (I, 14) repeats Dowden's statement and adds that she tried to reconcile father and son. Blunden (p. 17) gives a more favourable picture of her but makes no analysis. Hughes (p. 5) comments: "She played in the drama of her son's life a minor and unavailing part."

19. Whoever told Dowden (I, 52) that Graham grew up in the Shelley house, and that he and Shelley "were like brothers," must surely have exaggerated. There is no reference to Graham being in the household in Shelley's letters, or in the later reminiscences of his sisters. Nor does the tone of Shelley's letters to Graham imply so intimate a relationship.

20. Elizabeth, born May 10, 1794; Mary, born June 9, 1797; Hellen, born Sept. 26, 1799; Margaret, born Jan. 20, 1801. Shelley's younger brother, John, was born on Mar. 15, 1806. Another sister, also named Hellen (born Jan. 29, 1796) died at the age of four months. (Ingpen, p. 25.) Percy Bysshe, the eldest, was born on Aug. 4, 1792.

21. Hellen Shelley to Lady Jane Shelley, 1856–1857, quoted in: Hogg, I, 24. For other similar letters, see: *ibid.,* pp. 21–30. Hogg does not give exact dates for these letters. Lady Jane Shelley was the wife of Shelley's son, Sir Percy Florence Shelley.

22. Hogg, 1, 47.

23. Medwin, p. 68. Shelley, in later years, condemned hunting; see his letter to Hogg of Oct. 20, 1821, *Shelley at Oxford,* p. 64.

24. Dowden, I, 78; from Lucas's own recollections given to the Horsham minister, Dr. Sadler.

25. Hellen Shelley to Lady Jane Shelley, 1856–1857, Hogg, I, 22, 25.

26. For an account of this school, see: Ingpen, pp. 34–38. Before going to Syon House, Shelley had received private instruction in Latin from a Welsh clergyman. (Medwin, p. 14.)

27. The Medwin and Shelley families were related: Medwin's grandfather was first cousin to Sir Bysshe Shelley's first wife; and his mother, first cousin to Shelley's mother. (Medwin, p. 13.) Medwin's father was a Horsham attorney and steward to the Duke of Norfolk. See below.

28. *Ibid.,* p. 17.

29. *Autobiography of Sir John Rennie* (London, 1875), pp. 1–2. (The autobiography was written in 1867.)

30. Dowden, I, 16 n., quoting recollection by W. C. Gellibrand as given in *Athenaeum,* May 3, 1884, p. 567.

31. Hogg, I, 30.

32. According to *Webster's Collegiate Dictionary:* "An apparatus show-ing the positions and motions of bodies in the solar system by balls moved by wheelwork." Named after Charles Boyle, 4th Earl of Orrery. Walker's "transparent" orrery apparently was rather special; see: *An Epitome of Astronomy . . . as Illustrated by the . . . Transparent Orrery, invented by A. Walker and as lectured upon by his son* (London, 1812).

33. Medwin, p. 28; see also White, I, 23. For further information on Walker see: Dowden, I, 17 f.; White, I, 22–24, 565 f.; Hughes, pp. 9–10. Professor White uses one of Walker's scientific tracts and a syllabus of his lectures as evidence that some of Shelley's scientific ideas, which were thought by Professor Carl Grabo (*A Newton Among Poets*) to come from later reading in science, probably originated in these early talks by Walker. Walker also lectured at Eton when Shelley was there. His two-volume *System of Familiar Philosophy in Twelve Lectures* (London, 1802) pro-vides a popular compendium of the scientific knowledge of the time in physics, chemistry and astronomy. See below, ch. VII, n. 93.

34. *Hellas,* ll. 197–210; *On the Devil and Devils, Works,* VII, 97. As the idea of other inhabited planets was popular at the time, Shelley need not have taken it from Walker alone.

35. Quoted in: Hogg, I, 23.

36. I do not mean by this to countenance the absurd theory that the roots for Shelley's radical philosophy were to be found in his experiences at Syon House, a favorite supposition with those who feel that a radical philosophy has to be accounted for by psychological aberrations (whereas a conservative one is the result of "normal" development). Shelley's social philosophy was, as we shall see, based on a rational analysis of the condi-tions of the age and would have taken place whether he had gone to Syon House or not. The point is that his treatment there laid psychological pat-terns which made the development of this philosophy easier.

37. To Charles Ollier, June 11, 1821, *Works,* X, 275. A publisher had brought out a pirated edition of *Queen Mab* (see below, ch. VII, n. 127); Shelley expressed relief that he had had the "delicacy" to omit the "foolish dedication."

38. On July 30, 1810, Shelley gave a speech at Eton and apparently left for Field Place shortly after, but whether before or after his eighteenth birthday (Aug. 4) I do not find recorded. Dowden, in a letter to Richard Garnett, "thinks" Shelley left on July 30, but is not sure. (*Letters About Shelley,* p. 98.)

39. Rees Howell Gronow, *Reminiscences and Recollections* (London, 1889, 1900), 1, 154.

40. Letter by Andrew Amos, *Athenaeum,* Apr. 15, 1848; reprinted in: White, II, 494–495.

41. From a letter by Walter S. Halliday, Feb. 27, 1857; quoted in: Hogg, I, 41 f.

42. Letter from W. H. Merle, *Athenaeum,* Mar. 4, 1848, quoted in: White, II, 492.

43. On rowing, see: Dowden, I, 25 n.; on hunting (duck hunting with spears), see: Ingpen, pp. 61–62.

44. Gronow, I, 155; Shelley's poem of 1821, "The Boat on the Serchio," ll. 76–83.

45. W. H. Merle (not to be confused with Joseph Gibbons Merle; see below) informs us that "Shelley in his days of trial was not 'a small boy.' " (White, II, 491.) Whether this signifies that he was bullied also in his later years at Eton or simply that he was, while in the lower forms, tall for his age, Merle does not state, and, perhaps, indeed, forty years later, did not remember.

46. To J. T. T. Tisdall, Jan. 10, 1809, *Works,* VII, 289–290. This letter was dated 1808 by Professor R. Warwick Bond (followed by the Julian editors), but it should almost certainly be 1809. (See: Hughes, p. 25 n.) The letters to Tisdall are all clearly of the same period; and Shelley frequently misdated letters in the first month of a new year. Shelley's account of his shooting prowess in this letter seems at variance with that by Medwin quoted above.

47. To the same, Apr. 7, 1809, *ibid.,* pp. 291–292.

48. Letter from Charles William Packe, *Shelley Memorials,* p. 6. Packe's story that Shelley received £40 for *Zastrozzi* has been doubted, but as Shelley told Byron's physician Polidori some six years later that he had received £30 for it, the story probably had some basis in fact. (*The Diary of Dr. John William Polidori,* ed. by W. M. Rossetti [London, 1911] p. 107.) On the other hand, however, although Shelley confidently expected to receive "at least £60" for his second novel, *St. Irvyne* (to Graham, Apr. 1, 1810, *Works,* VIII, 5.), Stockdale, the publisher, informs us that it put him in £300 debt (by 1827, plus interest), which the Shelley family refused to pay. (*Stockdale's Budget,* Jan. 3, 1827, p. 26.)

49. For the dating of these works, see below, nn. 115, 117, 125, 131.

50. Medwin, p. 44. One would gather from Medwin's comments that although Shelley was now approaching literature of a higher type than the "penny dreadfuls" which until that time had been his favorite fare, he was, nevertheless, approaching it with something of the same tastes in mind. Thus his delight in Southey's *Thalaba* was doubtless evoked by its horrorific motifs, and his dislike for Wordsworth was, conversely, due to the lack of such stimulation (expressly condemned in the Preface to the *Lyrical Ballads*): "Wordsworth's writings were at that time by no means to his taste . . . he wanted something more exciting." (*Ibid.*)

51. *Ibid.,* p. 50. On Shelley's interest in Condorcet, see the next chapter. How much or what of Franklin he read we do not know. He numbers him among prominent deists—along with Voltaire, Hume, and Rousseau—in a letter to his father on Feb. 6, 1811 (*Works,* VIII, 51), and when he told Elizabeth Hitchener in Apr., 1812, to post his *Declaration of Rights* broadside in farmhouses, he added: "It was by a similar expedient that Franklin promulgated his commercial opinions among the Americans." (*Works,* VIII, 308.)

52. Medwin, pp. 37, 50.

53. Dowden, I, 25.

54. Rennie, p. 2.

55. Hogg, I, 35–36 (quoting Mary Shelley), 93; Mary Shelley, Note on *The Revolt of Islam, Works,* I, 409; Medwin, p. 33.

56. Hogg, I, 313–314. See also below, ch. II, n. 106.

57. Lind, *DNB.*

58. *Ibid., Letters About Shelley,* p. 132.

59. Hughes, p. 28.

60. Medwin, p. 47.

61. *The Journal of Harriet Grove for 1809–1810,* ed. by Roger Ingpen (privately printed, 12 copies, 1932). Professor White consulted the manuscript journal and has quoted extensively from it. (White, I, 65 f., 578, 582.)

62. On the extent of the correspondence and possible early relationships, see: White, I, 63; on the probable nature of the correspondence, see n. 65 below.

63. "Melody to a Scene of Former Times," *Posthumous Fragments of Margaret Nicholson, Works,* I, 52, 416.

64. White, I, 63.

65. To Hellen Shelley, Feb. 16, 1857, Hogg, II, 155. Grove indicates that the official breaking of the engagement took place in the fall of 1810 as a result of Shelley's letters to Harriet and this view has been generally accepted. But this correspondence, as I have noted, ended in Sept., 1809, and a poem by Shelley enclosed in a letter of Apr. 22, 1810, to his friend Graham implies that the affair had been over for some time:

> For there a youth with darkened brow
> His long-lost love is heard to mourn. (*Works,* VIII, 7.)

And that it was considered as ended at least by Apr. is indicated also in another poem written during Harriet's visit that month, "Song"—"Come [Harriet]! sweet is the hour"—in *Original Poetry, Works,* I, 10. As late as Aug., however, he had apparently not given up hope of subversion by remote control, for he then ordered a copy of Locke's *Essay concerning Human Understanding* to be sent to her (a favorite weapon later against Elizabeth Hitchener). (To Graham, Aug. 13, 1810, White, II, 455.) But in the "Melody to a Scene of Former Times," noted above, published by the middle of Nov., 1810, he wrote:

> And Heaven does know I love thee still,
> Does know the fruitless sick'ning thrill,
> When reason's judgment vainly strove
> To blot thee from my memory.

Thus, in Nov. or Oct. (see ch. II, n. 75 below) he writes of a previous attempt to enforce a break with Harriet. That Grove is right in his statement that the break occurred as a result of impieties in Shelley's correspondence is indicated by the similar nature of Shelley's correspondence during these years with the young poetess, Felicia Hemans (Medwin p. 59), and later with Harriet Westbrook and Elizabeth Hitchener, but Grove's remembrance of happy days at Field Place during the Apr., 1810, visit and the later definite break in the winter of 1810–1811 (see below) may have made him think the family edict came later than it did, as—forty-eight years later—he attempted to recollect the sequence of events.

66. White, I, 63.

67. See poem in letter to Graham, Apr. 22, 1810, noted above.

68. To Hogg, Jan. 6, 1811, *Works,* VIII, 36; to the same, Jan. 2, 1811, *ibid.,* p. 31. See below, ch. III, n. 19. The first intimation we have of the crisis is in the poem in *The Posthumous Fragments of Margaret Nicholson* noted above, poems written between Oct. 15 and Nov. 15 (see below, ch. II, n. 75):

> Art thou indeed forever gone,
> Forever, ever, lost to me?

In the succeeding months the crisis occupies the letters to Hogg, being noted first in letters on Dec. 20 and Dec. 23 (*ibid.,* pp. 24, 26), and the implication in them is that it is of recent origin. Mr. Walter Sidney Scott informs us that a letter which Hogg gives as of Jan. 3, and which also reflects the crisis, is dated in the manuscript "Dec. 8," although it was not posted until Jan. 4. (*Shelley at Oxford,* p. 15.) If Dec. 8 were really the date of composition, then this letter would be our first intimation of the depth of the crisis. But this dating is impossible as the letter is addressed to Hogg at Lincoln's Inn Fields, and Shelley did not know that Hogg was there until Dec. 20. (*Works,* VIII, 23.) Furthermore the letter continues arguments presented to Hogg in a letter of Jan. 2, in answer to one received from Hogg by Shelley on Dec. 30. (To Hogg, Dec. 28, 1810, Jan. 2, 1811, *Works,* VIII, 31–32.)

69. To Hogg, Jan. 2, 1811, *ibid.,* pp. 31–32.

70. To Hogg, Jan. 3, 1811, *Shelley at Oxford,* pp. 18–19. Harriet apparently gave as her excuse for the final break with Shelley and her engagement to another the religious differences previously raised by her family. Shelley may have suspected, as he did later, that the real reason for the break was financial. In 1816, he told the story to Byron's physician, John William Polidori, who recorded it in his journal: "He was betrothed from a boy to his cousin, for age; another came who had as much as he *would* have, and she left him 'because he was an atheist.' " (*The Diary of Dr. John William Polidori,* pp. 12–13.) As for Harriet Grove's side of the case, she told Shelley's sister Hellen that she "did not consider herself bound by a promise to Shelley, and that, had she done so, her father would not have persisted in his objection to their union." (Dowden, I, 49 n.) So that while Shelley may have exaggerated their "engagement" he was right in implying that the final decision lay with Harriet.

71. To Hogg, Jan. 11, 1811, *Works,* VIII, 39 and n. The text (see also: *Shelley at Oxford,* p. 21) reads "She is married," but, as Miss Grove was not actually married until the fall of 1811, Peacock suggested the emendation to "She married!" It seems to me, however, that the text should remain. Shelley is dramatizing the situation for Hogg's benefit, either by pretending that Harriet is already married or implying that she is as good as married, probably the former.

72. Shelley's two poems to Harriet in Apr., 1810, noted above, imply the hope that all may not be finally over, as does also the letter of Aug. 13 to Graham.

73. "The Indian Serenade," ll. 19–20; see also, ll. 17–18, and *Epipsychidion*, l. 591. The same psychological attitude is perhaps present also in "Ode to the West Wind," ll. 43–54. All of Shelley's love poetry, however, is not in this vein; for an expression of a more reciprocal passion see the preceding lines of *Epipsychidion* (560–587).

74. We might note also the incest theme of *The Cenci*. In spite of this interest in incest, Shelley did not intend to advocate incestuous relations in his own age. When Byron was accused of such a relationship with his half-sister, Augusta Leigh, Shelley appeared to be horrified at the charge and referred to it in a letter to Byron as "the only important calumny that ever was advanced against you." (Sept. 29, 1816, *Works*, IX, 198.) I presume, however, that Shelley did believe incest would be part of the general free love pattern in the egalitarian society of the future. In this rather liberal view he was anticipated by Diderot. ("Supplement to Bougainville's 'Voyage,'" *Diderot, Interpreter of Nature, Selected Writings*, ed. by Jonathan Kemp [New York, 1943], pp. 174–175, 187.)

75. Capt. Kennedy, quoted in: Hogg, II, 153.

76. To Hogg, Dec. 8, 1810, *Shelley at Oxford*, p. 17.

77. Timothy seemed to fear especially Shelley's influence on Elizabeth; see, for example: Shelley to Hogg, Apr. 24, 1811, *Works*, VIII, 70. Shelley was interested also in promoting a free love relationship between Elizabeth and Hogg. See letters to Hogg in 1811: Jan. 11 (*Shelley at Oxford*, pp. 20–21); Jan. 12 (*ibid.*, p. 22); Apr. 28 (*Works*, VIII, 77); *ca.* May 13 (*ibid.*, p. 84); May 17 (*Shelley at Oxford*, pp. 38–39); May 22 (*ibid.*, pp. 42–43); *ca.* July 28 (*Works*, VIII, 135); and Hogg's letter to Elizabeth on Aug. 22 (*The Athenians*, pp. 18–20). This project may at first seem at variance with Shelley's own incest drive but more probably it represents an unconscious and perhaps masochistic transference of these feelings to Hogg, with whom Shelley was emotionally intimate.

78. To Hogg, Jan. 11, [Apr. 25], 1811, *Works*, VIII, 39, 72. Shelley's implication in the Jan. 11 letter that his mother exaggerated his objections is nullified by his statement of proselytizing intent in the Apr. letter and in others. See his letters to Allen Etheridge and his sister Hellen, Dec. 16, 1811, *ibid.*, pp. 219–221.

79. For Hogg, see: the *DNB* and Sylva Norman, *After Shelley* (London, 1934), pp. vii–xlvi. *After Shelley* consists of letters by Hogg to Jane Williams with an introduction by Sylva Norman giving a sketch of the correspondents and their relationship. The letters reveal Hogg as a rather formal suitor bent on writing the opinions that he felt his beloved would like to hear. Some of his infrequent references to Shelley (remarkably few for the period of his travels through Shelley's haunts in Italy) strike the same ironic note as his biography; e.g. (p. 77): "I set out early this morning and saw near Tremadoc the house dear Shelley inhabited, called not improperly, under-the-cliff, Tan-yr-allt; there is the sea, and there are mountains and jagged rocks, but few of the necessaries of life; for a poet therefore, whom

the bees feed with honey while he sleeps, it may be good, but not for others." See also letters by Hogg in *Stockdale's Budget* (Jan. 10, 1811, p. 34), *The Athenians, Harriet and Mary, Shelley at Oxford,* R. Glynn Grylls, *Mary Shelley* (Oxford University Press, 1938), pp. 288–291; and references in *Letters of Mary W. Shelley.* Mary depicts him as becoming increasingly cynical and self-centered, e.g. "She [Jane Williams] had lived so unnatural a life under the iron rule of one [Hogg] who seems to think that warm pulses and kindly feelings and social intercourse, at least under his own roof, as vulgar and vicious impulses that no one with a proper moral sense and a gentlemanly education can possibly encourage." (To Leigh Hunt, Dec. 15, 1842, *Letters of Mary W. Shelley,* II, 178.)

80. Shelley's son, Sir Percy Florence Shelley, indicated to Hogg that he felt the book threw "discredit and ridicule on the memories of my father and mother," and demanded the right to see the material for the third volume before publication. (To Hogg, May 13, 1858, Grylls, p. 292.) Sir Percy Florence's wife, Lady Jane Shelley, attacked the book as a "fantastic caricature." (*Shelley Memorials,* p. viii.) She wrote to Leigh Hunt complaining of its "garbled and falsified letters" and asked him to contribute to the *Shelley Memorials.* (*Leigh Hunt's Letter on Hogg's Life of Shelley,* privately printed [Cedar Rapids, Iowa, 1927], pp. 9–11.) That these attacks were largely the result of pique over Hogg's indelicate handling of Shelley's love life is doubtless true, but the charge of falsification of letters has been amply demonstrated, and can be checked by a comparison of the text of letters as given by Hogg and as printed by later editors. (*Works,* VIII; *Shelley at Oxford; Harriet and Mary.*) In reply to her response, Hunt produced an unbalanced diatribe, whose vehemence made it unprintable but which revealed the extent of his indignation. (Hunt, *op. cit.,* pp. 13–25.) Of others who had known Shelley, Peacock was disturbed by Hogg's inaccuracies and gossip mongering, but apparently did not feel that the picture was fundamentally warped. (To Claire Clairmont, May 12, 1858, *Peacock's Works,* Halliford Edition, VIII, 249; and, Peacock, pp. 305–306.) Thornton Hunt, son of Leigh Hunt, assailed the book as a fundamental distortion in "Shelley, by One Who Knew Him" (1863), *Shelley and Keats . . .* ed. by Edmund Blunden (London, 1925), p. 48. Trelawny thought it "very interesting and admirably written." (To Claire Clairmont, *Letters of Edward John Trelawny* [Oxford University Press, 1909], p. 228; see also, pp. 232–233.) Shelley's Irish biographer, Denis Florence MacCarthy (*Shelley's Early Life*), revealed many inaccuracies in the work and pointed out that the apparently verbatim conversations of Shelley it records—forty-eight years later without the aid of notes—must be largely fiction. Of Shelley's two leading biographers, Dowden (I, 59) considered it "an admirable portrait," and White (I, 587) "in many respects the best account of Shelley by one who knew him"; and both use the book rather uncritically. Among modern critics, Humbert Wolfe, Carl Grabo, and Edmund Blunden have assailed it, Wolfe giving a detailed analysis of its faults and distortions. (Wolfe, Hogg, I, Introduction, vii–xxxi; Blunden, "Shelley is Expelled," *On Shelley* [Oxford University Press, 1938], p. 22; Grabo, pp. 19–20.)

81. Hogg, I, 190, 406. Hogg hastens in his preface to foreswear all

kinship with Shelley's views not only by his attacks on the radicals but by his praise of the Tories and his association of himself with them: "We Tories . . ." (*Ibid.,* p. 17.) And he was especially anxious on the point, as he had been (at least in his ethical and anti-religious thinking) as radical as Shelley when at Oxford. See: Frederick L. Jones, "Hogg and The Necessity of Atheism," *PMLA,* LII (1937), 423–426; "Shelley's Leonora," *MP,* XXXII (1935), 391–395. Hogg was sensitive also for fear it might be discovered that he was living with Jane Williams without legal tie (as she was unaware whether or not her first husband—*ante* Williams—had died). (*The Athenians,* p. 73.)

82. Hogg, I, 17. Hogg is mainly taking a dig at Leigh Hunt; cf., *ibid.,* p. 374.

83. Sept. 10, 1857. R. Glynn Grylls, *Mary Shelley* (*Oxford University Press,* 1938), p. 290.

84. Hogg, I, 46–47.

85. *Ibid.,* pp. 136, 82–83.

86. *Ibid.,* pp. 142–143.

87. *Works,* VIII, 55–56. Hogg, as MacCarthy (pp. 66–67) points out, omits this maturely written and reasoned letter in his account of Shelley at Oxford, as it would have contradicted his picture of Shelley, and inserts it, completely out of place, in his second volume.

88. Hogg, I, 132.

89. *Ibid.,* Introduction, p. ix.

90. *Ibid.,* p. 134.

91. See: White, I, 70–75.

92. Quoted in: Peck, I, 105–106. Peck prints "St. Ircoyne [sic]," but this, I presume, is a mistake in transcription. For Sharpe, see the *DNB;* for the poem on the State of Public Affairs, see: MacCarthy, pp. 100–106, 252–256, and H. Buxton Forman, *The Shelley Library* (London, 1886), pp. 20–22. Frank and Charlotte are featured in "Epithalamium" in *The Posthumous Fragments of Margaret Nicholson.* For more of Sharpe's comments, see: Peck, I, 110; II, 446; White, I, 595–596.

93. Merle, p. 701. On the identification of Merle as the author of "A Newspaper Editor's Reminiscences" in *Fraser's Magazine* for June, 1841, see: White, I, 48–50, 574–575. Merle states that he first met Shelley after Shelley had gone to Oxford, but he must be mistaken as Shelley refers to him in letters to Graham in Apr. and May, 1810. (*Works,* VIII, 8, 12.) He has perhaps confused Shelley's matriculation into Oxford (Apr. 10, 1810) with his actual taking up residence there in Oct.

94. Quoted in: Peck, I, 107; see also, pp. 60–62. When Miss Grant's *Memoirs of a Highland Lady* were written, I do not know, but it must have been many years before the publication date, 1898, as she died in 1830. Her general impressions are doubtless correct enough but her memory of facts is inaccurate. For instance, she states incorrectly that Timothy accompanied Shelley from Oxford on the occasion of his expulsion and that he was expelled for pasting up the aforementioned "squibs."

95. Quoted in: Montgomery, *loc. cit.*

96. *Stockdale's Budget,* Jan. 3, 1827, p. 26.

97. Hogg, I, 162–165; see also: to Hogg, Jan. 14, 1811, *Works,* VIII, 45–46.

98. Quoted in: Montgomery, *loc. cit.*

99. Quoted in: White, I, 74–75.

100. For an account of these, see: Blunden, "Shelley is Expelled," *On Shelley,* pp. 16–27; and (for an 1811 letter to an unknown correspondent): *The Athenians,* pp. 11–13. Scott, in his editorial note, guesses that either Elizabeth Shelley or Elizabeth Hitchener was the recipient of this letter. But, in it, Shelley is obviously trying to tone down his views (even to the point of casting reflections on atheists), and this he would have felt no need for in a letter either to his sister or Elizabeth Hitchener.

101. *Ibid.,* pp. 21–25.

102. Quoted in: Dowden, I, 123–124 n., 122. For the official college decree, which bears out Ridley's account of the reason given for the expulsion, see: Blunden, *op. cit.,* p. 27. See also: J. M. Rolleston to R. E. E. Mynors, March, 1811, *New Shelley Letters,* ed. by W. S. Scott (Yale University Press, 1949), p. 27.

103. Medwin, p. 88.

104. Hogg, 1, 169.

105. Walter S. Halliday to Lady Jane Shelley, Feb. 27, 1857, quoted in Hogg, I, 42.

106. Quoted in: Blunden, *op. cit.,* p. 33.

107. To Godwin, Jan. 10, 1812, *Works,* VIII, 239–240. See above, pp. 2–3. "Peculiar susceptibility" may be rendered, in present-day English, as "unusual sensitivity."

108. To Godwin, June 3, 1812, *Works,* VIII, 331.

109. In addition to these, Shelley also wrote, during this early period, a number of works no longer extant, including at least one play and a volume of poems. Rennie (p. 2) remembered Shelley writing "English and Latin" verse at Syon House. (For an example of the English verse, see "Verses on a Cat" and of the Latin [of the Eton period], "Epitaphium.") Hellen recalled that she and her brother produced a small book of verse which was printed but "bought up and destroyed." (Hogg, I, 26.) Amos, in his memories of Shelley's first years at Eton, tells of Shelley and himself "composing plays and acting them before the other lower boy." (Quoted in: White, II, 494.) Hellen remembered also that Shelley and Elizabeth "wrote a play secretly and sent it to Matthews, the comedian." (Hogg, I, 26.) (Hellen must have mixed up her comedians; Thomas Matthews, "actor and pantomimist" of Sadlers Wells, was not born until 1805 and I find no other recorded in the *DNB*.) In the spring of 1810, Shelley informed Graham that he had written a tragedy which he intended to submit to Covent Garden, while "my friend" had written a farce to be sent to the Lyceum. (*Works,* VIII, 8.) The farce may possibly be the same as the comedy of Hellen's recollection. We learn from Merle that Sir Bysshe supplied the means for printing "many of his fugitive pieces. These issued from the press of a printer at Horsham named Phillips." (Merle, p. 702.) As the Victor and Cazire volume was printed by "C. and W. Phillips" at Worthing (but, apparently with a residence at Horsham—see n. 125 below),

Merle may have it in mind or perhaps the lost volume by Hellen and Shelley. In any case his comment does not constitute sufficient evidence for us to posit the existence of a third volume. That the Hellen and Shelley volume was a reality in spite of Hellen's tender age at the time is indicated by the vividness of her recollection of it: "When I saw my name on the title page: 'H-ll-n Sh-ll-y,' I felt much more frightened than pleased. . . ." (Hogg, *loc. cit.*)

110. For the parody, see Shelley's "fiendmongering" letter to Graham, Apr. 23, 1810, *Works,* VIII, 9–11. Edith Birkhead, *The Tale of Terror* (London, 1921), pp. 120–121, and Grabo (p. 15) have argued that Shelley wrote the novels largely as a "lark."

111. To Godwin, Mar. 8, 1812, *Works,* VIII, 287. In fact as early as Dec. 18, 1810, Shelley was referring with scorn to his "wild romances." (To Stockdale, *ibid.,* p. 22.) And on Aug. 1, 1811, he speaks of "the imprudence of publishing a book so ill-digested as 'St. Irvyne.'" (To Stockdale, *ibid.,* p. 137.) And in 1817, as Leigh Hunt afterwards told Browning, Shelley "snatched it [*St. Irvyne*] out of my hands." (Hughes, p. 30.)

112. As we are informed by Medwin, p. 25. Two modern scholars have followed up Medwin's suggestion and explored the influence in detail. See: A. M. D. Hughes, "Shelley's *Zastrozzi* and *St. Irvyne,*" *MLR,* VII (Jan., 1912), 54–63; A. H. Koszul, "Quelques Sources des Romans de Shelley," *Revue Germanique,* I (Mar., 1905), 181–182. Shelley, however, did take a good deal also from Lewis direct; see: A. B. Young, "Shelley and M. G. Lewis," *MLR,* I (1906), 324.

113. Matthew Gregory Lewis, *The Monk* (London, n. d.), II, 157.

114. Hughes, *MLR,* VII, 61.

115. On Mar. 26, 1809, Shelley wrote to his Eton friend Tisdall that he was whiling away the time at Field Place by writing "Novels and Letters." (*Works,* VII, 291.) On May 7, 1809, he wrote to Longman and Company, publishers, informing them that he had "written a large portion of a Romance," and intended to finish it "before the end of July." (*Works,* VIII, 4.) By Mar. 23, 1810, we know that *Zastrozzi* had appeared (published not by Longmans but by "G. Wilkie and J. Robinson") because on that date Harriet Grove records receiving a copy. (White, I, 578.) In view of the fact that Longmans had previously published a horror novel to which Shelley was greatly indebted in *Zastrozzi* (*Zofloya*—Medwin, p. 25), it is probable that the novel he referred to in May, 1809, was *Zastrozzi* and that it was also included in the comment to Tisdall in Mar. The novel was probably completed in Aug. or Sept., 1809, sent to and turned down by Longmans, then sent to Wilkie and Robinson, who published it the following spring. (See also, n. 117, below.)

116. *Works,* V, 88–89.

117. On Apr. 1, 1810, Shelley writes of "my new Romance in three Volumes," for which he expected £60. (To Graham, *Works,* VIII, 5.) In letters on Apr. 23 and in Sept. he quotes poems which later appeared in *St. Irvyne.* (*Ibid.,* pp. 9, 15.) On Nov. 14, he returns *St. Irvyne* to Stockdale, who had been preparing it for the press. (*Ibid.,* p. 18.) By Dec. 10, *St. Irvyne* was published, for on that date, Shelley sent a copy of it to his

uncle, Robert Parker. (*Ibid.,* p. 22 n.) This sequence indicates that the "Romance" of the Apr. 1 letter was *St. Irvyne.* We know of no other "Romance" and presumably if there had been one in any kind of final shape, Shelley would have published it or attempted to publish it. The songs in the Apr. 23 and Sept. letters may indicate some work on the novel beyond Apr. 1, but Shelley's obvious disinterest in it as revealed in his letter to Stockdale on Nov. 14—when he cannot force himself even to make corrections in it—makes it likely that this work was minor. *Zastrozzi,* as we have seen, Shelley expected to finish by the end of July, 1809, and if he had been working on it since Mar. and had "a large portion" of it finished by May 7, it is likely, in view of the shortness of the novel, that it was finished by the late summer of 1809. And if he had most of *St. Irvyne* finished by Apr., 1810, the indication is that he had begun work on *St. Irvyne* shortly after completing *Zastrozzi,* projecting it at first as a three volume novel but later hastily putting what he had completed into one volume (with two plots—on which see below, n. 121). The probable dates of composition, then are: *Zastrozzi,* Mar.–Aug., 1809; *St. Irvyne,* Sept., 1809–Apr., 1810.

118. As he admits in a letter to Stockdale on Nov. 19, 1810 (*Works,* VIII, 19): "What I mean as 'Rosicrucian' is the elixir of eternal life which Ginotti has obtained, Mr. Godwin's romance of 'St. Leon' turns upon that superstition." See also: Medwin, p. 49, and Hughes, *MLR,* VII, 57.

119. On an estate near Field Place, perhaps that of the Duke of Norfolk, called "St. Irving's Hills," Charles Grove informs us, Shelley and he and Harriet Grove and Elizabeth Shelley went for moonlight walks in Apr., 1810. (Quoted by: Hogg, II, 154–155; cf. Dowden, I, 48 n., 49 n.) Dowden informs us that he saw a manuscript poem by Shelley to Harriet Grove, headed "February 28, 1805. To St. Irvyne." (Dowden, I, 48 n.) This, as he suggests, may be the date of an early childhood meeting which they later regarded as the beginning of their romance. In his letter of Apr. 22 to Graham, Shelley, as we have noted, copied a poem later used in *St. Irvyne;* in it he speaks of "St. Irvyne's glade" and "Irvyn's tower," near which a "youth with a dark'ned brow," who is clearly himself from his comments on the poem in the letter, "mourns" for his "long-lost love"— i.e. Harriet Grove. These personal stanzas were later omitted when he published the poem in the novel. In view of these associations, it is probable that the title of the novel came from the nearby estate and that it would be so recognized by Harriet and other friends.

120. Shelley may have got the "Chevalier," from Sir James Henry Lawrence, author of his favorite free love romance *The Empire of the Nairs,* who was commonly known as "Chevalier Lawrence," claiming to be a "Knight of Malta."

121. Forman (V, xii–xviii) suggests that *St. Irvyne* may have been translated from two German stories which Shelley tacked together. This theory, which was repeated by Dowden (I, 93–94) is repudiated in: F. W. Stokoe, *German Influence in the English Romantic Period* (Cambridge, 1926), pp. 148–150. It is possible that *St. Irvyne* consists of two originally separate novels which Shelley rather incongruously combined, but it is more likely that it is really one novel whose two plots would have been more elaborately (if not

more convincingly) tied together if the "three volume" length intimated in the Apr. 1, 1810, letter to Graham had materialized. A comparison of Shelley's descriptions of Ginotti and Nempere indicate that he really intended them for the same person (cf. Ginotti, *Works,* V, 120 f., 129 f.; Nempere, *ibid.,* p. 157 f.); Ginotti, we remember, met Wolfstein in his fatal tryst near the castle of St. Irvyne (*ibid.,* pp. 185, 198 f.); Nempere is greatly startled when Eloise mentions St. Irvyne (*ibid.,* p. 175). Eloise had a brother; he apparently died young and is mourned by her and her sister Marianne (*ibid.,* pp. 173, 178), but how this brother could be Wolfstein is hard to see, unless he had not really died. Nempere, in his youth, poisoned a fellow student. (*Ibid.,* p. 181.) Shelley perhaps originally intended this youth to be the brother of Eloise, and Nempere thus to be her brother's murderer; and apparently if the novel had continued, sister Marianne would have played something of a part. (*Ibid.,* pp. 156, 161, 173.)

When Stockdale protested the double death of Ginotti-Nempere, Shelley replied that "Mountfort did physically kill Ginotti, which must appear from the latter's paleness." (Nov. 17, 1810, *Works,* VIII, 19.) When Ginotti appears to Wolfstein in the final scene, his figure is "wasted almost to a skeleton," and his "cheek sunken and hollow." (*Works,* V, pp. 198–199.) What Shelley has in mind apparently is that Ginotti, can, like the Wandering Jew, undergo many torments without really dying; his body can apparently even endure the symptoms of physical death without bringing annihilation or release to the soul.

122. Hughes, *MLR,* VII, 62–63. See especially: to Stockdale, Dec. 18, 1810, *Works,* VIII, 22. In this letter Shelley informs Stockdale that he has "in preparation a Novel . . . principally constructed to convey metaphysical and political opinions by way of conversation." We hear no more of this novel unless it was the first form of the later (now lost) propaganda novel *Hubert Cauvin* (for which see below). It cannot, as Ingpen suggests (*ibid.*) be *Leonora* because Hogg was the sole author of *Leonora* (see below, ch. II, n. 166). The MS of the letter in the Huntington Library shows that Shelley first wrote "religious" and crossed this out for "political" (Ingpen to the contrary). Stockdale (*Budget,* Dec. 27, 1826, p. 18) informs us that Shelley would not even bother to correct the page proofs for *St. Irvyne.*

123. Shelley's opening chapter with its depiction of the bandits perhaps also owes something to Schiller's *Robbers,* which Peacock tells us was a favorite work of Shelley's. (Peacock, p. 328.)

124. Letter, Nov. 30, 1810, *Works,* VIII, 20.

125. The date of composition of the volume is given by the individual dates appended to each poem; the earliest is dated Oct., 1809, the latest, Aug., 1810. On Aug. 13, 1810, Shelley informed Graham that "Philipps the Horsham printer has undertaken our poetry,—1500 copies are to be taken off." (White, II, 455.) The book was printed by the firm of C. and W. Phillips at Worthing, some twenty miles from Horsham, but according to Stockdale, one, or perhaps both, Phillipses "resided in Horsham." (*Stockdale's Budget,* Dec. 13, 1826, p. 1.) Shelley informed J. J. Stockdale on Sept. 6, 1810 (*Works,* VIII, 14) that he had just received the last "proof impression" from his printer that morning. The work was published by

Stockdale, and he records receiving 1480 copies on Sept. 17. (Stockdale, *loc. cit.*) Shelley apparently gave a false name for his co-author: "The author told me that the poems were the joint production of himself and a friend, whose name was forgotten by me as soon as I heard it." (*Ibid.*, pp. 1–2.) Stockdale, whose memory for detail was good, would hardly have forgotten if Shelley had mentioned his sister as co-author. Stockdale's comment led Dowden (who had not seen the volume) to speculate that perhaps Shelley's youthful friend Graham had a hand in it. (Dowden, I, 52–54.) When a copy of the work finally turned up in 1898, Garnett identified Elizabeth as Cazire by the lines in the second "Letter," "To Miss —; from Miss —":

> For they're all alike, take them one with another,
> Begging pardon—with the exception of my brother.

(*Original Poetry*, by Victor and Cazire, ed. by Richard Garnett [London, 1898], p. xvi.)

126. Quoted in: White, *The Unextinguished Hearth* (Duke University Press, 1938), p. 32. For the bibliographical history of the volume, see: Garnett, *ed. cit.*, pp. v–xiii, and Thomas James Wise, *A Shelley Library* (London, 1924), pp. 29–30.

127. Hogg, I, 125–126, the poem beginning, "Cold, cold is the blast, when December is howling." The first five stanzas appear as a complete poem in the first "Song" in *Original Poetry*, and lines from the stanzas following it in Hogg, are used in two other "Songs": "Ah! sweet is the moonbeam that sleeps on yon fountain," and "Stern, stern is the voice of fate's fearful command."

128. The two "Songs" last mentioned in the note above. Garnett, apparently forgetting the excerpts in Hogg, assigns all three of these songs to Shelley. (Garnett, *ed. cit.*, p. xiv.) Peck (I, 32–34) accepts the first and second as by Shelley and omits mention of the third. White (I, 58) accepts the second and third but in his notes (p. 583) has qualms about the third.

129. *Works*, V, 115.

130. Stockdale informs us that "some short time" after the announcement of the poems for publication, he discovered that one of them was plagiarized from Lewis. He informed Shelley of his discovery and Shelley "expressed the warmest resentment at the imposition, practiced upon him, by his co-adjutor, and intreated me to destroy all the copies." This was presumably done, for Stockdale states that only "about one hundred, in the whole, have been put in circulation." (*Stockdale's Budget,* Dec. 13, 1826, p. 2.) The poem of Lewis's to which Stockdale referred was first identified as "The Black Canon of Elmham; or, St. Edmund's Eve," by A. B. Young, in "Shelley and M. G. Lewis," *MLR*, I (1906), 323. (It will be found in Lewis's *Tales of Terror* [London, 1801], pp. 104–110.) The other plagiarisms in the horror poems were pointed out in: Helene Richter, "Original Poetry by Victor and Cazire," *ESt*, XXVI (1899), 138–144; and: Young, *loc. cit.* Richter was the first to point out the "Revenge" and "Ghasta" parallels with *The Monk;* Garnett, *ed. cit.*, p. xxiii, noted that the first stanza of "Ghasta" was lifted from Chatterton's "Mynstrelles Song" (stanza four)

in *Aella*. (Medwin [p. 44] tells us of Shelley's early interest in Chatterton.) In 1929, Professor A. Koszul noted that the first stanza of one of the lyrics, the Song beginning "Oh! what is the gain of restless care," and learnedly labelled by the juvenile authors in the table of contents as "translated from the Italian," is taken from a "Song" in William Smyth's "English Lyrics." ("Another plagiarism in Shelley's 'Original Poetry by Victor and Cazire,'" *MLN*, XLIV [1929], 42–43.) And, as Koszul remarks, there are doubtless other plagiarisms as yet undetected. (For a possible candidate, see Ingpen, pp. 99–100.) We might note also that part of a poem appearing in *St. Irvyne*, "Ghosts of the dead! have I not heard your yelling" is lifted from Byron's "Lachin-y-Gair." (Forman, V, 185 n.; Jeaffreson, I, 166–167; *St. Irvyne, Works,* V, 123.)

All these plagiarisms cannot have been the work of Elizabeth. None of them occurs in poems definitely assignable to her but in poems probably by Shelley. A well-thumbed copy of Lewis's *Tales of Terror,* we hear, "marked throughout by childish characters, perhaps in the hand of Shelley" existed in the library of Field Place. (Peck, I, 30.) And Shelley's sister Hellen remembered the "great attraction" of Monk Lewis's poems for him. (Hogg, I, 26.) Hence, Elizabeth could hardly have inserted so much Lewis material—including a complete poem and a versification of a leading episode from *The Monk*—without Shelley's detecting it. Furthermore, Shelley appears to have taken the initiative in publishing the volume. Harriet Grove recorded, on Sept. 17, 1810, that Elizabeth was "offended" with the publication "and with reason." (Wise, p. 30.) So that apparently Elizabeth did not want the poems published, perhaps because she felt that her "Letters" were rather personal in tone or because she was aware of the plagiarisms. The indication is that Shelley perpetrated the plagiarisms either alone or with the connivance of Elizabeth and that he arranged for publication without consulting Elizabeth, or, at least, without her approval. It is improbable that either of the youthful authors—sixteen and eighteen respectively—regarded the matter very weightily. In fact, it seems likely that Shelley intended the insertion of a long poem by the famed Monk Lewis as a hoax (and apparently a successful one as the reviewers did not note it) and was indicating this in his title. Such a procedure would be in keeping with the practical joker spirit which he displayed so prominently in these months (and was soon to illustrate again in his next volume of poetry). When some weeks later (White, I, 58) he was confronted by Stockdale with the cold and legal fact of plagiarism, he then, perhaps with his tongue in his cheek, perhaps in actual fear, threw the blame on "Cazire" and offered to destroy the issue. He had not, as we have noted, told Stockdale the true identity of "Cazire."

131. *The Wandering Jew* presents a series of complex problems in dating, text, publication, and authorship.

DATING

Medwin (p. 39) informs us that he and Shelley in the winter of 1809–1810, began but did not finish a "wild and extravagant romance" called *The Nightmare*. He continues: "Shelley having abandoned prose for poetry, now formed a grand design, to write a metrical romance on the subject of the Wandering Jew. . . ." Medwin does not further specific the date, but "now" gives the impression of shortly after the abandonment of *The Nightmare* in the winter of 1809–1810. On Mar. 28, 1810, Harriet Grove records receiving "a part of B[ysshe]'s poem." (White, I, 583.) On Apr. 1, 1810, Shelley writes to Graham that he expects "a devil of a price for my Poem and at least £60 for my new romance." (*Works*, VIII, 5.) Both these references are probably to *The Wandering Jew*. The Poem sent in part to Harriet was apparently a long one and considered of some importance to be known simply as "Bysshe's poem"; this fits in with Medwin's comment on it as a "grand design." The "new romance" was, as we have seen, *St. Irvyne;* and at the head of chapters eight and ten of *St. Irvyne* are extracts from *The Wandering Jew,* showing that the two works were associated; and once more the poem is evidently a long one, to be published separately, and worth "a devil of a price." We know of no other poem of Shelley's of this period to fit these descriptions. The probability, therefore, is that *The Wandering Jew* was begun in Jan. or Feb., 1810, and by Apr. 1, apparently a fairly large part was completed (at least large enough to warrant sending it to Harriet Grove).

TEXT AND PUBLICATION

The London publishers having failed to consider the work either at "a devil of a price" or any other tangible sum, it was next dispatched to Ballantyne and Co. in Edinburgh (perhaps following a discouraging perusal by Thomas Campbell [Medwin, p. 40]). Ingpen (pp. 80–82), Peck (I, 38) and White (I, 61–62) indicate that Shelley also sent the poem or some other early poetry to Sir Walter Scott but the letter of Scott's upon which this belief was based (printed in: *The Diary of Frances Lady Shelley,* ed. by Richard Edgecombe [New York, 1913], II, 49–51) was not to Shelley but to a James Dusautoy. (See: *Letters of Sir Walter Scott,* ed. by Sir Herbert Grierson [London, 1932] II, 280 n.) When the poem was sent to Ballantyne, we do not exactly know, but Ballantyne's letter of rejection is dated Sept. 24, 1810 (*Stockdale's Budget,* Dec. 20, p. 9), and Shelley informed Stockdale that he had sent it to Ballantyne's "before I had the pleasure of knowing you." (Sept. 28, 1810. *Works,* VIII, 16.) As Shelley met Stockdale "early in the autumn of 1810" (*Budget,* p. 1), the poem was probably sent to Ballantyne's in the summer of 1810. On Sept. 28, Shelley offered the poem to Stockdale, intimating that he had requested Ballantyne to send it to him. (*Works,* VIII, 16.) On Nov. 14, he wrote in surprise that Stockdale had not received it and indicated his intention of again writing to Ballantyne. (*Ibid.,* p. 18.) On Nov. 19, he wrote: "If you have not yet got the 'Wandering Jew' from Mr. B. I will send you a MS copy which I possess." (*Ibid.,* p. 19.) And on Dec. 2: "Will you, if you have got two copies of the 'Wandering Jew' send one of them to me, as I have some corrections which I wish to make." (*Ibid.,* p. 21.)

Why Shelley expected Stockdale to have two copies is puzzling. This would imply that Shelley sent his manuscript copy—or had someone send it for him—to Stockdale, and expected that Stockdale might also have received the Ballantyne copy. Stockdale, however, asserts that he never received any copy (either from Ballantyne or from Shelley) and this statement, coming from a publisher with so clear a memory of Shelley's works submitted to him, we can take as probably correct. (*Budget,* p. 9.)

Shelley himself never published the poem and we have no further knowledge from him of the two manuscripts. The next we hear of the poem is in a notice in the June 20, 1829, issue of *The Edinburgh Literary Journal:*

THE POET SHELLEY

There has recently been put into our hands a manuscript volume, which we look upon as one of the most remarkable literary curiosities extant. *It is a poem in four cantos, by the late poet Shelley, and entirely written in his own hand.* It is entitled *The Wandering Jew,* and contains many passages of great power and beauty. It was composed upwards of twenty years ago, and brought by the poet to Edinburgh, which he visited about that period. It has since lain in the custody of a literary gentleman of this town, to whom it was then offered for publication.

(Quoted in: *The Wandering Jew,* ed. by Bertram Dobell [London, Published for The Shelley Society, 1887], p. xviii.) In the June 27 number, the editors stated that the manuscript had been given to the "literary gentleman" by Shelley "when he visited Edinburgh in 1811," and that he never requested its return. (*Ibid.,* p. xix.) The "literary gentleman" has been identified as James Ballantyne, brother of the publisher who refused the poem in 1810. (White, I, 580.) Shelley was not, in 1829, generally known to have visited Edinburgh in 1811, for no biographies giving that information had then appeared; so that Ballantyne's story was probably based on a genuine memory of an event; and Shelley probably did visit the Ballantynes in 1811 and either asked them to keep the manuscript—if they had not returned it—and reconsider it; or he may have brought with him a revised copy. The latter, I think, is the more likely. Shelley informed Stockdale, as we have seen, that he intended to revise the poem (Dec. 2, 1810, *Works,* VIII, 21); and that he did revise it appears from a comparison of the following passages, the first quoted in *St. Irvyne* (*Works,* V, 165), the second in the text of the poem as first published in full in *Fraser's Magazine* (for which see below):

> Then would cold shudderings seize his *brain,*
>> As gasping he labour'd for breath;
> The strange *gaze* of his *meteor* eye,
> Which, frenzied, and rolling dreadfully,
>> Glar'd with *hideous* gleam. . . .

> Then would cold shuddering seize his *frame,*
> As gasping he labour'd for breath.
> The strange *light* of his *gorgon* eye,
> *As,* frenzied and rolling dreadfully,
> *It* glared with *terrific* gleam. . . .
>> (*Wandering Jew,* II, 102 ff., my italics.)

As *St. Irvyne* was published in Dec., 1810, and probably largely written by Apr., the *St. Irvyne* version is presumably the earlier; hence the probability is that Shelley took a revised version with him to Edinburgh in 1811.

After the preliminary notice in its June 20 issue, the *Edinburgh Literary Journal* published a summary of the poem with quotations in its succeeding issues (June 27, July 4). And the editors gave a further excerpt in the Dec. 26 issue. (Adeline E. Glasheen and Francis J. Glasheen, "The Publication of 'The Wandering Jew,'" *MLR*, XXXVIII [Jan., 1943], 13.)

In its June, 1831, issue, *Fraser's Magazine*, ignoring the previous articles in the *Literary Journal*, announced that it would publish a "new poem" by Percy Bysshe Shelley and presented forthwith a lengthy essay on Shelley. (Reprinted in Dobell, *ed. cit.*, pp. 71–91.) In the following issue (July) the editors printed the poem, not in excerpts only as had the *Literary Journal*, but complete. They announced further that they had "the sanction of Mrs. Shelley" for so publishing. (Glasheen, p. 13.) When we compare the text as given in the *Literary Journal* excerpts with the parallel passages in *Fraser's*, the two show considerable differences, the *Fraser's* text being generally more condensed. These differences were thought by Dobell (*ed. cit.*, p. xxiii) to stem from different manuscripts, but it has recently been argued to have more likely been due to editorial cutting and tampering by the editors of *Fraser's*. (Glasheen, pp. 11–17.) This latter view is supported by the following declaration by the editor of the *Literary Journal* in his July 9, 1831, issue:

> The story of Shelley's poem is simply this. You remember our predecessor [Henry Glassford Bell] published a few extracts from it. The book was afterwards lent by him to a gentleman who was writing an essay on the genius of Shelley, with permission to make a few extracts. That person copied the whole poem, and transmitted it to Fraser. Upon our predecessor's remonstrance that the poem was Mrs. Shelley's property, he wrote to Fraser requesting him not to print it. The bibliopole, however, or his editor, persisted. (Quoted in Glasheen, p. 14.)

Hence, we have no complete text of *The Wandering Jew* as Shelley wrote it, and can judge the original verse only in the *Literary Journal* excerpts.

AUTHORSHIP

One more problem remains to be noted, namely Medwin's claim to have written a goodly portion of the poem. In 1823, Medwin published anonymously a work on the Wandering Jew Legend called *Ahasuerus, The Wanderer*. Examination of the volume reveals some stylistic similarities between it and Shelley's *The Wandering Jew* but no marked parallels in matter or treatment. (See also: Koszul, p. 31 n.) In his preface, although mentioning Shelley's note on the Wandering Jew in *Queen Mab*, Medwin does not refer to the poem *The Wandering Jew*. (Medwin, p. 489.) Nor does he refer to it in his biographical note on Shelley in his *Conversations of Lord Byron* (London, 1824), pp. 306–317. In the *Shelley Papers* (1833; first published in 1832, i.e. the year following *Fraser's* publication of *The Wandering Jew*), however, he informs us that he wrote the "first four" cantos "with the exception of a very few lines," and that the whole poem was in "six or seven cantos." "The part which I contributed I have still, and was surprised to find *totidem verbis* in Frasers Magazine." (*Shelley Papers,* pp. 7–8.) In his *Life of Shelley* (first published in 1847) Medwin informs us that "the first three cantos, with a few additions and alterations, [were] almost entirely mine," and that "seven or eight cantos" were written in all. He reiterated his claim to possession of the manuscript of his own contribution. (Medwin, p. 40.)

This attempt by Medwin to claim the bulk of the poem as his own was rejected by Dobell on the following grounds: Medwin's 1833 and 1847 accounts are inconsistent as he first states the whole poem to have been in "six or seven cantos" of which he did the "first four," and later that it was in "seven or eight cantos" of which he did the "first three"; Shelley in writing about the poem to Stockdale does not mention any collaborator (as he did with *Original Poetry*); but treats the poem as his own and alone expects to reap any profits from it; the editor of the *Edinburgh Literary Journal* said that the "manuscript volume" was in Shelley's handwriting; both *Fraser's* and the *Literary Journal* state the poem was complete in four cantos. (Dobell, *ed. cit.,* pp. xiii–xxxii.) To this we may add that Medwin did not mention the poem until it had been published by *Fraser's* and that his statement that the *Fraser's* text corresponded to his manuscript "totidem verbis" cannot be true in view of *Fraser's* revisions; in fact it seems doubtful that Medwin possessed such a manuscript either in 1832 or 1847 or at any time. Dobell concludes that "the original design was Shelley's (this even Medwin allows); that he wrote (possibly with some slight assistance from Medwin) the four cantos as we now have them; that some discussion may have taken place between them with regard to a continuation of the poem, but that Shelley ultimately decided not to extend it." (Dobell, *ed. cit.,* p. xxx.) And this is the conclusion indicated by the weight of the evidence. (For a different conclusion—but for reasons not given—see Forman's note to Medwin, p. 41. See also: Manfried Eimer, "Zu Shelley's Dichtung *The Wandering Jew," Anglia,* XXXVIII [1914], 433–476.)

132. The legend of the Wandering Jew had been given literary treatment many times before Shelley. (See: Moncure Daniel Conway, *The Wandering Jew* [New York, 1881].) Shelley, however, in view of his intense interest in *The Monk,* perhaps first became fascinated by him in the striking episode in that novel in which he features. (*The Monk,* II, 155 ff.) The story, however, is considerably complicated—as everything connected with *The Wandering Jew* seems to be—by the fact that in addition to *The Monk,* Shelley used two German sources, one of them a translation of Schubart's poem on the subject, the other of unknown origin. In a note to Canto III, l. 196 of *The Wandering Jew* he quotes a prose excerpt from a Wandering Jew story and comments: "I have endeavoured to deviate as little as possible from the extreme sublimity of the idea which the *style* of the German author, of which this is a translation, so forcibly impresses." (*Works,* IV, 376.) The original of this prose excerpt we do not know. When in 1813, he published *Queen Mab,* Shelley gave a second prose excerpt on

the same subject—the attempts of the Jew to achieve death—in the Notes, and commented that it was derived from "some German work, whose title I have vainly endeavoured to discover. I picked it up, dirty and torn, some years ago, in Lincoln's-Inn-Fields." (*Works*, I, 152.) This version is different from that in the *Wandering Jew* note and is identifiable as a translation of Schubart. The relationship of these two excerpts is puzzling and complex.

In 1823, in his Preface to *Ahasuerus, The Wanderer*, Medwin writes as follows:

> In one of the daily rides I was accustomed to take in the spring of 1822, at Pisa, with Lord Byron and Mr. Shelley, a juvenile production of the latter, published without his consent, happened to become the subject of conversation; in the course of which, Lord Byron asked Mr. Shelley why he had prefaced his note on the Wandering Jew, attached to the poem above alluded to, with an assurance that it was accidentally picked up in Lincoln's-inn-fields; his reply was, "ask M., he best can answer the inquiry."
>
> Though I perfectly remembered the circumstance of having given the note in question to Mr. Shelley, some fifteen years ago, I had a very vague recollection of what it contained, nor at this distance of time can I trace its origin. Whether it was translated by a German master who at that time attended me, from his own language, or was partly his composition, and partly mine, or what its real history is, I am at this moment entirely ignorant. (Medwin, p. 489.)

Medwin then quotes the fragment from the Note to *Queen Mab* in what Forman rightly calls a "considerably retrenched" version. (*Ibid.*, p. 490 n.) In 1839, Mary Shelley in her Note on *Queen Mab* repeated Shelley's story of having picked up the fragment in Lincoln's Inn Fields. (*Works*, I, 167.) In *The Shelley Papers* (first published in 1832) Medwin commented: "In the notes of 'Queen Mab' he gives the Legend, probably a translation from the German. . . ." In 1847, in his *Life of Shelley*, Medwin answered Mary: "Mrs. Shelley is strangely misinformed as to the history of the fragment, which I, not Shelley picked up in Lincoln's-Inn-Fields (as mentioned in my preface to *Ahasuerus*), and which was not found till some of the cantos [of *The Wandering Jew*] had been written." (Medwin, p. 42.) In 1858, in his *Life of Percy Bysshe Shelley*, Hogg stated that he had found "amongst Shelley's papers, a fragment of the fragment [in the *Queen Mab* version], in his handwriting," and this (the conclusion of the fragment containing a final paragraph omitted by Shelley) he prints. (Hogg, I, 122–123.)

Hogg casts ridicule on the story of Shelley's having found the fragment: "It is a common device to add to the interest of a romance by asserting that the MS was discovered in a cavern, in a casket; that it had long lain hidden in an old chest, or a tomb." And Byron, it would appear, was similarly skeptical.

The Schubart fragment quoted by Shelley in the Notes to *Queen Mab* was thought by Dowden (I, 44) to be "probably part of the *German*

Museum (a monthly periodical) for June, 1801, or some other journal which had reprinted it from the translation from Schubart given on its pp. 424–426." White (I, 580–581) however, identified it as from "*La Belle Assemblee, or Bell's Court and Fashionable Magazine,* for January, 1809, pp. 19–20."

My own impression is that the skepticism of Hogg and Byron was justified and that neither Shelley nor Medwin found any such fragment in Lincoln's Inn Fields or anywhere else. Medwin obviously had no recollection of so dramatic a discovery in 1823 or in 1832; in fact, all he remembered in 1823 was that he "had given the note" to Shelley, but had no other memory of it, and it was not until Mary (in 1839) reiterated Shelley's statement (which statement itself Medwin calmly passes over) of its romantic origin that Medwin (in 1847) hastened forward as the official snapper-up of previously unconsidered trifles. That any such dramatic discovery took place, as Medwin asserted, in 1809 is ruled out by Shelley's failure to mention it in the Preface or a note to *The Wandering Jew,* for it seems most unlikely that he would have failed to exploit so romantic an incident. Yet, it is reasonably certain that Shelley did know the *Bell's Court and Fashionable Magazine* version at the time of writing *The Wandering Jew.* The account in the poem of the misfortunes of the Jew are closer to that version than to the one he quotes in the *Wandering Jew* note; for example, the important "avenger" theme is not in the *Wandering Jew* note version but is in the *Bell's Court* version used in the Notes to *Queen Mab.* (Cf. *The Wandering Jew,* III, 126–127, and *Works,* I, 152.) In a letter to Hogg on Dec. 8, 1810, we find the following sentence: "Has vengeance in its armoury of wrath a punishment more dreadful!" (*Shelley at Oxford,* p. 17.) In the *Bell's Court* version we find: "Awful avenger in heaven, hast thou in thine armoury of wrath a punishment more dreadful." (Notes to *Queen Mab, Works,* I, 152.) Shelley, therefore, had definitely encountered the *Bell's Court* article by Dec., 1810, and almost certainly knew it during the writing of *The Wandering Jew.* Hence, his failure to mention the Lincoln's-Inn-Fields discovery in *The Wandering Jew* makes it reasonably certain that he came across the article by normal means. Why, if he knew of the article at the time, he did not quote it in the note, but used another version, we can only guess. It may simply be that he felt the *Bell's Court* version too close to his text in the poem. Nor do we know, as I have stated, the origin of the version that he did use. I suspect, however, that this was the version which Medwin informs us was translated by his German teacher and given to Shelley in 1809. In later years Medwin, having no word-for-word memory of this version thought that it was identical with the one used in the Notes to *Queen Mab.* When Shelley came to use the material in *Queen Mab,* he saw an opportunity, as Hogg intimates, of building up some romantic interest by inventing the tale of the Lincoln's Inn Fields discovery; and Medwin, in 1847, added to Shelley's fantasy by inserting himself, in true Medwinian style, into the role of protagonist.

The Wandering Jew story, regardless of the origin of the fragment, had a considerable influence on Shelley. In addition to *The Wandering Jew* and *Queen Mab,* the character of the Jew appears in: "The Wandering

Jew's Soliloquy" (1810); *The Assassins* (1814); *Alastor* (1815; Medwin—p. 43—claims ll. 675–681 as a reference to him); *Hellas* (1821). As I note above Ginotti in *St. Irvyne* bears considerable resemblance to the Wandering Jew; both are mysterious wanderers tired of immortality and seeking release in death. And "Ghasta" in *Original Poetry* is said, in a learned note by the authors, to be "evidently" part of the Wandering Jew legend. (*Works*, I, 25.)

133. *The Wandering Jew*, III, 337–427; see *St. Irvyne, Works*, V, 182–184; see also: *Zastrozzi, ibid.*, p. 96. Dobell, *ed. cit.*, p. 97 gives the possible parallel with *The Monk* (first suggested by Medwin).

134. Medwin, p. 39.

CHAPTER II

1. Mary Shelley, Preface to *Shelley's Collected Poems*, 1839, *Works*, I, xi.

2. *Shelley Memorials*, p. 1.

3. *The Autobiography of Leigh Hunt*, ed. by Roger Ingpen (London, 1903), II, 28.

4. The woolen industry, once the most important in England, had traditionally been protected by parliamentary statutes, and this tradition was continued in the eighteenth century by the predominately Whig ministries of that period. In the late eighteenth and early nineteenth centuries, however, it was edged from its privileged position by the rapidly rising cotton industry, the Tory ministries failing to give it its customary protection. In this struggle the woolen manufacturers were supported by the sheep raisers. See: Paul Mantoux, *The Industrial Revolution in the Eighteenth Century* (New York, 1934), pp. 85–90; E. A. J. Johnson, *An Economic History of Modern England* (New York, 1939), pp. 52–56; Arnold Toynbee, *Lectures on the Industrial Revolution of the Eighteenth Century in England* (London, 1908), p. 59.

5. White, I, 3. We might note, too, that the semi-annual fairs held at Horsham were "principally for sheep and lambs." (Samuel Lewis, *A Topographical Dictionary of England* [London, 1835].) On the timber, see: Ingpen, pp. 460–462.

6. Ingpen, pp. 5–6.

7. Merle, p. 702. The picture is confirmed by Medwin (p. 11).

8. Oct. 13, 1811, *Works*, VIII, 155.

9. By William Albery (London, 1927), pp. 123–191.

10. *Ibid.*, p. 123.

11. *Ibid.*, p. 130.

12. *Ibid.*, p. 170.

13. *Ibid.*, p. 301.

14. White, I, 15.

15. Albery, pp. 259–260.

16. *Hansard*, XXXV, 913 (1817). (This work was entitled *The Parliamentary History of England* until 1803, when it became the *Parliamentary*

Debates, published under the superintendence of T. C. Hansard. I use the usual short title *Hansard* for all volumes of the work.)

17. But see Garnett's *DNB* article on Shelley.

18. Hogg, II, 156.

19. Letter to Leigh Hunt, Mar. 2, 1811, *Works,* VIII, 56; see also: Medwin, pp. 100–101.

20. Hogg, I, 129–130; see also: *ibid.,* p. 156.

21. As first pointed out in: MacCarthy, pp. 66–67.

22. Merle, pp. 705–706.

23. *An Address to the Irish People* [1812], *Works,* V, 227.

24. *Hansard,* XXXIII (1797–98), 644–735. For some account of these debates and the Whigs during this period see: William Harris, *The History of the Radical Party in Parliament* (London, 1885), pp. 45–68; George Macaulay Trevelyan, *Lord Grey of the Reform Bill* (London, 1920), pp. 73–97; George Stead Veitch, *The Genesis of Parliamentary Reform* (London, 1913), pp. 281–282, 331–333.

25. *Ibid.,* pp. 644 ff. For Grey, later the champion of the Reform Bill of 1832, see: Trevelyan. In 1817, Shelley sent Grey a copy of his first reform pamphlet. (*Works,* IX, 222 n.) *Hansard* reports in indirect discourse; hence some of the peculiarities of syntax.

26. *Hansard,* pp. 653 ff. Lord Erskine (1750–1823) was the leading liberal attorney of the Whigs. In 1792, he defended Paine and, as a consequence, lost his office as Attorney General; in the famous Treason Trials of 1794 he defended Hardy, Tooke, and Thelwall; he supported the Bill of 1806 for the abolition of the slave trade; from 1817–1820, he fought the renewed attempts of the Tories at dictatorship in the Seditious Meetings Bills, suspension of Habeas Corpus and the infamous Six Acts.

27. Shelley's reform pamphlets often echo the type of phrasing used in these Whig debates. Here, for example, cf.: *A Philosophical View of Reform* (*Works,* VII, 48): "He [the true patriot] will endeavour to rally round one standard the divided friends of liberty." See also, the letter to Hunt quoted below.

28. Cf.: *Prometheus Unbound,* I, 780–788 for a similar thought; e.g.:

> Thou shalt quell this horseman grim,
> Woundless though in heart or limb.

29. *Hansard,* p. 661. For similar sentiments see, e.g.: Preface to *The Revolt of Islam;* Preface to *Hellas.*

30. *Hansard,* pp. 662 ff.; cf.: *An Address to the People on the Death of Princess Charlotte, Works,* VI, 79; *A Philosophical View of Reform, Works,* VII, 22.

31. *Hansard,* pp. 670 ff.

32. *Ibid.,* pp. 681 ff.

33. *Ibid.,* pp. 689 ff.

34. *Ibid.,* pp. 699 ff.

35. *Ibid.,* p. 703. Shelley's views on the "anarchy-despotism" dilemma are approximately the same as those of Fox; e.g.: letter to Horace Smith, Apr. 11, 1822: ". . . anarchy is better than despotism: for this reason, that

the former is for a season, and the latter is eternal." (*Works,* X, 378.) Cf. also: *A Philosophical View of Reform:* "No friend of mankind and of his country can desire that such a crisis [i.e. a revolution] should suddenly arrive; but still less, once having arrived, can he hesitate under which banner to array his person and his powers." (*Works,* VII, 45.)

36. *Hansard,* p. 722. Shelley's ideas on the National Debt came largely from Cobbett (see my article: "Shelley, Cobbett and the National Debt," *JEGP,* XLII [April, 1943], 197–209), but no doubt his opposition to the Debt stems ultimately from Whig influence. For this later opposition to the debt, see: *An Address to the People on the Death of the Princess Charlotte, Works,* VI, 77–79; *A Philosophical View of Reform, Works,* VII, 21–41.

37. One can appreciate better the struggle of Mary Wollstonecraft when one notes the position on this subject even of such an advanced Whig as Fox: "And yet, why has it never been imagined that the right of election should be extended to women? Why! but because by the law of nations, and perhaps also by the law of nature, that their sex is dependent on ours." (*Hansard,* p. 727.) Fox was later attacked for this position by Jeremy Bentham: *Plan of Parliamentary Reform* [1817], *The Works of Jeremy Bentham* (Edinburgh, 1843), III, 463.

38. H. S. Doubleday and Lord Howard de Walden, eds., *The Complete Peerage* (London, 1936), IX, 633; Gerald Brenan and Edward Phillips Statham, *The House of Howard* (London, 1907), II, 632.

39. Brenan and Statham, pp. 629, 631.

40. *Hansard,* XI, 686–7; XVII, 410–411; W. J. Amherst, *The History of Catholic Emancipation* (London, 1886), II, 228.

41. Michael Roberts, *The Whig Party, 1807–1812* (London, 1939), p. 95.

42. Brenan and Statham, p. 633.

43. Albery, p. 245.

44. Edward Lascelles, *The Life of Charles James Fox* (Oxford University Press, 1936), p. 284.

45. *Ibid.,* pp. 284–285.

46. While it is probable that this poem is by Shelley and not by his sister Elizabeth (see p. 34 above) this is not certain. One of the poems which Hogg quotes as Elizabeth's (Hogg, I, 124–125) and the poem of Elizabeth's that Shelley enclosed in a letter to him on Jan. 11, 1811, (*Works,* VIII, 40) are radical and anti-imperialist, e.g.:

> All are brethren, and even the African bending
>   To the stroke of the hard-hearted Englishman's rod . . .

The authorship, however, is not of much consequence, as it is clear that brother and sister thought alike. "I like it very much," wrote Shelley of the poem quoted above in his Jan. 11 letter, "if a brother may be allowed to praise his sister."

47. Hogg, I, 155–156; Medwin, pp. 86–87. Of this letter Medwin remembers only that "it was a well written paper, and calculated to produce some effect." Some years later MacCarthy, acting on this hint from Medwin, found in *The Morning Chronicle* for Nov. 15, 1809, a letter in support of Grenville's candidacy, signed "A. M. Oxon." which may be Shelley's letter.

If so, it manifests considerable enthusiasm for Grenville. MacCarthy, pp. 23–25.

48. Grenville, however, was in favor of Catholic emancipation, "the only great public question," writes Trevelyan, "on which Grenville and the Foxite Whigs agreed." (Trevelyan, p. 132.) See also: Roberts, pp. 67–79, 312–316. Another reason for Shelley's support of Grenville was, doubtless, that Grenville had been Prime Minister of the 1806, "All the Talents" ministry that had granted his grandfather a baronetcy.

49. For Burdett, see: W. M. Patterson, *Sir Francis Burdett and His Times,* 2 vols. (London, 1931); Joseph Jackson, *The Public Career of Sir Francis Burdett* (Philadelphia, 1932).

50. *Hansard,* XIV, 1053.

51. The poem was by Elizabeth; see above, ch. I, n. 125.

52. *Works,* IV, 349.

53. Jackson, pp. 125–126.

54. Roberts, p. 236. The first real break between Burdett and the Whigs had come in May, 1809, when Burdett chaired a meeting of Reformers in the Crown and Anchor Tavern, at which vigorous attacks were delivered against the Whigs. (*Ibid.,* pp. 246–248.) This breach was further widened by Burdett's reform plan in June, and then by his defense of John Gale Jones and his subsequent imprisonment the following year.

55. To Catherine Nugent, Jan. 16, 1813, *Works,* IX, 41.

56. For an account of Finnerty, see: MacCarthy, pp. 77–94, 395–400; the *DNB;* and, for a discussion of his 1811 misadventures, *Hansard,* XX (1811), 723–743.

57. The Whigs took full advantage of the uproar engendered by Burdett and the reformers and made four attempts to vote the Perceval ministry out of office, on one occasion coming within 23 votes of doing so. (Roberts, pp. 144–148.)

58. MacCarthy, pp. 95–100.

59. *The Weekly Messenger,* Dublin, Mar. 7, 1812, quoted in: *ibid.,* p. 255: "Mr. Shelly, [sic] commiserating the sufferings of our distinguished countryman Mr. Finnerty, whose exertions in the cause of political freedom he much admired, wrote a very beautiful poem, the profits of which we understand, from *undoubted* authority, Mr. Shelly remitted to Mr. Finnerty; we have heard they amounted to nearly an hundred pounds." The "undoubted" authority was probably Shelley himself (perhaps via his Irish journalist friend John Lawless). This article was attacked two weeks later in a letter to *The Dublin Journal* (*ibid.,* pp. 256–260). See below, ch. IV, n. 80.

60. Quoted in: Dowden, I, 125 n.

61. White, I, 599–600.

62. The "Poetical Essay" still has to be chalked up as one of the unsolved mysteries of Shelley bibliography. That it was actually written is probable as Shelley would hardly have inserted advertisements for it unless he had written it; and it is almost certainly the "Poem" which Shelley, on Jan. 11, told Hogg he was trying to get published in Oxford (by Munday and Slatter). (*Works,* VIII, 40.) That it was actually printed, however, we

have no evidence, for there is no reference indicating that anyone actually saw a copy. It may, as MacCarthy suggests, be the same as another lost work, the poetical *Essay on Love,* sent to Godwin as exemplifying some of his views and acknowledged as received in Mar., 1811. (MacCarthy, p. 105.) Whether it was actually published or not, however, the story of its having netted £100 for Finnerty must be false, for some copies of a book with a sufficiently wide sale to have made this profit would have survived. It may be that Finnerty received some slight benefit from the sale of the *Margaret Nicholson* volume, which both Sharpe and Slatter agree independently was written to raise funds for him, and this the Dublin *Weekly Messenger* somehow confused with the "beautiful poem."

63. *Works,* VIII, 55–56. About two months after writing this letter Shelley paid Hunt a visit. (Walter Sidney Scott, ed. *Shelley at Oxford,* pp. 36–37.) The similar letter to *The Statesman,* which MacCarthy (pp. 63–65) apparently considered genuine, was a forgery by the notorious "Major Byron." (De Ricci, pp. 294–295.)

64. See: *State Trials,* compiled by T. B. Howell, XXXI (1823), 367–414. The trial took place on Feb. 22.

65. *Edinburgh Review,* XV (1810), 504–521.

66. *Ibid.,* pp. 520, 508.

67. For a good account of the controversy between Hunt and the *Edinburgh,* see: Michael Roberts, "Leigh Hunt's Place in the Reform Movement," *RES,* XI (1935), 58–65; a briefer account will be found in: Michael Roberts, *The Whig Party,* pp. 281–286.

68. As these left Whigs had already defied their party chiefs by associating themselves with Burdett on some issues, Shelley felt that there was a basis for a more permanent cooperation. For these Whigs, see: Roberts, pp. 242–250.

69. The Hampden Club was a kind of extension of Cartwright's earlier venture in political unity, The Friends of the People (Cartwright and his workers being the "people" and Grey and some other Whigs, the "friends"), which had faded out under the Pitt repression. The Hampden Club did not last long but it did succeed in getting some of the left Whigs and reformers together for a time. In 1817, Shelley sent ten copies of his first reform pamphlet to the London Hampden Club. (*Works,* IX, 222 n.) For the Hampden Club see: Veitch, pp. 344–345; *The Life and Correspondence of Major Cartwright,* ed. by F. D. Cartwright (London, 1826), I, 24, 380–383 (list of members); Roberts, pp. 292–294. For Byron's membership in the organization, see: *The Works of Lord Byron, Letters and Journals,* ed. by R. E. Prothero (London, 1901), V, 424; *Lord Byron's Correspondence,* ed. by John Murray (London, 1922), 11, 115.

70. Hogg, I, 71; on these works, see: below, and *Works,* I, 139.

71. Medwin, p. 50.

72. Letter to Elizabeth Hitchener, Feb. 14, 1812, *Works,* VIII, 275. In the *Proposals for an Association* written in the same month he writes: "The names of Paine and Lafayette will outlive the poetic aristocracy of an expatriated Jesuit [the Abbé Barruel] . . ." (*Works,* V, 263.) On Jan. 26, 1812, he wrote: "I have been busily engaged in an 'Address to the Irish,'

which will be printed as Paine's works were, and pasted on the walls of Dublin." (*Works,* VIII, 253.) In *A Refutation of Deism* (1813–1814) he gives evidence of having read Paine's anti-theological works. (*Works,* VI, 40 n.)

73. In an open letter to *The Examiner, Works,* X, 105–119.

74. The first indication of an interest in Mary Wollstonecraft comes in a letter to the publisher Thomas Hookham, July 29, 1812, when Shelley ordered a copy of *The Rights of Woman;* later Shelley became a steady reader of her works and a great admirer of her doctrines. The *Conciones ad Populum* is echoed in *Swellfoot the Tyrant* (1820) and many of Coleridge's ideas in this tract are close to Shelley's but the only indication of an early interest in Coleridge's revolutionary thought is the imitation of "The Devil's Thoughts" by Coleridge and Southey in "The Devil's Walk" (Jan., 1812). (See: my article, "Shelley and the *Conciones ad Populum,*" *MLN, LVII* [Dec., 1942], 673–674.)

75. *The Posthumous Fragments of Margaret Nicholson* were written shortly after Shelley arrived at Oxford. Slatter informs us that Shelley "soon [i.e. soon after his father had brought him to Slatter's shop on his first arrival at Oxford] put the parties to the test by writing some fugitive poetry, entitled 'posthumous Fragments of Margaret Nicholson,' a work almost still-born, and directing the profits to be applied to Peter Finnerty. The ease with which he composed many of the stanzas therein contained is truly astonishing. When surprised with a proof from the printers in the morning he would frequently start off his sofa, exclaiming that that had been his only bed; and on being informed that the men were waiting for more copy, he would sit down and write off a few stanzas, and send them to the press without even revising or reading them. This I have myself witnessed." (Quoted in: Montgomery, *loc. cit.*) Slatter's observations indicate that the poems were written at Oxford—even though the morning improvisations may be suspect—and were begun shortly after Shelley's arrival (the new term opened on Oct. 10, Sir Timothy leaving a few days later). On Nov. 17, the volume was advertised in the *Oxford University and City Herald* as "just published." (MacCarthy, p. 39.) By Nov. 30, Shelley's friend Graham, living in London, had received and acknowledged a copy. (To Graham, Nov. 30, 1810, *Works,* VIII, 20.) While, therefore, some of the poems included might have been of earlier composition, the bulk of them were composed between about Oct. 15 and Nov. 15.

Several fictions have been spread about the volume, some by Shelley and some by Hogg. Shelley, in his Nov. 30 letter, informed Graham that the book "sells wonderfully." This is contradicted by Slatter's statement that it was "almost still-born"; and in choosing between the statements of the publisher and the youthful author, I think we may take that of the publisher as preferable. In the same letter Shelley informs Graham that "the part of the Epithalamium which you mention (i.e. from the end of Satan's triumph) is the production of a friend's *mistress.*" (*Ibid.*) This startling revelation I take to be schoolboy horror-mongering; we know of nothing of either friend or mistress, or any friend of Shelley's who would be likely to possess a mistress.

Hogg informs us that the first poem—"condemning war in the lump; puling trash"—in the volume was not by Shelley but "by some rhymster of the day" who "confided" the manuscript to Shelley. (Hogg, I, 161.) We have no knowledge of any such rhymster, and Shelley in his Advertisement appended to the volume refers to this poem as "intimately connected with the dearest interests of universal happiness." (*Works,* I, 39.) It is the key poem in the volume and the only one thus selected for specific reference in the Advertisement. Further, we might note that Shelley himself, in his letter to Graham, represents the volume as his alone and that it was so taken by both Slatter and Sharpe (see above, p. 21). Hogg further states that the poems were re-written as parodies of radicalism by cutting and rejoining lines, written in part by Hogg. (Hogg, I, 158–163.) When Hogg wrote his account, the book was presumed lost; unfortunately for his story, however, copies later showed up; they reveal no indication of parody or of rejoined lines. (See MacCarthy, pp. 32–40.) Both these stories by Hogg fall so typically within his general pattern of ridiculing or toning down Shelley's radicalism and keeping himself in the clear ("We Tories . . .") that they may be safely rejected. Shelley may have done some parodying of his works and allowed Hogg to do some also as a minor amusement, but, if so, he did not include these efforts in the printed volume. The indication is that the whole volume was by Shelley and that its contents were generally intended seriously (especially the opening poem), although Shelley certainly has his tongue in his cheek in the "shocking" parts of the "Epithalamium."

76. *Works,* I, 39.

77. Ravaillac was the lover of Charlotte Corday (the assassin of Marat) and the poem indulges in considerable gory revelling in the assassination of tyrants (mingled with that tumescent sensuality—see especially ll. 82–90—which was to make the work "sell like wildfire").

78. See above, n. 46.

79. Quoted in: C. B. Roylance Kent, *The English Radicals* (London, 1899), p. 111.

80. Moncure Daniel Conway, *Life of Thomas Paine* (New York, 1893), I, 346. Paine's rise was a thorn in the flesh of the Whigs. "Those of them who would not follow Burke into the Tory camp found it impossible to dissociate themselves in the public mind from Tom Paine. For years he stuck to everything Liberal like a burr. Either you were for 'the good old King,' or else you were set down as a rebel and a Painite. The man in the street, as he gazed through the shop windows at Gillray's Cartoons, began to think of the Foxite Whigs as people in red caps of liberty intent on beheading George III and setting up a ragged Republic." (Trevelyan, p. 40.)

81. Thomas Paine, *The Rights of Man, The Life and Works of Thomas Paine,* Patriots edition (New Rochelle, New York, 1925), VI, 20.

82. *Ibid.,* p. 45: cf. the rise of the people in *The Revolt of Islam,* Canto V. I do not, of course, in these and similar parallels mean to imply that Shelley is directly copying Paine but only that the same revolutionary-republican attitudes pervade the works of both writers; and the main fountainhead of these attitudes in England was Paine.

83. *Ibid.,* p. 49. For Shelley's similar views on the masses of the French

Revolution, see: Preface to *The Revolt of Islam,* e.g.: "Can he who the day before was a trampled slave suddenly become liberal-minded, forbearing and independent?"; *A Philosophical View of Reform* (*Works,* VII, 13–14); *Proposals for an Association of Philanthropists* (*Works,* V, 264).

84. Paine, *op. cit.,* pp. 52–53, 104; cf.: Shelley, *Works,* VII, 12.

85. For a discussion of these parallels, see: W. M. Rossetti, "Shelley in 1812–13," *Fortnightly Review,* Jan., 1871, pp. 71–72; Peck, I, 236–248.

86. Paine, p. 149.

87. It was this second part, in which Paine made more specific application of his revolutionary principles, that called down the wrath of the British authorities. (Trevelyan, p. 38.)

88. Paine, pp. 234–235. For similar perspective in Shelley, see the prefaces to *The Revolt of Islam* and *Hellas.*

89. *Ibid.,* p. 241. For Shelley, see: *Declaration of Rights,* I–IV; for Godwin, see below, n. 118.

90. Paine, p. 243.

91. *Ibid.,* p. 255.

92. *Ibid.,* pp. 262–263.

93. Paine's *Works,* VII, 15.

94. *Ibid.,* p. 25.

95. *Ibid.,* p. 26.

96. *Ibid.,* pp. 87 ff.; see n. 36 above.

97. *Ibid.,* pp. 105–106; cf. also Shelley's *Proposals for an Association, Works,* V, 266–267, and *Prometheus Unbound,* I, 790 ff.

98. Medwin, p. 50. The beginning and conclusion of the passage from Condorcet, of which Medwin quotes the middle, run as follows:

> It is manifest that the improvement of the practice of medicine, become more efficacious in consequence of the progress of reason and social order, must in the end put a period to those general maladies resulting from climate, ailments and the nature of certain occupations. Nor would it be difficult to prove that this hope might be extended to almost every other malady, of which it is probable we shall hereafter discover the most remote causes. . . . Certainly man will not become immortal; but may not the distance between the moment in which he draws his first breath, and the common term when, in the course of nature, without malady or accident, he finds it impossible any longer to exist, be necessarily protracted?

Medwin (*ibid.*) also informs us that Shelley quoted similar ideas from Benjamin Franklin: "a time would come when mind will be predominant over matter, or, in other words, when a thorough knowledge of the human frame, and the perfection of medical science, will counteract the decay of nature." This comment (presumably from Franklin) brings up a rather curious point. Godwin in *Political Justice* writes: "It was in this sense that the celebrated Franklin conjectured that 'mind would one day become omnipotent over matter.' " And to this Godwin appends the following note: "I have no authority to quote for this expression but the conversation of

Doctor Price. I am happy to find upon enquiry, that Mr. William Morgan, the nephew of Dr. Price, and editor of his works, distinctly recollects to have heard it from his uncle." (William Godwin, *Enquiry Concerning Political Justice,* ed. by F. C. L. Priestley [University of Toronto Press, 1946], II, 503.) Then a few pages later (p. 520) Godwin again makes the quotation from Franklin and in a footnote refers to Condorcet's *Outlines* as another work containing similar theories on "extending the term of human life." On this occasion he explains that Franklin's thought might be taken to refer to the control of the mind over the body and hence to "maintaining the human body in perpetual youth and vigor." It seems fairly certain that Shelley had seen this passage in Godwin before his conversation with Medwin; the conjunction of the names of Franklin and Condorcet as theorists on longevity and the explanation of Franklin's thought in these terms can hardly be coincidence. And it was perhaps this reference to Condorcet which sent Shelley to his *Outlines* (for the passage from Condorcet that Medwin cites is not quoted by Godwin).

In *Proposals for an Association,* Shelley refers twice to Condorcet. First, he links him with D'Alembert and Boulanger as one who "contributed greatly to the extension and diffusion of knowledge" which "is incompatible with slavery." (*Works,* V, 264.) Then: "Helvetius and Condorcet established principles, but if they drew conclusions, their conclusions were unsystematical and devoid of the luminousness and energy of method:—they were little understood in the revolution. But this age of ours is not stationary. Philosophers have not developed the great principles of the human mind, that conclusions from them should be unprofitable and impractical." (*Ibid.,* p. 265.) Shelley, therefore, while agreeing with Condorcet's general theories ("principles") condemns him for not showing how these theories can be put into practice for the establishment of the new society he envisaged (i.e. draw up a plan of action as Paine had done). (It should, however, be noted that the rather derogatory tone of some of Shelley's comments on Condorcet and Helvétius as well as on Rousseau and Voltaire in the *Proposals* is probably due to the influence of the Abbé Barruel's *Memoirs Illustrating the History of Jacobinism* [London, 1798], II, 1–78. Shelley's "Voltaire was the flatterer of kings," for instance, is a direct echo: "Voltaire loved kings; their favor and their caresses were his delight." [Barruel, II, 1: on Rousseau, see p. 69; Condorcet, pp. 72–78.] For Shelley's reading in Barruel, see: Peck, I, 75–76, I, 111, 128–129, and: Peck, "Shelley and the Abbe Barruel," *PMLA,* XXXVI (1921), 347–353. The copy of Vol. I in the Berg Collection of the New York Public Library is inscribed on the title page "Percy B. Shelley, 1810." (See below, ch. VII, n. 137.) Following these Irish pamphlets, Shelley next refers to Condorcet's *Outlines* in his Notes on *Queen Mab.* (*Works,* I, 157.) These are the only direct references to Condorcet that I know of in Shelley. His great vision of ascending humanity, however, permeates much of Shelley's work from the Irish pamphlets to *Hellas,* and his theory of Utopian longevity appears in *Queen Mab,* IX, 57 ff.

99. *Outlines of an Historical View of the Progress of the Human Mind* (London, 1795), p. 4.

100. *Ibid.*, p. 316. For similar views in Godwin, see: *Political Justice*, I, 118–119, 274–275.

101. Condorcet, pp. 371–372.

102. Ford K. Brown, *The Life of William Godwin* (London, New York, 1926), pp. 58–59.

103. *Ibid.*, pp. 62–64. For further study of the influence of Godwin see F. C. L. Priestley, *ed. cit.*, III, 100–114.

104. William Hazlitt, "William Godwin," *The Spirit of the Age, Complete Works,* ed. by P. P. Howe (London, 1932), XI, 17.

105. Hogg, I, 313–314.

106. In his Jan. 10, 1812, letter to Godwin, Shelley claims to have first seen the work "more than two years" previously; in a letter of Jan. 16, 1812, he writes: "You will perceive that 'Zastrozzi' and 'St. Irvyne' were written prior to my acquaintance with your writings—the 'Essay on Love,' a little poem—since. I had, indeed, read 'St. Leon' before I wrote 'St. Irvyne,' but the reasonings had *then* made little impression." (*Works,* VIII, 240, 244.) *St. Irvyne* was probably written between the fall of 1809 and the spring of 1810; Shelley left Eton at the end of July or the beginning of Aug., 1810. Hence, while the implication in this letter to Godwin is that Shelley first read the work after the spring of 1810, this reading could have been still within the Eton period. The explanation, I suspect, is that Shelley, in the first letter is trying to impress Godwin as a long-standing admirer, whereas in the second he is trying to flatter him by stressing the change that Godwin's theories had made in his writings. That he had first seen the book during his Eton days is indicated also by the conversation with Medwin on Franklin and Condorcet, commented on in n. 98, above, for that conversation reveals a knowledge of *Political Justice* and it is implied by Medwin to have taken place about the time of the composition of *St. Irvyne.* (Medwin, p. 50.) After this first reading of Dr. Lind's copy, Shelley sent for a copy of his own. (To Stockdale, Nov. 19, 1810, *Works,* VIII, 19.)

107. I note, on Dec. 20, 1810, the following typically Godwinian thought: "*Man* is equal, and I am convinced that equality will be the attendant on a more advanced and ameliorated state of society." (To Hogg, *Works,* VIII, 25.) In the same letter, he suggests sending Hogg's *Leonora* to "Wilkie and Robinson," because "they published Godwin's works." On Jan. 16, 1811, he writes: "Alas! I must, with Godwin, say that in man, imperfect as he now exists, there is never a motive for action unmixed." (To Hogg, *Works,* VIII, 46.) On Jan. 11, he asserts his faith in "the perfectibility of man." (*Shelley at Oxford,* p. 20.) But skepticism on the practicality of Godwin's political perspectives is shown in a letter of *ca.* May 13, 1811: "Shall we take Godwin's criterion: Expediency? Oh! surely not. Any very satisfactory general reform is, I fear, impracticable." (To Hogg, *Works,* VIII, 83.) What Shelley's views on Godwin were in the earlier months of 1810 we do not know, as we have no letters for that period touching on political subjects.

108. To Elizabeth Hitchener, Nov. 26, 1811, *Works,* VIII, 205; see also: to the same, Dec. 26, 1811, *ibid.*, p. 226.

109. Hogg, II, 153. On dating this visit, see above, ch. I, n. 17.

110. The first influential work giving a false picture of the views of both Godwin and Shelley was Leslie Stephen's "Godwin and Shelley," *Hours in a Library* (New York and London, n.d.), III, 356–406, originally published in the *Cornhill Magazine* in 1879. Next came Dowden's essay, "Last Words on Shelley," *Transcripts and Studies* (London, 1888), pp. 75–111. H. N. Brailsford's *Shelley, Godwin and Their Circle* (London, New York, n.d.), while containing much of value presents an absurdly simplified view of Shelley's debt to Godwin, e.g.: "It would be no exaggeration to say that Godwin formed Shelley's mind, and that *Prometheus Unbound* and *Hellas* were the greatest of Godwin's works." (P. 174.) For a more detailed treatment of Godwin's influence on Shelley, see Priestley, *ed. cit.*, III, 108–112.

111. *Political Justice*, I, 5; III, 139. Priestley used the third (1798) edition for his text, collating the three versions in his notes. I depart from this text when that of the first (1793) or second (1796) editions seems to me to present the meaning more clearly, and indicate such departures. Here I use the text of the second edition. Shelley was acquainted with all three editions (*ibid.*, III, 109 n.) but seems to have preferred the first. (To Elizabeth Hitchener, Dec. 26, 1811, *Works*, VIII, 226.)

112. See: *Political Justice*, II, 520.

113. *Ibid.*, I, 92–93.

114. For Shelley, see: to Elizabeth Hitchener, July 25, 1811, *Works*, VIII, 130: "You say that equality is unattainable, so will I observe is perfection; yet they both symbolize in their nature, they both demand that an unremitting tendency towards themselves should be made."

115. *Political Justice*, I, 26.

116. *Ibid.*, III, 179.

117. *Ibid.*, II, 119.

118. *Ibid.*, I, 246; cf. also I, 124, where Godwin acknowledges his debt to Paine for the theory.

119. *Ibid.*, II, 453.

120. *Ibid.*, I, 15. *Cf.* Shelley, *Fragments on Reform, Works*, VI, 295; *Essay on Christianity, Works*, VI, 249.

121. *Ibid.*, I, 16.

122. *Ibid.*, I, 21–22.

123. *Ibid.*, II, 454.

124. *Ibid.*, II, 459–460. For one of Shelley's elaborations of the idea, see: *An Address to the People on the Death of Princess Charlotte, Works*, VI, 78–79. Shelley, of course, is not indebted only to Godwin in this passage (or in most of the others noted); a good deal of it comes from his own thinking and observations.

125. *Ibid.*, I, 206–207.

126. *Ibid.*, II, 435. Cf. Notes on *Queen Mab, Works*, I, 139: "There is no real wealth but the labour of man"; and: *A Philosophical View of Reform, Works*, VII, 36–39: "Labour and skill and the immediate wages of labour and skill is a property of the most sacred and indisputable right, and the foundation of all other property. . . . If however he takes by vio-

lence or appropriates to himself through fraudulent cunning, or receives from another property so acquired, his claim to that property is of a far inferior force."

127. *Ibid.*, II, 463–464; cf. *ibid.*, III, 180–181. Cf. Shelley, *An Address to the Irish People, Works,* V, 233–234; *The Assassins, Works,* VI, 162–163.

128. *Ibid.*, II, 292; cf. *ibid.*, II, 526–529, for a peculiar aspect of Godwin's final Utopia, namely an extension of the Condorcet notion of prolonging life into actual physical immortality in this state: "The men therefore whom we are supposing to exist, when the earth shall refuse itself to a more extended population, will probably cease to propagate. They will no longer have any motive, either of error or reason, to induce them. The whole will be a people of men, and not of children."

129. *Ibid.*, I, 384; III, 171. Cf. Notes on *Queen Mab, Works,* I, 144–146; *A Refutation of Deism, Works,* VI, 48 ff.

130. *Ibid.*, I, 450–451.

131. *Ibid.*, I, 426–427.

132. *Ibid.*, II, 474–475.

133. *Ibid.*, II, 540–541. Robert Owen, for a time at least, advocated a similar view and sent his writings to prominent and wealthy people.

134. *Ibid.*, I, 289.

135. *Ibid.*, I, 275.

136. To Godwin, Mar. 8, 1812, *Works,* VIII, 287; quoted above, p. 153f.

137. *Hymn to Intellectual Beauty* (1816).

138. To Elizabeth Hitchener, Jan. 26, 1812, *Works,* VIII, 254.

139. Medwin, p. 13. To this Medwin appends the following anecdote further to illustrate Sir Timothy's irreverence: "On one occasion when Sir Timothy and his son were walking in a street of Horsham they met the chaplain of the gaol in his canonicals just returned from administrating the last consolations of religion to a criminal, before his execution. 'Well,' exclaimed the baronet with a loud laugh, 'old soul-saver! how did you turn the rascal off?' "

140. To Timothy Shelley, Feb. 6, Feb. 17, 1811, *Works,* VIII, 50–52, 54–55; see also: to Hogg, Jan. 17, 1811, *ibid.,* p. 47.

141. Dowden, I, 5 n. Sadler was a clergyman at Horsham (*ibid.,* p. 10 n.), whom Sir Timothy thought of bringing to his own church at Warnham. Unitarianism was then the creed of advanced liberals. (See below, ch. V, n. 54.) On one occasion, Timothy was rash enough to refer to himself as "a Sceptic," and while this admission was not regarded seriously by Shelley or his uncle, Captain Pilfold, the fact that Timothy would make such a statement testifies to a desire to be considered "advanced" in his religious thinking. (To Hogg; May 15, 1811, *Works,* VIII, 86–87.)

142. For Paley see the *DNB.* For Sir Timothy's use of Paley to convert Shelley, see: Hogg, I, 184–185, 187. The effect of this proselytizing is revealed in a heavily scornful comment in a letter to Elizabeth Hitchener in Dec., 1811 (*Works,* VIII, 212): "Paley's 'Moral Philosophy' begins: 'Why am I *obliged* to keep my word? Because I desire Heaven and hate Hell.' *Obligation* and duty, therefore, are words of no value as the criteria of excellence.—So much for obedience—Parents and Children." That Shelley

read *Natural Theology* and also *Evidences of Christianity* is revealed in *A Refutation of Deism* (1813–1814). See above, p. 282, and *Works,* VI, 45–46, 29 n. Shelley's aversion to Paley, presumably induced by these paternal efforts at indoctrination, continued into the Preface to *Prometheus Unbound* (1819): "For my part I had rather be damned with Plato and Lord Bacon, than go to Heaven with Paley and Malthus." (*Works,* II, 174.) And this comment is repeated by Claire Clairmont in her journal for Nov. 8, 1820. (White, II, 602.) But Paley nevertheless influenced Shelley's early deistical thinking. (See n. 170, below.)

143. See above, p. 3.

144. To Hogg, May 17, 1811, *Shelley at Oxford,* p. 39.

145. See Medwin, p. 19 on Greenlaw. Shelley's early instruction in Latin came from a local clergyman, Evan Edwards; "A good old man," Medwin comments, "but of very limited intellects . . . whose preaching might have been edifying if his Welsh pronunciation had made it intelligible." (*Ibid.,* p. 14.)

146. Hughes, pp. 23–24, see also: White, I, 33.

147. To Godwin, June 11, 1812, *Works,* VIII, 337.

148. Medwin, pp. 50–51.

149. Loeb Classical Library edition (London; Cambridge, Mass., 1937), I, 179, 183. See also Dowden, I, 28–29, who quotes a section from Philemon Holland's translation of Pliny with the pious Philemon's gloss: "Here let Christians take heed, and be thankful to God for the light revealed unto them out of the holy scriptures." Shelley quotes from the "De Deo" (II, V) section of the *Natural History* in Notes on *Queen Mab,* and in *A Refutation of Deism, Works,* I, 150; VI, 29 n.

150. *Works,* VI, 30 n. For the Lucretius passage, see: Loeb Classical Library edition, p. 13. Lucretius continues: "For which reasons when we shall perceive that nothing can be created from nothing, then we shall at once more correctly understand from that principle what we are seeking, both the source from which each thing can be made and the manner in which everything be done without the working of gods."

151. Hogg, I, 163; see also: *ibid.,* I, 71: "We read together Hume's *Essays,* and some productions of Scottish metaphysicians of inferior ability." These latter probably included Dugald Stewart and Robert Forsyth (for both of whom see the *DNB*). Shelley refers to Stewart's *Outlines of Moral Philosophy* (a dull work in which I can see little that Shelley would have agreed with) in *A Refutation of Deism, Works,* VI, 45 n. In the Preface to *Prometheus Unbound* (*Works,* II, 174) he claims he has "what a Scotch philosopher characteristically calls a 'Passion for reforming the World.'" This quotation Rossetti has traced to Robert Forsyth's *Principles of Moral Science.* (*Note Books of Percy Bysshe Shelley,* ed. by H. Buxton Forman [Boston, 1911], I, 10 n.) We might note also that Shelley apparently sent a copy of *The Necessity of Atheism* to Stewart. (*Letters of Thomas J. Wise to John Henry Wrenn,* ed. by Fannie E. Ratchford [New York, 1944], p. 126 n.)

152. Hogg, I, 71.

153. For Volney, see below.

154. See: John Orr, *English Deism, Its Roots and Its Fruits* (Grand Rapids, Michigan, 1934), pp. 83–109.

155. *Works,* VIII, 51.

156. Hogg, I, 91. Hogg claims that Shelley informed him that this title referred to a kind of schoolboy office—"youths of the greatest hardihood might be considered as boys commissioned for executing the office of Lord High Atheist"—and, hence, had no theological connotation. But Dowden (I, 29) failed to find any trace of such an "office" at Eton, and, while Shelley may have received the title partly for his defiance of the masters (the Gods of Eton), it is probable, in view of Hogg's practice of toning down Shelley's views, that, as Rossetti suggests, the title also indicates anti-religious sentiments. (William Michael Rossetti, *A Memoir of Shelley* [London, 1886], p. 10.)

157. See above, p. 14.

158. *Works,* V, 100. On pp. 47–48 Zastrozzi argues confusedly on the subject of immortality—always the stumbling block to Shelley's entry to a complete materialism—rejecting the notion that immortality depends on moral conduct but believing in it as a natural phenomenon. (Cf. To Elizabeth Hitchener, June 20, 1811, *Works,* VIII, 108.) Matilda also ventures into atheistic thought; e.g.: pp. 52, 89.

159. *St. Irvyne, Works,* V, 176–177.

160. *Ibid.,* p. 199. See also p. 133 where Ginotti asks that his soul be allowed to rest "in the endless slumber of annihilation." (Cf.: to Hogg, Jan. 3, 1811, *Works,* VIII, 34.)

161. A. H. Koszul (pp. 27–28) argues that as atheistic ideas were used in other horror novels these views in Shelley's novels do not show that Shelley was anti-religious. But as Shelley's letters of 1810 also reveal anti-religious views, there can be little doubt that his motive was partly propagandistic.

162. See: *Works,* V, 47, 62, 90, 96 (Matilda's conversion; alas, too late) 177, 179. At least one of these anti-atheistical passages (p. 47), however, is ironical (in the style later used in *A Refutation of Deism*): "Thus sophistically argues Zastrozzi.—His soul, deadened by crime, could only entertain confused ideas of immortal happiness; for in proportion as human nature departs from virtue, so far are they [sic] also from being able clearly to contemplate the wonderful operations, the mysterious ways of Providence."

163. *Works,* IV, 351; see also: *The Wandering Jew,* ed. by Bertram Dobell, Shelley Society Publications, ser. 2, no. 2 (London, 1887), pp. xxi, xxii n.

164. Canto III, ll. 126–127.

165. *Works,* VIII, 23. Stockdale in his *Budget* for Jan. 3, 1827 (p. 26) tells us that he gave some "delicate hints" on Shelley's views to Timothy but to little effect, for he "was not the quickest in the world at comprehending anything less conspicuous than a pike-staff." (The object of his solicitations, we might note, was at the same time informing Hogg that "S[tockdale]'s skull is very thick.") Timothy, however, had understood more than Stockdale perceived, for he wrote, apparently in some anger, to his son. (*Works,* VIII, 23.)

166. See: Frederick L. Jones, "Shelley's *Leonora*," *MP*, XXXII (May, 1935), 392–393. The anti-religious character of *Leonora* is testified to by Slatter. (Montgomery, *loc. cit.*) In addition to the references given by Jones, see, for instance, Shelley's letter to Hogg, Jan. 3, 1811, *Shelley at Oxford*, p. 17. (On the dating of this letter see ch. I, n. 68.) In his comment on this letter in *Shelley at Oxford* (p. 19), Mr. Scott appears to believe that he has for the first time established Hogg's authorship of *Leonora*. He had, however, been preceded by Professor Jones.

167. Jones, *op. cit.*, pp. 392–394. Stockdale himself does not inform us that he received a manuscript from Hogg. This fact emerges from Hogg's indignant letter to him on Jan. 21, 1811: "The bare mention of the MS. with which I entrusted you . . ." (*Stockdale's Budget*, Jan. 10, 1827, p. 34.)

168. *Shelley at Oxford*, p. 16. On the date of receiving Hogg's letter, see: *Works*, VIII, 31–32; see also, ch. I, n. 68.

169. *Works*, VIII, 37. For this letter we have only Hogg's text, which reads, "your arguments against the non-existence of a deity." That this should be "existence" is clear from Shelley's argument which follows. In Shelley's letter for Jan. 12, Hogg's text reads, "you [Hogg] disbelieve not the existence of an eternal omnipresent Spirit." (*Ibid.*, p. 44.) The original manuscript reads, "you disbelieve the existence of an eternal & omnipresent spirit." (*Shelley at Oxford*, p. 22.) Hogg is covering up his youthful atheism.

170. *Shelley at Oxford*, pp. 20–23. For many of the deistic arguments in these letters Shelley, as Professor Hughes (pp. 64–65) interestingly demonstrates, was indebted to his later abhorred Paley.

171. *Stockdale's Budget*, Jan. 3, 1827, p. 26.

172. *Loc. cit.; ibid.*, Jan. 10, p. 34; to Hogg, Jan. 14, 1811, *Works*, VIII, 46. That Stockdale's feeling that Hogg had led Shelley astray was shared by others is evident from Shelley's denial of the accusation in a letter to Hogg's father in Apr., 1811. (*Works*, VIII, 63.) When Merle visited Shelley in the spring, he found him vehement on the subject: "I am vain enough, if it be vanity, to believe that there is not one of my friends from whom I have anything to learn, good or bad, on the subjects which excite my father's anxiety. If there be a seducer, it is myself." (Merle, p. 705.)

173. *Works*, VIII, 45–46. The correspondence with Wedgewood had been going on for some time; see, *ibid.*, pp. 25–35. Was Wedgewood perhaps the younger Josiah Wedgwood of the famed pottery family, a benefactor of Coleridge and a man of intellectual interests? See: Eliza Meteyard, *A Group of Englishmen (1795–1815), being records of the younger Wedgwoods and their friends* (London, 1871).

174. *Ibid.*, p. 47.

175. Shelley disagreed with this "argument," which seems to have continued the hedonistic trend of a previous letter (*Works*, VIII, 32), but admired the "cudgel" and the letter to Wedgewood.

176. *Ibid.*, p. 49. We might note, too, that on Jan. 11, he informed Hogg he would not return to Oxford for "a fortnight." (*Ibid.*, p. 40.)

177. MacCarthy, p. 108.
178. *Works*, VIII, 53.

AUTHORSHIP

179. The questions of dating and joint authorship are connected. Professor Jones gives the following points of evidence to establish joint authorship (Frederick L. Jones, "Hogg and *The Necessity of Atheism*," *PMLA*, LII [1937], 423–426): Medwin, who saw Shelley immediately after his expulsion states that the work "was the production of both"; Shelley's cousin, Charles Grove, who also was intimate with Shelley at the time, wrote, "Bysshe and Mr. Hogg published *their* little work. . . ." (my italics); C. J. Ridley, who was at University College with Shelley, wrote, "It has always been supposed that T. J. Hogg wrote the preface"; Phillip Bliss, a fellow of St. Johns College, left a notation at the time, "Mr. Shelley and Mr. Hogg were expelled from University college, for being the authors of a little pamphlet, entitled *The Necessity of Atheism*." On Mar. 29, Shelley wrote to his father: "You well know that a train of reasoning and not any great profligacy has induced me to disbelieve the scriptures:—this train *myself and my friend* pursued. . . . *We* therefore embodied our doubts on the subject and arranged them methodically in the form of 'The Necessity of Atheism'. . . ." (My italics.) In 1945 (*LTLS*, June 23, p. 295), Professor Jones pointed out that in a letter to Hogg on May 6, 1812, (first published in *The Athenians*, 1943, pp. 22–23) a local clergyman referred to "your little pamphlet" and "your arguments" which attempt to "make shipwreck of faith." And this letter bears out Stockdale's findings on Hogg's reputation for skepticism.

Against this evidence of dual authorship the following may be cited. Henry Slatter, in whose shop Shelley placed the pamphlets for sale and who discussed it with Shelley, does not mention Hogg. (*Ibid.*, p. 425.) Charles Kirkpatrick Sharpe presumed the work to be by Shelley alone. (Ingpen, pp. 192, 196 n.) Shelley, in writing to Godwin, on Jan. 10, 1812, treats the work as his own: "In the meantime I became, in the popular sense of the word 'God,' an Atheist. I printed a pamphlet, avowing my opinion, and its occasion. I distributed this anonymously to men of thought and learning, wishing that Reason should decide on the case at issue; it was never my intention to deny it." (*Works*, VIII, 241.) In the same month he told a similar story to Southey: "So he prints half a dozen papers which he entitled The Necessity of Atheism. . . ." (Southey to John Rickman, Jan. 6, 1812, White, I, 618.) In 1813, Shelley reprinted the pamphlet in one of the Notes to *Queen Mab* without any indication of joint authorship. Joseph Gibbons Merle, who visited Shelley in the period following his expulsion, believed it to be Shelley's work alone and received that impression from Shelley himself: "During a short absence from college he had written a small work, which he published under the appalling title of *The Necessity of Atheism*. . . . 'You know [Merle represents Shelley as saying] that I had not affixed my name to this work, but that I had never denied the authorship.'" (Merle, pp. 703–704.) In the same period he informed the young poet Janetta Philipps that he had been expelled from Oxford "as author of a metaphysical pamphlet." (May 16, 1811, *Works,* VIII, 88.) Stockdale, although suspicious of Hogg's influence on Shelley, represents Shelley as informing him of "*his* having completed a Metaphysical Essay, in support of atheism, and which *he* intended to promulgate throughout the university." (*Stockdale's Budget,* Jan. 3, 1827, p. 26; my italics.) And, finally, the "Advertisement" prefacing the *Necessity* speaks only of one "Author." (*Works,* V, 205.)

The four witnesses (Slatter, Sharpe, Merle, Stockdale) who believed the work to be by Shelley alone were not, however, on intimate terms with Shelley or Hogg; Shelley had already misled Slatter (as Professor Jones points out) into believing that *Leonora* was his and not Hogg's; Sharpe may have met Shelley but his condescending attitude as revealed in his letter (quoted above, p. 21) must have prevented any intimacy; Merle, Shelley had met through his friend Graham, but did not know well and was doubtless kept from a close relationship with him by his aggressive religious orthodoxy (which Merle parades in his article and which led to his break with Shelley; Merle, pp. 704–707); Janetta Philipps he had never met; and Stockdale, by the time of the composition of *The Necessity,* was suspect because of his malicious gossip about Hogg. Two of the witnesses who assert joint authorship, Medwin and Grove, were intimate with Shelley and were with him and Hogg immediately following their expulsion. One, Ridley, is reflecting the opinion of the college authorities, and Bliss, who belonged to another college, is really doing little more than recording the formal statement of expulsion. The weight of the evidence, then, as gathered from all witnesses is that the work was a joint production, but that the dual authorship was not revealed to outsiders.

To this let us add the evidence from Shelley and Hogg themselves. Shelley's letter to his father, written but four days after the expulsion, is specific in its attribution of joint authorship. Hogg's statement is no less definite. Hogg informs us that he and Shelley wrote together "a very careful analysis" based on the works of Locke and Hume. "Shelley had the custody of these papers, which were chiefly in his handwriting although they were the joint production of both in our common daily studies. From these and from a small part of them only, *he* made up a little book, and had it printed, I believe in the country, certainly not at Oxford." (Hogg, I, 163; my italics.) In his later accounts to Godwin and Southey, Shelley was dealing solely with his own career, and the revelation of Hogg's complicity was irrelevant and unnecessary. Nor is it surprising that he made no notation of Hogg's part in the Notes to *Queen Mab;* Hogg himself would have been only too anxious to have avoided such publicity in a work of a legally blasphemous and seditious character. What Hogg is covering up in his *Life of Shelley* is that, as Shelley's letters in Dec. and Jan. reveal, the central atheistical argument was his and that part of the writing was his also. That Hogg, indeed, was not averse to admitting this privately is indicated by the local clergyman's letter in which the work is taken as Hogg's own, although the clergyman was aware of his association with Shelley. (*The Athenians,* p. 25.) On the other hand, Shelley, having taken the initiative in printing the work, wished to alone assume public responsibility for it; hence the solitary "Author" of the Advertisement and his later comments.

DATING

Both Hogg's statement and the Dec.–Jan. letters show that the views expressed in the final work were the result of many weeks' incubation. The final draft, however, was probably composed, as both Ingpen (p. 188) and Jones argue, before Shelley's return to Oxford. Professor Jones bases his conclusion on the comment of Merle (quoted above) that it was written by Shelley "during a short absence from college" and on it being printed at Worthing. A member of the Worthing firm (C. and W. Phillips) later stated that Shelley "took great interest in the art of printing, and would often come in and spend hours in the printing office learning to set up the types . . ." (Ingpen, p. 189.) Hogg's statement "he had it printed, I believe, in the country" and Shelley's comment to both Godwin and Southey, "I printed," perhaps imply that the *Necessity of Atheism* was taken personally by Shelley to the press (and it may be that he set some of the type himself). If Shelley did take the work to the press, it must have been composed and printed before he left Horsham for Oxford, for while he could easily have gone over to Worthing from Horsham (*ca.* twenty miles) for a day, he could hardly have done so from Oxford (*ca.* ninety miles) during term time.

The evidence from Stockdale bears out this conclusion. Stockdale informs us that Shelley had expressed anti-religious sentiments, and that he had, in consequence, "given some gentle hints to his father." This presumably was the cause of Shelley's annoyance with him on Dec. 20. Next he made his investigations of Hogg and again communicated with Timothy. This news Shelley conveyed to Hogg on Jan. 14 and Hogg wrote to Stockdale in anger on Jan. 21 and 23. Shelley had, also, as we have seen, told Stockdale that he had "completed" *The Necessity of Atheism* and was going to distribute it at Oxford. Stockdale warned him that if he followed out his plans he would be expelled. Exactly when Shelley gave him this information, Stockdale, writing sixteen years later, did not remember. But on Jan. 30, Timothy wrote the following note to Stockdale: "I am so surprised on the receipt of your letter this morning that I cannot comprehend the meaning of the language you use. I shall be in London next week, and will then call on you." Timothy called and Stockdale "gave him such particulars as the urgency of the case required." A little later came "the news of the catastrophe, which I had too truly predicted." Stockdale had apparently not known on or about Jan. 14 of the existence of the *Necessity,* as it is mentioned neither in Shelley's letter of that date nor in Hogg's on Jan. 21 or 23, both of which center solely around the question of Stockdale's slanders on Hogg's character and the disclosure of his MS (*Leonora*). But Stockdale clearly did know of it on Jan. 29 when he wrote to Timothy. As Shelley, on about Jan. 23, told Hogg that he would be back in Oxford on Jan. 24 or 25 (and was definitely there by Jan. 28) and that he would go to London on the way, the indication is that he informed Stockdale about the *Necessity* on that occasion; and by then the *Necessity* was "completed." (*Stockdale's Budget,* Jan. 3, Jan. 10, Jan. 17, 1827, pp. 26, 34, 42.) Timothy, presumably after seeing Stockdale, wrote to Shelley from London enquiring anxiously about his religious views and Shelley replied (in a tone of mollifying irony) on Feb. 6. (*Works,* VIII, 50–52.)

Finally, if we place the date of composition later than Shelley's return to Oxford, this leaves very little time for the necessary procedures of mailing the manuscript to Worthing, its printing there, and the return of the books to Oxford, for the work was advertised on Feb. 9. The catalyzing arguments were perhaps those received from Hogg between Jan. 11 and Jan. 17, and the final draft was completed by Jan. 24 or 25, or at the latest, Jan. 27.

180. Percy Vaughan, *Early Shelley Pamphlets* (London, 1905), p. 17.

181. Locke, after demonstrating at length that all ideas come from sensation, backtracks on the question of God, arguing that His existence is obvious from an examination of ourselves and the world. (*Essay concerning Human Understanding,* Book IV, ch. 10; see Shelley's comment in his letter to Elizabeth Hitchener, June 11, 1811, *Works,* VIII, 101.) A good deal of the argument of *The Necessity of Atheism* is inherent in the first paragraph of Hume's essay *Of Miracles:* "It is acknowledged on all hands, says that learned prelate, that the authority, either of Scripture or tradition, is founded merely on the testimony of the apostles, who were eye witnesses of those miracles of our Saviour, by which he proved his divine mission. Our evidence, then, for the truth of the *Christian* religion, is less than the evidence for the truth of our senses; because even in the first authors of our religion, it was no greater; and it is evident it must diminish in passing from them to their disciples; nor can anyone rest such confidence in their testimony, as in the immediate objects of his senses." For comments on some possible general sources for Shelley's little essay see: Vaughan, pp. 19–20. Shelley refers to Hume's essay *Of Miracles* in the Notes to *Queen Mab, Works,* I, 154.

182. *Works,* V, 208.

183. *Works,* I, 147.

184. *Works,* V, 208.

185. David Hume, *Dialogues Concerning Natural Religion,* Part IX.

186. *Works,* V, 208.

187. *Ibid.,* 208–209. Cf. Hume, as cited in n. 181 above and in the conclusion of Part 1 of the essay *Of Miracles:* "When any one tells me, that he saw a dead man restored to life, I immediately consider with myself, whether it be more probable that this person should either deceive or be deceived, or that the fact he relates should really have happened."

188. *Works,* VIII, 51.

189. *Ibid.,* p. 52. Here Shelley is perhaps echoing Paine's *Age of Reason:* "They promised him ALL the Jews, ALL the Turks by anticipation, nine-tenths of the world beside, and Mahomet into the bargain. After this who can doubt the bountifulness of the Christian Mythology?" (*The Life and Works of Thomas Paine,* VIII, 16–17.)

190. *Works,* V, 209; see also p. 207: "They have attached a degree of criminality to disbelief . . ." and ch. VII, n. 160, below.

191. *Works,* V, 75. The extremity of the sentiment is, however, hastily

modified by a proposal of marriage (which sends Matilda into one of those ecstasies of bleating voluptuousness which were presumably intended to make the novel—like the "Epithalamium" in *Margaret Nicholson*—"sell like wildfire").

192. *Works,* V, 197. For other similarly daring passages see pp. 135–136, 138–139, 176–177, 194.

193. To Hogg, Jan. 12, 1811, *Shelley at Oxford,* p. 22. The emotional intensity of the second passage reflects Shelley's unbalance following his final rejection by Harriet Grove, as the rest of the letter reveals.

194. Jan. 23, 1811, *Works,* VIII, 48.

195. Medwin, pp. 37, 50.

196. *Ibid.,* p. 34.

197. Jan. 10, 1812, *Works,* VIII, 239.

198. To Godwin, June 3, 1812, *ibid.,* p. 331.

199. Carl Grabo, *A Newton Among Poets* (Chapel Hill, N. C., 1930), pp. 30 ff.

200. Hogg, I, 55–56.

201. See MacCarthy, pp. 28–30.

202. Medwin, p. 69.

203. A. N. Whitehead, *Science and The Modern World* (New York, 1927), p. 123.

204. Hogg, I, 47.

205. *Ibid.,* pp. 50–52.

CHAPTER III

1. *Works,* VIII, 59–60.

2. To Shelley, Apr. 5, 1811, Hogg, I, 187.

3. Enclosed with letter from Shelley to his father, *ca.* Apr., 1811, *Works,* VIII, 62. On the proposals Timothy has scrawled: "Fine fellows these to presume to offer proposals."

4. The failure to accept these proposals was the real turning point in the transactions. The essence of Timothy's position is revealed in the following sentences of his letter to his son on Apr. 5: "The disgrace which hangs over you is most serious, and though I have felt as a father, and sympathized in the misfortune which your criminal opinions and improper acts have begot; yet, you must know, that I have a duty to perform to my own character, as well as to your younger brothers and sisters. Above all, my feelings as a Christian require from me a decided and firm conduct towards you." (Ingpen, p. 217.) Timothy, that is to say, did have fatherly feelings toward his son but these were being overbalanced by his sense of family pride and duty. He gives the impression of a man of rather weak character compensating for his own inferiority feelings by an excessive display of authority—"I have a duty to perform to my own character." This becomes even more clear, if we contrast his attitude toward Shelley with that taken toward Hogg. Mr. Hogg placed the problem in the hands of a friend of his, a Mr. R. Clarke, an agent for the Earl of Bridgewater, then in London. The reasonableness displayed in a letter he wrote back to Mr.

Hogg contrasts markedly with the rigid authoritarianism of Timothy and his attorney Whitton: "It will blow over, I have no doubt, and Jefferson may be admitted into any of the Inns of Court. He cannot return to either of the Universities without a disavowal of his opinions: At his time of life that is not to be expected." (*Shelley at Oxford,* pp. 25–26. The first part of this letter—Hogg omits the conclusion—will be found in: Hogg, I, 195–196.)

5. Hogg, I, 182–185; Dowden, I, 129. Reading between the lines of Hogg's caricature of Timothy, he emerges as a rather kindly and bewildered man, greatly upset by his son's "disgrace."

6. On Apr. 11, Timothy told Whitton he had informed Shelley's cousin, John Grove, who had written urging more conciliatory measures, that he had "plac'd the business in your hands to guard my honour and character against Prosecution in the Courts," and he similarly informed Mr. Hogg's intermediary, Clarke, on Apr. 14. On Apr. 13, Whitton wrote to C. and W. Phillips, printers of *The Necessity of Atheism:* "I have been informed that a prosecution is intended against you." (Ingpen, pp. 231, 238, 194 n.) Clarke, however, did not take the threat of prosecution seriously, writing to Mr. Hogg on Apr. 6: "You need not be anxious, at all, I think, about any criminal prosecution: the Pamphlet is not of the kind to merit such a proceeding, I should apprehend.—It will blow over, I have no doubt. . . ." (*Shelley at Oxford,* p. 25.) Nor did Shelley himself take it seriously: "All danger about prosecution is over; it was *never* more than a hum." (To Hogg, May 15, 1811, *Works,* VIII, 86.) But there can be no doubt that the threat frightened Timothy and was largely responsible for his subsequent handling of the affair.

7. Apr. 17, 1811, *Works,* VIII, 65. A few weeks later when Merle visited Shelley at Field Place his determination was unchanged: "My first act, when in possession of my estate, shall be to divide it equally with my family. The world shall see how much more just is the reasoning man than the credulous believer." (Merle, p. 706.)

8. Ingpen, p. 249. (Ingpen was the first biographer of Shelley to have access to the Whitton papers, i.e. the legal papers of the Whittons which contained letters from Shelley, Whitton, Sir Bysshe, Sir Timothy, Peacock, Mary Shelley, and Byron, and which throw important new light on Shelley's years in England. Some of these papers are now in the library of Yale University.

9. To Whitton, Apr. 19, 1811, *Works,* VIII, 68. (My punctuation.)

10. Ingpen, pp. 253–254. Timothy here, we may note, places the blame for Shelley's actions on his radical readings, readings which had moved him beyond the respectable orbits of Whiggism and liberal Christianity into the outer wastes of republicanism and atheism. That he had mainly Godwin in mind is clear from a letter to Whitton of Oct. 27, 1811. (*Ibid.,* p. 348.)

11. Medwin, 100–101; C. H. Grove to Hellen Shelley, Feb. 16, 1857, Hogg, II, 156. I quote both accounts below.

12. Hogg, I, 197; Timothy Shelley to Whitton, Apr. 23, 1811, Sir Bysshe Shelley to Whitton, Apr. 15, 1811, Ingpen, pp. 255, 237, 262 n.; Shelley to Hogg, Apr. 24, Apr. 29, May 8, *Works,* VIII, 69–70, 79, 80.

13. To Hogg, Apr. 24, *ca.* May 13, May 15, *Works,* VIII, 70, 85; to Graham, n.d., *Works,* X, 416. On May 8, Shelley informed Hogg that he would be home "in the course of a few days"; the next datable letter is May 15, from Field Place, written just after his arrival; if we allow two or three days for the negotiations in conjunction with Pilfold, this would place the date of his departure at May 12 or 13. Shelley was perhaps also assisted in his negotiations by the Duke of Norfolk, whom he later thanked for his "friendly interposition in the spring." (Oct. 28, 1811, *ibid.,* p. 171.) On Pilfold, see: *DNB;* William Laird Clowes, *The Royal Navy* (London, 1900), V, 131; *The Dispatches and Letters of Vice Admiral Lord Viscount Nelson* (London, 1846), VII, 305; Medwin, p. 110. Pilfold was appointed a Companion of the Bath in 1815.

14. Timothy, according to *Alumni Oxonienses,* was *MP* for Horsham, 1790–1792 and for Shoreham, 1802–1818.

15. Medwin, pp. 100–102. Medwin lifts the Duke's speech from Hogg's 1832 articles without acknowledgment. The comment on the Duke renouncing his faith for political power refers to his change from Catholicism to Protestantism in order to be eligible (before his Dukedom) for election to the Commons. The Duke, however, remained a staunch advocate of Catholic emancipation.

16. Quoted in: Hogg, II, 156.

17. Merle, p. 705.

18. Shelley to Elizabeth Hitchener, Oct. 27, 1811, *Works,* VIII, 168; Southey to Shelley, 1820, *The Correspondence of Robert Southey with Caroline Bowles,* p. 359. Hellen later remembered Harriet as "a very handsome girl . . . with hair like a poet's dream." (Hogg, I, 32.)

19. *Works,* VIII, 42; Charles Grove to Hellen Shelley, Feb. 16, 1857; Hogg, II, 155. Grove's account runs as follows: "During the Christmas vacation of that year, and in January 1811, I spent part of it with Bysshe at Field Place, and when we returned to London, his sister Mary sent a letter of introduction with a present to her schoolfellow, Miss Westbrook, which Bysshe and I were to take to her. I recollect we did so, calling at Mr. Westbrook's house. I scarcely know how it came about, but from that time Bysshe corresponded with Miss Westbrook." Shelley arrived at Field Place for his vacation on about Dec. 15 (*Works,* VIII, 21–22); he left for Oxford on about Jan. 24, intending to stop over in London. (*Ibid.,* pp. 48–49.) If it was on this latter ocasion that he stopped to see Harriet in London, then he must have mailed her the copy of *St. Irvyne* (on Jan. 11) before delivering the letter of introduction, a procedure which seems unlikely. It is more probable that he accompanied Grove back to London between Jan. 1 and Jan. 11. On Jan. 2 he wrote to Hogg: "I am but just returned to Field Place from an inefficient effort," and informs him that he had left on Dec. 30. (*Ibid.,* pp. 31–32.) This "effort," he hints, was an attempt to win Harriet Grove back, and the implication is that he had been to Wiltshire to see her. But the vagueness of the phrasing is suspicious. It may be that he had been in London and did not wish Hogg to know that he had been there and had failed to visit him, Hogg being at Lincoln's Inn Fields until about Jan. 3. (*Ibid.,* pp. 33, 35.) If this were the case, it makes

it clear why Shelley had been able to be away from Field Place for four days; Timothy would certainly not have let him go off alone to Wiltshire to see Harriet Grove but would have let him accompany his cousin, Charles Grove, to London. There he may have made added pleas with some members of the Grove family to win Harriet Grove back to him, or he may simply be romanticizing for Hogg's benefit. As we know of no other visit to London, this occasion (Dec. 30–Jan. 2) is the most probable time for the first meeting with Harriet Westbrook. (My attention was called to the problem of specifically dating this meeting by Dr. Richard Hudson of the English Department, Indiana University, who kindly showed me a term paper he had once written on the subject.)

20. Hogg, *loc. cit.;* to Elizabeth Hitchener, Oct. 27, 1811, *Works,* VIII, 168–169; Harriet Shelley to Elizabeth Hitchener, Mar. 14, 1812, *Works,* VIII, 1812.

21. Ingpen, p. 516 n. Westbrook married a Miss Ann Elliott. In *Kent's Directory* [of London], 1781, I find listed: "John Elliott, Wine and Brandy Merchant, New Street, Covent-Garden," and in succeeding directories, "Elliot and Co., Brewers, Pimlico"; so perhaps Mrs. Westbrook also came from a family connected with the liquor trade.

22. *Ibid.,* pp. 515–516.

23. Henry B. Wheatley, *London, Past and Present* (London, 1891), II, 565. Although Wheatley states the coffeehouse was on Mount Street and Westbrook's business address was officially 78 Lower Grosvenor Street, the two are apparently identical. A map of London in 1806 ("exhibiting all the new buildings to the present year") shows Mount Street and Lower Grosvenor Street running parallel but one block apart, and between them at the corner of Charles Street (which formed one side of Grosvenor Square) is a single building, labelled "Mount," one entrance to which could have been in Grosvenor Street, the other in Mount Street. (Map appended to: B. Lambert, *The History and Survey of London and its Environs* [London, 1806], 4 vols.)

24. Ingpen, p. 516 n., states that "Sterne addressed many of his letters" from the Mount Coffee House (without stating whether he believed it to be the same house as that presided over later by Westbrook). But I find only one letter, addressed on Apr. 23, 1765, to Lady Workworth, in which Sterne states that he has "come forth from my lodgings to a coffee house, the nearest I could find to my dear Lady's house, and have called for a sheet of gilt paper. . . ." (*Letters of Laurence Sterne,* ed. by Lewis Perry Curtis [Oxford, 1935], p. 242.)

25. First two lines quoted in: Wheatley, *loc. cit.* John W. Draper, *William Mason, A Study in Eighteenth Century Culture* (New York University Press, 1924), pp. 259–260, informs us that Mason's *The Dean and the Squire* is a satire, from the Whig viewpoint, of Soame Jenyns' conservative *Disquisition on Government.* This may possibly mean that Westbrook's coffeehouse was a haunt of Whig liberals. Coffeehouses sometimes had a distinct political allegiance and clientele.

26. Ingpen, p. 516.

27. Chancery Papers relating to Shelley's children by Harriet, given in:

Medwin, p. 464; letter to Hogg, *Works,* VIII, 110–111. Westbrook may have retired as early as 1807, "the year in which he first appears as a rate payer in Chapel Street." "His house, No. 23, was of the rateable value of £16 which was about the average in 1807 for Chapel Street; his stables were subject to an additional rate of £4." (Edmund Blunden, *LTLS,* July 13, 1946, p. 331.)

28. Hogg, I, 270, 274; e.g. on Eliza—"a barmaid by origin, or at best a daughter of the house."

29. John Timbs, *Clubs and Club Life in London* (London, 1899), pp. 300–301, 304–305.

30. Pierce Egan, *Life in London* (London, 1821), pp. 181–183 (with Cruikshank's vivid illustration of the interior of a poorer coffeehouse).

31. Hogg, I, 274.

32. *Works,* VIII, 67.

33. Hogg tells us that he saw Harriet "for the first time" in Edinburgh after the elopement. (Hogg, I, 253.) And he was "presented" to Eliza by Harriet later in York. (*Ibid.,* p. 274.)

34. To Hogg, *Shelley at Oxford,* p. 27.

35. The school was first run by a Mrs. Fenning; later by Miss Hawkes. For its location, see: MacCarthy, p. xv. Shelley's anger at the modes of punishment at the school was remembered in later years by his sister Hellen. (Hogg, I, 27.)

36. To Hogg, *ca.* Apr. 25, *Works,* VIII, 72; to Elizabeth Hitchener, Oct. 27, 1811, *ibid.,* 169; Dowden, I, 149.

37. *Ibid.,* p. 76. Rossetti suggested that the "fiend" is intolerance (Ingpen, p. 271 n.); it is—in the light of the original text of some of Shelley's letters to Hogg—more probably Christianity.

38. To Hogg, May 8, 1811, *ibid.,* p. 82; to Hogg, n.d., *ibid.,* pp. 92–93; *Shelley at Oxford,* pp. 36, 39. The dating of this second letter is uncertain. Ingpen (*Works,* VIII, 92 n.) dates it May 18 on the following grounds. A dated letter of May 17 to Hogg (*ibid.,* p. 90) opens: "Your letters have never reached me"; the undated letter opens: "I found this moment all your letters. They were in Great Portland Street." The postmark, he believes, is "possibly . . . May 18." But there are difficulties in this dating. The postmark is evidently not clear because in his 1909 edition of Shelley's letters (*The Letters of Percy Bysshe Shelley,* I, 72 n.), Ingpen thought the postmark "possibly . . . May 12," and so dated it. Shelley's letter on May 17 is addressed from Field Place and one on May 19 (to Hogg) from Cuckfield. (*Works,* VIII, 94.) As the letter under question was written at the Westbrook house in London, this sequence would necessitate a flying visit to London from Field Place on May 18 and a return to Cuckfield the same day or the next day. And the tone of the letter gives no indication of such a trip, but implies that Shelley is living in London. Further, the May 19 letter to Hogg comments on a letter just received from Eliza apparently giving him news of events since his departure from London. (*Ibid.,* p. 95.) Finally, in a dated letter from London on May 8, to Hogg, he writes: "I have received very few of your letters; they have been sent to Portland Street, and I cannot recover them." (*Ibid.,* p. 80; *Shelley at Oxford,*

p. 36.) The letter under question gives me the impression of immediately following this letter rather than that of May 17. If so, there may have been two batches of lost letters from Hogg, a contingency which seems less unlikely when we keep the volume of their correspondence in mind and note that Shelley's letters to Hogg went astray also: "Strange! you have not received one of mine, and I have written to you almost every day during my stay in London." (May 19, *ibid.*, p. 94.)

The situation is further confused by Scott, who (*Shelley at Oxford*, p. 39) dates the letter under question "on 8th May," without stating his evidence, and then places it after the May 17 letter; further, the typography indicates a missing figure before the 8; so apparently Scott intended to date it May 18. The most likely dating for the letter is May 8 or shortly after, certainly before Shelley's departure from London for Field Place.

39. To Hogg, *ca.* May 13, *Works,* VIII, 85. The only extant letter in the correspondence by Eliza was addressed to Pilfold's. (Ingpen, p. 277.)

40. Mentioned in letter to Hogg of that date, *Works,* VIII, 95.

41. Ingpen, pp. 276–277.

42. Shelley received the Groves' invitation before he left London for Field Place, i.e. before May 15. (Charles Grove to Hellen Shelley, Feb. 16, 1857; Hogg, II, 156.) On June 16, Shelley told Hogg he had been "invited to Wales" but did not say by whom; on June 21, he wrote to Hogg: "Old Westbrook has invited me to accompany him and his daughters to a house they have at Aberystwith in Wales; I shall stay about a week; then I shall come to see you." (*Works,* VIII, 105, 110–111.) And Hogg was apparently under the impression that Shelley was going to Aberystwyth with the Westbrooks until he received a letter from the Groves' house near Rhayader. On July 25, Shelley, apparently in answer to his query, wrote: "I had, previously to my intention of coming to York, accepted an invitation from a cousin of mine here to stay a week or two; whence, I intend to proceed to Aberystwith, about thirty miles off." (*Ibid.*, p. 126.)

There is something queer about these two invitations to Wales coming so close together. Shelley's intention in accepting the Groves' invitation was probably—as he told Hogg—to get into the vicinity of the Westbrook home at Aberystwyth, and he probably arranged the invitation with that in mind. (Charles Grove indicates that the invitation was extended on Shelley's initiative.) He had, it seems to me, either received the Westbrooks' invitation previously, or knowing of the Westbrooks' plans, had used the Groves' invitation to secure one from the Westbrooks also. That both invitations should have come providentially is unlikely.

To Hogg, Shelley is clearly intent on playing up the romantic aspect of a vacation with Harriet and her family and so does not inform him of the Groves' invitation until it is unavoidable. His statements are, in any case, contradictory. He cannot, at the same time have intended to (a) visit the Westbrooks for a week and then proceed to York, and (b) spend one to two weeks with the Groves, then stay with the Westbrooks, and then go to York. The mystery is increased by the fact that we have no later references to the Westbrooks having been in Wales; Shelley's later letters give the impression that they had been in London all the time. On July 25, however, he informed Hogg that they are in "Condowell" and will proceed to Aberystwyth. (*Works*, VIII, 126.) I can find no trace of a "Condowell" either in Wales or England; and by Aug. 3, Shelley had received a letter from Harriet from London which must have been posted in that city by Aug. 1. (*Ibid.*, p. 138.)

43. *Works*, VIII, 116.

44. *Shelley at Oxford*, pp. 45, 46; *Works*, VIII, 123.

45. Hughes, pp. 95–97.

46. Letter, July 15, *Works*, VIII, 124. Cf. Shelley's comment to Elizabeth Hitchener on Aug. 10, when he had returned to London from Wales to plan the elopement: "Particular *business* occasioned my sudden return." (*Ibid.*, p. 139; my italics.) Professor White (I, 606) suggests the "business" in July had to do with the printing and distribution of a poem; but while this may have formed part of Shelley's activities it seems inadequate to account for the "violent nervous illness." The two "businesses" were probably similar. It is, in any case, inconceivable that Shelley should spend several days in London without visiting Harriet.

47. To Hogg, *ibid.*, pp. 126, 127, 129, Ingpen guesses the date of the letter to Hogg on pp. 126–127 as "July 25"; but this is too late a date, for Shelley's (dated) letter to Graham (p. 123) shows that he was at Rhayader at least by July 15, and this letter to Hogg is apparently the first to Hogg after a brief note announcing his arrival. (*Ibid.*) In that note he promised to write to Hogg on "Wednesday," and it is unlikely that he would wait ten days or more before doing so. The date is more likely July 16 (which was a Wednesday).

48. White, I, 150–151.

49. *Ca.* July 30, *Works*, VIII, 136.

50. *Ibid.*, pp. 138–139. This letter is undated by Shelley and had no postmarked date. Ingpen dates it "probably about August 3." This date is almost certainly correct. Shelley writes that he will "set off for London on Monday." This must have been Monday, Aug. 5, and not Monday Aug. 12, because he addressed a letter in London on Aug. 10, and had apparently been there several days. Nor can it have been Monday, July 28, because he addressed a letter from Cwm Elan on Aug. 1. (*Works*, VIII, 139, 137.) The letter, therefore, was written two or three days before Aug. 5 and would be received about two days later by Hogg.

51. Charles Grove to Hellen Shelley, Hogg, II, 156.

52. Shelley wrote to Elizabeth Hitchener on Aug. 10 from London that he intended to "be at Field Place tomorrow." This was to be but a brief visit, for he indicated that he would not see her then but probably would see her later in the month. (*Works*, VIII, 139.) However, he did not leave until Aug. 14 for on Aug. 15 he states that he had "left London yesterday" for Field Place and is back in London. On Aug. 19, he writes to Elizabeth Hitchener, apparently, as Dowden (I, 172 n.) surmised, from Field Place, and not, as Ingpen indicates (*Works*, VIII, 143), from London, for the letter bears no postmark as it would if it had gone through London, and Shelley writes as though he were in her vincinity. He indicates, too,

that he had recently called on her, and she had reported that this call had been a reason for gossip, people viewing it as a visit from a young aristocrat to a poor school teacher and not as a communion of two intellectually congenial spirits. This call cannot have been made later than Aug. 18, and probably took place a day or two earlier; Shelley, therefore, must have left London again on Aug. 16 or 17. And this fits, too, with his later statement to Elizabeth Hitchener that but "one short week" after "I saw you" he was married. (Oct. 8, *ibid.,* p. 152.) During this visit he saw Mr. Medwin at Horsham and borrowed the £25 from him, which annoyed Timothy, even though Medwin did not know what Shelley intended to use the money for. (To the Duke of Norfolk, Oct. 28, *ibid.,* p. 171; to Thomas Charles Medwin, Nov. 26, *ibid.,* p. 207.) That this visit lasted until almost the day of the elopement is indicated by the phrasing used to the Duke on Medwin's loan—"he was ignorant of the purposes to which I was *about to apply* the money" (my italics)—and by Charles Grove's statement: "When Bysshe finally *came to town to elope* with Miss W. . . ." (Hogg, II, 156; my italics.)

53. To Hogg, *ca.* Aug. 14 (or earlier), *Works,* VIII, 140.

54. To Hogg, Aug. 15, *Works,* VIII, 141–142. For his previous free love arguments, see: to Hogg, May 8, 1811, *Shelley at Oxford,* pp. 39–40. See also: to Hogg, *ca.* May 13, 1811, *Works,* VIII, 84.

55. Charles Grove to Hellen Shelley, Feb. 16, 1857, Hogg, II, 156–157. Dowden (I, 173) adds details not in this letter but for which he must, as White (I, 610) argues, have had a basic source. The date of the elopement is set by the following facts: on Aug. 26, Shelley sent a letter to his father from Houghton, near Durham, and he could only have reached that point if he had left London at least by the previous day (*Works,* VIII, 145); that he had not left earlier than the 25th we know because Timothy informed Whitton that he had borrowed money in London from a Mr. Dunn on "Sunday morning, ye 25th Aug." (Ingpen, p. 307.) Grove states that they went "in a hackney coach to the Green Dragon, in Gracechurch Street." Dowden, however (I, 173 n.), notes that the coaches started from the "Bull and Mouth" and so presumes that Grove was mistaken. This may be so, but Grove's notation seems so exact that it is possible that they did stay at the Green Dragon, purposely avoiding the Bull and Mouth in case of a search, until near the time for the departure of the coach. The Bull and Mouth was near St. Martins le Grand, only a short distance from Gracechurch Street. Coaches for Edinburgh left there at 11 a.m. and 7 p.m. daily. They left from other inns also but only early (6-7.30) in the morning. (*The Post Office Annual Directory for 1813.*) Shelley perhaps had intended to take the 11 a.m. coach, but Harriet apparently (Dowden, I, 173) was late.

56. Shelley chose Edinburgh for his honeymoon presumably because of the greater laxity of the Scottish marriage laws (which permitted the marriage of minors), but he was perhaps influenced also by Hogg, who had been considering a vacation in Scotland. (Hogg, I, 246–247.) On the coach he met a Scottish lawyer who told him how to go about getting

married in Edinburgh. (Hogg, I, 261.) They were married by the Reverend Joseph Robertson, who, apparently, showed them how to circumvent a six weeks residence rule. Seven years later Robertson was prosecuted for similar practices, sentenced to three months in prison and banished from Scotland. (Peck, I, 171–174; White, I, 611.)

Shelley and Harriet left London at 7 p.m. on Aug. 25; by midnight of Aug. 26, they were passing through York. (Hogg, I, 247.) It later took Hogg approximately thirty hours to go from York to Edinburgh, leaving York in the afternoon and arriving at Edinburgh late the next night. (Hogg, I, 247–251.) Hence Shelley and Harriet must have arrived in Edinburgh on the morning of Aug. 28. The marriage certificate is dated Aug. 28, and the marriage ceremony, which could not by law take place the same day, was performed on Aug. 29. (Ingpen, pp. 309–310.) (I note, in Arthur Groom, *Old London Coaching Inns and Their Successors* [London, n.d.], p. 13, that coaches travelled at about seven miles per hour; this would make the Edinburgh run approximately sixty hours, which fits in with the facts noted above.) Shelley later spent "three nights" on a coach travelling from York to Cuckfield in Sussex. (To Elizabeth Hitchener, *ca.* Oct. 18, 1811, *Works,* VIII, 161.)

57. This had also apparently been the theme of her previous letter to Shelley received on May 19. See, Shelley to Hogg, May 19, 1811, *Works,* VIII, 95. In the trial for the custody of the children of Shelley and Harriet in 1817, the accusation was made that it was by Eliza's "active concurrence, and it may be said by her management," that Shelley and Harriet eloped. (Brief by Shelley's lawyer, Wetherell, quoted in: Dowden, II, 83.) Hogg (I, 274) was of a similar opinion: "Eliza intended, guided, and ruled Harriet from her earliest infancy; she doubtless had married her, had made the match, had put her up to everything that was to be said or done, as Shelley's letters plainly show."

58. To Timothy Shelley, Aug. 26, 1811, Ingpen, pp. 301–302. Hogg had a similar impression. (Hogg, I, 270.)

59. To Elizabeth Hitchener, Mar. 14, 1812, *Works,* VIII, 294. (Harriet's letters are included in Shelley's *Works.*) See also Hogg's description of Harriet. (Hogg, I, 265.)

60. Section of letter to Elizabeth Hitchener added by Harriet, Jan. 29, 1812, *Works,* VIII, 263. Cf. Hogg, I, 274.

61. Reminiscences of a Mrs. Field, formerly a pupil at the school. (Dowden I, 149.)

62. Oct. 27, 1811, *Works,* VIII, 169.

63. White, I, 609–610.

64. Oct. 8, 1811, *Works,* VIII, 152.

65. *Ibid.,* pp. 141–142; White, I, 609.

66. Aug. 19, 1811, *ibid.,* p. 143; Merle, p. 706:

I am one of these aristocrats. In me, although as it were a living outcast from my parent's bosom, the same machinery of oppression is preparing, in order that I also in my turn may become an oppressor. But my father deceives himself. My first act, when in possession of my estate, shall be to divide it equally with my family. The world shall see how much more just is the reasoning man than the credulous believer.

67. Jan. 10, Jan. 28, 1812, *Works,* VIII, 241, 257.

68. Letters to Hogg, Nov., 1811, *Harriet and Mary,* pp. 15–16, 25, 22, 20. These letters are undated and, as they did not go through London, without postmark, but they clearly come in the days and weeks immediately following Shelley's arrival in Keswick early in Nov. The sequence as given by Scott (*ibid.,* pp. 13 ff.) follows that of Ingpen in his early edition of Shelley's letters and not Ingpen's later sequencing as given in *Works,* VIII, 177 ff., which appears to be more exact.

69. Dec. 15, Nov. 24, Nov. 12, 1811, *Works,* VIII, 218, 201, 184–185.

70. Nov., 1811, *Harriet and Mary,* p. 30.

71. *A Discourse on the Manners of the Antient Greeks Relative to the Subject of Love,* ed. by Roger Ingpen (London, 1931), p. 14.

72. This is deducible from the *ca.* Aug. 3 letter to Hogg, especially if we remember Shelley's motives in that letter for playing down his own initiative: "She asked my advice; resistance was the answer . . . in consequence of my advice she has thrown herself on my protection." The advice was probably not only to "resist" but to run away with Shelley. Shelley, we might note, did not want Hogg to know that he had been in London with Harriet in July, for Hogg had been expecting him in York and Shelley did not wish him to think that his failure to go there was due to the influence of Harriet. Hence, in this letter he is implying that this "advice" had either been given by letter or in London in Apr. But the wording implies a fairly recent happening and one that can hardly all— including the attempted "mollifying" of Mr. Westbrook—have taken place by correspondence.

73. Hogg had previously advised Timothy Shelley to arrange a marriage for his son. (Hogg, I, 183.)

74. Shelley indicates to Elizabeth Hitchener that this proposal came immediately before the elopement, but this (see following n.) was not so. He had seen Elizabeth Hitchener on about Aug. 17 and had not apparently told her anything of Harriet; hence he did not later want to hurt her feelings by letting her know that he had by that time made his proposal. (Oct. 27, 1811, *Works,* VIII, 169.)

75. On about Aug. 3, Shelley wrote to inform Hogg of his plan for running away with Harriet; Hogg answered by urging him to marry if he intended to go through with the scheme. (To Hogg, Aug. 15, *ibid.,* p. 142.) In the Aug. 14 letter, immediately after the sentence, "My arguments have been *yours,*" Shelley added: "They have been urged by the force of the gratitude which this occasion excited"—in explanation for his departure from his free love creed. (*Ibid.,* p. 140.) Shelley, that is to say, had proposed marriage to Harriet, using Hogg's arguments as the basis for his proposal. (He had previously used the word "gratitude" in regard to Harriet in his *ca.* Aug. 3, letter.)

76. Southey, a few months later got the impression from Harriet and

Shelley that her family had disapproved of the elopement. (Southey to John Rickman, Jan. 6, 1812, quoted in White, I, 619.) But someone must have planned matters. The day that Shelley and Harriet were in London, they were chaperoned by Charles Grove; the succeeding two and a half days were spent in continuous travel in a coach, passing without a stop even through York, native habitat of the beloved Hogg; the day the couple arrived in Edinburgh they obtained a license and Shelley duly informed their landlord that they were not yet married. (Peacock, p. 320.) This sequence clearly shows planning and agreement in advance. That Westbrook put up no money is stated by Hogg (I, 270) and is indicated also by Shelley's borrowing £25 from Medwin before the elopement; £10 from a Mr. Dunn on the morning of the elopement (Ingpen, p. 307); £10 requested from Hogg en route (*Works,* VIII, 145); and his lack of funds in the early days in Edinburgh (when he was rescued from poverty by his uncle, Capt. Pilfold). (Hogg, I, 269–270.)

77. That the final decision came by mail Shelley informed Elizabeth Hitchener—"She wrote to me. I came to London"—and, as this fits in with other factors previously noted, it is probably true.

78. This, I presume, is what he had in mind when he told Hogg, on *ca.* Aug. 3, that whether he came to York "now" or "in three weeks" depended on Harriet, i.e. if Harriet did not consent to his scheme he would come alone to York and live with Hogg but if she consented he would have to wait for his allowance. (For the date of the allowance see letter to Hogg, Aug. 25, *Works,* VIII, 145.) He had no money in Wales (to Hogg, July 30, *ibid.,* p. 136), and he cannot have anticipated borrowing the £25. If this is what he had in mind, he is either using the term "three weeks" in a loose sense or he believed that he could obtain the allowance a week in advance (which is perhaps what he was trying to do at Field Place).

79. Hogg, I, 264–265. That Harriet actually translated in so brief a time (Aug. 28 to the end of Sept.) two full volumes, as Hogg contends, is doubtful. The novel was *Claire d'Albe* by Marie (Ristaud) Cottin, which, according to the British Museum Catalogue, had been translated previously in 1808.

80. *Ibid.,* p. 255.

81. *Ibid.,* II, 1.

82. *Ibid.,* I, 280.

83. Peacock, p. 338.

84. Hogg, I, 270.

85. Dec., 1811, *Harriet and Mary,* p. 23.

86. Oct. 27, 1811, *Works,* VIII, 169.

87. Shelley sent a letter to his father from Edinburgh on Sept. 27, urging that funds be mailed to him "immediately"; his next letter is from York and is also to his father, announcing his change of residence, and is postmarked Oct. 5 (*ibid.,* pp. 149–151); this, in view of his need for cash, I presume he would send immediately on arriving at York. Hence, Oct. 5 is the probable date of arrival. On Pilfold, see Hogg, I, 269–270. The Oct. 5 letter, it is interesting to note, is addressed in Hogg's handwriting; Shelley

apparently feared his father would not open a letter if he saw that it was from his son.

88. On Oct. 18, he informed Elizabeth Hitchener that he had "arrived this morning" at Cuckfield after three days and nights on a coach. (*Works,* VIII, 161.)

89. Letters from Whitton to Timothy Shelley and Sir Bysshe Shelley, Aug. 26, 1811, Ingpen, pp. 301–303. Shelley noted in his Aug. 15 letter to Hogg that Timothy was in London "wondering possibly about my London business" (*Works,* VIII, 142), and Whitton's letter to Timothy implies previous consultation.

90. Whitton to Sir Bysshe, Aug. 26, 1811, Ingpen, p. 303.

91. *Works,* VIII; 145 postmarked, Houghton, Aug. 26. Houghton is about 250 miles north of London. Shelley does not mention Harriet but Timothy doubtless presumed her presence as his instructions to Whitton show that he was aware of his son's interest in her.

92. Ingpen, p. 307. Elizabeth Hitchener wrote to Shelley on Nov. 12 that Capt. Pilfold "tells me he believes they have not made you a Ward of Chancery, say if you think they have." (*Letters of Elizabeth Hitchener to Percy Bysshe Shelley* [New York, 1926], p. 23.)

93. Ingpen, pp. 307–308; Shelley to Whitton, *Works,* VIII, 162.

94. *Stockdale's Budget,* Jan. 31, 1827, p. 59.

95. Thomas de Quincey, "Notes on Gilfillan's Literary Portraits," *Collected Writings,* ed. by David Mason (Edinburgh, 1890), XI, 367–368. See also the comment of the Earl of Chichester (above, p. 169): "I hear that he has married a Servant, or some person of very low birth." "An Oxford Collegian," writing to the *Anti-Jacobin Review* in Feb., 1812, on Shelley's career, commented: "Report says that our ex-collegian, on being discountenanced by his friends, ran off with a young lady of no fortune, to Scotland, after very sudden acquaintance and has married her." (Quoted in: White, I, 590.)

96. Sept. 15, 1811, *Works,* VIII, 148.

97. *Ca.* Oct. 15, 1811, *ibid.,* p. 156.

98. Oct. 26, 1811, Ingpen, p. 347. The facts on the Graham story are as follows. In an undated letter written immediately after his return to Field Place on May 15, 1811, Shelley wrote to Graham: "We had a letter this morning addressed to my father accusing him and my mother of getting drunk, etc. the latter of being more intimate with *you* than with my father himself. We all laughed heartily . . ." (*Works,* X, 416.) In a verse letter to Graham, clearly written about the same time (*Works,* III, 92–94), he handles the rumor in high mock style:

> All fairly may acquit your soul,
> Though your life's pulses fiercely roll,
> Of having let one wild wish glow
> Of cornuting old Killjoy's brow.

We hear no more of the incident—a letter of Aug. 30 shows him still friendly with Graham (*Works,* VIII, 147)—until on Oct. 22 he wrote to his mother from Capt. Pilfold's accusing her of attempting to marry off his sister Elizabeth to Graham in order to "shield *yourself* from that suspicion which at length has fallen on you." On the same day, he wrote to Elizabeth urging her to "speak truth" if challenged. (*Ibid.,* pp. 163–164.) On Oct. 25, Timothy wrote to Whitton: "He would not regard any language against his mother or sister. He accuses me of Libel and the thought of everything that could be bad. . . ." (Ingpen, p. 348.) On Oct. 26, Shelley wrote to his father: "Did Graham, the music-master, or did he not ward off a threatened action for libel?" (*Ibid.,* p. 166.) On Oct. 27, Timothy, writing to Whitton, dismissed the story as "too absurd and ridiculous for a thought." (Ingpen, p. 349.) Shelley told the story (or one like it) to Elizabeth Hitchener (Oct. 27, *Works,* VIII, 169), and to his cousin Charles Grove: "Graham's business is at length made public. I little suspected my Mother of such baseness tho' I knew her intentions and counteracted them." (Oct. 29, *ibid.,* p. 173.) The last we hear of the business is in a letter to Timothy on Dec. 22: "I know not what may be the precise state of that affair . . . but I cannot consider myself blameable for having interfered." (*Ibid.,* p. 222.)

The episode goes through two stages, one in the spring, in which the story is taken as a joke by all concerned, including Shelley; one in the fall, in which Shelley makes it the basis for an accusation. My own feeling is that, most probably, Shelley himself wrote—in a spirit of semi-malevolent buffoonery—the accusing letter in May (a procedure in keeping with his penchant for pseudonymous letter writing), and that he either invented the story or elaborated it from some gossip he had picked up at Pilfold's. His somewhat different use of it in the fall I take to be another example of his manic reaction to frustration. His father's attempt to tame him by cutting off his income and the subsequent bitter humiliation of having to beg at Field Place had reduced him to a frenzy in which he struck out recklessly (the Syon House psychological pattern), building up a fantasy until he half convinced himself of its truth and then carrying it out in action. (Timothy, witnessing the phenomenon, evidently regarded him as on the verge of insanity.) The reason for the resurrection of this particular fantasy was perhaps the projected match between Graham and Elizabeth, of whom he was extremely jealous. And the story told to Elizabeth Hitchener and the Groves—John Grove had previously been considered as a suitor for Elizabeth—may have dealt rather with his mother's attempts to make this match than with the supposed liaison. The cryptic references in these letters can be taken either way. By Dec., however, the agitation had receded, and the letter to his father implies a retreat.

99. Oct. 13, 1811, *Works,* VIII, 154–155; the visit is noted by Timothy to Whitton, Oct. 23. (Ingpen, p. 338.)

100. Shelley to Whitton, Oct. 20, 1811, *Works,* VIII, 161; to Thomas Charles Medwin, Oct. 21, 1811, *ibid.,* p. 162; Ingpen, pp. 338–339; Whitton to Shelley, Oct. 24, 1811, *ibid.,* pp. 344–345.

101. *Works,* VIII, 162.

102. Timothy told Whitton that he had heard that Pilfold had accompanied Shelley to London. (Oct. 27, Ingpen, p. 349.) Whether Pilfold

stayed for the whole of Shelley's visit or only made an overnight trip on the 22nd–23rd we do not know, but the latter seems more likely.

103. The marriage settlement has more the flavor of a Westbrook than a Shelley production, and Shelley's having Medwin address it to them shows that he intended to discuss it with them. Perhaps Westbrook demanded it as a condition for supplying an allowance. Whether Shelley stayed with the Westbrooks or only gave their address as a mailing address we do not know. In a letter to his mother apparently written on the morning of the 22nd just before leaving for London he told her to "write to me at Mr. Westbrooks, 23 Chapel Street, Grosvenor Square," but then crossed out the address. (*Ibid.,* p. 164.) A letter to Whitton on "Tuesday evening, Oct. 22" is addressed from the Turk's Head Coffee House in the Strand (formerly a favorite haunt of Samuel Johnson's), which is a good distance from Chapel Street but not far from Whitton's office. So presumably he stayed there on the night of the 22nd. But whether he later stayed at the Westbrooks or not he must have called there to get Medwin's reply to his request on the marriage settlement.

104. Hogg, I, 273.

105. Shelley must have seen Eliza in London, for as she arrived in York but one day ahead of him (*ibid.,* p. 275)—i.e. Oct. 25—she must have left one day ahead also. Hence she was in London during the first two or three days of Shelley's stay there and presumably was consulted on the marriage settlement. Shelley must have known on the 24th or 25th that all was not well in York for a letter mailed by Whitton to Shelley in London on the 24th was forwarded to Harriet's new address in York. (Ingpen, p. 345.) Hence Shelley knew before he left London that Harriet and Hogg were no longer at the same address. He or Eliza, therefore, must have received a letter from Harriet, and it was perhaps after consultation on this letter that Eliza decided to leave a day early. Hogg had "urged" his "suit" immediately on Shelley's departure from York (i.e. Oct. 15) and on the day preceding Shelley's arrival (i.e. the day of Eliza's arrival) had confessed himself to be in the wrong. (To Elizabeth Hitchener, Nov. 14, 1811, *Works,* VIII, 188.)

106. Timothy Shelley to Whitton, Oct. 27, Ingpen, p. 348.

107. Whitton to Shelley, Oct. 24, 1811, Ingpen, pp. 344–345; Shelley to the Duke of Norfolk, *Works,* VIII, 171–172.

108. Hogg, I, 277.

109. Feb. 24, 1812, *Works,* VIII, 277.

110. E.g. to Elizabeth Hitchener, Jan. 2, 1812, *ibid.,* p. 231: "Eliza, her sister is a very amiable girl," and to Hogg, May 8, 1811, *ibid.,* p. 82.

111. The exact day of departure we do not know. Shelley addressed a letter from York on Oct. 29. (*Ibid.,* p. 172.) His first letters to Hogg from Keswick are undated and, as they did not go through the London post office, bear no postmark. (Hogg, I, 283.) A letter to Elizabeth Hitchener apparently written shortly after his arrival is undated but postmarked "Nov. 11," presumably in London, and so was probably mailed on Nov. 9 or 10. (*Works,* VIII, 178–180.)

112. *Ibid.*, p. 179.
113. To Elizabeth Hitchener, Nov. 14, *Works,* VIII, 188.
114. To Elizabeth Hitchener, *ca.* Nov. 8, *ibid.,* p. 180.
115. Hogg's letters have unfortunately not been preserved (or, at any rate, have not been published), but we can gather their tenor from Shelley's replies and from phrases quoted from them in letters to Elizabeth Hitchener. (Nov. 14, Nov. 24, Dec. 15, *ibid.,* pp. 187, 201, 217.)
116. *Ca.* Nov. 6; *ca.* Nov. 12, *Harriet and Mary,* pp. 13, 21; for approximate datings of these letters, see *Works,* VIII, 177, 187. The original text was first published in *Harriet and Mary* (1944); previously we had known the letters only in Hogg's mangled version.

Scott (*ibid.,* pp. 9, 66–82) revives Jeaffreson's argument (I, 407–435) that there was no seduction attempt, and that Shelley either had a hallucination or was misled by Eliza and Harriet. But both these arguments are ruled out by the text which Scott himself prints, for that text reveals that the subject at issue, as accepted by both Shelley and Hogg, was the physical possession of Harriet and not a mere "flirtation" or "indiscretion." We might note too that Harriet and Elizabeth Hitchener also corresponded on the question (to Harriet, Dec. 20, 1811, *Letters of Elizabeth Hitchener,* p. 32), and that Shelley informed not only Elizabeth Hitchener but Southey and Hookham that Hogg had attempted to "seduce" Harriet. (Southey to Shelley, 1820, *The Correspondence of Robert Southey with Caroline Bowles,* p. 364; Peck, II, 410.)

In support of his views Scott produces two pieces of evidence (previously produced by Jeaffreson): the dedicatory lines of Shelley's *Essay on Friendship*—"I once had a friend, whom an inextricable multitude of circumstance has forced me to treat with apparent neglect"—which Hogg takes as referring to himself, and the passage in *The Revolt of Islam* (1817) in which the hero Laon encounters an old friend:

> Then, suddenly, I knew it was the youth
> In whom its earliest hopes my spirit found;
> But envious tongues had stained his spotless truth,
> And thoughtless pride his love in silence bound,
> And shame and sorrow mine in toils had wound,
> Whilst he was innocent, and I deluded.   (V, v)

The dedicatory lines, however, according to Ingpen, are "not in the MS., and were probably written by Hogg" (*Works,* VII, 358), so that the essay does not refer to Hogg at all; and if we assume that *The Revolt of Islam* passage refers to Hogg, this does not indicate that Shelley had been deceived but only that some six years later (when his hatred of the Westbrooks was extreme) he liked to believe that he had. As to what actually happened, the letters written at the time are more important as evidence than Shelley's later views.

117. *Ca.* Nov. 15–19, *Harriet and Mary,* pp. 30, 28; *Works,* VIII, 191.
118. *Ca.* Nov. 12, *Harriet and Mary,* p. 22; *Works,* VIII, 186.
119. *Ca.* Nov. 8, *Harriet and Mary,* p. 18; *Works,* VIII, 181. Dots in MS.
120. Dec. 15, 1811, *Works,* VIII, 218.

121. *Ca.* Nov. 8, *Works,* VIII, 179.

122. Based, in part, on interview with Wardell B. Pomeroy and material in: Alfred C. Kinsey, Wardell B. Pomeroy, Clyde E. Martin, *Sexual Behavior in the Human Male* (Philadelphia and London, 1948), pp. 610–666. There is evidence of early homosexual tendencies also in *An Essay on Friendship.* (*Works,* VII, 143–144.) Edward Carpenter in *The Psychology of the Poet Shelley* (London, 1925) argued a strong (but repressed and unconscious) homosexual component in Shelley and based his psychological analysis on this assumption. The resulting study is, in my judgment, false in its fundamental concept of Shelley (as predominantly homosexual) but contains many interesting insights into his character and works. Stephen Spender in reviewing the letters in *Harriet and Mary* (*New Statesman and Nation,* XXVIII [Nov. 25, 1944], p. 355) implied that they express homosexual feelings. Shelley's basic revulsion of homosexuality, however, is clear from his later condemnation of Byron: "He associates with wretches who seem almost to have lost the gait and physiognomy of man, and who do not scruple to avow practices which are not only not named, but I believe seldom even conceived in England." (To Peacock, Dec. 22, 1818, *Works,* X, 12.)

123. *A Discourse on the Manners of the Antient Greeks,* p. 16.

124. *Ibid.,* p. 13.

125. *Ibid.,* p. 15.

126. *Ibid.,* p. 14.

127. Nov. 30, 1811, *Works,* VIII, 208.

128. Oct. 28, 1811, *ibid.,* p. 171.

129. Quoted in: MacCarthy, p. 120.

130. De Quincey, p. 368. De Quincey's memory of time sequence, after thirty-four years, is not accurate. The Duke cannot have made these preparations for the Shelleys' reception before they arrived as he did not know as late as Nov. 7 that they were leaving for Keswick; but De Quincey is right on the fact of the Duke's interest and activities. The extent of his interest is revealed in his journal entries. (Quoted in MacCarthy, pp. 119–121.)

131. MacCarthy, pp. 119–120.

132. For Calvert see: "The Last of the Calverts," *Cornhill Magazine,* n.s. XIV (May, 1890), 497–501. Shelley was much struck by Calvert at Greystoke. (To Elizabeth Hitchener, *ca.* Dec. 10, *Works,* VIII, 209.) Within two days of his return to Keswick Shelley went (apparently by invitation) to see him. (Dec. 11, *ibid.,* p. 213.) He later (Dec. 26) found that Calvert "knows every thing that relates to my family and myself." (*Ibid.,* pp. 223–224.) Just before leaving Keswick for Ireland, Shelley, Harriet, and Eliza stayed with the Calverts. (Jan. 29, *ibid.,* p. 260.)

133. Gerald Brenan and Edward Phillips Statham, *The House of Howard* (London, 1907), II, 630–641.

134. To Elizabeth Hitchener, Jan. 29, 1812, *Works,* VIII, 262.

135. To Elizabeth Hitchener, Aug. 19, 1811, *ibid.,* pp. 143–144.

136. See, for instance, Thackeray's story of the Prince Regent and his brothers getting the Duke helplessly drunk. ("George The Fourth," *The*

Four Georges, Prose Works, ed. by Walter Jerrold [London, 1902], X, 406–407.) See also, Albery, *op. cit.,* pp. 121–122, on his eating and drinking habits.

137. See, for instance, Merle's accounts of his conversation. (Merle, pp. 705–706.)

138. Dec. 23, 1811, *Works,* VIII, 222.

139. On Calvert, see letter to Elizabeth Hitchener, *ca.* Dec. 10, 1811, *ibid.,* p. 209; on the other guests, see: to the same, Dec. 11, *ibid.,* p. 211. For an account of these guests, see: MacCarthy, pp. 120–123.

140. MacCarthy, p. 121.

141. *Works,* VIII, 215–216.

142. Ingpen, p. 365.

143. Dec. 23, *Works,* VIII, 222.

144. Quoted in: to Elizabeth Hitchener, Jan. 26, 1812; and, to Godwin, Jan. 28, 1812, *Works,* VIII, 253, 259.

145. Quoted in: Jack Simmons, *Southey* (London, 1945), p. 136.

146. Letter to Grosvenor Bedford, Jan. 4, 1812, *Life and Correspondence of Robert Southey,* ed. by C. C. Southey (London, 1850), III, 325.

147. *Wat Tyler, The Poetical Works of Robert Southey* (London, 1837), II, 25. *Wat Tyler* was written in 1794, accepted by a publisher but was not then printed. In 1817 a pirated edition was brought out by the parliamentary reformer William Sherwin; Southey sought an injunction to stop the sale but was refused. William Smith, a left Whig, attacked Southey in the Commons and Southey answered in his *Letter to William Smith,* and was in turn answered by Hazlitt in *The Examiner.* Byron, in a letter to his publisher Murray, attacked Southey for attempting to "bring to the stake (for such would he do) men who think as he thought, and for no reason but because they think so still, when he has found it convenient to think otherwise." (Simmons, pp. 42, 158–161.)

148. Robert Southey, "Army and Navy Reforms" (1810), *Essays, Moral and Political* (London, 1832), I, 44.

149. "Of Sir Francis Burdett's Motion for Parliamentary Reform" (1810), *ibid.,* p. 11. Southey's remarks on Burdett enraged Shelley. See: Letter to Elizabeth Hitchener, Jan. 20, 1812, *Works,* VIII, 246. For Southey's defense of sinecures see: "On the Economical Reformers" (1811), *Essays,* pp. 53–55. Southey's views on these matters were paralleled by those of his former comrades in radicalism, Wordsworth and Coleridge.

150. De Quincey, p. 368: "Southey, made aware of the interest taken in Shelley by the Duke of Norfolk, with his usual kindness, immediately called upon him."

151. To John Rickman (M.P.), Jan. 6, 1812, quoted in: White, I, 618–620. In examining the MS. of this letter (in the Huntington Library) I note an error in transcription. The published text (which White derived from Orlo Williams, *Life and Letters of John Rickman* [Boston and New York, 1912], pp. 158–160) reads (White, p. 619): ". . . he had a sister at school who was old enough for an example." This should read: "for a disciple." See also Southey's letter to Grosvenor Bedford, Jan. 4, 1812, noted above, which is quoted in part in: Dowden, I, 211.

152. Jan. 16, 1812, *Works,* VIII, 244.

153. To Southey, Mar. 7, 1816, *Works,* IX, 146–147; to Elizabeth Hitchener, Jan. 20, Feb. 3, 1812, *Works,* VIII, 246, 268. Shelley's comments to Elizabeth Hitchener on Southey as a man are tinged by his abhorrence of his views and his letter to Southey in 1816 is affected by his desire to have Southey react favorably to *Alastor* (which he had sent to him). The true picture lies in between. Shelley, I suspect, was deeply touched by Southey's kindness and developed a sincere admiration for his personal qualities, which, although shaken as he became increasingly disillusioned on Southey's philosophy, was still present when he left Keswick, his final remarks to Elizabeth Hitchener notwithstanding. His condemnation of Southey's views is no more violent than that of the average liberal opinion of the day, in fact less violent than Hazlitt's (e.g. "Mr. Coleridge and Mr. Southey," *Works,* ed. by P. P. Howe, XIX, 196–198, 154 n.).

154. To Elizabeth Hitchener, Jan. 26, 1812, *ibid.,* p. 254; to Southey, June 26, 1820, *Works,* X, 178: "We parted, I think, with feelings of mutual kindness."

155. See: Kenneth Neill Cameron, "Shelley vs. Southey: New Light on an Old Quarrel," *PMLA,* LVII (June, 1942), 489–512.

156. Quoted in: John Ashton, *Social England Under the Regency* (New York, 1890), I, 52–55. For the *Morning Chronicle* account see: Ingpen, p. 289.

157. June 20, 1811, *Works,* VIII, 108–109.

158. Charles Grove to Hellen Shelley, Feb. 25, 1857, quoted in: Hogg, II, 158. For two other burlesques on the fête, one by the renowned "Peter Pindar" (John Wolcott), see: Forman, *The Shelley Library,* p. 23. For four lines of Shelley's poem that have survived (quoted from memory by Grove), see: *Works,* III, 92.

159. See below, ch. VII, n. 2.

160. To Elizabeth Hitchener, Jan. 2, Jan. 7, 1812, *Works,* VIII, 231, 236. See above, Ch. I, n. 122.

161. Dowden apparently made enquiries about the manuscript but was unable to find it. (Dowden, I, 199.)

162. For the text of the ballad, see: *The Complete Poetical Works of Samuel Taylor Coleridge,* ed. by Ernest Hartley Coleridge (Oxford, 1912), I, 319–323. For Porson and the history of the ballad, see: *The Poetical Works of Robert Southey* (London, 1838), III, 83–86. For Byron's "The Devil's Drive," see: *The Works of Lord Byron,* ed. by Ernest Hartley Coleridge (London, 1904), I, 30 n.; VII, 21–34.

163. *Works,* VIII, 249–251.

164. For a comparison of Shelley's ballad with that of Southey's and Coleridge's see: William Michael Rossetti, "Shelley in 1812–13," *The Fortnightly Review,* n.s. IX (1871), 72–77; and Peck, I, 248–250.

165. *The Devil's Walk,* xx, xiv.

166. To Elizabeth Hitchener, July 26, 1811, *Works,* VIII, 132.

167. To the same, Aug. 10, 1811, *ibid.,* pp. 139–140.

168. *Ibid.,* p. 225.

169. To the same, Jan. 7, 1812, *ibid.,* p. 234; see also: *A Philosophical View of Reform, Works,* VII, 45, 53.

170. To Janetta Philipps, *ca.* May 1811, *ibid.,* p. 89.

171. To Hogg, Apr. 26, 1811, *Shelley at Oxford,* p. 29.

172. To Hogg, May 8, 1811, *ibid.,* p. 37.

173. To Elizabeth Hitchener, June 11, 1811, *Works,* VIII, 102.

174. For Shelley's later interest in Spinoza, see below, p. 408. Whether he had read Spinoza at this time we do not know. He refers to Spinoza in a letter to Hogg on Jan. 12, 1811 (*ibid.,* p. 44), but the theory which he there attributes to him—of a "fortuitous concourse of atoms"—is Lucretius's and not Spinoza's. The source of the error may lie in the brief article "Atheist" in Nicholson's *British Encyclopedia:* "He attributes everything to a fortuituous concourse of atoms . . . in the year 1619, Spinoza was burned to death for having avowed his adherence to the opinion of atheism." Shelley was acquainted with this encyclopedia (Notes to *Queen Mab, Works,* I, 135 n.) and would hardly omit to note the article on atheism.

175. To Elizabeth Hitchener, June 11, 1811, *ibid.,* pp. 102–103.

176. To Hogg, Apr. 26, 1811, *Shelley at Oxford,* p. 31.

177. To Elizabeth Hitchener, June 20, 1811, *Works,* VIII, 108. Cf. *Zastrozzi, Works,* V, 48. For a later, and opposite, view, see: *On a Future State, Works,* VI, 205–209.

178. To the same, Jan. 7, 1812, *ibid.,* pp. 130–131.

179. To the same, Nov. 20, 1811, *ibid.,* pp. 195–196.

180. *Ca.* May, 1811, *Works,* VIII, 89.

181. To Hogg, May 8, 1811, *Shelley at Oxford,* pp. 39–40.

182. To the same, *ca.* May 13, 1811, *Works,* VIII, 84.

183. To Elizabeth Hitchener, Nov. 26, 1811, *ibid.,* p. 204.

184. To the same, Oct. 8, 1811, *ibid.,* p. 152; to William Godwin, Jan. 28, 1812, *ibid.,* p. 257: "My peculiar reasons were considerations of the unequally weighty burden of disgrace and hatred which a resistance to this system would entail upon my companion. A man, in such a case, is a man of gallantry and spirit—a woman loses all claim to respect and politeness."

185. To Elizabeth Hitchener, Oct. 8, Nov. 26, 1811, *ibid.,* pp. 152, 204. For the expression of similar views in 1809 and 1810 in *Zastrozzi* and *St. Irvyne,* see above, pp. 78–79.

186. *Works,* I, 141.

187. Letter to Shelley, 1820, *The Correspondence of Robert Southey with Caroline Bowles,* ed. by Edward Dowden (London, 1881), p. 364.

188. Carl Grabo, *A Newton Among Poets,* pp. 30, 177. See also above, pp. 247–248, and below, pp. 393–394.

189. To Elizabeth Hitchener, Nov. 26, 1811, *Works,* VIII, 203.

190. *Lord Byron and his Contemporaries* (Philadelphia, 1828), pp. 161–163.

191. "Shelley—by One Who Knew Him," *Shelley and Keats as they struck their Contemporaries,* ed. by Edmund Blunden (London, 1925), pp. 50–52. (First published in *The Atlantic Monthly,* Feb., 1863.)

192. Dec. 13, 1811, *Works,* VIII, 215.

193. *Ibid.*

194. Hogg, I, 313.

195. Trelawny, p. 194.

196. H. F. B. Brett-Smith, *Biographical Introduction, The Works of*

Thomas Love Peacock (London, 1934), I, cxcvi; Merle, p. 706; see also p. 704.

197. Thornton Hunt, pp. 30–31.

198. *Ibid.,* p. 44; *Epipsychidion,* ll. 256 ff.

199. See, e.g. White, I, 107, 595. But see also: Peck, I, 107; II, 191, 446, and Grabo, p. 341. Peck's speculations on Shelley and a "Miss Burton" have been satisfactorily demolished by White's (*ibid.*) demonstration that she must have been about fifty or sixty years of age.

200. Edmund Blunden, "Leigh Hunt's Eldest Son," *Essays by Divers Hands, being the Transactions of the Royal Society of Literature* (Oxford University Press, 1942), n.s. XIX, 53–75.

201. See: Kenneth Neill Cameron, "The Planet-Tempest Passage in *Epipsychidion,*" *PMLA,* LXIII (Sept., 1948), 950–972.

202. Medwin, pp. 233–234; for Williams's portrait see: White, I, frontispiece.

203. *The Examiner,* Jan. 5, 1812, p. 11. The correspondent is basing his figures on Patrick Colquhoun's well-known *Treatise on the Police of the Metropolis.*

204. Notes to *Queen Mab, Works,* I, 142.

CHAPTER IV

1. To Elizabeth Hitchener, *Works,* VIII, 212, 214. On Dec. 26, he informed her that he had upheld the Irish cause and Catholic emancipation in an argument with Southey. (*Ibid.,* p. 223.)

2. Michael Roberts, *The Whig Party,* p. 95.

3. Shelley returned from Greystoke on Dec. 8 or 9 (MacCarthy, p. 121); on Dec. 11, he wrote to tell Elizabeth Hitchener of his projected trip to Ireland; on Jan. 20, he informed her that his uncle, Capt. Pilfold, was sending him £50 and that he had "previously written to request the D[uke] of Norfolk to lend me £100"; on Jan. 26, he wrote to her again: "All is now prepared for Ireland, except the arrival of our £100, daily expected from Whitton the attorney. (By-the-bye, my father has allowed me £200 per ann. . . .)" (*Works,* VIII, 212, 214, 248, 253.) This latter £100 is apparently not that from the Duke, but, as the mention of Whitton indicates, from his father. As there is no further reference to the Duke's £100, I presume that he declined the loan. We might note, too, that Shelley mailed at least one copy of the *Address to the Irish People* under the frank of the Duke. (To Elizabeth Hitchener, *ca.* Feb. 20, 1812, *ibid.,* p. 276.)

4. Quoted in: G. Locker-Lampson, *A Consideration of the State of Ireland in the Nineteenth Century* (London, 1907), p. 10.

5. Edward Raymond Turner, *Ireland and England in the Past and at Present* (New York, 1919), p. 90.

6. See, for instance: Constantia Maxwell, *Dublin Under the Georges, 1714–1830* (London, 1936), ch. 4.

7. For an account of these events, see: Locker-Lampson, pp. 27–34; Turner, pp. 95–102.

8. Locker-Lampson, p. 32.

9. Frank MacDermot, *Theobald Wolfe Tone* (London, 1939), p. 78.

10. *Ibid.,* pp. 70, 80, 254.

11. *Ibid.,* p. 81.

12. For Rowan, see: *Autobiography of Archibald Hamilton Rowan* (Dublin, 1840), and Harold Nicolson, *The Desire to Please: A Story of Hamilton Rowan and the United Irishmen* (New York, 1943).

13. Nicholson, pp. 93–94, 99.

14. *DNB* account.

15. Locker-Lampson, pp. 53–54.

16. Byron, for instance: *Don Juan,* Dedication, xi–xiv (from which I quote the above line), the "Epigrams" and "The Irish Avatar."

17. See: Locker-Lampson, pp. 67–73; Turner, pp. 108–113.

18. Denis Gwynn, *Daniel O'Connell, The Irish Liberator* (London, n.d.), p. 97.

19. *Ibid.,* pp. 102–105. Cf. Shelley's letter to Elizabeth Hitchener, Mar. 14, 1812, *Works,* VIII, 297.

20. Gwynn, p. 101.

21. *Ibid.,* p. 100.

22. *Ibid.*

23. *Ibid.,* p. 101.

24. *Works,* VIII, 246. Shelley probably began the address but a day or so before writing this letter. The first we hear of the Irish trip is on Dec. 11 just after his return from Greystoke, so presumably he had not been at work on it before that time. Between Dec. 11 and Jan. 10, he is occupied with his essays, *Hubert Cauvin* and the "Enquiry into the causes of the failure of the French Revolution to benefit mankind." (*Works,* VIII, 212, 225, 231, 235–236, 241.) In the Jan. 20 letter, he quotes a passage from the *Address,* as I note below, and this passage occurs on p. 4 of a twenty-two-page pamphlet. (First edition as in Henry E. Huntington Library.) He may, of course, have written beyond this passage by Jan. 20, but if he had written much beyond it, it is probable that he would have indicated to Elizabeth Hitchener more of the general nature of the work. As it is he simply says: "After describing their miseries I select you a passage which may give you some idea of my views." He left Keswick on Feb. 2 or 3 and arrived in Dublin on Feb. 12. On Feb. 14, he informed Elizabeth Hitchener that a printed copy of the address would be sent to her "in a few posts" (*Works,* VIII, 270); but it was not until Feb. 20 that he sent her the "first sheet" as it came off the press. (As the *Address* is an octavo in half-sheets, this probably refers to the first half-sheet, i.e. the first eight pages of text.) (*Ibid.,* p. 276.) The printing was completed on the afternoon of Feb. 24, for in the morning of that day when he wrote to Elizabeth Hitchener he did not mention it but stated that he was going to the printers, and on the same day he sent a copy to Godwin. (*Ibid.,* pp. 276–279.) From the Post-script to the *Address* we learn that the Postscript itself was written after his arrival in Ireland and the *Address* itself in England. (*Works,* V, 246.) That this postscript was written either on or later than Feb. 18 is shown by Shelley's reference in it to a newspaper article of that date. (MacCarthy,

p. 225.) The bulk of the work, therefore, must have been written between *ca.* Jan. 15 and Feb. 2, but revision could have taken place up to Feb. 20; and that some revision did take place is clear from a comparison of the passage in the *Address* quoted in the Jan. 20 letter to Elizabeth Hitchener with the passage as printed in the *Address* itself. (*Works,* VIII, 247; V, 219.)

25. *Works,* VIII, 247.
26. To Elizabeth Hitchener, Jan. 26, 1812, *ibid.,* p. 254.
27. *Ibid.,* p. 258.
28. Feb. 24, 1812, *ibid.,* p. 279.
29. *An Address to the Irish People, Works,* V, 218.
30. *Ibid.,* p. 222.
31. *Ibid.,* pp. 223–224.
32. *Ibid.,* p. 224.
33. *Ibid.,* p. 227. O'Connell praised the Prince Regent as late as Dec. 26, 1811; at the Feb. 28 meeting—at which Shelley spoke—he is decidedly hesitant in his comments: "Of the Prince I shall say nothing—uncertainty as to present circumstances—reliance on the past, and the lingering and dutiful affection in a heart devoted to the friend of Ireland restrain me." (*The Life and Speeches of Daniel O'Connell,* ed. by John O'Connell [Dublin, 1846], I, 129, 151.) But by June, disillusionment with the Regent had spread so far that O'Connell read a resolution against him, and commented unfavorably on him in a speech. (*Ibid.,* pp. 168–182; Gwynn, pp. 107–108).
34. *Works,* V, 228.
35. *Ibid.,* p. 238.
36. *Ibid.,* p. 231.
37. John O'Connell, *op. cit.,* I, 150, speech, Feb. 28, 1812.
38. Gwynn, p. 101.
39. *Works,* V, 239.
40. *Ibid.,* pp. 238–239. The Spanish campaign, as we noted, came under attack also in *The Devil's Walk.*
41. *Ibid.,* p. 242.
42. *Ibid.,* pp. 237–238. Shelley is here partly echoing the creed of Tone's United Irishmen. (Peck, II, 341.)
43. *Ibid.,* pp. 233–234.
44. *Ibid.,* p. 233.
45. *Ibid.,* p. 236; cf.: letter to Godwin, Mar. 18, 1812, *Works,* VIII, 301; *The Revolt of Islam,* IX, xxvi; Preface to *Hellas, Works,* III, 9; *A Philosophical View of Reform, Works,* VII, 42–43.
46. *Works,* V, 240.
47. See n. 24 above.
48. Quoted in: MacCarthy, pp. 149–150.
49. To Elizabeth Hitchener, Jan. 20, 1812, *Works,* VIII, 249.
50. To the same, Feb. 27, 1812, *Works,* VIII, 283–284, 286 (Harriet's note, added to Shelley's letter).
51. *Ibid.,* p. 283.
52. In *The Dublin Evening Post,* Feb. 25, 29, Mar. 3, 1812, MacCarthy, pp. 149–150.

53. To Elizabeth Hitchener, Feb. 27, 1812, *Works*, VIII, 283; [John Anster] "Life and Writings of Percy Bysshe Shelley," *North British Review*, VIII (1847), 237: "A poor man offered the pamphlet for a few pence— its price, stated on the title page, was five-pence. On being asked how he got it, he said a parcel of them were given him by a young gentleman, who told him to get what he could for them—at all events to distribute them." Anster (for whom, see the *DNB*), according to Dowden (I, 258 n.), received this information from Catherine Nugent (for whom, see above, pp. 144–145). MacCarthy (pp. 171–172) states that the man who distributed the pamphlets was probably Shelley's Irish servant, Daniel Healey.

54. Quoted in MacCarthy, p. 253.

55. Harriet Shelley to Elizabeth Hitchener, Mar. 18, 1812, *Works*, VIII, 300: "He has not many of his first 'Address,' having taken great pains to circulate them through this city."

56. Peck, II, 341–343.

57. *Works*, VIII, 282. First printed in Rowan's *Autobiography* (1840), pp. 388–389.

58. Nicolson, pp. 185–186.

59. *Works*, VIII, 285.

60. To Elizabeth Hitchener, Mar. 14, 1812, *Works*, VIII, 297.

61. William Fagan, *The Life and Times of Daniel O'Connell* (London, 1847), I, 87.

62. Gwynn, p. 183.

63. Thomas Wyse, *Historical Sketch of the Late Catholic Association* (London, 1829), I, 404.

64. *Ibid.*, p. 402. For more on Lawless, see the *DNB* and Webb's *Compendium of Irish Biography*.

65. *Works*, VIII, 291.

66. To Elizabeth Hitchener, Mar. 14, 1812, *ibid.*, p. 297. See also Harriet's comments in a letter of Mar. 10: "Has Percy mentioned to you a very amiable man of the name of Lawless? He is very much attached to the cause, yet dare not act." (*Ibid.*, pp. 292–293.)

67. John Lawless, *A Compendium of the History of Ireland from the Earliest Period to the Reign of George I* (Dublin, 1814). Shelley took his contribution back with him to England and there, after perusal by Elizabeth Hitchener (Harriet Shelley to Catherine Nugent, Aug. 11, 1812, *Works*, IX, 16) it was apparently lost. Lawless does not appear in this work as a republican or radical but essentially as an Irish nationalist: "We take up our pen with an ardent wish to avenge the insults against the religion, the honour, and courage of our country" (p. 519). He is opposed to atheism and deism and for the uniting of all religious sects; he supports parliamentary reform and is against the use of violence.

68. Later when Shelley returned to Ireland, he stayed in Lawless's house in Dublin; the Shelleys' interest in him continued until at least the fall of 1813. See: Harriet Shelley to Catherine Nugent, June 7, 1812, June 30, 1812, Aug. 11, 1812, *Works*, VIII, 333; IX, 4, 16; Shelley to Thomas Hookham, Mar. 6, 1813, *Works*, IX, 53. Hogg informs us that Lawless spoke of Shelley "with uniform, unvarying kindness and respect." (Hogg,

I, 407.) On May 3, 1813, Lawless wrote to Hogg inquiring after the Shelleys. (*Harriet and Mary,* p. 32.) Later in the same year the Shelleys heard that Lawless was in prison and were writing to Ireland for information. (Harriet Shelley to Catherine Nugent, May 21, 1813, Oct. 11, 1813. *Works,* IX, 67, 78.) By the time of this latter letter, it would appear that Shelley and Lawless had quarrelled, apparently over Shelley's treatment of his Irish servant, Daniel Healey. (Harriet Shelley to Catherine Nugent, Nov. 23, 1813, *Works,* IX, 80.) In 1842, Frederick William Conway, editor of the *Dublin Evening Post* stated that Shelley had been "made the pecuniary dupe of a person not less sincere in his politics, but in money matters less honest." (Quoted in: MacCarthy, p. 304.) This, MacCarthy presumes to be a reference to Lawless, but, as he points out, Lawless and Conway "had life-long difficulties," so that too much reliance should not perhaps be put on the statement.

69. *Works,* VIII, 299.

70. Alfred Webb, "Harriet Shelley and Catherine Nugent," *The Nation,* XLVIII (June 6, 13, 1889), 464, 486. Webb, whose father was acquainted with Catherine Nugent, was loaned letters to her from Harriet Shelley. These he copied in a notebook and added letters and notes about Catherine Nugent and the Newmans. In 1889, he published the letters from Harriet Shelley in *The Nation* and added some comments on Catherine Nugent. The notebook later was passed to Dowden, who made use of it in his life of Shelley, and, in 1947, via Dowden's granddaughter, to the late Professor Newman I. White, who sent it to me in photostat. Most of the information in it will be found in *The Nation* as cited; the connection with the United Irishmen, I take from the notebook. The originals of Harriet Shelley's letters are at present in the Henry E. Huntington Library.

71. Gwynn, p. 106.

72. Quoted in MacCarthy, pp. 232–233.

73. *Life and Speeches of Daniel O'Connell,* p. 146. (See pp. 142–152 for the whole of O'Connell's speech.)

74. *Ibid.,* pp. 150–151.

75. MacCarthy, p. 247.

76. *Ibid.,* p. 241. It seems curious that Shelley was granted the floor at so large and important a meeting simply by "requesting" it. Perhaps he had made arrangements previously with the chairman, who would probably have been glad enough to have him speak on the grounds that he was the son of an English Member of Parliament. But he cannot have made arrangements much in advance, because on the day preceding the meeting, he makes no mention of it in a letter to Elizabeth Hitchener in which he speaks at length of his activities in Ireland. (*Works,* VIII, 283–285.)

77. *Ibid.,* pp. 242–243; for a brief account of the speech in *The Freeman's Journal* see *ibid.,* p. 240.

78. To Elizabeth Hitchener, *Works,* VIII, 297. Shelley's claim in this letter that he "spoke for more than an hour" must be false. The newspaper accounts do not reflect a speech of more than ten or fifteen minutes, and the brief comment of the government spy noted below indicates a short speech. Furthermore, Shelley, appearing late in the evening, after the long main

speech by O'Connell, and other secondary speeches, would not have been granted time for an hour's speech.

79. MacCarthy, p. 240.

80. MacCarthy, p. 251. It occurs to me, however, that this letter, ostensibly attacking Shelley, may have been written by Shelley himself in order to arouse a controversy. Such an action would have been in line with what Hogg tells us of his writing pseudonymous letters from Oxford to unsuspecting divines in a spirit of Christian naïveté.

81. *Ibid.,* p. 239.

82. On Feb. 14, Shelley wrote to Elizabeth Hitchener that the *Address* would "soon come out" and would "be instantly followed by another." (*Works,* VIII, 274.) On Feb. 20, when sending her "the first sheet" of the *Address,* he again said that it would be "followed by another" and that this second pamphlet would be of the same length as the *Address.* (*Ibid.,* p. 276.) On Feb. 25, he told Rowan "in the course of a few days I shall print another small pamphlet." (*Ibid.,* p. 282.) On Feb. 27, he informed Elizabeth Hitchener that "on Monday [March 2] my next book makes its appearance." (*Ibid.,* p. 284.) (Feb. 27 in 1812 was a Tue. and the following Mon. was Mar. 2, as Ingpen correctly interpolates here; the note in *Works,* V, 303 giving Mar. 4 as Mon. is incorrect.) MacCarthy (p. 172), followed by White (I, 209), states that the pamphlet was published on Mar. 2, but we have no evidence beyond Shelley's anticipation to show that it was. We know, however, that it had been published by Mar. 8, for on that date Shelley sent a copy to Godwin. (*Ibid.,* p. 289.) Shelley, as we have seen, was still working on the *Address* as late as Feb. 18; that he had not completed the *Proposals* by Feb. 20 is shown by the fact that he then thought it would be as long as the *Address* whereas it is only about half as long. By Feb. 27, he had either sent it to the printer or expected very shortly to do so.

83. Note to Elizabeth Hitchener, *ca.* Feb. 20, 1812, *Works,* VIII, 276.

84. *Works,* V, 253–257; see also: to William Godwin, Feb. 24, 1812, *Works,* VIII, 279.

85. *Works,* V, 254.

86. *Ibid.,* p. 255.

87. *Life and Speeches of Daniel O'Connell,* I, 138.

88. *Works,* V, 256.

89. *Ibid.,* p. 268.

90. *Ibid.,* p. 258.

91. *Ibid.,* pp. 256–258.

92. *Ibid.,* p. 261.

93. *Works,* V, 264–265; cf. Preface to *The Revolt of Islam, Works,* I, 241–242, and *A Philosophical View of Reform, Works,* VII, 13–14, 53–54.

94. *Ibid.,* p. 265.

95. *Ibid.,* p. 257; to Elizabeth Hitchener, Feb. 27, 1812, *Works,* VIII, 284.

96. *Works,* V, p. 266.

97. William Michael Rossetti, "Shelley in 1812–13," *Fortnightly Review* (Jan., 1871), pp. 71–72.

98. *Works,* V, 273, 274. On Godwin see above, pp. 62–64.

99. *Ibid.,* VIII, 272.

100. For a brief account of the revolution, see: Herbert Ingram Priestly, *The Mexican Nation* (New York, 1923), pp. 225–230.

101. Southey's lines "Written immediately after reading the speech of Robert Emmet." The part of the poem on Ireland in the letter to Elizabeth Hitchener on Feb. 14 (*Works,* VIII, 271) is given in prose form, although it is clearly, as Dowden points out (I, 247–248), blank verse and later appeared in *Queen Mab,* IX, 23–37. See also: *Works,* III, 322. Dowden (I, 268) thinks the poem on Emmet may have been written later in Wales, but it was probably among those given to a printer before Shelley left Dublin. See below, ch. VII, nn. 2, 4. Only the two final stanzas have been published; the first five, however, exist in manuscript. (*Works,* III, 322.)

102. *Works,* VIII, 280.

103. Quoted in: Hogg, I, 321–322.

104. Mar. 8, *Works,* VIII, 287–288.

105. Mar. 14, Hogg, I, 327–329.

106. Mar. 18, 1812, *Works,* VIII, 300–301.

107. *Ca.* Apr. 16, 1812, *ibid.,* p. 308.

108. To William Godwin, Jan. 28, 1812, *Works,* VIII, 259 (after speaking of his Irish plans): "I will say no more of *Wales* at present. We have determined next summer to receive a most dear friend [Elizabeth Hitchener], of whom I shall speak hereafter, in some romantic spot." See, also: to Elizabeth Hitchener, Jan. 26, 1812, *ibid.,* p. 253. By Mar. 18, he had decided to leave on Apr. 7; he actually left on Apr. 4. (Harriet Shelley to Elizabeth Hitchener, Mar. 18, 1812, *Works,* VIII, 300.)

109. *Ibid.,* p. 292.

110. *Ibid.,* p. 300.

111. To Elizabeth Hitchener, Mar. 10, 1812, *ibid.,* pp. 290–291.

112. Harriet Shelley to Elizabeth Hitchener, Mar. 18, *ibid.,* p. 298.

113. *Ibid.,* p. 303.

114. To Elizabeth Hitchener, Mar. 10, 1812, *ibid.,* p. 292.

115. To the same, Feb. 27, 1812, *ibid.,* pp. 284–285.

116. O'Connell's son, for instance, although deprecating his anti-religious sentiments, commented, "It was a generous and a Christian impulse that impelled him to attend the meeting in question. . . ."—and, as we have seen, paid high tribute to his political acumen. (*Life and Speeches of Daniel O'Connell,* I, 135, 138.) (John O'Connell, *ibid.,* I, 135, 126, followed by Gwynn, p. 106, wrongly supposes that Shelley spoke at the aggregate meeting of Dec. 26, 1811, instead of the next meeting on Feb. 28, 1812.) See also T. C. Luby, *The Life and Times of Daniel O'Connell,* n.d., pp. 308–309: "Some observations of his [Shelley's] remain, which—along with a certain visionary wildness . . . show manifest signs of a heart and imagination and intellect better able to realize the peculiar features and difficulties of the Irish question, than Englishmen in general, even those of the highest intellect, or even many of our Irishmen, could boast of. At all events, he was able to see clearly that emancipation, gained by itself, would in any sense worth speaking of, profit only the 'higher orders of the Catholic persuasion,'

and also had sufficient insight to perceive that, in a consideration of Ireland's grievances and obstacles to prosperity, the paramount grievance and obstacle even of those days was the thrice-accursed Union. The observations of Shelley are worth quoting here: . . ." (Quotes from *Proposals,* "It is my opinion . . . blood in England." *Works,* V, 254–255.)

117. MacCarthy, pp. 253–255.

CHAPTER V

1. To Godwin, Mar. 8, 1812, *Works,* VIII, 289.

2. George Macaulay Trevelyan, *Lord Grey of the Reform Bill* (London, New York, Toronto, 1929), p. 74.

3. George Stead Veitch, *The Genesis of Parliamentary Reform* (London, 1913), p. 7. One hundred and thirty boroughs had less than 300 voters apiece, 51 had less than 50. (*Ibid.*)

4. J. L. and Barbara Hammond, *The Town Labourer,* 1760–1832 (London, New York, 1917), p. 85.

5. *Ibid.,* pp. 157–163.

6. *Ibid.,* p. 72.

7. *Ibid.,* pp. 72–73. The pamphlet turned out to be a publication of the Religious Tract Society.

8. Frank Ongley Darvall, *Popular Disturbances and Public Order in Regency England* (London, 1934), pp. 5–6.

9. *Ibid.,* p. 73.

10. To Elizabeth Hitchener, Dec. 26, 1811, *Works,* VIII, 225.

11. *Hansard,* XXI (1812), 17, 25–27; see also: M. W. Patterson, *Sir Francis Burdett and His Times* (London, 1931), I, 315–316.

12. *Cobbett's Weekly Political Register,* XXI (Feb. 29), 282.

13. John Ashton, *Social England Under the Regency* (London, 1890), I, 103–108.

14. *Hansard,* XXI (1812), 971–974.

15. *Ibid.,* XXI, 1264–1292; XXII, 1–2 (the Petition of the Frame Work Knitters was "ordered to lie upon the table"); XXII, 122–146.

16. *Cobbett's Political Register,* XXI, 492–511, 523–538. Cobbett's predominant role in this important change of strategy is attested by the other reformers. See: Samuel Bamford, *Passages in the Life of a Radical* (London, 1844), I, 7, and: *Memoirs of Henry Hunt, Esq. Written by himself in His Majesty's Jail at Ilchester* (London, 1820), p. vii.

17. Darvall, pp. 100–101. See also, *ibid.,* ch. 15, "The Danger of Revolution."

18. *The Examiner,* Apr. 5, 1812, p. 231.

19. F. D. Cartwright, *The Life and Correspondence of Major Cartwright* (London, 1826), II, 24, 380–383.

20. *Hansard,* XXII, 500.

21. *Ibid.,* p. 651.

22. *Ibid.,* p. 1147.

23. *The Examiner,* May 10, 1812, p. 289. In the May 24 issue a corre-spondent took the editors severely to task for their remarks on Burdett. (*Ibid.,* pp. 333–334.)

24. *Hansard,* XXII, 1149.

25. Ashton, I, 118.

26. *Cobbett's Political Register,* XXI (May 23, 1812), 671; *The Exami-ner,* May 24, p. 335. The political difference between the two journals is interestingly illustrated in their different attitudes on Bellingham. Cobbett, while deprecating the assassination, was sympathetic towards him for the injustice he had received from the government; to *The Examiner* (May 17, p. 314) he was simply "the wretched assassin."

27. *Hansard,* XXIII, 358.

28. *Ibid.,* pp. 794–800.

29. *Ibid.,* pp. 855–858.

30. *The Examiner* (July 12, pp. 445–447) noted the following toasts drunk at the banquet: "The People, the source of all Power" ("drunk three times three, the band playing 'Liberty Hall'"); "A free Press and free Discussion"; "Success to the South American Patriots"; "May the oppres-sion of the People of Ireland speedily be removed"; "Arms in the hands of free men"; "the Navy—May promotion be gained by merit, and not by Borough Interest."

31. White, I, 230.

32. Mar. 10, 1812, *Works,* VIII, 292.

33. To Elizabeth Hitchener, *ca.* Apr. 16, 1812, *ibid.,* pp. 307–308; to Timothy Shelley, Apr. 24, 1812, *ibid.,* p. 311; to Thomas Charles Medwin, Apr. 25, 1812, *ibid.,* pp. 314–315; for the marriage certificate see Ingpen, p. 309.

34. Ingpen, p. 390.

35. To Elizabeth Hitchener, *ca.* Apr. 16, 1812, *Works,* VIII, 308.

36. *Ibid.,* pp. 308–309. For Marr, see *Annual Register,* 1811, pp. 138–139.

37. *Ibid.,* p. 325. "General Sir James Henry Craig (1748–1812), for-merly Governor of Canada, was supposed to have employed Captain John Henry 'to go to Boston to find out how the minds of the People were then affected, and whether they would be inclined to break the Union.' Great Britain and America were on the point of hostilities. . . ." (*Ibid.,* n.)

38. Original of letter in the Huntington Library shows the position of this comment.

39. Ingpen, pp. 383–384.

40. *Works,* VIII, 333.

41. *Ibid.,* pp. 298–299.

42. MacCarthy, pp. 314–315. MacCarthy discovered these letters in the Public Records Office and was the first to publish them. The Secretary of State at the time was Richard Ryder; Sidmouth was not appointed until June, 1812.

43. *Ibid.,* pp. 310–311.

44. *Ibid.,* pp. 312-313. Timothy Shelley was member for New Shore-

ham, not the Rape of Bramber. Horsham, however, was in the Rape of
Bramber. ("Rape, n. Any of six administrative divisions of Sussex [from
1086; etym. dub.]." *Concise Oxford Dictionary.*)

45. *Ibid.,* p. 321.

46. Cobbett, for instance, when Bentham suggested agitation for female
suffrage, claimed that the suggestion would "render" the whole reform
movement "ridiculous." (*Political Register,* XXX [1818], 359.) Fox, in the
Whig reform debate of 1797, as we have noted, also cast ridicule on the
notion of extending votes to women. Even Shelley, strong advocate of
women's rights as he was, feared that the demand was inexpedient as part
of a practical reform platform. (*A Philosophical View of Reform* [1820],
Works, VII, 44.)

47. Merle, p. 709.

48. To Godwin, July 5, 1812, *Works,* IX, 5–6.

49. Hogg, II, 57.

50. Aug. 11, 1812, *Works,* IX, 16.

51. To Shelley, *ca.* June 8, *ca.* July 13, Oct. 23, 1811; *Letters of Elizabeth Hitchener to Percy Bysshe Shelley,* ed. by W. E. Peck (New York,
1926), pp. 5–6, 11, 18.

52. Dowden, I, 314. See also: Medwin, p. 118 n.; Forman's comments.

53. To Elizabeth Hitchener, Jan. 29, 1812, *Works,* VIII, 261–262.

54. *Gentleman's Magazine,* n.s. IV (July, 1867), 116. "In continental
literature," the article continues, "Mr. Hookham was as great as Mr. Murray
is now in travels, and his name was familiar to everybody in Europe who
took an interest in any literary subject." For a biographical sketch see:
Works, VIII, xxxii–xxxv; on the library, see: William Tinsley, *Random
Recollections of an Old Publisher* (London, 1900), I, 69–75. The Unitarians
were in the forefront of many radical causes in the late eighteenth and
early nineteenth centuries. See: Raymond V. Holt, *The Unitarian Contribution to Social Progress in England* (London, 1838). Holt lists as Unitarians:
Jeremy Bentham, Major Cartwright, Mary Wollstonecraft, William Hazlitt,
Joseph Priestley. Shelley, too, was perhaps subjected to Unitarian ideas as a
boy as a result of Timothy's interest in the sect. (See above, pp. 71, 324.)

55. *Works,* IX, 9–10.

56. Dowden, I, 292. Dowden informs us in a note that Mrs. Blackmore
gave the information to Mathilde Blind, a Victorian Shelley scholar, who
brought out an edition of his poems in 1872.

57. Harriet Shelley to Catherine Nugent, Aug. 4, 1812, *Works,* IX,
15; to Hookham, Aug. 18, 1812, *ibid.,* p. 18: "In the first place I send you
50 copies of the 'Letter.'" According to the printer "Shelley had about
fifty copies as they were printed" and no more. But these letters reveal a
total of at least 79, unless Shelley did not actually send Hookham 25 copies
as promised on July 29. He does not, we may note, say on Aug. 18, "I send
you 50 copies more" but simply, "I send you 50 copies," as though this was
the first large batch to be sent. It seems strange that, if the pamphlet actually
came off the press on July 29, Shelley does not mention it to Godwin in a
letter of that date (*Works,* IX, 10–14); but it was certainly, as Harriet's

letter tells us, printed by Aug. 4. Perhaps Godwin did not approve. Dowden (I, 291) states that copies were sent to "some private friends of the author," and that one was sent to Lord Sidmouth, but he does not give the source of this information.

58. John Roberts Chanter, *Sketches of the Literary History of Barnstaple* (Barnstaple, 1866), pp. 55–56. Syle was not only the leading printer in Barnstaple but a man of literary interests. Between 1797 and 1824 he printed twenty-one books and other items; in 1823, he was editor of the *Barnstaple Miscellany* and, in 1824, of *The Universal Medley,* both of them apparently literary periodical anthologies. (*Ibid.,* pp. 47–49, 82–83.) Barnstaple "in 1809 and for many years subsequently" supported a theatre. (*Ibid.,* p. 43.) So it was something of a cultural as well as an industrial and political center. The Shelley material in Chanter is reprinted in MacCarthy, pp. 345–348.

59. Dowden, I, 297 n.

60. Peck, I, 270–272. This letter and other material connected with the incident were discovered in the Public Records Office by William Michael Rossetti and first published by him in: "Shelley in 1812–13," *Fortnightly Review,* n.s. IX (Jan., 1871), 68 ff. The letter was re-transcribed more exactly from the original by Peck. Mrs. Blackmore remembered Dan's name as Healey. Dowden is probably right in taking this as his real name and Hill as an assumed name given when he was arrested. (Dowden, I, 295 n.) Healey, perhaps fearing deportation, avoids all mention of Ireland, even implying that he had lived with Shelley in Sackville Street, London, instead of Dublin.

61. Rossetti, p. 77.

62. *Ibid.,* pp. 77–78.

63. *Ibid.,* pp. 78–79.

64. *Cobbett's Political Register,* XXI (Apr. 18, 1812), 493–495.

65. Darvall, p. 96.

66. *Cobbett's Political Register,* XXI (May 23, 1812), 667.

67. Hammonds, p. 258.

68. Darvall, p. 277.

69. "In Nottingham it [the spy system] was handled by the Town Clerk." *Ibid.,* p. 292. On Oliver, the first great labor spy, see: J. L. and Barbara Hammond, *The Skilled Labourer,* 1760–1832 (London, 1919), pp. 341–378.

70. Shelley was, however, able to pay 15 shillings per week whereby Dan was granted "certain immunities and privileges." (Dowden, I, 297, again quoting Mrs. Blackmore's recollections.)

71. Following a pitched battle around the Cartwright mill in Yorkshire two wounded Luddites were carried to a neighbouring inn for questioning. "Among other eager amateur detectives who tried to worm out of these men some of the secrets of the Luddites was the Rev. Hammond Robertson, a fiery Anglican parson immortalised in the pages of *Shirley.* It is said that just before the end John Booth, one of the victims, a tinner's apprentice and the son of a local preacher from Huddersfield, making a last

effort to rise, beckoned to Robertson. 'Can you keep a secret?' he said. 'I can,' eagerly replied the hopeful cleric. 'So can I,' flashed back the Luddite, turning over to die." (Darvall, p. 117.)

72. Dan apparently covered up also for Elizabeth Hitchener (who had perhaps become aware of her "watch") by representing her to his inquisitors as a sister of Harriet.

73. Hughes, p. 156, from papers in the records office discovered by Barbara Hammond. Professor Hughes informs me that, in answer to a query made at my request, Mrs. Hammond stated that the material he quotes represents her discovery in toto.

74. Both the present Sir Francis Burdett and Mrs. W. M. Patterson, widow of Burdett's biographer, inform me that they have no knowledge of the letters.

75. To Catherine Nugent, Aug. 4, 1812, *Works,* IX, 15.

76. *Hansard,* XXIII (July 23, 1812), 1192: *"Earl Stanhope* objected to the Bill, that it was founded in its preamble and its clauses upon expediency and expediency alone, and did not recognize the right of religious worship, which he contended to be the inalienable right of man." Shelley must have greatly admired Stanhope, for he was one of the old Foxite leaders in the Lords who had continued a fight for liberal principles, and was also an intellectual leader and inventor of note.

77. July 29, *Works,* IX, 14.

78. See: Patterson, I, 320–321, and (for a different viewpoint) G. D. H. Cole, *The Life of William Cobbett* (London, 1924), pp. 156–159.

79. July 12, p. 435.

80. Pp. 479, 466.

81. To Hogg, Feb. 7, 1813, *Works,* IX, 45. See also: to Elizabeth Hitchener, Aug. 10, 1811, *Works,* VIII, 139–140.

82. Medwin, p. 116.

83. Dowden (I, 284–285) gives a brief account of both poems. See above, pp. 234–235.

84. Dowden, I, 289. The third part of the *Rights of Man* will be found in: *The Life and Works of Thomas Paine,* Patriots Edition (New York, 1925), IX, 205 ff. For Eaton, see the *DNB.*

85. Hughes, p. 148.

86. T. B. Howell, *A Complete Collection of State Trials* (London, 1823), XXXI, 928–929.

87. *Ibid.,* p. 940.

88. *Ibid.,* pp. 938–947.

89. *Ibid.,* p. 949.

90. *Ibid.,* p. 958.

91. *Cobbett's Political Register,* XXI (June 13, 1812), 750 ff. On the preceding pages the scene at the pillory is described. In the next issue (June 20, June 27, pp. 790–793, 814) and again on July 11 (XXII, 52–55) Cobbett continued his defense of Eaton. I note only general similarities between his defense and Shelley's and see no evidence that Shelley had read his articles. In fact, Shelley, in Wales and Devon, would not normally have seen the *Political Register* for these months unless someone had mailed it to

him, and his comment in the Advertisement (*Works*, V, 281) implies ignorance of any other defense. But it is interesting that Eaton's two most vigorous champions were Shelley and Cobbett.

92. *The Examiner*, May 31, 1812, quoted in: Peck, I, 265–266. Peck also quotes an interesting account of the pillory scene from Crabb Robinson, who commented: "The whole affair was an additional proof of the folly of the Ministers, who ought to have known that such an exhibition would be a triumph to the cause they meant to render infamous."

93. To Godwin, *Works*, VIII, 337.

94. June 18, 1812, *ibid.*, p. 339.

95. See above, n. 57.

96. *Hansard*, XXIII (1812), 820. Shelley's version, taken, as he informs us (*Works*, V, 279), from *The Globe*, differs slightly from that in *Hansard*.

97. *Works*, V, 284.

98. *Ibid.*, p. 287.

99. See Hughes, p. 148.

100. *Works*, V, 287–288.

101. *Ibid.*, p. 290. In working this passage into the Notes on *Queen Mab*, Shelley prefaced this comment with: "Milton's poem alone will give permanency to the remembrance of its absurdities." (*Works*, I, 153.) For a later development of the idea, see: *On the Devil, and Devils, Works*, VII, 90–92.

102. *Ibid.*, p. 293.

103. *Ibid.*, pp. 292–293. For the debt to Holbach, see: Notes on *Queen Mab, Works*, I, 150.

104. "On Marriage," *Works*, VII, 150.

105. H. Buxton Forman, *The Shelley Library*, p. 34; J. M. Robertson, *A History of Freethought in the Nineteenth Century* (London, 1929), pp. 430–433. Bennett (1818–1882) was prosecuted by Anthony Comstock for his anti-religious activities.

106. *Shelley on Blasphemy, being his Letter to Lord Ellenborough* (London, 1883), pp. 4–5. The Introduction is unsigned, but may have been by Joseph Mazzini Wheeler. (Forman, *ibid.*)

CHAPTER VI

1. *Hansard*, XIV (May 11, 1809), 489.

2. *Ibid.*, p. 491.

3. *Cobbett's Political Register*, XV (May 20, 1809), 737–738.

4. *Hansard*, XIV (June 15, 1809), 1061.

5. Michael Roberts, *The Whig Party*, pp. 287–288.

6. *DNB* entry on Madocks. For an interesting account of Tremadoc see: Samuel Lewis, *A Topographical Dictionary of Wales* (London, 1840).

7. *Gentleman's Magazine*, LXXXI (Sept., 1811), 279.

8. *Ibid.*, p. 380.

9. White, I, 258.

10. Medwin, p. 119. Medwin first gave this account of his talks with

Madocks in *The Athenaeum* in 1832 (i.e. within ten years of the meeting), reprinted in 1833 in *The Shelley Papers,* pp. 18–20. This earlier account does not differ materially from that in his *Life of Shelley* (1847).

11. Quoted in: *Works,* VII, 326–327.

12. *North Wales Gazette,* Apr. 2, 1812, quoted in *ibid.,* pp. 329–330.

13. Ingpen, pp. 396 n., 633–634; White, I, 255–256, 643–644. The physician was Dr. William Roberts of Carnarvon, later mayor of the town. He states that Shelley later paid the debt for which he was arrested. (Ingpen, p. 634.)

14. C. Kegan Paul, *William Godwin, His Friends and Contemporaries* (London, 1876), II, 212. Paul and Dowden had access to Godwin's MS letters and journals which are at present in the possession of Lord Abinger. In 1948, Lord Abinger made them available in microfilm to the late Professor Newman I. White. I cannot find the basis for White's statement that Shelley spent two or three days in Sussex before this date. (White, I, 259.) We know that he was in Sussex early in Nov. (See n. 47 below.)

15. Dowden, I, 304–305.

16. See: to Godwin, Jan. 3, 1812, *Works,* VIII, 232–233; to Elizabeth Hitchener, Jan. 7, 1812, *ibid.,* p. 234; to Godwin, July 29, 1812, *Works,* IX, 10.

17. Paul, I, 24–25.

18. *Ibid.,* p. 26.

19. *Ibid.,* p. 61.

20. William Godwin, *Cursory Strictures on the Charge Delivered by Lord Justice Eyre to the Grand Jury, Oct. 2, 1794* (London, 1794), pp. 22–23 (reprinted from the *Chronicle,* Oct. 22, 1794). For a summary of Godwin's letter and some account of the trial see: Paul, I, 129–137. The previous year Godwin had similarly protested the government's deportation of two Scottish radicals, Muir and Palmer. (Paul, I, 120–123.)

21. William Godwin, *Memoirs of Mary Wollstonecraft* (London, 1927), ed. by W. Clark Durant, p. 101. The *Memoirs* were first published in 1798.

22. To T. Wedgewood, Apr. 19, 1797, Paul, I, 235.

23. *Memoirs of Mary Wollstonecraft,* pp. 113–124.

24. *Political Justice,* ed. by Priestley (1946), III, 81–100. In his Preface to *St. Leon* (1799) Godwin noted some minor changes in his views. In *Thoughts Occasioned by the Perusal of Dr. Par's Spital Sermon* (1801) he contended that his basic political philosophy was unchanged and attacked those who had turned from revolutionaries into Tories, claiming (pp. 7–8) that their renegacy was the result of the Pitt terror: "We must look elsewhere than in the naked convictions of the understanding, for the principles of their conduct." *Thoughts on Man* (1831) reveals no basic change.

25. *Essay on Sepulchres* (London, 1809), p. vi.

26. Paul, II, 158–162. Godwin suggested that the Duke of Norfolk might contribute but his name is not on the final list.

27. *Ibid.,* p. 153.

28. Harriet Shelley to Catherine Nugent, Oct.–Nov., 1812. *Works,* IX, 24; Shelley to Fanny Imlay, Dec. 10, 1812, *ibid.,* p. 31.

29. *Ibid.,* p. 24. Claire Clairmont, then fifteen years of age, "was only at home for two nights during the six weeks Shelley spent in London." (Paul, II, 213.)

30. Dowden, I, 304.

31. *Essay on Sepulchres,* pp. 5–6.

32. "Of the Material Universe," *Thoughts on Man* (London, 1831), pp. 448–449.

33. "Of Difference in Opinion," *The Enquirer* (London, 1797), p. 322.

34. Paul, I, 26, 357–358.

35. *Political Justice,* I, 127 ff., 177; "Of Self-love and Benevolence," *Thoughts on Man,* pp. 205–225; *Works,* I, 145.

36. For Godwin's views, see *The Enquirer,* p. 228 ff.

37. William Godwin, *Letter of Advice to a Young American on the Course of Studies it might be most Advantageous for him to Pursue* (London, 1818), p. 13: "Even French literature was worthy of some notice in these times; and Montaigne is entitled to rank with some of the best English prose writers his contemporaries." Shelley, *A Philosophical View of Reform, Works,* VII, 13–14: "The French were what their literature is (excluding Montaigne and Rousseau and some few leaders of the . . .) weak, superficial, vain. . . ." The *Letter* to the Young American, as Mr. Jack Marken of the English Department of Indiana University has pointed out to me, was reprinted, along with five brief, personal letters to the same (unknown) correspondent, in: *The Analectic Magazine,* XIV (1819), 230–243. See also: Osborne Earle, *The Reputation and Influence of William Godwin in America* (Unpublished Harvard Thesis, 1938), pp. 425–426.

38. Paul, II, 209.

39. William Godwin, *Letters of Verax to the Editor of the Morning Chronicle* (London, 1815). There is, it seems to me, a certain undercurrent of sympathy for Napoleon running through these letters as well as opposition to the British government's war policy.

40. Dec. 27, 1812, *Works,* IX, 37.

41. Hunt's campaign, featured by the use of troops against the electorate, had taken place a few months earlier. (*Cobbett's Political Register,* XXII [July 4, 1812], 27–31, and succeeding issues.)

42. P. 655.

43. Jan. 16, 1813, *Works,* IX, 41.

44. Dowden, I, 280–281; *Works,* IX, 33–36; cf. the reading recommended in Godwin's *Letter to a Young American,* as noted above. See also: Godwin's letter to Shelley on Dec. 10, 1812, where he makes similar recommendations. He specifically advises the study of history. Shelley, in submitting his book list to Hookham on Dec. 17, states that he had "determined to apply" himself to the study of "that record of crimes and miseries—History." (*Shelley Memorials,* pp. 45–48; *Works,* IX, 33.) The comment has sometimes been used to indicate a general aversion to historical study; but Shelley was well read in history, both ancient and modern.

45. Dowden, I, 316. Shelley is unable to give any adequate excuse to Fanny Godwin, in a letter to her on Dec. 10, for their precipitate departure: "But had you been placed in a situation where you might justly have bal-

anced all our embarrassments, qualms and fluctuations . . ." (*Works,* IX, 31.)

46. To Catherine Nugent, Oct.–Nov., 1812, *ibid.,* p. 24.

47. John Bedwell to John Evans, Nov. 5, 1812: "Mr. Shelley is just returned here from Sussex." (White, I, 256.)

48. Shelley to John Williams, Nov. 7, 1812, *Works,* IX, 23.

49. Hogg, I, 368. Shelley informed Williams on Nov. 7, that he intended to call upon the Duke that day.

50. To Catherine Nugent, Oct.–Nov., 1812, *Works,* IX, 24.

51. White, I, 261.

52. *Biographical Introduction, The Works of Thomas Love Peacock,* ed. by H. F. B. Brett-Smith (London, 1934), xlix–l.

53. Quoted in: Dowden, I, 307.

54. Hogg, I, 366.

55. To Hogg, Feb. 7, 1813, *Works,* IX, 44–45; see also: Dec. 3, Dec. 27, 1812, *ibid.,* pp. 27, 37–38.

56. Hogg, II, 58.

57. Nov. 14, *Works,* IX, 25.

58. Merle, pp. 709–710.

59. Shelley to John Williams, Mar. 30, 1813; *Works,* IX, 58–59; John Pilfold to John Williams, July 6, 1814, *ibid.,* p. 60 n.

60. Merle, p. 710.

61. *Letters from Elizabeth Hitchener to Percy Bysshe Shelley,* ed. by Bertram Dobell (London and New York, 1908), xli–xlii; Ingpen, pp. 555–556. She later returned to England, kept a school at Edmonton, and died in 1822. The £100 annuity which Shelley promised her when she left was apparently never paid; after her death (but a few months before Shelley's own), her executor claimed £100 from Sir Timothy which she had loaned Shelley in June, 1812—i.e. just before she joined the Shelley household in Devon—and which had not been repaid. (Ingpen, pp. 552–553.) Peck's theory (in his Introduction to his edition of Elizabeth Hitchener's letters), accepted by Robert Metcalf Smith, *The Shelley Legend* (New York, 1945), p. 154 n., that she was an adventuress pursuing Shelley for his money, is, as White (I, 605) notes, inconsistent with the known facts.

62. *Works,* IX, 27–28.

63. Hogg, II, 55.

64. To Catherine Nugent, Aug. 4, 1812, *Works,* IX, 15.

65. To John Williams, Mar. 30, 1813, *ibid.,* p. 59. Harriet added a postscript to this letter which reveals that she had read it; and the letter to Hogg concludes: "Write soon, for your letters amuse us ALL."

66. Dowden, I, 314–315. If we compare these lines with her sentiments in her first letter to Shelley, quoted above—"I so rarely meet anyone possessing the requisites for intellectual pleasure"—it is reasonably sure that Dowden's conjecture, shared by Forman (Medwin, p. 118 n.), that these lines refer to Shelley is correct. We have two indications of Shelley's later attitude towards Elizabeth Hitchener. She is almost certainly included in the melodramatic line in *Epipsychidion* (270), "Others were wise, but

honeyed words betray." And Medwin tells us of Shelley, in Italy, quoting a line from an ode of hers on the rights of women—"All, all are men— women and all!"—and "laughing till the tears ran down his cheeks." (Medwin, pp. 117–118.) She is not referred to in his later letters or in the journals (except to record her name as a topic of conversation—*Journal*, Oct. 7, 1814, p. 18).

67. Dowden, I, 319–320.

68. To John Evans, [? Dec., 1812], *Works*, IX, 30; see also: to John Evans, Dec. 3, 1812, *ibid*., pp. 29–30.

69. To Hookham, Jan. 2, Jan. 26, 1813, *ibid*., pp. 40–42.

70. For an account of the trials see: J. L. and Barbara Hammond, *The Skilled Labourer 1760–1832*, pp. 323–332; and Darvall, pp. 129–130.

71. *Works*, IX, 43.

72. Quoted in: *Shelley-Leigh Hunt, How Friendship Made History*, ed. by R. Brimley Johnson (London, 1928), pp. 215–216. I note other attacks on the Regent in *The Examiner* in these months on Jan. 5, pp. 65–66; Mar. 8, pp. 145–146, 157–158; Mar. 15, pp. 161–162, 173; Mar. 29, p. 193; Apr. 19, p. 241.

73. *The Examiner*, Dec. 13, 1812, p. 792.

74. *The Examiner*, Dec. 20, 1812, p. 808.

75. *Works*, IX, 37–38.

76. *The Autobiography of Leigh Hunt*, ed. by Roger Ingpen (London, 1903), II, 13.

77. *Works*, IX, 46–47.

78. *Ibid*., p. 49. Hookham, however, had already sent the £20 to the Hunts' defence fund; but he made a personal loan of £20 to Shelley. (Shelley to Hookham, Mar. 6, 1813, *ibid*., p. 53.)

79. *Ibid*., p. 50.

80. *Ibid*., p. 52–53.

81. *Ibid*., p. 55; Hogg, I, 389.

82. Dowden, I, 354–355.

83. Medwin, *Shelley Papers*, pp. 18–20. See also: Medwin, 116–117. Medwin is almost certainly wrong in stating that Shelley made a deposition before Madocks. Mrs. Williams stated that Madocks was not at Tremadoc during Shelley's stay there (Dowden, I, 357 n.), and this is borne out by the fact that Shelley never in his letters or recorded conversations gives any indication of a meeting with Madocks, an event which, if it had taken place, he could hardly have failed to note. Madocks may have told Medwin that he took the deposition from him but it is more likely that this item was supplied by Medwin in order to lend importance to the interview. It is interesting that in 1832 Medwin wrote: "I had a long conversation with Mr. Maddocks . . ."; by 1847 this had grown to: "I knew Mr. Maddocks well, and had many conversations with him. . . ." (*Shelley Papers*, p. 18; Medwin, p. 116.)

84. Hogg, I, 389.

85. Peacock, pp. 322–323.

86. Dowden, I, 355 n. But if Harriet later became sceptical, apparently

Eliza did not, and is said, "often in after years [to have] related the circumstance as a frightful fact." (*Shelley Memorials,* p. 56.) Lady Shelley gives no authority for the statement.

87. Dowden, I, 356–357. Margaret L. Croft, "A Strange Adventure of Shelley's," *The Century Magazine,* n.s. XLVIII (Oct., 1905), 905–909, and Margaret L. Woods (née Croft?), "Shelley at Tan-yr-allt," *The Nineteenth Century,* LXX (Nov., 1911), 900–902, claimed that the assassin was a local character called Robin Pant Ifan who confessed that he had staged the incident in order to frighten Shelley in retaliation for Shelley's having shot some diseased sheep. This theory, although accepted by Ingpen (pp. 399–400), Peck (I, 291–292), Grabo (pp. 100–101), and others, was disproved by White (I, 282, 649–650) by the simple procedure of looking up Robin's death certificate and finding that he was three years of age at the time of the alleged assault. Blunden (p. 86) and Hughes (pp. 178–179) accept White's argument as eliminating Robin but still feel that an actual attack took place.

88. Dowden, I, 357 n.

89. White, I, 284–285.

90. Two more theories might be mentioned, Hogg's (I, 390–391), followed by Rossetti (*Memoir of Shelley,* pp. 40–41), that Dan Healey was trying to frighten his master, and MacCarthy's (pp. 363–364) that Elizabeth Hitchener was seeking revenge. But Dan was at the door while Shelley was struggling with the sword in the window, and, if he had heard Dan cry out threats against Harriet and Eliza he would have recognized his voice. Nor can one imagine Elizabeth Hitchener embarking on a one-night terrorizing expedition from Sussex to Wales. A further theory that either of them hired an assistant is possible but has no evidence to support it, and is subject to the general criticism of the actuality of the alleged happenings. (See below.)

91. Jeaffreson (II, 145–160), who had legal training, made a thorough, though typically malevolent, analysis of most of the evidence available to him.

92. White, I, 282–283.

93. Dowden, I, 227. See also: Shelley's and Harriet's comments in their letter to Elizabeth Hitchener, Jan. 26, 1812, *Works,* VIII, 253, 256. On Dowden's suggestion (*ibid.*) that this Keswick episode might have been partly due to Shelley's use of laudanum, see n. 95 below.

94. White, I, 284–285; see also: Dowden, I, 357: "Leeson's cruel assertion that Shelley invented the entire story as an excuse for escaping from his creditors in Tremadoc, is sufficiently disproved—if disproof were needed—by the state of nervous excitement in which Shelley was found the next morning by Williams. . . ." On this, see below.

95. To Elizabeth Hitchener, Jan. 20, 1812: ". . . a terrible headache I have had. I have been obliged, by an accession of nervous attack, to take a quantity of laudanum, which I did very unwillingly and reluctantly, and which I should not have done, had I been alone:—I am now quite recovered." (*Works,* VIII, 245.) The reference to laudanum apparently

alarmed Elizabeth Hitchener, for in his answer to her reply he informed her that his "health is re-established" and that he hopes "to be compelled to [have] recourse to laudanum no more." (Jan. 29, 1812, *ibid.,* p. 262.) He used laudanum in 1814 during the marriage crisis, and in later years—as one would take morphine today—when in physical pain, but there is no evidence of addiction. (Peacock, p. 336 and note.)

For a discussion of the effects of opiate addiction, see: Charles E. Terry and Mildred Pellens, *The Opium Problem* (New York, 1928), and Alfred R. Lindesmith, *Opiate Addiction* (Principia Press, 1947). Terry and Pellens (pp. 452, 459) are of the opinion that a "hallucinated state" can develop in "some" addicts after many years of addiction. Lindesmith (p. 24), on the other hand, states flatly, "The notion that narcotics produce hallucinations or dreams is completely false"; and, in an interview, stated that whatever this experience of Shelley's indicated it could have had no basis in his laudanum taking. See also: Elisabeth Schneider, "The 'Dream' of *Kubla Khan,*" *PMLA,* LX (Sept., 1945), 784–801. On this and other problems connected with the episode, I consulted also with Dr. Julius I. Steinfeld, Physician in Charge at The Forest Sanitarium, Des Plaines, Ill.

96. Hogg, I, 265, 347: II, 29–30; Shelley to John Williams, Nov. 7, 1812, *Works,* IX, 23. One of the maids, however, was perhaps a replacement for Dan who at the date of this letter was still in jail. Harriet, in the letter quoted above, we may note, referred to their "servants."

97. To Mrs. Hooper, London, Dec. 19, 1812, *Works,* IX, 26. (This date must be incorrect as Shelley had left London on Nov. 13.) William Roberts to T. L. Peacock, June 12, 1844, Ingpen, p. 634.

98. See above, pp. 215–216.

99. To Hookham, Dec. 3, 1812, *Works,* IX, 29.

100. *Works,* IX, 43–44. "Teased," I note, is always used by Shelley and others at the time, in the sense of a serious aggravation. Thus Keats's "teased out of thought" means "tortured," "tormented" out of thought, a strength of meaning missed by modern readers. See: *OED.*

101. That Shelley had been expected to return from Ireland to Tremadoc is indicated in Eliza Westbrook's letter to John Williams, *ca.* Mar. 21, 1813, White, II, 498–499, and is implied also in Shelley's letter to Williams, Mar. 21, 1813, *Works,* IX, 57.

102. For the history of these MSS see below, ch. VII, n. 2.

103. The paranoid pattern is present also in an early phobia that his father intended to send him to a madhouse (which may have had some basis in fact but which was melodramatized), and a later fear that he had contracted elephantiasis (1813). For the first of these, see: Hogg, I, 35–36 (quoting Mary Shelley); *Diary of Dr. John William Polidori,* June 1, 1816, p. 112; for the second, see Hogg, II, 39; Peacock, p. 326; Dowden, I, 373.

104. On the Williams story, see: Peacock, pp. 341–343; for some analysis of the Pisa incident, see: White, II, 178, 589.

105. Shelley to Hookham, undated, *Works,* IX, 56–57. The letter opens: "Harriet related to you the mysterious events which caused our departure from Tanyralt." Harriet's letter is dated Mar. 12 and Shelley seems to be

writing a week or ten days later, perhaps just before leaving Dublin for Killarney on Mar. 21 or 22. (See: Eliza Westbrook to John Williams, White, II, 498.)

106. Hogg, I, 407.

107. White, II, 498.

108. Shelley expected Hookham to publish the poem, but he did not do so. Hookham and Shelley were reported by Hookham's nephew to have quarreled over *Queen Mab.* (*Works,* VIII, xxxiii.)

109. To Hogg, Mar. 31, 1813, *Works,* IX, 61.

110. Hogg, II, 2.

111. May 21, 1813, *Works,* IX, 67.

112. Such, at least, was Hogg's impression. (Hogg, *loc. cit.*)

113. S. Girdlestone to John Williams, Sept. [1812], White, II, 499–500.

114. Hogg, II, 5.

115. To Catherine Nugent, *Works,* IX, 67.

116. Shelley to Timothy Shelley, May 18, 1813, *ibid.,* p. 66.

117. *Ibid.*

118. Harriet Shelley to Catherine Nugent, June 22, 1813, *ibid.,* p. 72. See also following note.

119. Timothy Shelley to Shelley, May 26, 1813, *ibid.,* p. 68 n. This letter makes it apparent that Timothy's lettter in response to Shelley's of May 18 and Shelley's reply to Timothy have been lost. We have the first and last letters only in the exchange, but from them and from Harriet's of June 22, we can gather the nature of the missing two. That Timothy's now missing reply to Shelley's May 18 letter was dictated by Whitton is indicated by Whitton's entry in his minute book for May 20: "Letter to Mr. Shelley advising on the letter to P. B." (Ingpen, p. 404 n.)

120. *Works,* IX, 68.

121. William Albery, *A Parliamentary History of Horsham,* p. 123.

122. *Works,* IX, 70.

123. Shelley to Thomas Charles Medwin, July 6, 1813, *ibid.,* p. 74; to Hogg, July 9, 1813. Something of their conversation is probably reflected in Harriet's letter to Catherine Nugent on Aug. 8, quoted below. The "great personage" is most likely the Duke of Norfolk, Medwin's political patron.

124. £600 to Munday and Slatter at Oxford, borrowed to assist a needy author in publishing a work on the history and politics of Sweden (Ingpen, pp. 144, 629–632); £300 to Stockdale for the printing of *St. Irvyne* (*Stockdale's Budget,* Jan. 3, 1827, p. 26); £100 to Elizabeth Hitchener (Ingpen, pp. 552–553); £400 to merchants and individuals at Tremadoc (Shelley to John Williams, Mar. 21, 1813, *Works,* IX, 57)—this presumably included a debt of £100 to Owen Williams and £6 to William Roberts (Ingpen, pp. 633–635); £350 to Madocks's estate (White, I, 275, II, 500–502); about £500 for the purchase of and repair to a carriage. This last sum is uncertain; but one, T. Charters, claimed £532, 11s. 6d for "coachmakers work done for him [Shelley] up to Novr. 1815" and in Nov., 1813 Shelley had a repair bill on the carriage of £20 (Ingpen, pp. 636–638); nor is the exact amount of Stockdale's bill ascertainable as his 1827 estimate included

interest; but it is clear from the above figures alone (and there may have been other debts of which we have no record) that Shelley's debts by his twenty-first birthday must have run well over £2000.

125. Hogg, II, 51–52; see preceding note. Hogg's account makes it clear that the carriage was purchased in London before Shelley left for Bracknell about the middle of July (see below) and hence before his twenty-first birthday.

126. To Catherine Nugent, Aug. 8, 1813, *Works,* IX, 76.

127. The Bailiffs hunting Shelley for this bill on one occasion seized upon Hogg by mistake: ". . . two ill-looking fellows burst abruptly into the room; one of them locked the door, and set his back against it, telling me that he arrested me; that I was his prisoner. He was a short, stout man. The other, a long lean fellow, showed me a writ, and presented me with a copy of it.

'What does all this mean?' I asked.

'You know very well, you are Mr. Percy Bysshe Shelley!'

'You are pleased to say that I am.'

'We know very well that you are the defendant; you need not try to persuade us that you are not!'

'Then I will not try!'

"Upon this the bailiffs became rather insolent, and were inclined to be abusive." (Hogg, II, 51.)

The episode is interesting as revealing the continual financial harassment that must have been at this time a daily part of Shelley's (and Harriet's) existence.

128. The root ideas of the school are traceable to Rousseau's *Essay on the Origin of Inequality Among Mankind* but for its specific development, see: Lord Monboddo, *Antient Metaphysics; or, The Science of Universals* (London and Edinburgh, 1789), III, 84 ff.; V, 27–29 (anti-clothes and pronudist), 97, 36 (anti-liquor), 177 (anti-meat), 178–192 (on sexual excesses and venereal disease), 192–193 (against smoky air, opium, and tobacco), 51–52 (against excessive wealth and war).

129. *Ibid.,* V, 237–238.

130. Hogg, II, 14–15. Hogg informs us also that Mrs. Newton used to spend several hours nude in her study each day as a health measure. (*Ibid.,* pp. 15–16.)

131. *The Monthly Magazine or British Register,* XXXIII (1812), pp. 18–22, 107–109, 318–321, 408–409. See also Peacock's humorous account of his doctrines in: Peacock, pp. 324–325. The *Three Enigmas* is an elaborate attempt to show that an allegory he presumed inherent in the signs of the zodiac is vegetarian. Newton had retired to Weymouth by 1821, for it was there (*ibid.,* p. 5 n.) that he wrote this latter work. The New York Public Library copy of *The Return to Nature* is inscribed: "To Mrs. Burney, with the author's compliments and best wishes. Weymouth, 25 August, 1827." He died at Weymouth in 1837. (White, I, 657.)

132. To Clio Rickman, Dec. 24, 1812, *Works,* IX, 36.

133. *Mémoires . . . de Général Lafayette Publiés par sa Famille.* (Paris

and London, 1837), II, 429–431. He is probably also the same De Boinville who assisted Fanny Burney in Paris in 1812. *Diary and Letters of Madame D'Arblay* (London, 1905), VI, 64, 68.

134. *Mémoires . . . ,* p. 430. For more on De Boinville's mission see: *ibid.,* pp. 475–480; and: Thomas Constable, *Memoir of the Reverend Charles A. Chastel de Boinville* (London, 1880), 8–9.

135. Constable, *loc. cit.*

136. Wilberforce to Manning, Oct. 18, 1809: "I have often thought it might do much good, if Collin's excellent work on the management of the negroes were generally circulated." Robert Isaac Wilberforce and Samuel Wilberforce, *The Life of William Wilberforce* (London, 1839), III, 481. James Stephens in *Slavery of the British West India Colonies Delineated* (London, 1823), made use of Collins' book (*Practical Rules for the Management and Medical Treatment of Negro Slaves in the Sugar Colonies*) and was assailed for recommending it in: Alexander Barclay, *A Practical View of the Present State of Slavery in the West Indies* (London, 1827). As Collins had "large estates" on St. Vincent's and was said to have been "very popular among the black population" (Constable, pp. 10, 13), he was probably the author of the book. The book is noted in: Lowell Joseph Ragatz, *A Guide for the Study of British Caribbean History, 1763–1834* (U. S. Government Printing Office, Washington, 1932), p. 448: "A Professional Planter, *Practical Rules . . .*" (London, 1803). The author was resident of the West Indies for twenty years and urges humanitarian reforms.

137. *The Lafayette Letters in the Bostonian Society,* ed. and tr. by Horace H. Morse, Boston Society Publications, IV, ser. 2, 1924, p. 37. Lafayette refers to De Boinville also in two later letters, Jan. 23, 1810, (*ibid.,* p. 141), and Mar. 8, 1812, (*ibid.,* pp. 155–156), in the latter of which he speaks of him as "my former aide-de-camp, whose fortune has been lost, but who is familiar with business and knows much of the world."

138. Constable, pp. 10–11, quoting (as in the above references also) from the Reverend Charles A. Chastel de Boinville.

139. Hogg, II, 107.

140. Peacock, pp. 323–324.

141. *The Examiner,* Jan. 5, 1812, pp. 11–12. See also the issues of Jan. 19 (pp. 43–44) and Feb. 16 (pp. 108–110).

142. To Peacock, Apr. 6, 1819, *Works,* X, 45–46. On Apr. 20, 1820, he wrote to Peacock: "Do you ever see the Boinvilles now? Or Newton? If so, tell them, especially Mrs. Boinville, that I have not forgotten them." (*Ibid.,* p. 160.) He inquires about them as late as Mar. 21, 1821. (To Peacock, *ibid.,* p. 249). In Aug., 1819, he asked Peacock whether or not the Boinvilles were "included in the list of *conviti* at the monthly symposium" (*Works,* X, 73), indicating that he considered them intellectually worthy of Peacock, Hunt, Hogg, etc. (See: *The Athenians,* for a general impression of the group.)

143. Sept. 20, 1843, *Letters of Mary W. Shelley,* II, 201.

144. To Thomas Hookham, Dec. 3, 1812, *Works,* IX, 28.

145. "Jefferson's Memoirs," Peacock's *Works* (Halliford Edition), IX, 187. Peacock gives a remarkably acute picture of the struggle between Jefferson and Hamilton and an excellent summary of Jefferson's principles.

146. In the 1810 edition of *The Genius of the Thames,* Peacock included a long note on Zoroastrianism which he omitted from the 1812 edition. (Peacock's *Works,* VI, 370–375.) His intended epic narrative *Ahrimanes* (which influenced Shelley's *The Revolt of Islam*) has a Zoroastrianism framework. For his satirizing of Newton, see: Peacock, 324–325.

147. To Hookham, Aug. 18, 1812, *Works,* IX, 19. Although Shelley's general attack is justified, he does not do justice to the anti-war sentiment in Peacock's poem, *The Genius of the Thames,* on which he is commenting.

148. Mrs. Newton to Hogg, Oct. 21, 1813. (Hogg, II, 115.)

149. Peacock was an admirer of Cobbett's economic reform plans which Shelley took up in *An Address to the People on the Death of the Princess Charlotte* and *A Philosophical View of Reform.* See: Kenneth Neill Cameron, "Shelley, Cobbett and the National Debt," *JEGP,* XLII (Apr., 1943), 197–209. Peacock's views can be most pleasantly assimilated from his witty *Paper Money Lyrics.*

150. Shelley had, of course, studied the classics at Eton and Oxford, but they had later, as he was more and more absorbed by his humanitarian perspectives, seemed of minor and even reactionary import, e.g.: "I do not see how one of the truths of Political Justice rests on the excellence of ancient literature. . . . Throughout the whole of their literature runs a vein of thought similar to that which you have so justly censured in Helvetius. . . . Their politics sprang from the same narrow and corrupted source." (To Godwin, July 29, 1812, *Works,* IX, 12–13. Godwin—*Political Justice,* I, 279–281—attacks Helvétius for a cynical and pessimistic attitude towards the achievement of "fundamental reform.") After Shelley met Godwin in the fall of 1812, however, he ordered a number of classical works on Godwin's recommendation. (Godwin to Shelley, Dec. 10, 1812, *Shelley Memorials,* pp. 46–47; Shelley to Hookham, Dec. 17, 1812, and to Rickman, Dec. 24, 1812, *Works,* IX, 33–36.) But it is not until Shelley is in Edinburgh in the fall of 1813, with Peacock as his companion, that we first detect a note of genuine enthusiasm for the classics: "I have for some time given myself to study. I have read 'Tacitus,' many of Cicero's philosophical works (who is, in my estimation, one of the most admirable characters the world ever produced) and Homer's 'Odyssey.' " (To Hogg, Nov. 26, 1813, *ibid.,* p. 81; see also: Peacock's *Works,* I, liii–lv.)

151. Ianthe was probably born either late on June 27 or early on June 28. On June 27, Shelley dropped notes to Hogg and Williams on routine matters but did not mention the birth; on June 28, he wrote to Thomas Charles Medwin: "I am happy to inform you that Mrs. Shelley has been safely delivered of a little girl and is now rapidly recovering. (*Works,* IX, 72–73.)

152. Oct. 20, 1813, *ibid.,* p. 79.

153. See, for example, the bill on repairs to the carriage. (Ingpen, pp. 636–638.)

154. Hogg, II, 21; Shelley to Hookham, Aug. 18, 1812, *Works,* IX, 20. Holbach's *System of Nature* is not a work on "perfectibility" but an exposition of materialism. Hogg, however, probably had little recollection in 1855–1858 of the exact nature of the book, but remembered only that it was

by one of the French philosophers whose works he associated with the perfectibilian theme.

155. Hogg, I, 146. On Mar. 14, 1812, Harriet wrote to Elizabeth
Hitchener from Dublin: "You do not know that we have forsworn meat,
and adopted the Pythagorean system. About a fortnight has elapsed since
the change. . . ." (*Works,* VIII, 295–296.) When Catherine Nugent first
met the Shelleys in Mar., 1812, they were vegetarians (Shelley talking "as a
man believing in the metempsychosis"), but on one occasion they "mur-
dered" a chicken for their guest. ([John Anster], *North British Review,*
III [1847], 126–127; Harriet Shelley to Catherine Nugent, *Works,* VIII,
299.) Hogg (II, 81–82) states that it was not "until the spring of 1813 that
he [Shelley] entered upon a full and exact course of vegetable diet," although he had previously "fed much on pulse [beans, peas, etc.] at different
periods." But the evidence of Harriet's letter of Mar. 14, and the observations of Catherine Nugent that an actual vegetarian regime had been begun
a year previously is of more consequence than Hogg's recollection some
forty-five years later, especially as Hogg was in Shelley's company between
Mar., 1812, and the spring of 1813 only during two or three weeks (late
Oct. to mid Nov.), and then apparently only on a few occasions. That
Shelley had informed Hogg of his vegetarianism during his visit in London
in Nov., 1812, is clear from his letter to Hogg on Dec. 27: "I continue
vegetable; Harriet means to be slightly animal until the arrival of spring.
My health is much improved by it. . . ." (*Works,* IX, 38.)

On Apr. 16, 1812, Harriet informed Catherine Nugent that they had
a meal including meat after being without food for thirty-six hours on the
crossing from Ireland, but this is stated apologetically, implying a trans-
gression (as was the previous murder of the fowl). (*Works,* VIII, 310.)
There may, however, later have been some fluctuations, for on May 21,
1813, Harriet (then eight months pregnant) wrote to Catherine Nugent,
"we have all taken to the vegetable regimen again," which seems to imply
that they had "all" been off it for a time. (*Ibid.,* p. 67.) We might note
also that the poet of *Alastor* (1815) was a vegetarian (l. 101), and that the
new society proclaimed in *The Revolt of Islam* ([1817], V, LI, 5) is
vegetarian. But I fail to find any similar stipulation laid down for the new
order in *Prometheus Unbound* (1819) or *Hellas* (1821).

156. *Works,* IX, 81.

157. Howard Williams, *The Ethics of Diet* (London, 1883), pp. 169–
172, 162–163, 134–137, 130–131, 18–19.

158. See n. 128 above. Monboddo's views on marriage will be found
in *Of the Origin and Progress of Language* (Edinburgh, 1774), I, 447–454.

159. *Ibid.,* pp. 269–289; *Antient Metaphysics,* III, 175; Peacock, *Melincourt;* see especially ch. 6 and its notes, and chs. 21 and 22 (Sir Oran's election to Parliament).

160. Plutarch, "Of Eating of Flesh," *Plutarch's Morals* (Boston, 1878),
V, 3–13.

161. For Lambe, see the *DNB.* Newton's *The Return to Nature* may
be found reprinted in: *The Pamphleteer,* XIX (1822), 497–530; XX (1822),
97–118. Lambe and Newton were friends, and in 1818 Lambe's daughter

married the son of Mrs. de Boinville. (Constable, p. 24.) Shelley also advocated the use of distilled water. (*A Vindication of Natural Diet, Works,* VI, 9 n.)

162. Joseph Ritson, *An Essay on Abstinence from Animal Food as a Moral Duty* (London, 1802), pp. 95, 86.

163. Rousseau's *Emile,* quoted in: Williams, p. 162.

164. *Ibid.,* p. 206.

165. *Works,* IX, 36. In a note to *A Vindication of Natural Diet,* Shelley refers to "Trotter on the Nervous Temperament," as the source for the statement that a habitual drunkard cannot gradually break off but must do so completely and at once. The passage will be found in *A View of the Nervous Temperament* (Troy, New York, 1808), p. 323. Trotter deals with the subject in more detail in *An Essay, Medical, Philosophical, and Chemical on Drunkenness* (Philadelphia, 1813), pp. 176–178. As the *Vindication* was almost certainly written in Nov., 1812, at Tanyrallt (see n. 173 below), Shelley is probably here remembering a reading of Trotter's book at Newton's (whom he first met on Nov. 5) or a discussion of it with Newton. Shelley gives no page number in his reference as he does with other works. Shelley, we might note, in previous years took alcoholic drinks. Hogg (I, 87; II, 82) informs us that he drank some wine at Oxford, and a bacchanalic note to a fellow student has survived: "Dear Roe: At ½ past 4 or 5 o'clock there will be wine Poetry in my room. Will you honor me with your Co." (*Works,* X, 415.) Merle (p. 705), we remember, found him drinking "brandy-and-water" in the Swan "taproom" at Horsham in the late spring of 1811.

166. *On Drunkenness,* p. 12.

167. See n. 165 above.

168. *The Nervous Temperament,* pp. 34–36, 234, 51, 323, 294.

169. *Ibid.,* pp. 279, 280, 286, 290, 175, 92.

170. White, I, 326.

171. To Elizabeth Hitchener, Jan. 20, 1812, *Works,* VIII, 245. Shelley, however, contrary to Trotter's advice took laudanum for these attacks, although only as a temporary measure. (To the same, Jan. 29, 1812, *ibid.,* p. 262.) His description of "nervous" symptoms in a letter to Godwin on Dec. 7, 1817, reads almost like a case history out of Trotter. (*Works,* IX, 258–259.)

172. See, for instance, the description of the spasm in: [Thornton Hunt], *Shelley by One Who Knew Him, Shelley and Keats,* ed. by Edmund Blunden (London, 1925), p. 14.

173. The *Vindication* title page reads, in part, "A Vindication of Natural Diet. Being one in a series of Notes to Queen Mab, A Philosophical Poem," and is dated, London, 1813. *Queen Mab* is also dated on the title page 1813; a letter from Harriet to Catherine Nugent on May 21 (*Works,* IX, 67) indicates that the printing had then begun and Hogg (II, 44) indicates that it was in circulation before Shelley left London for Bracknell (in the middle of July). We thus have two texts of the *Vindication,* one a separate pamphlet, one as part of a long Note to *Queen Mab.* The reference to *Queen Mab* on the title page of the *Vindication,* with the correct designation "A

Philosophical Poem," naturally led scholars to believe that it was published later than *Queen Mab,* and so it was assumed by Ingpen and others, but David Lee Clark ("The Date and Sources of Shelley's *A Vindication of Natural Diet," SP,* XXXVI [Jan., 1939], 70–71) argues the contrary on the following grounds: (a) in the concluding sentence of the appendix to the *Vindication* (omitted in the Note) Shelley states that "the author and his wife have lived on vegetables for eight months"; as this diet began on about Mar. 1, 1812, this statement places the date of composition as Oct.–Nov., 1812; (b) Shelley's letters to Hookham show that he was preparing the Notes to *Queen Mab* in Feb. and Mar., 1813, after sending him the MS of the poem itself, and it is likely that many of these Notes were being reworked from material already on hand; (c) Hogg's "impression" was that the *Vindication* was published prior to *Queen Mab* (Hogg, II, 83–84); (d) the Note contains a paragraph on "unnatural" evils other than meat eating which is not in the *Vindication.* To this evidence we might add that an examination of grammatical and stylistic changes between the texts indicates that the Note and not the *Vindication* represents the revised text, for this text exhibits a consistent series of grammatical and stylistic corrections. Thus, the Note text grammatically corrects "possess" to "possesses," "lay" to "lie," and omits two redundant "that's." And these changes all go in one direction, i.e. from the *Vindication* to the *Queen Mab* text and never vice versa. So, too, with the stylistic changes. In the *Vindication* Shelley writes: "There is no exception, except man be one . . ."; in the Note this is changed to: "There is no exception, unless man be one"; "that broods" is changed to "which broods" to avoid a repetition of "that" within the sentence. Other stylistic changes are designed to make the meaning more exact. For instance, "There is no other species of animals in which this analogy exists" is amended to "There is no other species of animals, which live on different foods, in which. . . ." In a passage quoted from Newton two minute mistakes are corrected in the Note, "the" to "this," and "the" to "these." (For these and other emendations, see the Notes to the *Vindication, Works,* VI, 347–348. The significance of the emendations, however, can be ascertained only by an actual collation of the complete context in each case.)

The evidence thus shows that the *Vindication* text was the earlier, i.e. it was earlier than Feb.–Mar., 1813, when the *Queen Mab* Notes were being prepared. The "eight months" reference in the *Vindication* text certainly indicates Oct.–Nov., 1812, as the general period of composition. As Shelley, however, did not meet Newton until Nov. 5, and the Newton influence is so strong in the work, and it was published by the same firm that published Newton's *The Return to Nature,* we are reasonably safe in dating it later than this. It may have been written before Shelley left London for Tanyrallt on Nov. 13, or later in the month at Tanyrallt. It must, in any case, have been set up in type before Mar., 1813, or Shelley would have incorporated the changes of the Note version in it. Hence the indication for date of composition is Nov. 5–30, 1812, and of publication early in 1813, which latter conjecture is in agreement with Hogg's impression that it preceded the printing of *Queen Mab.* Shelley, however, apparently did not expect that it would precede *Queen Mab* by too long a period as he would hardly have referred to *Queen Mab* on its title page if he had anticipated a very long time lapse between the two. His plans for *Queen Mab* were doubtless delayed by his work on the Tremadoc embankment.

174. This work remained in manuscript until 1929 when Ingpen published it from a MS derived from Shelley's descendants. (*Works,* VI, 335–344.) A reference in a note, "See Queen Mab, p. 223" (*Works,* VI, 340 n.), shows that it was composed later than the publication of *Queen Mab* (*ca.* June, 1813), and the use of similar source material to that in the *Vindication,* the Note in *Queen Mab,* and *A Refutation of Deism* indicates that it was written in the 1813–1814 period and not later. A more precise indication is perhaps to be found in a letter from Shelley to Hogg from Edinburgh on Nov. 26, 1813: "I have translated the two Essays of Plutarch, περὶ σαρκοφαγίας, which we read together. They are very excellent. I intend to comment upon them, and to reason in my preface concerning the Orphic and Pythagorian system of diet." (*Works,* IX, 81–82.) This, Ingpen (*ibid.*) takes to be a reference to *A Refutation of Deism* apparently on the ground that Shelley there includes a paragraph on vegetarianism and quotes from Plutarch. But the same quotation from Plutarch is to be found in the *Queen Mab* Note (*Works,* VI, 51 n.; I, 164–165); and it is much more likely that Shelley is referring to *The Vegetable System of Diet* than to *A Refutation of Deism.* A discussion of the vegetarian doctrines of the Orphic and Pythagorian sects, based on metempsychosis, is appropriate to a treatise on vegetarianism but not to an essay on atheism. (When Catherine Nugent first met Shelley, he was, as we have noted, a "Pythagorian" and "spoke as a man believing in the metempsychosis.") The indication of the available evidence is that the *Vegetable System* was written in the fall of 1813, Shelley perhaps intending it as fairly elaborate restatement of his vegetarian position, but later—perhaps under the humorous probings of Peacock, who was then with him in Edinburgh—abandoned it.

175. *Works,* VI, 5–6. For parallels with Newton, see: *ibid.,* pp. 347–348; with Ritson, see: Clark, pp. 72–76.

176. *Works,* I, 159. Shelley himself, Hogg (II, 83) informs us, dressed thinly, never wearing an overcoat "even in coldest weather."

177. Ritson, pp. 12–21; for Newton, see: *The Pamphleteer,* XIX, 507–508.

178. Quoted in: Williams, pp. 172, 18–19.

179. *Works,* VI, 13–14.

180. *Works,* VI, 19–20, where Shelley quotes Newton on "Old Parr." For other parallels in Shelley's list, see: Clark, p. 74. "Patrick O'Neale" also comes from Ritson (p. 72), who quotes his case from Rousseau's *Emile.* Ritson also (pp. 42–43) gives Rousseau as his authority for the argument that as young children do not like meat it is not "natural" to man, an argument Shelley (p. 9) repeats. Ritson (p. 43 n.) states that out of 17,814 children born, nearly 7,500 die in the first five years; this also, Shelley repeats (p. 17 n.). Shelley for some reason was clearly anxious to hide his indebtedness to Ritson, never referring to him, and when taking material from him, citing the sources given by Ritson as though they were his orig-

inals. Thus, Shelley (p. 19) gives *Emile* as his source for the Patrick
O'Neale example.

181. *Works,* VI, 337–338.

182. *Ibid.,* pp. 339, 15. Cf.: Newton, *The Pamphleteer,* XIX, 529: "A
general deterioration of the humours has been transmitted, by slow degrees
and in a long descent, from father to son. . . ."

183. *Works,* VI, p. 15.

184. *Ibid.,* p. 335.

185. *Ibid.,* pp. 341–342; my italics.

186. "Dinner by the Amateurs of Vegetable Diet (Extracted from an
Old Paper)," *The London Magazine and Theatrical Enquirer,* July, 1821,
quoted in: White, *The Unextinguished Hearth,* pp. 267–268. Shelley in the
Vindication (Works, VI, 12) had stated: "In April, 1814, a statement will
be given, that sixty persons, all having lived more than three years on
vegetables and water, are then in *perfect health.*" This skit is a humorous
representation of a banquet which might have celebrated such an event,
and begins: "On the 14th of April, 1814, sixty persons, who had lived for
three years on vegetables and pure water, met for the purpose of felicitating
each other on the circumstances of their still being alive." Newton is represented as president, Shelley as vice-president:

> The president gave, "A return to nature, or success to vegetable
> regimen," drank three times three—Song: "Peas, Beans, and Cab-
> bage." . . . Mr. P.B.S. then gave, "the memory of Nebuchadnezzar,
> and may all kings, like him, be speedily sent to graze with their
> brother brutes." This toast excited much commotion, but was drank
> at last, without the adjunct, which it was deemed prudent to omit.

The skit is unsigned, but as White indicates, the author is almost certainly
either Hogg or Peacock. White himself favors Hogg; Hughes (p. 164 n.)
"suspects" Peacock. The satirical style, especially the use of verse and Greek
quotations, seems to me to indicate Peacock rather than Hogg. Hogg was
himself an ardent vegetarian for a period and, while he later made mild
fun of some vegetarians, always seems to have considered the doctrine
worthy of serious consideration. (Hogg's vegetarianism was a cause of alarm
to his family, and the family clergyman, William Terrot, undertook to
remonstrate with him: "But this new system of eating vegetables, in which
it does not appear to us how your conscience can be concerned, though I
pretend not to judge, has hung on your Mother as a sort of indication
that your determination was to deviate from all the old established ways
of the world, & I have reason to say that it has hurt her & your Father very
much, in addition to the old business." To Hogg, undated but apparently
written in the spring of 1813, *The Athenians,* p. 24.) Hogg's comments on
the subject in his life of Shelley (II, 81–91, 111) do not exhibit the (typically
Peacockian) cynical acidity of this skit. (One of Hogg's stories on Newton,
we might note in passing, is demonstrably false. Newton, he informs us
[II, 92], had given a copy of *The Return to Nature* to Horne Tooke. When
Tooke died and his library was up for sale, Newton, feeling sure that the
book would certainly have been enriched by annotations by the great man,

"commissioned a friend, who was to attend the sale, to purchase it for him, and to go as far as fifty guineas." Then, feeling this might not suffice, authorized him to go as high as 200 guineas. The climax of the story is that the friend returned from the sale having purchased the book for eighteen pence, not only unannotated but with the pages uncut. Unfortunately for Hogg there exists in the Huntington Library—and perhaps in others also— a *Catalogue of the Valuable Library late the property of John Horne Tooke, sold by auction by King and Lockée, May 26, 1813 and 3 following days,* in which the purchaser and price for each item have been added. Opposite "Newton, John Frank, *The Return to Nature,*" is the notation: sold to Valpy—a well-known publisher—for five shillings.)

187. See, for instance, their list of publications as given in the back pages of Shelley's *Vindication.*

188. Frederick L. Jones, "Unpublished Fragments by Shelley and Mary," *SP,* XLV (July, 1948), 476.

CHAPTER VII

1. *Works,* VIII, 214.

2. It has been generally accepted (e.g. White, I, 279) that Shelley received the poems from Ireland before leaving Tremadoc, but a close reading of the letters of Shelley and Harriet, including their comments on the related problems of the manuscripts of *Queen Mab* and *Biblical Extracts,* makes it appear more probable that he had not.

On Jan. 20, 1812, and again on Jan. 26, Shelley informed Elizabeth Hitchener from Keswick that he would print the "younger poems" in Dublin, and that he would print there also his essays on metaphysics, the "address to the Irish," and Hubert Cauvin, the first two printed "expensively," the latter two "cheaply." (*Works,* VIII, 249, 253.) Of these, so far as we know, only the address was actually printed in Ireland, but we learn from a letter from Harriet to Catherine Nugent on June 7, 1812, that the poems were sent to a printer in Dublin (*ibid.,* p. 333) and apparently some of them set up in type. The printer was "very slow," and by June 30, Shelley was thinking of sending Dan Healey back to Dublin to see about them. (Harriet to Catherine Nugent, *Works,* IX, 4.) On July 29, Shelley informed Hookham that he was working on "poems" and "essays" which he would send to him when completed. (*Ibid.,* pp. 9–10.) By Aug. 4 the poems had still not arrived and we learn that the trouble is that the printer "refuses to go on with his poems until he is paid," an "unusual" demand, Harriet thinks; but apparently the printer thought otherwise (aided, perhaps, by an edict for "expensive" printing). (Harriet to Catherine Nugent, *ibid.,* pp. 14–15.) Shelley next thought of sending Lawless after the poems (and, in view of the constant association of Lawless's name with the project, perhaps it was he who had suggested the printer). Hookham, having, in the meantime, apparently expressed an interest in the poems and essays, is informed that Shelley would like to have a volume of essays ready by Nov., "but, all my MSS now being in

Dublin, and from peculiar circumstances not immediately available, I do not know whether I can." (Aug. 18, *ibid.,* pp. 18–19.) By the fall, the situation had become desperate: "Percy says he wishes you to go to Stockdale's, and get all his manuscript poems and other pieces. I am afraid you will be obliged to use a little manoeuvre to get them. In the first place, you can say you wish to look at them, and then you may be able to steal them away from him. I leave it all to you . . ." (Harriet to Catherine Nugent, *ibid.,* pp. 24–25, written within a few weeks of Shelley's arrival in London on Oct. 4; see above, p. 191.)

From these last two letters we learn that the printer (R. and J. Stockdale, Jr., 62 Abbey St.—no relation to the London Stockdale who had published *St. Irvyne* and *Original Poetry*) not only had Shelley's poems in his possession but "other pieces" and "essays" as well. The essays were doubtless the "metaphysical essays" and the "other pieces" may refer to them only or also include *Hubert Cauvin* and two other works that Shelley contemplated in Dublin: a selection from Paine's works and a selection from the "moral sayings of Jesus Christ." (To Elizabeth Hitchener, Feb. 14, Feb. 27, *Works,* VIII, 275, 285.) We hear no more of the Paine selections, but the "moral sayings" were doubtless (as Ingpen suggests—*ibid.,* p. 285 n.) the same as a work known as "Biblical Extracts," which Shelley informed Hookham on Jan. 2, 1813, would make a small booklet about the size of Godwin's *Essay on Sepulchres.* (*Works,* IX, 40.) By Nov. 14, nothing had been heard from Catherine Nugent, so that when Shelley left London in that month for Tremadoc the situation was that the Stockdales were holding on to his poems and "other pieces," and stubbornly demanding their money before they would either "proceed" further or return the manuscripts.

The theory that the Stockdales did later return the manuscripts is based on an undated, unaddressed note from Shelley to Hookham apparently written immediately after a letter of Dec. 17 instructing Hookham to send him a box of books: "I write hastily again today because I hear from Ireland of my MSS. You can include it in the box of books." (*Ibid.,* p. 35.) The implication in this note is that Shelley had heard that the MSS were being sent from Ireland to Hookham in London and he was to forward them to Shelley. But a following letter on Jan. 2 to Hookham—who had in the meantime replied—does not mention the arrival of the manuscripts, an omission which, in view of their importance in the preceding correspondence, can only mean that they had not arrived. Furthermore, they had apparently not been received by Hookham either, for the letter contains a characterization of the "Poems" which implies that Hookham had enquired about their nature but did not have them in his possession. In a letter to Catherine Nugent on Jan. 16 Harriet simply remarks: "Eliza and Percy desire their kind regards to you, with many thanks for your embassy to Stockdale, who will hear from Mr. S. soon." (*Ibid.,* p. 41.) The impression which I derive from this comment is that Miss Nugent had not been able to retrieve the manuscripts, but that Stockdale had perhaps made some counter-proposal on which Shelley was to communicate to him. If she had actually been able to retrieve them, one would expect a more elaborate comment of congratulations, for their recovery had been a key point in the preceding correspondence. Nor would one expect Stockdale to release them without some guarantee of payment, and Shelley at Tremadoc, head over heels in debt, had no means of payment. By Jan. 31, the "box" from Hookham had still not arrived. (*Ibid.,* p. 43.) A letter to Hookham on Feb. 19 still makes no reference to receipt of any manuscripts (*ibid.,* p. 47), and it was only after his arrival in Ireland that Shelley commented, while sending *Queen Mab* to Hookham: "I *have* many other poems which shall also be sent." (*Ibid.,* p. 57; my italics.) This is the first statement of an actual possession of the manuscripts of the poems. The indication is, therefore, that Stockdale did not release the manuscripts until Shelley made personal contact with him in Dublin. Shelley received £20 from Hookham before leaving for Ireland and £100 from Owen Williams, brother of John Williams, apparently soon after arriving in Dublin. (To Hookham, Mar. 6, 1813, *Works,* IX, 53; to John Williams, *ca.* Mar. 9, 1813, *ibid.,* p. 54; Hugh Owen to T. L. Peacock, Dec. 12, 1844, Ingpen, p. 635.) These loans perhaps explain how he was able to overcome Stockdale's resistance.

If, therefore, as this evidence indicates, Shelley did not receive the manuscripts from Stockdale at Tremadoc, the note to Hookham of *ca.* Dec. 17 cannot mean that he had received definite word that the manuscripts were on the way. Nor does he specifically say this, although he seems to be implying it. The probability is that he had heard from Miss Nugent that the Stockdales were prepared to make some kind of deal, which he perhaps hoped would result in the speedy release of the manuscripts, but which, in fact, did not. In the meantime he wished to keep up Hookham's interest and so overstated the case (with not untypical dramatic insinuation).

That Stockdale released not only the poems but the essays also is made likely by the fact that some of these essays were almost certainly used in the Notes to *Queen Mab.* (See below, n. 100.) Whether Stockdale also had a manuscript of the *Biblical Extracts* is not clear, but, in any case, Shelley must have possessed a second copy, as he did not of the poems; so that tracing the vicissitudes of the *Extracts* does not assist in determining the fate of the manuscript at Stockdale's. (In future years, we may note, Shelley was careful to make copies for his poems.) On Dec. 17, 1812, when he had still not received his manuscripts from Ireland, he wrote to Hookham: "You will receive the 'Biblical Extracts' in a day or two by the twopenny post. I confide them to the care of a person going to London. Would not Daniel I. Eaton publish them?" (*Works,* IX, 33.) By Jan. 2, Hookham had evidently received the *Extracts,* for on that date Shelley instructs him to send them to the press. (*Ibid.,* p. 40.) Shelley, furthermore, hoped that they would be printed by the end of the month, for on Jan. 31 Harriet informed Hookham that "Mr. Shelley hopes to find some copies [i.e. printed copies] of the Biblical Extracts in the Box." (*Ibid.,* p. 43.) According to a note in the *Shelley Memorials* (p. 48), the *Extracts* were never published, and, as Lady Shelley had contact with Hookham, he was perhaps the source of this statement.

In addition to the above references to the *Extracts* we have one more, in an undated note apparently to Hookham: "You will receive a parcel directed to me at your house. Open it and you will find the Essay on Atheism; Queen Mab, and the Biblical Extracts. Keep the former for yourself (it is the only one I have) and send the others carefully packed by the Mail: directed to be forwarded with care and speed. If you have got anything new on Paine's Works send it with them. Oh! and is God Save the King done. My loyal soul pants for its arrival." This note Shelley heads: "Tanyralt, Tremadoc, Carnarvonshire for letters. Tanyralt, Tremadoc, Carnarvonshire, to be left at Capel Curig Inn for Parcels." R. H. Hill in *The Shelley Correspondence in the Bodleian Library* (Oxford, 1926), p. 8, dates the note "between Feb. 19 and Mar. 3, 1813," and Ingpen (*Works,* IX, 48) places it in this position in his sequencing of the letters. The Mar. 3 limit is based on the fact that Shelley left Tremadoc on Mar. 3 or 4; the Feb. 19 limit is presumably based on Shelley's statement to Hookham on that date that he had finished *Queen Mab*. Shelley, however, did not actually send *Queen Mab* to Hookham until *ca.* Mar. 21; so that it is more likely that this note refers to an earlier draft (for evidence of revision see n. 27 below) than to the completed poem. Further, the directions for mailing indicate a letter sent to Hookham shortly after Shelley's arrival at Tremadoc. It was most probably written between the middle of Nov. when Shelley arrived at Tremadoc and Dec. 3 when he wrote to Hookham: "The parcel is not yet arrived. I own I am rather anxious concerning it . . . when does God save . . ." (*Works,* IX, 28–29.) Shelley received this parcel, I presume, before Dec. 17, and perhaps (see n. 22 below) by Dec. 10, revised or polished the *Extracts,* and sent them back to Hookham a few days later. ("God Save the King" does not seem to be a work by Shelley, as White [I, 279–280] suggested, but simply one that Hookham had told him about during his London visit, perhaps one that Hookham was himself publishing.) Who originally shipped the parcel containing the *Queen Mab* manuscript, etc., to Hookham we cannot tell, but a probable hypothesis is that Shelley had, in his haste of departure from London, left it and the other material with Godwin, and that he later directed Godwin to send them to Hookham, so that Hookham could look through the manuscript drafts of *Queen Mab* and the *Extracts* and keep the copy of the *Necessity of Atheism.* Godwin had the manuscript of *Queen Mab* at least as late as Oct. 31 (Dowden, I, 340), and when Shelley left London suddenly on Nov. 13, he broke an engagement to meet Godwin that evening. (See above, pp. 197–198.) The manuscripts of *Extracts* and *Queen Mab* were duly forwarded to Shelley and *The Necessity of Atheism* was kept by Hookham; Shelley returned the *Extracts* to Hookham for printing and kept *Queen Mab* for further work. Hookham's copy of *The Necessity of Atheism* is now in the Bodleian. (Hill, *loc. cit.*)

For an attempted reconstruction of the *Biblical Extracts,* see: Bennett Weaver, "Shelley's *Biblical Extracts:* a Lost Book," *Papers of the Michigan Academy of Science, Arts and Letters,* XX (1935), 523–538. See also: *Note Books of Percy Bysshe Shelley,* ed. by H. Buxton Forman (Boston, 1911), II, 117–119. Weaver concludes, from a tabular study of Biblical passages in Shelley's other works, that the "core of the compilation" would have been from the Sermon on the Mount, and that the *Old Testament* section "might have included Job and Ecclesiastes entire, a considerable selection from Psalms, and those chapters from Isaiah which are spiritually the most imaginative or which are warmest with the essential social passion of the prophets." Shelley would doubtless have used those sayings of Christ which would best illustrate his concept of him as a "reformer" of a "moral and humane" character in contrast both to the reactionary nature of the Church and the "sanguinary deity of the Jews." (*A Letter to Lord Ellenborough, Works*, V, 289.) Some of the *Old Testament Extracts* stressing this "sanguinary deity" did later, I suspect, find their way into the notes to *A Refutation of Deism*. (*Works*, VI, 34–35.) Even this use of the Bible, however, troubled Shelley, and he intended to write an anti-religious preface to the *Extracts* as an antidote to "Biblical poison." (To Hookham, Jan. 2, 1813, *Works*, IX, 40.)

3. Shelley's use of two poems—the Dedication to Harriet and "Falsehood and Vice"—in the *Queen Mab* volume indicates, as Dowden (I, 348–349) notes, that Shelley had "already abandoned his intention of printing the shorter pieces." (And Dowden could have noted also part of another poem—"To Harriet"—in the *Queen Mab* volume; see below, n. 4.) *Queen Mab* was in the press in May. (Harriet Shelley to Catherine Nugent, May 21, 1813, *Works*, IX, 67.)

4. All the poems and fragments of poems from the volume so far published may be found as follows: (1) *Works*, III, 70–78 (a group of juvenile poems, 1809–1810, including the more mature *Wandering Jew's Soliloquy*). (I give the dating throughout from *Works*, as Ingpen, the editor, was permitted to see the MS book and presumably found the poems dated therein. Editor's Preface, *Works*, III, [v].) (2) *Ibid.*, pp. 88–90 (two poems "On an Icicle" and "Bigotry's Victim" inclosed in letters to Hogg, Jan. 6 and Apr. 28, 1811; see also *Works*, VIII, 36–37, 78–79, and *Shelley at Oxford*, pp. 34–35). (3) *Ibid.*, pp. 91–92 ("From the Marseilles Hymn"; for complete version, see: *Works*, IV, 341–343; stanza IV was included in a letter to Graham, June, 1811, *Works*, VIII, 110). (4) *Ibid.*, pp. 95–112 (poems of 1812–1813, with the exception of fragments of *Zeinab and Kathema*, which is dated 1811 by Ingpen. Ingpen dates *A Tale of Society as it is*, 1811, but it is included in a letter of Jan. 7, 1812, to Elizabeth Hitchener with the comment: "It is the overflowings of the mind this morning." *Works*, VIII, 236). (5) *Works*, I, 204 ("The pale, the cold, and the moony smile," included in the *Alastor* volume in a revised text; the earlier text has not been printed). (6) *Ibid.*, pp. 136–138 ("Falsehood and Vice" included in Notes to *Queen Mab*). *Ibid.*, p. 65 (dedicatory poem, used as dedication to *Queen Mab*). *Ibid.*, p. 157 (ll. 58–69 of *To Harriet* included in Notes to *Queen Mab*; see: *Works*, III, for complete poem).

In addition, for descriptions of poems unpublished or published only in fragment see: *Works*, III, 318 ("an unpublished poem 'Mary' in four sections"); Dowden, I, 268 ("The Tombs," suggested date, spring, 1812); *ibid.*, pp. 283–285, 293 n. ("The Voyage" and "Retrospect of Times of Old"; suggested dates, Aug., 1812); *ibid.*, pp. 345–348 (various minor poems including "a series of poems in unrhymed stanzas," fragments from some of which will be found in *Works*, III, 111, plus an account of the longer narratives *Henry and Louisa* and *Zeinab and Kathema,* both apparently dated 1811). Taking the poems and fragments in *Works* together with those described by Dowden we arrive at a total of at least thirty-three poems in the volume, including one—"The Cowardly and Infamous Bombardment of Copenhagen"—by Elizabeth Shelley. (To Hogg, Jan. 11, 1811, *Works,* VIII, 40; see also *Works,* III, 316.) Of these, the long narratives described by Dowden and the smaller poems in *Works,* III, 70–78, 88–90, 95–99, plus, perhaps, "On Robert Emmet's Tomb," *ibid.,* p. 104, and some of the "poems in unrhymed stanzas" presumably made up the original volume as left with the Stockdales in Dublin, because the rest of the poems in the MS book were written following Shelley's return to England. Shelley himself only published three of the poems and part of another: "Falsehood and Vice," the Dedication, and ll. 58–69 of "To Harriet" in the *Queen Mab* volume, and "The pale, the cold, and the moony smile" in the *Alastor* volume (1816). The poems included in the letters to Hogg (*Works,* III, 316 ff.) appeared first in Hogg's *Life of Shelley* (1858); the poems included in letters to Elizabeth Hitchener, plus "Eyes: A Fragment," appeared in Rossetti's edition of Shelley's poems in 1870 (*Works,* III, 317 ff.); the fourth stanza of the translation of the "Marseillaise" appeared first in Forman's edition of Shelley's poetical works in 1876. (*Ibid.,* p. 320.) Following Dowden, the next scholar to be allowed use of the MS volume was Bertram Dobell who first printed "The Wandering Jew's Soliloquy" in his edition of *The Wandering Jew* in 1887. A. Koszul in 1910 was allowed to transcribe from it the full translation of the "Marseillaise" for his *La Jeunesse de Shelley* (pp. 401–404). Ingpen was allowed to check the text of the poems which had been previously printed for use in *Works,* III (1927), but was apparently not allowed to transcribe the others. (*Works,* III [v].) Mr. William C. H. Esdaile, Shelley's great-grandson, informed me in the summer of 1949 that the MS volume was still in his possession. Dowden inspected the volume in 1884 and copied it for his own use although he was only allowed to print the biographical poems. (Dowden, I, viii; *Letters About Shelley,* pp. 106–107; *Letters of Edward Dowden and His Correspondents* [New York, 1914], pp. 206, 226.)

One other poem on which Shelley was apparently engaged at this time, but which is not in the Esdaile MS volume, should be noted. This is *Sadak the Wanderer,* a fragment of which was printed in *LTLS,* May 16, 1936, p. 424. The story will be found under the title "Sadak and Kalasrade" in: Sir Charles Morell, *The Tales of the Genii* (London, 1764), II, 93–256. The plot concerns the attempts of Sadak to get his wife Kalasrade back from the Sultan Amurath who has had her carried off to his seraglio. It is, thus, akin to *Zeinab and Kathema* and anticipatory of *The Revolt of Islam.*

5. Jan. 2, 1813, *Works,* IX, 40.

6. Jan. 26, 1813, *ibid.,* p. 42. Dowden, I, 344–345. Dowden states that the material in the volume intended for publication by Hookham contained 2,822 lines. Of these, according to my reckoning, only 975 have been printed. Dowden, following an earlier text of Shelley's letter to Hookham, read 2,600 instead of 2,800 and condescendingly noted Shelley's "char-

acteristic error in reckoning." Hill, however, in checking the MS, reads it as probably 2,800. (Hill, p. 6.)

7. To Elizabeth Hitchener, Jan. 26, 1812, *Works,* VIII, 254: "My volume of Poetry will be I fear an inferior production: it will be valuable only to philosophical and reflecting minds who love to trace the early state of human feelings and opinions,—who can make allowances for some bad versification." Shelley, here, is, of course, referring only to the earlier poems in the volume, probably with the narratives, *Henry and Louisa* and *Zeinab and Kathema* mainly in mind.

"I remember you advising me not to publish my first blights on Hampstead Heath." Keats to Shelley, Aug., 1820, *Works,* X, 195 n.

8. Dowden, I, 347.

9. *Works,* VIII, 236–238; *Works,* III, 97.

10. See above, pp. 152, 177–178.

11. Dowden, I, 268, 345, 348, 285, 346–347. For Volney, see above, pp. 243–244. Shelley wrote to Hookham on Aug. 18, 1812, that he considered "the conclusion of 'Palmyra' the finest piece of poetry I have ever read" (*Works,* IX, 20), and indicated that he had but recently received it from Hookham. He may, however, have read the poem (originally published in 1805) by Feb. 14, 1812, because there are apparently echoes from its concluding stanzas in a blank verse poem included in a letter to Elizabeth Hitchener on that date. (*Works,* VIII, 271; *Works,* III, 104–105.) This poem was later, in revised form, inserted in *Queen Mab,* IX, 23 ff. Shelley writes:

> every wave might seem
> An instrument in Time the giant's grasp,
> To burst the barriers of Eternity.
> Proceed, thou giant, conquering and to conquer!
> March on thy lonely way.—The nations fall
> Beneath thy noiseless footstep; pyramids
> That for millenniums have defied the blast,
> And laughed at lightnings, thou dost crush to nought.
> Yon Monarch, in his solitary pomp,
> Is but the fungus of a winter day
> That thy light footstep presses into dust.
> Thou art a conquerer, Time! All things give way
> Before thee but the 'fixed and virtuous will';
> The sacred sympathy of soul which was
> When thou wert not, which *shall be* when thou perishest.

Peacock writes:

> So swift is Time's colossal stride
> Above the wrecks of human pride. . . .
>
> But Time still shakes, with giant-tread,
> The marble city of the dead,
> That crushed at last, a shapeless heap,
> Beneath the drifted sands shall sleep. . . .

His mantle dark oblivion flings
Around the monuments of kings. . . .

But ne'er shall earthly time throw down
The immortal pile that virtue wears.

(Peacock's final lines on "Necessity's mysterious sway" perhaps also found
their echoes in *Queen Mab.*) *A Retrospect of Times of Old,* Dowden
thought, was "probably" written in July–Aug., 1812, in Devon.

12. *Works,* I, 204; from the *Alastor* volume version. Dowden (I, 349)
quotes the first stanza from the Esdaile MS version and it differs from
the *Alastor* volume version only in the change of "stormy night" to "starless
night." This probably indicates only minor revision in the other stanzas
also, so that we are reasonably safe in taking the stanza quoted as representative of Shelley's growing lyrical talents in 1812–1813.

13. Dowden (I, 317 n.) informs us that the poem is in eight stanzas,
of which he prints four. The final line quoted echoes Godwin's advice to
Shelley in Dublin. (See above, pp. 153–154.) The poem is interesting also
as anticipating Shelley's use of the Spenserian stanza for a radical theme
in *The Revolt of Islam,* e.g.:

That Reason's flag may over Freedom's field,
Symbol of bloodless victory, wave unfurled,
A meteor sign of love effulgent o'er the world.

14. The *Alastor* hero is anticipated also in *St. Irvyne.* See: Frederick L.
Jones, "*Alastor* Foreshadowed in *St. Irvyne,*" *PMLA,* XLIX (1934), 969–
971.

15. *Ca.,* Oct. 27, 1811, *Works,* VIII, 169.

16. See: Kenneth Neill Cameron, "The Planet-Tempest Passage in
Epipsychidion," *PMLA,* LXIII (Sept., 1948), 950–972 for some discussion
of these later problems.

17. So, too, in the "each floweret" of l. 15. Shelley, however, according
to Dowden (I, 348), made "some differences in phrasing" when preparing
to use the Dedication for *Queen Mab.*

18. *Works,* VIII, 213.

19. To Elizabeth Hitchener, Dec. 26, 1811, *ibid.,* p. 225.

20. *Ibid.,* p. 231.

21. *Works,* IX, 19.

22. Godwin's diary, quoted in: Dowden, I, 340. On Dec. 10, Godwin
wrote to Shelley, doubtless with *Queen Mab* in mind: "*You* have what
appears to me a false taste in poetry. You love a perpetual sparkle and glittering, such as are to be found in Darwin, and Southey, and Scott, and
Campbell." (*Shelley Memorials,* p. 48.) This is in answer to a letter to
Shelley apparently no longer extant. Godwin had presumably returned the
Queen Mab MS to Shelley between Oct. 31 and Dec. 10, perhaps, as I suggested in note 2, via Hookham.

23. *Works,* IX, 47; to Hookham, *ca.* Mar. 21, 1813 (on dating see
above, pp. 369–370, *ibid.,* p. 56; Harriet Shelley to Catherine Nugent, May
21, 1813, *ibid.,* p. 67: "Mr. Shelley continues perfectly well, and his Poem of

'Queen Mab' is begun [apparently, to be printed], tho' it must not be published under pain of death, because it is too much against every existing establishment. It is to be privately distributed to his friends, and some copies sent over to America." Hookham had apparently refused to publish *Queen Mab* under his name, and he and Shelley "quarrelled" over the poem, Hookham's nephew, Edward Hookham, informed Ingpen. (*Works,* VIII, xxxiii.) Shelley had told Hogg on Feb. 7 that "'Mab' has gone on but slowly, although she is nearly finished." (*Ibid.,* p. 44.) Hence, the poem was, in the main, completed in Feb., but revision was possible until May.

Hogg (II, 44), in describing the reception of the poem (calling on his memory some thirty-five years later), implies that it was distributed during Shelley's visit to London in Oct.–Nov., 1812, which is clearly wrong. What Hogg is probably correct in, however, is that it was printed and distributed while Shelley was in London, and, hence, his statements make it probable that it came out before Shelley's departure for Bracknell in the middle of July, 1813, which is what one would expect if it was in the press by May 21. Hogg is apparently, in the passage, describing the Newton-Boinville set to which Shelley became attached in the spring and early summer of 1813. Hogg (*loc. cit.*) confirms Harriet's statement that the poem was to be privately distributed. (See also: Preface to *Alastor, Works,* I, 174, and Shelley's letter to *The Examiner,* June 22, 1821, *Works,* X, 280. For a list of some of the recipients, see: White, I, 653.) To whom the copies were to be sent in America we do not know. The first American edition of *Queen Mab* came out in 1831 edited by Frances Wright and Robert Dale Owen (son of Robert Owen); an 1821 edition, bearing an American imprint was published in England, the imprint being used to avoid prosecution. (Forman, *A Shelley Library,* pp. 50–51, 53–54; White, *The Unextinguished Hearth,* p. 368; George T. Goodspeed, "The 'First American' Queen Mab," *The Colophon* [New York, 1939], New Graphic Series, no. 1, pp. 25–32; Goodspeed argues plausibly that the work was printed in London by William Benbow.) Shelley informed Hookham on Aug. 18, 1812, that he had procured a work from America dealing with "the actual state of republicanized Ireland." It was perhaps to the sender of this work— presumably a radical bookseller—that Shelley intended to mail copies of *Queen Mab.*

24. Medwin, p. 62: ". . . Queen Mab, which Shelley says was written at 18, in 1809. . . ." *Ibid.,* p. 91: "He reverted to his Queen Mab, commenced a year and a half before, and converted what was a mere imaginative poem into a systematic attack on the institutions of society." *Ibid.,* p. 93: "Intimate and confidential as we were, Shelley never showed me a line of Queen Mab. . . ." How, if Shelley never showed him a line of the poem, Medwin was so intimately acquainted with the nature of its revision, he does not explain. I suspect that his only basis for the 1809 story was Shelley's own false statement (see following note) that it was written at the age of eighteen. Medwin seems to think that Shelley was eighteen in 1809. Another by-product of this typically Medwinian flight is his theory (p. 48) that the Dedication of *Queen Mab* was to Harriet Grove and not Harriet Shelley. Shelley himself informs us that it was dedicated to Harriet

Shelley (to Charles Ollier, June 11, 1821, *Works,* X, 275); so that speculation on the point is unnecessary.

Shelley, as we have noted, included some lines—on the "giant time"—in
a letter to Elizabeth Hitchener from Dublin on Feb. 14, 1812, and these
were later used in *Queen Mab.* (IX, 23–37.) This, Hughes (p. 174 n.)
considers to indicate that Shelley was at that date engaged on the composition of *Queen Mab.* But the lines constitute a complete poem in themselves and there is no reason to suppose that Shelley originally intended
them as part of *Queen Mab.* See also n. 27, below.

25. To the Editor of "The Examiner," June 22, 1821, *Works,* X, 280.
Shelley, here, annoyed at a piratical reprint of the poem is interested in
representing it as an immature work; hence, his exaggeration of his youth
at the time of composition. For other similar statements, see: Hughes, p.
174 n.

26. For instance, Dowden (I, 285) points out that both *A Retrospect
of Times of Old* and *The Voyage,* written, he believes, in July–Aug., 1812,
have much in common with *Queen Mab,* but, from his comments, it is
clear that Shelley did not attempt to incorporate them into the larger poem.
And if he did not attempt to incorporate comparatively recent work of this
nature, it is most unlikely that he would have incorporated even earlier
work. So, too, apparently with *The Crisis* and *To Liberty. (Ibid.,* pp. 345,
346–348.) We might note, too, that the Ahaseurus scene (Canto VII) does
not embody material from *The Wandering Jew* or *The Wandering Jew's
Soliloquy* but is a completely new treatment. The verse forms of *Queen
Mab,* he intimates to Hogg, who was familiar with his earlier verse, was a
new medium for him (Feb. 7, 1813, *Works,* IX, 44), and, hence, would not
have been suitable for the incorporation of earlier material, at least on
any extensive scale. And the generally unvaried technical level of *Queen
Mab*—of a much higher quality than most of the earlier verse—in itself
makes any patchwork theory untenable. There is no evidence to support
Dowden's conjecture (I, 110–111), followed by Hughes (pp. 174–175),
that Shelley made use of the now lost *Essay on the Existing State of Things,*
written at Oxford. Indeed, a comparison of the blank verse of *Queen Mab*
with the blank verse of "War" in the *Margaret Nicholson* volume, as representative of Shelley's powers in this medium during his Oxford period,
makes such a conjecture most unlikely.

27. On Aug. 18, 1812, Shelley, as we have seen, wrote to Hookham:
"I enclose also by way of specimen all that I have written of a little poem
begun since my arrival in England. I conceive I have matter enough for
six more cantos. . . . The Past, the Present, and the Future are the grand
and comprehensive topics of this Poem. I have not yet half exhausted the
second of them." (*Works,* IX, 19.) The section of *Queen Mab* dealing
with the Present begins with Canto IV and runs through VII; halfway
through the Present would put us at about the middle of Canto V. Yet at
the beginning of Canto IV there occurs a passage (ll. 34–70) clearly descriptive of the burning of Moscow and Napoleon's subsequent retreat. The news
of the retreat did not reach London until late in Nov., and the battles
involved are commented on by Shelley in a letter to Hogg from Tremadoc

on Dec. 27. (See below, n. 63.) This passage must, therefore, have been written in Nov. or later. And this dating is borne out also by the opening lines of the Canto which are apparently descriptive of Welsh mountain scenery in winter. As Shelley was halfway through the Present in Aug.— and his statement must be true because he sent the material to Hookham— this passage must have been inserted later, apparently with the thought that it made a good dramatic opening to the Present, with its stress on the horrors of war and dictatorship.

Halfway through the Present, as the poem now stands, brings us, to be exact, to Canto V, l. 133, or a total of roughly 400 lines of material on the Present. But Shelley informed Hookham that he planned six more cantos. And on Jan. 26, 1813, he further informed him that "Queen Mab will be in ten cantos and contain about 2800 lines." (*Ibid.*, p. 42.) As it now stands, it is in nine cantos of roughly 250 lines each with a total of 2,289 lines. Hence, the poem is about 500 lines short of Shelley's original plan. But 500 lines would mean two extra cantos and not one. The cantos originally, therefore, must have been divided differently than in the final product, apparently averaging about 280 lines apiece. The probability is that when Shelley said he was halfway through the Present in Aug., he had completed Canto IV and had six more to go. But this redivision of the cantos implies more revision than is at first apparent, for the cantos as they now exist are (as I point out below) accurately divided. Thus, for instance, Canto IV deals with the evils of political tyranny and Canto V with the evils of Commerce. Hence, Shelley could not simply take the first 250 lines, say, of an originally longer Canto IV, end the Canto with them, and begin V, or he would overlap the subject matter of IV into the subject matter of V. He could not, that is to say, when he decided on a poem of 2,300 lines and nine cantos instead of one of 2800 and ten cantos, achieve his new scheme by a simple process of cutting up his existing material. He would have to rearrange and rewrite. And this rearranging and rewriting is implied in his letter to Hogg on Feb. 7: " 'Mab' has gone on but slowly, although she is nearly finished. . . . With some restrictions, I have taken your advice, though I have not been able to bring myself to rhyme. The didactic is in blank heroic verse, and the descriptive in blank lyrical measure. . . . Since I wrote the above, I have finished the rough sketch of my poem. As I have not abated an iota of the infidelity or cosmopolicy of it, sufficient will remain, exclusively of innumerable faults, invisible to partial eyes, to make it very unpopular." (*Ibid.*, pp. 44–45.) Shelley, therefore, had written the poem in "rough sketch" first; and this "rough sketch," I would gather from the comment "sufficient will remain," had originally been of greater length and had, by Feb. 7, been cut down. What Shelley decided to cut out of the poem we do not know, but he refused to leave out any of the anti-religious or politically radical material (of which Hogg had apparently complained). Whether he had previously sent Hogg a copy of the "rough sketch" in an earlier stage or had only given him a detailed description of it, is not clear, but if he had actually sent it to him, then it cannot originally have been written in its combination of blank verse and "blank lyrical measure" but was perhaps all in blank verse. In any case, Shelley gives the impression on Feb. 7 of having decided on this particular combination of verse forms rather recently.

Finally, we have evidence of revision in the lines in *Queen Mab* IX, 23–37 included in a letter to Elizabeth Hitchener on Feb. 14, 1812. (*Works,* VIII, 271.) These lines, Shelley has rewritten (and improved) in preparing them for insertion in the longer poem. That he had not originally written them as part of *Queen Mab* is indicated by the fact that he only arrived at about the end of Canto IV by Aug. when he wrote to Hookham, and by the fact, also, that he only used those of them in *Queen Mab* (omitting the opening and concluding lines) that were appropriate to the passage in the longer poem.

28. In addition to such minor or hypothetical works as *The Devil's Walk* or the *Poetical Essay on the Existing State of Things,* and the juvenile poems reputedly published by Sir Bysshe and the juvenile plays at Eton. Shelley had apparently been writing pretty consistently from about the age of twelve. The Eton plays were written in the lower forms. (Andrew Amos to *The Athenaeum,* White, II, 494.)

29. Notes to *Queen Mab, Works,* I, 135, 159, 143. (*Rees Cyclopaedia* was not published until 1819; Shelley must be referring to Rees's edition of *Chambers's Cyclopaedia.*)

30. Speech at a meeting of The Shelley Society, Apr. 14, 1886, following address on "The Vicissitudes of *Queen Mab,*" by H. Buxton Forman: *Note Book of The Shelley Society* (London, 1886), p. 31. Shaw appears to have been one of the leading members of The Shelley Society, and spoke on several other occasions. On Dec. 15, 1886, he spoke on Rossetti's paper on *Prometheus Unbound,* pointing out that Shelley's ultimate society was anarchistic, and (correctly) doubting Rossetti's interpretation of Demogorgon as Eternity. On Mar. 9, 1887, he spoke against the society's high estimation of *The Cenci,* giving his own (strangely obtuse) view that it was simply "an accumulation of horrors." On Apr. 13, 1887, he attacked an anti-socialist paper on *The Revolt of Islam* and was followed by Edward Aveling (the son-in-law of Karl Marx), the two of them forming a team which sent the speaker into a chagrined retreat: "He had not expected to meet an audience of such pronounced socialistic sympathies, much less to see such well known socialists as Dr. Aveling and Mr. Shaw among them." On June 8, 1887, following a paper by Edward Silsbee he made the shrewd (and much needed comment): "He [Silsbee] contended that Shelley's 'poetic melancholy' proved a lack of humour; on the contrary Shelley had a large fund of humour, but the fact of his taking so serious a view of life and life's work kept the humour away from his poetry." (*Ibid.,* pp. 121–122, 184–185, 193–194, 197.) Shaw was asked to speak at the Shelley centenary celebrations at Horsham in 1892 but preferred instead a "proletarian celebration of Shelley in the easterly parish of St. Luke's." See his witty and penetrative essay on Shelley written on this occasion: "Shaming the Devil About Shelley," *Collected Works* (New York, 1932), XXIX, 248–259. In numerous passages in his works, Shaw testifies to the influence of Shelley upon him.

31. In spite of more judicious estimates in recent years (e.g. by Grabo

and White), the spirit of the detractors still predominates in the textbooks, anthologies, and other popular accounts. The comment in *The Oxford Companion to English Literature* that it is "a crude and juvenile production" is typical: or, to take another example, at random, that in Cunliffe, Pyre, and Young's *Century Readings*—"a frantic poetical drama [?] interesting only for its revolutionary doctrines."

32. Sir William Jones, "Speech on the Reformation of Parliament," *Works* (London, 1799), VI, 719.

33. London, 1795, p. 4. See above, pp. 59–61.

34. When the States General was summoned in 1789, Volney was elected as representative from Anjou. When he found that he could not there adequately forward his republican and democratic principles, he resigned, and was later elected to the Constituent Assembly, where he served during the first years of the Revolution. In 1793 he was imprisoned by the Jacobins for his anti-extremist views, but was released after the overthrow of Robespierre the following year, and appointed professor of history at the Ecole Normale.

35. Medwin, p. 92; Hogg, I, 373. Hogg also saw the book in Shelley's lodgings in London during his visits there in Nov., 1812, when Shelley was working on *Queen Mab*. (*Ibid.*, II, 3.) Shelley, himself, does not anywhere mention Volney, but Mary Shelley in *Frankenstein*, which was written the same year as *The Revolt of Islam*, writes: "The book from which Felix instructed Safie was Volney's *Ruins of Empires*. . . . He had chosen this work, he said, because the declamatory style was framed in imitation of the eastern authors. Through this work I obtained a cursory knowledge of history, and a view of the several empires at present existing in the world; it gave me an insight into the manners, governments, and religions of the different nations of the earth." (*Frankenstein, or The Modern Prometheus* [Everyman edition, n.d.], p. 123.)

36. See: Kenneth Neill Cameron, "A Major Source of *The Revolt of Islam*," *PMLA*, LVI (Mar., 1941), 175–206. For the influence of Volney on *Queen Mab* see: L. Kellner, "Shelley's Queen Mab and Volney's Les Ruines," *ESt*, XXII (1896), 9–40. Kellner's parallels are repeated in: Peck, I, 303–338. See also: Albert Elmer Hancock, *The French Revolution and the English Poets* (New York, 1899) pp. 54–62.

37. Volney's *Ruins* (Dublin, 1811), pp. 17–19.

38. *Ibid.*, p. 60. Apparently (Peck, I, 316) echoed by Shelley; *Queen Mab*, II, 100–101:

> The thronging thousands, to a passing view,
> Seemed like an anthill's citizens.

39. *Ibid.*, p. 92.

40. See: E. Koeppel, "Shelley's 'Queen Mab' and Sir William Jones' 'Palace of Fortune,'" *ESt*, XXVIII (1900), 46–48.

41. For some of these, see: Warner Taylor, "The Sources of Shelley's 'Queen Mab,'" *SR*, XIV (1906), 324–351; Peck, I, 303–338; Carlos Baker, "Spenser, the Eighteenth Century, and Shelley's 'Queen Mab'," *MLQ*, II (Mar., 1941), 81–98; and Baker, pp. 21–40.

42. Feb. 7, 1813, *Works,* IX, 44. See also: Mary Shelley, "Note on *Queen Mab,*" *Works,* I, 167.

43. To Shelley, Dec. 10, 1812, *Shelley Memorials,* p. 48.

44. Shelley's early enthusiasm for the *Essay on Man* (to Hogg, Jan. 3, 1811, *Works,* VIII, 33) was, as we shall note, still very much alive during the composition of *Queen Mab.* For his reading in Darwin, see: Carl Grabo, *A Newton Among Poets.* Shelley read Darwin as early as July, 1811, (*Works,* VIII, 135), and put his *Temple of Nature* and *Zoonomia* in his book lists for Rickman and Hookham in Dec., 1812. (*Works,* IX, 34, 36.) Shelley, as we have noted, made use of both Rees's, Chambers's, and Nicholson's encyclopedias.

45. Erasmus Darwin, *The Temple of Nature,* I, 65–68. Shelley, however, was, as a reviewer in *The Edinburgh Review* (CXXXIII [Apr., 1871], 448) pointed out, also influenced by Collins' temple of Freedom in his *Ode to Liberty,* a poem which left an imprint on much of Shelley's work including his own *Ode to Liberty* (1820) and *Hellas* (1821).

46. "Spallanzani's works," are included in the book list to Rickman, Dec. 24, 1812, *Works,* IX, 36. (Marjorie Nicolson, *The Microscope and English Imagination, Smith College Studies in Modern Languages,* XVI, No. 4, July, 1935.)

47. *Queen Mab,* II, 73, 226–230; III, 233–234; *Essay on Man,* I, 209–210; *The Seasons,* II, 287–313. (Thomson's passage is singled out for comment by Marjorie Nicolson, p. 68.) Shelley quotes from *The Seasons,* I, 990–992, at the opening of Ch. XIII of *Zastrozzi.* (*Works,* V, 73.) Peacock (p. 421 n.) informs us of his interest in Thomson's *Castle of Indolence,* which appears in his reading list for 1815. (*Journal,* p. 48.) For further evidence of the influence of Thomson, see Baker's article cited above.

48. *Essay on Man,* I, 233 ff. See also the passage in *The Seasons* cited above.

49. Monboddo, *Antient Metaphysics* (Edinburgh, 1789), I, 244: "But the earth, air and water swarm with such prodigious numbers of the lesser animals, that I do believe we have not yet half the number of the species of them. Beside those that are visible to the naked eye, glasses discover a new world of them; for we find that there is no part of any animal or vegetable substance, dead or alive, in which we cannot discover, by the help of good microscopes, life and motion, in various forms and figures. The vegetable life still abounds more, and multiplies much faster. . . ." On Shelley's reading of Monboddo, see above p. 218.

Sir William Drummond, *Academical Questions* (London, 1805), I, 252: "Nature is active throughout the whole universe; and the germs of life are scattered everywhere in the infinite mass. Some are nourished and developed, while others must continue in their present state, until motion necessarily place them in situations fit for their growth and expansion."

Hogg, visiting Shelley in Nov., 1812 (Hogg, II, 3), notes that Drummond's *Academical Questions* was one of the books that Harriet was then reading aloud in place of those she had previously read at Edinburgh and York. It is possible that Shelley first came across the work as part of Southey's "course of Berkeley" (Southey to Grosvenor Bedford, Jan. 4,

1812, Dowden, I, 211) at Keswick in the winter of 1811–1812. His first reference to Drummond is a request to Clio Rickman for his *Essay on a Punic Inscription* on Dec. 24, 1812. (*Works,* IX, 36.) He had, however, previously received Drummond's *Oedipus Judaicus* from Hookham, and on Jan. 24, 1813, he commented to him: "I do not think Sir W. Drummond's arguments have much weight. His Oedipus has completely failed in making me a convert." (*Ibid.,* p. 42.) With some of Drummond's arguments in this work, however, Shelley would have been in agreement; for instance his mockery of those who take all Old Testament statements literally: "a material and local God, who dwelt in a box made of shittim wood"; "They find it quite simple, that the triune Jehovah should dine on veal cutlets at Abraham's table." (William Drummond, *The Oedipus Judaicus* (London, 1811), p. ii.) The first of these, Shelley is perhaps echoing in *A Refutation of Deism* (*Works,* VI, 34): "When the chief of this obscure and brutal horde of assassins asserts that the God of the Universe was enclosed in a box of shittim wood . . ." What Shelley objected to doubtless was Drummond's continuing argument that Jehovah and his anthropomorphic passions must all be considered purely as allegorical, for this would weaken his favorite "Eternal Avenger" theme. In the Notes to *Queen Mab,* Shelley attacks Drummond's rejection of atheism in his *Academical Questions.* (*Works,* I, 150–151.) And it seems likely that the comment to Hookham includes the *Academical Questions* as well as the *Oedipus.* As neither book is in Shelley's book list to Hookham on Dec. 17, probably Hookham had loaned him one or both of them before he left London on Nov. 13. In *A Refutation of Deism* (written probably in the fall of 1813), Shelley notes with approval Drummond's argument that "Power cannot be at once the principle and attribute of being," utilizing it for his own atheistic objectives. (*Academical Questions,* p. 5; *Works,* VI, 55.) He considers Drummond as an anti-Christian in his open letter to *The Examiner* on Richard Carlile, Nov. 3, 1819 (*Works,* X, 112–113); but it was Drummond who convinced him of the inadequacy of the materialist theories of matter and knowledge. ("Of Life"—*ca.* 1819—*Works,* VI, 195.) For some account of Drummond's influence on Shelley, see: G. S. Brett, "Shelley's Relations to Berkeley and Drummond," *Studies in English by Members of University College, Toronto* (Toronto, 1931), pp. 170–202.

Shelley could also have found a great deal of material on microorganisms in Darwin's *Temple of Nature* in the Additional Notes, Spontaneous Vitality of Microscopic Animals. Darwin (p. 13) gives tables of "microscopic animals" and the different characteristics of each. The general concept of abounding life also dominates Darwin's *The Botanical Garden.*

50. Quoted by Marjorie Nicolson, p. 80. Cf. Shelley to Elizabeth Hitchener, Nov. 11, 1811, *Works,* VIII, 202.

51. *Antient Metaphysics,* I, 83, 85, 245.

52. *Academical Questions,* I, 322. Drummond gives his outline of Leibnitz's system on pp. 322–326.

53. *The System of the World,* tr. by Henry H. Harte (Dublin, 1830), II, 342.

54. James Parkinson, *Organic Remains of a Former World* (London,

1811), III, 449; I, 270. Parkinson views the earth as having gone through five creative stages, each corresponding to the "day" of the Genesis account, and each under divine supervision: (a) the separation of "the granitic and other primary rocks" from the water; (b) "the creation of vegetables"; (c) the creation of birds and fishes; (d) the creation of land animals; (e) the creation of man. (*Ibid.,* III, pp. 449–451.) Shelley was introduced to *Organic Remains* by Elizabeth Hitchener. (To Elizabeth Hitchener, Dec. 26, 1811, Feb. 14, 1812, *Works,* VIII, 226, 275.) He refers to Cuvier's anatomical theories in *A Vindication of Natural Diet* and *A Refutation of Deism* (*Works,* VI, 8, 51), but not to his geological or evolutionary theories; for which, see his *Essay on the Theory of the Earth* (New York, 1818), in which he argues that fossil remains indicate the existence of previous stages of the world, some before man, some after, all destroyed by sudden catastrophes. For some discussion of Parkinson, Darwin and other advocates of the catastrophic school, see: Grabo, *A Newton Among Poets,* pp. 175–180. The most influential early catastrophic theory—on religious rather than scientific grounds—was that propounded in Thomas Burnet's *Sacred History of the Earth,* for an account of which, see: Basil Willey, *The Eighteenth Century Background* (New York and London, 1941), pp. 27–34. Shelley may have learned something of Burnet's views from his friend Newton (see below, n. 94), and seen similar views in Monboddo (e.g.: *On the Origin and Progress of Language,* I, 212–213). The geological catastrophic theory appears (as Grabo notes) in *Prometheus Unbound,* IV, 287–316. Byron's "Darkness" and Mary Shelley's *The Last Man* are interesting extensions of it into the future.

55. *The Temple of Nature,* Additional Notes, p. 45.

56. That Shelley was thinking of vast time sequences here is clear from his Notes, *Works,* I, 143.

57. Nov. 23, 1811, *Works,* VIII, 198. I note the following in Holbach as perhaps representing Shelley's view (Parkinson to the contrary): "There have been perhaps men upon earth from all eternity; but at different periods they may have been nearly annihilated, together with their sciences and their arts; those who have outlived these periodical revolutions, each time founded a new race of men, who by dint of time, labour and experience have been by degrees withdrawn from oblivion by the inventions of the primitive races." (*The System of Nature,* tr. by H. D. Robinson (Boston, 1889), I, 176.) See: *The Necessity of Atheism* (*Works,* V, 208), and *A Refutation of Deism* (*Works,* VI, 47–48), which seem to imply a view similar to Holbach's. But see also, *Prometheus Unbound,* IV, 296–298, where Shelley speaks of vast cities in the remote past whose inhabitants were "mortal, but not human." The origin of man presented a difficult problem to the pre-Darwinian materialists, for to admit his creation meant to admit a Creator, and yet geology was demonstrating periods showing no trace of human life. Monboddo (e.g. *Antient Metaphysics,* V, 3–4, *Of the Origin and Progress of Language,* I, 269) has some interesting speculations on the Orang-utan as an earlier form of the human species; and it is perhaps this kind of thinking that Shelley has in mind in his "mortal, but not human" creatures of the past.

58. See above, n. 11.

59. *The Ruins,* pp. 77–78.

60. To Hookham, Nov., 1812: "If you have got anything new of Paine's works send it with them." (*Works,* IX, 48; on dating this letter see n. 2 above.)

61. *Wat Tyler,* Act I. Tyler's concluding speech of this act may have later found an echo in "Men of England:"

> your hard toil
> Manures their fertile fields—you plough the earth,
> You sow the corn, you reap the ripen'd harvest,—
> They riot on the produce.

62. Campbell, *The Pleasures of Hope,* I, 498 f. Kozsul (p. 154 n.) suggested an influence of Campbell on *Queen Mab. Wat Tyler,* Act I, concluding speech. Shelley could find the same sentiment placed with vigor in Samuel Jackson Pratt, *Cottage Pictures, or The Poor* (London, 1805), to which he refers in the Notes to *Queen Mab* (*Works,* I, 163):

> Ask we the CAUSE why earth supplies in vain,
> Th' abundant herbage and luxuriant grain;
> Why, when the golden sheaves like mountains rise,—
> Bending as if in homage to the skies—
> Those golden sheaves refuse their aid to yield,
> To such alone as sow and reap the field.

Pratt's sentiments on Famine as a goad to revolution may have blended with a similar sentiment in Coleridge (see above, p. 318) to influence *Swellfoot the Tyrant.* (Pratt, pp. 35–36, 53, 75.)

63. Grabo (*The Magic Plant,* p. 109) first notes the reference to the burning of Moscow, news of which reached London in the middle of Oct. (*The Courier,* Oct. 15.) Shelley, however, also speaks of the death of soldiers in the cold and snow. The first news of the retreat did not reach London until the middle of Nov. and it was not until late Nov. and early Dec. that speculation of a possible destruction of the army in the cold began. (*The Examiner,* Nov. 15, p. 726; Nov. 22, p. 743; Nov. 29, p. 762; Dec. 6, p. 780.) On Dec. 27 Shelley commented to Hogg: "With respect to those victories in the north; if they tend towards peace they are good; if otherwise, they are bad. This is the standard by which I shall ultimately measure my approbation of them. At the same time I cannot but say that the first impression that they made on me was one of horror and regret." (*Works,* IX, 37.) It is this reaction of "horror and regret" that dominates the passage in the poem. Shelley's sardonic reference to "the conqueror" in line 47 is perhaps echoed from the first Russian communique on the burning of the city, and other parts of his description seem to have been influenced by it. The "haughty conqueror," we are there informed, found himself "possessed merely of bare walls, containing within their circuit neither inhabitants nor provisions"; "He entered Russia with 300,000 men . . . The half of this multifarious army has been destroyed." (*The Examiner,* Oct. 25, 1812, pp. 674–675.) Shelley was perhaps influenced also by the French

communique of the previous week on the same subject, which gave a vivid description of the fire, e.g.: "Five-sixths of the houses were built of wood; the fire spread with a prodigious rapidity; it was an ocean of flame. . . . Thirty thousand sick and wounded Russians have been burnt." (*Ibid.*, p. 658.) The French in this bulletin, I note, refer to themselves as "conquerors"; as does *The Examiner* (ironically) on Dec. 13 (p. 813).

64. *A Vindication of the Rights of Woman* (London, 1891), pp. 225, 230, 232; Godwin, *The Enquirer* (London, 1797), pp. 2–4 and *passim*. For a present-day expression of similar sentiments see: Auden's "Ode: to my Pupils."

65. Aug. 10, 1811. *Works*, VIII, 139–140.

66. See above, n. 62.

67. Mar. 18, 1812, *Works*, VIII, 301. For the influence of Gray on the *Queen Mab* passage, and on Shelley, see: Baker, p. 27. The indebtedness to Gray was pointed out by a reviewer in *The Edinburgh Review*, CXXXIII (Apr., 1871), 448, and has been periodically rediscovered.

68. Feb. 7, 1813, *Works*, IX, 45; plus comment to Hookham, Dec. 17, 1812, *ibid.*, p. 33: "Any works except those absolutely cosmopolitical or antiChristian I shall not want until I write for."

69. *The System of Nature*, tr. by H. D. Robinson (Boston, 1889), p. 33 n.: "This was the decided opinion of Plato, who says, 'Matter and necessity are the same thing; this necessity is the mother of the world.'" According to the title page of this edition, the notes are by Diderot. The phrase is repeated by Mary Shelley, *The Last Man* (London, 1826), III, 192. The indebtedness to Holbach was first noted in: Albert Elmer Hancock, *The French Revolution and The English Poets*, pp. 63–64. Hancock also notes that Shelley's description of Necessity—

> A Spirit of activity and life
> That knows no term, cessation, or decay—

probably echoes Holbach: "Nature acts and exists necessarily; nature is an active living whole whose parts necessarily concur to maintain activity, life, and existence."

70. For example, *A Refutation of Deism*, *Works*, VI, 46–48. See also *The Necessity of Atheism*, *Works*, V, 208.

71. *Works*, I, 146.

72. *Essay on Man*, I, 267 ff.; to Hogg, Jan. 3, 1811, *Shelley at Oxford*, p. 16. (On dating this letter see above, p. 297.)

73. *Works*, I, 154: "Prayer may be considered under two points of view; as an endeavour to change the intentions of God, or as a formal testimony of our obedience. But the former case supposes that the caprices of a limited intelligence can occasionally instruct the Creator of the World how to regulate the universe; and the latter, a certain degree of servility analogous to the loyalty demanded by earthly tyrants."

74. *Works*, IX, 11.

75. Godwin, *Thoughts on Man* (London, 1831), 436–450. Shelley's fragmentary essay "On Life," in which he declares his conversion from

materialism to idealism has been generally misunderstood. He is not rejecting rationalism and accepting intuitive mysticism, as one would gather from some commentators, but is only rejecting one aspect of materialist doctrine, namely its theory of the nature of matter. Matter, he now came to believe—and he is largely echoing Drummond and Godwin—was a spiritual and not a material substance. But whether one considered it as one or the other made no difference to the operations of natural law. Necessity (Demogorgon) in *Prometheus Unbound* is still the ruling force both in society and nature.

76. *The Ruins*, p. 143. See Peck, I, 330. See also: Kenneth Neill Cameron, "A Major Source of *The Revolt of Islam*," *PMLA*, LVI, 191–192.

77. *Essay on Man*, I, 237 ff.

78. Jan. 2, 1812, *Works*, VIII, 227–228.

79. *Works*, I, 135. For a similar argument, see: Thomas Paine, *The Age of Reason, Theological Works of Thomas Paine* (New York, n. d.), pp. 15, 41–45.

80. June 11, 1811, *Works*, VIII, 101–103.

81. *The Ruins*, ch. XXI.

82. An echo of Darwin's *Temple of Nature*, IV, 66: "And one great Slaughter-house the warring world." (Grabo, *A Newton Among Poets*, p. 23.)

83. *The Pleasures of Hope*, I, 485 f. *The Pleasures of Hope*, Part I, is largely a poetic rendering of the Whig anti-war and anti-dictatorship creed of the 1790's. Its anti-imperialist sentiment is very similar to that in *An Address to the Irish People* or *A Vindication of Natural Diet*, its humanitarian indignation and overall philosophy of man and nature to some degree foreshadow *Queen Mab* (see, for instance, Part I, ll. 488–502), and so, too, with its confident assertion of future victory.

84. *Works*, V, 289.

85. *Works*, I, 153.

86. Apr. 24, 1811, *Shelley at Oxford*, p. 27–28; see also: Merle, p. 706.

87. This work was reprinted in London in an English translation in 1813, having been previously published in Edinburgh in 1799. Holbach had as a sub-title *Ecce Homo*, and this the English translator, George Houston, used as the title. (J. M. Robertson, *A History of Freethought in the Nineteenth Century* [London, 1921], p. 61.)

88. *Ecce Homo! or A Critical Enquiry into the History of Jesus Christ* (London, 1813), pp. 131, 148. Holbach was anticipated in this attitude by the English deist Thomas Woolston; see, for example, his *A Sixth Discourse on the Miracles of Our Saviour* (London, 1729). Woolston anticipates both Holbach and Samuel Butler in his theory that Christ was not dead when removed from the cross, and, hence, never arose from the dead. Both Woolston and Holbach treat the miracles, in a spirit of ribald derisiveness, as fakes. I know of no evidence that Shelley had read Woolston.

89. *Political Justice*, II, 519–527, 520 n. (reference to Condorcet).

90. *Works*, VI, 295; cf. *Works*, VII, 43.

91. Hogg, I, 50–51.

92. (London, [1852]), p. 98. Grant goes on to show, from the calculations of Lagrange and Laplace, that "such a condition cannot possibly exist."

93. *A System of Familiar Philosophy in Twelve Lectures, being the course usually read by Mr. A. Walker* (London, 1802), I, 15–16. The argument is restated in II, 165–166; and in Plate III, figure twelve, we have a representation of the earth straightening out under bombardment of light particles from the sun. Walker does not state the prevalent (and correct) theory of the earth's ultimate return to its present position without achieving actual perpendicularity.

94. Quoted in: Israel James Kapstein, "Shelley and Cabanis," *PMLA*, LII (1937), 242–243. Newton could have found the theory in Thomas Burnet's *Sacred Theory of the Earth.* (Kapstein, *loc. cit.;* Basil Willey, *The Eighteenth Century Background,* p. 31.)

95. Feb. 19, 1813, *Works*, IX, 47–48.

96. Shelley had but recently read in Newton (*The Return to Nature, The Pamphleteer,* XIX [1822], 506) comments on the discovery of the skeleton of a mammoth in Siberia as indicating a warm climate there in past ages—a type of argument used in the Note (*Works,* I, 143)—and perhaps it was Newton, too, who had informed him of Laplace's theories. Following his request, on Feb. 19, for material on the Precession of the Equinoxes, Shelley in the Notes to *Queen Mab* adds to the comment that "this progress is not merely an oscillation, as has been surmised by some late astronomers," as a footnote—"Laplace, Systême du Monde." (*Ibid.*) On Nov. 26, he writes to Hogg from Edinburgh: "I am now studying Laplace, 'Systeme du Monde,' and am determined not to relax until I have attained considerable proficiency in the physical sciences." (*Works,* IX, 81.) In *A Refutation of Deism* (*Works,* VI, 49) he writes: "The anomalous motions of the heavenly bodies, their unequal velocities and frequent aberrations, are corrected by that gravitation by which they are caused. The illustrious Laplace has shewn that the approach of the Moon to the Earth, and the Earth to the Sun, is only a secular equation of a very long period, which has its maximum and minimum." It seems probable that Shelley had not read (and certainly had not studied) Laplace before writing the Notes to *Queen Mab* (it will be noted that he gives neither page nor chapter reference in his footnote—as he does on the same page to Cabanis), but that he had studied him before writing *A Refutation of Deism,* and Laplace had convinced him that the oscillation hypothesis was correct. Laplace explains the oscillation of the earth partly in terms of the gravitational effects of the sun and the moon and this is apparently the section that Shelley has in mind. (Chapter XIII, "Of the Precession of the Equinoxes," etc.; see, for instance, pp. 187–188, 192–193.)

97. *Antient Metaphysics,* III, 119, 195, 201.

98. The perspective in these lines of a long period of gradual advancement is consistent with that developed in the Irish pamphlets, e.g. "we can expect little amendment in our own time . . . we must be content to lay the foundation of liberty and happiness by virtue and wisdom." (*An Address to the Irish People, Works,* V, 236.) Or, somewhat more specif-

ically: "I propose an association which shall have for its immediate objects, Catholic Emancipation and the Repeal of the Act of Union between Great Britain and Ireland; and grounding on the removal of these grievances, an annihilation or palliation, of whatever moral or political evil it may be within the compass of human power to assuage or eradicate." (*Proposals for an Association, ibid.,* p. 253.) The same perspective is inherent in the letter to Hunt from Oxford (Mar. 2, 1811, *Works,* VIII, 55–56), and in that of Mar. 18, 1812, to Godwin from Dublin: "I will look to events in which it will be impossible that I can share, and make myself the cause of an effect which will take place ages after I have mouldered in the dust." (*Ibid.,* p. 301.) First, to bring about elementary political reforms (in the case of Ireland, Catholic emancipation and repeal of the Union Act), then to advance to a democratic republic, and, finally, to an egalitarian society; such was Shelley's concept; and it is the concept of his later as well as his earlier political thinking, as a brief consultation of *A Philosophical View of Reform* will reveal (even the revolutionary Preface to *Hellas* speaks of "generations" of effort). On the other hand two passages in the earlier works seem to assume a more rapid change. The first is in the conclusion of *A Letter to Lord Ellenborough:* "The time is rapidly approaching, I hope that you, my Lord, may live to behold its arrival, when the Mahometan, the Jew, the Christian, the Deist, and the Atheist, will live together in one community, equally sharing the benefits which arise from its association, and united in the bonds of charity and brotherly love." (*Works,* V, 294.) The second passage is in *Queen Mab* (III, 233 ff.):

> Man like these passive things,
> Thy [Necessity's] will unconsciously fulfilleth,
> Like theirs, his age of endless peace,
> Which time is fast maturing,
> Will swiftly, surely, come;
> And the unbounded frame which thou pervadest,
> Will be without a flaw
> Marring its perfect symmetry.

It is presumably on these passages that the generally accepted idea that Shelley expected a rapid transformation of society has been based. But it is necessary to see these passages in their relation to Shelley's overall political theory. And this theory—of gradual change—is often enough and clearly enough expressed in his writings to be unmistakable, and is, moreover, in accordance with the views of Godwin, Paine, Condorcet, Volney, and others from whom Shelley derived his basic concepts. In neither of these two passages is Shelley giving a political judgement for the guidance of others. The hope that Ellenborough, then over sixty years of age, might live to witness the advent of the new age, is obviously not intended to be taken literally but is in the nature of a rhetorical warning to a representative of the unyielding Tory hierarchy. The transformation envisioned in the *Queen Mab* passage is rapid only in the perspectives of Necessity and the universe, and is expressive of an emotional hope legitimate enough in such a passage. (And the same is presumably true of the fragment of "The

Crisis," which seems to deal with the same subject.) When Shelley, in the conclusion, is speaking of man and his actions in the present, the emphasis is on the "gradual paths."

99. The first two notes are on astronomical points: the appearance of the sun beyond the earth's atmosphere, and the "plurality of worlds." To the statement in the second note that Sirius is "54,224,000,000,000 miles from the earth," Shelley adds the footnote: "See Nicholson's Encyclopedia, art. Light." The article on light in Nicholson's *British Encyclopedia,* however, does not give the distance of Sirius from the earth, but simply states that "light takes many years to travel" between the two bodies. The article "Star" informs us that Sirius is 2,000,000,000 miles from the earth. Shelley must, therefore, have used some other source here. On the other hand, the first note, which contains no footnote reference, is partly paraphrased from Nicholson's article on light. The third note (to IV, 178–179) is in two parts; the first, a quotation on the soldier from Godwin's *Enquirer*—"a man whose business it is to kill those who never offended him"—a passage which re-emerges in *The Mask of Anarchy* and *A Philosophical View of Reform* (*Works,* VII, 47–49, 54). (See: *The Enquirer,* London, 1797, Essay V, "Of Trades and Professions," pp. 234–236.) The second part of the note is taken up by the poem "Falsehood and Vice," already considered.

Notes four, five, and six (V, 1–2, 4–6, 58) consist of quotations from, respectively, *Ecclesiastes,* the *Iliad* and Lucretius, *De Rerum Natura* (the opening of Book II), that from Homer perhaps later influencing the *Ode to the West Wind.* Note seven (V, 93–94) is the essay on labor economics. Eight (V, 112) is a comment on a lady driven mad by religion. (I note a similar comment in Darwin, *Temple of Nature,* IV, 87.) Nine (V, 189) is the essay on free love. Ten (VI, 45–46) is the note on the perpendicularity of the poles already commented upon. Eleven (VI, 171–173) is a quotation from Holbach's *Système de la Nature* on the operations of Necessity in nature and society. Twelve (VI, 198) is the essay on Necessity. Thirteen (VII, 13) consists of the reprint of *The Necessity of Atheism* and a series of quotations, paraphrases, and comments: Sir Isaac Newton (with interpretative comment which would have startled Sir Isaac); Bacon (a précis of his remarks on atheism and superstition); Holbach (a long anti-religious passage); Pliny (the *de Deo* passage Shelley read and liked at Eton); Sir William Drummond (a reference to Drummond's anti-atheism argument, with vigorous rebuttal); Spinoza (the passage, from the *Theological-Political Treatise* [*Works,* London, 1889, p. 25] on the theme "Nature herself is the power of God under another name"). Note fourteen (VII, 67) is a quotation on the Wandering Jew (see above, ch. I, n. 132). Fifteen, the second main anti-religious note, is an essay attaching the theories of Christian theology, some of it restating arguments from *The Necessity of Atheism* (but in a more mature style), some paragraphs taken (with minor changes) from *A Letter to Lord Ellenborough* (*Works,* I, 153 "The vulgar . . ." to 154 *"If God has spoken, why is the universe not convinced?"* parallel, *Works,* V, 289–291, 292–293). Note sixteen is a brief comment on the Humean doctrine, "Time is our consciousness of the succession of ideas in our mind" (largely lifted from *Political Justice,* I, 411–413), and concludes with some lines from "To Harriet" (*Works,* III, 107) beginning "Dark flood of time." Seventeen, the final note, is a reprint of *A Vindication of Natural Diet* (see above, ch. VI, n. 173), concluding with a quotation from Plutarch against meat eating.

100. On these essays, written in 1811, see above pp. 115, 379–381. Some of the material from them—e.g. that on the effects of the French Revolution—as I have suggested, probably was used in the Irish pamphlets. Three of the *Queen Mab* Notes—on love, on necessity, and on labor and value—almost certainly contain further material from them. The evidence on the dating of the Notes is as follows.

In regard to the Notes as a whole the first we hear is in a letter from Shelley to Hookham, Feb. 19, 1813: "Queen Mab is finished and transcribed. I am now preparing the Notes which shall be long and philosophical." (*Works,* IX, 47.) On Feb. 26 occurred the alleged assassination at Tanyrallt; on Mar. 5 Shelley left for Ireland; on Mar. 9 he arrived in Dublin; on about Mar. 21 he wrote to Hookham: "I send you my poem. . . . The notes are preparing and shall be forwarded before the completion of the printing of the Poem. . . . The notes will be long, philosophical, and anti-Christian." (*Ibid.,* pp. 56–57.) On Mar. 21 Shelley left Dublin for Killarney, but after some five days there left again on hearing of Hogg's arrival in Dublin, and then proceeded to England. As he had taken "a considerable number of books" with him to Killarney (Hogg, II, 2), the implication is that he had gone there in order to work on the Notes in quiet. But in view of his short time there, it is unlikely that he finished the Notes there or that they were, as he had promised Hookham, mailed from Ireland. He probably took what he had finished of them with him to London, where he arrived on Apr. 5. By May 21, as we have seen, *Queen Mab* was in the press, and as the volume was out before the middle of July, the Notes too must have been in the press at the same time or but shortly after.

In addition to these general indications of dating there is evidence to be derived from the individual Notes. The first two notes, on astronomical data, must, as they comment specifically on the text, have been written after the completion of the poem, either in the "rough sketch" that Shelley mentioned to Hogg on Feb. 7, 1813, or in the final draft that he sent to Hookham on Mar. 21. As it was on Feb. 19 that he first informed Hookham that he was working on the Notes, the probability is that these two notes, and all the others which are genuine information notes arising out of the text and not separate essays were not begun until at least Feb. 7.

The inclusion in the third Note of the poem "Falsehood and Vice" from the Esdaile MS book shows that Shelley was doing some work on the Notes certainly later than Mar. 21 (when he informed Hookham he would send him the poems) and probably later than Apr. 5, when he arrived back in London, for it was probably not until after personal consultation with Hookham that he finally decided to give up the scheme of publishing the volume of poems. And the inclusion of the lines from "To Harriet" in the sixteenth note supports this conclusion.

The seventh note, that on labor, is probably of early origin. As I indicate below, it echoes sentiments in letters of the summer of 1811 and its paraphrasing of *Political Justice* would seem more symptomatic of the early enthusiasm for that work which Shelley was exhibiting during the opening months of 1811 than of his later assimilation and re-expression of its doctrines. The reference in it to the "fete" and the "show and pomp of courts" may have been inspired by the Prince Regent's fete of June 19, 1811, which Shelley refers to in his letter of June 20 to Elizabeth Hitchener (*Works,* VIII, 108–109), and on which he composed a political satire. (See above, p. 114 f.) It was on Aug. 1, 1811, that Shelley informed Stockdale that he was "at present engaged in completing a series of moral and metaphysical essays." (*Ibid.,* p. 137.)

The ninth Note, on love, is perhaps, in part, also a product of this earlier period, for it exhibits the same dependence on Godwin, and its free love doctrines are characteristic of the letters of 1811; but, if so, it must have been revised for it contains indication (see p. 270 above) of the influence of Sir James Lawrence, and Shelley did not read Lawrence until the spring of 1812. (To Lawrence, Aug. 17, 1812, *Works,* IX, 17.)

The tenth note, on the perpendicularity of the poles, was apparently being written in Feb., 1813, for on Feb. 19, Shelley asks Hookham to "collect all possible documents" on the question for him. (*Ibid.,* pp. 47–48.) The note contains a page reference to Cabanis, whose works Shelley requested on Dec. 17 (*Ibid.,* p. 34) but which did not arrive until sometime after Jan. 31. (See above, n. 2.) As it contains no specific reference to Laplace (see n. 96 above) or to any other documents on the subject, I presume that Shelley did not wait to hear further from Hookham before going ahead to compose it.

The eleventh note consists of a quotation from Holbach's *Le Système de la Nature;* the same work is quoted in the thirteenth note (that containing *The Necessity of Atheism*); and its influence is clear in the fifteenth note, that containing some material from *A Letter to Lord Ellenborough.* On June 3, 1812, Shelley informed Godwin that he had "just finished reading" the *Système;* on July 29 he commented on it as "a book of uncommon powers"; on Aug. 18 he informed Hookham that he was translating it. (*Works,* VIII, 331–332; IX, 11, 20.) During these months, too, he was composing *A Letter to Lord Ellenborough;* and in the letter of Aug. 18 he speaks of plans for "a vol. of essays, moral and *religious.*" In the light of these facts, it seems probable that this Holbach material and the second anti-religious essay (n. 15), containing Holbach influence and reminiscent in its tone of the *Letter to Lord Ellenborough,* represents work originally done in July–Aug., 1812, some of it perhaps being originally written for the *Letter* but later omitted, and some of it intended for the volume of essays. This is indicated also by the footnote to the note: "Since writing this note, I have reason to suspect that Jesus was an ambitious man, who aspired to the throne of Judea." As we have already seen, the attitude in the text of *Queen Mab* toward Christ is hostile, and expresses the same view as this footnote, but that in the note is the same as the "meek reformer" approach of the *Letter.* The indication, therefore, is that Shelley in this note is embodying material of the previous summer without revision and simply (perhaps hastily) tacking on a footnote. The note, that is to say, was written earlier than the text, the footnote to the note, later. Of the quotations in the thirteenth note, aside from that from Holbach, that from Pliny is from early (Eton) reading, those from Drummond (see above, n. 49) and Spinoza from recent reading. (Spinoza is on the Dec. 17 book list, *Works*, IX, 34; and the *Tractatus,* from which the quotation is taken, is specifically requested on Jan. 2, *ibid.,* pp. 39–40; and see below n. 131.)

The twelfth note, on Necessity, is, as we shall see, directly dependent on Godwin, and may represent more of the 1811 essay material. The fourteenth note is the Wandering Jew excerpt from *La Belle Assemblee* for Jan., 1809. (See above, ch. I, n. 132.) The final note is the reprint of *A Vindication of Natural Diet,* which, as we have seen, was probably written in Nov., 1812. The note version is identical except for the addition of one paragraph and stylistic and grammatical changes. (See above, ch. VI, n. 173.)

The Notes therefore, consist of material written at different periods: *The Necessity of Atheism,* Jan.–Feb., 1811 (see above, ch. III, n. 179); three of the "moral and metaphysical essays" of the summer of 1811; an antireligious essay of July–Aug., 1812; *A Vindication of Natural Diet,* Nov., 1812; three short notes on scientific questions, Feb.–Mar., 1813; a series of quotations and paraphrases, in part from earlier reading. When, therefore, Shelley informed Hookham on Feb. 18, 1813, that he was "preparing" the Notes, he perhaps used the word advisedly. Most of the Notes were already written. Some revision certainly took place, as *A Vindication of Natural Diet* (and perhaps the note on free love) reveals, but that this was not extensive is indicated by the failure to change the comment on Christ in the fifteenth note into line with the attitude in the poem.

101. "Of Avarice and Profusion," *The Enquirer* (1797), pp. 177–178. The passage crops up again in *A Philosophical View of Reform* (1819–1820): "Not that the poor have rigidly worked twenty hours, but that the worth of the labour of twenty hours now, in food and clothing, is equivalent to the worth of ten hours then." (*Works,* VII, 30.) Shelley, in the conclusion of the note, quotes from the same *Enquirer* essay. To the phrase, "employments are lucrative in an inverse ratio to their usefulness," he adds the footnote: "See Rousseau, 'De l'Inegalite parmi les Hommes,' note 7." But his source is really, once again, Godwin's essay. Rousseau's note 7 to his essay on inequality has nothing to do with this subject but deals with the life span of the horse. Shelley, as his note further informs us, had also been following Godwin's treatment of the subject in *Political Justice,* Book VIII, Ch. II. In Ch. VII of the same book, Godwin, in touching again on the argument, has a reference to Rousseau which Shelley might possibly have misread as connecting him with the theory. (*Political Justice,* II, 491.) I find no reference to the theory in any of Rousseau's notes. (Compare Shelley's use of Ritson in *A Vindication of Natural Diet;* see above, p. 377 f.)

102. Cf., to Elizabeth Hitchener, July 25, 1811: "You say that equality is unattainable, so will I observe is perfection; yet they both symbolize in their nature, they both demand that an unremitting tendency towards themselves should be made; and, the nearer society approaches towards this point the happier will it be." (*Works,* VIII, 130. See also, letter of July 26, *ibid.,* p. 132.)

103. "Of Avarice and Profusion," *The Enquirer,* p. 176.

104. II, 494.

105. See above, p. 62.

106. See above, pp. 120–121.

107. See, for instance, *The History of the Decline and Fall of the Roman Empire* (Boston, 1850), I, 549: "It was their [the Church fathers'] favorite opinion, that if Adam had preserved his obedience to the Creator, he would have lived forever in a state of virgin purity, and that some harmless mode of vegetation might have peopled paradise with a race of innocent and immortal beings. The use of marriage was permitted only to his fallen posterity, as a necessary expedient to continue the human species, and as a restraint, however imperfect, on the natural licentiousness of desire." Shelley (like Byron—"sapping a solemn creed with solemn sneer") obviously took considerable delight in Gibbon's famed fifteenth chapter (on the early Church).

108. See above, p. 126. Shelley follows the theory of the inheritability of venereal disease (as, less excusably, did Ibsen many years later) in accordance with the general concept of the inheritance of disease as stated in his *Vindication of Natural Diet.*

109. *Political Justice,* III, 219–220; II, 507–510. (Priestley's text is difficult to follow here; I have collated it with copies of the first and second editions.)

110. *Works,* IX, 17.

111. *A Vindication of the Rights of Woman* (London, 1891), p. 212.

112. *Ibid.,* p. 56.

113. *Ibid.,* pp. 250, 118–119.

114. *History of Human Marriage* (New York, 1922), I, 184–187, 111, 133–141, 198–206.

115. James Lawrence, *The Empire of the Nairs, or The Rights of Women: An Utopian Romance* (London, 1813), I, 5–12. For the influence of this book on Shelley, see: W. E. Peck, "Shelley's indebtedness to Sir [James] Lawrence," *MLN,* XL (1925), 246–249; Walter Graham, "Shelley and *The Empire of the Nairs,*" *PMLA,* XL (1925), 881–891; Hughes, pp. 213–215.

116. *Ibid.,* p. 39.

117. Sir James Lawrence, "Love: an Allegory," *The Etonian Out of Bounds, or Poetry and Prose* (London, 1828), I, 145–170.

118. Priestley, Introduction, *Political Justice,* III, 86–87.

119. Oct. 8, 1811, *Works,* VIII, 152.

120. Aug. 18, 1812, *Works,* IX, 17.

121. Hogg, I, 71, 163–164. For the influence of Hume on Shelley's views on necessity, see: Frank B. Evans, "Shelley, Godwin, Hume, and the Doctrine of Necessity," *SP,* XXXVII (1940), 632–640.

122. For the influence of Hume on Godwin, see: Evans, and Priestley's Introduction, *Political Justice,* III, 3–114, *passim.*

123. *Political Justice,* I, 362 ff.; e.g. (p. 372): "When the science of the material universe was in its infancy, men were sufficiently prompt to refer events to accident and chance; but the further they have extended their

enquiries and observation, the more reason they have found to conclude that every thing takes place according to necessary and universal laws. The case is exactly parallel with respect to mind. . . ."

124. *Ibid.,* p. 378.

125. *Ibid.,* II, 323–324. See also, *ibid.,* I, 179, 371, 393; II, 375. Shelley's reference in this passage to "the crime of Damiens" is taken from *ibid.,* I, 13, 153.

126. Book IV, chs. VII and VIII, "Of Free Will and Necessity," and "Inferences from the Doctrine of Necessity;" e.g. the cautious comment (I, 383): "The virtuous man, in proportion to his improvement, will be under the constant influence of fixed and invariable principles; and such a being as we conceive God to be, can never in any one instance have exercised this liberty, that is, can never have acted in a foolish and tyrannical manner."

127. The future history of *Queen Mab,* during Shelley's lifetime is, briefly, as follows. Some time after the publication of the poem Shelley revised Cantos, I, II, VIII, and IX, making his revisions (essentially minor) in two printed copies of the poem. Cantos I and II he published in 1816 under the title "The Daemon of the World" in the *Alastor* volume, in which volume he published also the attack on religion from *Queen Mab,* VI, 72–101 under the title "Superstition." (See: Forman, *The Shelley Library,* pp. 36–44; Thomas J. Wise, *A Shelley Library* [London, 1924], pp. 38–40.)

In Jan., 1817, when the Westbrooks were suing to deprive Shelley of the custody of his children by Harriet, one of the charges they made, to demonstrate his unsuitableness as a parent, was the writing of *Queen Mab:* "And your Orators show that the said Percy Bysshe Shelley avows himself to be an atheist and that since his said Marriage he has written and published a certain work called *Queen Mab* with notes and other works and that he has therein blasphemously derided the truth of the Christian Revelation and denied the existence of God as the Creator of the Universe." (Quoted in Medwin, Appendix III, p. 464.) In Nov. of the same year Shelley informed a correspondent that although he now felt that the poem contained weaknesses "in imagery and language and a connected plan," he still adhered to its "doctrines of equality and liberty and disinterestedness, and entire unbelief in religion of any sort." (To Waller, Nov. 22, 1817, *Verse and Prose,* ed. by Sir John C. E. Shelley-Rolls and Roger Ingpen [London, 1934], p. 129.) In the spring of 1821 William Clarke and Richard Carlile brought out pirated editions of the poem. (Forman, *The Shelley Library,* pp. 46–50; White, II, 304; White, *The Unextinguished Hearth,* pp. 95–97.) On June 11, 1821, Shelley wrote from Italy asking his publisher Charles Ollier to protest the piracy on the ground that the poem was "better fitted to injure than to serve the cause which it advocates." (*Works,* X, 274.) On June 16 he wrote to his friend John Gisborne: "You may imagine how much I am amused. For the sake of a dignified appearance, however, and really because I wish to protest against all the bad poetry in it, I have given order to say it is all done against my desire." (*Ibid.,* p. 278.) On Sept. 14 he wrote to his friend Horace Smith: "If you happen to have bought a copy of Clarke's edition of 'Queen Mab' for me, I should like very well to see it.—I really hardly know what this poem is about. I am afraid it is rather rough." (*Ibid.,* p. 325. Shortly afterward he received a copy. *Journal,* Feb. 12, 1839, p. 207.) On June 22, he wrote to Leigh Hunt, as Editor of *The Examiner* (which published the letter):

> Having heard that a poem, entitled "Queen Mab," has been surreptitiously published in London, and that legal proceedings have been instituted against the publisher, I request the favour of your insertion of the following explanation of the affair as it relates to me.
>
> A poem, entitled "Queen Mab," was written by me at the age of eighteen, I dare say in a sufficiently intemperate spirit—but even then was not intended for publication, and a few copies only were struck off, to be distributed among my personal friends. I have not seen this production for several years; I doubt not but that it is perfectly worthless in point of literary composition; and that in all that concerns moral and political speculation, as well as in the subtler discriminations of metaphysical and religious doctrine, it is still more crude and immature. I am a devoted enemy to religious, political, and domestic oppression; and I regret this publication, not so much from literary vanity, as because I fear it is better fitted to injure than to serve the cause of freedom. I have directed my solicitor to apply to Chancery for an injunction to restrain the sale; but after the precedent of Mr. Southey's "Wat Tyler" (a poem, written, I believe, at the same age, and with the same unreflecting enthusiasm), with little hopes of success.
>
> Whilst I exonerate myself from all share in having divulged opinions hostile to existing sanctions, under the form, whatever it may be, which they assume in this poem, it is scarcely necessary for me to protest against this system of inculcating the truth of Christianity and the excellence of Monarchy however true or however excellent they may be, by such equivocal arguments as confiscation, and imprisonment, and invective, and slander, and the insolent violation of the most sacred ties of nature and society. (*Ibid.,* pp. 280–281.)

It has been considered, on the basis of this letter, that Shelley in later years "repudiated" *Queen Mab* and its doctrines; and this argument has been used to support the prevalent but false theory that Shelley in his later years grew more conservative. But in the same year in which he wrote this letter he was reiterating the revolutionary political doctrine of *Queen Mab* in his Preface to *Hellas,* its free love doctrines in *Epipsychidion* and its anti-religious doctrines in *On the Devil, and Devils.* Shelley, therefore, is not repudiating the ideas of *Queen Mab.* What he is troubled about, as the above correspondence shows, was, first, that some of its crudities of style (he had radically changed his poetic style in the intervening years) might injure his reputation, and, second, that its outspoken radicalism might be used to "injure" the reform movement as represented by *The Examiner* group with which he was then identified in the public mind. The work had been used against him at the trial, and these pirated editions were, as he foresaw, used by the Tory reviewers for further attacks. (White, II, 356.) These attacks he attempts to offset by exaggerating his youth at the time of composition and the "privacy" of its distribution. But at the same time he indicates his continued hostility to "religious, political and domestic oppression," i.e. to the Christian church, to the monarchical-aristocratic form of government, and to marriage. And perhaps when he again saw a copy and scanned its truly powerful passages he would have found that its stylistic "roughness" was not so marked as he had feared. His friend Williams, reading the poem the following year, was delighted with it and apparently regarded its views as similar to those Shelley was then expressing: "Sunday, June 30 [1822]. Read some of Shelley's *Queen Mab*— an astonishing work. The enthusiasm of his spirit breaks out in some admirable passages in the poetry, and the notes are as subtle and elegant as he could now write." (Williams's *Journal,* p. 67.)

128. White, I, 294; II, 304, 408; Medwin, pp. 97–98; Shaw, "Shaming the Devil About Shelley" *The Collected Works,* Ayot St. Lawrence Edition (New York, 1932), XXIX, 257. *Queen Mab* was influential also on the young German radicals; Frederick Engels, for instance, began a translation. (Ernest Rose, *JEGP,* XXVI (1927), 141.)

In 1841 Edward Moxon, who published *Queen Mab* complete in Mary Shelley's one volume edition of Shelley's poems in 1839, was tried on the charge that "he did falsely and maliciously publish a scandalous, impious, profane and malicious libel concerning the Holy Scriptures, and of and concerning Almighty God." (Newman I. White, "Literature and the Law of Libel," *SP,* XXII (Jan., 1925), 34–47.)

129. Hogg, II, 119. The duplication of references in readings—from Holbach, Drummond, Spinoza, Sir Isaac Newton—with those in the Notes to *Queen Mab* indicates a work of the same general period. The reference to Laplace, as we have seen (n. 96 above), indicates composition in the latter months of 1813. (See also ch. VI, n. 174.) *The Refutation of Deism* was reprinted anonymously in *The Theological Enquirer,* Mar. and Apr., 1815. (Bertram Dobell, "Shelleyana," *The Athenaeum,* Mar. 7, 1885, p. 313; Wise, *A Shelley Library,* p. 42; White, *The Unextinguished Hearth,* pp. 45–46, 395.) Extracts from it were printed, under Shelley's name, in a radical periodical, *The Model Republic,* in 1843, apparently from a copy that Shelley had given to Hookham. (Forman, *A Shelley Library,* p. 61; *Works,* VI, 349.) Some of the new classical references, e.g. to Suetonius, Tacitus, Euripides, may indicate influence from Peacock, who was with Shelley in Edinburgh in the fall of 1813. Tacitus and Euripides appear on Shelley's book order list for Dec. 17, 1812, *Works,* IX, 36.

In 1948, Professor Frederick L. Jones published from a notebook of Mary Shelley's the first section of Shelley's fragment *On Miracles* (for the second section see: *Works,* VII, 147–148) in *SP,* XLV, 473–475, a fragment which he believed to represent "a first draft of a part of *A Refutation of Deism.*" But, although the subject of miracles is briefly mentioned in the *Refutation* (*Works,* VI, 39–40)—as well as in *The Necessity of Atheism* and the Notes to *Queen Mab* (*Works,* V, 208–209, *Works,* I, 154–155)—the argument of the *Refutation* does not call for so elaborate a discussion of the subject as we find in this essay. In fact, such a discussion would be disproportionately out of place. The *Essay on Miracles*—as we may now call it—is a completely separate work, probably written at a somewhat later date. (See: James A. Notopoulos, "The Dating of Shelley's Prose," *PMLA,* LVIII [June, 1943], 496–497.) Its opening sentence indicates its nature: "At your request I shall endeavour to state, in the form of remarks on Leslie's short method with the Deists, a few of the most obvious reasons for considering that system of opinions most erroneously called the Christian religion as false." The reference is to the Reverend Charles Leslie's *A Short and Easy Method with the Deists . . . in a Letter to a Friend* first published in 1698 and many times reprinted. Leslie's "method" is to attempt to establish the existence of a providential God—in distinction from the remote deity of the deists—by asserting the truth of miracles. This he tried to do by claiming that the miracles of the Bible were adequately witnessed and often have a continuing tradition, in feasts, etc. Shelley's *Essay on Miracles* is a systematic attack on Leslie, also written in the form of a letter (and, hence, on this ground also, unsuitable for insertion in *A Refutation of Deism*).

130. Perhaps the most extraordinary form that this tendency has thus far assumed is the argument by Frederick L. Jones that *The Refutation of Deism* is Shelley's announcement of his conversion to Christianity (a conversion flanked at one end by the Notes to *Queen Mab* and at the other by *The Revolt of Islam*). Frederick L. Jones, "Shelley's *On Life*," *PMLA,* LXII (Sept. 1947), 781.

131. Neither Medwin nor Hogg mentions Spinoza as among Shelley's early reading, and Shelley's own first references to him in a letter of Jan. 12, 1811, indicates that he had not read him. (See above, p. 350.) Shelley included "Spinoza" in his book order list on Dec. 17, 1812, and on Jan. 3, 1813, informed Hookham, presumably in reply to his enquiry, that he wished the *Tractatus Theologico-Politicus* and the *Opera Posthuma.* (*Works,* IX, 34, 39.) That he received the *Tractatus* we know for he quotes it in the Notes to *Queen Mab* (*Works,* I, 151) and again (the same quotation on the identity of the power of God and nature) in *A Refutation of Deism.* (*Works,* VI, 56.) In the fall of 1817 he was translating Spinoza (probably, as White, I, 736, argues, the *Tractatus*); in 1820, Mary Shelley was translating Spinoza, with some help from Shelley; in the fall of 1821, Shelley and Edward Ellerker Williams continued the translation, named by Williams as the *Tractatus.* (*Journal,* pp. 85, 127–128, 130–131, 134, 161; Williams's *Journal,* pp. 25–26.) The impression from Williams is that the *Tractatus* was completed or almost completed; but only a few pages have ever been published. (*Works,* VII, 272–274.)

132. *Theological-Political Treatise, The Chief Works of Benedict de Spinoza,* tr. by R. H. M. Elwes (London, 1889), I, 5.

133. *Ibid.,* p. 19; see also pp. 44–45, 81–83; and n. 131 above.

134. See n. 121 above and *Works,* I, 144. The theory is implied, although not developed in its general concepts, in *The Necessity of Atheism* (*Works,* V, 208), in a passage probably by Hogg, Shelley having rejected it (by implication) in a letter of Jan. 12, 1811. (*Works,* VIII, 44.) (He reverses

his position in a letter of Jan. 2, 1812, *ibid.,* p. 227.) See also pp. 74, 76–77, above.

135. *Works,* V, 208–209, and Shelley's letter to his father, Feb. 6, 1811, *Works,* VIII, 51.

136. See John M. Robertson, *A Short History of Freethought* (London, 1899), pp. 296 f.

137. On Holbach and his collaborators, see *ibid.,* pp. 348–351. Shelley must have read of *The System of Nature* in Barruel's *Memoirs Illustrating the History of Jacobinism* while at Oxford, where Barruel was a "favorite book." (Hogg, I, 376; letter to Leigh Hunt, Mar. 2, 1811, *Works,* VIII, 56.) Barruel (I, 337–345, II, 159–204) gives long descriptions of "the Club of Holbach," containing Diderot, Boulanger, and Helvétius, and mentions the *System of Nature* and *Christianity Unveiled* as products of the Club. He thinks, however, that the *System of Nature* was written by Diderot (I, 177) and *Christianity Unveiled* by Damilaville (I, 340) as "Boulanger," and does not know the author of *Good Sense* (I, 149–150, 144–145, 340). It may well have been Barruel that sent Shelley searching for a copy of *The System of Nature* and, perhaps, also for Helvétius. (Barruel, I, 152, quotes Helvétius on free love and has other comments on him; Shelley was reading Helvétius in the summer of 1811. To Hogg, May 19, 1811; to Elizabeth Hitchener, July 15, 1811, *Works,* VIII, 94, 124. Shelley's comments on Helvétius and others in the *Address to the Irish People* were also, as we have noted, influenced by Barruel. I fail to note much influence of Helvétius on Shelley, but the following from *De L'Esprit, or Essays on the Mind* [London, 1809], p. 181—". . . the Turks, who admit into their religion the doctrines of necessity, a principle destructive to all religion . . ."— is perhaps echoed in the Notes to *Queen Mab* [*Works,* I, 145]: "The doctrine of Necessity tends . . . utterly to destroy religion." Shelley agreed with Godwin's attack on Helvétius's pessimism [see below] and would have disliked his doctrines of self-interest as much as he disliked those of Holbach.) As Hogg does not mention the *System of Nature* as among Shelley's "favorites" at Oxford and, indeed, seems to have no knowledge of it (Hogg, I, 358), and as it is not mentioned in Shelley's letters to Hogg in 1811, it is probable that Shelley had not read it until after the break with Hogg in the fall of 1811. His first actual reference to the work is in a letter to Godwin on June 3, 1812 (*Works,* VIII, 331–332): "I have just finished reading 'La Systeme de la Nature,' par M. Mirabaud. Do you know the real author? It appears to me a work of uncommon powers." Godwin was, in fact, well acquainted with the book (although he apparently did not know that Holbach was the author), for it was the work which had first shaken his own religious belief. (Kegan Paul, *William Godwin,* I, 26.) The Godwin of 1812, however, probably looked back upon it with some apprehension (it does not appear in his recommended reading to the "young American" or to Shelley), and apparently replied with some strictures against it, fearing its influence on his already not too acquiescent disciple, for on July 29 Shelley answered: "To begin with Helvetius. I have read La Systeme de la Nature. I suspect this to be Helvetius's by your charges against it. It is a book of uncommon powers, yet too obnoxious to

accusations of sensuality and selfishness." (*Works*, IX, 11; see also pp. 12–13. Godwin has apparently attacked Holbach for the pessimism on social progress with which he had charged Helvétius, a strange charge to bring against Holbach. *Political Justice*, I, 279–282.) Once Shelley encountered the book it had an immediate and powerful effect on him. On Aug. 18, he informed Hookham that he was beginning a translation of it and it is possible that this was the French work which Hogg noted him as translating in the fall. (See above, pp. 223, 373.) It became a major influence on *Queen Mab*, written during and immediately after Shelley's reading of it, and then on *A Refutation of Deism*.

138. Baron d'Holbach, *The System of Nature*, tr. by H. D. Robinson (Boston, 1889), I, 11–15.

139. *Ibid.*, p. 33; cf. *Queen Mab*, VI, 146–149.

140. *Works*, VI, 54 n.

141. *Ibid.*, pp. 33–34.

142. *Ibid.;* for the original passage, see: *Common Sense, or Natural Ideas Opposed to Supernatural* (New York, 1795), p. 5.

143. *Common Sense*, p. 7.

144. For some account of the English free-thought movement in this period see: J. M. Robertson, *A History of Freethought in the Nineteenth Century*, pp. 1–21, 59–110. Hone's three trials for blasphemy, published by himself, make highly entertaining reading. Shelley subscribed to his defence fund in 1817. (*Works*, IX, 278.)

145. Thomas Paine, *The Age of Reason, The Life and Works of Thomas Paine*, ed. by William M. Van der Weyde (New Rochelle, N. Y., 1925), VIII, 16–17. The conclusion of the passage seems to be echoed in Shelley's letter to his father on Feb. 6, 1811, *Works*, VIII, 52.

146. *Christianity Unveiled* (London, 1819), pp. 31–33.

147. *The Ruins*, pp. 139–143.

148. See above, pp. 258–259, 402–403.

149. *The Age of Reason*, p. 92. In his Note to *Queen Mab*, VII, 135–136 (*Works*, I, 154–155) Shelley writes: "But even supposing that a man should raise a dead body to life before your eyes, and on this fact rest his claim to being considered the son of God;—the Humane Society restores drowned persons, and because it makes no mystery of the method it employs, its members are not mistaken for the sons of God."

150. *Ibid.*, p. 94.

151. *Ibid.*, p. 25; *A Refutation of Deism, Works*, VI, 34–35.

152. *Ibid.*, p. 4.

153. *Ibid.*, p. 73.

154. *Ibid.*, pp. 43, 108.

155. See above, p. 118.

156. *Works*, VI, 25.

157. Hogg, in speaking of Shelley's early enthusiasm for Hume's *Essays*, does not mention the *Dialogues*, but it is most unlikely that Shelley would not also read this famous skeptical work, which continues Hume's anti-religious arguments beyond the *Essays*. A comparison of Part II, of the *Dialogues* with *A Refutation of Deism* reveals several close parallels, some

of which I note below. We might note also that Shelley was apparently re-reading Hume in Edinburgh in Nov., 1813. (To Hogg, Nov. 26, 1813, *Works,* IX, 81.) In the same letter he informs Hogg that he had been reading "many of Cicero's philosophical works," and that he considered him "one of the most admirable characters the world ever produced." The reference doubtless includes another famous anti-religious dialogue, Cicero's *Dialogue on the Gods.*

The *Academical Questions* contains a long dialogue on materialism and idealism (between Hylas, Theophilus, and Eugenius). When Hylas, the materialist, has finished, Theophilus, the religious idealist, comments (p. 278): "To what direful conclusions do the doctrines of Hylas lead? I shudder at the thought. They leave the soul without the hope of futurity, the universe without a plan devised by wisdom, man without a judge, and nature without a God." Theophilus then attacks atheism and upholds a religious outlook. Shelley seems to have this comment of Theophilus and his subsequent arguments in mind in the conclusion of *A Refutation of Deism.* (*Works,* VI, 56–57.) In the Notes to *Queen Mab* he comments: "The consistent Newtonian is necessarily an atheist. See Sir W. Drummond's *Academical Questions,* chap. iii.—Sir W. seems to consider the atheism to which it leads, as a sufficient presumption of the falsehood of the system of gravitation: but surely it is more consistent with the good faith of philosophy to admit a deduction from facts than an hypothesis incapable of proof, although it might militate with the obstinate preconceptions of the mob. Had this author, instead of inveighing against the guilt and absurdity of atheism, demonstrated its falsehood, his conduct would have been more suited to the modesty of the sceptic and the toleration of the philosopher." (*Works,* I, 150–151.) A few months later he was at work on the *Refutation.* It seems likely that he was inspired to a defence of atheist doctrine by Drummond's defence of religious idealism and his fulminations against atheism. Drummond must have appeared to him at the time as the very type of inconsistent deist.

158. A very real possibility in view of the blasphemy trials of Eaton, Carlile, and Hone. Carlile was sentenced to prison for six years for publishing Paine's *Age of Reason,* and one of his printers to three years on the same charge.

159. *Works,* VI, 31.

160. *Ibid.,* p. 32; the argument is concluded on p. 39: "Intensity of belief, like that of every other passion, is precisely proportioned to the degrees of excitement"; "Belief is not an act of volition, nor can it be regulated by the mind." The argument appears in Shelley's letter to his father on Feb. 6, 1811 (*Works,* VIII, 50–52); then in *The Necessity of Atheism* (*Works,* V, 207–209); then in *An Address to the Irish People* (*ibid.,* p. 222); then in *A Letter to Lord Ellenborough* (*ibid.,* p. 285); and then in the Notes to *Queen Mab* (*Works,* I, 154).

161. *Works,* VI, 33, 36. Similar skits appear in *Queen Mab,* VII, 106–157; the Notes to *Queen Mab* (*Works,* I, 152), and in Shelley's later (1821) brilliant and neglected satire *On the Devil, and Devils.* (*Works,* VII, 89–90.)

162. *Works,* VI, 36–37.

163. *Ibid.,* p. 37.

164. *Ibid.,* p. 38.

165. *Ibid.,* p. 39. The argument on miracles appears in Shelley's letter to his father on Feb. 11, 1811, in *The Necessity of Atheism,* and in the Notes to *Queen Mab.* (*Works,* I, 154–155.) His most extended discussion of the subject appears in the *Essay on Miracles.* (See above, n. 129.)

166. *Works,* VI, 45 n. Shelley also refers to Paley's *Evidences of Christianity, ibid.,* pp. 29 n., 40 n.

167. *The Works of William Paley,* ed. by Edmund Paley (London, 1825), V, ch. 1.

168. *Works,* VI, 45.

169. Part II.

170. *The Ruins,* pp. 229–230.

171. *Works,* VI, 48. Hume, *Dialogues Concerning Natural Religion,* Part II.

172. *Ibid.,* p. 50. See *The Ruins,* pp. 220–221, 226; Darwin, *The Temple of Nature,* Additional Notes, pp. 87–91. See also Grabo, *A Newton Among Poets,* pp. 39–103 on the new concepts of matter prevalent in the science of the time, and pp. 118–158 on Shelley's later use of them in *Prometheus Unbound.* Shelley may also have got something of this (ultimately Newtonian) view of matter from his conversations with Godwin in the fall of 1812. See Godwin, *Thoughts on Man,* pp. 382 ff.

173. The Lawgiver in *The Ruins* argues that all the concepts of all the different religions, which are given *in extenso,* cannot represent one God.

174. *Works,* VI, 55. Shelley acknowledges his indebtedness to Hume. Holbach advanced a similar argument but without accepting Hume's subjective theory of causation. See, for instance, the chapter "On Motion" in *The System of Nature,* or the concept "The universe is a cause, it is not an effect," in *Common Sense* (p. 27).

175. In a letter to Leigh Hunt on Sept. 27, 1819, (*Works,* X, 87) Shelley tells us that he first came across the phrase, "Mind cannot create, it can only perceive," as a marginal note in a copy of Berkeley owned by Southey's friend Lloyd at Keswick (i.e. between Nov., 1811, and Feb., 1812). The argument appears again in the essay *On Life* (*ca.* 1819).

176. Cf., letter to Elizabeth Hitchener, Jan. 2, 1812, *Works,* VIII, 227, on Shelley's arguments to Southey on this point; and his earlier letter to her, June 11, 1811, *ibid.,* p. 102. For an apparently earlier draft of parts of Eusebes' final speech see: *Works,* VII, 281–285.

177. *Works,* VI, 57.

178. *Ibid.,* pp. 49–51.

INDEX

(Both text and notes are indexed; some items can be completed only if both text and note references are consulted. The letter "S" standing alone = Percy Bysshe Shelley; the letter "S" preceded by a first name = Shelley; e.g. Harriet S = Harriet Shelley. The indexing under Percy Bysshe Shelley is placed separately for convenience at the end of the general index. The full titles of major authors and works used are given on pp. 289–290 above and are not always repeated in the index.)

PERCY BYSSHE SHELLEY